REDISCOVERING ROSCOE

REDISCOVERING ROSCOE

THE FILMS OF "FATTY" ARBUCKLE

STEVE MASSA

BearManor Media

2020

Rediscovering Roscoe: The Films of "Fatty" Arbuckle

© 2020 Steve Massa

All rights reserved.

No portion of this publication may be reproduced, stored, and/or copied electronically (except for academic use as a source), nor transmitted in any form or by any means without the prior written permission of the publisher and/or author.

Published in the United States of America by:

BearManor Media
1317 Edgewater Dr. #110
Orlando, FL 32804

BearManorMedia.com

Printed in the United States.

Typesetting and layout by John Teehan

Cover design by Marlene Weisman

ISBN—978-1-62933-452-3

Mabel Normand has deadly aim with an udder from the other side of the fence in *Fatty and Mabel's Simple Life* (1915). Courtesy the Library of Congress.

To Sam Gill, the silent comedy "beacon" who has lit the way and charted the course for all the researchers who have followed his lead. For all your trailblazing and devoted passion, I want to offer the ultimate slapstick salute:

"Here's milk in your eye."

Table of Contents

Foreword by Dave Kehr 1

Introduction by Ben Model 3

Preface and Acknowlegements 7

Archives Key 11

Chapter 1: Beginnings 13

Chapter 2: Mack Sennett Films 31

Chapter 3: Keystone 1914 97

Chapter 4: Keystone 1915 187

Chapter 5: Keystone 1916 237

Chapter 6: Comique Comedies 269

Chapter 7: Starring Feature Films 345

Chapter 8: Banishment 391

Chapter 9: Reel Comedies, Inc. — Round One 401

Chapter 10: Reel Comedies, Inc. — Round Two 419

Chapter 11: The Mystery of "Biff Thrill
    Comedies." 441

Chapter 12: Enter William Goodrich 445

Chapter 13: Goodrich in Sound 483

Chapter 14: Vitaphone Shorts 563

Appendix 1: Seeing the Films Today 585

Appendix 2: "The Screen Must Have a
    Fat Comedian!" 591

Bibliography 663

About the Author 669

Index 671

Character shot of Roscoe during his stage days. Courtesy Marc Wanamaker/Bison Archives.

by Dave Kehr
Foreword

Roscoe "Fatty" Arbuckle looked like a sketch out of the Sunday funnies: the large, almost perfectly round head, bisected by a wide mouth that could leer or grin or lustily devour, perched atop an almost equally round body, the spherical qualities of the ensemble accentuated by a bowler hat. He was a large man, but not markedly obese. For all his bulk he was fast and graceful of movement, and many of the jokes in the early Keystone films—he started at Mack Sennett's pioneering comedy studio in 1913, after a career in vaudeville—depend on Arbuckle's surprising agility, as he ducks and dives and dashes to avoid the grasp of a pursuing policeman or the wrath of a jealous wife.

Arbuckle's body is that of both an overgrown infant and an adult sensualist, and he often shifts between the two connotations of his appearance for rich comic effect. He may approach a woman as an awkward, ungainly child, only to shoot a sudden look at the audience that bespeaks a happy, uninhibited lechery. He is also, like Chaplin and several other comedians of his age, an enthusiastic cross-dresser; with his corpulence poured into one of the tentlike bathing suits of the period, he could pass for a curvaceous Victorian woman of the sort only then going out of style.

Arbuckle's ambiguity—the ease with which he moved between infantile appetite and grown-up desire, between feminine coquetry and masculine aggression—made him one of the most subversive figures in a subversive genre. As Eileen Bowser wrote in her introduction to Steve Massa's 2013 book, *Lame Brains and Lunatics*, silent comedies were "a reverse mirror of the conventions of society. Where many feature films in this period taught a moral lesson, the short slapstick films mocked authority figures and family values, they were amoral and politically incorrect, and they tell us a lot about American life at the time." One look from Arbuckle was enough to undermine all the pieties that the church groups and social reform societies were attempting to impose on our unruly society in the early years of the 20th Century: he was a one-man anti-temperance league, a pleasure principal on two stout legs.

The prudes and the censors got their revenge, of course, on September 11, 1921, when Arbuckle was arrested for the rape and murder of Virginia Rappe, a twenty-eight-year-old actress who passed out during a party in Arbuckle's suite in a San Francisco hotel and died a few days later of peritonitis. It mattered little that Arbuckle was cleared of all charges after three trials—the real hanging judge was Will Hays, the first president of the organization that later became the Motion Picture Association of America, who used his industry-appointed position to issue a ban on all of Arbuckle's films. He would not appear on screen again for a decade, when he was finally allowed to return in 1932 for a series of shorts produced by Warner Brothers' Vitaphone unit. The new films were a success, but in a final twist of fate, Arbuckle died the same day Warners renewed his contract.

Someday it will be possible to write about Roscoe Arbuckle without mentioning the scandal that destroyed his career, and when that day comes Steve Massa will have made a major contribution to it, both with the lovingly-researched and perceptively-written volume you hold in your hands, and with the many programs of silent comedies that Steve (often with fellow silent comedy enthusiast Ben Model) has curated for institutions like The Library of Congress, The Museum of Modern Art, The Museum of the Moving Image, the Pordenone Silent Film Festival, and the Silent Clowns Film Series that Steve and Ben have long been organizing for the New York Public Library for the Performing Arts at Lincoln Center. Roscoe Arbuckle's artistry and humanity continue to live in his films and in these pages; the last laugh is his and ours.

New York, NY
January 2019

Dave Kehr wrote film criticism for the Chicago Reader *and* Chicago *magazine during the 1970s and early 1980s. In 1986 he became the principal film critic for the* Chicago Tribune, *where he worked until 1992, when he became a film critic for the* New York Daily News. *He then wrote a weekly DVD column for the* New York Times *until 2013. He is now a curator in the Film Department at the Museum of Modern Art where he has organized series such as* William Fox Presents, Seriously Funny: The Films of Leo McCarey, *and* Mexico at Midnight: Film Noir from Mexican Cinema's Golden Age, *as well as overseen restorations of neglected films like* Rosita *(1923) and* Forbidden Paradise *(1924). Collections of his criticism,* When Movies Mattered *and* Movies That Mattered, *have been published by University of Chicago Press, and he is also the author of* Italian Film Posters.

by Ben Model

Introduction

THE SO-CALLED "SILENT" ERA was more than the starting point of American film comedy. It was its Big Bang. Not only were the basics of screen comedy developed and established during that time—specifically from the early 'teens through 1929—but something else magical came from the cauldron of silent film comedy: the comedian/filmmaker.

There hasn't been another time in the many decades that have ensued after the advent of talking pictures when as many lead comics came to the fore, rapidly, with an innate understanding of the medium. More remarkable is that this occurred during a time when the form itself was still being established.

The silent comedy era gave us comedian/filmmakers Charlie Chaplin, Roscoe Arbuckle, Buster Keaton, Marcel Perez, Charles Parrott, Larry Semon, and to a certain extent Harold Lloyd and Stan Laurel. These are comedians whose films had an identifiable style to them, even when they were co-piloted by someone else—Eddie Cline (Keaton), Leo McCarey (Parrott/Chase), William Seiter (Perez). Harold Lloyd may not be credited as director on any of his films, but he knew what was the right way to do things, and a Harold Lloyd picture is a Harold Lloyd picture is a Harold Lloyd picture. A Laurel & Hardy comedy is a Laurel & Hardy comedy—even when the credited director is Edgar Kennedy (?!), as it is on *You're Darn Tootin'*. This continued with them into the sound era, and interviews with cast members on the L&H films claim that Stan was the main collaborator, calling the shots and spending time in the editing room. The same applies to Raymond Griffith. A similar argument could be made for Harry Langdon, considering that the style that he and Capra-Ripley-Edwards settled into ultimately reverted to the style of the vaudeville acts Langdon had been touring and headlining with for years.

These comedians just seemed to know what you could do with comedy in the medium of motion pictures. With no precedent to guide them whatsoever. None. And yet the choice of camera placement, the types of shots used for a particular kind of comedy action, the way certain gags are covered, the use of lighting, the sense of storytelling, cutting rhythms—it's something these comedians innately *got*, and more so than most of their contemporaries. They would come up with ideas for gags and the way they'd be shot or staged that no one else was doing and which, through today's eyes, seem more advanced or mature than a lot of the other silent comedy work being made at the time. All they

Roscoe directing Luke to put the bite on Al St John or Buster Keaton. Courtesy The Museum of Modern Art.

had to draw on was having performed a ten-to-twelve-minute slapstick act in vaudeville or music hall for months and months over a few years or more. It's truly amazing when you stop to think about it.

With the exception of Laurel & Hardy's films and Stan Laurel's contribution to them, talkies appeared to have thrown everyone a major curveball. The late silent Laurel & Hardy shorts had slowed their pacing to the point that shifting over to real-time speed and synch dialog turned out (thankfully) to be a natural next step. Lloyd did his best to adapt, adding more jokes, but gradually that remarkable or special thing that was *Speedy*, or *Kid Brother*, or *For Heaven's Sake*, that verve and agility he and his pictures were known for, could not work in sound film, and there was no second act (or third, depending how you score it) for him with pictures. Chaplin held off as long as he could—*because* he could—continuing to make the kind of pictures only he could in silent film until 1936. Keaton was stuck in a factory-like setting without creative control, with no room or motivation to innovate and get a handle on talking-picture comedies.

Instead of instinctively getting what sound film comedy was and what it could be, the leading comics of the silent screen did what they could do to continue working in pictures.

Except for Roscoe Arbuckle.

The shorts Roscoe was directing in the early 1930s have snap and tempo to them that don't have that draggy feel as do so many other comedy shorts from the time. It would be easy to blame the molasses-y timing and pacing on technology, or on the fact that many of the performers in early 1930s comedy shorts had been in silents for several years and were still moving and behaving a tad slower to compensate for the 35-50% speed-up of footage that everyone did in silent film.

But every Arbuckle-directed short I've seen from this time moves along at a brisk pace like a screwball comedy from the mid-1930s. I've actually had to remind myself after looking at something like *Bridge Wives*, or *Honeymoon Trio*, or *One Quiet Night* that these films were made in 1931 or 1932, and not in 1936 or 1937. He's not the credited director on the half-dozen shorts he starred in for Vitaphone, but these two-reelers exhibit the same sense of pacing and I'm sure he collaborated on the direction of them.

Arbuckle just seems to innately *know* what sound comedies could or should look like, and how to direct them.

These comedian-auteurs (if you'll pardon my French) are all people whose work has been viewed, known and rather available to some degree, either through theatrical screenings, 16mm and 8mm collector prints, TV packages, and in some cases home video. That is, with the exception of Mr. Arbuckle.

The history books—film history books, to be precise—have not been kind to Roscoe. Well, not so much unkind as they simply list him as being part of the Keystone comedians' stable. It is Keaton's contributions to the Comique shorts that is discussed, if the Comiques are on the table at the moment, usually within the context of the Keaton canon. There was a generation of film historians who in the 1950s, 1960s and 1970s wrote books on silent films and made compilation feature films who did not give credence to the films of Roscoe Arbuckle; books and films and documentaries that people like Steve Massa and I, and maybe you, grew up reading and watching.

Roscoe and cameraman during the making of *The Iron Mule* (1925). Courtesy Marilyn Slater.

It was certainly a revelation for me when Steve and I spent time screening the Arbuckle shorts held in the Museum of Modern Art's film archive during the early-to-mid-2000's. We were preparing for the Arbuckle retrospective that we co-organized with MoMA's Ron Magliozzi and which ran for two months to great reviews and audience turnouts in 2006. There were ways Roscoe handled camera placement—or consistently went with ideas his cameramen suggested—as well as types of gags, story and gag construction, cutting and especially direction that we'd notice in film after film. A directorial style, if you will.

There have always been books about the films of the major silent era comedians and comedian-filmmakers, books on Chaplin, Keaton, Lloyd, Langdon, Laurel & Hardy, either as individual studies or as a group. A number of books have been written and published about Arbuckle's life, with the infamous scandal as their centerpiece, but never on his work. Steve Massa has taken on the monumental task of researching and writing the book on the *films* of Roscoe Arbuckle that deserves to be on a shelf next to the other "The Films of…." tomes you have.

Here's hoping more and more of Arbuckle's films from 1909 to 1933 become available for fans to watch, study and enjoy, and that more of the missing ones turn up. And that your copy of this book will sustain a little wear in making many trips from a shelf to your desk or lap as you reference it in your own journey through Roscoe's film canon.

New York, NY
January 2019

Ben Model is a silent film accompanist and historian based in New York. He is a resident film accompanist for the Museum of Modern Art (New York, NY) and for the Library of Congress (Culpeper, VA), and regularly performs around the USA and internationally at historic theatres, museums, libraries, schools and universities. His recorded scores have been heard on numerous DVDs and Blu-rays released by Kino Lorber, Milestone Films, Thanhouser Company Film Preservation, Inc., and Undercrank Productions, as well as on Turner Classic Movies broadcasts. Undercrank Productions is Model's DVD label, and is dedicated to releasing obscure and overlooked gems of the silent era for home video and theatrical viewing. In addition to his music work, Model has co-programmed several silent film series for MoMA together with Steve Massa and with MoMA Film Curators Ron Magliozzi, Charles Silver and Dave Kehr. He is a Visiting Professor at Wesleyan University's College of Film and Moving Image. Model is also the archivist for the Ernie Kovacs and Edie Adams collections, and for Ediad Productions has curated DVD box sets of Kovacs' and Adams" television work released by Shout Factory. Online: silentfilmmusic.com and @silentfilmmusic

Preface and Acknowledgments

A FRESH LOOK AT THE FILMS of Roscoe "Fatty" Arbuckle has been long overdue. For almost one hundred years it's been impossible to separate the legend surrounding Arbuckle from his work as a filmmaker and comedian. In the wake of the famous scandal and trials his reputation was buried in the 1920s. Years later, when critics and film historians began re-examining silent comedy, the taint still remained, causing squeamishness about delving into his films. Routinely dismissed as "primitive," "vulgar," or "not funny in himself," until recently the films were rarely revived; the exception being his shorts with Buster Keaton, but anything found funny in those comedies was usually credited to Buster by modern commentators. More than enough has been written on the scandal and the media circus that followed. The time has come to focus on the films and give the man, who for a number of years was second only to Charlie Chaplin in popularity, his due. A large number of his films survive and reveal not only an immensely likeable clown, but an innovative comedy creator and sophisticated director.

Although I grew up hooked on silent comedies, I really didn't discover Roscoe's work until much later. Cutting my teeth on television programs like *Comedy Capers* and *Who's the Funny Man*—where silent two-reelers were condensed and repackaged for kids—his films weren't included (perhaps due to left over stigma from the scandal). As a teenager I got a steady diet of Chaplin and Keaton, but the only Arbuckle I saw at that time was Blackhawk Films' release of *Fatty's Magic Pants* (1914) and a cut down version of *Fatty and Mabel Adrift* (1916) in one of Robert Youngson's compilation features.

My first real look at Roscoe was thanks to film historian William K. Everson. In a 1983 all-Arbuckle evening at New York's Collective for Living Cinema, Professor Everson showed *The Waiter's Ball* (1916), his feature *Leap Year* (1922), and the comeback sound short *Buzzin' Around* (1933). Seeing the comedian from his first full flowering to his last hurrah was an eye opening experience, and I made sure thereafter to catch the couple of Arbuckle Comique shorts that were always a side bar in the perennial Buster Keaton Film Festivals.

The next dose of concentrated Arbuckle came in 1986 at the Museum of the Moving Image when Richard Koszarski programmed a two weekend series that included a large swatch of his Keystone shorts, the feature *The Life of the Party* (1920), and the entire

Early portrait of a spiffy-looking Roscoe.
Courtesy Marc Wanamaker/Bison Archives.

run of his Vitaphone sound two-reelers. Now I was a confirmed fan—impressed with his clean and precise direction, his amazing dexterity with props, the limitless variety of physical knockabout, and a certain sardonic strain of humor that ran through all the films.

Seeking out his films wherever I could, I was eventually able to screen rare items in the collections at the Library of Congress and New York's Museum of Modern Art. Having by that time begun programming and writing about silent comedy, I had the great good fortune to become involved in the production of the four-disc DVD release *The Forgotten Films of Roscoe "Fatty" Arbuckle*. Working alongside Robert Arkus, Andy Coryell, Bruce Lawton, David B. Pearson, Richard M. Roberts, Patricia Tobias, Brent Walker, and Robert Young Jr. as an advisor to producer Paul Gierucki, and providing commentary tracks and booklet notes, it was an immense thrill to help get such a large chunk of his work collected and available to the general public.

Not long after this in 2006, Ben Model and I teamed up with Ron Magliozzi, curator of film at the Museum of Modern Art, to mount a two-week retrospective devoted to Roscoe. At MoMA, with twelve programs and fifty-five films, we were able to cover his career in detail. Taking him from his very beginning to his reign as a comedy star, we also brought focus to his work as a director before and after his banning from the screen, and tied everything together with his final films. One of the great joys in doing this series was to get hard to see rarities like *The Gangsters*, *A Noise from the Deep* (both 1913), *A Bath House Beauty* (1914), *His Wife's Mistake* (1916), *Scraps of Paper* (1918), *Camping Out* (1919), *No Loafing* (1923), *Dynamite Doggie* (1925), and *Special Delivery* (1927) out of the vaults and up on the screen.

Work began on what would become this volume during that festival. Initially focusing on the overlooked Reel Comedies, Inc. shorts that he directed with Poodles Hanneford, Ned Sparks & Harry Tighe, and Al St John, after the series ended I moved on to profiling some of my other favorites with a vague idea of a book on his overall career. However I was soon sidetracked by other projects. While I had continued researching Arbuckle material it wasn't until I had finished and sent off the manuscript for my previous book, *Slapstick Divas: The Women of Silent Comedy*, that I came across my original Arbuckle notes and decided that it was finally time to proceed with a film-by-film study.

During the ensuing twelve years since the start there have been many people who have shared their love for, and insights on, the Arbuckle films, so there are numerous people to thank. I'd like to start with Sam Gill, who for many years has been a pillar of silent comedy research. Since setting the standard in the 1960s, he has become something of the Yoda of silent comedy history—sharing his vast store of knowledge and guiding young researchers. Sam's 1976 Arbuckle filmography (that originally came out with David Yallop's *The Day the Laughter Stopped*) is the inspiration and bones for this book. As the first charting of Roscoe's overall body of work, his filmography has been a valuable tool for all the Arbuckle research that has followed. I only hope that I've been able to successfully build upon what Sam started.

For guidance, encouragement, and inspiration I'm indebted to Eileen Bowser, Serge Bromberg, Kevin Brownlow, Elif Rongen-Kaynakci, Dave Kehr, Ron Magliozzi, Mike Mashon, Ben Model, Rob Stone, and Brent Walker. Extra thanks to Dave and Ben for their wonderful Foreword and Introduction.

The generosity of Robert Arkus, Peter Bagrov, John Bengtson, Eileen Bowser, Serge Bromberg, Kevin Brownlow, Rachel Del Gaudio, Louis Depres, Robert Farr, Richard Finegan, Mike Hawks, Sam Gill, Tom Lisanti, Dorinda Hartmann, Michael J. Hayde,

Luke supervises as Roscoe cranks their car outside the Balboa Studio.
Courtesy Marc Wanamaker/Bison Archives.

John Hillman, Mark Johnson, Nancy Kaufman, Elif Rongen-Kaynakci, Dave Kehr, Jim Kerkhoff, Robert James Kiss, Richard Koszarski, Crystal Kui, James Layton, Ron Magliozzi, Mike Mashon, Bruno Mestdagh, Peter Mintun, Ben Model, Tom Reeder, Jessica Rosner, Richard Simonton, Zoran Sinobad, Andrew Sholl, Annichen Skaren, Marilyn Slater, Larry Smith, Rob Stone, Ashley Swinnerton, Matt Vogel, Brent Walker, Marc Wanamaker, Jay Weissberg, George Willeman and Joseph Yranski, as well as Undercrank Productions and the Vitaphone Project in sharing research, photos, films, and other materials has been overwhelming and impossible to ever repay.

Sadly, no longer here to receive my thanks are Robert S. Birchard, William K. Everson, Cole Johnson, Jay Leyda, David Shepard, and Charles Silver, but I'm still benefitting from their influence and feel very lucky to have known them. Ron Hutchinson of the Vitaphone Project passed away unexpectedly while I was putting the finishing touches on this volume, so I'd like to give an individual nod to his unparalleled knowledge, enthusiasm, and generosity.

It would have been impossible for me to do this project without the special help of two extremely talented people: Robert Arkus and Marlene Weisman. As he did on *Lame Brains and Lunatics* and *Slapstick Divas* Rob oversaw the transferral and tweaking of this book's images, as well as providing photos from his own collection. His great ideas, superb eye and untiring work were an invaluable contribution and support, going well beyond the call of duty. As she did on *Slapstick Divas*, Marlene designed this fantastic cover. Always creating images that are striking and interesting, I couldn't wait to see what she would come up with for Roscoe. And of course, it's fantastic.

In addition to everyone mentioned above there are the friends, fellow researchers, and film lovers Mike Abadi, Joe Adamson, Mana Allen, Norbert Aping, Lisa Bradbury, Neil Brand, Geoff Brown, Rick De Croix, Kim Deith, John Del Gaudio, Dennis Doros, Joe Eckhardt, David Eickemeyer, Shane Fleming, Paul Gierucki, Valerio Greco, Bob Greenberg, Lisa Stein Haven, Geraldine Hawkins, Mark Heller, Tommie Hicks, Nelson Hughes, Pamela Hutchinson, Rob King, Leonard Maltin, Madeline Matz, Jon Mirsalis, Molly Model, Joe Moore, David Pierce, Jack Roth, Jeni Rymer, Uli Ruedel, Frank Scheide, Randy Skretvedt, Melinda Solan, Yair Solan, Tommy Stathes, David Stenn, Cathy Surowiec, Karl Tiedemann, Lorenzo Tremarelli, Lee Tsiantis, Ed Watz, Bill Weber, Steven Winer and Steve Zalusky.

As far as archives, libraries and research facilities I must first thank my colleagues in the Billy Rose Theatre Collection at the New York Public Library for the Performing Arts at Lincoln Center, especially Tom Lisanti, Jeremy McGraw, David Callahan, Doug Reside and Charlie Morrow. I also want to give big thanks to:

The Museum of Modern Art Department of Film: Dave Kehr, James Layton, Ron Magliozzi, Anne Morra, Rajendra Roy, Josh Siegel Ashley Swinnerton, Katie Trainor, and Peter Williamson.

The Library of Congress: Rob Stone, Mike Mashon, Rosemary Hanes, Dorinda Hartmann, Rachel Del Gaudio, Jenny Paxon, Lynanne Schweighhofer, Zoran Sinobad, Larry Smith, and George Willeman

George Eastman Museum: Nancy Kaufman, Anthony L'Abbate, and Jared Case

Bison Archives: Marc Wanamaker

Academy of Motion Picture Arts and Sciences, Margaret Herrick Library: Rachel Bernstein

EYE Filmmuseum, Netherlands: Elif Rongen-Kaynakci, Catherine Cormon, Mark Paul Meyer, Rixt Johnson, Marlene Labst, Dorette Schooteneijer, and Frederique Urlings

Thank you to Ben Ohmart, John Teehan, Michael J. Hayde, Sandra Grabman, and everyone at BearManor Media for the opportunity to make this volume a reality.

My most important thank you goes to my very patient wife and son, Susan Selig and David Massa, who have always put up with and encouraged my silent comedy obsession. Without their love and support, this study wouldn't have been possible.

Archives Key:

    ACAD – Academy Film Archive, Los Angeles.
    AUS – Filmarchiv Austria, Vienna.
    Berk – U.C. Berkeley Art Museum and Pacific Film Archive, Berkeley.
    BFI – British Film Institute/National Archive, London.
    BRUS – Cinematheque Royale de Belgique/Cinematek, Brussels.
    Buch – Archiva Nationala De Filme, Bucharest.
    Budapest – Hungarian National Film Archive, Budapest.
    CAN – National Film and Sound Archive of Australia, Canberra.
    CNC – Centre National de Cinema et de L'image Animee, Paris
    DAN – Danish Film Institute, Copenhagen.
    ESM – Filmoteca Espanola, Madrid.
    EYE – EYE Filmmuseum, Amsterdam.
    FRANC – Cinematheque Francaise/ Musee de Cinema, Paris.
    FRIU – Cineteca del Friuli, Gemona, Italy.
    GEM – Film Department/George Eastman Museum, Rochester, NY.
    GOS – Gosfilmofond, Moscow.
    ITAL – Fondazione Cineteca Italiana, Milan.
    LOC – Library of Congress, Washington, D.C.
    LOB – Lobster Films, Paris.
    MoMA – The Museum of Modern Art Department of Film, New York.
    MUN – Filmmuseum Munchen, Munich.
    NAZ – Fondazione Centro Sperimentale di Cinematografia – Cineteca Nazionale, Rome.
    NOR – Norwegian Film Institute, Oslo.
    OTT – National Film, Television and Sound Archives, Ottawa.
    QUB – Cinematheque Quebecoise, Montreal.
    UCLA – UCLA Film and Television Archive, Los Angeles.

Chapter 1
Beginnings

Early Life and Career

Roscoe Conklin Arbuckle was born on March 24, 1887 in Smith Center, Kansas on the Great Plains into an early life of poverty and drudgery. The family later moved to California and Roscoe, enamored of the theatre, made his debut at age eight when a replacement was needed for a touring company's local performance. After his mother's death when he was twelve Roscoe was frequently shunted around to various family members, but often fended for himself with multiple odd jobs—at first in hotels or restaurants, then more and more in the theatre. From singing "illustrated songs" with slides he graduated to touring

Roscoe (extreme right) and fellow future film comic Snub Pollard (fourth from left) when they were both members of Ferris Hartman's stage troupe circa 1912.

with various stock companies, where "on the road" in the U.S. and Asia from 1904 to 1913 Roscoe became a well-seasoned performer and comedian. In 1916 he gave this stage career itinerary to the April issue of *Picture Play*:

> *My first experience on the stage was in San Jose, California, in 1904, when I acted as a super on the stage at the request of a hypnotist, who wanted to demonstrate his hypnotic powers. I thought that I made a hit, and decided to take a chance myself. My first venture after this was a ballyhoo with a carnival company, which lasted less than a month.*
>
> *My next experience was a little different. It was singing illustrated songs in San Jose. This job lasted a year, and then I went to Frisco doing the same stunt. From there, I worked all through the Northwest. It was here that I met Leon Errol, the comedian, who persuaded me that I had a voice, ability, and that I would make a good actor. It was he that gave me my first part, and put on my first make-up.*
>
> *I then traveled all through the West with a singing act, working anything from single to quartet. I then put together another act in which I sang and danced. It was in Long Beach that I made my first hit, and it was also there that I met and married Minta Durfee. Naturally, I am still very fond of the town.*
>
> *Since 1908, I have made Los Angeles my headquarters, working from there, taking out little troupes into Arizona and Texas with some success.*

First Films 1909 - 1913

As a popular local performer Roscoe was in the right place at the time when the movies began taking hold in California around 1909. The pioneer Selig Polyscope Company had been formed by Colonel William Selig in Chicago in 1896. By 1908 they began shooting in Los Angeles, and the next year established a permanent West Coast unit under the direction of former stage director Francis Boggs. Selig is best known for its westerns—they established Tom Mix as a cowboy star in the mid-teens, but they also turned out a slew of comedies to round out their program line-up. Roscoe's first film would be a combination of the two genres.

Ben's Kid

Released July 1, 1909. Produced by the Selig Polyscope Co. Directed by Francis Boggs. Photographed by James Crosby. One reel. With Tom Santschi, Roscoe Arbuckle, Harry Todd.

Buck Minor was the most detested man in Wolf Hollow, partly because he was quarrelsome, and partly because he abused and neglected his little wife, Molly, whom all the camp adored. A little baby girl was the only bright spot in Molly's life. When Buck gets into a fight with a cowboy and is beaten in front of the whole camp, he decides to move on.

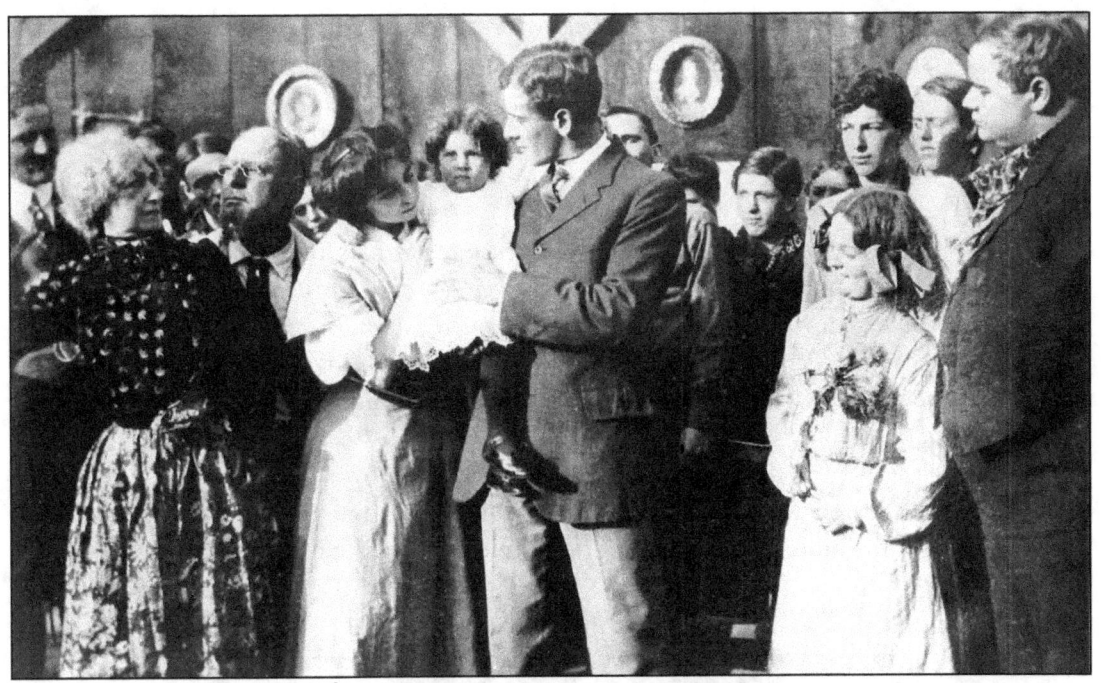

Tom Santschi (middle) in the happy ending of *Ben's Kid* (1909) with Roscoe on the right. Courtesy Sam Gill.

He informs Molly that they are leaving and she must leave the baby behind. When Molly clings to the baby and pleads to take it with them, Buck threatens to kill the child if she won't cooperate. They leave the baby in the cabin and Molly is forced on her horse crying.

Buck has written a note about the baby and on the trail they meet a woman from the camp. Buck gives her the note, which she takes to Judge Honk, the father of the camp and the dispenser of law and justice. A party is organized and quickly reaches the cabin where they find the abandoned baby. Taking it back to town they decide to "raffle off" the youngster—whoever draws the winning card becomes the kid's adopted daddy. Ben Brooks, a good-natured, big-hearted cowpuncher draws the lucky card. Ben has second thoughts, but the cheers of the rest of the bunch brace him up. The baby becomes known as "Ben's kid," and that night in the bunkhouse a half-dozen sleepy cowhands are trying to get some rest as Ben walks the floor with the crying baby. They all take turns trying to distract and entertain it—"Fatty" Carter, the heaviest weight on the range, even does an Indian war dance, but to no avail. In a panic that the kid is sick they send for Judge Honk, who arrives with mustard, and other old-fashioned remedies to bring order to the chaos.

Out on the trail Molly and her husband have traveled until the evening, when Molly puts her plan into action. When Buck falls asleep she sneaks to where the horses are tethered and mounts one to head homeward. Buck hears the sound of the hooves and takes off after her. She gets to the camp ahead of him, but just as she gets to the bunkhouse Buck catches up to her and bursts into the room. The men grab him but he breaks loose and fires at her. Luckily Ben spoils his aim, and the Judge is hit in the arm instead. Howling with pain the Judge orders the men to "hang the varmint" but Buck rushes off.

A year has passed and we find that Buck was caught and strung up. Molly, now a pretty widow, is persuaded to let Ben retain his title to the kid by marrying him. Mr. and Mrs. Brooks tie the knot, getting the good will and best wishes of the entire camp.

The June 1919 issue of *Photoplay* gave this recounting of Roscoe's first venture into movies:

> *It was eleven years ago, nearly, when the late Francis Boggs brought the first motion picture company to Los Angeles. Arbuckle was playing in a little theatre devoted to tabloid musical comedies when a friend who had just started a picture theatre induced him to call on Boggs with the result that he was engaged during his spare time at $5 a day to act in single reel productions.*

Roscoe was comic relief in *Ben's Kid* as "Fatty" Carter—that nickname from the very beginning—and his main scene was his efforts to entertain the crying infant.

The ill-fated Francis Boggs, who brought Roscoe to films.

Director Francis Boggs, the person responsible for bringing Roscoe to films, is a forgotten cinema pioneer, who headed the first film studio in Los Angeles. A stage veteran he joined Selig in Chicago in 1907. Directing all kinds of pictures, but mostly westerns, he went to L.A. in 1909 as general manager of the Western unit but was killed in 1911 when a crazed Japanese gardener at the studio (Frank Minnimatsu) opened fire on studio founder William Selig and Boggs. Selig survived, but Boggs succumbed to his injuries and sadly became a cinema footnote.

Two of Roscoe's fellow performers also became movie regulars. Tom Santschi was another stage performer who hooked up with the Selig Company. Starting in bit roles in 1908 he worked his way up to leading man, and even directed for the studio. In the mid-teens he branched out into features and had a huge success with William Farnum in *The Spoilers* (1914). He remained in demand in pictures such as *Little Robinson Crusoe* (1924), *Paths to Paradise* (1925), *3 Bad Men* (1926), and *Isle of Lost Men* (1928) until his death from a heart attack in 1931.

Harry Todd, like Roscoe, ended up a popular silent comedy player. A vaudevillian who entered films with Essanay in its early days, he joined Selig in 1909 only to return to Essanay the next year to become one of the leads in their successful *Snakeville* comedies. Todd played "Mustang Pete" opposite Margaret Joslin (his real-life wife), Victor Potel, and Augustus Carney as "Alkali Ike." When the series ended in 1916, Todd and Joslin passed through L-Ko before roosting at the fledgling Hal Roach Studio to support Harold Lloyd, Toto, and Stan Laurel. Todd played progressively smaller roles in features like *Fickle Women* (1920), *The Hurricane Kid* (1925), and *It Happened One Night* (1934) up to 1935.

The Billboard (July 3, 1909): "This is a story of rough life on the plains and recites the suffering and final happiness of the wife of a brutal outlaw and their child. It is thrilling and possesses deep pathos."

Moving Picture World (July 10, 1909): "A Selig Western drama which has all the go for which these dramas have become popular and which is reproduced with fidelity to the life environment depicted. The scene where the mother is forced to leave the little one behind is almost too realistic, and when the camp is informed of the circumstances the audience responds to the miner's attempts to straighten out the tangle. Then when the mother mounts her pony and starts back, with her cruel husband in hot pursuit, the audience holds its breath as it watches the race. What was done to the husband is agreed to be no more than he deserved, but, fortunately, the audience is spared the actual scene, which is at it should be. The imagination in most individuals is powerful enough to appreciate what is done under such circumstances without having the scene enacted before them. And the end is happy. Withal it is a satisfactory picture, having ample life and animation to satisfy the most exacting individual."

Mrs. Jones' Birthday

Released August 30, 1909. Produced by the Selig Polyscope Co. ½ reel. (Released with **Winning a Widow**). With Roscoe Arbuckle, Tom Santschi.

It was Mrs. Jones' birthday, and she, womanlike, did not fail to impress this upon her husband's mind as he departed at his customary early hour for work. Excited over the

Roscoe (right) has second thoughts about confronting irate husband Tom Santschi (left) in *Mrs. Jones' Birthday* (1909). Courtesy Sam Gill.

prospect of presenting his better half with a gift benefitting the occasion, he loses his balance as he steps out the front door and rolls pell-mell down a flight of six steps to the street. Picking himself up, he boards a street car, and arriving at his office he goes through his daily routine of business.

At the close of office hours he repairs to John Post & Co.'s crockery establishment, and after much cogitation and repeated questioning, purchases a rather handsome flower pot. Delighted with his choice and anticipating the caress he will receive in return, he takes a street car for home. As he seats himself he is accosted by an old friend. After a reminiscent talk Jones arrives and his destination and alights, forgetting the flower pot. The car speeds on. Poor Jones, recovering his wits and realizing that he dare not return home empty-handed, goes back to the same store and purchases another pot.

Again en route to the street car, while passing a grocery store, Jones is hailed by another old acquaintance. In the good fellowship of this accidental meeting, Jones absentmindedly places his wife's present on the rear end of the grocery wagon nearby. Thereupon the driver departs with his wagon and is out of sight before Jones realizes what has occurred. He gives chase, but to no avail. He glances nervously at his watch. Exasperated and overheated, he rushes back to the store, and to the amazement of the proprietor purchases his third flower pot.

This time he is determined to get safely home; no friend shall balk his way. His street car is in sight, when attention is attracted by a heated altercation between a lady and a taxicab driver, she claiming that she is being overcharged. Now Jones was ever of a chivalrous tendency, and, upon being requested to decide the dispute, proceeds to do so after first placing his precious parcel on the sidewalk near the cab. A few words, and with a satisfied feeling of having accomplished a heroic deed, Jones reaches for his flower pot, but to his consternation finds that the chauffeur has mistaken it for the property of the occupant of the taxicab, and pot and taxi were 'over the hills and far away.'

Half-crazed with his repeated misfortunes, he rushes back to the same store. The clerk is dumbfounded at the reappearance of this monomaniac on flower pots, but sells him another. Poor Jones, his very soul distorted by his anticipated reception of a late arrival home on this eventful day, dashes madly for his street car, when he us startled by a woman who clutches him, not too fondly, but too strongly, and screams into his ears "For God's sake, help me, my husband is killing my mother." Much against his will, unfortunate Mr. Jones is urged into an apartment house.

Inside the house he finds himself battling for life, while he is chased madly about the room by a fiend incarnate, who wields an axe with a dexterity so accurate that Jones decidedly disapproves of accuracy. The woman and her mother flee from the house while he, poor man, makes a hurried departure, smashing his pot, and screaming an athemas on all birthdays.

Bruised, tattered and heartsick, he again slowly wends his way to the now familiar store. "Another of the same kind please," he meekly requests. He at last gets on a car safely, although it is crowded. A workman enters carrying a package, places next to that of Jones' flower pot, and he takes a seat beside our friend. At last Jones reaches his destination, and grabbing the wrong parcel alights. He enters his dining room, much relieved, and inscribing a loving message to his wife, he places it beside what he believes to be his well-earned flower pot.

Calling Mrs. Jones he points with pride to his gift. She embraces him fondly after reading his words of affection, truly meant but unfortunately so inappropriate. For as she discloses the article so carefully wrapped, lo and behold! It is a workingman's teapot, black with soot. Poor Mrs. Jones, expectant all day, resents what she considers a practical joke, and belabors her husband with words well-nigh unspeakable, and leaves the room, vowing that henceforth he is no husband of hers and that she will return to her mother, never again to

Tom Santschi, leading man of numerous Selig films.

be called wife by such as Jones. He, amazed and crestfallen, and disgruntled with the world and himself, swears that birthdays should never exist.

It's said that Roscoe's comedy work on *Ben's Kid* so impressed Francis Boggs and the Selig people that this short was immediately put together for him and built around his talents. Although it's considered lost, the detailed synopsis provided by the studio (included here in total) gives a very strong impression of what the film was like, and as one reads it it's easy to see Roscoe as the harried Mr. Jones.

Moving Picture World (August 9, 1909): "A Selig which might well be called a chapter of errors. If all husbands have had similar experiences, it is too bad to harrow them up with the telling of this story. If they have not, perhaps it will be a warning to them to watch very carefully the birthdays and see that some appropriate gift is at home in time for the event. Not wait, as poor Jones did, until the fateful day arrives, and then have a series of unfortunate accidents overtake one and prevent him presenting the present he intended. It is a tale of woe, indeed, and the fact that Jones meant well, but was pursued by an unkind fate, is the interesting point of the story, and in the telling much dramatic ability is shown and much excellent acting is done. The technical qualities of the film serve to emphasize the picture, making it a pleasure to look at. There is too much truth in it to suit some men, but it is sometimes well to have such shortcomings illustrated, so that the man—the average man—can see what he does and take measures to overcome his characteristics."

Making It Pleasant for Him

Released November 29, 1909. Produced by the Selig Polyscope Co. ½ reel. (Released with ***Brought to Terms***). With Roscoe Arbuckle.

Miss Van Astorbilt is a widow lady with a retinue of servants. She has long promised one of her cousins, a large youth who lives on a farm near Lonesomhurst, L.I., to have him visit her in her New York home.

The long expected day arrives. We see Reuben receive a telegram: "Dear Cousin—Call down at 3, and we will make it pleasant for you." But Miss Van Astorbilt is called away. The servants are instructed to act for her. This does not suit the servants, as they are preparing for the yearly Housemaids' Masquerade: they resent Reuben's intrusion, but decide to obey Madam and make it pleasant for him. And they do, although not necessarily the way she had in mind.

Roscoe's next Selig appearance came three months after *Mrs. Jones Birthday*, and it seems that if it had not been for his busy theatre schedule he very likely would have become one of Selig's regular stable of stars like Tom Santschi, Hobart Bosworth, and George Hernandez. Of course fate had better plans for him, and it would only be three and a half years before he would emerge at the most popular comedy studio in the world.

Moving Picture World (December 11, 1909): "A comedy drama from Selig which clearly portrays the adventures of a country chap who falls into the hands of the servants of his city cousin who has instructed them to make it pleasant for him. No use trying to explain the different methods utilized in this interesting process. The most that can be said is that they succeed admirably in obeying the injunctions of their mistress, and the unsophisticated Rube has the time of his life."

Exhibitor ad for *Making It Pleasant for Him* (1909).

The Sanitarium

Released October 10, 1910. Produced by the Selig Polyscope Co. One reel. With George Hernandez, Hobart Bosworth, Nick Cogley, M.B. Curtis, Miss Williams, Roscoe Arbuckle.

Charley Wise is a young spendthrift who's hard up—owing his landlord as well as other creditors. To escape the heat Charley and his valet Pete decide to skip town and visit the country home of a rich old uncle. Upon arriving Charley finds that Uncle Jim and Aunt Sarah are just heading off on a trip to Europe, and Charley's timely arrival means it's unnecessary to close up the house as he's put in complete charge with Pete as his assistant. Once the old couple is off to Europe Charley heads to the racetrack and loses what little bankroll he had left. Pete hits upon a plan to open uncle's palatial home as a sanitarium and that way collect funds that health seekers are always willing to let loose of.

An ad is run in the papers, and the patients begin to flock. All suffering from all kinds of maladies to being outright looney, Charley is collecting in advance and making a fortune. All is going well until a telegram arrives from Uncle Jim saying that Aunt Sally lost a necklace and that they're coming home this evening to find it. In a panic Charley and Pete clear the house and even have to return all the money. No sooner has everyone gone but a second message arrives saying never mind—the necklace has been found and the oldsters are off to Europe. Sadly Charley is left as badly off as he started.

Roscoe continued to be busy on stage. The October 1, 1910 *San Francisco Dramatic Review* noted:

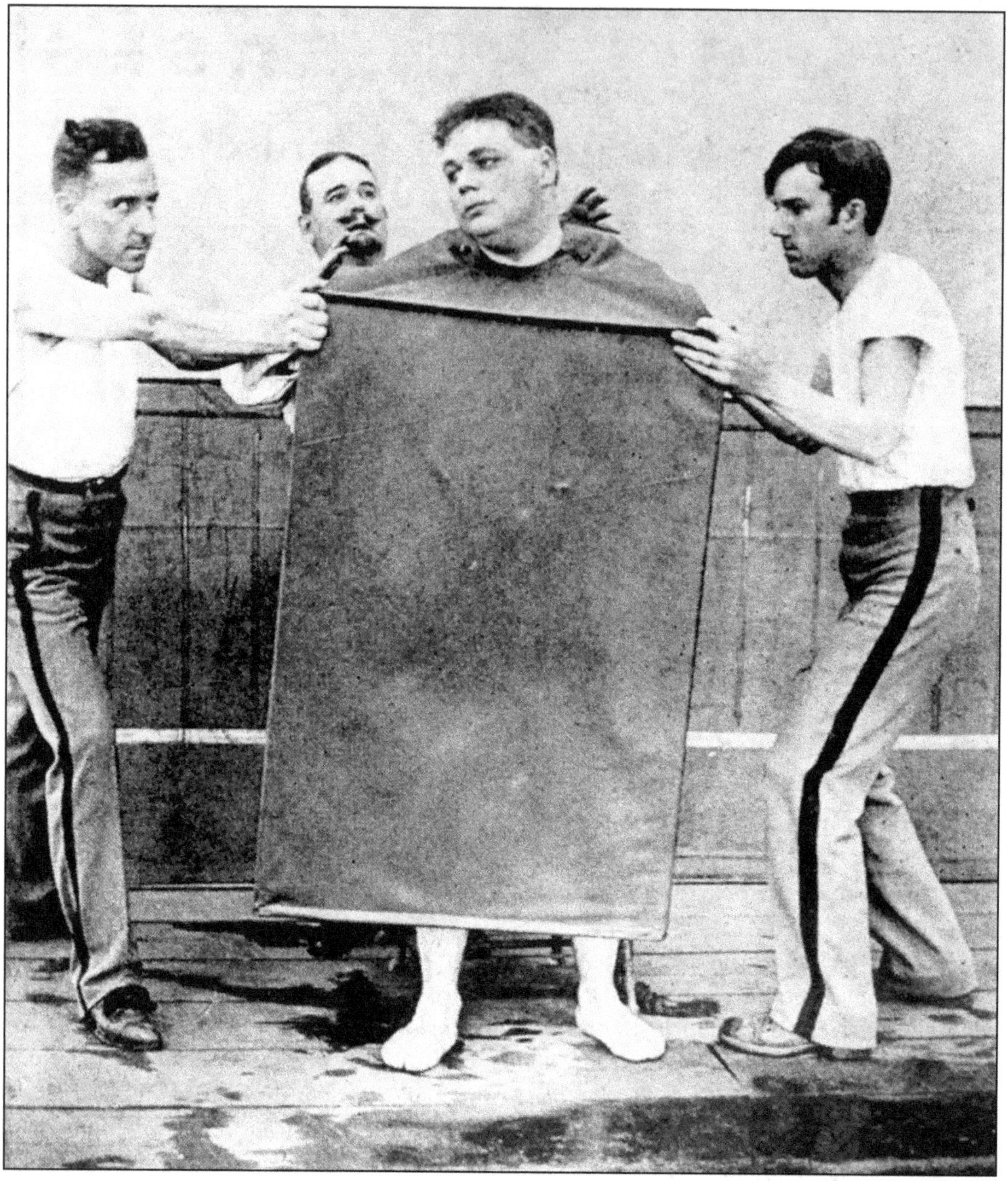

George Hernandez (back) treats Roscoe in *The Sanitarium* (1910). Courtesy Sam Gill.

Roscoe Arbuckle, late of the Princess Musical Comedy Co., played a special engagement in Strongheart at the Burbank Los Angeles, and stole the honors for comedy.

Almost a year went by before he worked again for Selig. This time he's not the lead, but one in the collection of loonies that shows up at George Hernandez's make-shift sanitarium. By this time the studio had developed a strong stock company of West Coast performers.

Two that were the most prominent in *The Sanitarium* are the previously mentioned George Hernandez and Hobart Bosworth. Hernandez was a short, and stout character player who was at home in dramas and westerns, as well as headlining in comedies like *Goody Goody Jones*, *The Millionaire Vagabonds* (both 1912), *A Cure for Carelessness* (1913), and *While Wifey is Away* (1914). Moving on from Selig, he kept busy in features for Triangle, Universal, and Fox right up to his death in 1922.

Hobart Bosworth, Uncle Jim in *The Sanitarium*, was a friend and neighbor of Roscoe's for many years, and was one of the grand old men of the silent American cinema. He came to films for Selig in 1908 from a long career on the stage. As early as 1903 he had achieved stardom on Broadway but due to reoccurring bouts of tuberculosis had to settle out West. After beginning to write scenarios he left Selig in 1913 and started his own company, Hobart Bosworth Productions. In addition to frequently starring in items like *Behind the Door* (1919), he wrote pictures, directed others, and produced many until 1921. From there he became an in demand character actor in big pictures like *Captain January* (1924), *The Big Parade* (1925), *My Best Girl* (1927), *Abraham Lincoln* (1930), and *Steamboat Round the Bend* (1935) making the transition to sound and working until 1942.

The Film Index (October 8, 1910): "Sunny Skies, invigorating breezes laden with the perfume of orange groves and the eucalyptus tree, and all the other beneficent influences that combine to make life a gladsome comedy in the aureate clime of southern California, have evidently put the members of Selig's Los Angeles stock company in the happy mood that finds expression in the desire to make the rest of the world laugh and enjoy the wholesome pleasures of life with them.

Their exuberant, exhilarant mood, in this especial instance, has vented itself in "The Sanitarium," one of those mirthful, silent farce comedies in which the fun is as furious as the action is brisk, and where humorous incident jostles against comical situation with a frequency that makes one's ribs complain loudly against the tyranny of laughter.

The characters in this farcical skit are in the charge of highly capable actors, the principal roles being sustained by such well known people on the legitimate stage as Hobart Bosworth, M.B. Curtis (of

Hobart Bosworth, grand old man of the early cinema.

'Sam'l of Posen" fame), and Miss Williams, the first and last mentioned being formerly prominent members of the Belasco stock company of San Francisco."

Moving Picture World (October 22, 1910): "The picture is acted with spirit and the personality of the Selig players pervades it so strongly that it is especially attractive. It is a comedy which develops its humor through unexpected situations and good acting, and the result is almost one continuous laugh."

The Nickelodeon (October 15, 1910): "The Sanitarium is a sure laugh-producer. The comedy is of a farcical helter-skelter variety; but the acting is good, the complications are swift and surprising; and the result is screamingly funny."

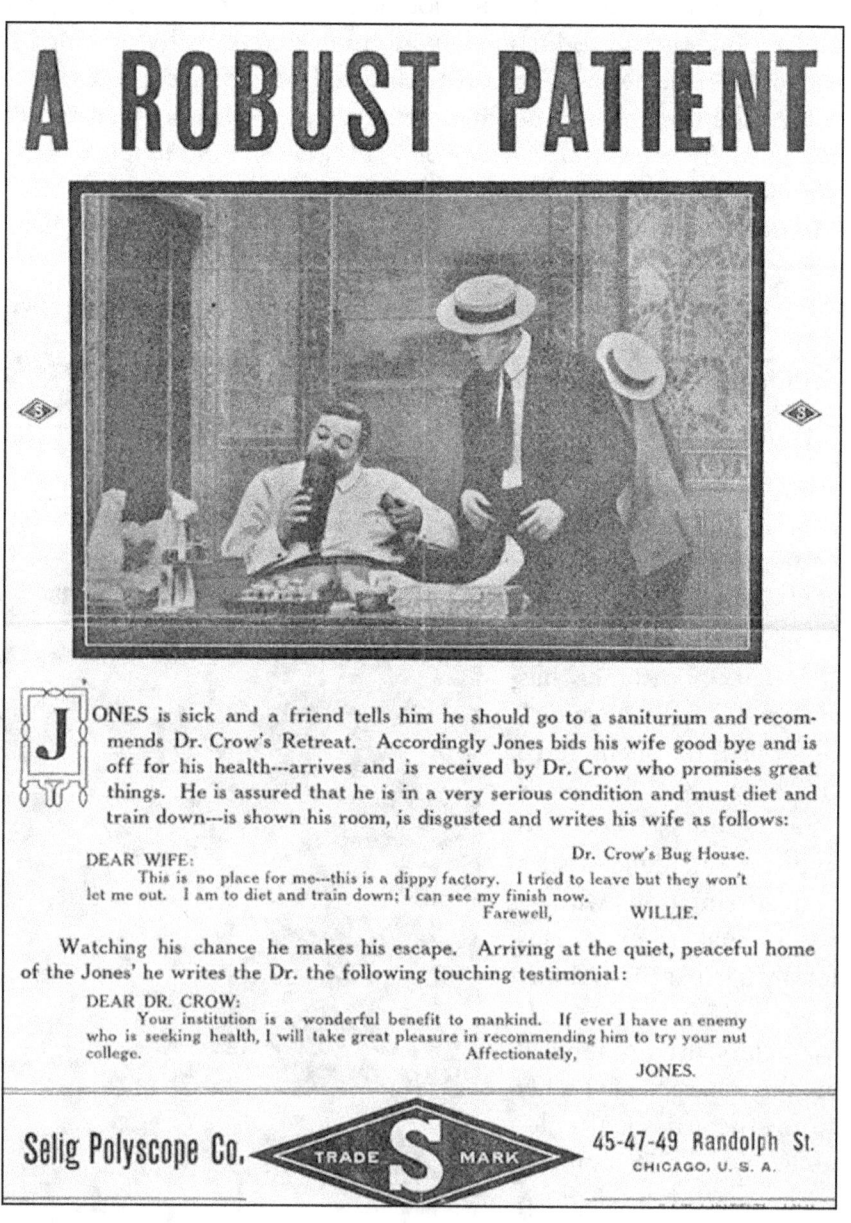

Roscoe and a large sandwich in the Selig Bulletin ad for *A Robust Patient* (1911).

A Robust Patient

Released January 23, 1911. Produced by the Selig Polyscope Co. One reel. With Roscoe Arbuckle, Nick Cogley.

Jones is sick and a friend tells him he should go to a sanitarium and recommends Dr. Crowe's Retreat. Accordingly Jones bids his wife goodbye and is off for his health—arrives and is received by Dr. Crowe who promises great things. He is assured that he is in a very serious condition and must diet and train down—is shown his room, is disgusted and writes his wife as follows:

"Dr. Crowe's Bughouse. Dear Wife: This is no place for me—this is a dippy factory. I tried to leave but they won't let me out. I am to diet and train down; I can see my finish now. Farwell—Willie."

Watching his chance he makes his escape. Arriving at the quiet, peaceful home of the Jones' he writes the Dr. the following touching testimonial:

"Dear Dr. Crowe: Your institution is a wonderful benefit to mankind. If I ever have an enemy who is seeking health, I will take great pleasure in recommending him to try your nut college. Affectionately, Jones.

A Robust Patient followed fairly quickly on the heels of *The Sanitarium*, and again used an insane asylum as a source for laughs but this time gave Roscoe the lead. This

Col. William Selig shares a smoke with one of his employees from the Selig Zoo. Courtesy Sam Gill.

missing film is the definite blueprint for Roscoe's later 1918 Comique short *Good Night Nurse,* where he would expand the story with an extra reel.

A reviewer in the February 11, 1911 *Nickelodeon* didn't like this film or find it funny, but did have a positive note:

> *One detail deserves commendation; in the restaurant scene the actor got away with a vast amount of food without any of the disgusting manners that photoplay comedians often bring to bear on such occasions. We expected to see it come here, but did not and are truly thankful.*

Moving Picture World (February 4, 1911): "A travesty upon sanitariums, which will undoubtedly appeal to a large number. The experiences of this robust patient are humorous, at any rate, and the vigorous way he takes of escaping from his thralldom will add zest to any program."

Motion Picture News (February 11, 1911): "A sturdy fellow feels unwell, bids his wife a fond farewell and sets off for a sanitarium. By a sad mischance he gets into a private lunatic asylum, where he is dieted, trained and all the rest. His trials and tribulations keep everyone laughing."

Alas! Poor Yorick

Released April 21, 1913. Produced by the Selig Polyscope Co. Directed & written by Colin Campbell. ½ reel. (Released with ***Canton, China***). With Wheeler Oakman, Thomas Santschi, Lillian Hayward, Hobart Bosworth, John Lancaster, Frank Clark, Frank Hayes, Roscoe Arbuckle.

At a sanitarium one harmless, but mentally deranged, patient imagines that he is the world's greatest tragedian. He escapes from the grounds. The various theatre managers are notified to be on the lookout for him. This results in numerous complications and many innocent but boastful actors find themselves detained without contracts.

Following his 1912 tour of Asia with the Ferris Hartman Company, Roscoe was back in California looking for work and accordingly stepped up his efforts to get on film. Returning to Selig, this appears to have been his first on screen appearance in female attire, although it's unclear, since the film is currently lost, whether he plays a male actor who's in drag or an actual actress with the acting company of the story. Roscoe in drag was a part of his regular stage repertoire, and it's said that when he heard about the part being open he showed up at Selig in full feminine regalia. The smallish part in this film led to bigger roles at Nestor and Keystone.

Moving Picture World (May 3, 1913): "A fairly amusing picture with a good situation that seemed to give entertainment to the audience. A man who thinks he is an actor has escaped from an asylum, and a well-known manager is notified by the authorities that he may receive a call. A real actor, "at liberty," is mistaken for the crank and has an unpleasant quarter of an hour, but is given a meal ticket. Thomas Santschi plays the crank, and Wheeler Oakman the actor, and both do well. The author and producer is Colin Campbell. The photography is fair."

Tom Santschi and George Hernandez (middle) act away as Roscoe in drag reacts from the left in *Alas! Poor Yorick* (1913). Courtesy Sam Gill.

Almost a Rescue

Released August 8, 1913. Produced by the Nestor Film Co. Distributed by Universal Pictures. Directed by Al Christie. One reel. With Donald McDonald, Roscoe Arbuckle, Irene Hunt, Billie Bennett, Eddie Lyons, Lee Moran, Russell Bassett.

May and Maud Smith are two sisters living in a hall room at Mrs. Prune's. They are out of work and very despondent. So is Jimmie, who occupies the room next to the girls. They are all delinquent in their board bill, and Jimmie tries to steal up to his room without the landlady seeing him, but Mrs. Prune comes out and demands her rent. Jimmie shows her a letter showing that he has prospects of a job, but she wants her money and refuses to allow him in the dining room. He goes to his room and on the way meets the two girls, who were fortunate enough to have had enough money to pay part of their board and thus entitled to a meal. The girls attempt to smuggle Jimmie into the dining room, but the "untimely" appearance of Mrs. Prune frustrates their plan.

Jimmie is sitting in his room, disconsolate and hungry, when he hears voices in the adjoining room. He listens at the door and hears one of the girls exclaim "Here is a way out of our difficulties," and then "It's the only way. Let us dye together." Jimmie does not stop for more, but rushes away for help.

Al Christie and his Nestor Company circa 1915. Courtesy Robert S. Birchard.

And in the meantime—the girls had been reading an advertisement in the newspaper—a want ad—which calls for "two sisters for vaudeville; must have blonde hair, etc." and which brought forth the remarks Jimmie had heard. They decide it is their last hope to relieve their pressing need of money.

Jimmie fails to find a policeman, so rushes to a detective agency and informs Hawkeye, the detective, that two girls are about to commit suicide. Jimmie and Hawkeye, with the latter's "fussies" watch the house, see one of the girls come out and follow her to a drugstore. They are convinced that she has gone to buy the poison. Hawkeye send Jimmie for a doctor, while he and his men follow the girl back to the house. Jimmie arrives about the same time with the doctor, and they all enter the house and creep upstairs to the girl's door. When they burst into their room, they find the girls dying their hair. Explanations ensue, and the disgusted detective leaves with a glaring look from his "hawkeye" meant to wither the frightened Jimmie.

At the moment this is Roscoe's only confirmed appearance for the Nestor Company. As mentioned before he had increased his efforts to obtain film work, and Nestor was a good place for fledgling movie comics. Founded in 1907 by Bayonne, New Jersey businessman David Horsley as Centaur Films, around 1910 it morphed into Nestor and its director and outstanding talent was Al Christie. Christie became one of the biggest names in silent comedy, and although it doesn't have quite the same ring as Mack Sennett or Hal Roach, for thirty years he produced high-quality comedies. At first Christie was turning out a steady stream of little westerns and comedies, having his first success with a 1911 series of live-action Mutt and Jeff shorts. In order to fly under the radar of the Motion Picture Patents Trust the company moved from Bayonne to California.

Distribution through Universal kept them busy turning out an average of two one-reelers a week, so Christie was always on the lookout for talent. Roscoe told the September 1914 *Motion Picture Magazine* that he had been introduced to Christie "by Robert Leonard, a close personal friend." Robert Z. Leonard had come from the stage and became a popular movie actor at Universal and Selig (where he and Roscoe may have gotten friendly). By 1913 he was directing at "Big U," and a recommendation from him would have carried weight with Christie. Leonard later became one of the staff directors at MGM from the 1920s into the 1950s, and was a champion of Buster Keaton during his days of Hollywood "exile"—giving him good roles in *New Moon* (1940) and *In the Good Old Summertime* (1949).

Roscoe's teammates in *Almost a Rescue* included Eddie Lyons and Lee Moran, who at Nestor became the most popular team in silent comedy before Laurel & Hardy. Other stars developed by Christie were Billie Rhodes, Neal Burns, Dorothy Devore, Jimmie Adams, Billy Dooley, and Bobby Vernon. *Almost a Rescue* was released August 8, 1913, about three months after Roscoe's Sennett debut in *The Gangsters*, and it's possible that he did more work for Nestor that's undocumented and lost.

In a side note, another performer who passed through Nestor was Charley Chase, in his real name of Charles Parrott, who appeared in at least *Sophie of the Films #4* (June 26, 1914) on his way to working with Roscoe at Keystone.

Moving Picture World (August 9, 1913): "A lively burlesque farce that has several astonishing situations and makes a good deal of laughter. It deals with some young people (two girls and a man) in a theatrical boarding house in New York, who, it happens, are unable to pay their board bills. The man misunderstands an overheard conversation of the girls and gets some burlesque sleuths on the job with comical results. It is cleverly acted and will amuse."

Luke and Roscoe outside the Keystone Studio main gate. Character comic Harry Booker watches from the other side of the car.

Chapter 2
Mack Sennett Films

ROSCOE'S EARLIEST MOVIE WORK was sporadic, due to his flourishing stage career:

> I worked in Ferris Hartman's Opera Company in 1912; Mr. Hartman is now associated with me in the production of Keystone comedies, you know. Late in 1912, I left his company for a tour of the Orient, which was a big success. I visited Honolulu, Japan, China, Philippines, and Siam, and returned to Los Angeles the last February, 1913.
>
> It was while rehearsing an act for my wife and myself that someone told me that Fred Mace was leaving the Keystone Company, and that there was a good opening. I went and interviewed Mack Sennett, who immediately put me on salary. My first picture was "The Gangsters."

His movie career began in earnest in April of 1913 with the joining of Sennett's Keystone Company. There he appeared in a one-reeler almost every week, and learned film basics from Sennett and Henry "Pathé" Lehrman—two of the most important pioneers of American silent comedy. Roscoe's screen persona rapidly solidified into a moon-faced, innocent, fun-loving fat boy, and while perhaps never as complex a character as Chaplin or Keaton's, he became a huge draw and was loved all over the world. Right off the bat he became known as "The Keystone Fat Boy" and just plain "Fatty." Not surprisingly, Roscoe loathed the moniker, but was stuck with it for the rest of his life.

By 1914 he was directing his shorts himself, and from the beginning showed an easy mastery of setting up and shooting physical action in a clean and precise manner. Soon, in shorts like *That Little Band of Gold* and *Fatty's Tintype Tangle* (both 1915), he was using better developed stories, although the main purpose of his films was to showcase his prowess as a fun-maker. Incredibly light and fast on his feet, he took tremendous falls, and had a dexterity with props that was truly amazing. Since his arrival at Keystone Roscoe had worked frequently with Mabel Normand. In 1915 they were the most popular stars on the lot and their teamwork became official—leading to a series that included *Mabel and Fatty's Married Life*, *Wished on Mabel*, and more. Their films were a slapstick version of the Mr. & Mrs. Sidney Drew comedies as, despite the generous helpings of knockabout,

Roscoe as director still managed to include sly digs and satirical observations on marriage and male-female relationships.

Roscoe became invaluable to the Sennett organization. Besides being big at the box-office, shorts like *Fatty and Mabel Adrift* (1916) show him to be the most skillful director on the lot, and as early as August of 1914 whenever Sennett would be away on business Roscoe would take over as director-general of the Keystone plant. In 1916 he had the opportunity to work away from the Sennett lot at Triangle's East Coast studio and there made his most mature shorts yet—*The Waiter's Ball, His Wife's Mistake*, and particularly *He Did and He Didn't* (with its combination of dramatic feature lighting, camera work, and adult situations rarely seen in a comedy short). This taste of creative freedom made him realize that to continue to develop, artistically and financially, he had to leave Sennett.

1913

The Gangsters

Released May 29, 1913. Produced by Mack Sennett for the Keystone Film Co. Distributed by the Mutual Film Corp. Directed by Henry Lehrman. Working title: **The Feud**. One reel. Extant: MoMA. With Roscoe Arbuckle, Fred Mace, Evelyn Quick (Jewel Carmen), Nick Cogley, Rube Miller, Bill Hauber, Charles Avery, Edgar Kennedy, Grover Ligon.

The local gang leader has an "understanding" with the police force, so it's live and let live until officer Roscoe makes time with the leader's "moll." Swearing vengeance, the gang starts a campaign where every cop they see is de-pants and beaten up, starting with Roscoe. He gets his revenge by putting a dummy officer on a barge in the canal, and when the gang goes after it the real police close in and a battle royal takes place in the water.

Since this is Roscoe's first comedy for Sennett we're lucky that the Museum of Modern Art in New York has a beautiful 35mm print of this milestone in his career. For many years much misinformation has been written about this film—mostly stating that Roscoe had only a small part, and was really more or less a glorified extra. All of this couldn't be further from the truth. Roscoe really co-stars in this film with Fred Mace, and even has more footage and business than Mace. Roscoe takes focus whenever he's on the screen, and it's amazing that his "Fatty" character is already well developed at this early date. It seems that he understood what was needed for acting on the screen from the beginning, as he's very relaxed and underplays his scenes in his usual manner.

Like Charlie Chaplin, Roscoe's first Sennett comedies were directed by Henry "Pathé" Lehrman (more on him in *Help! Help! Hydrophobia*). His co-star is Fred Mace, who was, along with Mabel Normand, Ford Sterling, and Mack Sennett, one of the original Keystone stars. He started working in films in 1909 for the Biograph Company after a long career on stage where he happened to work with Sennett, who began headlining Mace in his early Biograph directorial efforts such as *Josh's Suicide* (1911) and *Algy the Watchman* (1912). Becoming a comedy sensation at Keystone, after *The Gangsters* he moved out to do his own series for Majestic and Apollo (opening the debate that Arbuckle had been hired to replace Mace), but didn't have the same kind of success. Having never developed a regular

Thug Fred Mace (center) is about to lambast Roscoe as fellow officers Nick Cogley, Bill Hauber, Grover Ligon, and Charles Avery try to intervene in *The Gangsters* (1913). Courtesy the Academy of Motion Picture Arts and Sciences.

The overlooked Fred Mace. Author's collection.

comic persona, Mace was a versatile character comic, adept at playing everything from punch drunk prizefighters to effeminate mama's boys. A return to the Sennett fold in 1915 didn't jump start his career again, and he died of a stroke in early 1916 while planning a new film venture.

The Gangsters' attractive blonde leading lady is Evelyn Quick, who appeared in many 1912-1913 Keystones such as *The Professor's Daughter* and *A Strong Revenge* (both 1913). Not long after the release of this film Ms. Quick was involved in a case as one of a number of underage girls who were entertaining men at the Vernon and Venice Country Clubs. For some reason this sent Sennett and the bulk of the Keystone male comics to location shooting in Mexico until the whole thing blew over. After appearing in some L-Ko Comedies like *The Jailbird's Last Flight* and *Ignatz's Icy Injury* (both 1916), she changed her name to Jewel Carmen and became a popular foil for Douglas Fairbanks in four features that included *Flirting with Fate* and *American Aristocracy* (both 1916). She married director Roland West, and appeared in his *Nobody* (1921) and *The Bat* (1926), which was her last picture. Later a business partner with West (by then her ex-husband) and his girlfriend Thelma Todd in the restaurant Thelma Todd's Sidewalk Café, she retired from the public eye after the investigation into Todd's mysterious death, and died in her eighties in 1984.

Moving Picture World (May 5, 1913): "An amusing burlesque of gang fighters. The police go after them, one by one, and each guardian of the peace is caught and despoiled of his clothing and compelled to return to the station."

Moving Picture World: (May 31, 1913): "Fred Mace appears as the leader of a gang of toughs, who make things lively for the police force. A pastime of the gang is stripping trousers from the members of the force. This renders the film a little rough for presentation in some houses."

Passions, He Had Three

Released June 5, 1913. Produced by Mack Sennett for the Keystone Film Co. Distributed by the Mutual Film Corp. Directed by Henry Lehrman. Working title: **Country Boy**. ½ reel. (Released with **Help! Help! Hydrophobia!**). With Roscoe Arbuckle, Beatrice Van, Charles Avery, Nick Cogley, Alice Davenport, Rube Miller.

Henry is a big, fat country boy with three passions. He likes eggs, milk and girls. He steals the eggs from their nests, sucks their contents, and refills the shells with water. When the family sit down to breakfast and shells are broken the crime is discovered and Farmer Jones places a big bear trap, covered with straw, in front of the nests. Henry sees this done, however, and says nothing.

Henry weighs about 260 pounds. The Jones' cow, Loretta, seems suddenly to have gone dry. Of course Henry does not tell them that he has been making secret visits to Loretta with a cup.

Henry is also in love with Jenny Brown. Si Black is also enamored of the fair Jenny. Si only weighs about 102 pounds, and when the rivals become engaged in a physical conflict it looks dark for Si until he practices a new kind of Jui Jitsu on the stomach of his foe. For the nonce Henry accepts defeat, but turns the tables on Si when he lures him to the concealed

Roscoe is caught sucking eggs by Nick Cogley, Beatrice Van, Alice Davenport, Rube Miller, and Charles Avery in *Passions, He Had Three* (1913). Courtesy the Academy of Motion Picture Arts and Sciences.

bear trap and pushes him onto it. The jaws close upon poor Si's legs, and Henry calls everyone to come and see the captured egg thief.

Passions, He Had Three was only Roscoe's second appearance for Mack Sennett but he was already making a definite impression. In the editorial *A Contrast in Comedy*, from the

July 26, 1913 issue of *Exhibitors' Times*, the writer "R.R." talks about a recent experience of seeing an average "thriller" at a cinema where he and the audience were:

> *…bored—exceedingly bored. I reached for my hat, and my eye sought the nearest exit.*
>
> *Suddenly I stopped. On the screen a shaking, mirth-provoking mountain of rotundity in the shape of a country yokel was solemnly piercing and sucking an egg, after which he carefully replaced it in its nest. They were showing Keystone's "Passions—He Had Three." Our corpulent rustic had three passions: eggs, milk and—what could be more logical? —girls. The fun bubbled. It gurgled. It effervesced. It squeezed rapturous chuckles out of the spectators. The delicious buffoonery of that fat rascal made us fairly wriggle for joy. Humor emanated from every crease of his double chin and from every dimple of his inflated cheeks. The story was slight. You could hardly call it a story. It was a winsome episode of farm life, with the farmer's pretty daughter and a dried up little rival involved, not forgetting the eggs, the milk and Fatty. It had the smell of the soil. The sincere, homely good-humor was contagious and snuggled right into the hearts of the onlookers. A veritable oasis in this desert of long drawn-out, stupid series of chases and counter-chases labeled "melodrama," its only fault was its brevity.*
>
> *It was a splendid example of those comedies which depend upon their character delineation and apparent spontaneity for their humor, in contrast to that class wherein a carefully thought-out plan of action is made to serve the same purpose. What one attains by its rugged fun and characterization the other accomplishes by ingenuity or charm of plot. Both methods have been*

"Keystone Fat Boy" portrait of Roscoe.

> *used and abused by motion picture producers. For, it is a truism that a good comedy, free of horse-play and suggestiveness, is a mighty hard thing to do—much harder than a straight drama.*

The author goes on to talk about the July 12, 1913 Vitagraph comedy *The Moulding* as an example of a successful example of the more "sophisticated" mode of comedy, and says in summation:

> *In the two photo plays quoted we have what may be regarded as examples of each class of the one and split-reel comedies as nearly ideal as we have approached at present. It seems that producers these days are having a hard time turning out original comedies that are free of the taint of European sensualism and Western horse-play. A comedy that is fresh, wholesome and not insipid is a rarity. Too often we find the they-love-they-quarrel-they-kiss kind hashed and rehashed with sickening regularity to fit various studio personalities.*
>
> *In "Passions—He Had Three," there is the broad Falstaffian fun with the human touch of "The Merry Wives of Windsor" and portions of Moliere. Of course, the motion picture director is laboring under the great handicap in being unable to produce (at present) sparkling dialogue, so he attempts to overcome this by rapid action and clever pantomime. The natural result is that novelty and adroitness of plot are what must be sought after.*

Moving Picture World (June 7, 1913): "The fat boy again appears in this. The milking scene will not appeal to refined audiences. There is not much motive to the story, which appears on the same reel with above (*Help! Help! Hydrophobia!*)"

Help! Help! Hydrophobia

Released June 5, 1913. Produced by Mack Sennett for the Keystone Film Co. Distributed by the Mutual Film Corp. Directed by Henry Lehrman. Working title: **The Chemist**. ½ reel (released with **Passions He Had Three**). With Roscoe Arbuckle, Beatrice Van, Nick Cogley.

The professor does not approve of his daughter's suitor. His disapproval is so marked that it is finally noticed by said swain—Jim Brown—when he is kicked out of the house by the father of his lady love, and he resolves to be careful in the future and not be subjected to further indignities.

The professor has been experimenting with germs, and discovers some new and deadly ones which he exhibits to some of his medical friends. The germs have been raised in a culture of milk, and when the professor escorts his guests to the door the milk bottle and the cup are left on the table.

Unfortunately Jim Brown seized this particular moment to make a call on his lady love, accompanied by his dog, making his entrance through an open window. The dog is thirsty, so he innocently pours milk into the cup and gives it to the animal. The professor,

Beatrice Van, Roscoe, and pup in *Help! Help! Hydrophobia* (1913). Courtesy Sam Gill.

returning, sees what is taking place, and crying: "The dog is full of deadly germs," runs away. The dog, attracted by the queerly acting, screaming man, runs after him, and soon there is tremendous excitement, half the town running with the professor, and the others running after him and the dog. After many narrow escapes from the deadly teeth of the dog, the professor reaches a place of safety.

Although generally dismissed today as a sort of second-string Mack Sennett, Henry Lehrman was an important pioneer of American silent comedy and one of the biggest comedy producers of the teens. By all accounts he was also a callous individual who was nicknamed "Suicide" by the comics who worked for him due to the cavalier way he had of putting them in physical danger. Having Lehrman as your first film director must have been something like a baptism of fire for Roscoe and Chaplin, but they both became excellent comedy directors in their own right, as did other Lehrman fledglings like Jack White and Norman Taurog.

Lehrman had been born in Austria in 1883, and later spun dubious accounts of a wealthy steel manufacturer father and having been a lieutenant in the Austrian army. But according to legend he was working as either a movie usher or a streetcar conductor in New York when he presented himself at the Biograph Studio as a director from the Pathé Frères company of France. It was soon apparent to everyone that he had never been inside a studio before, leading D.W. Griffith to dub him "Pathé," but he was kept on and soon became Mack Sennett's right-hand man—first in the comedies Sennett directed at Biograph, and then in the formation of Keystone, where Lehrman was influential in creating the studio's style and maintaining the output.

Roscoe would work under Lehrman's direction sporadically, until the latter left Sennett's employ in early 1914. Going to his own units like L-Ko (Lehrman Knock-Out) and Fox Sunshine Comedies, Lehrman would remain friendly with Roscoe, and their paths would continue to cross. In 1919 it was announced that Roscoe would share a studio that Lehrman had constructed in Culver City, and Roscoe did end up renting space. More ominously it was Lehrman's long-time girlfriend, Virginia Rappe, who died after Roscoe's 1921 Labor Day party, leading to Lehrman grand-standing in the press and calling for Arbuckle's blood. His egocentric nature and continual clashes with his backers led to

Lehrman's bankruptcy in the early 1920s and the end of his glory days as a producer. Later he bounced around from job to job, directing shorts and mostly program features, eventually finding a berth as a sort of jack-of-all-trades trouble-shooter and advisor for Darryl F. Zanuck at 20th Century-Fox. He died in 1946 and was buried next to Virginia Rappe.

Moving Picture World (June 7, 1913): "Some mad dogs and a scared fat boy combine to bring about a series of wild happenings in this half reel. Trained Boston bulldogs are employed to good advantage in this."

Silent comedy pioneer and innovator Henry Lehrman.

The Waiter's Picnic

Released June 7, 1913. Produced by Mack Sennett for the Keystone Film Co. Distributed by the Mutual Film Corp. Directed by Mack Sennett. Working title: ***The Chef***. One reel. With Ford Sterling, Mabel Normand, Roscoe Arbuckle, Nick Cogley, Bert Hunn, Bill Hauber, Max Asher, Alice Davenport.

Louis, the chef, and Oscar, the head waiter, are in love with Mabel, the pretty cashier. The Waiter's Picnic is held, and Mabel is the cause of much trouble between Louis and Oscar. Mabel accidentally falls over a high bank and Louis, in attempting to rescue her, falls over too. Oscar and the other picnickers rush to the scene, and by means of a human rope pull Mabel up. Louis is left to his fate, but by superhuman efforts manages to near the top, when Oscar pushes him back again.

That night the headwaiter makes things as unpleasant as possible for the chef, and the latter retaliates by sending out some weird concoctions from his kitchen, causing the patrons to heap maledictions upon Oscar. The chef finally decides to gain a terrible revenge by killing his rival, so he prepares a seemingly appetizing dish, which is liberally sprinkled with poison. It looks so good that the headwaiter presents it to Mabel, who is about to go home, and she wraps a napkin about it and goes out.

Louis waits until the poison should have taken effect and then enters the dining room to gaze at his dead enemy. He is surprised to see Oscar serenely walking about, and when he learns what has occurred he bolts for the door and rushes madly down the street. Police and pedestrians attempt to stop the supposed mad man, but he bowls over every one in his path and continues on his flight, pursued by a howling mob. He arrives at Mabel's home in time

Alice Davenport and Mabel Normand can't believe that Ford Sterling's ear is being gnawed on in *The Waiter's Picnic* (1913). Courtesy The Museum of Modern Art.

to prevent the family eating the poisoned food, and then falls into the hands of Oscar who administers a well merited beating.

The Waiter's Picnic marks the momentous occasion of the first on-screen pairing of Roscoe and Mabel Normand, who would not only become his important screen partner but a life-long friend. The most famous woman of silent comedy, who was both clown and leading lady, Mabel began her career as a model for commercial ads, lantern slides, and photo-postcards. Being in New York with the fledgling movie industry all around her it was only a matter of time before she ended up in films. This occurred in 1910 for the Vitagraph and Biograph companies where her spontaneous and spunky personality soon made her an audience favorite. When Sennett set up his own studio in 1912 Mabel became "the sugar on the Keystone grapefruit."

At the time that Roscoe joined the outfit in 1913 Mabel was something new in comedy heroines—pretty and sweet per regulation but with an independence and feistiness that enabled her to give back as good as she got in any slapstick proceeding. Onscreen Roscoe and Mabel had an instant rapport, and in twenty-six screen appearances together they went from playing innocent farm boy and girlfriend to more middle-class husband and wives. Their last film together would be 1916's *The Bright Lights*, and while they'd have success in features ironically both of their careers were seriously hampered by scandal.

Their lives also ended far too early—and just three years apart. But luckily films like *A Noise from the Deep* (1913), *The Sea Nymphs* (1914), *That Little Band of Gold* (1915), and *Fatty and Mabel Adrift* (1916) survive so they can be seen at their peak.

Moving Picture World (June 21, 1913): "This full reel Keystone offering shows us a waiter's picnic at the beginning. Mabel falls from a cliff and Ford has a hard time rescuing her. The scene shifts to a hotel where she is cashier and he is chef. He "doctors" the food ordered by a rival. Some amusement in this, but it is not exceptionally good."

A Bandit

Released June 23, 1913. Produced by Mack Sennett for the Keystone Film Co. Distributed by the Mutual Film Corp. Directed by Mack Sennett. ½ reel. Shot in Tijuana, Mexico. Extant: LOB. (Released with **Peeping Pete**). With Roscoe Arbuckle, Nick Cogley, Beatrice Van, Bill Hauber, Charles Avery, Bert Hunn, Rube Miller, Arthur Tavares.

Willy is a rather effeminate young man, and is abused by the town bully. He suspects that the bully is a coward at heart, so he disguises himself as a bandit and shoots up the town. Everybody, including the sheriff, flees in terror, and their consternation is ludicrous when they discover that the terrible bandit is none other than harmless Willy.

The leading lady in this and three other of Roscoe's first Sennett comedies was the blonde and pretty Beatrice Van. With no previous acting experience she became an

Roscoe, Nick Cogley (right of middle) and other townsfolk keep an eye on the titular *A Bandit* (1913). Courtesy the Lobster Collection.

Beatrice Van as the star of the American Film Company's *Beauty Comedies* such as 1915's *When His Dough Was Cake*.

ingénue at Keystone and would eventually become a busy screen writer. In 1978 she told film historian Sam Gill:

> After being an extra in several films, I was given the chance to play the lead in several split-reel pictures, the first one playing opposite Roscoe Arbuckle. I recall the film was titled "Passions, He Had Three" although at the time, I don't think any of these pictures were given titles, only after they were made and released.

After a very brief stint with Sennett she moved on to Universal where she appeared in many of their Powers, Nestor, and Victor brand comedies, in addition to dramas for Rex and Bison. Soon she was headlining the American Film Manufacturing Co.'s *Beauty Comedies*, but by the end of the teens her focus had changed to writing.

In the 1920s she was a full-time screenwriter, penning features for Bessie Love, Doris May, Reginald Denny, and Laura La Plante, as well as shorts for Mr. & Mrs. Carter De Haven, the *Fighting Blood* series, *Bill Grimm's Progress*, and Fox's *O. Henry Stories*. She even had a run at the Hal Roach Studio on shorts such as *Along Came Auntie*, and Mabel Normand's *Raggedy Rose* (both 1926). When sound arrived she remained busy, writing the dialogue for the 1930 version of the musical *No, No Nanette*, and worked with Roscoe again when she provided scripts for two of the *Gay Girls* two-reelers he directed, *Take Em and Shake Em* (1931) and *Gigolettes* (1932), for RKO-Pathé. Her career eventually wound down and she retired after the Bela Lugosi thriller feature *Night of Terror* (1933) and the Andy Clyde short *Super Snooper* (1934).

As mentioned in the entry for *The Gangsters*, the arrest of the teenage Evelyn Quick sent Mack Sennett and a unit scurrying to Tijuana, Mexico for a couple of weeks. Beatrice Van was part of this group and was told that they were going on location to San Diego, but they ended up "south of the border." Van later elaborated to Sam Gill:

> *It was not until we reached Tijuana, and after Mabel and I were settled into our room, that Mabel explained the real reason we were in Mexico rather than San Diego. Mabel said that an underage girl who had been working at Keystone—a girl by the name of Evelyn Quick—had had sexual relations with several of the males among the Keystone comedians, that she had been arrested by the police, and was "naming names" as Mabel explained it.*

Van added that Mabel, angry about being hijacked to Mexico, refused to work, so Van got to be the female lead. Three, and perhaps four, shorts were made during this Mexican stay—the Henry Lehrman-directed *Out and In* (June 19, 1913), *A Bandit* (June 23, 1913), *Peeping Pete* (June 23, 1913), and maybe *Rastus and the Game Cock*. Beatrice Van remembered a fourth film, and although *Rastus* was released later on July 3, 1913, it seems likely as its main event is a cockfight, which were illegal in California. The Evelyn Quick incident soon blew over and the unit returned to Hollywood.

Moving Picture World (June 28, 1913): "This, on the same reel with above (*Peeping Pete*), is about equal merit. The fat man with flirting proclivities, is pursued by a rival made up as a bandit. The plot is very slight indeed."

Peeping Pete

Released June 23, 1913. Produced by Mack Sennett for the Keystone Film Co. Distributed by the Mutual Film Corp. Directed by Mack Sennett. Working title **The Peep Hole**. ½ reel. Shot in Tijuana, Mexico. Extant: LOB. (Released with **A Bandit**). With Mack Sennett, Ford Sterling, Roscoe Arbuckle, Nick Cogley, Beatrice Van, Charles Avery, Edgar Kennedy, Bill Hauber, Bert Hunn, Arthur Tavares, Rube Miller, Hank Mann.

Mack Sennett ignores wife Roscoe's pleadings in *Peeping Pete* (1913). Courtesy the Lobster Collection.

Jack and Pete are the terrors of the town. Pete is bored with his large wife and peeps through a knothole in the fence as Mrs. Jack is combing her hair. Jack catches him and resents this. After many threats, much stalking, and some shooting at each other, the men finally come together, and to the surprise of the people, sit down and have a drink together.

Peeping Pete is Roscoe's first Keystone outing in drag, playing the overweight and neglected wife of Mack Sennett's fence-hole peeper. He spends most of the short taking some tremendous falls while trying to get away from the firing gunmen, especially when "she" is shot in the rear-end while doing her laundry.

Mack Sennett shares the lead with Ford Sterling, and acquits himself very well as actor and director. Sennett always liked to portray himself as a just a country boob or an unsophisticated ex-boilermaker. Many of his former employees later played into this myth, practically painting him as some kind of film comedy idiot savant. The truth is that Sennett had much experience in different levels of show business before he even entered the movies. He learned filmmaking from D.W. Griffith and Frank Powell, and for about twenty years was a savvy producer who had his finger on the pulse of what audiences found funny (or at least his derrière, as it was said that if he rocked in his rocking chair while previewing a film it was funny—if he didn't, it wasn't).

Besides his eye for talent, Sennett's major accomplishment was that he took the principles of the early French comedies and set up the first assembly-line to mass produce Hollywood slapstick shorts. There he created the template for the genre and established most of the big comics of the era, almost all of whom, like Roscoe, would eventually leave him for greater fame and fortune.

Moving Picture World (June 28, 1913): "A half reel in which Ford Sterling and Mack Sennett appear as "bad men." One rouses the ire of the other by peeping through a knothole at a woman making her toilet. Fairly amusing."

For the Love of Mabel

Released June 30, 1913. Produced by Mack Sennett for the Keystone Film Co. Distributed by the Mutual Film Corp. Directed by Henry Lehrman. Working title: ***The Melo-Drama***. One reel. With Mabel Normand, Roscoe Arbuckle, Charles Avery.

Mabel loves her fat sweetheart Bob. Harry, a desperate lover, captures Bob and ties him to a fence and presents him with a dynamite bomb with a burning fuse. Mabel so indignantly spurns Harry that he ties her to the other side of the fence. After a series of thrilling burlesque melodramatics, the villain is thwarted so that Mabel and Bob are saved.

A key member of the early Keystone stock company was the 5'4" Charles Avery. Chicago-born and a long-time stage veteran—Avery had spent twelve years under the management of Charles Frohman, playing large roles in *Charley's Aunt* and *The*

Mabel Normand scuffles with Charles Avery (left) and Dave Anderson (behind) in a re-release lobby card from *For the Love of Mabel* (1913). Courtesy Sam Gill.

The born old Charles Avery.

Clansman, and supporting the stars William Faversham and W.H. Crane. He became a member of the Biograph company under D.W. Griffith in 1907, and appeared in many of Sennett's first directorial efforts for the company such as *The Brave Hunter, Algy the Watchman, The Would-Be Shriner,* and *Katchem Kate* (all 1912).

Avery worked at Bison and Nestor before becoming an early Keystone regular in 1912. Appearing constantly in support he began directing in 1915, helming many of Syd Chaplin's *Gussle* comedies and the *Hogan* series starring Charlie Murray, as well as *Beating Hearts and Carpets, A Submarine Pirate* (both 1915), and *A Modern Enoch Arden* (1916). Leaving Keystone in 1916 to direct at L-Ko, he also directed shorts for Triangle, Roach, Universal, Romayne, and Vitagraph that included *The Bookworm Turns* (1917), *A Kaiser There Was* (1919), and *The Applicant* (1921). Near the end of his career he returned to acting with small roles in features such as *The Blackbird* (1926), *The Rambling Ranger,* and *The Western Rover* (both 1927). Avery may have been a suicide when he died at fifty-three in 1926.

Auburn New York Citizen (August 22, 1913): "Keystone breaks loose again in another reel of nonsense. The spurned lover catches the lucky one, ties him to a fence along with a lighted dynamite bomb. Mabel throws the villain down so hard that she is tied to the other side of the fence. The couple are rescued after a series of indescribable incidents."

Rastus and the Game Cock

Released July 3, 1913. Produced by Mack Sennett for the Keystone Film Co. Distributed by the Mutual Film Corp. Directed by Mack Sennett. Working title: **The Cock Fight**. One reel. May have been shot in Tijuana, Mexico. Extant: LOC, CAN. With Ford Sterling, Nick Cogley, Charles Avery, Mack Sennett, Bill Hauber, Rube Miller, Bert Hunn, Charles Avery, Edgar Kennedy, Roscoe Arbuckle.

Rastus wants to go to the cockfight, so he steals a chicken and sells it to his wife. It is then discovered that Rastus has unintentionally stolen the wrong chicken—the champion game one, and Rastus tries to get back the fowl in order to win the reward offered. He barely saves it from the descending axe, but in the end there are so many claimants for the reward that the owner of the chicken refuses to pay anyone.

British Keystone poster featuring Ford Sterling.

Edgar Kennedy gives Roscoe a hard time in *A Bath House Beauty* (1914).

As you would expect from the title character's name this is a blackface comedy with most of the cast "corked-up", although Roscoe isn't and appears as his usual self in a small bit watching the cockfight. Ethnic stereotypes were a staple at Keystone—not just black characters, but Irish, German, and Jewish. In fact, half of the very first Keystone program of split-reelers was *Cohen Collects a Debt* (1912) with Ford Sterling as the title Jewish character. Sterling routinely played Jewish or German types in shorts like *Hoffmeyer's Legacy* (1912), *Toplitsky and Co.*, and *Cohen Saves the Flag* (both 1913). Roscoe spent time blacked up in films such as *That Minstrel Man* (1914), and treaded into Jewish territory with *The Riot*, *His Sister's Kids* (both 1913), and *Rebecca's Wedding Day* (1914). The studio also made fun of policemen, country rubes, ministers, criminals, scholars, and race car drivers, so in its attitude that everyone and everything was fair game for laughs Keystone was an equal opportunity abuser.

Spectating at the cock fight along with Roscoe was Edgar Kennedy, who was a fixture in practically every Keystone short during this period. Later famous for his "slow-burn," where he would get aggravated and rub his bald dome of a head, at this point Kennedy was learning the movie business and was young, trim, and even sports a full head of hair. After an early career as a boxer, he toured on stage in musical comedies, and made his film debut in Chicago for Selig in *Brown of Harvard* (1911). Still occasionally boxing, his entrée at Keystone is said to have come through Fred Mace who at the time was arranging bouts for Kennedy. Edgar told a somewhat different story in the May 31, 1933 issue of *Film Daily*:

> *My next hunch was to become a movie actor. So I went to the Mack Sennett studio and pestered the casting director until he almost had me arrested. Finally he told me that I'd never make an actor in a thousand years. That burned me up. So I told him that if I wasn't a good actor, I was still a good fighter and could lick any fourteen men in his or any other studio. Mack Sennett overheard the boastful remark. With a funny grin on his face he told me to report for work in the morning.*
>
> *I was there bright and early. Sennett had set the "stage" for me. It was a prizefight ring and on benches around it sat fourteen of the ugliest bruisers I had ever seen. They had been recruited from the labor gang. Everyone from the studio was there to see the fun. "There you are pug," said Sennett. "Lick the fourteen of them and you can work for me."*
>
> *Well, I don't like to appear conceited, but I went to work for Sennett the next day as a Keystone Cop.*

Between 1913 and 1919 he appeared in over sixty Sennett films that included *Bangville Police* (1913), *The Star Boarder* (1914), *Fatty's Tintype Tangle* (1915), and *Hearts and Flowers* (1919).

In 1917 he began making the rounds of the other comedy units like L-Ko, Fox, Educational, and Arrow Mirthquake shorts, and appeared in features such as *Skirts* (1921), *Paths to Paradise* (1925), *The Better 'Ole*, and *Oh What a Nurse!* (both 1926). He even directed shorts at Fox, Sennett, and Universal—*Step Lively, Please* (1922), *The Marriage Circus* (1925), *Olga's Boatman*, and *Do or Diet* (both 1926) are just a few. In 1928 Kennedy joined the Hal Roach Studio where his short-fused and long-suffering persona really developed, and some of his most memorable Roach appearances are *Leave 'Em Laughing*, *Limousine Love* (both 1928), *A Pair of Tights*, *Hurdy Gurdy*, and *Dad's Day* (all 1929).

1931 saw him begin his popular series of *Average Man* two-reelers for RKO which continued for seventeen years until his death. Between the shorts he was busy in features such as *Duck Soup*, *Diplomaniacs* (both 1933), *A Star is Born* (1937), and *Anchors Away* (1945). At the very end of his career he became part of the Preston Sturges' stock company and had excellent roles tailored to his talents in *The Sin of Harold Diddlebock* (1947) and

Unfaithfully Yours (1948). In demand to the very end, the only thing that stopped Edgar from going on to be a hit on television was the throat cancer that killed him at fifty-seven in 1948.

Daily News (Frederick, Maryland) (July 21, 1913): "A reel that is real funny."

Safe in Jail

Released July 7, 1913. Produced by Mack Sennett for the Keystone Film Co. Distributed by the Mutual Film Corp. Directed by Mack Sennett. Working title: **The Constable**. One reel. Extant: LOC. With Ford Sterling, Edgar Kennedy, Raymond Hatton, Roscoe Arbuckle, Charles Avery, Bert Hunn, Arthur Tavares.

The sheriff captures a couple of desperate characters, and places them in jail. During the night they escape and burglarize the sheriff's home, and then return to the lockup. In the morning the sheriff, having no evidence against the prisoners, releases them. The sheriff's wife discovers the loss of her jewelry, and the Deputy Sheriff goes in quest of the unknown thieves. He finds the erstwhile guests of the jail dividing the "swag" and captures them, and again they are landed safe in jail.

Roscoe makes his second drag appearance at Keystone only two weeks after the first in *Peeping Pete*. This time he's the hulking wife of little Charles Avery, and the pair show up in the big night scene where the entire town turns out in a panic over the escaped burglars.

The more than expressive Ford Sterling was the star of *Safe in Jail* (1913) and the King of the Keystone lot when Roscoe arrived. Author's collection.

Moving Picture World (July 12, 1913): "Lovers of the particular brand of nonsense put out by this enterprising company will rock in their seats over this jail burlesque. Fred Sterling keeps the merriment going for the entire reel. The night scene was a lively one, with both men and women running about in night attire. Low comedy of the most successful kind."

The Telltale Light

Released July 10, 1913. Produced by Mack Sennett for the Keystone Film Co. Distributed by the Mutual Film Corp. Directed by Mack Sennett. Working title: ***The Mirror***. One reel. With Mabel Normand, Roscoe Arbuckle.

The Anti-Spooning League captures Mabel and her sweetheart Fatty. Mabel and Fatty discover that the Leaguers are not averse to flirting themselves, and they decide to expose them. Securing a big electric searchlight, they explore the dark recesses of the park at night and turn the light upon numerous spooning couples who prove to be Leaguers who are practicing what they preach—against.

Mabel Normand and Roscoe cuddling but not quite "spooning."
Courtesy The Museum of Modern Art.

"Spooning" was a very topical subject in 1913, and would remain a popular source for movie comedy material into the 1930s and films like *Hips, Hips, Hooray* (1934). The subject would especially rear its angry head in park comedies where there would frequently be a big sign that would say "No Spooning Allowed," in addition to a police force that had nothing better to do than to harass would-be lovers. Movie theatres, trains, or any other kind of public place would also be no-no spots for movie spooning.

An official definition of spooning is "a form of cuddling in which the man embraces the woman from the back and they fit together like spoons," but in silent comedy spooning there's not that much physical contract—usually the lover's plans are thwarted before they get that far. 1915's *Mabel, Fatty and the Law* may be the quintessential spooning comedy since most of its screen time is devoted to the various couple's spooning and its aftermaths.

Moving Picture World (July 12, 1913): "In this reel kissing and spooning run riot. The Anti-Spooning Club winds up with everybody practicing the art of osculation. Mabel turns a searchlight on everyone in turn. This reel, as may be imagined, is not of an elevating type, and we did not consider it very amusing, but it will undoubtedly appeal to certain audiences."

Love and Rubbish

Released July 14, 1913. Produced by Mack Sennett for the Keystone Film Co. Distributed by the Mutual Film Corp. Directed by Henry Lehrman. Working title: ***Park Sweepers***. One reel. Extant: MoMA, BFI. With Ford Sterling, Charles Avery, Roscoe

The Echo Park bridge—scene of many Keystone "crimes" in shorts like *Love and Rubbish* (1913).

Arbuckle, Henry Lehrman, Bill Hauber, Virginia Kirtley, Dave Anderson, Edgar Kennedy, Paul Jacobs, John Rand.

Two park cleaners try to flirt with pretty girls, but they are repulsed. They secure fine clothes and get back on the job—of flirting again. They make the mistake of picking out the sweetheart of the park superintendent, and a battle royal ensues. This lady is a widow, with a little child. The child is seen to hide in an empty barrel, but gets out again and wanders away. One of the park cleaners, running from the wrath of the superintendent, hides in the barrel, which is carried away, pursued by those that think the child is in it. The barrel has a rough time, but the park cleaner is finally rescued.

A standard plot in numerous Henry Lehrman-directed films is "mayhem in a park." It was cheap and easy to go to one of the nearby parks—Echo or Hollenbeck—set the comedians loose at each other and see what developed. This time it's Ford Sterling and Charles Avery as park cleaners battling over territory and pretty women. In many of Lehrman's later comedies like *Love and Surgery* (1914) or *Wet and Warmer* (1920) the comedy leads would meet and have some kind of altercation in a park. Then in the second reel the now enemies would meet again in another location—say a hospital or boarding house—and finish the battle royal which had started in the park. Roscoe appears very briefly in this entry, looking like he had an extra five minutes while going from one location to another.

Moving Picture World (July 19, 1913): "Ford Sterling appears in this as Mr. Fickle. He flirts with women in the park and starts considerable trouble. His rival rides downhill in a barrel into the lake. The children thumbing their noses was a bad piece of business in an otherwise fairly good reel. Many exhibitors will prefer to cut this out."

A Noise from the Deep

Released July 17, 1913. Produced by Mack Sennett for the Keystone Film Co. Distributed by the Mutual Film Corp. Directed by Mack Sennett. Working title: *A New Trick*. One reel. Extant: MoMA. With Mabel Normand, Roscoe Arbuckle, Arthur Tavares, Nick Cogley, Edgar Kennedy, Al St John, Charles Avery, Alice Davenport, Bill Hauber, Charles Inslee.

Mabel falls into the water. Her sweetheart rescues her while the man her father favors runs for help. A boy is bribed to blow into a hose, the other end of which is concealed under the water. While the rescuers are diving for the body which is supposed to lie under the bubbles, Mabel and her lover are married.

A Noise from the Deep is often considered to have the first use of a thrown Keystone pie, but like most "firsts" it's difficult to absolutely verify. As in 1913's *Bangville Police* a very rural version of the Keystone Cops turns up at the climax, this time on horseback, to perform some very risky and dangerous looking stunts. Some of the horses even stumble and fall, taking their riders down with them.

This short gives a very good look at the neglected supporting player Arthur Tavares, who plays Roscoe's namby-pamby rival. Coming to Keystone in 1912 he regularly played cops and rivals, until he moved over to Sterling Comedies in 1914. Often playing leads in their "B" unit shorts without Ford Sterling, he also was busy in Essanay's *George Ade Fables*

A re-release lobby card for *A Noise from the Deep* (1913) with Roscoe, Mabel Normand, and Arthur Tavares. Courtesy Sam Gill.

shorts and in Mutual's Vogue Comedies with Rube Miller. After features that include *The Spanish Jade* (1915), *Ramona* (1916), *Hungry Eyes* (1918), and *Fortune's Mask* (1922) he stopped acting to become a film editor. Bridging silents into sound he edited *So Big* (1924), *Men of Steel* (1926), *The Good-Bye Kiss* (1928) for his old boss Mack Sennett, and the Spanish version of *Dracula* (1931). His last known work was in 1936, and he passed away in Los Angeles in 1954.

Moving Picture World (July 26, 1913): "This is one of the screamingly funny concoctions which made this company famous as a purveyor of nonsense. It begins with throwing pies and then Mabel and her lover go bicycling. Mabel falls into the lake and the lover flees for help. The fat boy, Bob, saves her. This is but the beginning of the fun. A hose is employed to gurgle in the water which makes everyone think Mabel is still in the lake. The police force comes to the rescue on bucking bronchos. Very funny and free from coarseness of any kind."

New York Dramatic Mirror (July 23, 1913): "An uproarious farce beggaring description of its grotesque acting. The impersonators of the successful suitor and of the constabulary mounted on the bucking bronchos, make one of the most side-splitting films seen in a long time."

Love and Courage

Released July 21, 1913. Produced by Mack Sennett for the Keystone Film Co. Distributed by the Mutual Film Corp. Directed by Henry Lehrman. Working titles: **Rubes**. ½ reel. (Released with *The Peddler*). With Roscoe Arbuckle, Mabel Normand, Charles Avery.

Mabel loves her big fat admirer, who has ludicrous encounters with his little rival.

One of Henry Lehrman's responsibilities at Keystone was making sure that the release schedule was filled, and this sometimes meant that he shot off-the-cuff little "quota quickies." The split reel length was perfect for something that could be shot briskly and economically in a park or other nearby location. Little is known about the missing *Love and Courage*, but it has the earmarks of possibly being something the crew and actors might have set out on with a rough idea and saw what developed for five minutes of screen time.

Of course this type of extemporaneous shooting helped give silent comedies the spontaneity for which they're prized today. Even as the shorts got longer, moving on to two reels, things stayed pretty loose. Frank Capra, a busy Sennett writer in the mid-1920s, said that the plot of an average two-reeler was often just a clothesline to hang gags on. Roscoe occasionally talked about how he worked behind the camera and is quoted as saying:

Roscoe lunching on Charles Avery's finger in *Love and Courage* (1913).

> "Not a scrap of scenario paper in my studio," he admitted. "I wouldn't know what to do with a manuscript in my hand. I plan out the pictures, and we rehearse them—that's all."
>
> – ***Film Fun***, 1916

> "We use more mental effort on a two-reel Keystone than is usually put on a five-reel feature," he said. "We have no scenario, no manuscript. Have to just sit down and think of a situation, and then build up to it and away from it. Our first run averages 4,000 to 5,000 feet, and then we cut to two reels, jumping from laugh to laugh as quickly as possible. I tell you the strain is awful. I take four or five days off after each film to regain my weight, or I'd never be able to do it."
>
> "That's right," said Mabel sympathetically, eating a green apple. "He'd never be able to do it; he gets so weak."
>
> – ***New York Tribune***, February 20, 1916

Moving Picture World (July 26, 1913): "Mabel's lovers become involved in a running fight. There are touches of vulgarity in this which might well have been avoided."

Professor Bean's Removal

Released July 31, 1913. Produced by Mack Sennett for the Keystone Film Co. Distributed by the Mutual Film Corp. Directed by Henry Lehrman. Working title: ***House Moving***. One reel. With Ford Sterling, Mabel Normand, Roscoe Arbuckle.

Prof. Bean and his daughter are enthusiastic cornetists, to the distress of the neighbors. Their efforts to have the noise stopped meets with no success, as Prof. Bean and Mabel put them all to rout. The landlord takes a hand, accompanied by the police, but Prof. Bean and his trusty gun convinces them that discretion is the better part of valor. The other tenants threaten to move, and in desperation the landlord places the house on automobile trucks and moves it away in the dead of night. The Professor and Mabel are awakened by being thrown out of their beds by the jolting of the house and, rushing to the door, find themselves moving rapidly down the street.

Although this film is at the moment considered lost, photos survive that show Roscoe playing the harassed landlord in an uncharacteristic mustache. During his first year with Keystone he turned up in occasional character roles. As the older Jewish doctor in *His Sister's Kids* he sports a beard, and stills from missing titles such as *The Riot*, *A Small Town Act*, *He Would a Hunting Go*, and *Wine* (all 1913) show a variety of mustaches and thick eyebrows. By the beginning of 1914 his boyish "Fatty" persona had become such a popular screen icon that the variations ended.

The Professor Bean of the title is played by Ford Sterling, a frequent screen mate of Roscoe's in 1913 and 1914. One of the original "Keystone Four," Sterling got so big that he left for his own company in 1914. Today the majority of silent comedy aficionados and scholars scratch their heads on the subject of Sterling. Seen now as a joke that's lost its original context—much of what he was about was a spoof on well-known melodramatic

Mabel Normand and Ford Sterling are surprised by their suddenly mobile home in *Professor Bean's Removal* (1913). Courtesy The Museum of Modern Art.

clichés and characters, so his exaggerated, semaphore-like gestures and huge faces were accepted as parody. In 1914 the Sterling Film Company was formed by Universal to film his misadventures, but the venture didn't last long and by 1915 Ford was back in the Sennett fold.

Some of his best-known shorts include *Our Dare-Devil Chief*, *Court House Crooks* (both 1915), *His Torpedoed Love* (1917), *Hearts and Flowers* (1919), as well as the lead as the Kaiser in the Sennett feature *Yankee Doodle in Berlin* (1919). Leaving the Sennett organization for good in 1920, he made a few starring shorts for Special Pictures Corp., and began free-lancing as a supporting character actor in features such as *Hollywood* (1923), *He Who Gets Slapped* (1924), and *Gentlemen Prefer Blondes* (1927). Having adapted to a more subtle performing style than that of his early Keystone days he even had the lead in *The Show-Off* (1926), and made a good transition to sound pictures like *Her Majesty Love* (1931) and *Alice in Wonderland* (1933). He also starred in sound shorts for Christie, Paramount, and RKO, but was besieged by health problems and died in 1939.

Moving Picture World (August 9, 1913): "Quite an amusing number, in the rough style of this company's well-known nonsense. Mabel and Ford are so violently on their trombones that the neighbors move the house one evening. An actual moving house is shown, and it is some time before the audience learns what is going on. Something new and different, without any particular offensiveness."

New York Dramatic Mirror (August 13, 1913): "An exceedingly funny farce, acted with characteristic animation by the new company. It is well photographed. A real house is actually employed in the transportation."

The Riot

Released August 11, 1913. Produced by Mack Sennett for the Keystone Film Co. Distributed by the Mutual Film Corp. Directed by Mack Sennett. One reel. Extant: BFI. With Roscoe Arbuckle, Mabel Normand, Paul Jacobs, Edgar Kennedy, Alice Davenport, Charles Inslee, Al St John, Bill Hauber, Charles Avery, Nick Cogley, Gordon Griffith, Virginia Kirtley, Hank Mann.

Mabel Normand is not quite sure that tiger is really deceased in *The Riot* (1913).
Courtesy the George Eastman Museum.

The Jewish shopkeeper chastises the Kelly kids. Mrs. Kelly upholds the fighting reputation of the race. Kelly reinforces his wife, and his Irish neighbors take a hand. The Jews rally to the defense of their fellowman, and a riot takes place. Stones and bricks fairly rain down on the combatants. The police are called out, but they cannot cope with the riot, in which bombs are now being thrown. The militia is ordered to the scene, but it is not until the fire department arrives with its hose and pours powerful streams of water on the mob that the fighters are stopped.

The Riot is another Keystone ethnic picture, this time with warring Irish and Jewish families, where Roscoe is the head of the Jewish contingent. In addition to the usual Keystone riff-raff there's one of the most important players in Roscoe's films—Al St John. Although busy in movies non-stop for forty years, today he's one of the most overlooked and underappreciated comedians of the silent era.

The son of Roscoe's older sister Nora, Al was born in 1893. Roscoe was six years older and is supposed to have lived with Nora and her husband Walter St. John when Al was little (one can only imagine what their roughhouse playing was like). Al followed his uncle into show business—dancing and performing bicycle stunts. Practically the minute after Roscoe started working at Keystone in 1913 Al was there too. Articles and interviews in the teens and twenties continually credit Al with having been one of the original Keystone Cops, and while this is hard to verify, it seems definite that outside of Edgar Kennedy Al

Frank Hayes (middle) is caught between Al St John (right) and Mai Wells in *The Grab Bag Bride* (1917). Courtesy The Museum of Modern Art.

appeared in more shorts between 1913 and 1915 than anyone else on the lot. He turns up everywhere—as a cop, waiter, bellboy, etc., even in blackface.

Al's best roles were in Roscoe's films and the character that developed was something like an evil gremlin's country cousin as Fatty's chief rival and nemesis. Long and lean, with legs like steel spring coils ready to bounce him straight up in the air, Al was always ready to take offense and was bloodthirsty in his revenge. Some of his most memorable Keystones are *Shot in the Excitement* (1914), *Fatty's Faithful Fido* (1915), and *Fatty and Mabel Adrift* (1916). Eventually assisting Roscoe in the direction of the films, he would go along and continue this dual function when Arbuckle left Sennett and went to Comique.

Two popular kid actors were also part of the cast. Gordon Griffith was part of a busy acting family that was made up of his mother and father Katherine and Harry, as well as his siblings Graham and Gertrude. Gordon started working at Keystone in 1913, with *The Riot* being one of his first films. Besides appearing with Roscoe in *His Sister's Kids* (1913) and *A Bath House Beauty* (1914), Gordon had prominent roles in *Little Billy's Triumph*, *How Villains are Made*, and *The Star Boarder* (all 1914). In 1915 he shared the lead with Hobart Bosworth in the baseball comedy feature *Little Sunset*, and was a busy kid actor through the 1920s, with his most outstanding roles being playing the young Tarzan in *Tarzan of the Apes* and *The Romance of Tarzan* (both 1918), and Tom Sawyer in William Desmond Taylor's *Huckleberry Finn* (1920). When his roles began dwindling in the 1930s he became an assistant director, and eventually an associate producer on titles such as *The Jolson Story* (1946), *Never Wave at a Wac* (1953), and *Alexander the Great* (1956). He died of heart attack in Hollywood in 1958.

Paul Jacobs was a blonde, curly-headed three-year-old who was discovered by Henry Lehrman and ended up headlining in the Keystone's series of kid shorts as "Little Billy." Starting in bits parts he was soon starred in outings like *The New Baby* and *Willie Minds the Dog* (both 1913), and thanks to his popularity titles like *Little Billy's Strategy* and *Little Billy's City Cousin* (both 1914) were built around him. When Fred Balshofer, Ford Sterling, and Henry Lehrman set up Sterling Pictures, Jacobs jumped ship and did "Little Billy" for them, sometimes opposite Sterling in shorts like *Sergeant Hoffmeyer* and *Papa's Boy* (both 1914), but mostly in his own pictures that included *A Rural Affair*, *Carmen's Romance* (both 1914), *Billie was a Right Smart Boy*, and *Playmates* (both 1915). After his time with Sterling he did a few shorts for L-Ko, and appeared in features until 1918, and as an adult worked as a writer, even on movie magazines like *The Film Spectator*.

Moving Picture World (August 16, 1913): "Here is a full reel given over to a free-for-all fight, in which bricks and bombs are thrown and the police, fire department and militia respond to quell the riot. It all begins over Cohen's saleslady, whose parcels are opened by the Irish children. A race war ensues and the situations contain a lot of harmless amusement, free from vulgarity."

Variety (March 13, 1914): "After "The Gangsters" (Mutual four-reel dramatic feature) and its heaviness, the light Keystone struck the house as very funny. "The Riot" is really a funny picture, albeit the Keystone crowd rely so much on "falls." It was a riot between the Irish and the Jews, with the two crowds throwing bricks at one another, the Jews finally routing their enemies with bombs while the militia and fire department were called into the finish to disperse both. The audience laughed uproariously at many of the situations."

Mabel's New Hero

Released August 28, 1913. Produced by Mack Sennett for the Keystone Film Co. Distributed by the Mutual Film Corp. Directed by Mack Sennett. Working title: ***The Balloon***. Extant: MoMA, Berk, QUB, LOB. One reel. With Mabel Normand, Roscoe Arbuckle, Charles Inslee, Virginia Kirtley, Evelyn Quick, Bernard Harris, Edgar Kennedy, Charles Avery.

Roscoe and Mabel, along with her girlfriends, go to the beach. While they are changing Roscoe discovers a masher peeping at Mabel's silhouette through her dressing room window. Roscoe gives him the what-for, but he stays around bugging the other girls and finally gets his revenge when he lets Mabel loose in a balloon. The Keystone cops are called and help Roscoe bring Mabel back to earth.

Mabel Normand on the beach during the making of 1913's *Mabel's New Hero*.
Courtesy of Robert S. Birchard.

Every beach comedy short needs a masher, and the masher that causes all the problems in *Mabel's New Hero* for Roscoe, Mabel, and the other girls is Charles Inslee. A busy character actor on whom there's very little information, Inslee entered films in the early days, and after working at Edison joined Biograph in 1908, even appearing in D.W. Griffith's first directorial effort *The Adventures of Dolly*. Playing all types of roles, it's said that Inslee was temperamental and frequently fought with Griffith, even coming to physical blows. In 1909 he went to the Bison Company, often playing Indians in shorts like *A True Indian's Heart* (1909), and having worked with Mack Sennett at Biograph he turned up at Keystone in 1913.

A versatile performer who was equally at home with or without a toupee, Inslee was busy playing rivals to Roscoe and Ford Sterling in shorts like *A Muddy Romance, The Bowling Match, The Gusher* (all 1913), and *Making a Living* (1914). Leaving Keystone in 1914 for Sterling Comedies, he soon moved to L-Ko, Kalem, and ended up at Essanay to support Charlie Chaplin in *Work, A Woman, The Bank,* and *A Night in the Show* (all 1915). The rest of his career saw him working with Billy West, back at L-Ko, and on the Hal Roach lot with Harold Lloyd. After the 1921 features *Cold Steel* and *Desperate Trails*, his last known appearance was the Hoot Gibson two-reeler *The Man Who Woke Up* (1921) before disappearing from films.

Minta Durfee (right) chaperones Mabel Normand and Charles Inslee in the Keystone *A Muddy Romance* (1913). Courtesy The Museum of Modern Art.

Moving Picture World (September 6, 1913): "A full reel comedy containing much that is genuinely funny, but also many broad, suggestive situations which will not commend it to the best houses; in fact, much of it is unfit for presentation anywhere."

Fatty's Day Off

Released September 1, 1913. Produced by Mack Sennett for the Keystone Film Co. Distributed by the Mutual Film Corp. Directed by Wilfred Lucas. Working title: ***The Invalid***. ½ reel. (Released with **Los Angeles Harbor**). Extant: LOC, CAN. With Roscoe Arbuckle, Charles Avery, Grover Ligon, Fred Gamble, Bill Hauber.

Fatty takes his girl to the beach, gets "in bad" with two mischievous boys, and they proceed to make the day "enjoyable" for him. After a fruitless chase, in which he loses his breath, not to mention his hat and temper, he seeks quiet in a summer garden. His tormentors tie a string to his rolling chair, and after a wild dash, in which they carry sundry persons and things before them, dump poor Fatty in the lake. With the assistance of the entire police force he is hauled out and sent home, a wetter but wiser man.

A mash-up at the beach caused when Fatty gets on the wrong side of a couple of mischievous boys—the most aggressive one played by the diminutive and forty year-old

Fatty's Day Off (1913) is ruined by the antics of some prankish boys.

Grover Ligon was a charter member of the Keystone rank and file.

Charles Avery. Lots of fast and furious action, with similarities to the 1912 early Keystone *At Coney Island*, where Mabel, Mack, and Ford Sterling frolic and fight on the various Coney attractions, and Charlie Chaplin's *His New Profession* (1914), where he pushes a gout-ridden man around in a wheelchair. The use of Roscoe's character name in this film's title is a good indication of his growing popularity with audiences. Up to this point at Keystone only Mabel Normand had been so highlighted, but titles like *Fatty at San Diego*, *Fatty Joins the Force*, and *Fatty's Flirtation* proliferated as his career soared.

The wheelchair-bound fellow is played by Grover Ligon. One of the stalwarts of the early Keystones, Ligon was not only an actor but also a stuntman, assistant director, make-up expert, and auto trick driver. He began his career with Biograph in 1911, and was with Sennett during his heyday of 1913-1917. Tall, thin, and with a big bald head, Ligon is always easy to spot in surviving shorts like *Mabel's Dramatic Career* (1913), *Caught in a Cabaret* (1914), *The Knockout* (1914), *Hash House Mashers* (1915), and *The Surf Girl* (1916). While he would return to the Sennett films on and off during the 1920s and 1930s, he was also in numerous Larry Semon shorts like *The Show* (1922) and *The Dome Doctor* (1925), as well as many features. He was in the Sennett reunion short *Keystone Hotel* (1935), but finally retired from films in 1938. Ligon did very well in real estate and died at age eighty in 1965.

Moving Picture World (September 6, 1913): "The fat boy takes a very reckless ride in a wheel chair, winding up by falling off a pier. Good comedy without offensive situations."

New York Dramatic Mirror (September 10, 1913): "To those who enjoy this sort of horseplay the burlesque will be acceptable."

Mabel's Dramatic Career

Released September 8, 1913. Produced by Mack Sennett for the Keystone Film Co. Distributed by the Mutual Film Corp. Directed by Mack Sennett. Working title: **The Actress**. One reel. Extant: MoMA, UCLA, ACAD, BFI, LOC, DAN. With Mabel Normand, Mack Sennett, Ford Sterling, Roscoe Arbuckle, Virginia Kirtley, Alice Davenport, Paul Jacobs, Charles Inslee, Charles Avery, Dave Anderson, Edgar Kennedy, Billy Gilbert, Hank Mann, Grover Ligon, Bert Hunn, Bill Hauber.

Zeke falls in love with Mabel, his mother's hired girl. He presents her with an engagement ring, but his fickle attentions soon turn when Lola, a beautiful city girl, pays a

Roscoe giving an out of the frame Mack Sennett a sidelong look in 1913's *Mabel's Dramatic Career*.

visit to the farm. Her heart "busted" at his perfidy, Mabel leaves the house, and her going is assisted by Zeke, who pushes her out the door. He throws his heart, and incidentally Mabel's engagement ring at the city girl's feet, but she in turn, "busts" his dream by laughing at his uncouth avowal of love. Meanwhile, the "hired help" has fallen into a job with a moving picture company and after many years has become an acknowledged "movie" queen and favorite, besides the wife of the director. Our friend Zeke, mourning his first love, stumbles into a picture house one night and to his at first amazement and then horror, finds his beloved "hired girl" in the clutches of the "villyon." Her boob lover follows her through many narrow escapes and tight situations until at last, beside himself, he shoots up the villain; also the audience. Following Mabel's persecutor to his home, he is about to "pop" him through the window when he sees the "villain" surrounded by Mabel and their children. Standing and taking this in he is drenched by a pail of dirty water thrown from an upper window, and retires disgusted from the scene.

As the wronged sweetheart of country ape Mack Sennett, Mabel finds that the best revenge is finding stardom and family happiness through the movies. The film is a particular treat for early film historians and fans as it not only gives a behind-the-scenes look at the Sennett studio, but also offers a good depiction of what the average neighborhood cinema was like in 1913. This is where Roscoe turns up, as a more than patient movie patron who tries to get fellow viewer Sennett to calm down and let them all watch the show.

More than any other film, *Mabel's Dramatic Career* is probably most responsible for giving the impression that Mack Sennett was a terrible actor. Admittedly it's one of his worst performances—unsubtle and way over the top—and unfortunately it's ended up being one of his most commonly seen roles. Although not the greatest performer he was capable of much better than this. Examples of his best performances include *The Manicure Lady* (1911), *The Would-Be-Shriner*, *Tomboy Bessie* (both 1912), *A Strong Revenge*, *Their First Execution* (both 1913), and *My Valet* (1915). The cliché is that he always played the country boob, but he was more often than not an average put upon Joe. Of course once Keystone really got rolling he tapered off his onscreen appearances.

Moving Picture World (September 27, 1913): "Good humor and extreme vulgarity are closely intermingled in this. Much of the latter can be cut out. It is difficult to see why a

Mabel Normand overreacts to Ford Sterling's villainy in *Mabel's Dramatic Career* (1913). Courtesy The Museum of Modern Art.

company with such splendid opportunities for appealing to all houses should appeal only to the less particular one."

The Gypsy Queen

Released September 11, 1913. Produced by Mack Sennett for the Keystone Film Co. Distributed by the Mutual Film Corp. Directed by Mack Sennett. Working title: **The Gypsy**. One reel. With Mabel Normand, Roscoe Arbuckle, Charles Inslee, Edgar Kennedy, Virginia Kirtley, Bill Hauber, Dave Anderson, Arthur Tavares.

Mabel is a Gypsy queen who is enamored of Fatty. When he spurns her for another woman she has him tied to a tree. A snake is then let loose to take care of him, while Mabel does her best to keep rescuers from freeing him.

Parody was Keystone's stock in trade, and in practically all of their films there was some element that spoofed serious dramatic pictures. Often they would make fun of specific movie genres such as Victorian melodramas in *Barney Oldfield's Race for a Life* (1913), would use the "Keystone sleuths" to skewer detective films in *A Bear Escape* (1912)

Mabel Normand reads Roscoe's palm as Dave Anderson, Charles Avery, Bill Hauber and others look on in *The Gypsy Queen* (1913). Courtesy the George Eastman Museum.

and *The Sleuth's Last Stand* (1913), or they would roast the popular civil war dramas of producer Thomas Ince with shorts such as *The Battle of Who Run*, and *Cohen Saves the Flag* (both 1913).

Melodramas about gypsies and gypsy life were big on the stage and in popular fiction—operas like *The Bohemian Girl* or the novel *Romany Rye*—that were full of titled children being kidnapped, murders, or other skullduggery. This lost short seems to be the Keystone contribution, and one hopes that it will eventually be found, if just to see Mabel as the "Gypsy Queen."

Roscoe would be fond of his own genre parodies, starting with the melodrama of the villain that lures the country girl to the big city in shorts like *Leading Lizzie Astray* (1914) and *The Bright Lights* (1916). He would go on to do more out and out burlesques in *The Moonshiners* (1916), *Out West*, *Moonshine* (both 1918), and would reach his peak with *The Iron Mule* and *Curses* (both 1925).

Moving Picture World (September 13, 1913): "A good burlesque offering, free from offense, in which Mabel Normand appears as the Gypsy queen. The fat boy is tied to a tree and as the live snake crawls toward him Mabel hatches up schemes for stopping the approaching rescuers. Quite laughable in places. A full reel number."

The Fatal Taxicab

Released September 18, 1913. Produced by Mack Sennett for the Keystone Film Co. Distributed by the Mutual Film Corp. Directed by Mack Sennett. Working title: **The Taxicab**. One reel. Extant: clips. With Mabel Normand, Ford Sterling, Roscoe Arbuckle, Charles Inslee, Bill Hauber, Hank Mann, Charles Avery, Edgar Kennedy, Billy Gilbert.

Egbert Throckmorton, father of nine, and a deep-dyed villain, forces his attentions on Mabel, pretty girl. Her "best feller" objects, and is pushed in the lake by the deep-dyed one. The Keystone Police Force are summoned. The villain escapes in a taxi, pursued by our hero, both followed by the police in an 1842 model speed demon. During the chase a running fire of shots takes place and the taxi, containing desperate Egbert topples over a precipice and lands safely in a tree. Fatty, our hero, his sweetheart, and the police surround the tree. He repels them by throwing deadly bombs from his vantage seat in the treed taxi, until one daring officer secures an ax and chops the tree to the ground, bringing down tree, taxi and villain.

Another melodrama spoof, this time with a wildly mustached Ford Sterling as a top-hatted European villain. A surviving chunk of this short shows Mabel performing a moving vehicle transfer as she's plucked from Roscoe's auto by the passing Sterling. In addition to the leap from car to car, Mabel also slugs the amorous Sterling as they're driving across the Echo Park bridge and then does her own dive out of the moving auto into the lake below. Roscoe, having been in pursuit on foot, hurls himself off the bridge to save her in the water. The clip ends with Sterling's careening car going over a steep cliff.

One of the vital cogs in the Keystone fun factory machinery, in addition to being an important ingredient in Roscoe's early films, was Bill Hauber. One of the top comedy stuntmen of the silent era, Hauber came from an acrobatic and circus background to join Keystone in 1913, and spent three years, often in cop uniform, as the daredevil

Ford Sterling and henchmen (Charles Inslee on the left) up to no good in *The Fatal Taxicab* (1913).

Bill Hauber—silent screen daredevil and stunt comic extraordinaire.

extraordinaire of the lot. After brief sojourns at Fox and working with Roscoe again at Comique, he became Larry Semon's stunt double. From 1918 to 1925 Hauber performed the stunts for which Semon became famous—swinging from water towers, diving headfirst from the top of silos into vats of goo, etc. When Hauber moved on Semon's career went into a tailspin and he died bankrupt in 1928. Hauber didn't long outlive his former boss, as he died the next year in a plane crash while working out stunts for a feature.

Moving Picture World (October 4, 1913): "A typical amusing offering of the burlesque type, in which Sterling, Mabel and the Fat Boy come into a new series of adventures. The Italian Count is pursued by the Keystone police. His auto falls over a cliff and lodges in a tree. Nothing offensive in this, but some rattling good nonsense with which to enliven a program."

When Dreams Come True

Released September 22, 1913. Produced by Mack Sennett for the Keystone Film Co. Distributed by the Mutual Film Corp. Directed by Mack Sennett. Working title: *The Snake*. One reel. Extant: GEM. With Ford Sterling, Mabel Normand, Roscoe Arbuckle, Hank Mann, Alice Davenport, Charles Avery, Charles Inslee, Emma Clifton, Dave Anderson.

The peddler insists upon going off on his bi-monthly bat, in spite of his wife's remonstrations. In the saloon where he acquires his agreeable sensations he meets a snake

The first appearance of Roscoe's "Fatty the tough" persona turns up in *When Dreams Come True* (1913). Courtesy the Library of Congress.

charmer—who leaves his suitcase full of snakes next to the peddler's bag. Of course the bags get mixed and the peddler returns home, nicely lighted up, with the suitcase of snakes. He is put to bed by his faithful wife—who presently brings in the suitcase and slams it on the bureau with such impatience that it bursts open. She is barely out of the room when snakes begin to emerge and scatter—real live snakes of the diamond-back rattler species. The partly-sobered man finds one between his knees on the bed—gently swaying towards his face. Another hangs from the chandelier with a gas-globe at the end of its tail. The whole room is alive with them.

The wife comes in—nearly faints—rushes out for help. Fatty responds—takes one look—falls out of the door on the rebound. Two policemen come in with drawn revolvers—and go out with a squirming rattlesnake coiled about each gasping neck. The husband, in his nightshirt—now crazed with physical repulsion—runs from the house and down the road with a mass of wriggling rattlers around his neck. Runs up the steep-pitched roof of a barn—and jumps off. Tears along the road—into a spooning country-couple, locked in each other's arms—scares them speechless. Runs out upon a bridge—leaps from the rail into the river—and finds Br'er Snake amiably swimming toward him in the water. Then his wife appears running out on the bridge—grabs his hair and keeps him afloat until the police rescue them.

Roscoe's participation in *When Dreams Come True* consists of a cameo in the tough guy version of his screen persona (derby, long-sleeved T-shirt, and loping walk) when Mabel summons him for help after she finds her bedroom full of snakes. Arriving all cocky to take care of the situation, he's soon falling all over himself to beat a hasty retreat from the serpentine epidemic.

The scenes with the snakes make quite an impression, and were highlighted in an editorial about special effects. The September 20, 1913 issue of the Mutual Pictures' house publication *Reel Life* used the film as an example of something that seems like it couldn't be "faked:"

> *Another is the sort of thing which is done in a new Keystone Mabel Normand comedy, called "When Dreams Come True," which will appear after Sept. 22nd. It represents "the morning after" when a husband who has spent a convivial night is sleeping off the effects in bed while his devoted wife ministers to him. Presently, someone comes in and leaves a large basket upon the bureau—going quickly out and closing the door. As you wonder what is to happen next, the lid of the basket comes off—and about thirty live rattlesnakes slide out of it onto the floor. They squirm into every corner of the room. One hangs from the chandelier and tickles the dozing man with its rattles. Another coils up between his knees, gently swaying its head back and forth as the man wakes up and looks at it in horror. During the next ten minutes, about every person who enters the room goes out of it shrieking, writhing, with one or more living snakes coiled about him.*
>
> *We cannot, of course, review the entire play in an editorial—but we can and do emphasize the point that in no other method of dramatic representation would it be possible to show actual living snakes in any such way as this. There is no doubt whatever in the spectator's mind as to*

Ford Sterling rigs up a deck in a nitrate print of *A Game of Poker* (1913). Courtesy EYE Filmmuseum.

the snakes being real, or as to their being the deadly poisonous, diamond-backed variety of rattlesnake. There is no question whatever that any person finding himself in the same room with such a lot of squirmers—or feeling their slimy coils about his neck—would do exactly as the people do in this roaring little comedy. But just how it is done, the Editor will not attempt to explain until he finds out himself.

This short is an excellent example of the kind of story in which Ford Sterling particularly thrived. Sterling's broad grimaces and gestures register best when he's confronted with extreme situations—say, when he's strapped in the live electric chair in *Their First Execution* (1913), hanging for dear life onto a safe that's been dynamited into orbit in *Only a Messenger Boy* (1915), or when, as in this film, when he wakes up surrounded by a roomful of live wriggling and writhing snakes.

Moving Picture World (October 4, 1913): "This burlesque offering is of rather coarse humor and will perhaps not appeal to all audiences. The suitcase full of live snakes creates havoc in Sterling's bedroom. He dashes out in his night clothes and there is much rough and tumble excitement, in which the snakes play a large part."

Mother's Boy

Released September 25, 1913. Produced by Mack Sennett for the Keystone Film Co. Distributed by the Mutual Film Corp. Directed by Henry Lehrman. Working title: ***The Bears***. One reel. With Roscoe Arbuckle, Nick Cogley, Alice Davenport, Billy Gilbert, Edgar Kennedy, Al St John, Bill Hauber, Charles Avery, George Jeske.

Fatty is his mother's pet. His father, the police inspector, longs to chastise his lazy son, but the mother protects her darling. Two girls are in love with Fatty, and the disappointed one orders one of her suitors to thrash Fatty. A furious fight results when two bears butt in and chase the fighters up a telephone post. Amusing situations arise before they are rescued.

This short is not known to exist and according to the reviews and descriptions it may be the first use of the gag where Roscoe sets his bed on fire and lackadaisically tries to put it out with tea cups full of water. This routine features prominently in the openings of *Fatty's Plucky Pup* (1915) and *The Rough House* (1917). "Pathé" Lehrman was the director, and seems to have been fond of having people running around on telephone wires for a big climax. He uses this again in some of his comedies for L-Ko, most notably in the surviving Billie Ritchie short *Live Wires and Love Sparks* (1916). Roscoe also reuses the gag at the end of *Their Ups and Downs* (1914), *Fatty's Tintype Tangle* (1915) and *The Garage* (1920).

Roscoe's disgruntled father is Nick Cogley, who first worked with the large comedian at Selig in *The Sanitarium* (1910) and *A Robust Patient* (1911). This bald, heavy-set character actor, who was always busy at Keystone playing fathers, sheriffs, police chiefs, and other authority figures, came from a long stage career that encompassed light opera and supporting stars such as Delia Fox and Lillian Russell. Like Roscoe he got his start in films with Selig in 1909, and stayed there for three years. His Sennett tenure began in 1913 when he appeared in seminal Keystones like *A Strong Revenge*, *Bangville Police*, *That Ragtime Band*, and *Zuzu, the Band Leader*. The stint with Sennett lasted until 1917, and during that time besides breaking a leg he also directed and wrote scenarios.

A bear has Roscoe up a telephone pole in *Mother's Boy* (1913).

Selig Pictures portrait of Nick Cogley. Courtesy Sam Gill.

Branching out into features he worked with his old teammate Mabel Normand in *Sis Hopkins* (1919), in addition to other pictures like *The Little Shepherd of Kingdom Come* (1920). He supported comic Will Rogers in *Jes Call Me Jim*, *Honest Hutch*, *Guile of Women* (all 1920), *Boys Will Be Boys*, and *An Unwilling Hero* (both 1921). The Normand and the Rogers' features were for Goldwyn, and at the same time the producer put out a series of two-reelers, *The Adventures and Emotions of Edgar Pomeroy*, based on stories by Booth Tarkington. Cogley was a regular in the series that included titles such as *Edgar's Hamlet* (1920) and *Edgar's Feast Day* (1921). By the mid-1920s the pace of Cogley's career slowed down, but he continued turning up in small parts until 1934, and passed away two years later.

Moving Picture World (September 27, 1913): "The fat boy smokes a cigarette in bed and sets the house on fire. Later several love affairs develop; a neighborhood row ensues; two bears chase the combatants up a telephone pole. The fat boy hangs out on the wires with a remarkable indifference to life and limb. Later the police force appears and the officers climb the pole. A good rough and tumble number, free from offense."

Two Old Tars

Released October 20, 1913. Produced by Mack Sennett for the Keystone Film Co. Distributed by the Mutual Film Corp. Directed by Henry Lehrman. Working titles: **Yachting**, **The Sea Dogs**. One reel. With Roscoe Arbuckle, Nick Cogley, Lucille Ward.

Two old tars, retired from service, live alone in a cottage by the sea. They sail along on an even keel, until a buxom and comely widow projects herself on the scene. This causes one of the old tars to break one of the unwritten laws and fall in love with her. The other old fellow objects strenuously.

This release gave Roscoe a change-of-pace character role as an old sea dog, and teamed him with ace Keystone supporting player Nick Cogley. The widow who causes strife for the two salts is played by Lucille Ward, a neglected performer who had an almost fifty year career on stage and in films. The first fifteen was spent in vaudeville, musical comedy, stock, and taking over the lead in the show *Tillie's Nightmare* after Marie Dressler. The heavy-set character actress made her film debut in 1912 and worked at Imp, supported Peter Lang at Lubin in entries like *Auntie's Affinity* (1913), not to mention Ford Sterling

Lucille Ward's flirting with old salt Nick Cogley causes conflict in *Two Old Tars* (1913).

at Sterling Pictures in *Snookie's Flirtation* (1914) and others. After finding a regular berth at Keystone and American, in *Beauty Comedies* such as *Art and Arthur* (1916), she spent the next thirty years doing all kinds of bits and occasional nice parts in features like *Oh, Doctor!* (1925), and shorts until 1944.

Moving Picture World (October 25, 1913): "One of the Keystone laugh producers which would make a confirmed dyspeptic forget his troubles. The rescue of the drowning man with a derrick was the most ludicrous, and the antics of the police force also brought laughter. A good release."

A Quiet Little Wedding

Released October 23, 1913. Produced by Mack Sennett for the Keystone Film Co. Distributed by the Mutual Film Corp. Directed by Wilfred Lucas. Working title: **Interrupted Wedding**. One reel. With Roscoe Arbuckle, Minta Durfee, Charles Avery, Billy Gilbert, Edgar Kennedy, Charles Inslee, Rube Miller, Hank Mann, Bill Hauber, Peggy Pearce, Virginia Kirtley, Emma Clifton.

The scene is laid for Fatty and a homely maid to be one. The guests are there and the ceremony begins when Fatty's rival appears and breaks up the wedding. A pie battle ensues where the rival is the victor and carries the bride away. Fatty follows in pursuit and the climax takes place on a high cliff, which the bride falls off of and lands unscathed in Fatty's arms.

A Quiet Little Wedding is the earliest known film appearance of Roscoe's wife Minta Durfee. Like his nephew Al St. John, Minta turned up very quickly on the Sennett employee ledgers, but spent the bulk of her career a bit in the shadow of her more famous husband. Although a pretty redhead Minta wasn't an ingénue, but a talented character comedienne who always brought interesting choices and details to her characterizations. Even in this debut performance she appears comically as Roscoe's unattractive fiancé. Born Araminta Durfee in Los Angeles in 1889, she began her career on stage as a singer and dancer with the Morosco Stock Company, and was an "end girl" (a dancer on the extreme left or right in the line) in the shows of Clarence Kolb and Max Dill. In 1908 she began an engagement at the Byde-A-Wyle Theatre in Long Beach, CA. where she met Roscoe and married him a few months later.

For the next few years the pair toured around the world with stock companies run by Walter C. Reed and Ferris Hartman, and when Roscoe was hired by Sennett in 1913 Minta soon followed suit. Although she worked frequently with her hubby she made the rounds with everyone else at the studio—as Mabel Normand's mother in *A Muddy Romance* (1913), Charlie Chaplin's love interests in items like *Cruel, Cruel Love*, and *The Star Boarder* (both 1914), plus played Mrs. Walrus to Chester Conklin and Mrs. Ambrose to Mack Swain in opuses such as *It's a Bird* and *Ambrose's First Falsehood* (both 1915). Her red hair photographed dark in black and white, and although slim and slender she was a no-nonsense love interest that swung a deadly left. In *The Knockout* (1914) she holds her own against Al St. John, so much so that when she's "rescued" by Roscoe it's really Al that needs the rescuing.

Minta later said that for doing a stunt for director Wilfred Lucas where she hung from the root of a tree over a three hundred-foot cliff, Lucas gave her a gift of a puppy. It appears to have been from the making of this film as it's directed by Lucas, plus photos show, and reviews talk about, the cliff and tree hanging at the climax. The puppy was named Luke by Minta and Roscoe in honor of Lucas, and would soon become an active member of the Arbuckle screen family.

Moving Picture World (October 25, 1913): "A typical Keystone offering, not quite as funny as some, but containing many humorous spots. It starts with the marriage of the Fat Boy to a homely maiden. The rejected rival begins to stir up things and brings on much excitement, winding up with the principals on a high cliff, the bride having fallen over and become entangled in a tree."

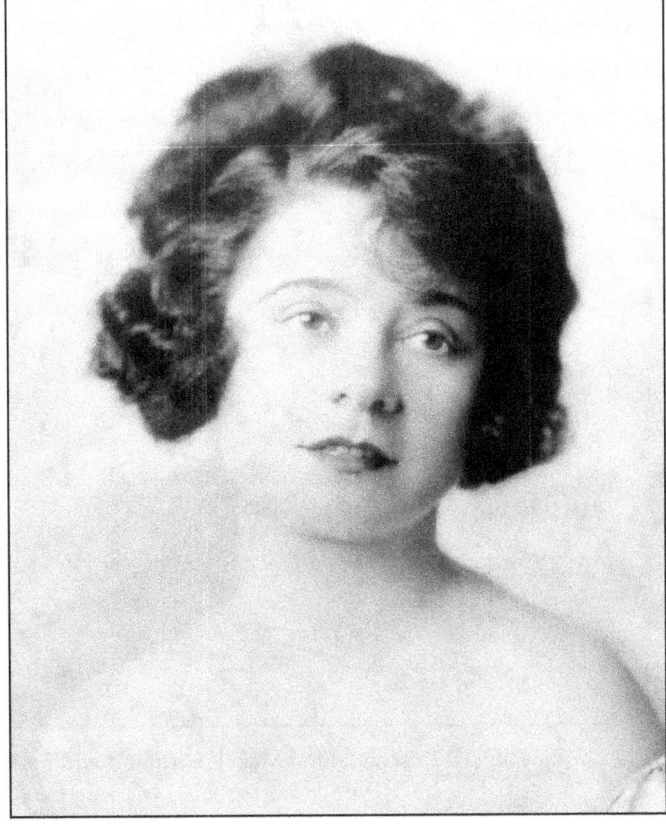

Now that villain Charles Inslee (right) is out of commission Roscoe and Minta Durfee can proceed with *A Quiet Little Wedding* (1913). Courtesy the Academy of Motion Picture Arts and Sciences.

An early portrait of Minta Durfee. Courtesy Marc Wannamaker/Bison Archives.

The Speed Kings

Released October 30, 1913. Produced by Mack Sennett for the Keystone Film Co. Distributed by the Mutual Film Corp. Directed by Wilfred Lucas. (a.k.a. ***The Speed King*** and ***Teddy Tetzlaff and Earl Cooper, Speed Kings***). One reel. Extant: LOC, LOB, ACAD, FRIU. With Mabel Normand, Ford Sterling, Earl Cooper, Teddy Tetzlaff, Barney Oldfield, Roscoe Arbuckle, Paul Jacobs, Edgar Kennedy, F. Richard Jones, Henry Lehrman, Ralph de Palma, Spencer Wishart, Billy Gilbert, Bert Hunn.

Mabel's father wants her to go out with racer Earl Cooper but she prefers his rival Teddy Tetzlaff. Her father decides to sabotage his car so he can't win the big race. Mabel and father watch the race in a peaceful way until Mabel runs up to the track to say hello to Teddy and gets into a fight with a track official. Father comes to her rescue and they go back to watch the finish. Earl Cooper finally wins, but Mabel still wants Tetzlaff. The film ends with father and the track official renewing their battle.

Arbuckle has the small part of the track official who gets into an all-out war with Ford Sterling. A very slight short in terms of comedy content, but with fascinating footage of the crowds and goings-on at the racetrack. Scenes in the bleachers have Sterling and Mabel Normand watching the race surrounded by Keystoners like an amazingly young F. Richard Jones and little Paul Jacobs (who disappears and reappears in different shots). A little background on the race was given in the November 1, 1913 *Motion Picture News*:

Race official Roscoe telling Mabel Normand and Ford Sterling to get off the track in *The Speed Kings* (1913). Courtesy Robert Arkus.

A Keystone comedy, "Speed King," just finished, shows Santa Monica and the Coronada races. Earl Cooper, winner of both, is used in this subject, as well as his Stutz No. 8, present holder of the world's road race record. Teddy Tetzlaff, another world's speed champion, is also used, along with Barney Oldfield, Ralph de Palma, Spencer Wishart, and several more of the racing celebrities of this and foreign countries.

Moving Picture World (November 15, 1913): "Mabel has a great time with her admirers, including Ford Sterling and Teddy Tetzlaff, at the auto races. Many views of cars in action at Santa Monica are shown. The racing scenes get ahead of the plot in interest."

Fatty at San Diego

Released November 3, 1913. Produced by Mack Sennett for the Keystone Film Co. Distributed by the Mutual Film Corp. Directed by George Nichols. Working title: ***A Jealous Husband***. One reel. With Roscoe Arbuckle, Minta Durfee, Phyllis Allen, Nick Cogley, Billy Gilbert, Charles Inslee, Bert Hunn, Peggy Pearce, Charles Avery.

Phyllis Allen buys Roscoe's grandiose tale of heroics in *Fatty at San Diego* (1913).

Fatty induces his wife to let him take a day off to go to the celebration at San Diego. He has a wonderful time, flirting with the girls, breaking up a parade, and fighting with the police force. After falling into the fountain with them, he escapes with the crowd after him by leaping into the river. Here he rescues a little boy and becomes a hero. He goes home to his wife in a bedraggled condition, tells of the rescue and is set upon a pedestal. As a reward his wife takes him to the movies, but there they see a newsreel that has captured his misadventures flirting and fighting in the fountain. Wifie of course becomes irate, and beats him all the way home.

This lost film seems to be Roscoe's first use of a plot that would turn up again later in *A Reckless Romeo* (1917) and *Never Again* (1924) —although the latter time Al St John plays the hubby while Roscoe's behind the camera. It also seems to have influenced Laurel & Hardy, as their *Sons of the Desert* (1933) follows a similar story.

Moving Picture World (November 15, 1913): "Some nonsensical stunts are pulled off in the southern California city during the Cabrillo celebration, a parade being the chief feature of interest. Fatty's dip in the fountain, while being pursued by the irate husband, was very funny and the reel will please many observers immensely."

The Milk We Drink

Released November 10, 1913. Produced by Mack Sennett for the Keystone Film Co. Distributed by the Mutual Film Corp. Directed by Wilfred Lucas. ½ reel educational subject. (Released with **A Small Town Act**). With Roscoe Arbuckle.

The first part of this film shows the old way of getting milk, and then switches to the modern methods. The "modern" however, does not refer to the very latest. The stalls and pastures are shown, and there is the most scrupulous cleanliness throughout. Each consignment of milk is thoroughly tested in laboratories for tuberculosis germs. Also shown is the method of pasteurization.

As a sidebar to his comedy assembly-line, Mack Sennett would also produce little split-reel actualities, which would provide variety for a theatre's shorts line-up. Most had an educational bent that told the audience how something was done, or how a product was made, while others would be travelogues and show highlights of an area or event. Perhaps the best known title of these films is *Olives and their Oil* (1914), which came out with Charlie Chaplin's first film *Making a Living*. Sometimes the shorts would be purely actualities, and others would incorporate Sennett's stars who would add a little bit of comedy to the proceedings. Other studios such as Selig and Vitagraph produced these as well, and Mack turned them out regularly until early 1915, but would return to doing a few like *The Trail of the Swordfish* (1931) and *Freaks of the Deep* (1932) in the early days of sound.

Moving Picture World (November 8, 1913): "An educational subject, depicting the changes in the manner dairy work is done. The dairy was not as modern in some respect as others shown on the screen, but the pictures are interesting. On the same reel with above (**A Small Town Act**)."

Roscoe with an unidentified girl and calf in *The Milk We Drink* (1913).
Courtesy the Academy of Motion Picture Arts and Sciences.

A Small Town Act

Released November 10, 1913. Produced by Mack Sennett for the Keystone Film Co. Distributed by the Mutual Film Corp. Directed by George Nichols. Working title: ***The Rajah***. ½ reel (a.k.a. ***Small Time Act***). (Released with ***The Milk We Drink***). With Ford Sterling, Roscoe Arbuckle.

Ford Sterling has his work cut out for him when he has to fill in for all the acts in the vaudeville show at the local tank town theatre.

Show business was a ripe source for silent comedy antics, especially since almost all of the participants had long backgrounds on the stage and knew too well the ups and downs of touring and playing in little tank town theatres. Director George Nichols came from the stage, having been based in San Francisco in the early part of his life, and after starting in movies with Edison he joined the Biograph Company in 1908. For three years he acted in shorts like *Lines of White on a Sullen Sea* (1909), *An Arcadian Maid* (1910), and *What Shall We Do with Our Old* (1911), while working as a directorial assistant to D.W. Griffith. After that he made the rounds as a director, working at Thanhouser, Gem, and Lubin before Keystone.

On the Sennett lot he directed numerous shorts with Roscoe, Charlie Chaplin, and Charlie Murray that included *Fatty's Flirtation* (1913), *The Under Sheriff*, *Mabel's Bear*

Theatre manager Roscoe is less than impressed with Ford Sterling's abilities in *A Small Town Act* (1913). Courtesy the Academy of Motion Picture Arts and Sciences.

Busy director and character actor George Nichols.

Escape, *The Star Boarder*, *Finnegan's Bomb*, and *When Reuben Fooled the Bandits* (all 1914). After this he directed at Sterling, L-Ko, Majestic, but finished the directorial phase of his career at Selig in 1916. He became a character actor in feature films and was extremely busy—supporting Mabel Normand in her features *Mickey* (1918), *When Doctors Disagree* (1919), *Pinto* (1920), *Molly 'O* (1921), *Suzanna* (1923), and *The Extra Girl* (1923), plus appeared in silent classics like *Hearts of the World* (1918), *A Romance of Happy Valley* (1919), *The Goose Woman* (1925), *The Eagle* (1925), and *The Wedding March* (1928). He died at sixty-two in 1927.

Moving Picture World (November 8, 1913): "An amusing half reel in which Ford Sterling gives burlesque imitations of a tight rope walker, a juggler, a prize fighter and a magician. Of course, trouble ensues with his audience and some laughter is created by the situations."

Wine

Released November 13, 1913. Produced by Mack Sennett for the Keystone Film Co. Distributed by the Mutual Film Corp. Directed by George Nichols. One reel. With Roscoe Arbuckle, Ford Sterling, Minta Durfee, Charles Inslee, Dot Farley, Bill Hauber.

Wine (1913) sees Roscoe, Dot Farley, Charles Inslee, Bill Hauber, and other diners stand at attention to Ford Sterling's reactions.

Fatty is employed bottling wine for a hotel; it does not matter what age wine the customer requires, Fatty takes it out of the same barrel. One customer requires older wine, and Fatty, to make the wine appear old, catches flies and puts them in the bottle. The trick is detected, and Fatty has a bad time.

This is a part educational and part comedy subject. The exploration of a vineyard, along with its wine manufacturing and transportation, is supplemented with the antics of Roscoe as a waiter serving wine to connoisseur Ford Sterling.

Moving Picture World (November 29, 1913): "As a half-reel subject, dealing exclusively with the manufacture of wine from grapes, this would be very acceptable. The vineyard scenes and the transporting of the grapes to the wine press were well shown, but the comedy scenes at the end were very poor from every point of view."

Motion Picture News (November 1913): "The first part of this picture is very good. The process the grapes pass through from the time they leave the field until they become wine is shown clearly. A 4,000-acre farm is chosen for the pictures, and interesting figures are given to show the amount of wine produced.

Fatty Joins the Force

Released November 24, 1913. Produced by Mack Sennett for the Keystone Film Co. Distributed by the Mutual Film Corp. Directed by George Nichols. Working title: **Freak Coward**. One reel. Extant: FRIULI, Buch, GEM, LOB, ACAD, QUB. With Roscoe Arbuckle, Dot Farley, Edgar Kennedy, Minta Durfee, George Nichols, Billy White, Charles Avery, George Jeske, Harry De Roy, Mack Swain, Bill Hauber, Hank Mann, Bert Hunn, Billy Gilbert, Jack White, Lou Breslow.

Fatty accidentally saves the police chief's daughter from drowning and as a reward is made a cop. While on duty one warm day he goes in for a swim. Some boys that he had chased earlier in the day cut his trousers into strips and steal the rest of his clothes. Donning his trousers he starts to cover his beat, but is pursued as a lunatic and eventually locked up in his own jail.

Yet another variation of Roscoe in uniform, which also includes *The Gangsters* (1913), *In the Clutches of a Gang*, and *A Brand New Hero* (both 1914). In this version Fatty's main opponents are an unruly group of boys, two of which would go on to have sizeable careers in film comedy.

Jack White, the kid seen smearing the pie in Roscoe's face, became the boy wonder of silent comedy and is today its forgotten mogul, who produced quality comedy shorts for more than ten years. He got his start in pictures at Keystone in 1912, and in 1983 talked about working at Sennett and on *Fatty Joins the Force*:

> *At Sennett, I was really an office boy, but they also put make-up on my face to play kid parts. Fatty Arbuckle was a Keystone cop and played bits. We called him the "cheese of police."*
>
> *In the film, I was hiding in the bushes. He had done something that bothered me and I had an opportunity to hit him with whatever I could find. Just*

Officer Roscoe with future producer/director Jack White (right) in *Fatty Joins the Force* (1913).

then, a baker went by with an apron and pies in the apron. I took one and hit Arbuckle in the face.

I was about thirteen years old and had just graduated grammar school. The director, Daddy Nichols, was an older gentleman. Everybody was an actor as far as he was concerned. Nichols originated pie throwing, but no one ever heard of him.

– Behind the Three Stooges: The White Brothers,
Director's Guild of America, 1990

White was eventually fired by Sennett for inadvertently delivering a rival job offer to star Ford Sterling:

> *Mack heard I had delivered the message that lost him Ford Sterling and thought that I had done it knowingly, which I hadn't. I thought I was doing a friend a favor. Mr. Sennett called me in and said "As of Saturday your employment here is terminated." I had to look it up in the dictionary—what the hell is terminated?*

White immediately got a job with Sterling Comedies, and spent the next few years working for Henry Lehrman—learning editing at L-Ko and directing Fox comedies by age nineteen. At Fox he met and formed a partnership with comic Lloyd Hamilton, and became a full-fledged producer at age twenty-one when they began distributing their shorts through Educational Pictures in 1920.

The 1920s were his glory days—producing shorts with Lloyd Hamilton, Lige Conley, Lupino Lane, Al St. John, and Johnny Arthur, a number of them directed by Roscoe under his pseudonym of William Goodrich. When sound arrived White plowed ahead with Jack White All-Talking Comedies like *Zip! Boom! Bang!* and *Look Out Below* (both

Jack White (center) in the early 1920s surrounded by Lloyd Hamilton (extreme left), Educational Pictures founder E.W. Hammons, E. H. Allen, and director Fred Hibbard (a.k.a. Fishback). Courtesy Cole Johnson.

1929), but the changes in the industry combined with the depression, a nasty divorce, and nervous exhaustion led to the filing of bankruptcy that was the end of his company. Although only in his early thirties White was never able to regain his footing in the film business. He mostly worked on and off for his brother Jules (who had apprenticed under Jack in the 1920s) at the Columbia Pictures Shorts Department, writing and occasionally directing the Three Stooges and Andy Clyde into the 1950s. White died in 1984 at age eighty-seven.

Another of the boys, Lou Breslow, became a busy comedy writer, and even directed and produced for television. After a few film appearances as a kid he joined the industry in the late 1920s writing Fox shorts and features such as *Mum's the Word* (1927), *Plastered in Paris*, and *The Farmer's Daughter* (both 1928). Besides being busy writing in the 1930s he also directed a few shorts, most notably the Three Stooges' *Punch Drunks* (1934), and some of the better known features he wrote include *Hollywood Cavalcade* (1939), Laurel & Hardy's *Great Guns* (1941), and *A Haunting We Will Go* (1942), *Murder He Says* (1945), and *Bedtime for Bonzo* (1951). The bulk of his career was spent at Fox, and he was later very involved in writing and producing for television. *Playhouse 90*, *Leave It to Beaver*, and *My Three Sons* all benefitted from his years of experience. Married for many years to silent comedy ingénue Marion Byron, Breslow retired in the 1960s and passed away in 1987.

Moving Picture World (November 29, 1913): "In this number the Fat Boy saves a drowning child and is rewarded with a place on the police force. The boys steal his clothes while he is bathing and much excitement follows. The humor of this is not as strong as in other offerings by this company."

The Woman Haters

Released December 1, 1913. Produced by Mack Sennett for the Keystone Film Co. Distributed by the Mutual Film Corp. Directed by Henry Lehrman. Working title: **Yachting**. One reel. With Roscoe Arbuckle, Nick Cogley.

Two old salts make a pact to stay away from women, but new ladies who move in across the hall put their anti-female agreement in peril.

This lost film seems to be a sequel to the equally lost *Two Old Tars* from October 20th, with Roscoe and Nick Cogley repeating their roles as two battling salts, and again directed by Henry Lehrman.

Moving Picture World (December 6, 1913): "Two old salts, batching it together, become acquainted with their lady neighbors. Gossip ensues and a row follows, in which the women pull hair and there is a general mixup. This is fairly amusing."

Ride for a Bride

Released December 8, 1913. Produced by Mack Sennett for the Keystone Film Co. Distributed by the Mutual Film Corp. Directed by George Nichols. Working title: **The Golf Ball**. One reel. With Roscoe Arbuckle, Virginia Kirtley, Edgar Kennedy, Charles Avery.

The Woman Haters (1913) has old salts Roscoe and Nick Cogley return in a sequel to *Two Old Tars* (1913).

Aftermath of an auto wreck with Roscoe, Charles Avery, and Edgar Kennedy from *Ride for a Bride* (1913).

Surviving photos show that the plot involved a golf game and auto problems.

A regular leading lady of the 1913 and 1914 Keystone product was Virginia Kirtley. A pretty blonde from Missouri, she began her career on stage in Los Angeles and made her film debut with the small Angelus Motion Picture Company before moving on to Carl Laemmle's Imp. In 1913 she ended up at Keystone in shorts like *Mabel's New Hero* and *A Quiet Little Wedding* (both 1913) playing attractive friends of the leading lady or their rival, but soon graduated to female lead in *He Would a Hunting Go* (1913), *In the Clutches of a Gang* (1914), and Charlie Chaplin's inaugural picture *Making a Living* (1914).

Moving over to the American Film Manufacturing Company, she headlined in their *Beauty* brand of comedies, appearing with the likes of Webster Campbell, Joe Harris, Fred Gamble, and Irving Cummings in shorts that included *Brass Buttons* (1914), *Mrs. Cook's Cooking*, and *When the Firebell Rang* (both 1915). She soon went over to Selig and Horsley, where she did mostly dramas, but in 1916 she began writing stories for Eddie Lyons and Lee Moran's one-reelers. Virginia put Eddie and Lee through their comical paces in *With the Spirits Help*, *Two Small Town Romeos* (both 1916), *To Be or Not To Be Married*, and *The Night Cap* (both 1917). She also married Eddie Lyons in 1916 and retired. Sadly Lyons died in 1926, and she did make one more appearance—in 1928's *The Midnight Adventure*. After marrying screen comic Eddie Fetherston she re-retired and died in 1956.

Arizona Republican (March 4, 1914): "The closer is another one of those screamingly funny Keystone comedies, entitled 'A Ride for a Bride,' a guaranteed sixty-laughs-a-minute production. To see it and not forget your troubles is a sure sign that you need a trip to the mental renovator."

Leading lady and writer Virginia Kirtley. Author's collection.

Fatty's Flirtation

Released December 18, 1913. Produced by Mack Sennett for the Keystone Film Co. Distributed by the Mutual Film Corp. Directed by George Nichols. Working title: ***The Masher***. ½ reel. (Released with ***Protecting San Francisco from Fire***). With Roscoe Arbuckle, Mabel Normand, Minta Durfee, Hank Mann, George Jeske, Frank Cooley.

Roscoe not making much of an impression on Mabel Normand in *Fatty's Flirtation* (1913). Courtesy the George Eastman Museum.

Fatty flirts with every girl he sees, including even his friend's wife. The police take a hand and Fatty suffers in diverse ways.

Early flirtations in a park comedy that would be the blueprint for later re-workings like *Fatty's Jonah Day* (1914), *Fatty's Chance Acquaintance,* and *Wished on Mabel* (1915), with even some of the same locations and actors. A duo of support in this short and in many of the 1913 and 1914 Keystones are Hank Mann and Frank Cooley.

Of the pair, Hank Mann is definitely the best known—becoming a star comic and headlining for a number of different producers. Considered the "comedian's comedian" of the silent era thanks to his underplayed style and dry wit. After some stage experience, and working as a painter near the studio, Mann joined Keystone as an extra in 1912. Playing many cops and other supporting bits, he left Keystone in 1914 and following a brief stint at Sterling Comedies made a name for himself at L-Ko. There he developed his bashful personality and signature brush mustache and bowl haircut. He returned to Sennett as a star for shorts like *His Bread and Butter* and *Hearts and Sparks* (both 1916), but was off again—this time for a series at Fox in entries like *There's Many a Fool* and *The Cloud Puncher* (both 1917) which were directed by Charles Parrott.

The peak of Hank's career was his series of comedies for producer Morris Schlank. Starting in 1919 as one-reelers they expanded to two, and numerous examples such as *The Bill Poster*, *Mystic Mush*, and *Broken Bubbles* (all 1920) were made and circulated on the states' rights market for many years. While these films were playing Hank couldn't appear in his trademark persona for other producers, so he worked behind the scenes as a gag writer for Lloyd Hamilton, Jack White Comedies, Christie Comedies, and features like *The Better 'Ole* and *Kid Boots* (both 1926). Studio "A" features such as *The Boob* (1926) and *Spite Marriage* (1929) provided him supporting character roles, and when sound came in he continued in small bits. His most memorable later work was two appearances with Charlie Chaplin—first as the suspicious boxer in *City Lights* (1931) and as a Keystone storm trooper in *The Great Dictator* (1940). Hank was still getting laughs as late as 1960 with *Man of a Thousand Faces* (1957) and *Rock-a-Bye Baby* (1958), and died in 1971.

Hank Mann at the beginning of his long screen career.

Frank Cooley is an overlooked performer and director who appeared briefly in some of the 1913 and 1914 Keystones before moving on. A stage performer since 1888, he entered pictures with Universal in 1911. Always easy to spot thanks to his big bald head, some of his other Keystone appearances include *A Flirt's Mistake*, *Double Crossed*, and *Mabel's Strange Predicament* (all 1914). That year he joined the American Film Manufacturing Company as a director and worked on comedies, dramas, and westerns such as *Mrs. Cook's Cooking*, *Life's Staircase* (both 1915), and *Wild Jim, Reformer* (1916). After leaving films for a few years he returned as a character actor in the mid-1920s, with supporting roles in the features *The First Year* (1926), *Wanted: A Coward* (1927), and *The Love Trap* (1929). He again left the screen with the arrival of sound and died in 1941.

Moving Picture World (December 20, 1913): "Fatty flirts with a girl, who slaps him and gets the police after him. A half reel with one or two amusing spots in it."

His Sister's Kids

Released December 20, 1913. Produced by Mack Sennett for the Keystone Film Co. Distributed by the Mutual Film Corp. Directed by George Nichols. Working title: **The Doctor's Cat**. One reel. Extant: LOC, ACAD. With Roscoe Arbuckle, Minta Durfee, Gordon Griffith, Jack White, Ford Sterling, Hank Mann, Al St John, Charles Avery, Virginia Kirtley, Rube Miller.

Roscoe is aghast to find out that all the commotion was caused by a cat, and Hank Mann, Bill Hauber, Mack Swain, Rube Miller, Jack White, Minta Durfee, and Gordon Griffith second his motion in *His Sister's Kids* (1913). Courtesy The Museum of Modern Art.

Roscoe is a well-to-do Jewish doctor whose sister comes to visit. She brings along her two trouble-maker sons, and leaves Roscoe to take care of them. They disrupt Roscoe's business, and when the youngest pretends to be trapped down the sewer the Keystone Cops are called to the rescue.

A change of pace for Roscoe, who's very good in a more character role that has him playing older and wearing a goatee. Gordon Griffith and future director/producer Jack White play the troublesome nephews. There are dynamite location shots of Arbuckle and the Cops running and cavorting in real traffic, and the footage looks like it was really grabbed on the sly. The January 3, 1914 *Motion Picture News* reported:

> ### Keystone "Cops" Cause Excitement
> Broadway, Los Angeles' most congested thoroughfare, was recently put at the disposal of the Keystone Company for the making of a picture entitled "His Sister's Kids." In the production the Keystone police were directed to make a chase down this thoroughfare at the busiest time of the day. The city traffic police mistook a fleeing player for an escaped lunatic and there was a genuine struggle in their attempts to capture him.

> *A large crowd gathered, and a bystander was about to turn in a riot call when it was discovered that it was the Keystone Company at work. Meanwhile the Keystone police, coming at full speed, had a hazardous time of it threading their way through the traffic. One of them was hit by a street car and two others had narrow escapes from being run down by autos.*

Besides the kids and the usual Keystone riff-raff, Ford Sterling turns up in a cameo as the police chief in the short scene in the station house.

Motion Picture World (December 20, 1913): "The doctor's life is made miserable by his sister's children, who put the cat down a manhole. The police force is required to recover it. Some fair amusement in this."

Some Nerve

Released December 25, 1913. Produced by Mack Sennett for the Keystone Film Co. Distributed by the Mutual Film Corp. Directed by Mack Sennett. Working title: **The Flirt**. One reel. With Ford Sterling, Roscoe Arbuckle, Dot Farley, George Nichols, Peggy Pearce.

A scheming girl gets Ford Sterling into a compromising situation, where of course he gets caught and ends up in hot water with his jealous wife.

Ford Sterling's jealous spouse is played by Dot Farley—one of America's first important screen comediennes. Starting on stage at the age of three, when she was known as "Chicago's Little Dot," vocal problems led her to enter films with Essanay in 1910. Moving through Essanay, American, and the St. Louis Motion Picture Co., Farley hit Keystone in early 1913 and quickly became the company's chief character woman. From

A disgruntled Ford Sterling gives Peggy Pearce and George Nichols the eye in 1913's *Some Nerve*.

The versatile and neglected slapstick diva Dot Farley.

the beginning of her career Farley was a versatile clown who played a succession of burlesque country girls, homely old maids, and flirtatious vamps. At Keystone she often played Mrs. Sterling or Mrs. Mace in outings like *A Strong Revenge*, *Hide and Seek*, *A Fishy Affair*, and *The Man Next Door* (all 1913). She also had a penchant for crossing her eyes for comic effect, as she does in surviving photos for this film or when she played Sterling's cock-eyed bride in *On His Wedding Day* (1913). This talent came in handy when she later played Ben Turpin's mother in *A Small Town Idol* (1921), *Where's My Wandering Boy This Evening?* (1923), and *Romeo and Juliet* (1924).

Never able to stay with one company for very long, the list of studios and little units she worked for is head-spinning—Frontier Films, Albuquerque Film Manufacturing Co., Kuku Comedies, Fox, Clover Comedies, Universal, and more—and some of these outfits she even wrote comedies for and played in dramas. By the 1920s she had settled into being a crack character comedienne for hire in shorts and features that included *So Big* (1924), *A Woman of the World* (1925), *The Grand Duchess and the Waiter* (1926), and *McFadden's Flats* (1927). Sound didn't faze her one bit and she went on doing small parts, making every second count, in titles like *The Women* (1939), *Cat People* (1942), *Hail the Conquering Hero* (1944), and *The Sin of Harold Diddlebock* (1947), but she's best remembered for her stint as Edgar Kennedy's mother-in-law in his long-running *Average Man* two-reelers. She retired after 1950's *The File on Thelma Jordan*, and died at ninety in 1971.

Moving Picture World (December 27, 1913): "This is the usual nonsensical offering, with the addition of a very pretty girl and a good character part. Ford Sterling goes through more of his emotional comedy and succeeds in bringing out many laughs. Pleasing nonsense."

He Would A Hunting Go

Released December 29, 1913. Produced by Mack Sennett for the Keystone Film Co. Distributed by the Mutual Film Corp. Directed by George Nichols. Working title: **Hunting Story**. One reel. With Roscoe Arbuckle, Hank Mann, Grover Ligon, Virginia Kirtley, Billy Gilbert, Frank Opperman.

Roscoe surrounded by cops and mud in *He Would a Hunting Go* (1913). Billy Rose Theater Division, the New York Public Library for the Performing Arts.

The foreign Count fancies himself as a sportsman, and ventured out alone. A sham bear caused a fall over a cliff and a complete wreck of his reputation.

The plot of a posturing foreigner who fancies himself a brave hunter and is proved to be inept and a coward was very popular around 1910-1915. This production seems to be a specific remake of the Mack Sennett-directed and starring Biograph comedy *The Brave Hunter* (1912), where Mack played the count and Mabel Normand the girl that he was trying to impress. Other examples of the genre includes L-Ko's *The Baron's Bear Escape* (1914) with Henry Bergman as a German nobleperson, and Keystone's own *A Bear Affair* (1915) where David Morris puts on airs for Cecile Arnold and her rich mother Louise Fazenda.

Moving Picture World (December 27, 1913): "In this the Fat Boy appears as a count. The scenes occur in the vicinity of a hunting lodge. He is pursued by a fake bear and the situations become very amusing. There is also quite an element of suspense in this burlesque number. A pleasing offering."

Mabel Normand after hitting what looks like Phyllis Allen with some kind of dessert in *A Misplaced Foot* (1914). Courtesy The Museum of Modern Art.

Chapter 3
Keystone 1914

A Misplaced Foot

Released January 1, 1914. Produced by Mack Sennett for the Keystone Film Co. Distributed by the Mutual Film Corp. Directed by Wilfred Lucas. Working title: **Comedy of Errors**. 2/3 reel (Released with *A Glimpse of Los Angeles*). With Mabel Normand, Roscoe Arbuckle, Minta Durfee.

At a dinner party Mabel has a foot flirtation under the table which leads to all kinds of complications.

This split-reeler follows the misadventures of Mabel's feet under a table, and is part of the subgenre of foot-oriented films that was popular at the time. Starting with Max Linder's 1910 *Le Soulier trop petit* (*Max's Feet Are Pinched*), similar shorts are *Pumps* and *A Reluctant Cinderella* (both 1913) where the heroines are wearing too tight and uncomfortable shoes at fancy soirees which they take off—only to lose them and suffer much social embarrassment. The best known pedal extremity film is Marcel Perez's Italian-made *Amor Pedestre* (*Love Afoot*, 1914), which showcases his sophistication and ingenuity as a director with a clever version of a love triangle soap opera that is entirely performed by the actor's feet.

Besides giving the Arbuckle's the puppy that would become Luke, Wilfred Lucas also directed Roscoe in this and four other shorts when he was hired by Sennett in 1913 to initiate a third directorial unit. Born in Ontario, Canada in 1871, Lucas started his career in grand opera, and then moved into theatre where he toured with his own company, appeared in *Quo Vadis*, and in addition to being a leading man also directed. During his stock company days he had been a friend of D.W. Griffith's and this proved to be his ticket into movies. He joined Griffith's troupe at Biograph in 1908 and was a strong leading man in shorts such as *His Trust*, *The Lonedale Operator* (both 1911), *The Transformation of Mike*, and *The Massacre* (both 1912) until 1912. He spent the first part of 1913 working for Universal's Rex brand, and as he had started directing films while at Biograph he both acted and directed while at Rex, but he wasn't there long as he was tapped by Mack Sennett.

In his six months of working for the "King of Comedy," Lucas piloted shorts like *Get Rich Quick*, *Cohen's Outing*, *Willie Minds the Dog* (all 1913), and *A Glimpse of Los Angeles* (1914), as well as acted in *Billy Dodges Bills*, *Their Husbands* (both 1913), and *Baffles*,

Director and matinee idol Wilfred Lucas.

Gentleman Burglar (1914). After Keystone he moved around—directed at Universal in tandem with Bess Meredyth (whom he married), and returned to D.W. Griffith's aegis as part of his Fine Arts Company. By the time the 1920s rolled around Lucas became a supporting character player and still occasionally directed. In sound films he remained busy, although many of his roles were uncredited, and made a return to comedy films with appearances in many Hal Roach films such as *Pardon Us* (1931), *The Devil's Brother* (1933), and *A Chump at Oxford* (1940). Lucas worked right up to his death in 1940.

Moving Picture World (January 10, 1914): "A half reel comedy, in which Mabel indulges in a flirtation with her feet, under the table. The situations are only fairly amusing."

The Under Sheriff

Released January 8, 1914. Produced by Mack Sennett for the Keystone Film Co. Distributed by the Mutual Film Corp. Directed by George Nichols. Working title: ***The Sheriff***. One reel. With Roscoe Arbuckle, George Nichols, Minta Durfee, Alice Davenport, Frank Opperman, Mack Swain, Phyllis Allen, Charles Avery, Bert Hunn.

Deputy Fatty flirts with his boss' wife, which puts him in bad with the sheriff and the wife's disapproving mother.

In this short Roscoe flirts with his own wife Minta, as the sheriff's wife, and her battle-axe mother is played by Alice Davenport. This early member of the Keystone stock company was the perennial mother-in-law at the studio. Having started her stage career at age five, she spent twenty-five years in stock companies and vaudeville. Her 1893—1896 marriage to actor Harry Davenport (later Dr. Meade in 1939's *Gone with the Wind*) left her with the last name and two daughters—Ann and Dorothy (later Mrs. Wallace Reid). After brief stints at Nestor and Horsley she joined Keystone when the company hit the West Coast in 1912 around the time of *Stolen Glory*, and remained an important player through 1919.

Almost always turning up as the no-nonsense mother or mother-in-law of Mabel Normand or Roscoe, she could also be flirty wives or stage-struck matrons. Sennett actress Dixie Chene told historian Sam Gill that there were a lot of underage girls at Keystone, and not only was Davenport called "Mother Davenport" by the girls, but that she and

A re-release lobby card for *The Under Sheriff* (1914) with Roscoe, Frank Opperman, and Alice Davenport in conflict. Courtesy Sam Gill.

Phyllis Allen watched out for the teens as far as the men on the lot. Having moonlighted a bit for Kalem and Rolin, Ms. Davenport left Sennett for good in 1919 to become a regular in Fox Sunshine Comedies supporting the likes of Slim Summerville, Ethel Teare, and Al St John. Less active in the 1920s, her feature appearances include *Skirts* (1921), *Unmarried Wives* (1924), *Night Life of Hollywood* (1924), and *The Dude Wrangler* (1930).

Norwich Morning Bulletin (January 28, 1914): "'The Under Sheriff' is the title of a very funny Keystone comedy with Fatty, the comedian, causing roars of laughter throughout the entire picture."

A Flirt's Mistake

Released January 12, 1914. Produced by Mack Sennett for the Keystone Film Co. Distributed by the Mutual Film Corp. Directed by George Nichols. Working title: *The Hindoo*. ½ reel. Extant: LOB. (Released with *Moscow and its Environs*). Extant. With Roscoe Arbuckle, Minta Durfee, Edgar Kennedy, Frank Cooley, George Nichols, Bill Hauber, George Jeske, Virginia Kirtley.

Edgar Kennedy is not the damsel that Roscoe expected which illustrates
A Flirt's Mistake (1914). Courtesy the Lobster Collection.

Fatty is a confirmed flirt—even when he's out walking with his wife he can't not make a pass at other women. In the park a foreign rajah is besieged by mashers as they mistake him for a woman from the back because of his flowing robes and umbrella. Much angered by this unwanted attention, the rajah swears death to the next flirt. Fatty has snuck out to the park to get away from Minta's watchful gaze, and sees the rajah from a distance. Assuming he's a woman, Fatty makes the mistake of accosting the sultan, who first beats Fatty with his umbrella and then takes after him with his gun blazing.

Fatty hightails it home, followed by the rajah, who chases Fatty and Minta from room to room. Minta calls to a cop outside for help, and three show up but have a hard time with the magnate themselves. After hiding in the closet Fatty finally subdues the irate caliph, and the police drag him off. When Minta finds out that all of this was caused by Fatty flirting again, she lets him have it worse than the rajah did.

In his shorts Roscoe is always a terrible flirt—ready to ditch his overbearing wife for a pretty face as in *Fatty's Chance Acquaintance* (1915), or as in this short where he has the attractive Minta for his wife but just can't help it. Like *A Flirt's Mistake*, his wandering attentions often lead to dire consequences. Roscoe's flirting with the gang leader's girl in *The Gangsters* (1913) causes total war between the gang and the police force, and thanks to his unwanted attentions to Alice Lake in *A Reckless Romeo* (1917) he gets pounded by her beau Al St John, as well as the incident being captured on film so that his wife and mother-in-law can see it and have at him.

Roscoe's more than ready to flirt with house maids, his wife's friends, chum's girlfriends, neighbor's wives, or burly rajahs in *Fatty's Flirtations* (1913), *A Robust Romeo*, *Fatty's Wine Party* (both 1914), *Mabel, Fatty and the Law*, *Fickle Fatty's Fall* (both 1915), *The Rough House*, and *Coney Island* (both 1917). Problems due to flirting also reared their ugly heads in his directorial efforts like *Never Again* (1924), *Peaceful Oscar* (1927), *Marriage Rows*, and *That's My Line* (both 1931).

Rockford Morning Star (February 1, 1914): "For the laughing part of the program the management has secured the latest Keystone cure for the blues, 'A Flirt's Mistake' with Fatty, a great favorite with motion picture fans, in the comedy character."

Arizona Republican (April 1, 1914): "To complete this program of excellence, a furiously funny Keystone Komedy Knockout is added just by way of extremely good measure. It is entitled 'A Flirt's Mistake' and features the famously laughable Fat Boy in fifteen minutes of excruciating mirth."

In the Clutches of a Gang

Released January 17, 1914. Produced by Mack Sennett for the Keystone Film Co. Distributed by the Mutual Film Corp. Directed by George Nichols. Working title: ***The Disguised Mayor***. Two reels. With Ford Sterling, Hank Mann, Roscoe Arbuckle, Rube

Iconic and much used *In the Clutches of a Gang* (1914) image with Ford Sterling, Edgar Kennedy, Al St John, Hank Mann, Rube Miller, Roscoe, and others.

Miller, Al St John, Edgar Kennedy, George Jeske, Marvin Cox, George Nichols, Virginia Kirtley.

After inadvertently arresting the mayor, Police Chief Teheezal and his uniformed squad must nab a gang of thugs who have been terrorizing the town or lose their jobs.

This is a legendary title, which also has an iconic photograph that's been used over and over with police chief Ford Sterling mugging on the telephone while a line-up of cops that includes Roscoe, Rube Miller, Hank Mann, Al St John, George Jeske, Edgar Kennedy, and others stands by. Unfortunately the film itself is lost, and is a much hoped for rediscovery as it's an important missing piece of the Keystone mythology.

In the photo line-up, and always touted as one of the original Keystone Cops, is George Jeske, who was something of a jack-of-all-trades in the early days of Keystone, working as a bit player, cop, stunt man, and gag writer. Joining the organization in 1913 he was very busy all over the lot, but left in 1914 to fulfill the same functions with the Sterling Film Company. It's said that after Ford Sterling got fired from his own company Jeske was used to double the comic to shoot linking material for unreleased footage. He returned to Sennett to do his multi-functions until 1919, and then made a jump to directing with some of Billy Franey's one-reelers for Reelcraft such as *The Water Plug*, *Play Hooky*, and *Dry Cleaned* (all 1920).

Silent and sound comedy worker bee George Jeske.

A step up in the right direction was made when he landed at the Hal Roach Studio and began helming the anything-for-a-laugh shorts of Snub Pollard, Paul Parrott, and Stan Laurel. This was the peak of his film career, and shorts like *Bowled Over*, *Oranges and Lemons* (both 1923), and *The Big Idea* (1924) are some of his best films. After directing a few 1926 two-reelers for producer Samuel Bischoff he concentrated on and penned shorts for Mack Sennett, Educational, and especially the RKO misadventures of Leon Errol and Edgar Kennedy until 1946.

Moving Picture World (January 10, 1914): "Another of those thoroughly enjoyable burlesque pictures, in which nothing occurs that is to be taken seriously. Ford Sterling as Chief Teheezal has more than the usual amount of trouble. The arrest of the mayor and the scenes on the raft were highly amusing. A very successful nonsense offering."

The Bioscope (October 15, 1914): "This is a two-reel feature of first importance, recording the astounding efforts of the famous Keystone police to round up a gang of crooks, their enthusiasm involving the Mayor in dire disaster. It is a film which shows these remarkable comedians to the best advantage."

Rebecca's Wedding Day

Released January 24, 1914. Produced by Mack Sennett for the Keystone Film Co. Distributed by the Mutual Film Corp. Directed by George Nichols. Working title: ***The Sisters***. One reel. With Roscoe Arbuckle, Billy Gilbert, Minta Durfee, Phyllis Allen, Virginia Kirtley, Frank Opperman, Edgar Kennedy, Mack Sennett, Charles Parrott.

Rebecca is a large Jewish girl who is all set to be married, but instead gets waylaid and experiences complications thanks to a couple of thieves.

Roscoe appears again in drag, this time as a hefty Jewess, and the potshots the film took at the religion caused outcry and cancellation of screenings in various parts of the country. In Chicago:

Roscoe looking alluring and all ready for *Rebecca's Wedding Day* (1914). Courtesy Robert Arkus.

> *The recently formed Anti-Defamation League and other Jewish societies, organized to prevent caricaturing of the Jewish race, exercised their powers of censorship one day last week when Major Funkhouser agreed to suppress a picture reel entitled "Rebecca's Wedding." A committee of Jewish women who viewed the film declared that its purpose was to create laughter by making women of that race appear ridiculous.*
> – **Moving Picture World**, February 7, 1914

The Major Funkhouser referred to was the second deputy of the Chicago police force, and in charge of the city's ten person censor board with "the power to revoke the license of any film which has been granted on the judgement of his subordinates." At the time Metellus Lucullus Cicero Funkhouser was a colorful and well-known figure, and was even parodied in the 1915 Nestor short *Pruning the Movies* as "Major Bunk." In this surviving film Bunk and his band of bluenosers descend on a studio projection room and cut out all kinds of "objectionable" items in an underworld drama—flowers are substituted for knives and prunes for cocaine—until the film makes absolutely no sense.

Charles Parrott (left) and Billy Gilbert (right) making off with bride Roscoe in *Rebecca's Wedding Day* (1914).

Early 1914 saw suits filed against the Chicago board by the World Film Corporation, H & H Film Service, and the Mutual Film Corporation concerning films the studio organizations felt were unjustly banned. The Mutual concern (distributor of Keystone comedies) had this to say about the situation:

> "Rebecca's Wedding Day" is condemned because Rebecca weighs 300 pounds and falls through the bottom of a cab on the way to the church. Had Rebecca been Irish or German there would have been no objection, but Mr. Funkhouser says the picture ridicules the Jewish race. Jewish citizens of high intelligence who have seen the picture see nothing but the real humor in the picture and enjoy it as they enjoy the Potash and Perlmutter stories.
> – **Moving Picture World**, March 7, 1914

Chicago wasn't the only middle-western town to raise objections:

> The Citizen's Commission of Milwaukee, Wis., made public announcement that the reason it stopped the exhibition of the Keystone comedy "Rebecca's Wedding Day," was because the direct representation of a religious organization was held up to ridicule. The statement by President C. B. Radley also said "The actions incident to the hiring of a bridegroom for a ponderously fat daughter becomes decidedly vulgar."
> – **Motion Picture News**, February 28, 1914

Unfortunately at the moment the depiction of Rebecca and her misadventures isn't known to exist for modern audiences to decide if the outcry on the film was justified or due to overt sensitivity.

Moving Picture World (January 24, 1914): "The Fat Boy impersonates a Yiddish girl in this. The characterizations are full of a rough type, but the complications are quite funny and will no doubt please many observers."

Making a Living

Released February 2, 1914. Produced by Mack Sennett for the Keystone Film Co. Distributed by the Mutual Film Corp. Directed by Henry Lehrman. Working title: The Reporters. One reel. Extant: MoMA, LOB, EYE, ACAD, BFI, UCLA, DAN, FRIU. With Charlie Chaplin, Henry Lehrman, Virginia Kirtley, Alice Davenport, Harry McCoy, Chester Conklin, Emma Clifton, Billy Gilbert, Charles Inslee, Eddie Nolan, Beverly Griffith, Grover Ligon, Edgar Kennedy, Roscoe Arbuckle.

A down on his luck sharper borrows money from a friend, and then ends up stealing the fellow's girl. The sharper looks for a job at the friend's newspaper. In order to impress the editor and get a position he steals the story and photographs the friend has done of a dramatic auto accident. Taking off for the newspaper office, the sharper is chased by the wronged friend. Despite running up and down stairs, and through occupied apartments, the sharper gets to the paper first and passes off the scoop as his own. After the newspaper

Emma Clifton panics as Roscoe can be seen in the crowd out the window in *Making a Living* (1914). Courtesy Robert Arkus.

comes out with the story, the friend has no recourse but to attack the sharper, and they fight in the busy street traffic until they're swept away on the front catcher of a speeding streetcar.

Making a Living is famous as the film debut of Charlie Chaplin. Recently recruited by Mack Sennett from the Fred Karno music hall company, Chaplin appears in a very British stage outfit—a long coat, top hat, droopy mustache, and monocle. His persona of the little tramp would arrive in Chaplin's next two pictures—*Kid Auto Races in Venice* and *Mabel's Strange Predicament* (both 1914).

Roscoe's participation was previously unknown, but a recent 35mm showing of the film revealed him in a fleeting cameo. In the scene where Chaplin and Henry Lehrman have run into a sleeping woman's apartment, and her excitable husband returns to battle Lehrman (whom he suspects of compromising his missus), the frantic woman (Emma Clifton) is watching the battle as a crowd can be seen gathering through the window. Very recognizable in the middle of the outside group is Arbuckle in his "Roscoe the tough" character wearing a black T-shirt, white suspenders, and derby. It appears that he's in costume for *Twixt Love and Fire* (February 23, 1914) which was released two weeks after *Making a Living*.

Blink and Roscoe's gone, but considering the Keystone policy of putting anyone not busy at the moment into service, it's possible that there are more of these unknown little Arbuckle cameos.

Moving Picture World (February 7, 1914): "The clever player who takes the role of nervy and very nifty sharper in this picture is a comedian of the first water, who acts like one of Nature's own naturals. It is so full of action that it is indescribable, but so much of it is fresh and unexpected fun that a laugh will be going all the time almost. It is foolish funny stuff that will make even the sober minded laugh, but people out for an evening's good time will howl."

A Robust Romeo

Released February 12, 1914. Produced by Mack Sennett for the Keystone Film Co. Distributed by the Mutual Film Corp. Directed by George Nichols. Working title: ***The Wolf***. One reel. With Roscoe Arbuckle, Emma Clifton, Frank Opperman.

Fatty secretly loves his neighbor's wife, but unfortunately they are discovered by her enraged husband. Fatty, to get over the shock, retires to the mountains, and the husband and wife also do the same thing to get away from the local gossip. Unknown to each other they

Frank Opperman lets the brick do his talking to Roscoe and Emma Clifton in *A Robust Romeo* (1914). Courtesy Sam Gill.

Emma Clifton and Roscoe sneak a meeting in *A Robust Romeo* (1914).
Courtesy the George Eastman Museum.

have secured apartments in the same hotel, and the greatest surprise of all is when they meet. The husband believes it is part of a plot on the part of his wife, and vows vengeance.

Another missing film, which portrayed Roscoe as a lothario caught in a triangle with Emma Clifton and her older husband Frank Opperman. Clifton was a Keystone ingénue that resembled a plump Mabel Normand. The daughter of screenwriters Wallace C. Clifton and Emma Bell, she started her acting career after visiting her uncle at the Lubin Studio in 1912. Coming West with the company she joined Keystone in 1913, and after a brief stay where she was leading lady in shorts like *Double Crossed* and *Between Showers* (both 1914), she soon defected to Sterling Comedies. There she supported star Ford Sterling in outings such as *Love and Vengeance*, *The Fatal Wedding*, and *A Shooting Match* (all 1914) before leaving the screen.

Although just one of their regular one-reelers, Sennett sent the company on location for the second part of the film:

> *Keystone recently sent one of its seven companies to the top of Mt. San Antonio to get snow backgrounds for the picture "A Robust Romeo." The peak, known to Californians as "Old Baldy," rises over 10,000 feet and is a landmark of southern California. The company went nearly to the top*

and worked in over four feet of snow—with one of the players running about in the ice in bare feet and pajamas, this latter feat being called for in an unfeeling scenario. Great difficulty was experienced in reaching the top because of impassable trails and the heavy going. Matters were further complicated by lack of communication, the company being completely cut off from the rest of the world and having no word from the home studio for over three days.

– **Reel Life**, February 14, 1914

Although this is a missing film and impossible to check—it seems very likely that the poor player described above as running around with bare feet and pajamas in the snow and ice was probably Roscoe.

Illustrated Films Monthly (March 1914): "Fatty comes in for a rather warm time, and wishes that he had not been so ardent in his lovemaking."

'Twixt Love and Fire

Released February 23, 1914. Produced by Mack Sennett for the Keystone Film Co. Distributed by the Mutual Film Corp. Directed by George Nichols. Working titles: **The Finnish** and **His Finnish**. One reel. Extant: LOC, AUS. With Roscoe Arbuckle, Edgar Kennedy, Peggy Pearce, Charles Avery, Frank Opperman, Dixie Chene, Alice Davenport, Harry McCoy, Hank Mann.

Edgar is the very jealous type and has a row with his wife Peggy about her flirting before going off to work. Icemen Charles and Fatty arrive to make their deliveries, and as Charles is going up to breakfast and flirt with Peggy he leaves Fatty outside to act as a lookout and whistle if Edgar is coming. Fatty instead whistles to scare Charles so he can flirt with her himself. An angry Charles and Fatty begin fighting in Peggy's apartment, and when Edgar calls during the scuffle he hears the men in the background, leading him to come running with guns blazing. In the meantime Fatty's gone back to his lookout post, and when he sees Edgar coming he whistles like crazy. Charles thinks he's being tricked again and ignores the whistling, so he gets shot at and run off by Edgar.

Eventually Charles returns, but by accident throws a cigarette butt in a pile of papers, which sets the entire building on fire. Fatty's in the apartment with Peggy when the fire's raging. Edgar runs into the burning building and shoots through the door, repeatedly hitting Fatty in the behind as he runs back and forth like a shooting gallery figure. Finally Fatty makes his escape from the apartment window by hanging from a sheet, but leaves Peggy in the fire. Edgar rescues her, and when they get outside he begins to battle with Fatty. Ultimately the pair gets hosed down by the attending firemen.

Long thought lost, 'Twixt Love and Fire was recently rediscovered and recovered by Library of Congress moving image curator Rob Stone from an unidentified European print. Roscoe turns up in the "Fatty the tough" version of his basic character—clad in a derby, black long –sleeved T-shirt, and pants with suspenders. Variations on this persona also are seen in When Dreams Come True (1913), The Knockout (1914), and Fatty's Faithful Fido (1915). In Twixt Love and Fire Roscoe's main support are the Keystone

Peggy Pearce giving iceman Roscoe a cold look in the recently rediscovered *'Twixt Love and Fire* (1914). Courtesy the George Eastman Museum.

Peggy Pearce in the 1914 Sterling Comedy *Snookie's Disguise*. Courtesy the Library of Congress.

regulars Charles Avery, Edgar Kennedy, and Peggy Pearce. Avery has much more to do than usual—he often has a small bit and then disappears, but in this he's Fatty's sidekick through the entire film—whereas Kennedy does his normal routine as the gruff and jealous husband.

Everyone's love interest, Peggy Pearce, was one of the most beautiful leading ladies of silent comedy. She wasn't funny on her own but added a lot of appeal to the comedies with her warm personality and striking looks. Very busy in the teens, she began her career at Biograph in 1913, and soon ended up at Keystone where she worked with Roscoe, Ford Sterling, and Charlie Chaplin. Like Hank Mann and others, Peggy moved to the Sterling Film Co. and L-Ko for items such as *Love and Sour Notes* and *Poor But Dishonest* (both 1915), but then returned to Sennett in 1916. She later did shorts and features for Triangle, and in one of her last films was support for Louise Glaum in *Sex* (1920).

Moving Picture World (February 28, 1914): "One of Mack Sennett's burlesque comedies with a fire scene which is good as far as it goes, and it was still going when the picture was finished. It was quite laughable in spots, however, and well produced. The acting was done in the Sennett style. It will please the public."

Motion Picture News (March 7, 1914): "How can you tell the story of a Keystone picture? There really is no story, at least hardly ever, but there is always the greatest amount of comedy obtainable in 100 feet of film. A flirtatious wife and her two icemen friends certainly cause the husband, and later themselves, considerable anguish."

A Film Johnnie

Released March 2, 1914. Produced by Mack Sennett for the Keystone Film Co. Distributed by the Mutual Film Corp. Directed by George Nichols. Working title: ***A Movie Bug***. Extant: LOC, LOB, UCLA, BFI, EYE, ACAD. One reel. With Charlie Chaplin, Peggy Pearce, Edgar Kennedy, Hampton Del Ruth, Roscoe Arbuckle, Ford Sterling, Henry Lehrman, Minta Durfee, Hank Mann, George Jeske, Billy Gilbert, Harry McCoy, Frank Opperman, Bill Hauber, George Nichols, Grover Ligon, Bert Hunn.

Charlie is a movie fan who gets completely carried away by the film when he goes to his local cinema, much to the annoyance of his fellow viewers. He's especially taken with Peggy Pearce on the screen and causes so much trouble that he's thrown out of the theatre. Charlie decides to go to the Keystone Studio, and gets there to see everyone arriving. He follows them in, and of course does nothing but get in the way and cause problems. Finally he finds his love Peggy, but when they're shooting a dramatic scene where she's being throttled it's too much for Charlie to stand and he rushes in and "saves her." Spoiling the take, Peggy, the irate director, and all the crew chase and abuse Charlie until he pulls out a pistol and begins

Charlie Chaplin literally puts a touch on Roscoe in *A Film Johnnie* (1914).

firing. Disgusted, he leaves the studio, but when the company heads out to take advantage of a real fire for their film's climax, Charlie follows and again disrupts the shooting. Everything descends into total chaos, and when Charlie finally gets soaked by the local firemen he decides that Peggy is not worth all the trouble.

This was Roscoe's first appearance with Charlie Chaplin, and it's just a brief cameo. Roscoe is seen in his street clothes arriving at the studio with Minta, Ford Sterling, and Henry Lehrman. As Arbuckle walks toward the studio Charlie stops him and converses with him as he checks out the width of Roscoe's stomach. Roscoe gives Charlie a once-over, and slips a coin into his hand before going on his way.

The most exciting aspect of *A Film Johnnie* is the great look it gives behind the scenes at Keystone, especially the large shooting stage. Also the scene where the cast and crew head out to make use of the real nearby fire gives an impression of what it must have been like when they really did that. Besides Roscoe in his civvies we also get to see Ford Sterling and Henry Lehrman au natural, and there are funny bits contributed by Edgar Kennedy as the harried movie director and Harry McCoy as a fey movie patron who's annoyed by Charlie in the opening sequence.

Moving Picture World (March 7, 1914): "Edgar English's work in this picture will keep it amusing. There are many good situations, fresh and laughable, and the offering ought to be welcome everywhere as a lightener of the program. Camera work helps a lot."

Tango Tangles

Released March 9, 1914. Produced by Mack Sennett for the Keystone Film Co. Distributed by the Mutual Film Corp. Directed by Mack Sennett. Working title: ***A Midnight Dance***. ¾ reel. (Released with **Washing Our Clothes**). Extant: MoMA, BFI, GEH, UCLA, ACAD, LOB, EYE, DAN. With Charlie Chaplin, Ford Sterling, Roscoe Arbuckle, Edgar Kennedy, Chester Conklin, Peggy Page, Frank Opperman, Charles Avery, Al St John, Bill Hauber, Glen Cavender, Eva Nelson, Hank Mann, Alice Davenport, Rube Miller, George Jeske, Harry McCoy, Minta Durfee, Peggy Pearce, Bert Hunn, David Morris.

Charlie, more than a bit in his cups, shows up at a dance hall and starts flirting with the hatcheck girl. The clarinetist and bandleader of the dance hall's house band are also sweet on the girl, and the three of them have a rivalry for her attentions.

Charlie takes her on the dance floor and is followed by the bandleader, and they proceed to battle it out as the crowd watches. The clarinetist sneaks in and gets the girl, but the other two meet in the cloakroom and resume their fight. Finally, both exhausted, the bandleader gives up the girl, and Charlie gives him one last blow before passing out himself.

A little impromptu film, where scenes shot on location on the actual dance floor of the Venice Dance Hall on Abbott Kinney Pier in Venice, California (with real people as background) are intercut with scenes shot back at the Sennett Studio in Edendale. Roscoe, Charlie, and Ford Sterling are involved in a three-way fight over hatcheck girl Peggy Page. Out of their usual comic make-ups, Chaplin and Sterling furiously try to out mug each other, and of the three Roscoe comes off best—underplaying the suspicious clarinetist and doing his usual thing. He even tries to stop Sterling's mugging by picking up little Charles Avery and holding him over his head as a weapon ready to be used. Practically everyone

Orchestra leader Ford Sterling annoys Roscoe to no end in 1914's *Tango Tangles*. Courtesy Robert Arkus.

else who was employed at Keystone at the time comes dancing by at some point (even Al St John and Chester Conklin who are dancing together as a convict and his jailer).

The Bioscope (August 27, 1914): "Jealousy in a dance room ends in a fight which is engaged in by the dancers, musicians, and attendants."

His Favorite Pastime

Released March 16, 1914. Produced by Mack Sennett for the Keystone Film Co. Distributed by the Mutual Film Corp. Directed by George Nichols. Working title: ***The Drunk***. (Re-issued by W.H. Productions as ***His Reckless Fling***) One reel. Extant: LOC, GEM, UCLA, LOB, EYE, DAN. With Charlie Chaplin, Roscoe Arbuckle, Peggy Pearce, Frank Opperman, Edgar Kennedy, Harry McCoy, Bill Hauber, Billy Gilbert, Rube Miller, Bert Hunn, George Jeske, Hampton Del Ruth.

Charlie is having a few drinks in a bar where he pestered by a shabby bum trying to cadge a drink. Charlie leads him on, pretending to give him a drink but always handing him an empty glass. Charlie leaves the bar as a cab pulls up outside with a society woman and her black maid inside. Charlie flirts with the young woman but is sent off when her gruff older husband shows up.

Charlie Chaplin toys with barfly Roscoe in the opening of *His Favorite Pastime* (1914). Courtesy Robert Arkus.

Returning to the bar Charlie gets in a scuffle with the husband. Taking it on the lam Charlie sees the pretty wife's cab leave so he takes off after it on a streetcar. Following it to her house he enters and looks for her. Turns out that it was only the black maid in the cab, and she's sitting in a room busy with sewing with a cover on her head. Charlie enters the room, and thinking it's the wife embraces her. The housemaid screams and attacks him, and at that point the lady of the house comes in and finds her drunken admirer in the hallway. Her husband also arrives and assumes that Charlie is his wife's lover. The husband and Charlie battle it out while the house staff forms an audience. Finally the worse for wear Charlie is ejected from the premises and staggers away.

His Favorite Pastime was Charlie Chaplin's seventh film, and at this point his character of the little tramp was really starting to make inroads into the public's consciousness and affections. Roscoe appears here in a cameo as the shabby bum in the bar trying to get a drink, but according to movie mythology he contributed an important element to the creation of Chaplin's screen image. Here's David Robinson's telling in his 1985 biography *Chaplin: His Life and Art*:

> The tramp costume, which was to be little modified in its twenty-two year career, was apparently created almost spontaneously, without

premeditation. The legend is that it was concocted one rainy afternoon in the communal male dressing room at Keystone, where Chaplin borrowed Fatty Arbuckle's voluminous trousers, tiny Charles Avery's jacket, Ford Sterling's size fourteen shoes which he was obliged to wear on the wrong feet to keep them from falling off, a too-small derby belonging to Arbuckle's father-in-law, and a moustache intended for Mack Swain's use, which he trimmed to toothbrush size.

In his 1964 autobiography Chaplin says that after being told to "Put on a comedy make-up. Anything will do," he did go and borrow the above clothing, but he doesn't say who he borrowed the items from (Chaplin rarely admitted who he borrowed things from). While the creation of his costume sounds like something a publicity agent dreamt up, Fred Goodwins, who later worked for Chaplin and wrote about it in a series of articles for the British magazine *Red Letter*, had this to report in the May 6, 1916 entry where he describes himself and Chaplin going through items in the comedian's office:

> *Then he proceeded to unearth a number of photographs from the recesses of his trunk. Many of them were of famous folk. All of them were signed. I noticed one from Roscoe Arbuckle ("Fatty" of the Keystone Co.) which read, "To dear old Charlie. What would you had done without my trousers?*
>
> *I asked Charlie what Roscoe had meant by that, and he told me how, when he first "broke into" the picture game, he had been compelled to gather up bits of wardrobe from various members of the company, because they needed him in a hurry, and he had no time to go down town and make a careful selection at the second-hand dealers.*

Roscoe's pants, already popular on himself, became even more iconic on Chaplin's person.

While Charlie was growing more popular, the regular Keystone supporting crew was keeping busy doing anything and everything that was needed to put over laughs. On hand here are Edgar Kennedy, Billy Gilbert, Bill Hauber, Rube Miller, and as Peggy Pearce's outraged husband who trounces Chaplin within an inch of his life, Frank Opperman. A Houston, Texas-born stage actor, whose twenty-eight-year career on the boards included appearing in Shakespeare with Edwin Booth and Minnie Madden Fiske, and playing Fagin in *Oliver Twist*, Opperman entered films in 1910 as part of D.W. Griffith's Biograph Company. While he appeared in many of the maestro's dramas such as *Ramona* (1910), *The Old Actor* (1912), *The Battle of Elderbush Gulch* (1913), and *Judith of Bethulia* (1914), he also played in Mack Sennett-directed comedies like *Helen's Marriage*, *A Close Call*, *Neighbors*, and *Katchem Kate* (all 1912).

He turned up in the very early Keystones *The Beating He Needed*, *Stolen Glory*, and *The Ambitious Butler* (all 1912), but headed over to Bison and Biograph before coming back to Sennett in 1913. Working frequently with Roscoe, he specialized in fathers, farmers, sheriffs, irate husbands, boarding house proprietors, and other authority figures. Some of their films together are *He Would a Hunting Go* (1913), *The Under Sheriff*, *The Knockout*, *Those Country Kids* (all 1914), *Fatty's New Role*, and *The Little Teacher* (both

Frank Opperman gets chummy with Roscoe in 1914's *Fatty Again*. Courtesy Sam Gill.

1915). Opperman also appeared in Triangle comedies until 1917 when he bought an olive grove in Fallbrook, California. He retired from the screen and died in 1922.

Moving Picture World (March 21, 1914): "One of the few farcical comedies in photoplays that gets continuous laughter. The comedian, whose favorite pastime is drinking highballs, is clever, in fact the best one Mack Sennett has sprung on the public. He is a new one and deserves mention. The situations in this offering are finely handled. This is a real comedy."

Motion Picture News (March 28, 1914): "If there is an audience anywhere outside of a blind asylum that does not roar when they see this comedy they cannot be in full possession of their wits. It is absolutely the funniest thing the Keystone Company has ever put out, and this is not written by a press agent. Charles Chaplin, the English comedian, and Velma Pearce play the leads. Mr. Chaplin has introduced a number of funny actions that are original to the American stage. His adventures in a saloon are unique to say the least."

A Rural Demon

Released March 19, 1914. Produced by Mack Sennett for the Keystone Film Co. Distributed by the Mutual Film Corp. Directed by Henry Lehrman & Mack Sennett. Working title: ***A Horse***. One reel. With Roscoe Arbuckle, Eva Nelson, Charles Avery.

Eva Nelson and Charles Avery have a laugh at Roscoe's expense in *A Rural Demon* (1914). Courtesy the George Eastman Museum.

A barnyard story full of chases, fractious fowls, and a lit bomb on the back of a man whose explosion throws everyone into the river.

Roscoe's leading lady in *A Rural Demon* is the forgotten comedienne Eva Nelson. Little is known about Nelson, but she was Texas-born and a dancer in vaudeville and musical comedies before she joined Keystone in 1914. Appearing to have been discovered by Henry Lehrman, during her brief time at the Sennett studio she frequently worked with Roscoe and Charlie Chaplin in shorts like *Cruel, Cruel Love*, *A Bath House Beauty*, and *Mabel's Married Life* (all 1914). As part of the group that left Keystone to be part of Lehrman's new L-Ko Company she usually worked in support of Billie Ritchie.

Sadly the bulk of the L-Kos are lost and unavailable, but Nelson is very good in the surviving *Live Wires and Love Sparks* (1916) as Ritchie's put upon wife who hatches a scheme and gets her revenge. Her other L-Ko titles include *Almost a Scandal*, *Stolen Hearts and Nickels* (both 1915), and *Billie's Waterloo* (1916). When Lehrman moved over to Fox Sunshine Comedies, Nelson turned up in a few and then disappeared from the screen.

Moving Picture World (March 21, 1914): "Here is one of Mack Sennett's comedy pictures. It is a hummer in every way. It has a regular rural twang and never hesitates from start to finish. It embraces all kinds of characters, including a fractious goose. There is a bomb effect, a chase and a wind-up where everybody gets soaked but the cameraman, in the river. If you want a good laugh see it."

Motion Picture New (March 28, 1914): "A typical Keystone, full of action, no story, yet always provocative of mirth. A bomb, lighted on the back of a man causes everyone to fly at his approach. A trained horse registers some good work."

Barnyard Flirtations

Released March 28, 1914. Produced by Mack Sennett for the Keystone Film Co. Distributed by the Mutual Film Corp. Directed by Roscoe Arbuckle. Working title: ***The Farmer's Toe***. One reel. Extant: LOC. With Roscoe Arbuckle.

Director Arbuckle lining up a shot. Courtesy Marc Wannamaker/Bison Archives.

Fatty is the village policeman who is engaged to catch the thief who has been stealing his future father-in-law's eggs. The plans to capture the crook backfire and puts Fatty into a compromising situation with the farmer's wife.

By the end of 1913 Mack Sennett was getting busier and busier dealing with studio business and administrative duties, so he began curtailing his on-screen appearances and directing, and began giving his star comics the opportunity to supervise their own films. Mabel Normand was the first, who starting with the December 27, 1913 short *The Champion* began calling the shots behind the scenes as well as in front of the camera. Ford Sterling was next at the beginning of 1914 with *Double Crossed*, and then it was Roscoe's turn with *Barnyard Flirtations*. Having been trained by Sennett and Lehrman, two of the best comedy directors in the business, Arbuckle took to directing like a fish to water, and eventually became the best and most sophisticated director on the lot.

Moving Picture World (April 4, 1914): "Of all the rough and tumble comedies ever made this one swipes the palm. The entire cast of principals as well as their support must be made up of acrobats, even the young lady who plays the farmer's daughter. She certainly earns her salary. This picture was rewarded with the heartiest laughter from the reviewers, and it was spontaneous. Mack Sennett can certainly dig up funny ones and put them over. Exhibitors you can book this "for fun."

The Bioscope (August 27, 1914): "Mr. Wurzel misses his eggs and engages the village policeman, then decides upon a ruse which unexpectedly reveals his buxom wife as a flirt and the reason of the cop's non-success."

The Chicken Chaser

Released April 2, 1914. Produced by Mack Sennett for the Keystone Film Co. Distributed by the Mutual Film Corp. Directed by Roscoe Arbuckle. Working title: **New Yard Lovers**. (re-released by W.H. Productions as **Fatty Chases Chickens**) One reel. With Roscoe Arbuckle, Charles Avery, Bill Hauber, Edward Cline, Chester Conklin, Hank Mann.

Fatty, a hired man, is in love with the farmer's daughter, but unluckily is suspected of stealing chickens. The guilty party turns out to be his rival for the girl.

One of Roscoe's many rural frolics, this time with a young Eddie Cline among the cast. Besides being one of the great film comedy collaborators, Cline was said to have been one of the nicest and easiest going guys in the business—which came in handy when he directed W. C. Fields in five pictures. Cline started in films as an extra, and landed at Keystone where he did bit parts and became an assistant to director Dell Henderson. Soon he was directing with Hampton Del Ruth, then on his own with films such as *A Bedroom Blunder* (1917) and *Hearts and Flowers* (1919), before moving over to Fox Sunshine Comedies. In 1920 he hooked up with Buster Keaton, and was his collaborator on seventeen shorts and his first feature *The Three Ages* (1923). Following his work with Buster, Cline returned to shorts for Sennett, while doing occasional features for Jackie Coogan and others. In sound he famously worked with Fields, Wheeler & Woolsey, and Olsen & Johnson, directing classics like *Million Dollar Legs* (1932), *So This Is Africa* (1933), *The Bank Dick* (1940), and *Crazy House* (1943). He finished his career doing *Maggie and*

Roscoe in a famous Keystone Comedies publicity composite.

Jiggs programmers for Monogram, plus contributing to the TV shows of Buster Keaton and Spike Jones.

Motion Picture News (April 11, 1914): "A typical Keystone comedy containing a great assortment of brick-throwing, tumbling, etc. This hero loved two varieties of chickens, both made trouble for him."

The Bioscope (October 1, 1914): "Mr. Roscoe Arbuckle, who seems to be made of watch springs and elastic, provides mirth during the entire length of a very amusing film."

A Bath House Beauty

Released April 13, 1914. Produced by Mack Sennett for the Keystone Film Co. Distributed by the Mutual Film Corp. Directed by Roscoe Arbuckle. Working title: **Bathing Picture**. One reel. Extant: MoMA. With Roscoe Arbuckle, Minta Durfee, Gordon Griffith, Edgar Kennedy, Charles Avery, Charles Murray, Hank Mann, Ted Edwards, Charles Lakin.

Fatty goes to the beach with his wife and son, but his flirting ways with a girl leads to her jealous and gun-toting boyfriend going after him. Disguised as a female bather Fatty flees throughout the amusement area and onto the roller coaster.

A break-neck paced hanky-panky at the beach short, which incorporates favorite Arbuckle routines such as drag in a ladies' bathing suit and chases on and around the rides of an amusement park. Something of a dry run for 1917's *Coney Island*, Fatty is bored with the domesticity of his family, and is ready to indulge in a little extra-curricular flirtation, which always leads to dire and animated consequences.

Moving Picture World (April 18, 1914): "Talk about actions and stunts to produce comedy, it is all incorporated in this picture. The strenuousness indulged in by the cast certainly kept the cameraman awake. The seashore resort scenes are hummers, taking in all the various devices. The facility with which they are engrafted in the plot does credit to the director. It causes hilarious laughter."

Roscoe getting the worst from Minta Durfee and Gordon Griffith in *A Bath House Beauty* (1914). Courtesy The Museum of Modern Art.

Motion Picture News (April 18, 1914): "The novelty of continued chases through a number of switchbacks, scenic railways, Ferris wheels and skating rinks provoke much mirth."

The Bioscope (August 13, 1914): "Strenuous action and farcical scenes on the seashore make up a bustling comic."

When Hazel Met the Villain

Released April 23, 1914. Produced by Mack Sennett for the Keystone Film Co. Distributed by the Mutual Film Corp. Directed by Roscoe Arbuckle. Working title: **Burglar's Union**. One reel. With Roscoe Arbuckle, Phyllis Allen.

For rejecting the villain's advances Hazel is tied to the railroad tracks. Fatty, the hero, has to overcome various obstacles and curious animals in his race to rescue her.

Descriptions of this lost film make it sound like a re-tread of 1912's *Barney Oldfield's Race for a Life*, except without Barney Oldfield and his auto coming in as the deus ex machina to rescue the girl on the tracks. In this version Roscoe as the hero appears to be on his own to surmount the obstacles in his way to save the heroine. This basic plotline would be dusted off numerous times for comedies. To begin with it was used as a satire of stage melodramas, and as time went on it would return in pictures like *Teddy at the Throttle* (1917) as a tongue-in-cheek parody of itself and of early movies.

Phyllis Allen has a grizzly experience in *When Hazel Met the Villain* (1914).
Courtesy the George Eastman Museum.

The Bioscope (August 27, 1914): "In return for a refusal, Hazel is bound to the line. Here she is entertained by a bear and other animals. The hero attempts a rescue, but his horse unseats him and, beating the flying tanker, does the brave deed himself."

The Bowery Boys

Released April 25, 1914. Produced by Mack Sennett for the Keystone Film Co. Distributed by the Mutual Film Corp. Directed by George Nichols. Working title: ***Trouble***. One reel. With Roscoe Arbuckle, Charles Avery.

Fatty is the heroine in a jewel heist story where the cops cause their usual complications.

Crooks, jail breaks, and robberies were common elements in the Keystone universe. Shady shenanigans were often the stock-in-trade of a large part of its general riff-raff and lower-class characters. While players like Hank Mann, Fred Mace, Joe Bordeaux, and even Al St John sometimes turned up as low-life thugs, Roscoe was always on the good side of the law. Frequently he would be an inept cop, or, as in this missing short, in drag as a heroine who would be a prime target for kidnapping and ransom. Some of the titles that have Roscoe involved with miscreants or underworld figures include *Safe in Jail* (1913), *A Brand New Hero, Leading Lizzie Astray* (both 1914), *The Bright Lights,* and *He Did and He Didn't* (both 1916).

Roscoe is the heroine in need of rescue in *The Bowery Boys* (1914). Courtesy The Museum of Modern Art.

The Bioscope (September 10, 1914): Burlesque jewel-stealing drama with Fatty as the lovely heroine and the "police" as usual, always in the way."

A Suspended Ordeal

Released May 9, 1914. Produced by Mack Sennett for the Keystone Film Co. Distributed by the Mutual Film Corp. Directed by Roscoe Arbuckle. Working title: **Hung by a Hook**. One reel. With Roscoe Arbuckle, Minta Durfee.

Fatty is a cop, who gets involved in a mix-up with another cop and their wives.

Very little information exists on this missing film, but it appears to be a reworking of the 1913 Keystone *A Life in the Balance*.

"Oh, it's great to be a comedian—if there's a hospital handy!"

Roscoe had just reached his first year's anniversary at Keystone, and had even lived to celebrate it. A year later Mack Sennett would reminisce in the May 1915 issue of *Photoplay*:

> *We got him in the beginning because he was the rare combination of fat and perfect athlete. Arbuckle is a wonderful athlete in spite of his weight.*

Minta Durfee seems to be saying the wrong thing to Roscoe's superior officer in *A Suspended Ordeal* (1914). Courtesy The Museum of Modern Art.

> *We got him on account of the falls he could make. Every week he has been developing. I can see the difference in every picture we turn out. He began as a rough "faller" and has become a finished artist. And he is still going.*

During his first twelve months with Sennett Roscoe had done a glossary's worth of assorted tumbles and falls, dodged bullets, been drug from carriages, dumped off cliffs, hit with various flying objects, ran barefoot in the snow, was singed by fire, and nearly blown up with dynamite. Or as Roscoe put it:

> *Yes, I have done my worst in "Two Old Tars," A Noise from the Deep, ""The Riot," and "The Gangsters." But outside of falling on my ear, being chased by bears and surrounded by snakes, or doing forty-five-foot dives off the long wharf at Santa Monica, my work has been rather uneventful.*
> – **Motion Picture**, September, 1914

Having to be an engineer to plan his stunts and a tip-top athlete to survive them, Roscoe elaborated a bit more in the April 1916 *Photoplay* article *Why Aren't We Killed?*:

> *We figure it out on paper, and if it looks as if it will work we do it. That's all there is to it. Now and then it doesn't work, and we either have to plan it a different way, or do it over again until we get it. Naturally I figure pretty carefully, because I don't want to roll off a roof more than seven or eight times just for a foot or two of film.*
> Then you don't figure on what will happen if you miss?
> *Certainly not. First of all, you can't clutter up the place with a lot of lifesaving apparatus, and next of all, if you begin to think about what will happen if you miss, you are pretty sure to miss.*
> Then it isn't a question of tricks?
> "Each one of Arbuckle's three hundred and eighty-five pounds got mad."
> *Say—if you, or anyone else, can show me a way that I can seem to fall through a roof, or into a river, and not do it, or even do it slow so that I can land gently, you can have just about half of my salary. Our stuff cannot be faked. When people see it they know they are seeing real stunts. Of course, now and then we do a trick film, but everyone knows it's a trick when they see it—there's no bunk about it.*
> *No, the only times I have been injured in the least, is when I have loafed on the job. A child or a drunk can fall all over itself and never be hurt. It is because they simply let go and flop. The same rule works with me. If I go right after the stuff, we get a real picture and I don't get a scratch. If I happen to be lazy, we usually have to do the scene over again, and I get a few bruises as a result.*

Bantam-weight boxer Al McNeil seems to be getting the worst while roughhousing with Roscoe.

Moving Picture World (May 23, 1914): "This Keystone comedy is decidedly laughable, the humor is of the rollicking variety with a bit of farce mixed up with it."

The Water Dog

Released May 18, 1914. Produced by Mack Sennett for the Keystone Film Co. Distributed by the Mutual Film Corp. Directed by Roscoe Arbuckle. One reel. Extant: BFI. With Roscoe Arbuckle, Alice Davenport, Minta Durfee, Baby Doris Baker, Charles Avery, Grover Ligon, Harry Russell.

Fatty is eating dinner at a diner, and then hooks up with his sweetie Alice. At the same time a nanny in charge of a little girl and her dog gives the kid money for an ice cream. Fatty

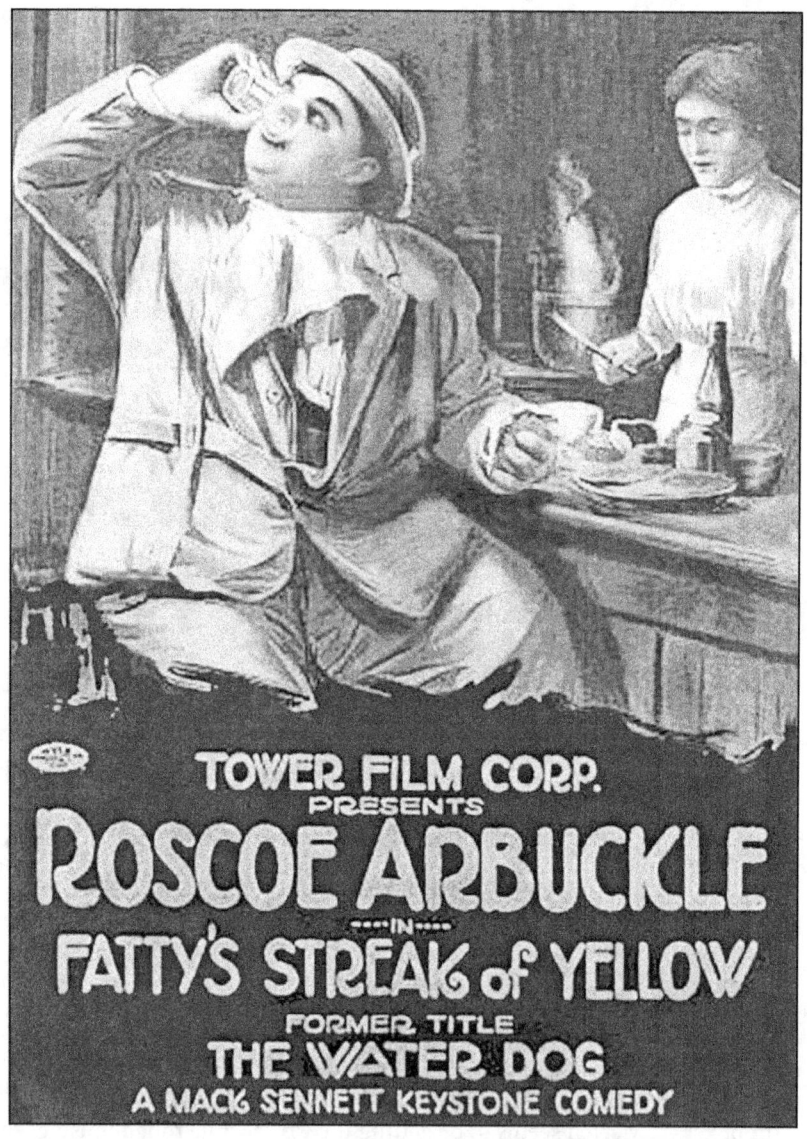

Tower Film Corporation's reissue poster for 1914's *The Water Dog*.

and Alice are spooning on the beach. The nanny's beau shows up and they spoon on the beach too, and neglect the little girl. When the nanny's fella goes to buy ice cream cones Fatty goes over and flirts with her. When the guy comes back with the cones he sees Fatty making time with his girl, so he alerts Alice who gives Fatty the what-for. In the meantime the neglected little girl and her dog have gone to sleep on a rock on the beach. All the various sweeties have patched things up, but the tide has come and trapped the little girl on the rock. The Keystone Cops are called who pile into boats, etc., with their usual inept results. In the excitement Fatty falls off a pier and has to be pulled out of the water. The little girls' tiny dog runs and gets a bigger dog who plunges into the surf and brings the kid to shore.

Kids and animals played an important part in the Keystone film universe from the very beginning, and *The Water Dog* displays both groups prominently. Comedies where children were key plot elements, such as *Hide and Seek* (1913), led Henry Lehrman to initiate a series of "Keystone Kids."

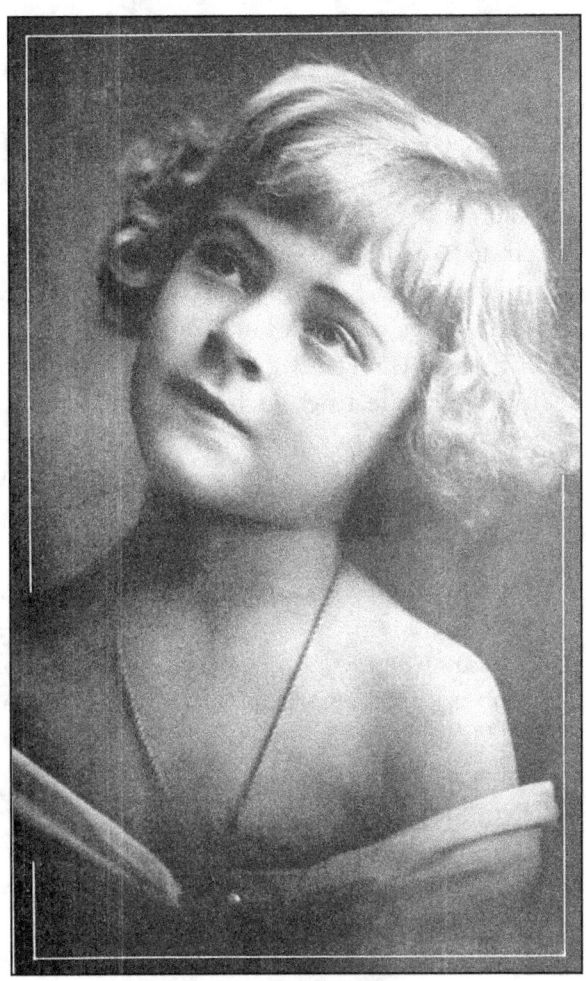

Popular child actress Doris Baker.

The casts included child actors Gordon Griffith, Thelma Salter, Charlotte Fitzgerald, Matty Roubert, and Paul Jacobs. After films like *Just Kids* and *Our Children* (both 1913), Jacobs became the star as "Little Billy," and headlined in *Little Billy's Triumph* and *Little Billy's City Cousin* (both 1914) before defecting to Sterling Comedies.

The Water Dog's neglected little girl was played by Doris Baker, a busy child actress who had been appearing in Pacific Coast vaudeville. Having made her film debut for the Powers Picture Play company in 1913, she made the rounds in shorts at studios such as Lubin, Bison, and Universal brands like Nestor, Imp, and Rex. Most of her screen work was in dramas, but besides *The Water Dog* she turned up in *Court House Crooks* (1915) for Keystone. Moving on to features films like *Glory* (1917) with the team of Kolb & Dill she played Juanita Hansen as a child, and was one of the orphans in *Little Orphant Annie* (1918) with Colleen Moore. Her career slowed down in the 1920s, with a few features like *The Secret Gift* and *Youth's Desire* (both 1920), in addition to appearing again with Colleen Moore in *Ella Cinders* (1926). Her later film appearances were as a chorus girl in the musicals *Happy Days* (1929) and *George White's 1935 Scandals* (1935), and she passed away at ninety-one in 1998.

Like kids, animals were also much in use on the lot. A short like *A Little Hero* (1913) is practically a forerunner of Hal Roach's later *Dippy-Doo-Dad* comedies, as Mabel Normand turns up at the beginning and end of a story about her little dog's attempt to protect a new canary from the jaws of the family cat. Roscoe would soon make his dog Luke a popular Keystone player, and Sennett himself would eventually develop a couple of animal stars.

In 1916 Teddy the Great Dane became a studio regular. Owned by Joseph E. Simpkins, and nicknamed "Keystone Teddy," he appeared in numerous shorts like *Teddy at the Throttle*, *A Dog Catcher's Love* (both 1917), *Down on the Farm* (1920), *Bow Wow* (1922), and *The Extra Girl* (1923). In addition to a few shorts for Century Comedies he also turned up in dramatic features such as *Stella Maris* (1918), *The Stranger's Banquet* (1922), and Jackie Coogan's *A Boy of Flanders* (1924), before dying of old age at fourteen in 1925.

Sennett's other feral Barrymore was Pepper, a dark Maltese cat, who was said to have been a stray kitten who just showed up on the lot one day and was adopted by the producer. Eventually billed as "the Sarah Bernhardt of Alley Cats," her earliest appearance may be the aforementioned *A Little Hero* (1913). She frequently worked with Louise Fazenda, and her titles include *A Bedroom Blunder* (1917), *The Kitchen Lady* (1918), *Reilly's Wash Day* (1919), *Down on the Farm* (1920), and *On a Summer's Day* (1921).

Moving Picture World (May 30, 1914): "A lively comedy with a plot which serves for the filming of a big human interest climax when a clever little girl swimmer is piloted safely back to shore from a rock in the ocean by a well-trained dog. The photography is excellent."

Motion Picture News (May 30, 1914): "Directed and acted by Roscoe Arbuckle, "The Fat Boy." The maid's lover and her mistress get mixed up, so the maid steals her mistress's lover. Two dogs do some clever work."

The Bioscope (October 22, 1914): "This clever film introduces the Keystone police, a remarkably clever and attractive little child actress, and two dogs, who achieve a rescue of the little girl from the sea, which should rouse any audience to enthusiasm. It is an excellent combination of farce and excitement, and beautifully photographed."

The Alarm

Released May 28, 1914. Produced by Mack Sennett for the Keystone Film Co. Distributed by the Mutual Film Corp. Directed by Roscoe Arbuckle. Working title: **Fireman's Picnic**. 2 reels. With Roscoe Arbuckle, Mabel Normand.

The chief of police and the chief of the fire department are rivals for the same girl. At the country fair they go through all kinds of foolish encounters to see who is the best, and their antics are continued throughout the picture. The picture ends with a wild chase where a firetruck winds up over a cliff and Fatty, the fire chief, is pulling the whole police force behind him by means of a rope. After the police the whole town is tearing in pursuit.

This is the first two-reeler directed by Roscoe, but sadly it's not known to exist. It sounds like an elaborate production, as the June 27, 1914 *Moving Picture World* reported that "there is a runaway in which a fire engine goes over a bluff."

Roscoe taking a break from *The Alarm* (1914) to pose on the firetruck with a friend and his dog.

Motion Picture News (June 27, 1914): "The first reel of this offering is below the usual Keystone standard, but what the first reel lacks the second reel amply supplies in regard to humor. The Keystone fat boy, Roscoe Arbuckle, is the important member of the cast. Whenever he appears he is good for a laugh from all."

Moving Picture World (June 27, 1914): "Keystone hasn't turned out anything funnier than this two-part farce in a long while, if ever. As usual, it is rough and tumble, helter-skelter; but the spirits of laughs is behind what goes on in it, especially of the second reel. As an offering to the public it is first class, there can be no doubt at all about it. But it is so full that it would be hard to give a compressive account of it. Roscoe Arbuckle is the author and director. It's a scream."

The Knockout

Released June 11, 1914. Produced by Mack Sennett for the Keystone Film Co. Distributed by the Mutual Film Corp. Directed by Mack Sennett. Working title: **Fighting Demon**. Two reels. (Reissued by W. H. Productions in 1919 as *The Pugilist*) Extant: FRIU, DAN, LOC, MoMA, BFI, CAN, UCLA, LOB, ACAD, EYE. With Roscoe Arbuckle, Minta

Minta Durfee, Al St John, and Roscoe have a confrontation in a reissue lobby card for *The Knockout* (1914). Courtesy Annichen Skaren.

Durfee, Edgar Kennedy, Charles Chaplin, Al St John, Hank Mann, Grover Ligon, Mack Swain, Frank Opperman, Mack Sennett, Charles Lakin, Charles Avery, Rube Miller, Slim Summerville, Charles Parrott, Edwin Frazee, Glen Cavender, Harry McCoy, Wallace MacDonald, Alice Howell, Eddie Nolan, Dan Albert, Frankie Dolan, Luke, James Bryant.

Two hungry tramps come to town, and to get money for food they convince the local theatre owner that one of them is the famous boxer Cyclone Flynn, and get the owner to set up an exhibition fight with all challengers. At the same time Fatty and Minta's romance is being interrupted by a jealous Al with slaps, kicks, and thrown bricks. After being routed by Fatty, Al, impressed with his fighting prowess, convinces him to accept the challenge and fight Cyclone Flynn.

But after Fatty agrees to fight the real Cyclone Flynn happens into town, trounces the imposters, and decides to do the exhibition fight himself. With Al and his gang's help Fatty goes into training—breaking chains and lifting 500 pound weights like they were nothing.

In the evening Minta dresses as a boy so she can come to the fight. Everyone files in for the bout, including a cowboy-type with pistols who tells Fatty "I'm betting heavy on you, so win or I'll kill you," and brandishes one of the pistols to prove he means business. The fight begins with a very spritely referee, who has trouble staying out of the way of the punches. When things look bad for Fatty he grabs the westerners pistols and begins firing at and chasing Cyclone Flynn, out of the theatre and over the roofs, and into a fancy society ballroom.

The Keystone Cops were called at the beginning of the fracas and they're soon on the scene following the boxers as they run here and there. Finally Fatty runs out of bullets and is roped by the cops, but he beats them in a tug of war and drags them down the street to a pier where he sends them all into the drink for the big climax.

The Knockout has Roscoe returning to Mack Sennett's direction in a two-reeler that makes up for a lack of subtlety with an abundance of speed and frenetic action. Interesting directorial touches include an angry Roscoe walking closer and closer to the camera until his distorted countenance fills up the screen, and later when Roscoe's going to change his trousers he notices the camera and motions for it to raise up so his lower extremities are out of camera range. The best-known item of this short is Charlie Chaplin's cameo as the balletic referee that's pure English music hall, with Charlie getting most of the punches himself.

During the big action chase sequence Roscoe and Edgar Kennedy are seen running through the big mansion ballroom set from *Tillie's Punctured Romance* (1914). Roscoe is notably absent from the cast of *Tillie*, which is often attributed to Marie Dressler not wanting to be upstaged by another hefty performer who looked better in a dress than she did. In a 1964 television interview with the Canadian Broadcasting Corporation Buster Keaton talked about Roscoe having directed parts of *Tillie* ("Arbuckle directed 'bout half of that picture"), which is likely something Roscoe told him. So far no information has turned up to corroborate Buster's statement. Brent Walker, author of *Mack Sennett's Fun Factory* (McFarland, 2010) the definitive study of all things Sennett, offers:

> *I never came across evidence to substantiate Buster's claims that Roscoe directed any of Tillie. However, since it was a large project being produced*

Roscoe, Al St John, Charles Lakin, and others workout in *The Knockout* (1914). Courtesy Annichen Skaren.

sort of piece-meal, unofficially (since Mutual didn't request a feature) around the standard one and two reel units schedules, it definitely seems possible that Roscoe could have directed a scene or two, or that other Keystone directors might have. I can't imagine that Sennett actually had time to direct the entire thing.

At any rate Roscoe's working behind the scenes on *Tillie* is a possibility, and it's hoped that perhaps someday some kind of definitive information will turn up.

Moving Picture World (July 4, 1914): "Roscoe Arbuckle, ably supported, makes barrels of fun in this two-reel comedy release. In its early stages, the story has a particularly well-connected plot, but things go to smash a little in this line when a big chase is introduced in the second reel. This chase, as well as a comedy prize fight, is unusually funny."

Motion Picture News (June 27, 1914): "Roscoe Arbuckle assumes the leading role. The comedy is not as good as most Keystones, although hilarious in parts. The usual brick throwing and the chase play prominent parts."

Fatty and the Heiress

Released June 25, 1914. Produced by Mack Sennett for the Keystone Film Co. Distributed by the Mutual Film Corp. Directed by Roscoe Arbuckle. Working titles: ***Marrying Money*** and ***Love and Money***. Two reels. Extant: LOC. With Roscoe Arbuckle, Phyllis Allen, Minta Durfee, Charles Bennett, Gordon Griffith, Charles Avery, Billie Bennett, Charles Parrott.

Fatty is in love with a beautiful poor girl, but when he hears about a homely girl that has inherited a fortune he gets rid of the pretty girl and marries the ugly one. Sadly he finds that he has been tricked—she's not rich but is still homely. In his desperation he makes an attempt to poison her, but when the film ends Fatty is still a husband—and a badly disillusioned one.

The murderous side of the Fatty character is explored in this short. Disappointed in his love match with Phyllis Allen, Fatty doesn't know what to do until he sees a newspaper placard about an incident where a wife was killed with poisoned candy. Fatty decides to try that himself, and after getting a box of candy goes to chemist Charles Bennett's shop. Luckily Bennett is suspicious and gives him something phony, and after Fatty dusts the candy with the powder he gets a kid to deliver it to Phyllis. It's only due to Bennett's suspicion that the murder doesn't occur—Fatty's intent was real.

Roscoe getting a bad idea from the placard in *Fatty and the Heiress* (1914).
Courtesy the Library of Congress.

Roscoe putting his *Fatty and the Heiress* (1914) plot in motion with Charles Bennett. Courtesy the Library of Congress.

Charles Bennett, who plays the wise apothecary, was one of the most seriously experienced actors to work for Keystone. During an extensive stage career he had worked with Edwin Booth, William Collier, and John Drew. He also appeared under the aegis of famous directors such as Dion Boucicault, A.M. Palmer, and Augustin Daly. Entering films in 1909, Bennett worked for Essanay and Edison before joining Vitagraph's West Coast Company, where he stayed for three years.

Bennett only spent five months in 1914 at Keystone, and during that time he played older authority figures in *The Property Man*, *Mabel's Blunder*, *Cursed by his Beauty*, and *His Talented Wife*. His best known role during his Keystone days was as Marie Dressler's rich uncle in *Tillie's Punctured Romance* (1914). Moving over to Biograph, he later returned to Sennett for shorts like *Teddy at the Throttle* and *Whose Baby?* (both 1917), as well as Triangle Komedies such as *Won By a Fowl*, *Done in Oil*, and *Hobbled Hearts* (all 1917). Bennett retired from films in the early 1920s and became a lawyer.

The Bioscope (January 21, 1915): "His attempts to poison his wife lead to indescribable scenes, packed with typical "Keystone" fun."

Fatty's Finish

Released July 2, 1914. Produced by Mack Sennett for the Keystone Film Co. Distributed by the Mutual Film Corp. Directed by Roscoe Arbuckle. Working title: ***Fatty's Flirtation***. One reel. Extant: LOC. With Roscoe Arbuckle, Phyllis Allen, Bill Hauber, Mack Swain, Hank Mann, Grover Ligon, Charles Avery, Ford Sterling, Charles Bennett, Alice Howell, Al St John, Harry McCoy, Chester Conklin, Dixie Chene, Charles Murray.

Fatty's on his way to a dinner engagement with a friend when he meets and picks up a girl. Turns out that she's the wife of his friend, and everything finally hits the fan—leading to a chase with all the participants and the police.

Supporting Roscoe in *Fatty's Finish* is Phyllis Allen, a memorable Mack Sennett performer who worked with Arbuckle many times in shorts such as *Fatty at San Diego* (1913), *Rebecca's Wedding Day*, *Fatty and the Heiress*, *The Rounders* (all 1914), and *Fatty's Plucky Pup* (1915).

At 5'8' and one hundred and eighty pounds Allen specializes in battleaxes and domineering wives. Born on Staten Island in New York, she was a long-time stage veteran, and a vaudeville headliner with an act called *The Dazzler*, plus a talented singer and pianist. After making her film debut for Selig in 1910, she was in residence on the Sennett lot from 1913 to 1916, and besides appearing with Roscoe she frequently supported the Chaplins (Charlie and Syd), Mack Swain, and the rest of the motley Keystone crew.

An irked Phyllis Allen ready to bring about *Fatty's Finish* (1914). Courtesy the Library of Congress.

In 1916 she began working in Fox Comedies, and made the rounds to practically all the Hollywood comedy units like Universal, Gale Henry's Model Comedies, and Vitagraph in titles such as *The Headwaiter, Her First Flame* (both 1919), and *Footprints* (1920). She even had a return engagement with Charlie Chaplin for *Pay Day* (1922) and *The Pilgrim* (1923). Also appearing in features on the order of *White Youth* (1920), she retired in 1928 and died in 1938.

Motion Picture News (July 18, 1914): "Roscoe Arbuckle takes the part of a flirt in this comedy. He tries to become acquainted with various young girls, but does not succeed. The result is a chase in which the police force are prominent. The reel keeps one in a continual laugh."

The Bioscope (November 19, 1914): "Having made an appointment to meet a friend at a café, Fatty spends the day looking for a pleasant partner for supper. He meets many ladies, but they seem to be animated with the desire to see how often and how high they can make Fatty bounce. Disaster reaches its climax when he discovers that one of the ladies is the wife of his friend. Mr. Roscoe Arbuckle plays this amusing farce with all his customary humor and even more than his customary agility."

Love and Bullets

Released July 4, 1914. Produced by Mack Sennett for the Keystone Film Co. Distributed by the Mutual Film Corp. Director unknown. Working title: **The Assassin**. One reel. Extant: UCLA. With Charles Murray, Minta Durfee, Edgar Kennedy, Wallace MacDonald, Alice Davenport, Slim Summerville, Fred Fishback, Charles Bennett, Roscoe Arbuckle, Billy Gilbert, Bill Hauber.

Charlie Murray pretends to hire a hitman to kill him so he can get sympathy and win favor of the fair Minta, the only trouble is hitman Edgar Kennedy wants Minta for himself and plans to kill Charlie for real.

Roscoe has what's basically a guest cameo in this Charlie Murray-starring short, while his wife Minta Durfee is the leading lady as Charlie's girl. Charlie Murray is said to have started his performing career at age ten and worked his way up through circuses, not to mention pony and medicine shows. He hit big time vaudeville when he teamed up with Ollie Mack and became Murray & Mack—an Irish Weber & Fields. The pair starred in successful shows like *Shooting the Chutes* and *The Sunny Side of Broadway*, and had been a team for twenty years when they split in 1910.

It didn't take Murray long to find his way into the infant film industry, and by 1912 he was one of the leading comics at Biograph, where he worked with the directors Dell Henderson and Edward Dillon. At Biograph he created his screen persona of the layabout Irishman named "Skelley," which he essentially played for the rest of his career. Working with the stock company of Gus Pixley, Sylvia Ashton, David Morris, and Gus Alexander, Murray's shorts for Biograph included *Getting Rid of Trouble* (1912), *Father's Chicken Dinner, Oh, Sammy* (both 1913), and *Skelley's Skeleton* (1914). In 1914 Murray migrated to Keystone, where "Skelley" was renamed "Hogan," and he continued his antics for the next few years.

Moving Picture World (July 25, 1914): "A farce in which a comically contrived mystery mixes a touch of bugaboo feeling with its fun in a way that helps not a little. It is

Hitman Edgar Kennedy flanked by his henchmen Fred Fishback (left) and Slim Summerville (right) in *Love and Bullets* (1914). Courtesy Jessica Rosner.

Long-time comedy veteran Charles Murray. Author's collection.

a somewhat different kind of offering from what we have been used to from Keystone or any other studio and will, we think, be amply acceptable. A good offering."

Motion Picture News (July 25, 1914): "Not as good as most of the Keystones. A man is lovesick and seeks advice from a trouble mender who causes a lot of trouble without mending it. Plenty of slapstick action appears."

A Sky Pirate

Released July 18, 1914. Produced by Mack Sennett for the Keystone Film Co. Distributed by the Mutual Film Corp. Directed by Roscoe Arbuckle. Working title: ***Up in the Air***. One reel. Extant. With Roscoe Arbuckle, Edgar Kennedy, Bill Hauber, Billy Gilbert.

Fatty is an heiress who is kidnapped in an airplane by villain Edgar Kennedy. In the big action climax two cars of cops are pursuing Edgar and Fatty's plane, as Edgar drops bombs on them. Miss Fatty knocks Edgar out and jumps off the plane. She lands in a lake, and all the pursuers jump in to save her. The plane turns upside-down dropping the unconscious Edgar into the lake and into the arms of the cops.

Airplanes were a novelty in the early Twentieth Century, and movies were quick to put them to use. Sennett had started incorporating planes in his films with 1912's famous

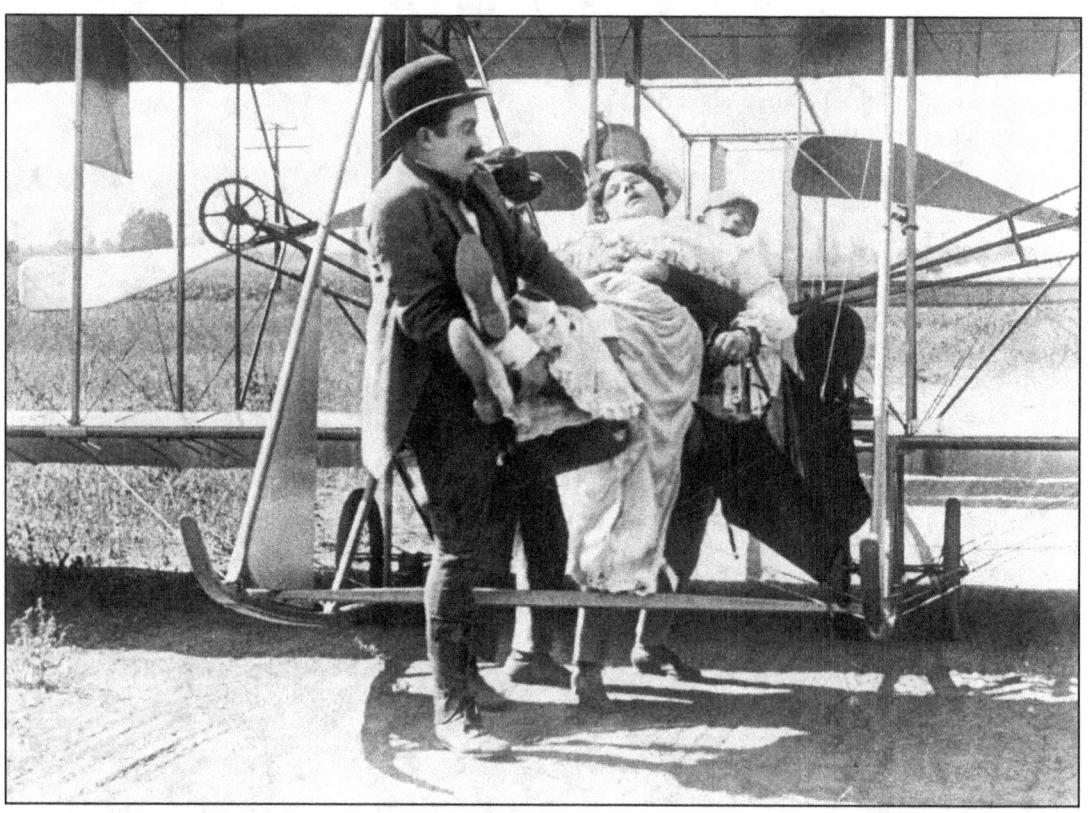

An unconscious Roscoe is trundled onto a biplane by villain Edgar Kennedy (left) with help from his minion Billy Gilbert (right) in 1914's *A Sky Pirate*. Courtesy the George Eastman Museum.

A Dash through the Clouds, where Mabel Normand and pilot Phillip Parmalee fly to the rescue of Mabel's boyfriend Fred Mace. In Europe, clowns like Max Linder and Marcel Perez took turns in the air, and Sennett continued with *Ups and Downs* (1913), *When Love Took Wings* (195), *Wings and Wheels*, and *Dizzy Heights and Daring Hearts* (both 1916). The September 5, 1915 *Moving Picture World* even noted a new studio acquisition:

> *A new monoplane has been added to the equipment of the Keystone Studios. The aviator in charge is Jose Muera.*

As items of speed planes were ideal for movie chases, as in the climax of this short where villain Edgar Kennedy whizzes away with heroine Roscoe and has two cars in hot pursuit. The early biplanes continued to be popular in shorts of the 1920s like *The Aero-Nut* (1920), many Larry Semon shorts like *The Cloudhopper* (1925), and Charley Chase's *Us* (1927), and reached their movie apogee in aviation features such as *Wings* (1927), *Lilac Time* (1928), and *Hell's Angels* (1930).

Motion Picture News (August 15, 1914): "One of the best of the recent comedies with Roscoe Arbuckle playing the charming heiress. Part of the action takes place in an aeroplane supposed to be high in the air. In the end both the heiress and the villain fall from the aircraft. A laugh throughout."

The Bioscope (December 3, 1914): "Mr. Roscoe Arbuckle is always funny, and his originality is as striking as his matchless energy. As the beautiful young heiress abducted by aeroplane he is at his best, and this film is one of the most humorous of the Keystone series."

Those Happy Days

Released July 23, 1914. Produced by Mack Sennett for the Keystone Film Co. Distributed by the Mutual Film Corp. Directed by Roscoe Arbuckle. Working title: **Cast Adrift**. One reel. Extant: BUCH. With Roscoe Arbuckle, Al St John.

Fatty is an amorous trombonist, who is the victim of his rival's tall tales. He ends up kidnapping the wrong woman which leads to a police chase on land and sea.

As an amorous trombonist Roscoe does his bit in the Keystone tradition of making fun of music and musicians. In the early days of the company it was usually done by Ford Sterling in entries such as *That Ragtime Band*, *Professor Bean's Removal*, and *Zuzu, the Bandleader* (all 1913). Other musical interludes include *Tango Tangles*, *The Fatal High C*, *His Musical Career* (all 1914), and *A One Night Stand* (1915).

After two years' worth of comedies the iconography of Keystone films had become well-known around the world. The look of the Sennett comics with their big moustaches, beards, and eyebrows, in addition to their mis-matched clothing, became the standard for the other comedy studios. Nearby parks such as Echo and Hollenbeck were familiar parts of the silent comedy landscape, as well as other locations around the studio which turned up in countless shorts. Minta Durfee later filled in author Stuart Oderman on some of the background on this:

Al St John putting a damper on Roscoe's trombone solo in *Those Happy Days* (1914). Courtesy Sam Gill.

Sennett used to film us around here. Effie Street. Hyperion. Manzanita. Blanche Sweet used to live a few streets away with her grandmother, and Slim Summerville used to have rooms in a hotel across the street from Taix's restaurant. You know why so many of these same houses were used in Sennett films over and over again? Because Mr. Sennett paid these people very well. If they shot in front of your house, you received ten dollars a day. If they went around your house, you received twenty-five dollars a day. And if they went inside your house, you received fifty dollars a day, but he wasn't responsible for the condition of the furniture. Ten dollars a day in those days was good money and twenty-five dollars a day on a steady basis could pay off your mortgage in less than two years. Some of the owners were hired as street extras. They received one dollar a day plus a box-lunch.

– **Films in Review,** August/September, 1985

Motion Picture News (August 15, 1914): "A sidesplitting slapstick picture with Roscoe Arbuckle playing the lead. This time he is the victim of a rival's tale-telling. The police force are prominent and many of the laughs are produced by their actions in the water."

The Bioscope (December 17, 1914): "Mr. Roscoe Arbuckle, with the assistance of a trombone, gives a strenuous gymnastic entertainment in the best Keystone manner. It is a certain laughter-maker, and will be a record success."

That Minstrel Man

Released August 17, 1914. Produced by Mack Sennett for the Keystone Film Co. Distributed by the Mutual Film Corp. Directed by Roscoe Arbuckle. Working title: *Fanny's Jewels*. One reel. With Roscoe Arbuckle, Ford Sterling, Al St John, Frank Hayes.

In drag and blackface, Fatty is Belle, the "Queen of the Minstrel Show," with many admirers. When she loses her beloved pearl necklace on stage thanks to a magician it results in a riot.

Another missing film, that sounds very politically incorrect as most of the cast is in blackface as the performers of a minstrel show. The August 22, 1914 *Motion Picture News* reported:

> *Roscoe Arbuckle made everyone on the Los Angeles downtown streets sit up and take notice on a day this week when he staged a regular Dockstader minstrel parade with a band of twenty-six, and sixty in the march. The*

Frank Hayes and Roscoe sport a darker hue in 1914's *That Minstrel Man*.
Courtesy The Museum of Modern Art.

picture will be used in one of the early Keystone releases, "Queen of the Ebony Club." Arbuckle was "the Queen" of the parade, and as a big, fat and shiny mammy he was some attraction.

Motion Picture News (September 5, 1914): "Roscoe Arbuckle appears as a negress in this picture, and a funny one he makes. All the rest of the characters are darkies. In the minstrel show the negress creates a disturbance and breaks it up. Nothing offensive is in this sidesplitter.

Bioscope (January 7, 1915): "Comedy, in which all the artistes are blacked up, Roscoe Arbuckle ably taking the part of a fat and over-dressed coloured lady. Some very humorous scenes at the minstrel show, also a comical chase after the purloiner of a necklace."

Those Country Kids

Released August 20, 1914. Produced by Mack Sennett for the Keystone Film Co. Distributed by the Mutual Film Corp. Directed by Roscoe Arbuckle. Working title: **The Rural Rivals**. One reel. Extant: LOC, BFI. With Roscoe Arbuckle, Mabel Normand, Al St John, Alice Davenport, Frank Opperman, Josef Swickard, Frank Hayes, Billy Gilbert, Slim Summerville, Fritz Schade.

Fatty and Mabel are a couple of farm sweethearts. They decide to get hitched and run off with their parents and a country version of the Keystone Cops in hot pursuit.

A very enjoyable comedy, sort of a dry run for the later *Fatty and Mabel's Simple Life* (1915) and *Fatty and Mabel Adrift* (1916). The basic premise was even reworked as the

Roscoe peeking over a fence in 1914's *Those Country Kids*.

first reel of *Love* (1919), with the parental problems and dunkings down the well enlarged. The second half of this original version features a thrilling climactic buggy race.

Character actor Josef Swickard is featured as Mabel's decrepit grandfather. Born in Germany, Swickard toured on stage in stock companies for over fifteen years before entering films at Keystone in 1912. During a break in 1912 and 1913 he worked at Thanhouser and Majestic, before he returned to the Sennett lot in 1914. Specializing in authority figures he was very busy in shorts like *Lover's Luck*, *His Talented Wife*, *The Noise of Bombs* (all 1914), *Willful Ambrose*, *A Versatile Villain* (both 1915), *An Oily Scoundrel*, and *Haystacks and Steeples* (both 1916).

He migrated to Fox comedies in 1917, and then moved into features where he became an important supporting player in big films such as *A Tale of Two Cities* (1917), *The Four Horsemen of the Apocalypse* (1921), *Don Juan* (1926), *Old San Francisco*, and *Senorita* (both 1927). His later work included serials like *The Golden Stallion* (1927), *Eagle of the Night* (1928), and *The Lost City* (1935), and bits in features such as *The Crusades* (1935) and *You Can't Take It with You* (1938). Swickard passed away in Hollywood at age seventy in 1940.

Motion Picture News (September 5, 1914): "An excellent farce featuring Mabel Normand and Roscoe Arbuckle, the Keystone fat boy. The usual chase is a feature of this picture and it is unusually funny. A fight in the parson's house puts an end to the picture with all the participants exhausted."

Bioscope (July 8, 1915): "Fatty as a lover of a country girl who didn't like a quiet life, and his unique method of discomforting his rival, opposed by her parents. The elopement in peril of parents, rival, and the police is one of the best Keystone episodes."

Fatty's Gift

Released August 24, 1914. Produced by Mack Sennett for the Keystone Film Co. Distributed by the Mutual Film Corp. Directed by Roscoe Arbuckle. Working title: **His Baby** and **His Wife's Baby**. One reel. With Roscoe Arbuckle, Minta Durfee, Coy Watson Jr., Wallace MacDonald, Rube Miller.

Fatty has a roving eye, and flirts with his son's nursemaid when she's out walking the baby in the park. While they're courting, the pram with the baby rolls away. In the ensuing panic to find it the Keystone police force is called, and eventually everyone ends up in the lake.

The infant in this "lost baby in the park" story was played by Coy Watson Jr., who recounted, in his book *The Keystone Kid* (Santa Monica Press, 2001), being upset by Roscoe (which really upset his mother):

> I played Arbuckle's baby in a picture called "Fatty's Gift." Fatty's real wife, Minta Durfee, played my mother. It turned out to be a bad experience for me. Mom told me that I was doing great and everything was fine until the director (Roscoe) wanted me to cry in a scene.
>
> "You were in a good mood and didn't feel like crying," Mom recalled. "I started onto the set to tell the director that if I waved goodbye to you and

Roscoe mistaking Wallace MacDonald for nurse maid Minta Durfee in *Fatty's Gift* (1914). Courtesy the Academy of Motion Picture Arts and Sciences.

started to leave you would possibly cry. But, before I got to the director, that fool Fatty yelled, "I'll make him cry," and he leaned over the crib, yelled and growled right in your face. I was six feet away and he even scared me! You began to cry all right and you cried hard. They got their scene but you were very upset and wouldn't stop crying."

Young Coy didn't appear to be permanently scarred by Roscoe's extreme directorial technique as he soon became one of the busiest child actors of the silent era. Coy and his family lived next door to the Sennett Studio and in addition to appearing there all the time he also worked with Lloyd Hamilton, Larry Semon, Mary Pickford, Jackie Coogan, and William Haines. He even headlined in the *Campbell Comedies* shorts *A Nick-of-*

Coy Watson Jr. (right) doing a little angling with Lloyd Hamilton from 1922's *No Luck*. Courtesy Sam Gill.

Time Hero, Assorted Heroes (both 1921), and *Schoolday Love* (1922), and had memorable feature bits in *Quality Street* (1927) and *Show People* (1928).

His entire family (including eight sisters and brothers) worked in pictures, with his father Coy Sr. busy as a movie cowboy, bit player, assistant, and wire effects master, and his uncle William Watson a comedy director at Sennett, Fox, Universal, Christie, and Educational. Coy's youngest brother Bobs Watson became a bit of a star with his performances in *Boys Town* (1938) and *On Borrowed Time* (1939). When he got older Coy stopped performing, but always being an avid still photographer, he became a cameraman for newsreels and California TV stations. Known as "The Keystone Kid," he passed away in 2009 at age ninety-six.

Bioscope (December 16, 1915): "Roscoe Arbuckle in a typical and highly amusing Keystone farce."

The Masquerader

Released August 27, 1914. Produced by Mack Sennett for the Keystone Film Co. Distributed by the Mutual Film Corp. Directed by Charles Chaplin. Working titles: **Queen of the Movies** and **Charlie Fools the Keystone**. One reel. Extant: FRIU, DAN, GEM, LOC, MoMA, BFI, UCLA, ACAD, QUB, LOB, ITAL, EYE. With Charles Chaplin,

Charlie Chaplin setting his sights on Roscoe's bottle of beer in *The Masquerader* (1914). Courtesy Robert Arkus.

Charles Murray, Mabel Normand, Roscoe Arbuckle, Chester Conklin, Jess Dandy, Minta Durfee, Frank Opperman, Harry McCoy, Charles Parrott, Billy Gilbert, Dan Albert, Glen Cavender, Cecile Arnold, Vivian Edwards, Dixie Chene, Frankie Dolan.

On a typical day at the Keystone Studio Charlie Chaplin is killing time outside the main gate chatting with Mabel Normand when the task master head director grabs him by the ear and drags him inside to get to work. In the dressing room, Charlie has to share space with Fatty Arbuckle and tries to steal his bottle of beer. When he finally gets to the set he's instructed by the director to foil a knife wielding villain from attacking a baby. While waiting to come on, Charlie flirts with a couple of pretty actresses and continually misses his cue and ruins take after take. In utter frustration the director fires him and has to have him physically ejected from the studio. Later a beautiful and elegant actress arrives at the studio and is welcomed inside. All the men show great interest, particularly the head director. He's gives her the men's dressing room, much to their objection, and then makes a play for "her" by chasing her around the room. After he leaves Charlie goes back to his usual make-up and costume, and when the director and other actors see him it leads to a battle and chase around the lot. Getting hit with a flying brick Charlie is knocked down the studio's well, and it's decided to leave him there to let him flounder.

A chronicle of Charlie Chaplin's misadventures on the Keystone lot—disrupting all the various busy companies—until he finally gets fired. Coming back disguised as a mysterious lady, he has all the men fascinated by him, particularly Charlie Murray's tough director. Like Roscoe, Chaplin was a master of female drag, and did it on numerous occasions. Roscoe turns up briefly in this picture as Charlie's dressing room mate, where they compete over space, stinky feet, and a bottle of beer. Like the earlier *Mabel's Dramatic Career* (1913) and *A Film Johnnie* (1914), *The Masquerader* is a veritable guided tour of the Sennett lot, with appearances by all its main stars such as Roscoe, Mabel Normand, Charlie Murray, and Chester Conklin.

A silent comedy icon and one of Keystone's most representative clowns, Chester Conklin came from a background on stage and working as a circus clown. He joined Keystone in 1913, but went off to Majestic Comedies until Sennett promised him better roles back at Keystone. He spent the teens as one of the studio's most familiar faces—where he alternated between his villainous persona of "Walrus" and the more put-upon bumbler "Fishface" in shorts such as *Between Showers* (1914), *When Ambrose Dared Walrus*, *A Bird's a Bird*, *Droppington's Family Tree* (all 1915), *Dizzy Heights and Daring Hearts* (1916), *His Smothered Love*, and *The Village Chestnut* (both 1918).

Chester Conklin taking on the chin from Marvel Rae, Vera Steadman, and the other girls in 1918's *It Pays to Exercise*.

In 1919 Chester left Sennett for shorts at Fox Sunshine Comedies, Special Pictures, Punch Comedies, and the Tenneck Film Corporation. More importantly he moved into supporting roles in features, with some of the most noteworthy being *Greed* (1923), *A Woman of the World* (1925), *The Duchess of Buffalo* (1927), and *Taxi 13* (1928), in addition to being teamed with W.C. Fields for *Two Flaming Youths* (1927), *Tillie's Punctured Romance*, and *Fools for Luck* (both 1928). With the change to sound Conklin had a starring series of shorts for Paramount and some good roles in features like *Her Majesty Love* (1931) and *Hallelujah, I'm a Bum* (1933). But after Chaplin's *Modern Times* (1936) he began popping up in much smaller bits in many Columbia shorts and features such as *The Great Dictator* (1940), *The Palm Beach Story* (1942), *The Good Humor Man* (1950), *Son of Paleface* (1952), and *The Beast with a Million Eyes* (1955) until 1966. Conklin died in Van Nuys, California in 1971.

Bioscope (January 21, 1915): "Here we have Mr. Chaplin rehearsing for a cinematograph production in which he gives a really remarkable female impersonation. The make-up is no less successful than the characterization, and is further proof Mr. Chaplin's undoubted versatility. The humour, neatness and agility he displays in his stage business, make this one of the best films in which he has yet appeared."

His New Profession

Released August 31, 1914. Produced by Mack Sennett for the Keystone Film Co. Distributed by the Mutual Film Corp. Directed by Charles Chaplin. Working title: ***The Rolling Chair***. One reel. Extant: ACAD, CNC, DAN, EYE, FRIU, LOB, UCLA. With Charles Chaplin, Charles Parrott, Peggy Page, Jess Dandy, Glen Cavender, Cecile Arnold, Vivian Edwards, Roscoe Arbuckle, Charles Murray, Billy Gilbert, Bill Hauber, Dan Albert.

Charlie is enjoying reading the Police Gazette *in a park when a young man hires him to take care of his gouty and wheelchair-bound uncle so he can spend time with his girlfriend. Charlie immediately has problems pushing the old man around, and passing a bar decides that he needs a drink. When uncle won't fund the snort Charlie waits until he dozes off and takes a "help a cripple" sign and tin cup from another invalid. He patiently plants them on the sleeping uncle and soon a passerby donates some coins. With his new funds Charlie leaves uncle and heads back to the bar.*

While Charlie's having his drink the young man and his girlfriend come by and find uncle with the "help a cripple" sign. When the girl is amused this leads to an argument between the pair. A soused Charlie returns to the old man and strikes up a flirtation with the girl. The young man sees Charlie and the girl together, which starts a battle that almost sends uncle off a pier into the water, and gets the police involved. When uncle finally gets arrested Charlie is back on his own to enjoy his day in the park.

Another example of a brief Roscoe cameo, this time as the bartender in the bar where Charlie stops in for a quick snort. For many years this short wasn't included in the regular Arbuckle filmography, but was finally noted by author Bo Berglund in a 1979 *Classic Images* article.

Spending his time behind the bar and giving Charlie suspicious looks, Roscoe looks spiffy in a white shirt and black bow tie. The bar set is the same as in *A Brand New Hero*, the

Roscoe's behind the bar in *His New Profession* (1914), ready to serve Charlie Chaplin as Charles Murray, Billy Gilbert, and Glen Cavender stand by.

film that Roscoe was shooting at the same time that would be released five days after *His New Profession*. Other Keystone regulars in the bar are Glen Cavender, Billy Gilbert, and Charles Murray, the latter completely out of comedy make-up in a nice suit and straw boater.

Motion Picture News (September 12, 1914): "Charles Chaplain [sic] appears in this picture and, as usual, whenever he appears it is a laugh throughout. He gets a job wheeling a cripple around, but a pretty girl, a beggar and a furious young nephew cause his downfall and much merriment."

Moving Picture World (September 26, 1914): "Chas. Chaplain [sic] entertains the observer in this number with a lot of new eccentric comedy. The plot is only sufficient to hang a number of amusing antics on. Some of the situations are very funny and this will please the admirers of slapstick fun."

A Brand New Hero

Released September 5, 1914. Produced by Mack Sennett for the Keystone Film Co. Distributed by the Mutual Film Corp. Directed by Roscoe Arbuckle. Working title: ***The Chief's Daughter***. One reel. With Roscoe Arbuckle, Harry McCoy, Frank Hayes, Billy Gilbert.

Tramp Fatty saves the Police Chief's daughter from drowning, so he's rewarded with a position on the force. A rival cop dopes him so he'll fall asleep during a robbery.

Another missing film, which sounds like a variation on *The Gangsters* and *Fatty Joins the Force* (both 1913), with the tramp character of *Fatty's New Role* (1915) added for good measure.

As mentioned in the entry for *Rebecca's Wedding Day* (1913), Chicago's Censor Board, headed by Major Funkhouser, was one of the worst in the country. By the end of the year the October 3, 1914 *Motography* reported:

> *The Chicago Censor Board is growing to be more of a menace, and that instead of being less harsh in its rulings it is more drastic than ever before.*

The Chicago Tribune was making daily reports of what was being cut by the board, and on September 1 listed some trims made in this film:

Tramp Roscoe trying to get a drink from bartender Harry McCoy (right) under the eyes of Frank Hayes (left) in *A Brand New Hero* (1914). Courtesy Jessica Rosner.

Policemen shooting cigars; thieves putting loot into bag; officer putting mask on.

Pretty innocuous stuff, at least the uproar surrounding *Rebecca's Wedding Day* did make some sense because of the racial stereotyping. Another Keystone, *He Loved the Ladies*, had some cuts made on September 14th which sound a bit more suggestive than policemen shooting cigars or crooks stealing loot:

Two scenes showing girl's legs under table.

It's not unusual to come across a censored print today. Slapstick comedies were frequently trimmed for violence, so you'll see someone about to be kicked in the seat, or conked on the head, and suddenly there's a jump in the action and no payoff. You may see the person reacting in pain or acting dazed, but not the moment of contact. Projectionists would often keep the snipped footage, and the Library of Congress has inherited a few reels of censored cuts. In some cases these little clips are all that exist of certain films today.

Moving Picture World (September 26, 1914): "Roscoe Arbuckle, the Fat Boy, appears in this number as a tramp. He saves the girl from drowning in a pond and is given a job on the police force. A jealous officer dopes him and he sleeps during a robbery, but afterwards wakes up and captures the miscreants. Rapid-fire eccentric comedy of an amusing sort."

Motion Picture News (September 12, 1914): "In which Roscoe Arbuckle rescues the chief's daughter from the water and is created an officer of the force. Numerous times do villainous rivals plot his downfall but he comes through with flying colors. A good many laughs in this."

The Rounders

Released September 7, 1914. Produced by Mack Sennett for the Keystone Film Co. Distributed by the Mutual Film Corp. Directed by Charles Chaplin & Roscoe Arbuckle. Working title: **The Two Drunks**. One reel. Extant: QUB, FRIUL, DAN, GEM, LOC, MoMA, CAN, BFI, UCLA, ACAD, LOB, EYE. With Charles Chaplin, Roscoe Arbuckle, Minta Durfee, Phyllis Allen, Al St John, Dixie Chene, Jess Dandy, Charles Parrott, Wallace MacDonald, Edward Cline, Billy Gilbert, Bill Hauber, Cecile Arnold.

Mr. Full and Mr. Fuller live in the same hotel, and both come home completely swazzled. Their wives are waiting and let them have it. Mrs. Fuller is beating her large husband so badly that Mrs. Full sends her hubby over to stop the bloodbath. When he interrupts the scene she turns her wrath on him, which brings Mrs. Full over to stop her. As the wives have it out on each other the husbands discover that they are lodge brothers and sneak back out on the town together. Ending up in a fancy café they disrupt the diners, and when their hot-on-their-trails wives show up it turns into a major melee. Fleeing the establishment, the drunken pair head to the park and commandeer a rowboat to sail to a safe distance on the lake. Followed by their wives and an angry crowd, they settled down to nap as their leaking boat sinks under the water.

In their last screen appearance together Roscoe and Chaplin make a great team—their opposite physicalities complement each other, as do their innate sense of comic timing and ability for roughhouse comedy. In addition to nice supporting roles for Phyllis

Revelers Charlie Chaplin and Roscoe discover that they're lodge brothers in 1914's *The Rounders*. Courtesy Robert Arkus.

Allen and Minta Durfee as their distraught wives, there's great physical business, such as Charlie standing on the back tails of his coat so he can't stand up straight, and the sequence of the drunken pair disrupting the restaurant is practically a dry run for Charlie and Harry Myers in the nightclub scene in *City Lights* (1931).

The pretty blonde sitting in the apartment house lobby who gets flirted with by Charlie and sat on by Roscoe is Cecile Arnold, an ingénue who appeared in over thirty Keystones from 1914 to 1917. As a flirtatious other woman she supported Chaplin, Chester Conklin, Charlie Murray, and Syd Chaplin in shorts like *His Musical Career*, *His Second Childhood* (both 1914), *Hushing the Scandal* (1915), and *Her Nature Dance* (1917). Her stint with Sennett was interrupted by appearances in the *Ziegfeld Follies* and the musical show *Robinson Crusoe*. After her return to Keystone she often used the last name Arly, worked mostly on one-reel comedies, and married Sennett assistant director Frank "Duke" Reynolds. When Reynolds joined the military in 1917 Cecile left the screen.

Motion Picture News (September 19, 1914): "Charles Chapman [sic] and Roscoe Arbuckle are the fun provokers in this farce, but it is really the tough handling they receive from their wives when they return home in a slightly intoxicated state that makes the merriment."

The Bioscope (February 18, 1915): "Comedy, which depends for its success more upon vigorous action than upon story, and enables Chaplin and "Fatty," as two jovial roysterers, to furnish a capital sketch. They go home, to neighboring flats, and indulge in many noisy antics, which cause a row between the wives of the pair. The manner in which they sneak out while the women are wrangling, and their subsequent exploits are farcical in the extreme. Splendidly photographed and staged throughout the length."

Bombs and Bangs

Released September 17, 1914. Produced by Mack Sennett for the Keystone Film Co. Distributed by the Mutual Film Corp. Directed by Roscoe Arbuckle. Working title: ***The Sleep Walker***. One reel. With Roscoe Arbuckle, Alice Howell, Rube Miller.

Fatty in drag plays the hefty heroine, a farmer's daughter, who often sleepwalks through town. One night when she picks up a lit bomb meant for her hard-hearted mother it causes a total panic. The final explosion gets the right man.

In this missing rural one-reeler Roscoe has support from two important 1914 Keystone players. Alice Howell was a gifted performer with a unique style that combined feminine delicacy with out and out roughhouse. Coming from a background of musical

Rube Miller uses Alice Howell as an arm rest in *Bombs and Bangs* (1914). Author's collection.

shows and vaudeville, she began working as an extra at Keystone in 1914. Very quickly she worked her way up to featured character roles such as in this and Charlie Chaplin's *Laughing Gas* (1914), and in 1915 moved over to Henry Lehrman's L-KO Comedies. Starting as support for star Billie Ritchie, she soon began headlining in her own one-reelers and by 1917 had worked her way up to full stardom.

The character she developed was that of a slightly addled working-class girl (beanery waitress, maid, etc.) and while attractive, her get-up emphasized the eccentric. A round kewpie-doll face, with large eyes and bee-stung lips, was topped off with a mountain of frizzy hair piled high on her head that resembled smoke billowing from an active volcano. Her starring career continued with Century, Reelcraft, and Universal, but she retired young in 1926. Having socked her earnings into California real estate, she spent her retirement comfortably managing her shrewd investments, and died in 1961.

Rube Miller was a busy comedy creator in the teens, very active as a performer and director, who completely disappeared from films around 1921. Having an unusual face like a carved totem, Miller spent his youth with circuses like Ringling Brothers and Forepaugh & Sells doing aerial work and clowning. He joined Keystone in 1912, and was ubiquitous as a supporting actor and stuntman. Frequently a Keystone cop, by 1914 he worked his way up to directing and starred in his own one-reel items like *A Fatal Sweet Tooth* and *Hard Cider* (both 1914).

Miller moved on from Keystone to Kriterion and Kalem, where he directed and acted, including some of Kalem's Ham & Bud entries. In 1915 he settled in at Mutual's Vogue Comedies to star in and direct two years of two-reelers like *Rube's Hotel Tangle*, *Germantic Love*, and *Doctoring a Leak* (all 1916), some co-starring Ben Turpin. From here he went on to direct and appear in a number of L-KO comedies, and ended up working with Roscoe again in the Comique shorts *The Hayseed* and *Back Stage* (both 1919). After a couple of isolated appearances for Reelcraft and the independent Gate City Productions he left films. His later trail is hard to follow, possibly appearing with various circuses or wild west shows, and it seems that he died in 1944.

The Bioscope (March 18, 1915): "With Mr. Arbuckle as a truculent and hefty farmeress, and a sleep-walking heroine who perambulates the neighboring roofs and spires holding a smoking bomb, one is assured of plenty of hilarious fun, and the exploits of a twopenny-coloured villain, and his shocking end will create laughter whenever they are seen."

Moving Picture World (September 19, 1914): "A number of "rube" characters appear in this. The chief feature is where the girl sleepwalker carries a lighted bomb through the town, causing much excitement. This is fairly amusing."

Lover's Luck

Released September 19, 1914. Produced by Mack Sennett for the Keystone Film Co. Distributed by the Mutual Film Corp. Directed by Roscoe Arbuckle. Working title: *The Three Lovers*. One reel. Extant: MoMA, BFI, FRANC. With Roscoe Arbuckle, Minta Durfee, Frank Hayes, Josef Swickard, Phyllis Allen, Al St John, Alice Howell, Slim Summerville, Billy Gilbert, Grover Ligon, Billie Bennett, Harry Russell, Luke.

Frank Hayes' presence causes Roscoe's hat to defy gravity in 1914's *Lover's Luck*.
Courtesy the George Eastman Museum.

Fatty's and Minta are in love, but her father insists on Al to be her husband. When the country constable gets caught in Fatty's widowed mother's kitchen he hides in her closet to avoid detection. When Fatty and Minta end up hiding there too and discover him they force him to marry them on the spot or reveal his predicament.

Lover's Luck is a good illustration of Roscoe's generosity in giving ample screen time to his fellow performers. Minta, Al, Phyllis Allen, and particularly string-bean Frank Hayes get plenty of business and attention. Plus Alice Howell, Billy Gilbert, and Slim Summerville also turn up as part of a group of lower-class neighbors who are snooping on and watching the antics of the principals with great relish (these were the days before television). All in all, the film confirms this statement from the April 1918 *Photoplay*:

> *Roscoe Arbuckle, like Charlie Chaplin, likes to dope out his funny stunts right in front of the camera, even if it's not in operation, but "Fatty" is more generous with his footage so far as his colleagues are concerned—he lets them "get" the laugh if it improves the completed product.*

Moving Picture World (October 3, 1914): "Works up to a grand and general knockabout of human beings that is astonishing. The picture is vulgar, perhaps a bit more so than usual. It is sure to make laughter in the many, loud and often, and even the few will laugh more. It is good as an offering to the public, but not so good as the best Keystones are."

Bioscope (April 8, 1915): "Our popular friend Fatty is again deeply in love, but the lady's father strongly objects to him as a son-in-law The sheriff is eventually compelled to perform the marriage by moral persuasion of a kind that makes a sufficiently diverting comedy."

Fatty's Debut

Released September 29, 1914. Produced by Mack Sennett for the Keystone Film Co. Distributed by the Mutual Film Corp. Directed by Roscoe Arbuckle. Working title: *Saving Lizzie*. One reel. With Roscoe Arbuckle, Glen Cavender.

Fatty's wife and mother-in-law are at home impatiently waiting for him so they can go to the theatre, when he comes in with a happy snootful. He manages to take a bath, dress, and go to the show with the family. There he ends up on stage as part of the performance, where he not only saves the heroine from the villain but brings the curtain down on the entire company.

Basically a dry run of 1915's *That Little Band of Gold*, but without the expanded subplot of Ford Sterling and his two girlfriends that leads to the break-up of Roscoe and Mabel Normand's not-so-happy home. In this original streamlined version more emphasis is put

Fatty's Debut (1914) details Roscoe's method of getting sober. Courtesy The Museum of Modern Art.

Glen Cavender (right) and the other actors have to deal with Roscoe making *Fatty's Debut* (1914). Courtesy The Museum of Modern Art.

on the drunken Roscoe disrupting the show. The "Fatty" character is often three sheets to the wind, whether he's a tramp, put upon hubby, or man about town in shorts like *The Rounders* (1914), *Fatty's Tintype Tangle* (1915), *A Reckless Romeo* (1917), and *Good Night, Nurse* (1918).

Moving Picture World (September 26, 1914): "Fatty comes home in a mild state of intoxication. He takes a bath, with considerable difficulty, and goes to the theatre with his wife and her mother. Here he butts into the play, saves the heroine from the villain, and cleans up the entire company. This is well photographed and has some amusing business in it."

Motion Picture News (October 10, 1914): "Roscoe Arbuckle is the funmaker in this laughable farce. He keeps his wife and mother-in-law waiting to go to the theatre and when he does arrive he is tipsy. A forced plunge into cold water sobers him up a bit, and they start off to the show. But Fatty gets in the wrong door and breaks up the performance when he makes his lively appearance on the stage."

The Bioscope (March 11, 1915): "The inimitable Fatty spends his time during the major portions of this film, endeavouring to attain to such a state of sobriety as will allow him to dress for the theatre, whither he is accompanied by his wife and mother-in-law. The latter portion is devoted to his appearance behind the scenes and on the stage, but, however, he is engaged Mr. Arbuckle is well able to hold the attention and rouse the mirth of the most exacting audience, and this film will be one of his most popular efforts."

Fatty Again

Released October 3, 1914. Produced by Mack Sennett for the Keystone Film Co. Distributed by the Mutual Film Corp. Directed by Roscoe Arbuckle. Working title: **The Star**. (Re-released by W.H. Productions as *Fatty the Fourflusher*). One reel. Extant: BFI, GEM. With Roscoe Arbuckle, Minta Durfee, Frank Opperman, Phyllis Allen, Wallace MacDonald, Frank Hayes, Joe Bordeaux, Jess Dandy, Charles Bennett, Chester Conklin, Charles Murray, Billie Bennett, Dixie Chene.

Fatty lives in a boarding house and is in love with Minta, the owner's daughter. Sadly, he is also out of a job and behind in his rent. In addition to having the food taken away from him at dinner, he's told that if he doesn't pay up—out he goes. A letter arrives from Fatty's former boss (signed David Tabasco) saying that he can have his old job back at $5 a week. Fatty changes the $5 to $50 a week and lets the boarding house crew "find" the letter. Now he's treated like royalty—his room is fixed up, he's fussed over at dinner, etc. When Fatty goes out to work his rival for Minta follows him, and discovers that Fatty's wonderful job is that of a carnival barker at a cheap sideshow. The rival then brings the boarding house crew to the sideshow, and Fatty's jig is up. After the ensuing melee the last shot has Fatty taking off for the highlands.

This short is a remake of a 1912 Sennett-directed Biograph one-reeler, *The Leading Man*, which starred Dell Henderson in the Arbuckle role. In addition to cameos at the

Minta Durfee, Frank Opperman, Phyllis Allen, Dixie Chene, and Frank Hayes watch Roscoe get the lion's share of dinner in *Fatty Again* (1914). Courtesy The Museum of Modern Art.

sideshow by Sennett stars Charlie Murray and Chester Conklin, this comedy gives a good look at leading man Wallace MacDonald.

Many Keystones needed a handsome young rival for the comic lead, and MacDonald got his first screen experience doing this in shorts like *Love and Bullets* and *A Fatal Sweet Tooth* (both 1914). He quickly moved on to the Navajo Film Co., L-Ko, Mutual, American Beauty, and Vitagraph, acted in features like *The Sea Hawk* (1924), *The Rogue Song* (1930), and *Island of Doomed Men* (1940), and re-lived his Keystone days when he directed Fox Imperial and Educational Cameo Comedy shorts like *A Silly Sailor*, *A Low Necker* (both 1927), *Cook, Papa, Cook*, and *Wife Trouble* (both 1928).

The 1930s saw him writing screenplays and in 1936 he became a busy producer for Columbia's B-movie unit, and turned out something like one hundred and nine features until 1959 that included *The Face Behind the Mask* (1941), *My Name is Julia Ross* (1946), *Harem Girl* (1952), and *Call 2455, Death Row* (1955).

Moving Picture World (October 17, 1914): "Fatty experiences several reverses of fortunes in this boarding house story. He is first ejected for failure to pay his board. He then fixes up a postal card offering himself a handsome salary and is warmly welcomed back by the girl's parents. When the truth becomes known that he is really a sideshow barker, they again turn on him. This is true to certain phases of life and quite amusing throughout."

Joe Bordeaux and Roscoe as side-show barkers in *Fatty Again* (1914).
Courtesy The Museum of Modern Art.

Motion Picture News (October 3, 1914): "Uproarious farce featuring that ever popular and funny comedian, Roscoe Arbuckle, as Fatty. The scenes of Fatty's troubles and mishaps and ultimate successful handling of a difficult situation will keep the audience in a continual peal of side-splitting merriment."

Their Ups and Downs

Released October 5, 1914. Produced by Mack Sennett for the Keystone Film Co. Distributed by the Mutual Film Corp. Directed by Roscoe Arbuckle. Working title: **The Balloon**. One reel. With Roscoe Arbuckle, Billie Bennett.

Fatty gives his sweetheart a bunch of balloons which causes her to have a wild ride in the air over the city. She finally ends up stranded on some telephone lines, from which she has to be rescued by her large lover.

Like *Mother's Boy* (1913) and *Fatty's Tintype Tangle* (1915), *Their Ups and Downs* is another example of Roscoe's fondness for a big climax that has characters bouncing and running around on telephone wires.

Their Ups and Downs (1914) sees Billie Bennett and Roscoe having their ups in the telephone wires.

His lighter-than-air sweetheart is played by Billie Bennett, a small dark-haired actress who specialized in domineering spouses, and would do as much for Roscoe in *Fatty's Chance Acquaintance* (1915) and "Smiling Bill" Parsons in *Bill's Opportunity* (1919). After fifteen years on the stage, she started in pictures in 1912 at the United States Motion Picture Company, and appeared in Universal's Joker and Nestor Comedies, where she first appeared with Roscoe in 1913's *Almost a Rescue*. Eventually taking up residence with Keystone, from 1914 to 1916 she was in shorts like *Leading Lizzie Astray*, *"Curses!" They Remarked* (both 1914), *Peanuts and Bullets*, *Love in Armor* (both 1915), and *Hearts and Sparks* (1916). She later did yeoman service for Fox and Strand Comedies, and branched into supporting roles in features like *Robin Hood* (1922), *Lady Windermere's Fan* (1925), and *One Romantic Night* (1930) before leaving films in 1930.

Bennett's film career may have ended in 1930 but not her work in Hollywood. In 1934 she was picked by MGM "fixer" Eddie Mannix to run the high-class film industry bordello Mae's. This was a whore house with women who were look-a-likes for movie stars like Claudette Colbert, Carole Lombard, Irene Dunne, etc. The girls would make-up, dress, and even "play" the role of their big screen representation. Located in an exclusive part of Los Angeles, its clientele included Clark Gable, Mickey Rooney, and even director Garson Kanin. Bennett, who's quoted as saying "My all-time best paying customer was Groucho Marx," passed away in 1951.

Moving Picture World (October 10, 1914): "The adventures of the flirtatious Fatty and his sweetheart will serve to amuse the multitudes very much. The girl's ride with the balloons in her hands was a capital feature and their predicament in the telegraph wires was funny also. A particularly good number of the nonsensical type."

Motion Picture News (October 24, 1914): "This is a real sidesplitter with Roscoe Arbuckle in the leading role. Midway in the picture his sweetheart who is about one tenth his size, is carried up in the air by a bunch of balloons. By an excellent double exposure she may be seen floating over a large city."

The Bioscope (March 25, 1915): "A film showing the Keystone comedians at their best."

Zip, the Dodger

Released October 17, 1914. Produced by Mack Sennett for the Keystone Film Co. Distributed by the Mutual Film Corp. Directed by Roscoe Arbuckle. Working title: **The African Dodger**. One reel. Extant: LOC. With Roscoe Arbuckle, Minta Durfee, Wallace MacDonald, Phyllis Allen, Josef Swickard, Billy Gilbert, Bill Hauber, Harry McCoy, Charles Avery, Eddie Nolan, Charles Parrott, Billie Bennett, Charles Lakin, Slim Summerville, Grover Ligon, Frankie Dolan.

Zip is engaged by the proprietor of a sideshow to undertake the extremely onerous duties of a "dodger." His occupation consists of sticking his head through a sheet, while the more boisterous amusement seekers endeavor to hit him, at the rate of "three balls a penny." Zip has aspirations higher than his present situation, and when he picks up a wallet containing a card, bearing the name of a "prune magnate," he makes good use of his opportunity, and establishes himself firmly in the affections of a dainty young lady. This earns the deadly

The happy baseball target of 1914's *Zip, the Dodger*. Courtesy of the Library of Congress.

hate of her sweetheart, who gets on his track and discovers his true identity. When Zip returns to his duties as a "dodger," the aforesaid maiden is brought by the rival to test her skill, and recognizing the alleged "prune magnate," she proceeds to throw the balls with unerring precision, helped to that end by the arrival of a baseball team, who administer cruel punishment. The film closes as Zip is getting badly mauled.

Fatty's pretty low in society in this entry as he's doing the "dodger" role in a carnival sideshow. This was usually a black person, as shown in the film when Fatty's late returning to his post and a blacked-up Billy Gilbert is lured to take over the job—he doesn't want to do it but the offered money overrides his good sense. Known as "The African Dodger," and much worse variations, this game was common in fairs, circuses, and carnivals in the U.S.A. from the late Nineteenth Century until the mid-1940s. The "dodger" would usually taunt the throwers, who would win prizes if they hit him. A not-quite-so-terrible variation on this was developed in 1911 and called "The African Dip," where the throwers would aim at a target that, when hit, would dump the person in a dunk tank. Eventually this was done into the 1960s with a white person in the dunk seat.

The year before *Zip, the Dodger* was made there was a well-reported incident in St. Louis where a carnival was unable to secure a dodger for hours because Baseball Hall of Fame pitcher Walter Johnson was rumored to be at the fair. Big baseball fan that he was,

Grover Ligon, Slim Summerville, Wallace MacDonald, and Minta Durfee all decide to see just how hard Roscoe's head is in *Zip, the Dodger* (1914). Courtesy the Library of Congress.

it seems likely that Roscoe had heard about this and used it as a germ for the story. In the film a number of professional ballplayers show up, and provide strong arms and expert marksmanship for the film's climax.

Moving Picture World (October 24, 1914): "The Fat Boy appears in this as the young man who dodges baseball at a resort concession. A colored boy is substituted while he pretends to be a young man of leisure, but the girl happens along later and discovers what Fatty's job really is. This is quite pleasing."

Motion Picture News (October 24, 1914): "Roscoe Arbuckle appears as the Dodger, who lends his face as a target for supposedly soft balls. He falls in love and informs the girl that he is a "prune magnate," but he is shown up in his true colors and a general roughhouse ends the picture which is a laugh throughout."

Lover's Post Office

Released November 2, 1914. Produced by Mack Sennett for the Keystone Film Co. Distributed by the Mutual Film Corp. Directed by Roscoe Arbuckle. One reel. With Roscoe Arbuckle, Minta Durfee, Al St John.

Fatty is in love with Minta, but her old father interferes with their courtship. The pair decides to elope, but when dad finds that the lovers are using an old tree trunk to leave love

What Al St John doesn't know will hurt him in *Lover's Post Office* (1914).

notes, he sets a trap and catches Fatty by the hand. They still manage to escape and end up happily married.

One of the many rural romances that were the stock-in-trade of Keystone. The area surrounding the studio was woodsy and undeveloped, so it provided ideal rustic settings for these kinds of stories.

This short seems to have been a very close re-telling of the 1909 Imp comedy *Love's Stratagem*. This, only the second Imp release, survives and concerns Florence Lawrence and her beau using an old tree trunk as a mailbox for their love notes, as Florence's crotchety father disapproves of her choice. After father puts his foot down, the downcast boyfriend gets a plan and the marriage is achieved for the fade-out. It may be that someone at Keystone had this short somewhere in their memory when the idea for this came up.

Of course the "borrowing" of older stories was standard practice in early movie days, as it seemed unlikely that anyone would ever see the original again.

Moving Picture World (November 14, 1914): "A reel of amusing nonsense, in which the lovers post their letters in a box in a tree. The old man gets wise and sets a snare, by which he catches Fatty's hand. The girl releases the snare and Fatty hooks the old man by the leg. This is well pictured and contains numerous laughs."

Pictures and the Picturegoer (August 14, 1915): "You all know Roscoe Arbuckle, our fat floppy friend of Keystone? Well, if you don't go out and see him in this film you'll miss a lot of fun—and Arbuckle. He is in love (as usual), and decides to elope, but his adored one's father gets wind of the arrangements and puts his foot down; but Fatty manages to escape with his girl and marry her."

An Incompetent Hero

Released November 12, 1914. Produced by Mack Sennett for the Keystone Film Co. Distributed by the Mutual Film Corp. Directed by Roscoe Arbuckle. Working title: *The Wrong Room*. One reel. Extant: LOC, UCLA. With Roscoe Arbuckle, Minta Durfee, Edgar Kennedy, Lucille Ward, Al St John, Josef Swickard, Ted Edwards, Dick Smith, Slim Summerville.

Roscoe heads for the open air as Lucille Ward pleads and Edgar Kennedy takes aim in *An Incompetent Hero* (1914). Courtesy the George Eastman Museum.

Fatty admires the young pianist and singer in the apartment across the way, and the notes he tosses her through the window enrages her husband, who does not appreciate his wife's talent and threatens Fatty. That same night a burglar gets into the pianist's apartment while her husband is out. Coming to the rescue, Fatty crosses from his window to hers on a clothes line. Although he has the worthy intention of chastising the thief, he also has the misfortune of entering the lady's bedroom just as her husband returns—and quite a commotion follows until the husband's bullets run out. In the meantime the burglar escapes to the cellar and from there makes a getaway.

During the making of this film the November 11, 1914 *Motion Picture News* had this to report about Roscoe's balancing prowess:

> Roscoe Arbuckle has been making an unusual comedy at the Keystone Studio in which he displays his ability at tight rope walking by escaping from his followers by walking a clothes line across a court of buildings from one six story window to another. Of course picture fans will think it is a clothes line, but instead a half inch steel wire was used to support the 315 pounds of Arbuckle.

Moving Picture World (November 21, 1914): "Fatty flirts with a married woman across the way. Later, when a burglar appears he crosses a rope in to her room. A rough-house ensues with some laughable moments in it. This is well photographed throughout."

Motion Picture News (November 21, 1914): "Fatty's charitable intentions are mistaken for another kind by the husband of the wife in the house next door. Uproarious situations lead to a very comical climax laid in a bedroom. It is funnily constructed, however, that it will not offend. A lot of slapstick work appears in this, which is as hilarious as usual."

Fatty's Jonah Day

Released November 16, 1914. Produced by Mack Sennett for the Keystone Film Co. Distributed by the Mutual Film Corp. Directed by Roscoe Arbuckle. Working title: **Park Troubles**. (Re-released as **Fatty's Hoodoo Day**). Extant: BFI, MoMA. With Roscoe Arbuckle, Norma Nichols, Frank Hayes, Al St John, Ted Edwards.

Fatty is sitting on a park bench excitingly reading the book "Three Weeks." His sweetheart Norma is on another bench with her father. When dad falls asleep, she joins Fatty on his bench. When she asks what he's so absorbed in he at first tries to hide it, but then they enjoy the book together. A rival suitor, whom Norma does not like, shows up and tries to cut in. At this point dad wakes up, and the rival points out to him just what book Fatty is reading with his daughter. Aghast the old man pulls her away and tells her that the rival is his choice for her. Fatty and the rival start battling, and when Fatty tosses a huge rock at the rival it hits Norma and knocks her out. Fatty thinks he's killed her, and dad gets a cop to arrest him for the "murder." Fatty breaks loose and is chased around the park while Norma comes to. Trapped on a bridge by the police, Norma sees Fatty dive into the lake and she dives in right after him to save him. After all this dad rebuffs the rival while Fatty and Norma settle in to finish reading "Three Weeks."

Roscoe's enjoying *Three Weeks* in *Fatty's Jonah Day* (1914). Courtesy Kim Deitch.

This short is nicely bookended with Roscoe reading the racy current novel (in 1914) *Three Weeks* by Elinor Glyn, and there's a strong morbid streak. Not only does the leading lady get beaned with a humongous rock, but Fatty, thinking that he's a "murderer," desperately does his best to elude the police and her father. Luckily it turns out that the girl was just dazed, but if this weren't a slapstick comedy the outcome probably wouldn't be happy

The lady in question is the attractive and overlooked Norma Nichols, who would later play his wife in *Fatty's Tintype Tangle* (1915). The sister of Marguerite Nichols, who was Mrs. Hal Roach, Norma was a pretty brunette who was a busy Keystone leading lady in 1914 and 1915 shorts such as *The Property Man*, *Dough and Dynamite* (both 1914), *Rum and Wall Paper*, and *Hogan's Wild Oat* (both 1915), where she also supported Charlie Chaplin, Chester Conklin, and Charlie Murray. On leaving Sennett she had a brief stint at Selig, and soon ended up at Kalem as the love interest for the scuzzy bums Ham & Bud in opuses that included *Ham Agrees with Sherman*, *Ham and the Masked Marvel*, and *The Tank Town Troupe* (all 1916).

After a few features such as *The Tides of Barnegat* (1917) and *The Legion of Death* (1918), as well as supporting Ruth Roland in the Pathé serial *Broadway Bob* (1920), she became part of the Vanity Fair Girls. This beauty squad supported comic Eddie Boland in Hal Roach one-reelers like *Mamma's Boy*, *The Sleepyhead* (both 1920), *Oh, Promise*

Norma Nichols joins Roscoe in his reading in *Fatty's Jonah Day* (1914). Author's collection.

Me (1921), and *The Man Haters* (1922). She's also said to have spent some time in her brother-in-law Roach's scenario department in the early 1920s. Following a brief spell working with comic Larry Semon in shorts like *The Bakery*, *The Rent Collector*, *The Fall Guy*, and *The Bell Hop* (all 1921), and the feature *The Call of Home* (1922), she retired from the screen.

Moving Picture World (November 28, 1914): "Fatty is reading "Three Weeks" with a girl in the park when a rival appears. Trouble of course follows, in which two policemen participate. There is a dive from the park bridge and other stunts of this sort. This is a success of its type and well photographed."

Motion Picture News (November 21, 1914): "Fatty sits reading "Three Weeks." A girl whose father happens to have fallen asleep comes and reads with him. The jealous lover arrives on the scene and summons father, and then a side-splitting mix-up ensues, including a few dives off a bridge. In the finale Fatty and the girl resume their book in quiet."

Fatty's Wine Party

Released November 21, 1914. Produced by Mack Sennett for the Keystone Film Co. Distributed by the Mutual Film Corp. Directed by Roscoe Arbuckle. Working title: **Only a Dollar**. One reel. Extant: LOC, BFI. (Reissued by W. H. Productions in 1918 as **Fatty's Wild Night**). With Roscoe Arbuckle, Mabel Normand, Syd Chaplin, Mack Swain, Frank Hayes, Phyllis Allen, Al St John, Harry McCoy, Joe Bordeaux, Alice Davenport, Fritz Schade, Cecile Arnold, Edwin Frazee, Billy Gilbert.

Syd Chaplin, Frank Hayes, Mabel Normand, Phyllis Allen, Roscoe, and Mack Swain in the melee that was *Fatty's Wine Party* (1914). Author's collection.

Fatty, in need of money, borrows a dollar from a friend who is waiting to take his girlfriend Mabel out to a party. As Fatty walks away with his dollar he runs into Mabel who rushes up to his side and kisses him. This is seen by her boyfriend, who lent Fatty the dollar, and two of his friends. They then see Fatty and Mabel go into a restaurant, though Fatty because of his shortness of funds was reluctant to go in. Once inside they have fun until they notice Mabel's boyfriend and his two buddies coming in. They order wine, and then disappear leaving a bill of $27.50 for Fatty to pay. Since he only has the dollar he's unable to do so, so he is beaten up and kicked out to the amusement of the three buddies. But just as they are laughing the hardest Mabel takes Fatty's side and turns the tables on them.

Fatty's Wine Party was Sydney Chaplin's introduction to movie audiences, and the role of the head waiter was perfect to take advantage of his hard-earned music hall skills of juggling dishes, and of course impressive tumbles and falls. As the older half-brother of the astronomically famous Charlie, Syd's work has always been overshadowed by that of his sibling, but the "other Chaplin" was a talented comic and neglected behind-the-scenes comedy creator.

The son of Hannah Hill and a mysterious Mr. Hawks, Sydney was adopted by Charles Chaplin Sr., and together he and young Charlie survived poverty, their mother's mental illness, and periodic stays in the public workhouse. Finding the stage as his ticket to success, by 1906 he was hired by the prestigious Fred Karno Company—where he played lead roles and created new sketches. He even managed to get Karno to hire his younger brother.

Portrait of "the other Chaplin"—Syd Chaplin.

Six years later Charlie returned the favor by getting Syd in to replace him at Keystone. After this initial short with Roscoe (they never appeared together again) Syd followed with a couple more supporting roles and then scored his first starring short with *Gussle the Golfer* (1914). The screen persona devised by Syd was that of Reggie Gussle, a bourgeois bounder with a padded-out rear-end, that was firmly in the Billie Ritchie/Jimmy Aubrey Karno refugee mold. Gussle's misadventures lasted through entries like *Gussle's Backward Way* to *No One to Guide Him* (both 1915), and his last Sennett film was the three-reel Triangle opus *A Submarine Pirate* (1915).

After the stint at Keystone, Syd took a break from performing to oversee Charlie's business dealings with Mutual, First National, and United Artists, as well as the building of his own studio. By the late teens Syd was turning up in Charlie's films like *A Dog's Life* and *Shoulder Arms* (both 1918). He produced and directed his own feature *King, Queen, Joker* (1921), did some supporting work, and then became a star with the 1925 filming of the famous play *Charley's Aunt*. This led to a series of starring farces for Warner Brothers that included *The Man on the Box* (1925), *The Better 'Ole* (1926), and *The Missing Link* (1927). After finishing his Warners' contract Syd made only one more film, *A Little Bit of Fluff* (1928) in England (released as *Skirts* in America), and having amassed a sizeable fortune of his own spent the latter part of his life traveling around the U.S. and living near Charlie in Europe.

Moving Picture World (November 28, 1914): "Roscoe and Mabel go to a restaurant. Syd Chaplin, a new Keystone star, is introduced as a waiter and does some amusing stunts. He juggles the food and plates and falls on the kitchen floor in pleasing fashion. The Fat Boy, being unable to pay for the dinner, is stripped of his coat and shirt. This is well photographed and amusing."

Motion Picture News (November 28, 1914): "This picture is a roar from beginning to end. Syd Chaplin makes his first appearance for this company and is excruciatingly funny as a waiter. Roscoe Arbuckle and Mabel Normand also appear."

The Sea Nymphs

Released November 23, 1914. Produced by Mack Sennett for the Keystone Film Co. Distributed by the Mutual Film Corp. Directed by Mack Sennett. Working title: **Catalina Story**. Two reels (Reissued by W. H. Productions in 1918 as **His Diving Beauty**). Extant: GEM, DAN, MUN. With Mabel Normand, Roscoe Arbuckle, Mack Swain, Minta Durfee, Charles Avery, Alice Davenport, James Bryant, Harry McCoy, Bill Hauber.

Fatty, with wife, mother-in-law, and impediments in the shape of numerous band boxes, bags, and bundles, goes for an outing at Santa Catalina Islands. On the steamer he sees charming Mabel and is badly smitten. Mabel is traveling with the parental necessity—a very insignificant looking father with side whiskers. Fatty not knowing the relationship decides that he will interfere with that "old duck who is flirting with a young chicken," and accosting the old duck on the deck, he pitches him overboard. Then he goes in quest of Mabel and is enjoying his solitary innings—when he finds out who the man is he has uncerimoniously flung into the briny deep.

Father is rescued, and they land at Santa Catalina. It's here that Ambrose, chronic masher, puts in an appearance, and is introduced by father to Mabel. Everybody prepares to go in bathing. Fatty, who is something of a schemer, contrives to get his mother-in-law and Ambrose locked up in the same compartment in the bathing pavilion and he and Mabel run away into the surf, where they have a great swim and feed the seals. Meanwhile, the frantic mother-in-law is rescued from her unconventional tete-a-tete with Ambrose. Mabel's father enlists the muscle of the latter, who is jealous of his plump rival, and together they attack Fatty. The latter does them up, however, then he and Mabel proceed to give a diving exhibition. Mrs. Fatty and mother-in-law witness this thrilling program, executed off the end of a plank vibrating from the end of the high pier. Mabel excels in the dolphin plunge. The crowd on shore cheer loudly—all except Fatty's immediate family, who are saving their strength for future punishment. Fatty gets his—and the siren Mabel is hastily cloaked and dragged off by her father.

Roscoe has a dust-up with wife Minta Durfee (right) and mother-in-law Alice Davenport (left) on the way to Catalina in *The Sea Nymphs* (1914). Courtesy Sam Gill.

Fairly elaborate two-reeler made on a location trip to Catalina that's really just an excuse to showcase Mabel's figure as she does a selection of dives in a one-piece bathing suit. Sennett really hit upon something when he first filmed Mabel in her swimwear in *The Diving Girl* (1911) and *The Water Nymph* (1912), and kept her at the beach in *Mabel's Lover* (1912) and *Mabel's New Hero* (1913). He basically came up with a more refined version of the "French Postcard," and moved on to the logical conclusion that if one girl in swimwear could cause a sensation—a bevy of them would become an industry standard. And they did—hence the Sennett Bathing Beauties were born, and like his Keystone Cops every comedy production unit had to have their own group of girls. There were the L-Ko Girls, Fox Sunshine Beauties, and the Vanity Fair Girls, not to mention all the unnamed squads from the smaller companies who would show up to frolic for moviegoers at the drop of a hat, regardless of any plot logic, simply because they were an expected ingredient.

According to the October 24, 1914 *Motion Picture News,* Mabel and her bathing suit attracted more than just viewers in the theatres:

> *In the making of a two-reel comedy featuring Roscoe Arbuckle and Mabel Normand, the Keystone players secured the services of a very excellent*

actor in the person of Big Ben, a tame seal that makes its home on the coast of Catalina Islands, where the company was working, and Director Mack Sennett immediately changed the story in order to give the seal a good part. The picture is entitled "The Water Nymphs—Fatty and Mabel," and the negative and first print is now on its way to the New York laboratories of the company.

Moving Picture World (November 28, 1914): "A two-reel number with the Fat Boy and Mabel in the cast. Their flirtation starts on a boat heading for Catalina and is continued, with startling interruptions, on that island resort. The various characters visit the bath houses and their troubles continue. Ambrose, a chance acquaintance, is locked in a room with one of the women, and Mabel dons a bathing suit and does some high diving. She also feeds the sea lions. Two reels of entertaining nonsense without very much plot, but containing some pleasing resort views."

Motography (November 28, 1914): "Fatty neglects his wife, and even his mother-in-law, when he spies the attractive Mabel. The girl's father takes a dislike to her stout friend, and introduces Ambrose into the love race. Fatty manages to have his mother-in-law and Ambrose locked in a dressing room while he and Mabel give a diving exhibition. Mabel's father enlists the muscle of Ambrose, and together they attack Fatty but without making any impression on him. Had the angry parent been wise he would have sought the aid of Fatty's wife and her mother who grow impatient at his flirtation, and demonstrate to the crowd how big men should be whipped."

Mabel Normand ready to hit the surf in *The Sea Nymphs* (1914).

Leading Lizzie Astray

Released November 30, 1914. Produced by Mack Sennett for the Keystone Film Co. Distributed by the Mutual Film Corp. Directed by Roscoe Arbuckle. Working title: ***The Country Girl***. One reel. Extant: Friuli, UCLA, LOB. With Roscoe Arbuckle, Minta Durfee, Ed J. Brady, Mack Swain, Charles Parrott, Edgar Kennedy, Glen Cavender, Frank Hayes,

Roscoe and Minta Durfee make up at the end of *Leading Lizzie Astray* (1914). Courtesy the Library of Congress.

Harry McCoy, Al St John, Billie Bennett, Fritz Schade, Billy Gilbert, Grover Ligon, Charles Lakin, Dixie Chene, Slim Summerville, Phyllis Allen, Joe Bordeaux, Vivian Edwards, Dan Albert, Cecile Arnold, Ted Edwards.

A city-slicker driving through the country gets a flat tire. The neighboring farmer and his family help get the car back in order, but while this is happening the slicker makes a play for the farmer's daughter. Although she's engaged to farmhand Fatty, she's won over by the city man and agrees to meet and go away with him. Breaking things off with Fatty she packs her bags and goes to the city with the sport. Once they arrive in the city he takes her to a seedy bar and keeps her there against her will.

Meanwhile back in the country, Fatty says goodbye to the farmer and his wife and sets out to find his girl. Minta is caught trying to escape and is forced to entertain the rowdy bar patrons. When Fatty arrives he spots the chauffeur and car outside the dive, and goes in looking for Minta. When he finds that she's being manhandled all hell breaks loose, and Fatty, with the help of a couple of partying westerners, picks up a piano and lays waste to the bad guys. Minta is rescued, and she repledges her devotion to Fatty for the happy fade-out.

A slapstick variation on the classic "country girl led astray to the big city" melodrama, Roscoe would use this same plot for his 1916 Fort Lee-made two-reeler *The Bright Lights*. On hand in this one-reel version are Keystone regulars such as Edgar Kennedy, Fritz Schade, Billie Bennett, Glen Cavender, Mack Swain, and Charles Parrott, but the city-slicker villain is played by Ed Brady, a specialist in dramatic heavies. A graduate of musical

Early composite of long-time character heavy Ed Brady.

comedy, vaudeville and stock companies, Brady started in films in 1913 and cornered the market in sinister and unlikeable characters for Nestor, Powers, Rex, and Selig, sometimes with cowboy star Tom Mix. After this one time only appearance at Keystone, Brady worked as thugs and "characters" in all kinds of features, particularly westerns, right up to his death in 1942. He worked for Roscoe again in 1931's *Pete and Repeat,* and a few of his numerous titles are *Mantrap* (1926), *Son of Kong* (1933), *In Old Chicago* (1937), *Stagecoach* (1939), and *Sullivan's Travels* (1941).

The tallest denizen of the seedy Bon Ton Café is Slim Summerville. Previous to his joining Keystone in 1914, beanpole Slim had hoboed around the country and appeared in small theatre companies. After an early beginning at Sennett doing bits and stunts, he worked his way up to regular featured clown in support of Charlie Murray, Syd Chaplin, and Louise Fazenda. In 1916 Sennett teamed Slim with little Bobby Dunn in shorts like *The Winning Punch* (1916) and *Villa of the Movies* (1917), where they made a natural "Mutt & Jeff" combo playing opportunistic buddies not above doing dirt to each other to get ahead. Their partnership lasted for a number of years, continuing at Fox and a 1924 series of one-reelers at Universal.

In 1920 Summerville began concentrating on directing, and under his real first name of George helmed comedies for Fox, Joe Rock, and Universal all through the 1920s. At the same time he continued turning up in shorts and was support in features such as *The Beloved Rogue* (1927). Slim's career fared better than many other silent comics, as the arrival of sound gave it a shot in the arm. After his wonderful performance in *All Quiet on the Western Front* (1930) he starred in some talking shorts for Universal, but was generally a supporting player in "A" films and a star in "B's." Often teamed with ZaSu Pitts, he worked up until his death in 1946.

Two of the good-time girls in the bar are played by Dixie Chene and Vivian Edwards. Dixie Chene had been a dancer in vaudeville, touring in the act *Mary Jane and Buster Brown* with her older sister Hazel. She entered films in 1912 at Universal, and after a stint at Kay Bee she settled in for two years at Keystone, where, in addition to shorts such as *The Noise of Bombs* (1914) and *Giddy, Gay and Ticklish* (1915), she also worked with Roscoe in *The Masquerader, Fatty's Magic Pants* (both 1914), and *Fatty's Faithful Fido* (1915). Leaving Sennett for L-Ko, she returned to the stage in the late teens.

Vivian Edwards was a tall brunette who began appearing at Keystone in 1914, working with Chaplin in *The Property Man, The Face on the Barroom Floor, Those Love Pangs,* and others, in addition to supporting Charlie Murray in "Hogan" entries such as *Hogan's Mussy Job, Hogan, the Porter,* and *Hogan's Aristocratic Dream* (all 1915). Mostly turning up in small featured roles, she also appeared in a number of one-reel Triangle Komedies that were shot on the Sennett lot and supervised by Hampton Del Ruth like *Her Donkey Love* and *A Tuner of Note* (both 1917).

Moving Picture World (December 12, 1914): "We think that people will find this farce amusing. Most will laugh."

Motion Picture News (December 19, 1914): "One of the Fatty series of Keystone comedies, and one of the best of these yet issued. It is a burlesque of the story of the villain who takes a girl to the great city. Fatty goes to the rescue. The scenes in the "low dive" beggar description."

Bioscope (July 22, 1915): "As the hefty hero, Fatty pursues the villain who has lured poor Lizzie to the City, the latter being represented by a cabaret-saloon, and sets about the whole crowd. There are some riotous scenes during the exploits of the adipose comedian, two "shooting-up" miners on holiday provide an additional diversion. The final episode, where Fatty literally smashes the saloon, is ludicrous in the extreme, and ends a first-rare burlesque."

Shotguns that Kick

Released December 3, 1914. Produced by Mack Sennett for the Keystone Film Co. Distributed by the Mutual Film Corp. Directed by Roscoe Arbuckle. Working title: ***Fatty's Birthday Present***. One reel. Extant: CNC. With Roscoe Arbuckle, Frank Hayes, Minta Durfee, Peggy Page.

Fatty is a wiz with a shotgun, and proves his expertise by shooting an apple off his sweetheart's head. He later comes upon three crooks and is able to hold them off until the law arrives.

An extant, but unavailable short, on which there's very little information on, although it's known that Roscoe was supported by Frank Hayes, Minta Durfee, and Peggy Page.

One of the great but unsung character players of silent comedy, Frank Hayes was a string bean who often performed without his teeth in numerous Sennett comedies from 1914 on. A longtime stage veteran, Hayes played the occasional chief of the Keystone Cops, in addition to various fathers and farmers. He was also a specialist in drag as comic spinsters where he was hideous and hilarious. He did this for a wide variety of producers, such as in the Fox comedy *Who's Your Father?* (1918). Hayes plays an old crone who spreads the rumor that a foundling is actually the love-child of herself and hunky sheriff Tom Mix. Hayes appeared all over the silent comedy map with the likes of Larry Semon, Al St John, and Billy West, and was in demand for features such as *Heart's Haven* (1922) and Erich von Stroheim's *Greed* (1923) before his premature death from pneumonia in 1923.

Peggy Page is a mysterious ingénue who turned up in a number of 1914 Keystones such as *Tango Tangles, Mabel's Busy Day*, and *Those Love Pangs*. Some film historians believe that Miss Page was the ill-fated Helen Carruthers, another ingénue on the Sennett lot. It seems likely as both were listed in films at the studio at the same time, and the resemblance between the two on film and in photos is very strong. Besides shorts for Keystone and Essanay in 1915, Carruthers had a vaudeville act that failed, and unable to get work attempted suicide. In 1918 she married Baron Franciscus Gerard Zur Muhlen, a Dutch sugar merchant from Java, and fell to her death from a New York hotel window in 1925.

Moving Picture World (December 19, 1914): "Runs, tumbles and kicks of one kind in the shoulder and another in the back and some wonderful shooting of hats from one head to another make the backbone of this picture. Part of it is very funny, part is only vulgar."

Motion Picture News (December 19, 1914): "An excellent comedy introducing some decidedly novel situations, such as Fatty playing William Tell and shooting an apple from his sweetheart's head with a shotgun. At the conclusion of the story Fatty literally falls into a camp of three crooks, and holds them at bay until the sheriff and his men arrive."

Frank Hayes forces Roscoe to kiss Minta Durfee goodbye in 1914's *Shotguns that Kick*. Courtesy the George Eastman Museum.

Fatty's Magic Pants

Released December 14, 1914. Produced by Mack Sennett for the Keystone Film Co. Distributed by the Mutual Film Corp. Directed by Roscoe Arbuckle. Working title: ***The Borrowed Dress Suit***. One reel. (Reissued by W.H. Productions in 1918 as ***Fatty's Suitless Day***). Extant: LOC, MoMA, UCLA, ACAD, LOB. With Roscoe Arbuckle, Minta Durfee, Harry McCoy, Alice Davenport, Phyllis Allen, Charles Parrott, Slim Summerville, Edward Cline, Frank Opperman, Glen Cavender, Dixie Chene, Al St John, Bert Roach, Frank Opperman, Vivian Edwards.

Fatty sees a notice in the newspaper for a big benefit dance. All excited to go with his girl Minta, when his rival Harry comes by it's found that the dance is formal attire only. Since Fatty doesn't have the fancy clothes Minta decides to go with Harry. Bitterly disappointed the fat boy asks his washerwoman mother for fifty cents to rent a dress suit, but since he refuses to work for it she turns him down.

Harry lives next door, and when he cleans his suit in preparation for the evening's festivities he hangs it to dry on a clothesline between their houses. Fatty spies the hanging clothes and helps himself to them. That evening Minta's all dolled up and ready to go, but as Harry can't find his suit she goes to the ball with Fatty.

Fatty's Magic Pants (1914) amuse Charles Parrott but overwhelm Minta Durfee.
Courtesy Robert Arkus.

Fatty is a crowd pleaser with his athletic dancing, and when Harry dejectedly comes by he recognizes his suit on his large rival. When Minta and Fatty are taking a break, Harry sneaks in and cuts Fatty's pants and attaches a rope to them. When the moment is right Harry yanks the pants off Fatty, who has to scramble around to try and hide his lack of trousers. Finally the entire crowd sees him, and Harry pulls out a gun and chases Fatty around, causing total pandemonium. Whe Fatty escapes out a window he's arrested for indecent exposure by a cop who drags him off to the hoosegow.

For many years *Fatty's Magic Pants* was one of the most accessible of Roscoe's films as it was readily available through Blackhawk Films for home use. Although not one of his more innovative comedies, it's still a solid example of his work at the time and has a full brace of the Keystone supporting crew on display. Besides Minta Durfee, Alice Davenport, Phyllis Allen, Charles Parrott, and other

Portrait of Harry McCoy. Author's collection.

usual suspects, one of the major roles is taken by Harry McCoy, an important and versatile player in the Sennett menagerie. Born in Philadelphia, he began his stage career with the Corse Payton Stock Company, and spent eight years touring in vaudeville. Harry made his film debut for Universal's Joker Comedies, and while there was teamed with Max Asher in a series of *Mike & Jake* one-reelers. Also having stints with American and Selig, he moved to Keystone in 1913 and would remain through 1916.

McCoy's extreme versatility may be a reason that he's not better known today. Playing everything from young lovers, to heavies, to besotted barflies, this lack of a constant and consistent persona gave the public less to latch on to in comparison to a comic like Chester Conklin or Mack Swain. Included in the numerous films that McCoy appeared in with Roscoe are *Twixt Love and Fire*, *Fatty's Finish*, *Zip, the Dodger*, *Leading Lizzie Astray* (all 1914), *Mabel and Fatty's Wash Day*, and *Fatty's Chance Acquaintance* (both 1915). After 1917 McCoy moved around a lot, making comedies for Triangle, Fox Sunshine, supporting Roscoe again in *The Garage* (1920), and doing an early 1920s stint in CBC's *Hallroom Boy Comedies*.

Occasionally directing for series like the *McDougal Alley Kids* and writing for his old boss Sennett, he still continued as a performer in *Century Comedies* and in some of the Arrow comedies produced by Billy West such as *Stick Around* and *Hard-Hearted*

Husbands (both 1925). The arrival of sound found him behind the camera writing shorts for Educational and Columbia. McCoy died of a heart attack in 1937 at the age of forty-seven just after joining the Walt Disney organization as a writer and gag man.

Making his first appearance on the Sennett lot as one of the party guests is character comedian Bert Roach. After spending three years on stage working with Henry B. Harris in *Louisiana Lou* and *The Commuters*, he began his film career at Reliance, Majestic, and Keystone. He landed at L-Ko in 1916, becoming a mainstay of their crew in titles like *Live Wires and Love Sparks*, *Where Is My Husband?* (both 1916), *Beach Nuts*, and *Street Cars and Carbunkles* (both 1917). Making a name at L-Ko he moved to the Sennett lot for a three-year run as an ace supporting player in shorts such as *Sleuths* (1918), *Why Beaches are Popular* (1919), *The Gingham Girl* (1920), and *She Sighed by the Seaside* (1921), as well as the features *Yankee Doodle in Berlin* (1919) and *Down on the Farm* (1920).

From Sennett he began headlining in shorts for Universal. Besides his own starring entries he was paired with Neely Edwards for a series of *Nervy Ned* comedies, where Edwards was a gentleman tramp with Roach as his hobo valet. This eventually morphed into a domestic series when comedienne Alice Howell was added to the mix. Neely and Alice played a comfortable middle-class married couple with Bert gumming up their lives as their goofy butler. The peak of Roach's career was the late 1920s when he had prominent character roles in big features like *Tin Hats* (1926), *Tillie the Toiler* (1927), *The Crowd* (1928), and *The Last Warning* (1929). He made a good transition to sound with nice roles in *So Long Letty* (1929), *No, No, Nanette* (1930), and *Murders in the Rue Morgue* (1932), but he was soon demoted to unbilled walk-ons in films like *Saratoga* (1937), *Hellzapoppin* (1941), *My Sister Eileen* (1942), and *Duel in the Sun* (1946) until 1951.

Bioscope (June 17, 1915): "The genial "Fatty," unable to hire dress-clothes on the occasion of a fancy dress ball, purloins those of a rival, and promptly wins the hearts of all the fair damsels, until the foresaid rival trickily deprives him of his nether garments with disastrous results. Bright, amusing comic."

Fatty and Minnie He-Haw

Released December 21, 1914. Produced by Mack Sennett for the Keystone Film Co. Distributed by the Mutual Film Corp. Directed by Roscoe Arbuckle. Working title: **The Squaw's Man**. Two reels. Extant: GEH, ACAD, LOB. With Roscoe Arbuckle, Princess Minnie, Minta Durfee, Joseph Swickard, Harry McCoy, Frank Hayes, Slim Summerville, Bill Hauber, Billy Gilbert, Joe Bordeaux.

Fatty is stealing a ride on top of a freight train, when he is discovered and put off in the middle of the wilderness. Stumbling along, overcome by the heat, he collapses and is found and rescued by a very fat old Indian squaw. She falls for him, and to keep on good terms with the tribe he agrees to marry her. While the Indians are preparing the wedding feast Fatty helps out a girl who is having trouble with her horse. After she goes off an enraged Minnie drags Fatty back to the camp for the wedding. When fatty finds out that dog is the main course at the feast he makes his escape, and ends up in town at the Lost Hope Inn where the girl he met earlier is the daughter of the owner. While they are getting friendly his deserted Indian love comes looking for him and all hell breaks loose. Trying to escape Fatty gets on

Roscoe has sport with barfly Harry McCoy in *Fatty and Minnie He-Haw* (1914). Courtesy Sam Gill.

Minnie's horse which takes him back to the Indian camp where his almost in-laws decide to cook him at the stake. Princess Minnie arrives and, still in love with him, frees Fatty. Again he takes it on the lam, and although he out runs the tribe he ends up with a number of arrows in his posterior as a reminder of his Indian maid.

Roscoe's last release of 1914 takes him to the Wild West, a setting he would return to later in *Out West* (1918), *The Sheriff* (1918), *A Desert Hero* (1919), and his feature *The Round-Up* (1920). Princess Minnie, also known as Minnie Devereaux, Minnie Ha-Ha, and Indian Minnie, makes a funny and touching co-star. She works very well with Roscoe and is particularly funny when they have trouble kissing due to the prominence of their stomachs. Minnie was said to have been part of the tribe that lived on the grounds of Inceville and made her film debut in Thomas Ince-produced Broncho shorts such as *Old Mammy's Secret Code* (1913). After working with Roscoe she turned up in many other comedies such as Billy West's *The Slave* (1917), *The Son of a Gun* (1918) with Billie Ritchie, and the feature *Up in Mary's Attic* (1920), in addition to dramatic pictures like *The Coward* (1915) and *The Four Horsemen of the Apocalypse* (1921). She's said to have been a great friend of Mabel Normand's, with whom she appeared with in *Mickey* (1918) and *Suzanna* (1923). The October 24, 1914 *Motion Picture News* gives us a little background on this film's shooting:

1918's *Mickey* sees Mabel Normand in hot water with George Nichols in spite of Princess Minnie's efforts to hide her. Courtesy The Museum of Modern Art.

This week Roscoe Arbuckle is working opposite Minnie, the 350-pound Sioux squaw, of the tribe of Indians who live at the New York Motion Picture Company studio camp, in a western Indian comedy. More than two hundred Indians are used in some of the scenes, all of which are being made in the canyons and along the shore line beyond Santa Monica.

Moving Picture World (December 12, 1914): "A two-reel subject in which Roscoe Arbuckle, the Fat Boy, falls in with a tribe of Indians. The big squaw wants to wed him. The Indians apparently enjoyed the humor of the situation and there are some very entertaining scenes in this. Some of the humor is rather coarse. Fatty's ride on the broncho and the squaw's pursuit were laughable. The photography is excellent throughout."

Motion Picture News (December 26, 1914): "In which Roscoe Arbuckle gets into a world of trouble with an Indian squaw who desires his hand in marriage. He runs away from her, and takes refuge in a bar room, where he and a gentleman aptly termed "the last of the booze fighters" will surely create roars of laughter. This is another of the sidesplitting two-reelers that this company is turning out. It will be received with just as much enthusiasm as the others."

Harry McCoy (left) looks dubious as Alice Davenport throttles Mabel Normand and officer Joe Bordeaux arrests Roscoe in *Mabel and Fatty's Wash Day* (1915).

Chapter 4
Keystone 1915

Mabel and Fatty's Wash Day

Released January 14, 1915. Produced by Mack Sennett for the Keystone Film Co. Distributed by the Mutual Film Corp. Directed by Roscoe Arbuckle. Working title: ***Mabel's Flirtation***. (Reissued as ***Fatty's Flirtation***). Extant: Friuli, LOC, BFI, LOB. One reel. With Roscoe Arbuckle, Mabel Normand, Harry McCoy, Alice Davenport, Joe Bordeaux, James Bryant, Luke.

Mabel is busy slaving over the laundry while her husband relaxes in bed. When he refuses to help she throws water on him and lets him have it. Fatty is also doing the laundry at his house, while his henpecking wife berates him. Mabel and Fatty meet when they take their respective wash outside to hang up. When Fatty helps Mabel ring out her clothes her husband and his wife get jealous make a fuss.

Both couples go out for an afternoon walk in the park. Fatty is forced to read to his spouse, while Mabel and Harry argue and separate. Eventually Fatty's wife falls asleep, and seeing Mabel he sneaks off and asks her to go for a soda. Sitting down at the cafe he realizes that he doesn't have any money so he goes back and nabs his wife's purse. After he's gone she wakes up to find her purse missing, and when Harry walks by looking for Mabel and carrying her purse, the wife assumes he's stolen hers. She confronts him and calls the police, who take chase. Harry and Fatty's wife find Mabel and Fatty at the café and all hell breaks loose, with the cops chasing off Harry, and the wife laying waste to Fatty.

Although Roscoe and Mabel Normand had worked together frequently since 1913's *The Waiter's Picnic*, most memorably in *A Noise from the Deep* (1913) and *The Sea Nymphs* (1914), with this short the teamwork became more official and led to a whole string of slapstick treatises on domestic life that would include *Mabel and Fatty's Simple Life, Fatty and Mabel at the San Diego Exposition, Mabel, Fatty and the Law*, and *That Little Band of Gold* (all 1915).

Along with the regular supporting crew of Harry McCoy, Alice Davenport, Joe Bordeaux, and Luke, is James Bryant. Doing a small bit as the waiter at the Hollenbeck Park's stone pergola, Bryant was an Arbuckle sidekick and general assistant, who worked with the comedian from 1914 through the years with Keystone, Comique, and Reel Comedies. While material on Bryant is scarce, Buster Keaton gave this description of him in his autobiography:

Jimmy Bryant, who had been the anchor man for the Cops, was another doughty fellow who did not know how to take a fall. The fact is that Bryant did not even know how to turn a cartwheel, a trick most nine-year-old American boys learn quickly after they first turn a somersault. Jimmy, a heavy-set man with a bull neck, was the only Keystone cop who looked like a real policeman. Along with Al St John, Jimmy left Sennett to work with Roscoe when Arbuckle started making his own two-reelers.

I discovered just how much punishment Bryant was willing to absorb to stay in pictures in one of the earliest Arbuckle two-reelers I was in. I think it was called His Wedding Night.

This picture opened in a room above a general store where the girl is fitting her wedding dress on me, using me as a clothing form. The villain's roughnecks rush into the room to kidnap her. But she has just gone to the next room to get some pins. They mistake me for the bride-to-be because I have on the wedding dress, and carry me out the window and roll me down a slanting roof. On the street below Jimmy Bryant is waiting with a seagoing hack. As he waits to catch "the girl" in his arms he braces himself with one foot on the ground, the other on the step of the hack. I was supposed to

Roscoe wins a cigar from James Bryant in *Fatty at Coney Island* (1917). Courtesy the Lobster Collection.

fall on him headfirst. He was supposed to try and catch me, and miss. We seldom rehearsed bone-breaking scenes like that one. It was too easy for someone in the scene to be hurt or badly injured. Even if not put out of action the bruised man might dog his work the second time. For the same reason we tried to avoid retakes.

But Roscoe, who was directing, didn't like the way we did the scene. As we were getting ready for the repeat shot, Jimmy Bryant came over to me and whispered, "I don't know how to take off on this one or how to take this fall. So really hit me so it will look all right."

"I'll hit you all right," I said. "But be sure and get a good hold."

As I fell on him I shoved him with both feet as hard as I could. Jimmy hit the ground, going backwards, head over heels. He kept on going for about twenty feet, far out of camera range. Meanwhile, I had landed on the hack's two facing seats. One of the roughnecks, Joe Bordeaux, to make sure that the "bride-to-be" would not escape jumped off the slanting roof and landed on top of me.

Typically, it did not occur to anyone to ask Jimmy if he was hurt. But if someone had, he would not have complained. Later on, when I had my own company, I was able eventually to put him on the regular payroll as a $125-a-week cameraman. Jimmy was a puzzler. He was intelligent enough to learn all about the intricate film camera. But somehow he just never learned to fall properly and kept taking punishment like some battered old club fighter right to the end of his acting days.

Besides doing the camera work and appearing in Keaton's *The General* (1926), Bryant was said to have been Roscoe's secretary in the 1920s.

Bioscope (September 2, 1915): "A most amusing comedy, arising out of the troubles of Mabel and Fatty, who have to do the washing for their husband and wife, respectively."

Fatty and Mabel's Simple Life

Released January 18, 1915. Produced by Mack Sennett for the Keystone Film Co. Distributed by the Mutual Film Corp. Directed by Roscoe Arbuckle. Working title: **The Runaway Auto**. (Reissued as **The Joy Riders**). Extant: Friuli, LOC, MoMA. Two reels. With Roscoe Arbuckle, Mabel Normand, Al St John, Josef Swickard, Joe Bordeaux, Ted Edwards, Phyllis Allen, Billy Gilbert, Bobby Dunn.

Mabel is a happy farmer's daughter who loves poor farm hand Fatty. The local wealthy squire has a mortgage on the farm, so Mabel's father promises her hand in marriage to the squire's son to pay off the debt. When told of the plan Mabel refuses and is spanked and locked in her room. The minister is called to come and perform the ceremony, but from her window Mabel gives Fatty the lowdown so they decide to run off and get married. After much slapstick action they get away in an auto with father, the squire's son, and the rural police force in hot pursuit. Fatty and Mabel's car goes wild—chasing them around and backing Fatty up against a tree to bounce off his stomach before finally breaking down. When the

Glass slide from the original 1915 release of *Fatty and Mabel's Simple Life*. Courtesy Matt Vogel.

group catches up with the lovers an explosion from the car sends Mabel up into a tree. In the ensuing chaos of rescuing her most of the pursuers end up down a well as Fatty and Mabel sneak off with the minister and tie the knot.

An elaborate and fast paced short with plenty of farm hijinks and car chases, although one of the funniest moments is when old farmer Josef Swickard gives Al St John a swig from the bottle he's been constantly nipping from through the early part of the short and Al begins coughing and practically chokes to death as the booze takes his head off. The January 16, 1915 *Motion Picture News* touted the expansiveness of the production:

> *The entire Keystone company has taken part in the special feature January 18, two-reel release. This has been a very expensive picture to make because of the explosions staged in which two automobiles were blown to atoms. The final positive print is now being assembled, and as soon as projected at the studio the final title will be adopted, all members of the big stock company taking their part in selecting the name.*

Not only were two cars "blown to atoms" but Roscoe also described a trick effect of one of the cars bouncing off his stomach to *Photoplay* in April of 1916:

Mabel Normand trying to help Roscoe with his case of auto-indigestion in *Fatty and Mabel's Simple Life* (1915).

This was the picture called "Fatty and Mabel's Simple Life." In one scene I was backed against a tree by a runaway Ford. We had a man crouching down on the floor of the machine, working it from the pedals. All he had to guide him was a line on the ground. He would run the machine up to this line, at which time it was pressed close against me; then he would back up a few feet, and then run into me again. It gave the impression that the *machine was acting like a goat. Well, of course no one believed that the car was doing this without some sort of control, so it was a trick picture and yet it wasn't. But if that man ever had gone past the line I surely would have had an attack of indigestion.*

Lexington Leader (January 21, 1915): "'Fatty and Mabel's Simple Life'; Keystone extra special two-part comedy. Fatty, the farm hand, makes love to Mabel, him employer's daughter. The farmer objects to the match and his efforts to keep the young people from being together cause many complications to arise, affording a riot of fun."

Lakeland Evening Telegram (March 10, 1915, advertisement for the Majestic Theater): "A special Keystone is our good thing for today, the first of a series of bookings of Keystone specials. Now, folks, these features are not in the regular service; we pay real money for them, but you like the best, so it's up to us to give you want you want. FATTY AND MABEL'S SIMPLE LIFE. This is it, folks, our special two reeler. You think the single reels are funny. See this one and you'll be tickled to pieces."

Fatty and Mabel at the San Diego Exposition

Released January 23, 1915. Produced by Mack Sennett for the Keystone Film Co. Distributed by the Mutual Film Corp. Directed by Roscoe Arbuckle. Working title: *Fatty and Mabel at the Fair*. (Reissued by W.H. Productions in 1919 as *Fatty's Joy Ride*). One

A bickering Roscoe and Mabel Normand from *Fatty and Mabel at the San Diego Exposition* (1915). Author's collection.

reel. Extant: Friuli, LOB, LOC, ACAD. With Roscoe Arbuckle, Mabel Normand, Glen Cavender, Minta Durfee, Joe Bordeaux, Harry McCoy, Bill Hauber, Dora Rodgers, Edgar Kennedy, Billie Brockwell, Alice Davenport, Venice Hayes, Ted Edwards, Frank Hayes, Harry Gribbon, Vivian Edwards, Royal Hula Dancers.

At the San Diego Exposition Mabel and Fatty watch a military parade, and of course get mixed up in it. Next they rent a motorized cart, and after bickering they go their separate ways. Mabel watches a filmmaking exhibit and sees film being spooled on rollers while Fatty tries to flirt with an attractive woman by chasing her with the cart. He finally speaks to her and she lets him have it with a haymaker, so he gives up on her and goes in to see the Royal Hula Dancers.

Fatty's having a great time at the show, but Mabel, who's been busy fighting off her own masher, finds out that Fatty's in the theatre ogling the girls. She decides to catch him. Horrified by the native dancers, Mabel decides to make it hot for her full-figured husband. She covers her face and does a dance on stage, and when he runs up and joins her she confronts him in front of the whole audience. Although he beats a hasty retreat, the husband of the woman he harassed earlier comes after him with a pistol, and Fatty, the husband, and a cop all end up in the big fountain for a wet ending.

Always taking advantage of local events, Sennett wasn't about to miss out on the Panama-California Exposition. Sending cast and crew to San Diego's Balboa Park, Mack

Roscoe's overheated behavior leads to him being cooled down in the fountain in *Fatty and Mabel at the San Diego Exposition* (1915). Courtesy the Library of Congress.

not only got this comedy but also the actuality *A Glimpse of the San Diego Exposition*. Celebrating the opening of the Panama Canal, this 1915 to 1917 expo was an extended plug for San Diego as the first U.S. port of call for ships sailing north from the canal.

As a bickering married couple Roscoe and Mabel take in all the festivities, with lots of location footage, including a military parade, Hawaiian dancing girls, and Harry McCoy as a Charlie Chaplin imitator. The usual Keystone riff-raff turns up in reaction shots that were taken in front of the studio and then cut into location footage of Roscoe and Mabel disrupting the parade. Studio shots are also found in the hula dancer audience reactions, with Harry Gribbon working very hard to steal focus. And as Mabel's masher we get a good look at Joe Bordeaux "au natural" —without makeup and looking extremely suntanned.

Bioscope (December 23, 1915): "Mabel and Roscoe Arbuckle "see the sights" at the San Diego Exposition. Fairly effective comic."

Mabel, Fatty and the Law

Released January 28, 1915. Produced by Mack Sennett for the Keystone Film Co. Distributed by the Mutual Film Corp. Directed by Roscoe Arbuckle. Working title: ***No Flirting Allowed***. (Reissued by W.H. Productions in 1919 as ***Fatty's Spooning Days***). One

Under the eye of cop Frank Hayes, Mabel Normand (center), Harry Gribbon, Minta Durfee (right), and Roscoe leave the police station in *Mabel, Fatty and the Law* (1915). Courtesy Sam Gill.

reel. Extant: Friuli, LOC, MoMA, ACAD, LOB. With Roscoe Arbuckle, Mabel Normand, Harry Gribbon, Minta Durfee, Frank Hayes, Joe Bordeaux, James Bryant, Al St John, Bill Hauber, Edward Cline, Ollie Carlyle, Glen Cavender, Josef Swickard, Alice Davenport, Billie Bennett.

In a small city park where strict vigilance is maintained against flirting, Mabel, a young and pretty wife with an annoying husband innocently amuses herself with the harmless attentions of Fatty. Fatty relishes the situation all the more because this is one of those rare occasions when he has succeeded in escaping from the jail-like watchfulness of his wife. Meanwhile, Fatty's wife and Mabel's husband are carrying on a similar game. They are all discovered by the police and multiple arrests ensue. Both couples appear at the precinct house, where numerous complications make a reel full of fun.

Mabel's husband is played by Keystone newcomer Harry Gribbon. Nicknamed "Silk Hat Harry," Gribbon had a long stage career that started at age sixteen and went through vaudeville, legitimate shows like *Flo Flo* and the 1913 *Ziegfeld Follies*, as well as working for the Shuberts and George M. Cohan. Hired by Mack Sennett in 1915 from the Gayety Company at the Morosco Theatre, *Mabel, Fatty and the Law* was his first role with Sennett, but he soon moved to L-Ko, and then back to Sennett before bouncing around to stints at Fox, Christie, and Universal—all by 1921. He spent the early part of the 1920s back in vaudeville but returned to films as support in features such as *The Cameraman* and *Show People* (both 1928).

Harry Gribbon, Mabel Normand, and the ever-present Keystone "No Spooning" sign in *Mabel, Fatty and the Law* (1915). Courtesy Sam Gill.

Early sound was good for Harry as he headlined in Mack Sennett talkies from 1929 to 1932, and from there continued working in features and New York-made shorts for Vitaphone, RKO, and Educational. He later returned to Broadway in shows like *Mr. Big* (1941) and the mega-hit *Arsenic and Old Lace* (1943) in which he replaced John Alexander as Teddy Brewster. Sadly drinking ruined his career and health, and he died in the Motion Picture Home and Country Hospital in 1961.

Bioscope (September 16, 1915): "Although flirting is forbidden in the park, Mabel, anxious to escape from her bore of a husband, flirts with Fatty, whose one desire is to leave his wife to simpler pleasures. Mabel's husband and Fatty's wife also indulge in the harmless game. The police intervene, with sensational results. A delightful absurdity, excellently acted."

Fatty's New Role

Released February 2, 1915. Produced by Mack Sennett for the Keystone Film Co. Distributed by the Mutual Film Corp. Directed by Roscoe Arbuckle. Working title: German Saloon Story. One reel. Extant: Friuli, LOB, LOC, EYE. With Roscoe Arbuckle, Mack Swain, Slim Summerville, Luke, Glen Cavender, Frank Hayes, Fritz Schade, Frank Opperman, Charles Lakin, Edgar Kennedy, Bobby Dunn, Al St John, Joe Bordeaux.

Tramp Roscoe helping himself at the empty bar in *Fatty's New Role* (1915). Courtesy the Library of Congress.

Mack Swain (right) ready to wring hobo Roscoe's neck in 1915's *Fatty's New Role*. Courtesy the Library of Congress.

Fatty is a tramp. After waking up in a barn and brushing off the accumulated layers of dust for his morning toilette, he sees Schnitz's bar. Going in to get a refill and help himself to the free lunch, he's physically ejected by Schnitz when he can't pay. A group of patrons in the backroom see this and decide to play a joke on Schnitz. They show him a newspaper item about a mysterious man who's going around blowing up saloons, then they write a threatening note for Schnitz to find. In the meantime, a well-to-do gentleman has given Fatty some money and he buys a big round cheese. Schnitz is getting panicky as the note said that the stranger would return at three to blow up the bar, and it's almost three. Of course at this point Fatty walks in and takes out the big round cheese, which everyone assumes is a bomb and flees. Having the bar to himself Fatty helps himself to booze and a cigar. Schnitz runs and gets the cops, and when they arrive they realize it's a cheese for the fade-out.

Very interesting to see Roscoe in this very different role as a tramp, complete with an Emmett Kelly–type of stage hobo beard. Roscoe really shares the comedy honors in this short with Mack Swain, who plays the panic-struck Schnitz, proprietor of the bar. Coming from a long stage career, Swain started in films at Keystone in 1913, and from small roles quickly became a star with his character of "Ambrose" —a put upon everyman with dark-circled eyes and a brush mustache. Leaving Sennett in 1917 he continued playing Ambrose for L-Ko, Fox, and the independent Poppy Comedies and Perry Comedies.

Swain's career stalled in the early 1920s when, for reasons that are lost to history, he was blacklisted by an influential producer, but his old Keystone teammate Charlie Chaplin came to the rescue and made him part of his stock company in films such as *The Idle Class* (1921) and *The Pilgrim* (1923). In 1925, Swain began riding the wave of a comeback thanks to his hilarious performance in Chaplin's *The Gold Rush* (1925). He went on to features such as *Hands Up!* (1925), *My Best Girl* (1927), *Gentlemen Prefer Blondes* (1928), and *The Cohens and Kelly in Atlantic City* (1929), until his career petered out in the early 1930s and his death in 1935.

Bioscope (October 14, 1915): "Roscoe Arbuckle as a Lasky hobo is unmistakably funny, and his whole performance is one long scream."

Mabel and Fatty's Married Life

Released February 11, 1915. Produced by Mack Sennett for the Keystone Film Co. Distributed by the Mutual Film Corp. Directed by Roscoe Arbuckle. Working title: **Monkey Scare**. One reel. Extant: MoMA, Friuli, LOC, CAN, UCLA, LOB. With Roscoe Arbuckle, Mabel Normand, Glen Cavender, Al St John, Charles Lakin, Mae Busch, Joe Bordeaux, James Bryant, Harry "Dutch" Ward, Frank Hayes, Dan Albert.

Fatty and Mabel are in the park when an organ grinder's monkey startles them. In the ensuing altercation with the organ grinder he swears an oath of vengeance on them. On the way home Fatty runs into a business associate, and goes to talk with him. Mabel returns home and gets nervous when Fatty comes home to get something. She surprises him with a gun, scaring him and his friend. Finally Fatty goes off, but Mabel is still nervous about being alone. Looking out the window she sees the organ grinder and a pal skulking around the house, but she tries to ignore it.

She notices that someone is behind the drapes in the room. She calls Fatty's office in a panic, and then finds that the organ grinder has gotten into the house. Fatty's secretary alerts the Keystone Cops, who race to the rescue. Mabel's locked herself in a room and the interlopers are trying to break in. Fatty and his pal get wind of the situation and join the race to get there. The Cops finally arrive and find that it's the organ grinder's monkey behind the drapes, and his owner only wanted to get him back. Roscoe arrives to find that everything is alright, and has a good laugh at Mabel's expense.

Mabel and Fatty's Married Life (1915) includes Mabel using Roscoe for target practice.

Roscoe's business associate Charles Lakin (right) gets a bird's eye view of *Mabel and Fatty's Married Life* (1915). Courtesy the Library of Congress.

Mabel and Fatty's Married Life is a spoof of dramatic films like D.W. Griffith's 1909 *A Lonely Villa* (written by Sennett) and Lois Weber's *Suspense* (1913) which feature a woman trapped in an isolated house that is beset by burglars. Glen Cavender's menacing organ grinder is dressed and made up very much like the tramp (Sam Kaufman) in *Suspense*. Besides Mabel's scared reactions, there is some very funny rush to the rescue footage with Roscoe, Charles Lakin, and the cops.

The short is a real tour de force for Mabel, as she's the main focus and has some marvelous solo scenes where she's reacting to the moving drapes. Trying to tell herself that it's only her imagination, she works to concentrate on her sewing but finds it impossible. It's one of her most sustained pieces of pantomime in which she goes through a hilarious progression of stages of fear. Al St John is also shown to good advantage as the head of the three police officers. He has some very elaborate legwork as the petrified cop who has to check out the room, and his bit ends with him doing a spectacular leap behind an upright piano in one bound.

Roscoe's stereotypical Jewish business associate is played by Charles Lakin, a busy, but overlooked, silent comedy supporting player. Bearing a strong resemblance to fellow comedy regular Leo White, Lakin worked on stage in the act *Social Maids* before coming to Keystone in 1914. For the next three years he played a succession of cops, crooks, bartenders, waiters, henchmen, and desk clerks, often with Roscoe in titles like *A Bath*

House Beauty, *The Knockout*, *Leading Lizzie Astray* (all 1914), *Fatty's New Role*, *That Little Band of Gold*, *Fatty's Faithful Fido*, and *Fatty's Tintype Tangle* (all 1915).

Leaving Sennett, he moved through the silent comedy universe and worked at L-Ko, Hal Roach, and Fox Sunshine Comedies. Lakin's film career tapered off following a stint supporting his look-a-like Leo White, in a series of 1920-1921 *Pinnacle Comedies* for the Independent Film Association. He remained in California running a notions store and being a salesman for the Green Hills Cemetery, where he was buried in 1965.

Motion Picture News (February 20, 1915): "Featuring Roscoe Arbuckle and Mabel Normand in a very funny comedy in which Mabel in the absence of her husband is terrified to the point of collapse by the queer movements of a window curtain. Very cleverly put on and extremely laughable."

Moving Picture World (February 20, 1915): "A rapid-fire comedy number, full of amusing action. Fatty and Mabel offend an organ grinder traveling about with a monkey. The organ man gets his pal and plans revenge upon Mabel, who is alone at home. This is a good number and well photographed."

Hogan's Romance Upset

Released February 13, 1915. Produced by Mack Sennett for the Keystone Film Co. Distributed by the Mutual Film Corp. Directed by Charles Avery & Charles Murray. Working title: **The Pug**. One reel. Extant: Friuli, LOC, LOB. With Charles Murray, Bobby Dunn, Billie Brockwell, Josef Swickard, Billy Gilbert, Frank Hayes, Charles Lakin, Ted Edwards, James Bryant, Glen Cavender, Roscoe Arbuckle, Ford Sterling, Mack Swain, Al St John, Vivian Edwards.

Hogan attempts to make a lady's acquaintance, but a rival forestalls him. To get even, Hogan bores a hole in a boat the lady and her admirer have hired, but this plot is discovered, and Hogan has to settle things with his rival in a boxing match.

Roscoe has a cameo in this Charlie Murray comedy as a spectator watching Hogan's big fight. Having settled in at Keystone in 1914, Murray was busy turning out the misadventures of his layabout Irish character. Titles include *The Noise of Bombs* (1914), *Hogan's Mussy Job* (1915), *The Feathered Nest* (1916), *A Bedroom Blunder* (1917), *Reilly's Wash Day* (1919), and *Hard Knocks and Love Taps* (1921), where Murray played with Louise Fazenda, Slim Summerville, and Polly Moran. He remained one of Sennett's top stars until 1922, when he began freelancing in shorts and numerous features.

Some of his features are *The Wizard of Oz* (1925), *The Boob* (1926), *McFadden's Flats*, *The Gorilla* (both 1927), *Vamping Venus* (1928), and *Clancy in Wall Street* (1930). In 1926 he was first teamed with comic George Sidney in the film *The Cohens and Kellys*. Thinly adapted from the smash stage hit *Abie's Irish Rose*, its story of feuding Irish and Jewish families struck comic pay dirt and spawned six sequels. Becoming a popular team, he and Sidney were mismatched in many more features and shorts. Although he made a good transition to sound Murray's career slowed down in the 1930s. His last appearance was the Eddie Cline-directed feature *Breaking the Ice* (1938), and he passed away in 1941.

Roscoe, Ford Sterling, Al St John, Mack Swain, Glen Cavender, and others watch Charlie Murray get the worst in a boxing match in *Hogan's Romance Upset* (1915). Courtesy the Library of Congress.

Bioscope (October 21, 1915): "Chas. Murray in his popular "Hobo" role. His attempts to gain a lady's favor by daring deeds on the river and in the boxing ring are unsuccessful. The glove fight is a particularly funny episode."

A Glimpse of the San Diego Exposition

Released February 18, 1915. Produced by Mack Sennett for the Keystone Film Co. Distributed by the Mutual Film Corp. Directed by Mack Sennett. Working title: ***Educational of San Diego Exposition***. ½ reel. (Released with ***Ye Olden Grafter***). Extant: LOC. With Roscoe Arbuckle.

Views and sights of the 1915 San Diego Exposition.

A Keystone educational subject, made at the same time as *Fatty and Mabel at the San Diego Exposition*. In the midst of all the sightseeing Roscoe suddenly stumbles into the frame to make some faces at the camera and do a little business before going on his way.

Moving Picture World (March 6, 1915): "On same reel with above (*Ye Olden Grafter*). Very pleasing views of the beautiful exposition buildings at the San Diego Fair; also a view of the bridge coasting a quarter of a million."

Motion Picture News (March 6, 1915): "On the same reel as "Ye Olden Grafter." Very interesting views of the exposition grounds, including an entire miniature reproduction of the Panama Canal."

Fatty's Reckless Fling

Released March 4, 1915. Produced by Mack Sennett for the Keystone Film Co. Distributed by the Mutual Film Corp. Directed by Roscoe Arbuckle. Working title: ***Disappearing Bed Story***. One reel. Extant: Friuli, LOC, LOB. With Roscoe Arbuckle, Minta Durfee, Edgar Kennedy, Katherine Griffith, Ted Edwards, George Ovey, Frank Hayes, Grover Ligon, Glen Cavender, Harry McCoy, Billie Walsh, Venice Hayes.

When Fatty comes home in a drunken state his irate wife confiscates his pants and locks him in the apartment. Of course this doesn't deter his wandering, and without his pants he ventures out in his robe to a high stakes poker game going on across the hall. Fatty joins the game and wins big time, but doesn't get to keep the money long as the game gets raided.

Making his escape Fatty finds that his door is locked, and with bullets nipping him in the behind and his wife in the lobby, he ducks into the next door apartment. The woman inside is startled (particularly as Fatty has lost his robe and is pantless) and when her husband makes a return she hides Fatty in their slide out bed. He spots Fatty and the bed ends up crashing through the wall into the next apartment. That apartment is Fatty's and at this point his wife joins the melee. As the husband is letting Fatty have it the detective gets out of the poker room and starts firing more bullets. Pandemonium reigns until Fatty gets knocked into the bathtub, where he curls up under the water and decides to sleep it off.

This is another boarding house fracas, this time with a drunken Roscoe at odds with his controlling wife. A novel prop in this outing is the bed that slides in and out of

Roscoe forgets his poker face in *Fatty's Reckless Fling* (1915). Courtesy the Library of Congress.

Minta Durfee caught between Katherine Griffith and Roscoe in *Fatty's Reckless Fling* (1915). Courtesy the Library of Congress.

the wall. Roscoe, of course, makes the most of this item in the big climax, which finally crashes through the wall into the next apartment.

Roscoe's wife, who's more of a virago than usual, is played by Katherine Griffith, a busy character comedienne and mother of Keystone kid actor Gordon Griffith. Her husband Harry and other children Gertrude and Graham acted as well. Mrs. Griffith rarely appeared at Sennett, but she was a regular in Powers Comedies, usually playing the mother of Powers Kids Matty Roubert and Baby Early, and at L-Ko Comedies teamed with Dan Russell in shorts like *The Right Car but the Wrong Berth* (1916) and *Heart Sick at Sea* (1917). She had meaty roles in prestigious features such as Mary Pickford's *Pollyanna* (1920) and *Huckleberry Finn* (1921), but her career was cut short by her sudden death from a stroke on the set of the Marshall Neilan film *Penrod* (1922).

George Ovey, another comedy stalwart rarely seen on the Sennett lot, also turns up as one of Roscoe's poker playing buddies. A graduate of traveling stock companies and minstrel shows, Ovey made a handful of Keystone appearances which included *The Cannon Ball* (1915), and the feature *Oh! Mabel Behave* (made in 1915 but released in 1922) before he was discovered by producer David Horsley. Starting in 1915 Horsley formed Cub Comedies to feature Ovey. Developing the character of "Jerry," a pint-sized wheeler-dealer in a soup bowl derby, cutaway jacket, checkered trousers, and spats, Ovey spent over two years cranking out a ton of Jerry one-reelers before moving on to the lower budgeted Gaiety and Folly Comedies. The peak of Ovey's career was 1915 to 1919, with his later silent days spent in a few Jack White comedies and as character support in serials, low budget action features, and westerns. When sound arrived he did uncredited bit roles from 1931 right up to his death at seventy-one in 1951.

Bioscope (August 19, 1915): "Poor Fatty is mistreated by his wife, who, in order to prevent him leaving the house, hides his trousers. Fatty is equal to the occasion, however, and his subsequent adventures are ludicrous in the extreme. A most amusing Keystone."

New York Dramatic Mirror (March 10, 1915): "Since it is no longer a secret that Keystone farces are built around an idea, it would not be guessing too much to suppose that the subtitle "While Wifey's away, Hubby has an inclination to play" which characterizes this offering, also served as its inspiration. It is thoroughly laughable."

Fatty's Chance Acquaintance

Released March 8, 1915. Produced by Mack Sennett for the Keystone Film Co. Distributed by the Mutual Film Corp. Directed by Roscoe Arbuckle. Working title: ***Fatty's Wife's Husband***. One reel. (Reissued as ***Fatty's Flirtation***). Extant: Friuli, Acad, Queb, LOB, LOC, UCLA, EYE. With Roscoe Arbuckle, Billie Bennett, Minta Durfee, Harry McCoy, Frank Hayes, Ollie Carlyle, Billie Walsh, Glen Cavender, Ted Edwards, Grover Ligon.

Fatty makes the acquaintance of a smart little girl, who expresses a desire for refreshment. He "borrows" his wife's handbag, unaware that a pickpocket has already abstracted its contents, and unable to pay, has not only an unpleasant time with the waiter, but also his wife, who has tracked him to the refreshment booth.

Another mix-up in the park short, this time stolen by Frank Hayes as a cop hellbent on catching park mashers. His introductory close-up where he emerges from the bushes looking for miscreants is comic poetry.

The *In and Out of Los Angeles Studio* column in the March 20, 1915 *Motion Picture News* reported some difficulty while shooting this short:

> "Fatty's Chance Acquaintance" featuring Roscoe Arbuckle and Minta Durfee, supported by Billie Bennett, Harry McCoy and Frank Hayes, was the cause of much grief in the making. The car the players

Billie Bennett keeping Roscoe in line from *Fatty's Chance Acquaintance* (1915). Courtesy Jim Kerkhoff.

Roscoe wetting more than his whistle in *Fatty's Chance Acquaintance* (1915).
Courtesy the Library of Congress.

were riding in while near Oxnard became stuck in the mud. The car is still in Oxnard and will remain there until July.

Bioscope (August 26, 1915): "One of the stout man's best "flirtation" releases. The confusion which arises from the theft of his wife's handbag by a park thief, whose girl "Fatty" has made up to, provides a whole service of big laughs."

That Little Band of Gold

Released March 15, 1915. Produced by the Keystone Film Co. Distributed by the Mutual Film Corp. Directed by Roscoe Arbuckle. Working title: ***Before and After Marriage***. (Reissued by W.H. Productions as ***For Better or Worse***). Two Reels. Extant: LOC, FRIU, LOB . With Roscoe Arbuckle, Mabel Normand, Ford Sterling, Alice Davenport, Mae Emory, Charles Arling, Al St John, Charles Parrott, Glen Cavender, Frank Hayes, Ollie Carlyle, Edgar Kennedy, Slim Summerville, Grover Ligon, Bill Hauber, Charles Lakin, Ted Edwards, Edward Bilby, Vivian Edwards, Bobby Dunn, Fred Fishback, Mack Swain, Billie Walsh, Harry McCoy, Minta Durfee, Edward Cline, Billy Gilbert, Phyllis Allen.

Mabel and Fatty are a shy and awkward couple who marry at City Hall. Jumping ahead a bit they are now comfortably middle-class, but Fatty is taking Mabel for granted—

Roscoe turns out to be a less-than dutiful husband in *That Little Band of Gold* (1915).

stumbling home after having a few snorts, flirting with the maid, and having a tussle with his mother-in-law. Fatty is dragged to the opera by his spouse and runs into a pal there. He leaves the performance on an excuse and hooks up with the friend and his two lady companions for drinks. The woman that his pal favors takes a shine to Fatty, so the angry friend calls Mabel and gives her an anonymous tip that her husband is stepping out. Mabel and her mother show up at the restaurant and catch him in the act, and the next scene is back at City Hall, but this time getting a divorce. Outside afterwards they patch things up and run back in to re-marry.

That Little Band of Gold is something of a breakthrough in Roscoe's career. A redo of 1914's *Fatty's Debut*, but with an extra reel and much more character nuance,

Ford Sterling at the theatre with his object of desire Mae Emory in *That Little Band of Gold* (1915). Courtesy the Library of Congress.

director Arbuckle manages to get in all the requisite knockabout but includes sly digs and satirical observations on marriage and male-female relationships—something new in the usual slap-dash Keystone product. Mabel gives an essentially dramatic performance as the neglected and disappointed wife, and Roscoe brings out unlikeable aspects in his character—generally brusque and grumpy—even reprimanding Mabel when she slips and falls instead of helping her up.

Alice Davenport is very good as Mabel's concerned mother, and Ford Sterling, coming in mid-way as a special guest star, gives one of his funniest performances. Playing a carousing buddy of Roscoe's, he spends a great deal of the second reel actively ogling the zaftig Mae Emory. The real-life wife of comic Harry Gribbon, Emory had spent sixteen years on stage as an actress and singer in the *Ziegfeld Follies* and other shows, in addition to appearing on major vaudeville circuits with and without her husband. She and Gribbon made their film debuts with Keystone in 1915, and the statuesque Ms. Emory was often displayed as eye candy and played alluring "other women" as in *Teddy at the Throttle* (1917). She joined her husband in shorts at L-Ko, but returned to Sennett and soon retired to run a beauty parlor. She passed away in New York thirteen years before husband Harry in 1948.

Moving Picture World (March 20, 1915): "A two-reel farce subject which finds Ford Sterling again with his former associates Fatty and Mabel. The men take their ladies to the theatre, Fatty and Mabel having been married but a short time before. Ford then lures his corpulent friend into a restaurant where they wine and dine Ford's friends to the neglect of Fatty's wife. When Mabel appears, there is trouble. A divorce follows and then both repent and they marry again. This is a breezy number, but escapes anything of a decidedly risqué character. The photography is very fine."

Fatty's Faithful Fido

Released March 20, 1915. Produced by Mack Sennett for the Keystone Film Co. Distributed by the Mutual Film Corp. Directed by Roscoe Arbuckle. Working title: **Fatty the Tough**. (Reissued in England as **Fatty's Canine Friend**). One reel. Extant: Friuli, LOB, LOC, EYE. With Roscoe Arbuckle, Minta Durfee, Al St John, Frank Hayes, Charles Lakin, Joe Bordeaux, Charles Parrott, Ted Edwards, Edward Cline, Billie Walsh, Dan Albert, Grover Ligon, Harry McCoy, Venice Hayes, Luke.

Street tough Fatty and his dog Luke stop in at the Swift Foot Athletic Club. Preparations are happening for the evening's Grand Ball. While Fatty is checking in with his sweetheart

Al St John, Glen Cavender, Minta Durfee, Frank Hayes, and an upside-down Roscoe make the left to right line-up from *Fatty's Faithful Fido* (1915). Courtesy The Museum of Modern Art.

Minta rival Al tries to muscle in, but he's thrown out by Fatty. Outside Al tries to foist his attentions on Minta again which leads to all-out war between he and Fatty which includes flying bricks and boulders, and the conking of innocent bystanders like the Chinese laundry man. Finally, Fatty sics Luke on Al, who keeps the rival cornered until a neighborhood cat distracts him.

At the ball Fatty is a hit with his athletic dancing. Al shows up and starts trouble but is properly trounced by the fat man. Al hatches a plot and hires a couple of thugs to beat Fatty up. Al has marked Fatty with a chalk mark on his back, but when the thugs arrive the chalk mark has ended up on Al and they attack him. A riot breaks loose at the ball, and the fighting is so violent that Fatty, Al, and Luke crash through the floor and end up in the big washtub of the laundry below.

A very entertaining short featuring the street-tough version of the Fatty character, this time surrounded by pals and rivals at the rough social club. Even included is the neighborhood's Chinese laundry man One Lung, played with over the top racism by skinny Frank Hayes. The title role is essayed by Luke, Roscoe and Minta's bull terrier. Given to them by director Wilfred Lucas as a reward for Minta's brave stunting on *A Quiet Little Wedding* (1913), and named in his honor, Luke began turning up in brief bits in

Luke beat Rin-Tin-Tin to the punch as an action movie dog. Courtesy The Museum of Modern Art.

1914 shorts like *The Knockout* and *Lover's Luck*. Being a screen natural, his appearances became more regular in 1915 films such as *Mabel and Fatty's Wash Day* and *Fatty's New Role*, and soon he was featured in shorts like this one, *Fatty's Plucky Pup* (1915), and *Fatty and Mabel Adrift* (1916).

Besides having loads of personality and presence Luke was quite the movie stunt dog—able to climb ladders or leap from roof to roof in pursuit of Al St John or Joe Bordeaux. When Roscoe went to East Coast in 1916 to make films like *His Wife's Mistake* and *The Waiter's Ball* it appears that Luke was left in California, but after this hiatus he returns in *The Butcher Boy* (1917) and is prominent in other Comiques such as *The Cook*, *The Sheriff* (both 1918), *The Hayseed* (1919), and *The Garage* (1920). Popular with audiences, the trade magazines focused much attention on the canine comic:

> *"How about the four-footed member of your company—you must pay him an enormous salary to make him such a willing worker."*
> "My dog! Oh, he's a true artist and works for pure love of his art."
> *"What part of his art does he love best?"*
> "Biting Al St John and 'Buster' Keaton."
> *"Do you have any trouble teaching him his share of the business?"*
> "Very little. The only thing is to prevent him from overdoing it. Both boys wear stout leather union suits when there is to be a mix-up with the dog, and the instant they start to run he darts after them without being told. In the picture where he jumps off the pier we didn't bother about rehearsing him. It was a thirty-foot drop, but the instant one of the actors jumped he was right after him. It must have hurt when the dog struck the water, but he was always game for the next jump."
> – ***Moving Picture World***, March 8, 1919

The November 11, 1920 issue of *Picture Play* even gave Luke the opportunity to express his own feelings:

> *I am responsible for the laughs in Fatty Arbuckle's comedies. I don't have to rely on my weight to get me over either. I've been in a lot of comedies, and now that Fatty's in serious drama I'm going to play in some of them, although, in my opinion, some of these serious pictures have more hokum then the two-reelers. Aside from putting the laughs in his pictures, I have to hear Fatty singing his own compositions at home. I earn my money, friends, believe me.*

Luke wasn't in any of Roscoe's features, and his last known appearance was putting the bite on Buster Keaton in *The Scarecrow* (1920). After this he retired, and later was replaced by up and coming pups like Pal and Pete the pup for the Arbuckle-directed shorts *The New Sheriff* (1924) and *Dynamite Doggie* (1925). Luke passed away at age twelve in 1926.

Important human support came from Charles Parrott, later to be better known as Charley Chase. Parrott got his early experience in vaudeville specializing in comic monologues and songs. Breaking into films in 1914 with a brief stint at Nestor Films, he settled in at Keystone. His youthful and dapper appearance limited his onscreen roles in the exaggerated Sennett universe, so he began contributing gags and stories in addition to becoming an assistant director. By 1916 he was a full-fledged comedy director helming shorts such as *A Dash of Courage* (1916) on his own. At that time he left Keystone to become a veritable silent comedy bee—flying from studio flower to studio flower.

The places he lit included Foxfilm Comedies with Hank Mann, Billy West Comedies for King Bee and Bulls Eye, entries for L-Ko, Mr. & Mrs. Carter De Haven for Paramount, and even a couple of Lloyd Hamilton shorts for the fledgling Jack White Company. By 1921 he was in residence at the Hal Roach Studio and took over the Snub Pollard series. Before long Parrott became director-general of the Roach lot and helped develop Our Gang. When Harold Lloyd left the studio, Parrott was headlined in his own series of comedies and given the new name of Charley Chase. Becoming one of Roach's top stars, turning out silent comedy masterpieces like *His Wooden Wedding* (1925) and *Limousine Love* (1928), he made a strong leap to sound films and continued making quality two-reelers for Roach and Columbia until his death in 1940.

Charles Parrott (upper right) was in charge of the Bulls Eye comedy unit that featured Sid Smith (bottom right), Charles Dorety (left of Parrott), Evelyn Nelson, and James Parrott (right). Courtesy Robert S. Birchard.

Bioscope (September 9, 1915): "This subject is a revelation to those accustomed to Keystone whole-heartedness. There are a series of back-breaking falls, a roof chase in which the terrier shows remarkable "holding" powers—a great and wet—Keystone finish."

When Love Took Wings

Released April 1, 1915. Produced by Mack Sennett for the Keystone Film Co. Distributed by the Mutual Film Corp. Directed by Roscoe Arbuckle. Working title: ***Fatty's Fast Ride***. One reel. Extant: Friuli, LOB, LOC. With Roscoe Arbuckle, Ollie Carlyle, Al St John, Joe Bordeaux, Frank Hayes, Ted Edwards, Glen Cavender.

Roscoe and minister Ted Edwards react to Ollie Carlyle's shiny dome in *When Love Took Wings* (1915). Courtesy the Library of Congress.

Three love sick youths, supplied with a bicycle, automobile, and biplane, all attempt to marry the girl they all three love. The elopement is first tried by the bicyclist and he loses the bride-to-be when the auto driver overtakes him. But the sky pilot proves to be the swiftest, and after a thrilling race reaches the home of the parson. But when the flyer finds that his prospective bride is actually bald, he's happy to let his rival tie the knot with her.

Roscoe's leading lady in *When Love Took Wings* is Helen "Ollie" Carlyle, a Keystone ingénue of 1914 and 1915 who kept busy playing small roles like maids or party guests in shorts such as *Hogan's Mussy Job*, *Love in Armor*, *That Little Band of Gold*, *Gussle's Wayward Path*, and *My Valet* (all 1915). This appears to be her one female lead, where she causes much rivalry between Roscoe and Joe Bordeaux—that is until she's revealed to be bald at the end of the picture! Around this time Carlyle married Sennett scenario editor and production manager Hampton Del Ruth and retired from the screen, but after their 1920 divorce she returned to acting on the stage and made two final films, *Models and Wives* (1931) and *Forgotten Commandments* (1932), before her death at age forty in 1933.

The April 17, 1915 *Motion Pictures News* added:

Aviator DeLloyd Thompson was specially engaged for the making of this picture and made some wonderful loops and dives before the lens.

Motion Picture News (April 24, 1915): "The girl's wealth of raven tresses is one of the many reasons for her great popularity with her suitors. Their efforts to win her cause many amusing situations. When one of them discovers that the tresses are of the portable variety there is a sudden resignation, but one unfortunate victim is collared by dad, and forced to face the minister. Roscoe Arbuckle is seen as one of the ardent swains."

Pictures and the Picturegoer (November 20, 1915): "Love passions end in the disillusionment of the lady's beauty."

Wished on Mabel

Released April 19, 1915. Produced by Mack Sennett for the Keystone Film Co. Distributed by the Mutual Film Corp. Directed by Roscoe Arbuckle. Working title: **Golden Gate Park Story**. One reel. Extant: FRIU, LOB, LOC. With Roscoe Arbuckle, Mabel Normand, Alice Davenport, Joe Bordeaux, Edgar Kennedy, Glen Cavender, Billy Gilbert, James Leslie, Frankie Dolan.

Mabel and her mother are reading in the park when Fatty comes by and joins them. Although under the watchful eye of mama they manage to spoon a bit, and then sneak off on their own. Exploring the park they decide to play hide and seek. A tramp sleeping on a bench is woken up and told to move on by a patrolling cop (who then takes the bum's reclining spot on the bench). Wandering on, the bum comes upon Mabel's mother and after sitting beside her with a sob story steals her watch. When mother notices the missing watch she tells the cop, who vows to look for the culprit but lays back down and goes to sleep.

Fatty and Mabel are having a great time romping through the park until Fatty flicks a bee at Mabel which lands on her nose. In a panic he manages to flick it off her, but it lands on an innocent bystander. The tramp accidently drops the stolen watch on the ground, and when he tries to flirt with Mabel, Fatty takes care of him. Finding the watch on the ground Fatty gives it to Mabel as a present. The crook sees Mabel with the watch and tries to take it from her. Fatty stops him, and at that moment mother joins them and recognizes her watch. The crook takes off but is soon captured by the cop. With her watch returned, mother, Fatty, and Mabel head off for more fun.

Mabel Normand and Roscoe find that Alice Davenport makes three a crowd in *Wished on Mabel* (1915). Courtesy the George Eastman Museum.

Wished on Mabel was shot on location at Golden Gate Park, during a four-week trip to San Francisco. *Mabel and Fatty Viewing the World's Fair in San Francisco* was also made during this jaunt, although it's reported that the weather was so rainy that the actual shooting only consisted of nine days. Making for a very different backdrop than the usual Hollenbeck or Echo Parks, the huge Golden Gate Park is twenty percent larger than New York's Central Park, and is where masses of people were housed following the famous 1906 San Francisco earthquake.

Along with Roscoe and Mabel, the group taken to San Francisco included Alice Davenport, Edgar Kennedy, and Glen Cavender, not to mention two unsung supporting players who were integral parts of the Keystone universe. Joe Bordeaux was a ubiquitous face in Roscoe's Sennett films, more accurately a mug with his broken nose and jutting jaw. The short Canadian-born Bordeaux began his duties as Arbuckle's chauffeur, and was soon a general behind the scenes gofer as well as a busy bit player. In addition he was a property man for Keystone. Joe has probably his largest roles as the crook in this short and in *When Love Took Wings* (1915).

Leaving Sennett to go with Roscoe to Comique, he then made the rounds of the silent comedy units—playing in Larry Semon and Billy West films, as well as working as an assistant director at Fox Sunshine Comedies. Until 1940 he was busy in small bits in tons of shorts and features, a very few of which includes *The Soilers* (1923), *The White Sheep* (1924), *Spite Marriage* (1929), *Keystone Hotel* (1935), *Our Relations* (1936), and *The Great Dictator* (1940). In his later years he returned to the former Sennett lot, now Republic Studios, as a property man, and passed away in 1950.

Popping in for a minute as Edgar Kennedy's supervising officer is Billy Gilbert, known in silent comedy history circles as "the other Billy Gilbert" to differentiate him from the better-known sound film character-player Billy Gilbert (a.k.a. "Sneezing Billy Gilbert"). Small, with a standing-up patch of thick brown hair, this Billy Gilbert was a Los Angeles native who started his show business career at five years old, and was an all-around daredevil and roustabout who spent time as an aeronaut, high diver, jockey, acrobat, clown, and show manager. Around 1909 he worked at Coney Island in New York as a clown at the Steeplechase and a diver at Dreamland Pier. Back in California he joined Keystone right before Roscoe in February of 1913 and is considered one

Portrait of the silent comedy Billy Gilbert.

of the original Keystone Cops. Gilbert spent the bulk of 1913 to 1933 working for Sennett. Two brief forays from the studio stand out. The first was a short stint as a director for Harold Lloyd on some of his early glasses character one-reelers like *Rainbow Island*, *The Flirt*, *Pinched*, *Move On* (all 1917), and *The Tip* (1918). Lloyd wasn't happy with his work, and mentions him (although unnamed) in his 1928 autobiography *An American Comedy*:

> *I had to think up story and gags, direct and play the lead at the rate of a picture a week—a judgement, some might have thought, upon my willful head. I was desperate enough to take on a former Keystone cop actor as director. Then Pollard suggested Alf Goulding, another former member of Pollard's Lilliputians. Goulding was hired on the theory that if he was any good at all I would alternate him with the former Keystone actor, giving each a week to work out his story. Goulding proved to be innocent of any camera knowledge; but an old vaudevillian, he could pull gags out of the air, and thin air at that, and was a tremendous help. With his alternative, I had to supply the gags as well as virtually direct for the week he presided.*
>
> Not long after, Billy Gilbert returned to Sennett and Gilbert Pratt took his place.

Gilbert's other berth away from Sennett was working for Schiller Productions in Yonkers, New York in 1921. Morris and Julius Schiller were producing *Mirth Comedies* starring Marcel Perez and *Aladdin Comedies* that headlined Bud Duncan for Reelcraft release. Gilbert was teamed with Duncan in shorts such as *Stuck Up* and *All Wet* (both 1921) and also appeared in others like *Moving* and *Dry Water* (both 1921). Returning to California, he was back doing bits at Sennett and working behind the scenes. He also freelanced in other shorts for Fox, Joe Rock, and Weiss Brothers, and turned up in features such as *The Missing Link* (1927) and *Welcome Danger* (1929). Having spent much time as a property man, in 1930 he became chief property master at the Sennett Studio, and continued doing property when Mascot and Republic Pictures took over the lot (working with Joe Bordeaux). His last known screen appearance was in 1935's *Keystone Hotel*, and he died in 1961.

Bioscope (October 7, 1915): "Mabel and "Fatty" Arbuckle in a mildly amusing farce."

Mabel and Fatty Viewing the World's Fair in San Francisco

Released April 22, 1915. Produced by Mack Sennett for the Keystone Film Co. Distributed by the Mutual Film Corp. Directed by Roscoe Arbuckle. Working title: **The Frisco Story**. One reel. Extant: LOC, FRIU, MoMA, UCLA, ACAD, QUB, LOB. With Roscoe Arbuckle, Mabel Normand, James Rolph Jr., Mme. Ernestine Schumann-Heink.

Mabel and Fatty view the World's Fair and other sights in San Francisco.

Another Keystone educational, this time a newsreel of the Fair and San Francisco, which includes sights of the Battleship Oregon, the Ferry Building, City Hall, the convict ship Success, and the Tower of Jewels after dark with all its lighting effects. Mabel and Fatty look pretty prosperous out of their usual slapstick duds, but still indulge in a few bits

Roscoe and Mabel Normand greeted by Mayor John Rolph Jr. in *Mabel and Fatty Viewing the World's Fair in San Francisco* (1915). Courtesy Robert Arkus.

of business such as almost taking a tumble down stairs with Mayor John Rolph Jr., playing around with the pointy spikes of an iron maiden, and opera diva Mme. Schumann-Heink doing her best to prevent Roscoe from singing.

There's also chilling footage of the Hotel St. Francis six years before Roscoe's infamous 1921 Labor Day party.

Bioscope (October 7, 1915): "Mabel and Fatty viewing the World's Fair gives excellent views of the Panama Exposition."

Mabel's Wilful Way

Released May 1, 1915. Produced by Mack Sennett for the Keystone Film Co. Distributed by the Mutual Film Corp. Directed by Roscoe Arbuckle. Working title: ***Idora Park Story***. One reel. Extant: LOC, FRIU, UCLA, BFI, LOB. With Roscoe Arbuckle, Mabel Normand, Edgar Kennedy, Alice Davenport, Glen Cavender, Joe Bordeaux, Bobby Dunn, Ferris Hartman, James Leslie.

Mabel is saddled with her mother and father on a trip to the Idora Amusement Park. Father insists on sitting at the café listening to the boring music while mother gobbles green onions, so Mabel sneaks off to explore the park on her own. Fatty and Edgar are short funded pals who are checking out all the available girls, and soon get in bad with the cop on the beat. Mabel decides to get ice cream, but finds that she has no money and gets into a fight with the proprietor. The boys see the altercation and Fatty comes to her rescue. Although he has no money he's able to secretly snatch a bill from the cash register, and the problem is solved. Heading over to the zoo they have a great time feeding their cones to a bear. In the meantime Mabel's parents have noticed her absence, and split up to look for her.

Searching for Mabel, Dad wanders into the "Soak Em" gallery and gets beaned by baseballs thrown by Edgar. The old man gives chase which leads to a duel with their canes. Edgar jumps on the nearby carousel and Dad runs around and around after him. Mabel and Fatty decide to try the giant slide, which ends up with Mabel landing hard

Roscoe makes a bad impression on Mabel Normand's parents Glen Cavender and Alice Davenport in *Mabel's Wilful Way* (1915).

on her rear. On the next go she pushes Fatty before he's ready, and getting hurt she wants nothing else to do with him. Walking away she meets Edgar while Fatty has another run in with the cop.

Still looking for Mabel, Mother finds her parasol. Tired, she opens it and sits on a bench to rest. Fatty, seeing the parasol, thinks it's Mabel, but Mother thinks he's fresh and beats him with the umbrella. Mabel runs into her father and decides to introduce him to her new beau Edgar, which starts their fight all over again. Fatty helps Dad out, but when he brings Fatty over to meet the family, Mother goes after him as the masher. Finally, Fatty and Edgar are chased off by the cop, and Dad and Mom spank Mabel.

Another park comedy, with this one set in the Idora Amusement Park in Oakland, California. Built in 1904 it was quite a sumptuous park, and besides the slides, café, zoo, and galleries seen in the film, there was also a skating rink, amphitheater, ballpark, and bear grotto. It even had one of the first outdoor public address systems, but was torn down in 1929.

The usual Keystone flotsam and jetsam are on hand, with Alice Davenport munching green onions and Roscoe's stage mentor and film collaborator Ferris Hartman (see *The Waiter's Ball*) turning up at the "Soak Em" gallery. Mabel's father is played by Arbuckle regular Glen Cavender, said to have been Roscoe's physical trainer, who like Vernon Dent and Bud Jamison was one of the rocks of silent comedy who worked everywhere with practically everyone. He's also rumored to have had one of the most colorful backgrounds in silent comedy—allegedly spending a couple of years with Buffalo Bill Cody's Wild West

Ubiquitous comedy player Glen Cavender.

Show, and awarded the Legion of Honor for bravery in the Boxer Rebellion. Years later his former wife Hazel Deane told film historian Sam Gill that some of this was more colorful story than truth.

He had been in vaudeville, and his early film days were spent in Frontier Films for the St Louis Motion Picture Company and at Majestic in comedies like the surviving *The Flat Upstairs* (1912). Ending up at Keystone in 1914 he played all kinds of characters and assisted directed. In 1918 he became a lead in Fox Sunshine Comedies, playing a goofy everyman with a putty nose, usually opposite Jack Cooper. The 1920s saw him an integral part of the silent comedy universe, playing the comic heavy for the likes of Lloyd Hamilton, Stan Laurel, Lupino Lane, Bobby Dunn, and Dorothy Devore, at studios such as Century, Vitagraph, Educational, Arrow, and Jack White.

Features made use of him too, including *Keep Smiling* (1925), Roscoe's *Special Delivery* (1927), and most memorably as the Union captain in Buster Keaton's *The General* (1926). Sound found him equally busy, but in smaller parts, in shorts, features, and television. Besides bits in in *G-Men* (1935), *Meet John Doe* (1941), and *Yankee Doodle Dandy* (1942), he also worked in MGM's makeup department. Later on hand for many of the Keystone cop and Mack Sennett reunions, Cavender died at seventy-eight in 1962.

Bioscope (October 21, 1915): "Mabel Normand and Roscoe Arbuckle. One of their happiest efforts, staged in one of the great American Expositions and abounding in humorous episodes in the grounds and side shows."

Miss Fatty's Seaside Lovers

Released May 15, 1915. Produced by Mack Sennett for the Keystone Film Co. Distributed by the Mutual Film Corp. Directed by Roscoe Arbuckle. Working title: **By the Sea**. One reel. Extant: LOC, FRIU, GEM, BFI, UCLA, Acad, LOB. With Roscoe Arbuckle, Edgar Kennedy, Harold Lloyd, Walter C. Reed, Billie Bennett, Joe Bordeaux, Billy Gilbert.

Fatty is the young daughter of the millionaire Finnegan, the moth-ball magnate. The family arrives at a seaside hotel and three young swains decide they are going to court the wealthy girl. Flirtatious, rambunctious, and elephantine, she's an easy mark for the mashers, and their love play consists of kicking, slapping, and choking. Her poor parents, particularly when her father is trying to shave with a giant straight razor, get in the middle of the knockabout, so the heiress gets in her striped circus tent bathing suit and heads to the beach. Her trio of admirers follow, and when she falls asleep on a rock and gets trapped when the tide comes in, they outdo each other trying to come to the rescue. The smallest of the three

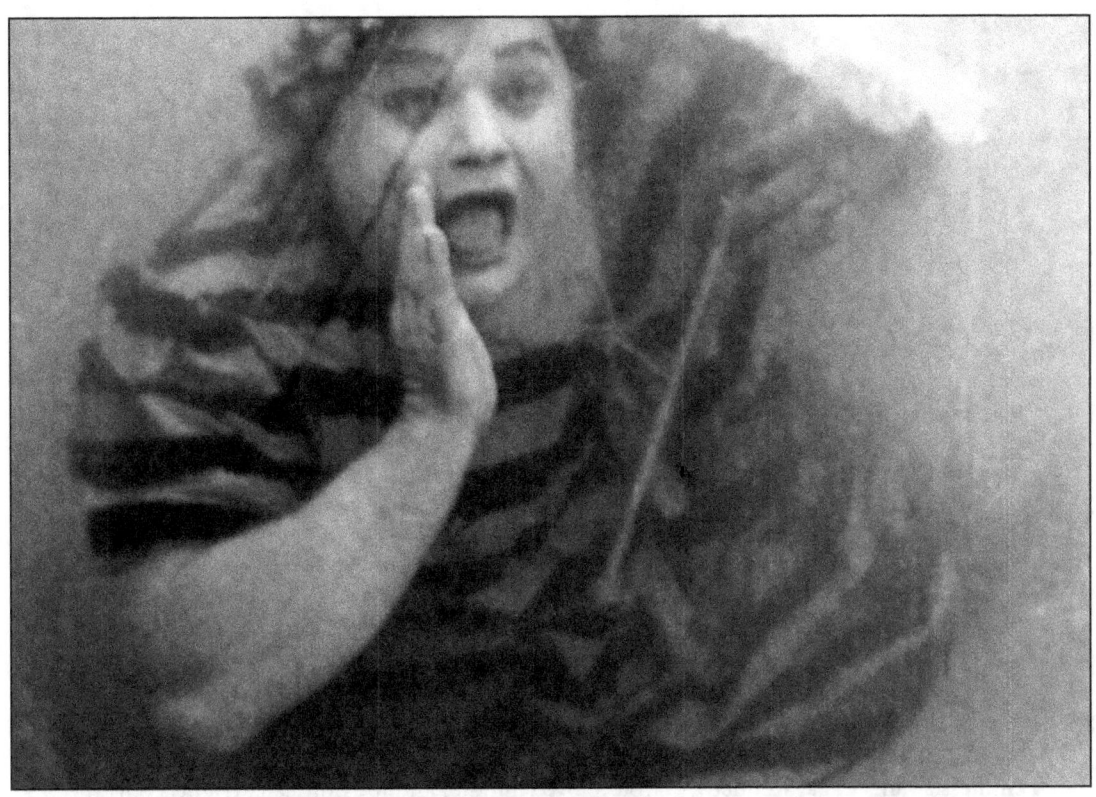

Roscoe not enjoying the surf in *Miss Fatty's Seaside Lovers* (1915). Courtesy the Library of Congress.

finally commands a rowboat and temporarily saves her as crabs are nipping at her toes, but she falls back in the water and finally staggers back to shore on her own.

A fast and funny little film that revels in the absurdity of Roscoe as the moth-ball heiress, *Miss Fatty's Seaside Lovers* gets attention today for the presence of Harold Lloyd as one of the trio of would-be lovers. Wanting to be a serious stage actor Lloyd was unimpressed with movies, but decided to work in them for the money. He began knocking around as an extra in 1913, and during this time struck up a friendship with fellow extra Hal Roach. When Roach received a small inheritance in 1914 he decided to set up his own production unit, and the first person he hired was Harold because "he was the best, hard-working actor I had ever seen." A few shorts were made, but while Roach was trying to sell them he and Lloyd had a falling out. Harold then went over to Keystone, and besides this film he can be seen in *Love, Loot, and Crash*, *Their Social Splash*, and *A Submarine Pirate* (all 1915). He mentions working with Roscoe in his 1928 autobiography:

> Once or twice I worked with Fatty Arbuckle, but with little success. Arbuckle had the star bumpers of the lot and he led them in person, taking Brodies that shook buildings. I could bump with any of them, but he surrounded himself with a group of regulars who knew his methods so well that they did not need to be told what to do, and weren't, leaving a new man to guess and flounder.

Penniless swains Edgar Kennedy, Harold Lloyd (middle) and Joe Bordeaux (right) court the titular heiress of *Miss Fatty's Seaside Lovers* (1915). Courtesy the Library of Congress.

His largest role at Sennett was as the young hero in *Court House Crooks* (1915), and despite the advice of star Ford Sterling that he should forget comedy and try to be a leading man like Bobby Harron, when Hal Roach came to him with a deal to star in comedies for Pathé Lloyd jumped at it. Roach and Lloyd came up with the character of Lonesome Luke, which eventually led to his "glasses character," and the rest is cinema history.

In addition to Lloyd, Edgar Kennedy and Billie Bennett are on hand, and Joe Bordeaux, as the smallest of the lovers, takes a great deal of punishment, as does Walter C. Reed as Roscoe's father. Reed is a forgotten figure who had a varied career in silent comedy in front of and behind the camera. In the early days he had his own West Coast theatrical troupe which Roscoe and Minta Durfee toured with before they entered movies. Known for his character of "Finnigan," it seems that Roscoe brought Reed to films with *Miss Fatty's Seaside Lovers*. During Sennett's Triangle era Reed assisted director Edwin Frazee, and then became a director of his own unit at Fox. His directorial career didn't go beyond Foxfilm Comedies such as *An Aerial Joyride*, *Social Pirates*, and *A Footlight Flame* (all 1917), but he would re-join Roscoe and work closely with him for many years.

Motion Picture News (June 5, 1915): "Roscoe Arbuckle dons the regalia of an heiress and succeeds in causing great commotion in a seaside hotel. Mr. Arbuckle also directed this, which is uproariously funny from start to finish as the Strand audience well testified."

Bioscope (November 25, 1915): "Roscoe Arbuckle makes a striking figure as a seaside-girl in this bright amusing comedy."

The Little Teacher

Released June 21, 1915. Produced by Mack Sennett for the Keystone Film Co. Distributed by the Mutual Film Corp. Directed by Mack Sennett. Working title: ***Small Town School***. (Reissued by W.H. Productions in 1918 as ***A Small Town Bully***). Two reels. Extant: LOC. With Mabel Normand, Owen Moore, Mack Sennett, Roscoe Arbuckle, Bobby Dunn, Joe Bordeaux, Frank Opperman, Frank Hayes, Hugh Fay, Billie Brockwell.

Mabel is a city girl who's the new teacher for a rural community. She arrives for her first day and meets her students (some of whom are in their thirties and playing children). The boys all make a big fuss over her. They also cause problems in the classroom and have to be punished. While Mabel struggles with her unruly pupils, her fiancé from the city arrives to try to renew their engagement. Things get worse in the classroom which includes pie-throwing and Mack wearing a dunce cone. The fiancé arrives at the schoolhouse amidst all the student unheavals, and Mabel tries to send him on his way. In addition to his getting hit with a wet towel, the class draws their teacher and her beau kissing on the blackboard.

After school while most of the boys fight, Mack admires the fiancé's fancy roadster. When two of the boys end up in the lake, Mabel dives in and saves them. In the meantime Mack is annoying the fiancé, who, to get away from him, goes into the classroom when Mabel is changing out of her wet clothes. The head of the school board comes in, and supposing the worst discharges Mabel. At that moment the mother of one of the saved boys comes by to thank Mabel, and explains why she was changing her clothes. All ends happily as the school board head is satisfied, and Mabel still has her beau.

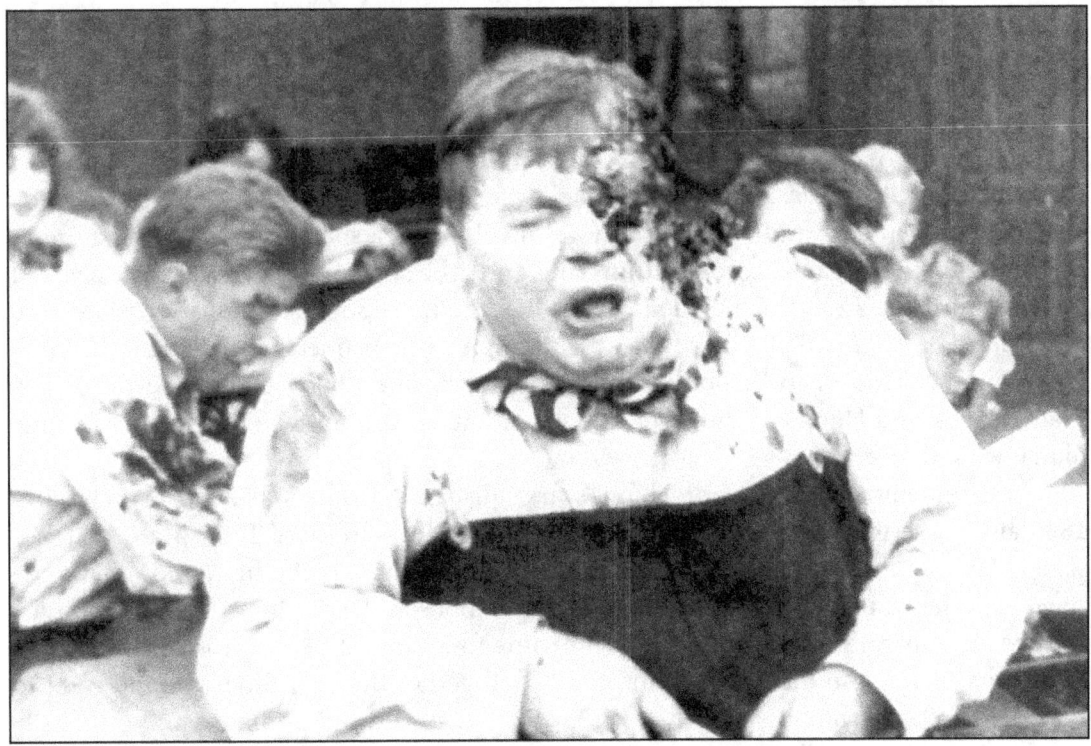

Roscoe gets a lesson in mud throwing from *The Little Teacher* (1915). Courtesy the Library of Congress.

Mack Sennett makes a confession to Owen Moore, Mabel Normand, and Billie Brockwell in *The Little Teacher* (1915). Courtesy The Museum of Modern Art.

Unfortunately not much of a short, with an overabundance of "rube" comedy. Mabel has very little to do, and Sennett gives his most annoying performance since 1913's *Mabel's Dramatic Career*. At this point Mack was focused behind the scenes on running his laugh factory, but would occasionally get involved on a specific film. Working under Sennett's direction again Roscoe is funny and gives the short whatever vitality it has, but it looks more like a Keystone made in 1912 than the more sophisticated shorts like *That Little Band of Gold* which Roscoe was turning out at the same time. Outside of Frank Opperman as head of the school, the other regulars like Bobby Dunn, Joe Bordeaux, Frank Hayes, and Hugh Fay don't get a chance to make an impression, nor does leading man Owen Moore.

Best-remembered as Mary Pickford's first husband, Moore was born in Ireland in 1886 and came to the U.S. at eleven. His entire family—brothers Tom, Matt, and Joe, sister Mary, and mother Mary—appeared in films. Owen was the first, and after some stage experience made his debut with Biograph in 1908. Dark-haired and dashing, he worked steadily for D.W. Griffith and at the same time started a secret romance with Ms. Pickford which led to their elopement in 1911. Together they left Biograph and went to Imp. Their relationship was stormy, with Moore having alcohol problems and physically abusing Mary. Eventually she returned to Biograph while he worked for Victor.

In April through June of 1915 Moore also had a stint at the Sennett Studio, working on shorts such as this, *Mabel, Lost and Won*, and *Stolen Magic*, as well as the feature *Oh, Mabel Behave* (finally edited and released in 1922). Although he occasionally appeared with Pickford in films like *Caprice* (1913), *Cinderella* (1914), and *Mistress Nell* (1915), their relationship was over by 1916, and when Mary was granted a divorce in 1920 she married Douglas Fairbanks. Moore was a popular player in the teens and early twenties, headlining in many comedies and dramas for Selznick, and working with Roscoe again as his leading man for *The Red Mill* (1927). By the late twenties his star began to fade, and after the changeover to sound his appearances became sporadic, with small roles in pictures like *As You Desire Me* (1932) and *She Done Him Wrong* (1933). His last role was in *A Star is Born* (1937), and he died of a heart attack at age fifty-two in 1939.

Motion Picture News (July 3, 1915): "An all-star Keystone cast help to make this picture a success. Mabel Normand is seen in the title role, while Mack Sennett and Roscoe Arbuckle are rubes. The work of Owen Moore is a weak spot, as it usually is. The new school teacher proves to be of "the marryin' sort" in spite of the school board's hopes. A comedy which is a sure laugh getter."

Fatty's Plucky Pup

Released June 28, 1915. Produced by Mack Sennett for the Keystone Film Co. Distributed by the Mutual Film Corp. Directed by Roscoe Arbuckle. Working title: **Dog and Villain Story** and **Foiled by Fido**. Two reels. Extant: FRIU, LOB, LOC. With Roscoe Arbuckle, Phyllis Allen, Edgar Kennedy, Joe Bordeaux, Al St John, Ted Edwards, Glen Cavender, Luke.

Fatty lays in bed smoking while his busy washer woman mother is working. Setting his bed on fire, he's very lackadaisical about putting it out, which sends his mother into a panic. Sent out to deliver her washings, he drops them in the mud and tries to clean up the clothes by spraying them with a hose. Fatty flirts over the fence with the neighbor girl, while at the same time two dogcatchers are after his dog Luke. Fatty rescues the dog from their clutches and lets all the other dogs out of their wagon for good measure.

Roscoe does Luke's toilette in an exhibitor ad for *Fatty's Plucky Pup* (1915).

After giving Luke a bath in his mother's laundry tub, Fatty, his girl, his mother, and Luke go on a day's outing to an amusement pier. Fatty gets involved with a shell game and takes all the hucksters' money. In retaliation, the shell game men team up with the dogcatchers and kidnap Fatty's girl. Luke's observes her abduction and follows the criminals to where they take the girl. They tie her up in a shack and set up a gun to shoot her when the clock hits three o'clock. Luke runs back to get Fatty and takes him to the shack where Lizzie is tied up. The cops are also alerted and are on their way. When Roscoe arrives he beats up the villains, as Luke tunnels into the shack and unties the girl. The crooks are rounded up by the police, and Luke and Fatty manage to save Lizzie for the fade-out.

After *Fatty's Plucky Pup* all of Roscoe's shorts (with the exception of 1916's three-reel *Fatty and Mabel Adrift*) would be two reels in length. This followed the industry norm where the important studios were putting out longer pictures. The first Keystone two-reeler was *Zuzu the Bandleader* in December of 1913. Before that everything had been a one or split-reeler. At first the longer films were referred to as "Two-reel Specials" but they soon became the standard, and while the one reel length remained for quite a while the split-reels disappeared except for newsreels or non-fiction items. The June 19, 1915 *Motography* told the industry about Sennett's change in his production output:

> **Keystone Announces Change**
> *From the executive offices of Kessel & Baumann, New York heads of the Keystone Film Company, comes the announcement that all single reel and semi-monthly releases will be discontinued after the week ending June 12. After that date all efforts of the Keystone organization will be concentrated on making Mack Sennett two-reel special features to be released twice a week.*

The memorable opening of this short has the lazy Fatty smoking in bed, as his mother slaves away at her washing, and sets his bed on fire. He lackadaisically and absent-mindedly tries to put it out with sporadic tea cups of water which he slowly goes in the other room to get and then walk back with (as the fire rages). Roscoe first used this routine in the lost *Mother's Boy* (1913) and then again in 1917's *The Rough House*.

Like *Fatty's Faithful Fido* (1915) this is another entry that gives the main focus to Luke, probably much to the delight of Roscoe's large kids following. The June 22, 1916 *Motography* surveyed kids' opinions in their column *What Children Want in Pictures*, and eight-year-old Keith Rogers had this to say:

> *I like war pictures best of all. "The Chocolate Soldier" was fine. I like comedy's like "Fatty's Plucky Pup." I do not like kissing pictures or where two fellows want the same girl.*

Seattle Daily Times (July 14, 1915): "'Fatty's Plucky Pup' is one of those extremely funny two-reel Keystone comedies that have made such a hit during the last few months that they have been released to the public. If you like excitement with comedy this picture will fill the bill. The pursuit of robbers by policemen, both in automobiles, presents some exciting moments."

Fatty's Tintype Tangle

Released July 26, 1915. Produced by Mack Sennett for the Keystone Film Co. Distributed by the Mutual Film Corp. Directed by Roscoe Arbuckle. Working title: ***Caught on the Screen***. Two reels. Extant: LOC, FRIU, ACAD, LOB, BFI. With Roscoe Arbuckle, Norma Nichols, Mai Wells, Louise Fazenda, Edgar Kennedy, Josef Swickard, Bobby Dunn, Glen Cavender, Frank Hayes, Joe Bordeaux, Grover Ligon, Charles Lakin, Ted Edwards.

Fatty's happily married to Norma, although he has to put up with his mother-in-law. Most of his time is spent on kitchen duties, in addition to helping his spouse comb her hair and lacing up his mother-in-law's corset. Getting fed up with the old lady, the end finally comes after Fatty takes a couple of drinks and rebels in the kitchen. Giving her the what-for he leaves the house, and wanders to the park to cool off. There he meets up with the wife of an Alaskan prospector, and a photographer takes an innocent photo of them in what appears to be a compromising position. The tough and jealous husband returns, and finding them together chases Fatty off. In the meantime Fatty's mother-in-law wanders by and gets possession of the "incriminating" photo.

The Alsakan tells Fatty to leave town before sundown, and more than happy to comply the fat man runs home and hurriedly begins to pack. Telling his wife that he's going on a business trip for a month, she decides to stay with her mother and rent the house for that time. It just so happen that the Alaskan and his missus are looking for a home to rent and end up with Fatty's.

Having missed the train out of town Fatty heads home and has a confrontation with the jealous Alaskan. Mrs. Alaskan calls the cops who rush over in their slapstick way (but never arrive). Fatty's wife, showing up at her mother's, finds the suggestive photo, and she and her mama rush back to the house. Chased from room to room by the gun-toting Alaskan, Fatty finally goes out the bedroom window and on to the telephone lines, where he runs and bounces around trying to dodge the bullets. He finally crashes through the roof of the house and back into the bedroom, and then he and his nemesis tumble out the window into an outside water trough where they are finally fished out by their respective wives.

Usually a terrible flirt, in this short Roscoe's a dutiful husband who does most of the kitchen work, and

The photo of Roscoe and Louise Fazenda that causes *Fatty's Tintype Tangle* (1915). Courtesy the Library of Congress.

Collage of Roscoe doing flapjack flips in *Fatty's Tintype Tangle* (1915).
Courtesy the Library of Congress and Robert Arkus.

even makes a game attempt to put up with his mother-in-law. Although he's completely innocent he still winds up in a suggestive photo with Louise Fazenda.

Best-known as a pig-tailed country bumpkin in numerous Mack Sennett comedies, Fazenda came from the stage and in 1913 began working in Universal's Joker Comedies alongside Max Asher and Gale Henry. By 1915 she was working at Keystone where she became a star, and would remain with the Sennett organization until 1921. At first she played a variety of roles, but soon became the country girl who was usually taken advantage of by conniving fellows like Ford Sterling or Charlie Murray. Louise roughhoused with the best of them, but besides being a wonderful comedian she was a fine actress who endowed her outlandish comedy roles with a lot of emotion.

After leaving Sennett she starred in shorts for Punch Comedies and Jack White, then made the jump to features in the mid-1920s. From supporting roles in films like *The Night Club* (1925) and *The Bat* (1926), she signed with Warner Brothers and starred in a string of pictures that included *Footloose Widows* (1926) and *A Sailor's Sweetheart* (1927). In sound films she continued in major supporting roles until 1939. Married to producer Hal Wallis, she retired and devoted herself to charity work until her death in 1962.

One of the joys of the Arbuckle films are the various kitchen scenes where Roscoe flips pancakes, vegetables, pots, knives, and what have you with deadly aim and in the greatest of ease. Although the final results always look easy, according to Roscoe in the April 1916 *Picture Play* it took a lot of time and hard work:

> *I spent just one week getting the kitchen scenes I was in alone. I used over ten thousand feet of film just for that. In one part of the play I had to toss a pancake up and catch it behind my back. I started at nine o'clock in the morning, did it on the first rehearsal, then started the camera and didn't get it till four-thirty. I'd hate to tell you how long it took me to catch the plate behind my back in "The Village Scandal!" I seldom rehearse since then.*

Moving Picture World (August 7, 1915): "A two-reel farce comedy with Roscoe Arbuckle and others of the inimitable Keystone stock company. The production is a scream from first to last; is almost free from any vulgarity, and can be highly recommended where a laugh is wanted."

Fickle Fatty's Fall

Released November 14, 1915. Produced by Mack Sennett for the Keystone Film Co. Distributed by the Triangle Film Corp. Directed by Roscoe Arbuckle. Working title: *Fatty's Way*. Two reels. With Roscoe Arbuckle, Minta Durfee, Phyllis Allen, Al St John, Glen Cavender, Ivy Crosthwaite, Fritz Schade, Bobby Dunn, Billy Gilbert.

Fatty is a boyish husband who throws the chef and the butcher boy out of the kitchen when he catches them fighting over the pretty maid. He then flirts with her himself, but gets caught by his wife and mother-in-law who promptly fire her. To punish Fatty they make him become the cook and maid for the household, but he finally rebels and runs off for a good time at the beach with the maid. The chef and butcher boy are at the beach too and begin

The triangle of maid Ivy Crosthwaite, hubby Roscoe, and wife Minta Durfee creates *Fickle Fatty's Fall* (1915). Courtesy Cole Johnson.

fighting again, and when his wife and mother-in-law show up Fatty and the maid try to take flight. Eventually everyone ends up in the water thanks to runaway autos, and Fatty manages to attach his mother-in-law to an anchor before he and the maid are rescued from the drink by some obliging cops.

Mack Sennett finished his distribution deal with the Mutual Film Corporation and in September of 1915 became part of the Triangle Film Corporation. Triangle was engineered by Harry Aitken, who had been president of Mutual, and united three of the biggest producers in Hollywood—Sennett, D.W. Griffith, and Thomas Ince. The companies really remained separate but were joined for strength in distribution. Key in Aitken's plan was the policy of block booking—exhibitors had to take the entire Triangle line-up to get Keystone comedies and Griffith dramas. Since the tent poles were films by these big three filmmakers the plan worked—for a while.

Aitken brought a new veneer of prestige to the Keystone films, and Sennett's first Triangle release was the four-reel short feature *My Valet* (1915), which headlined stage star Raymond Hitchcock as well as Mabel Normand, Fred Mace, and Sennett himself.

During the changeover from Mutual to Triangle three months had passed since *Fatty's Tintype Tangle*, an unheard of amount of time between Arbuckle pictures, as

A prosperous looking Roscoe in an original glass slide for *Fickle Fatty's Fall* (1915). Courtesy Matt Vogel.

Roscoe had always maintained an output of at least one film a month, and often even two or three. Roscoe's first Triangle short, *Fickle Fatty's Fall*, was the Sennett unit's fourth Triangle endeavor, and Arbuckle was soon back to his regular output schedule.

In addition to his usual stock company of Minta, nephew Al, Phyllis Allen, and Glen Cavender, Roscoe has a newer Triangle-Keystone actress playing the flirty maid. Ivy Crosthwaite had been a champion swimmer, and because of this had been an early Keystone bathing girl, appearing in the 1913 short *Their Husbands*. She returned in the Triangle period and became a leading lady in shorts such as *Fatty and the Broadway Stars*, *A Game Old Knight* (both 1915), and *By Stork Delivery* (1916). Married to Keystone assistant director Adolph Linkof, Crosthwaite eventually retired from films, and later managed a coffee shop at Los Angeles' Santa Fe Railroad offices.

Roscoe would return to this plot ten years later, substituting Lloyd Hamilton for himself, in *Peaceful Oscar* (1927). Right before this short's release, two items appeared in the trade magazines about the making of this missing comedy:

> *While making comedy scenes at Santa Monica, Roscoe Arbuckle called the police and did not know it until they arrived. The scenario called for a scene in which "Fatty" had to rush up to a telephone and wildly call for*

police assistance. Without realizing that the phone was a real one and not a "prop," Roscoe ran up to an outside phone used by a taxicab company, and on which the camera had been focused, and started calling for help and police. The scene was about finished for the third time when a patrol wagon loaded with patrolmen, who had been summoned by the excited central girl, dashed up. Explanations followed and later "Fatty" depleted his bankroll to the extent of purchasing something that caused corks to pop for a squad of thirsty officers.

– **Photoplayers Weekly**, October 16, 1915

Roscoe Arbuckle has just completed a two-reel beach comedy in which an automobile and an electric beach chair dash off a fifty foot pier into the ocean. The latter was occupied by Minta Durfee, who escaped drowning when Arbuckle dived in and saved her. The three-hundred-pound comedian has invented a new device to remove the water from the ears following swimming, and this will be used first in this subject. The device, operated by vacuum, will throw a stream ten feet.

– **Motion Picture News**, October 30, 1915

Moving Picture World (October 30, 1915): "A story of swift and thrilling adventure on the part of Roscoe Arbuckle, the more amusing that it is largely aquatic and offers some shapely young ladies as an added attraction to Roscoe's antics."

Variety (October 29, 1915): "'Fickle Fatty's Fall' was the two-reeler in which Mr. Arbuckle was starred. At times he was closely pushed for all honors in it by Alfred St. John as the butcher boy. It seemed all the tricks of the comic film trade had been compressed into this two-reeler, but they were kept within confines which did not destroy the class of the comedy, and the many situations forced laughter. At several points the action was so rapid, the laughs came in a stream. Ivy Crosthwaite in a union suit did some diving, and the exhibition of her figure in black outlines said that Kellerman has a rival, in part, at least."

The Village Scandal

Released December 12, 1915. Produced by Mack Sennett for the Keystone Film Co. Distributed by the Triangle Film Corp. Directed by Roscoe Arbuckle. Working title: **Eddie's Debut**. Two reels. Extant: clips. With Roscoe Arbuckle, Raymond Hitchcock, Flora Zabelle, Al St John, Harry McCoy, Grover Ligon, Frank Hayes, Pat Kelly, Joe Bordeaux.

A traveling magician comes to the small town where village belle Flora is the hotel waitress and sweetheart of Fatty. Infatuated with the elegant performer, she breaks it off with Fatty, who had lavished two years of savings on her and also put himself in debt for another two years. The torrents of tears that flow from the grief-stricken Fatty nearly drown his sympathetic landlady and cohorts. Later when Fatty finds Flora and the magician laughing at him he plots to get even.

For Roscoe's second Triangle release he was teamed with Raymond Hitchcock, a popular stage comic who had first appeared on Broadway in 1898. Hitchcock was a

Raymond Hitchcock protects Flora Zabelle from Roscoe and Al St John as Keystone flotsam and jetsam Grover Ligon, Frank Hayes, Pat Kelly, and Joe Bordeaux witness *The Village Scandal* (1915).

writer and producer as well, who headlined in his own annual *Hitchy-Koo* revues and shows such as *The Yankee Consul*, *The Man Who Owned Broadway*, and *The Red Widow*. Flora Zabelle who plays Fatty's love interest was Hitchcock's wife and long-time stage partner. The pair appears to have made their film debut in 1913 in some shorts for the Kinemacolor Company and in 1915 starred in the feature *The Ringtailed Rhinoceros* for Lubin. Hitchcock had also appeared in *My Valet* and *Stolen Magic* (both 1915) for Sennett, and continued to make occasional film appearances between his stage shows, including a couple of sound shorts, up to his death in 1929.

An illustration of the lengths Roscoe would go to get laughs and the risks it often involved was given to the June 1916 *Picture-Play Magazine* by fellow Sennett performer Chester Conklin in his article *Making People Laugh*:

> Of course, you are all aware of the large proportions of Roscoe Arbuckle, better known to picture followers as "Fatty." On account of a forced change in the ending of "The Village Scandal," one of the early Triangle releases he had to find a new finish with a punch to it, so he decided to roll off the roof of the country hotel, which was one of the buildings in the complete village erected for this picture. Right under the roof that he planned to roll off was a watering trough, just exactly large enough for him to get into without the

Raymond Hitchcock gets a poke from Mabel Normand in the 1915 Sennett feature *My Valet*.

use of a shoehorn, so he decided to fall into this. A miscalculation would mean several weeks in the hospital, but this did not faze Roscoe one bit. He climbed out on the roof, and after a hard tumble, rolled right off the edge and into the trough. His only remembrance of this occasion was a badly bruised hip. Of course it looked great in the picture, therefore got a tremendous laugh, and that was all Roscoe cared about.

Moving Picture World (November 13, 1915): "An amusing farce centering entirely upon the personality of popular Roscoe Arbuckle, although Raymond Hitchcock 'appears' only to be thrown in unfavorable contrast with the inimitable Roscoe."

Motion Picture News (November 20, 1915): "In a country town Fatty loses his girl when a traveling magician comes along.

The locale offers plenty of opportunities for the funmaking ability of the cast, which have been seized upon with the usual Keystone efficiency. The picture ends rather unexpectedly, but undoubtedly will be as well received in every house as it was at the Knickerbocker theatre."

Fatty and the Broadway Stars

Released December 19, 1915. Produced by Mack Sennett for the Keystone Film Co. Distributed by the Triangle Film Corp. Directed by Roscoe Arbuckle. Working title: *Fatty's Dream*. Two reels. Extant: NOR. With Roscoe Arbuckle, Weber & Fields, Polly Moran, Ivy Crosthwaite, Frank Hayes, Mack Sennett, Al St John, Wayland Trask, Slim Summerville, Harry Booker, Louis Hippe, Harry Gribbon, Joe Bordeaux, James Bryant, Sam Bernard, Chester Conklin, Nick Cogley, Hank Mann, Bobby Vernon, Mae Busch, Phyllis Allen, Minta Durfee, James Donnelly, William Collier, Bert Clark, Joe Jackson, Josef Swickard, Glen Cavender, Tom Kennedy, Fred Mace, Charles Murray, Mack Swain.

Fatty is janitor of the studio and is sweeping the entrance when the Broadway stars come trooping in for the day's work. He is always making a nuisance of himself—getting into people's way, stirring up dust and turning the hose on everyone. Finally he is discharged

Janitor Roscoe makes an impression on Mack Sennett (center) and William Collier Sr. (right) in *Fatty and the Broadway Stars* (1915). Courtesy Mike Hawks.

by the director and goes out to the front of the building, lights a cigarette and has a day dream. He imagines that the stage hands decide to strike and go to Mack Sennett's office and threaten him. Roscoe comes to the rescue and beats them up, so as a reward Sennett makes Fatty a director.

In the meantime the thwarted stage hands plot their revenge and set the studio on fire. Fatty sees himself rescuing several actors and actresses and even the director that had him discharged. Then he wakes up and finds that the "fire" is one under his seat that was started when his cigarette fell out of his sleeping mouth. Still believing that he saved the lives of the actors at the studio, when he sees some of the "rescued" coming out at the end of the day in their automobiles, they ignore him. Fatty shrugs his shoulders in acquiescence at the ingratitude of the stars, especially that of the comely young actress he had taken out while she was bound with ropes and encircled with flames.

As aforementioned, Sennett's joining of Griffith and Ince in Triangle was the brain child of producer Harry Aitken. Another of Aitken's schemes was the hiring of famous stage stars to give prestige to the Triangle product. Besides Raymond Hitchcock, names like DeWolf Hopper and Douglas Fairbanks went to work for D.W. Griffith, while Sennett got William Collier, Weber & Fields, Joe Jackson, and Sam Bernard. At this time Arbuckle and Mabel Normand were Sennett's biggest stars, so Roscoe was enlisted to introduce these stage personalities to movie audiences and drum up publicity for Triangle's ploy. The resulting picture gives a very entertaining tour behind the scenes of the studio, and Sennett pulled out all the stops, even building a half block's worth of ersatz studio expressly so it could be burnt down. The event was chronicled in the November 20, 1915 *Motion Picture News*:

> *The Keystone Film Company gave Edendale, a suburb of Los Angeles, the shock of its gay and fastidious life Sunday morning when a set a block in length and representing movie studio, garage and offices of an aeroplane company, was burned for scenes in a coming Roscoe Arbuckle Keystone subject. Every member of the Keystone stock company, together with many other others and companies of the Los Angeles Fire Department took part in the scenes. Every cameraman and all directors of the Keystone organization took part in the making of the scene. Roscoe Arbuckle rescued Mack Sennett when the exit of the building was practically filled with flames, then came little Sam Bernard overburdened with the body of Alice Davenport, whose weight amounts to far more than two hundred pounds, Lew Fields carried his little playmate, Joe Weber, out, and Joe then finding he had left his purse inside fought to return for it. Joe Jackson and his bicycle of miniature size blocked the exit of the burning building while he put the machine together. The streets and hills on both sides were covered with people watching the making of the scene, and the big crowds added much to the atmosphere.*

But none of these "Broadway Stars" fared too well on film; outside of Douglas Fairbanks, the majority of Aitken's stage imports hightailed it back to the footlights.

Janitor Roscoe second guessing the work of director Harry Booker (left) and cameraman Louis Hippe (right) in *Fatty and the Broadway Stars* (1915).

In early 2006 Ron Magliozzi, Ben Model and I were preparing our Arbuckle retrospective for the Museum of Modern Art, and got word that footage from the considered lost *Fatty and the Broadway Stars* had turned up at the National Library of Norway. After getting in touch we were told that the material needed extensive restoration and wouldn't be ready in time for our show, but they would keep us posted. That fall Ben was in Norway playing for the Stumfilm Dagere Festival and the Library invited him to see the preserved film. The six minutes of footage was all scrambled with shots completely out of sequence, and had only one (Norwegian) title card. To our excitement the Library invited us to unscramble the material. Armed with the film on DVD, an online editing program, plus the original shooting continuity, title list, and even tinting guide from the Sennett Collection at the Margaret Herrick Library, we were able to arrange the footage in sequence.

Our assembled version played at the Pordenone Silent Film Festival, Slapsticon, and the Silent Clowns Film Series in 2008. Much of the footage turned out to be from the second reel. Since then a two-minute long 9.5mm Pathé Baby abridgement has turned up with a few new shots, but is again mostly second reel material. Hopefully more will resurface, but at the moment there are at least six minutes of a previously thought lost Arbuckle film.

Moving Picture World (December 11, 1915): "Fatty and the Broadway Stars," two-reel Keystone, shows Roscoe Arbuckle in a "Happy Hooligan" character, trying to "help youse" among a group of Broadway stars, including Sam Bernard, Joe Weber, Lew Fields and William Collier—he used to "Willie." This is a change from the regular thing and highly amusing in spite of the efforts of the Broadway stars to be funny. The stars twinkled faintly now and then, but they were outshone by the huge full moon, the rotund Roscoe. Even Sennett surpassed them in psychological moments—it begins to look as though he will yet learn to be an actor, though it has seemed hopeless after all these years, and he has enough honors as a director. The story's chief merit is that it is something new."

Moving Picture World (December 18, 1915): "An excellent comedy which exploits the talents of a number of well-known stars, namely Weber & Fields, Sam Bernard, Joe Jackson and William Collier. Roscoe Arbuckle is of course the Fatty of the production, and after many vicissitudes goes to sleep and dreams a wonderful dream in which he is the hero of a studio fire."

Chapter 5
Keystone 1916

Fatty and Mabel Adrift

Released January 9, 1916. Produced by Mack Sennett for the Keystone Film Co. Distributed by the Triangle Film Corp. Directed by Roscoe Arbuckle. Assistant director Dave Anderson. Working title: ***House at Sea***. Three reels. Extant: Friuli, MoMA, UCLA, LOC, ACAD, Berk, LOB, DAN, EYE. With Roscoe Arbuckle, Mabel Normand, Al St John, Luke, Frank Hayes, Mai Wells, Glen Cavender, Wayland Trask, Joe Bordeaux, James Bryant.

Mabel and Fatty the farmhand are in love. When they marry Mabel's parents buy the newlyweds a house and lot at the beach. Al, who had hoped to marry Mabel himself, swears vengeance, and during a rainstorm on Mabel and Fatty's first night in their new home Al and some henchmen set the house out to sea. The pair wake up to find their love nest floating and filling up with water, so they send their dog Luke swimming out with a help message to Mabel's parents. The old couple alert the Keystone cops, and on their way to help run into the real estate man who sold them the property, who takes them on his speed boat. After much frantic action the newlyweds are saved, and Al's bad karma catches up with him.

Fatty and Mabel Adrift is one of the best and best-known of the Mabel and Fatty teamings, but this delightful and light-hearted short was made during a time of illness and emotional turmoil for Mabel Normand. After shooting had started on the picture Normand sustained a severe head injury and was hospitalized for a time in very serious condition. The often told version of the story has Mabel catching boyfriend Mack Sennett having a tryst with her friend Mae Busch. In the confrontation and confusion Mae is said to have picked up a vase and hit Mabel over the head with it. Another telling has the injured Mabel showing up afterward in the middle of the night at the Arbuckle's home—found by Roscoe and Minta in a coma on their porch moaning and bleeding profusely.

Whether or not these events are true, she was hospitalized with reports that she was dangerously ill, in a condition that was touch and go for several days. Shooting was suspended on *Adrift* and the studio put out a cover story that she was hurt shooting a burlesque wedding scene with Roscoe—that a boot that was thrown along with rice and shoes knocked her unconscious. Mabel's version for interviewers had a more comic spin. She told them that Arbuckle accidentally sat on her head while they were shooting a scene.

Luke patiently waits as Roscoe and Mabel Normand begin eating in *Fatty and Mabel Adrift* (1916).

As soon as Mabel was well enough filming resumed, and it's impossible to tell what was shot before or after. The picture was finished right before the holidays on December 17, 1915. At three reels it was a "Fatty and Mabel Special," and is excellently directed by Roscoe with immense charm and many clever and human touches. It opens with tableaus of Roscoe, Mabel and Al St John framed in heart-shaped cut-outs (of course Al's "heart" gets broken), and Cupid shoots an arrow that unites Fatty and Mabel. There's also a touching moment where Fatty gives Mabel a goodnight kiss, a realistically played funny scene about Mabel's first attempt at making biscuits, and a slam-bang climax with everyone mobilizing to the rescue. Roscoe also exercises his camera eye with some very pretty vistas, especially a shot of he and Luke fishing on the beach at twilight (the reeling in of a large and recalcitrant fish disrupts the pretty picture).

Besides stringbean Frank Hayes and the usual wrecking crew of Joe Bordeaux and Jimmy Bryant, sterling support is provided by Mai Wells and Wayland Trask. Mai Wells was an all-purpose character actress who specialized in spinsters, busy-body neighbors, and country wives. Beginning her career at age five in her parents' theatrical company, she appeared in David Belasco productions like *First Born*, and was also an accomplished singer and dancer. Moving to films in the very early teens, she appeared all over the silent comedy map working for Powers, Biograph, Edison, Reliance, Frontier, Éclair, and the Oz Film Company, where she played the witch Mombi in their features *His Majesty the Scarecrow of Oz* and *The New Wizard of Oz* (both 1914).

Making a move to Sennett for numerous 1915 -1917 Keystones-Triangle shorts, besides *Fatty and Mabel Adrift* she can be seen in *Fatty's Tintype Tangle* (1915) and *The Grab Bag Bride* (1917). Later she mostly turned up in small roles in features such as *The Breadth of the Gods* (1920), *Excuse Me* (1925), and *Blondes by Choice* (1927), but she's best remembered as the non-stop talking mother of bratty Dinky Dean Riesner in Charlie Chaplin's *The Pilgrim* (1923).

Hulking Wayland Trask plays Brutus Bombastic, the chief robber and bad guy for hire in the picture, and was a mid-teens Mack Sennett regular. Born and raised in New

Roscoe and Luke make a picturesque scene in *Fatty and Mabel Adrift* (1915).

York City he began his acting career there on stage in stock shows such as *The Truth Wagon* and *Welcome to Our City*, as well as spending time in the Olympic Minstrels. He began working at the Sennett Studio in 1915's *A Lover's Lost Control* and for the next three years essayed jealous husbands and oafish boyfriends in shorts such as *The Love Riot, Her Marble Heart* (both 1916), and *Friend Husband* (1918). On his way to becoming an integral supporting player like Vernon Dent or Bud Jamison he died in the 1918 influenza pandemic, with his last film being *Who's Little Wife Are You?* (1918).

New York Clipper (February 12, 1916): "Fatty and Mabel Adrift" has more laughs in its two reels than any five Broadway musical comedies that come to mind."

Moving Picture World (February 12, 1916): "Fatty and Mabel Adrift" for three reels under the conduct of Roscoe Arbuckle wins as no theatrical star of other days ever won in a Keystone comedy. The old theatrical stars are like some of the books we used to read—they were good enough once upon a time—but "Fatty" and "Mabel" are real screen artists of today, survivals of a natural selection that brings the fittest to the front. We need not concern ourselves about what they might have been in days gone by in some other art. They are interesting now, and they float about in a medium of expression with which they have long been on intimate terms."

He Did and He Didn't

Released January 30, 1916. Produced by Mack Sennett for the Keystone Film Co. Distributed by the Triangle Film Corp. Directed by Roscoe Arbuckle. Assistant directors Ferris Hartman & Dave Anderson. Working title: **Love and Lobsters**. Two reels. Extant: GEM, LOC, FRIU, UCLA, LOB, ACAD, EYE. Filmed at the Eastern Triangle Studio in Fort Lee, New Jersey. With Roscoe Arbuckle, Mabel Normand, William Jefferson, Al St John, Joe Bordeaux, James Bryant, G.A. Ely.

Roscoe and Mabel are a couple living in a richly furnished mansion. Roscoe is a well-to- do physician. Things begin to happen when Mabel's old school friend comes to see her. Their innocent pleasure in talking over old times is misunderstood by Roscoe, and he is fuming with jealousy and rage, but Mabel pays no attention to him.

Complications occur owing to the machinations of crooks. They send a hurry-up call to Roscoe saying that a patient is dying in a nearby town. When Roscoe finds that the address given to him is a vacant house he races back in his auto.

Meanwhile at the mansion Mabel goes to bed and finds a burglar under it. Her cries bring her school chum on the scene. He chases the burglar through the house, who finally makes a get-away through a window. When Roscoe returns he finds the school chum holding Mabel who has fainted. Assuming the worst Roscoe knocks the chum down several times and then turns on Mabel and chokes her. He leaves her unconscious but she suddenly comes to, grabs a gun, and follows him down the hall and shoots him dead.

At this point Roscoe wakes up and realizes it has all been a bad dream caused by the lobster dinner that they all had. Having gotten over his jealousy Roscoe patches things up with the school chum and they all have a good laugh.

Mabel Normand was able to finish *Fatty and Mabel Adrift* but she was still recovering from her head injury and wanted to put as much distance between herself and Mack

Roscoe and Mabel Normand keep crooks Al St John and Joe Bordeaux at bay in
He Did and He Didn't (1916). Courtesy Annichen Skaren.

Sennett as possible. At the same time, Roscoe, the most sophisticated director at Keystone, was itching to get out from under Sennett's thumb and flex his muscles to try new things. A deal was worked out for Mabel and Roscoe to relocate to the East Coast:

Mabel Normand Coming East
As soon as she recovers from her accident, Mabel Normand is coming east to locate permanently. She will be assigned to Keystone's Fort Lee studio and work with Roscoe Arbuckle.

– ***Variety***, October 1915

Triangle's Fort Lee, New Jersey studio had been built in 1913 as part of the Willat Film Manufacturing Company. It was sold to Charles Baumann and Ad Kessel Jr. (founders of the New York Motion Picture Company and Sennett's Keystone backers). Since Baumann and Kessel were officers of Triangle the studio was in the family and became known as the Willat-Triangle Studio. Triangle star Douglas Fairbanks also ventured East to make pictures like *The Habit of Happiness* and *American Aristocracy* (both 1916) there.

On December 26, 1915 Roscoe and Mabel left Los Angeles for New York. With them were Minta Durfee, Al St John, Ferris Hartman, Joe Bordeaux, and Jimmy Bryant. A *Chicago Post* reporter had this description of Mabel as they stopped there:

> Pretty Miss Normand is just recovering from a severe illness, so very severe, in fact, that she has lost her "pep." Tipping the scales at just ninety pounds, one couldn't imagine in her the sprightly Mabel whose antics with Fatty have made the Keystones what they are. In her smart seal coat with trimmings of blue fox and her close-fitting turban she looked not unlike the Mabel we

Mack Sennett's business manager George Stout (left) and head of publicity Frederick Palmer (right) see Roscoe, Mabel Normand, Ferris Hartman (right), and Joe Bordeaux (left of Roscoe) off on their trip to the East Coast. Courtesy Marc Wannamaker/Bison Archives.

know on the screen, but the deep shadows beneath her eyes told of her weeks of suffering. "But," said Mrs. Arbuckle, "she has picked up wonderfully in these four days out of Los Angeles, and we feel that three months in the East will restore the vim that is sadly missing." December 30, 1915

The group arrived in New York the next day and soon got to work at the Willat Studio. Away from Sennett's supervision Roscoe did very strong work during this stay in the East. Continuing with plenty of slapstick action, the resulting shorts were more cleverly choreographed and motivated, plus had stronger plots and better character development. *He Did and He Didn't*, with its dream plot structure, adult situations, and dramatic feature lighting, was without a doubt the most unusual film made on the trip, and the most unusual comedy Roscoe had made to date.

While the themes, settings, and camera work are more sophisticated Roscoe still gets in plenty of knockabout, particularly in the sequence of Al St John getting chased through the house. After years of working together, Arbuckle and Mabel have a remarkable ease in their domestic scenes and are completely convincing as a long-time married couple. Roscoe knew that he was venturing into new territory and talked about it in various statements to the press:

> *"You are breaking away from the slapstick stuff," commented someone from the far gloom of the room. "How'll Mack Sennett like that, huh?"*
>
> *"Well," he said calmly, "Mr. Sennett trusted me to come to New York and put on these plays. He knows what my ideas are along the newer lines of screen comedy."*
>
> – **Film Flashes**, 1916

> *It's a new theme and I want to go at it easily. I'm not trying to be "high-brow," or anything like that, but I am going to cut an awful lot of the slapstick out hereafter. If anyone gets kicked, or a pie thrown in his face, there's going to be a reason for it.*
>
> – **Picture-Play**, April 1916

Despite Roscoe's desire to move in new directions the original germ for the film may have come from an outside source. According to the February 4, 1916 *Variety*:

> *Incidentally there has been some discussion regarding this picture in film circles. According to certain folk who have the acquaintanceship of Sid Chaplin, that comedian is said to have had the idea for this comedy originally and to have outlined it to a party of picture players at a dinner at which Roscoe Arbuckle was one of the guests. Later, at another party, Arbuckle offered to let Chaplin in on the joke, and then told the English comedian that he had appropriated the idea and used it for a picture.*

William Jefferson in Kinemacolor's 1913 filming of *The Rivals*.

No matter who had the idea first, Roscoe would go on and remake the film in 1924 as *One Night It Rained*.

Being away from the Sennett lot and its regular stock company gave Roscoe the opportunity to take advantage of East Coast players. Perhaps the most important new edition, who plays Mabel's old beau in this picture, was William Winter Jefferson. As the son of the celebrated actor Joseph Jefferson, best known for his portrayal of Rip Van Winkle, the younger Jefferson grew up on stage performing with his famous father. While his older brother Thomas specialized in drama, William leaned to comedy in plays such as *The Rivals* and *The Senator Keeps House*. He entered the eastern film industry in the 1913 Mittenthal Studio crime drama *Wanted by the Police*, and moved on to other companies such as Biograph and Kinemacolor, where he starred in their three-reel version of *The Rivals* (1913).

A little known aspect of his career is that in 1915 he joined the World Comedy Stars Film Company and directed and starred in some of their one-reelers such as *The Magic Bottle* (1915). This series was shot at the Willat Studio where he would soon work with Roscoe. *He Did and He Didn't* was his first for Arbuckle and was followed by *The Bright Lights*, *His Wife's Mistake*, and *The Other Man* (all 1916). Also at the Willat he appeared in the Douglas Fairbanks feature *The Habit of Happiness* (1916). After his stint in these four shorts he and Roscoe remained friends, and the April 28, 1917 *Motion Picture News* credits Jefferson as writing *His Wedding Night* (1917) with Herbert Warren. But Jefferson later sued Roscoe for being dismissed from the cast of *The Butcher Boy* (more later). During the teens Jefferson was married to movie star Vivian Martin, but he left films in 1919 and retired from the stage in 1925. He later sold all his New York properties and moved to Honolulu, where he died in 1946.

According to the review in the February 4, 1916 *Variety* there was originally an unusual little informational prelude at the beginning of screenings of *He Did and He Didn't*:

> This two-reel Keystone comedy is preceded by a couple of hundred feet of the departure of Roscoe Arbuckle and Mabel Normand from Los Angeles, where the entire Keystone company took part in a farewell party at the railroad station. Then there is a leader to the picture which bears the information

that this picture is the first Keystone comedy that has been produced in the east since the arrival of the famous film favorites in this section.

Moving Picture World (February 12, 1916): "He Did and He Didn't," two reel Keystone, portraying the adventures of Fatty and Mabel, opens with a glimpse of their departure from the Pacific Slope for perilous New Jersey and incidentally, the Isle of Manhattan. They are soon in trouble as newly-weds through two unexpected visits, one from a former beau who knew Mabel "when she was a little girl" and one from a jumping-jack second-story man impersonated by Al St John.

The story, like other recent Keystones, preserves the animation of older releases, is replete with action for the "Hee-Haws," while offering an abundance of amusement for minds not primitive. The early scenes, almost purely those of mirthful mental revelation, depicting Fatty's state of mind, his boyish jealousy in a struggle with his big and kind heart, are a source of delight to intelligent members of the audience and make just as much of a hit with the "Hee-Haws." The improvement is welcome, and we all hope it has come to stay. "He Did and He Didn't" is none the less popular that some charming touches of artistry have been incorporated in its structure. A sure success."

Motion Picture News (February 12, 1916): "Such is this most recent of Keystones—an average number, nothing wildly funny, but cleverly done, very cleverly done, for as a nightmare it is handled realistically and the awakenings of the two dreamers comes as a surprise.

This is the first Triangle-Keystone made in the East, and Arbuckle, who directed, has paid particular attention to pretentious settings and good light effects as well as the element of comedy."

The Bright Lights

Released February 20, 1916. Produced by Mack Sennett for the Keystone Film Co. Distributed by the Triangle Film Corp. Directed by Roscoe Arbuckle. Assistant directors Ferris Hartman & Dave Anderson. Working title: ***The Lure of Broadway***. Two reels. Filmed at the Eastern Triangle Studio in Fort Lee, New Jersey. With Roscoe Arbuckle, Mabel Normand, William Jefferson, Al St John, Minta Durfee, Joe Bordeaux, James Bryant, G.A. Ely, Paddy Sullivan, Tommy Houck, Kid Broad, Eddie Kelly.

The manager of a small town hotel installs a cabaret in an attempt to achieve the standard set by restaurants in the large cities. His effort is ludicrous because of the fact that his talent is all recruited from the help in his hotel. Roscoe, the cook, is forced to appear in a dress suit and when Al St John appears from the bar there is a lively rivalry between the two for the applause of the crowd. Mabel, the waitress, vies with a professional dancer from the city.

Into this setting comes a polished sharper, who takes the innocent Mabel by storm. She listens with open mouth to his stories of life in the metropolis and when he convinces her that he can make her a star she willingly leaves the village with him. Roscoe, who has been in love with the waitress, realizes what her fate is likely to be and starts in pursuit. His search takes him to the Bowery just as an old sailor is being thrown out of a dive. From the sailor

After scouring the Bowery for types Roscoe ended up with (L-R) Paddy Sullivan, Tommy Houck, Kid Broad, and Eddie Kelly in *The Bright Lights* (1916). Courtesy of the Academy of Motion Picture Arts and Sciences.

Roscoe learns that Mabel is inside, practically a prisoner and forced to associate with thugs and the women of the dive. He plans a heroic rescue, but when his purposes become known he is promptly bounced.

Meanwhile the sailor has returned with reinforcements. Led by the persistent Roscoe they storm the dive. There is a free-for-all fight in the course of which Roscoe throws a member of the gang through a solid brick wall. This loosens the foundations and a shoe shop and Chinese laundry above drop into the dive. Mabel is found in an inner room, which she is only too glad to leave to return to the country with "Fatty."

The currently missing *The Bright Lights* was the second of Roscoe's East Coast productions to be shot at Triangle's Fort Lee, New Jersey studio. Originally titled *The Lure of Broadway*, Roscoe did a more elaborate remake of 1914's *Leading Lizzie Astray*, taking the cliche story of the country girl lured to the big city by a cad and pulling out all the stops—scouring the metropolitan area for "Bowery" types, and staging the collapse and destruction of a low-dive building. The March 4, 1916 *Moving Picture World* described Joe Bordeaux's role as a projectile:

> *Roscoe Arbuckle used Joe Bordeaux as a human battering ram at the Keystone studio in Fort Lee the other day and Joe still lives, although he was driven like a wedge through a 12-inch property wall with such force that a gap was opened up large enough to admit the bulky "Fatty" to a bowery dive, where his country sweetheart, Mabel Normand, was held a prisoner. This scene will furnish the big thrill in "The Bright Lights" when the new Keystone comedy is released to Triangle exhibitors. Joe says he'll be at the Knickerbocker the first night to see how he survived an experience for which they use 42-centimeter shells in the Champagne.*

Mabel Normand returned to California after this film, and Sennett set up her own studio, the Mabel Normand Film Company, to keep her from jumping ship and signing elsewhere. The plan wasn't a success—after making the troubled and delayed *Mickey* (ultimately released in 1918) the unit was dissolved and Normand signed with Samuel Goldwyn. *The Bright Lights* marked the last onscreen frolic of "Mabel and Fatty."

Motion Picture News (March 11, 1916): "Fatty and Mabel again and in a picture that well justifies and is benefited largely by their presence. It also shows Roscoe Arbuckle in the light of a master-comedy director for "The Bright Light," formerly known as "The Lure

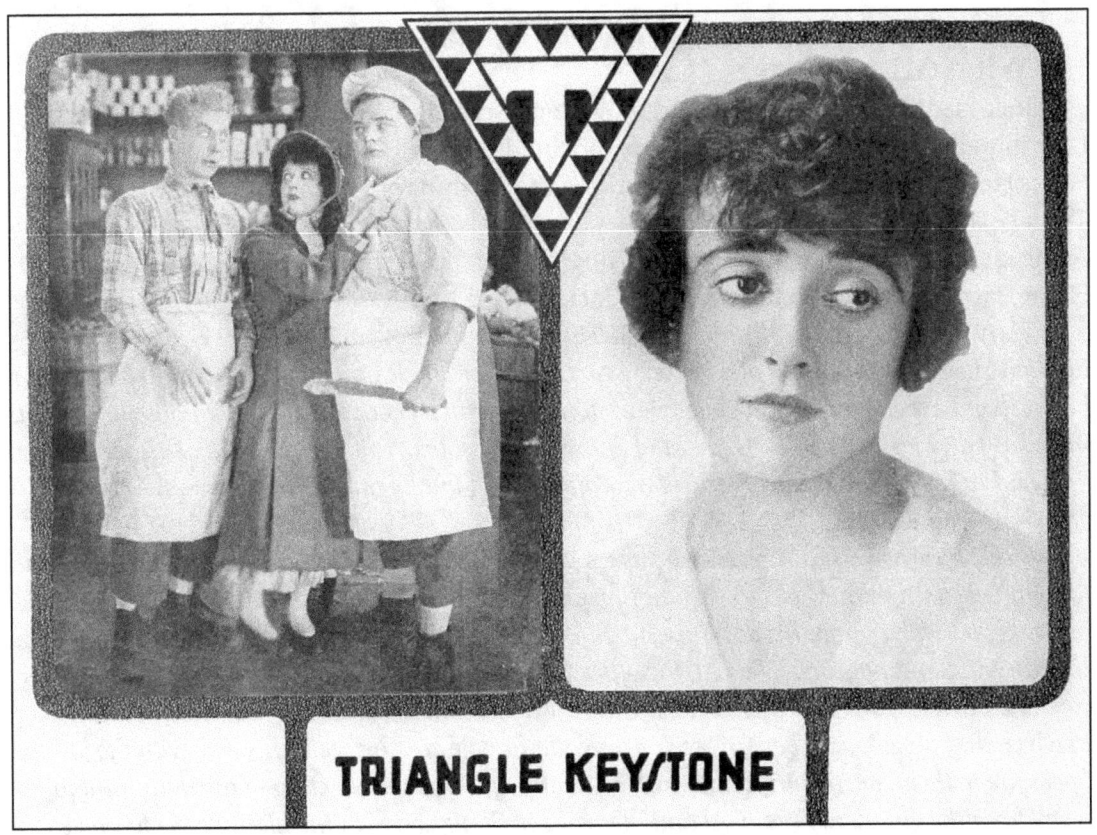

Exhibitor ad images of Mabel Normand, Al St John, and Roscoe from 1916's *The Bright Lights*.

of Broadway," was produced in New Jersey miles away from the western Keystone studio.

Evidently tired of a climax where the players merely swoop around in drunken flying machines or enjoy an eighty-mile-an-hour ride in a skidding automobile, Arbuckle has staged the most rough and tumble and at the same time one of the most breath-taking and craziest climaxes that ever saw the celluloid.

He does nothing more than wreck an entire building. A boisterous fight is staged and the fighters raise such a terrible rumpus that the two upper floors of the building fall in. This series of scenes mixes thrills and laughter most cleverly.

"The Bright Lights" amply demonstrates the ability of Fatty and Mabel to create a little pathos even in a slapstick comedy. It is their ability to do this that puts their pictures over in such excellent style.

In closing, "The Bright Lights" is not vulgar—it has nothing offensive—all after all is said in praise of Fatty and Mabel one must not forget that there is Al St John, who is one of the cleverest comedians that ever appeared in eccentric makeup."

Moving Picture World (March 11, 1916): "The Bright Lights" is one of the most strenuous offerings ever visualized by the Keystone Company, an amusing story to begin with, that of Fatty's sorrows when Mabel elopes from the local cabaret with a tempter to get a glimpse of Manhattan's Great White Way, and of his guileless pursuit… Fatty dominates by his irresistible humor and fine appreciation of what is amusing in human nature. The farce is headed for instantaneous and lasting success."

His Wife's Mistake

Released April 2, 1916. Produced by Mack Sennett for the Keystone Film Company. Distributed by the Triangle Film Corp. Directed by Roscoe Arbuckle. Assistant directors Ferris Hartman & Dave Anderson. Working title: ***The Wrong Mr. Stout***. Filmed at Eastern Triangle studios in Fort Lee, New Jersey. Two reels. Extant: LOC, UCLA. With Roscoe Arbuckle, Minta Durfee, Al St John, William Jefferson, Arthur Earle, Betty Gray, Horace Haine, James Bryant, Corinne Parquet, Jack Pollard.

Fatty gets a new job as the janitor of the Shortacre Building in New York. While performing his duties he enters the offices of a broker, I. Steele. The broker is out, but his wife, who knows that her husband expects a rich and eccentric customer in with a check for $10,000 to close an option, mistakes Fatty for this Mr. R. U. Stout of Showme, Missouri. Thinking to be of assistance to her husband in his business, Mrs. Steele is very affable and finally invites the supposed Mr. Stout to go to luncheon with her.

Steele returns with the necessary papers and is told by his office boy that his wife has gone to a gay café with the new janitor. The option expires in fifteen minutes, but Steele longs for blood and takes a revolver from his desk and starts for the restaurant. No sooner has he departed than the real Mr. Stout appears. With Al, the office boy, he goes in pursuit of the broker.

Meanwhile, Fatty and Mrs. Steele are having a pleasant meal, entirely unaware of the danger in which they are about to be. Mr. Steele arrives at the café, and on seeing his wife with the janitor opens fire in their general direction, which sets Fatty off on a lightning tour of the restaurant to get away from the gunman. Finally Al and the real Mr. Stout arrive in the nick of time to prevent a murder and to get the necessary papers taken care of before the expiration of the option.

Al St John spies on Roscoe and Betty Gray in *His Wife's Mistake* (1916). Courtesy Annichen Skaren.

Behind the "scenes" at Keystone-Triangle. Left to right: Joe Bordeau, Jimmy Bryant, "Doc" Willet, Ferris Hartman, "Fatty" Arbuckle and F. G. Schaefer.

The rarely screened *His Wife's Mistake* is an unsung gem in the Arbuckle cannon that follows Roscoe as he riffs and fools around as the janitor of a shopping arcade. There is lots of good physical business with Fatty mopping floors and trying to pick up a bar of soap that he's dropped. Besides manning a barber shop and ice cream parlor for their slapstick potential, he also does an extended routine involving a revolving door that predates Chaplin's *The Cure* (1917) by a year. All of this is done in a leisurely and playful manner, without a trace of being frenetic, which demonstrates Arbuckle's confidence and mastery of physical comedy.

Produced on a very lavish scale, the April 15, 1916 *Moving Picture World* reported:

> *An outlay of $33,000 for scenic effects alone is the total piled up by Roscoe Arbuckle at the eastern Triangle-Keystone studios, where he is putting the finishing touches on "His Wife's Mistake," a companion piece to "He Did and He Didn't" and "The Bright Lights." One set represents an office building with its arcade of booths and shops. Arbuckle is the new janitor who is mistaken by a broker's wife for a rich customer. They go to a popular café for luncheon, and here is where the star and his technical director, F. G. Schaefer, spent most of their money.*
>
> *Schaefer, who received his early training under the famous Stanford White, endeavored to reproduce the Moorish Room of the Café Boulevard in Paris. He ventures to boast that the Oriental interior with its fountains, balconies, etc., would outclass anything on Broadway if removed and made permanent there. Around the upper balcony is a series of mural paintings 125 feet in length and carrying out a Turkish harem scheme. This balcony required three weeks for the painting.*

Not one to waste a good thing, Roscoe also used the elaborate Café set in his next film *The Other Man*.

William Jefferson returns from *He Did and He Didn't* and *The Bright Lights* (both 1916) to play the excitable I. Steele, and other regulars from Roscoe's East Coast Keystones like Horace Haine, Betty Gray, and Corinne Parquet are also on hand. Generally overlooked in the cast is the very funny Jack Pollard who plays the fey "Percy Dovewings." Pollard (whose real name was John Cherry) was born in Australia, and began his career there on stage as a member of the touring juvenile troupe Pollard's Lilliputians. Like fellow alumni Snub and Daphne Pollard he used the company's name as his surname for a number of years. After coming to the U.S. he was busy in West Coast theatre, and that's likely where Roscoe knew him from. Most of his film work was done in 1915 in some Essanay one-reelers like *Street Fakirs*, *Mustaches and Bombs*, and *All Stuck Up* that were directed by a young Hal Roach and co-starred players such as Bud Jamison, Snub Pollard, Billy Armstrong, and Marta Golden when they weren't working in Charlie Chaplin's Essanay shorts. Afterwards Pollard's film work was sporadic, but as John Cherry he worked in many 1921 to 1944 Broadway shows like *Suzette* (1921), *Who Cares* (1930), and *I'd Rather Be Right* (1937). He died in 1968.

Moving Picture World (April 22, 1916): "A highly amusing story of mistaken identity with some gorgeous settings and Roscoe Arbuckle even funnier than ever."

Minta Durfee watches as Roscoe takes aim at Jack Pollard (right) in the big night spot of *His Wife's Mistake* (1916). Courtesy Marc Wanamaker/Bison Archives.

Moving Picture World (April 22, 1916): "His Wife's Mistake" confirms opinion expressed long ago that Roscoe Arbuckle is a whole play in himself. He has caught the idea of what gets the laugh and has developed it to a fine art. Yet all that he does is so intelligently performed that there is no evidence of effort. To the contrary, it has the appearance of spontaneity so rare in comedy of any kind. Nothing stagey, nothing artificial, mars his interpretation of stupidity, and nothing that offends. Even the farce has a story, and the concluding scenes are of a decorative wealth rarely seen in serious drama. "His Wife's Mistake" will rank high among the best of its kind."

The Other Man

Released on April 16, 1916. Produced by Mack Sennett for the Keystone Film Co. Distributed by the Triangle Film Corp. Directed by Roscoe Arbuckle, Assistant directors Ferris Hartman & Dave Anderson. Working title: **His Dual Role**. Two reels. Extant: clips. Filmed at the Eastern Triangle Studio at Fort Lee, New Jersey. With Roscoe Arbuckle, Irene Wallace, Horace Haine, Lillian Schaefer, Al St John, Minta Durfee, William Jefferson, Joe Bordeaux.

Roscoe writes of his love and announces that he will call on Irene with the ring and ask her parents' consent to their marriage. Father and mother are willing, but decide to give Roscoe a scare before accepting him as a son-in-law. Father assumes a gruff attitude but

Roscoe leads the dance for Minta Durfee (left), Al St John (left), Jimmy Bryant (right), and the ensemble of *The Other Man* (1916). Courtesy The Museum of Modern Art.

melts at the right time and Roscoe departs in high glee to prepare for a masked ball at which the engagement is to be announced. Irene jokes with him about his size but he warns her that he will fool her by the mystery of his disguise.

On the way home in his automobile Roscoe drives over a cliff and is taken to a hospital. There he is, out of his mind, as the guests begin to assemble at the ball. At about this time, however, a well-fed tramp who is the spitting image of Roscoe, is put to work in the kitchen by the cook, who is short of help. Irene wanders into the kitchen and immediately thinks the tramp is Roscoe in his costume. The tramp permits himself to be led to the buffet and later does a dance for the guests. One of the professional dancers is a crook, whose companion robs as she entertains. But her companion bungles the job and is spotted. Before he bounds away from his pursuers he slips a stolen necklace to his female accomplice.

At this point the real Roscoe arrives, clad in a hospital night shirt. He had awoke to find himself surrounded by beautiful nurses but fled at the suggestion of an operation. He leads the chase after the woman accomplice while the tramp is buffeted about during the pursuit of the crook on the grounds. Weary from his exertions the tramp sits down near a gutter spout just as Roscoe breaks into the room above. To avoid being caught with the goods, the woman crook drops the necklace down the spout. The tramp picks it up and gets the reward. As the returned Roscoe is being warmly welcomed by Irene, his double and Joe, the tramp's traveling pal, split fifty-fifty on the reward and hunt for the nearest restaurant.

Something of a variation on Mark Twain's *The Prince and the Pauper*, Roscoe plays dual roles in *The Other Man* (something he never did in any other film). He's an identical rich man and a tramp, and much of the action comes from all the mistaken identity situations that ensue. Although the film is currently missing it appears to have been a very elaborate production, with a car going over a cliff and the swanky restaurant set from *His Wife's Mistake* pressed into service again as the setting for the big masked ball.

One of Roscoe's core players in these East Coast shorts was character man Horace J. Haine. With a long and varied stage background—singing grand opera at the Metropolitan Opera and producing, stage managing, and performing at the Casino Theatre on Broadway—Haine made his film debut in 1915 for the Kalem Company. Very busy and versatile in Roscoe's ensemble, besides appearing in *The Other Man* he was the arcade manager in *His Wife's Mistake* (1916), Al St John's baggage handling boss in *The Moonshiners* (1916), and even had two roles in *The Waiter's Ball* (1916) —the bartender at the ballroom and the German diner lustily and aromatically eating his limburger cheese sandwich. After working for Roscoe he turned up in some New York-made features like *A Hungry Heart*, *Kidnapped* (both 1917), *The Woman of Lies* (1919), *The Truth* (1920), and *The Fifth Horseman* (1924) before going back to the stage. He died in 1940.

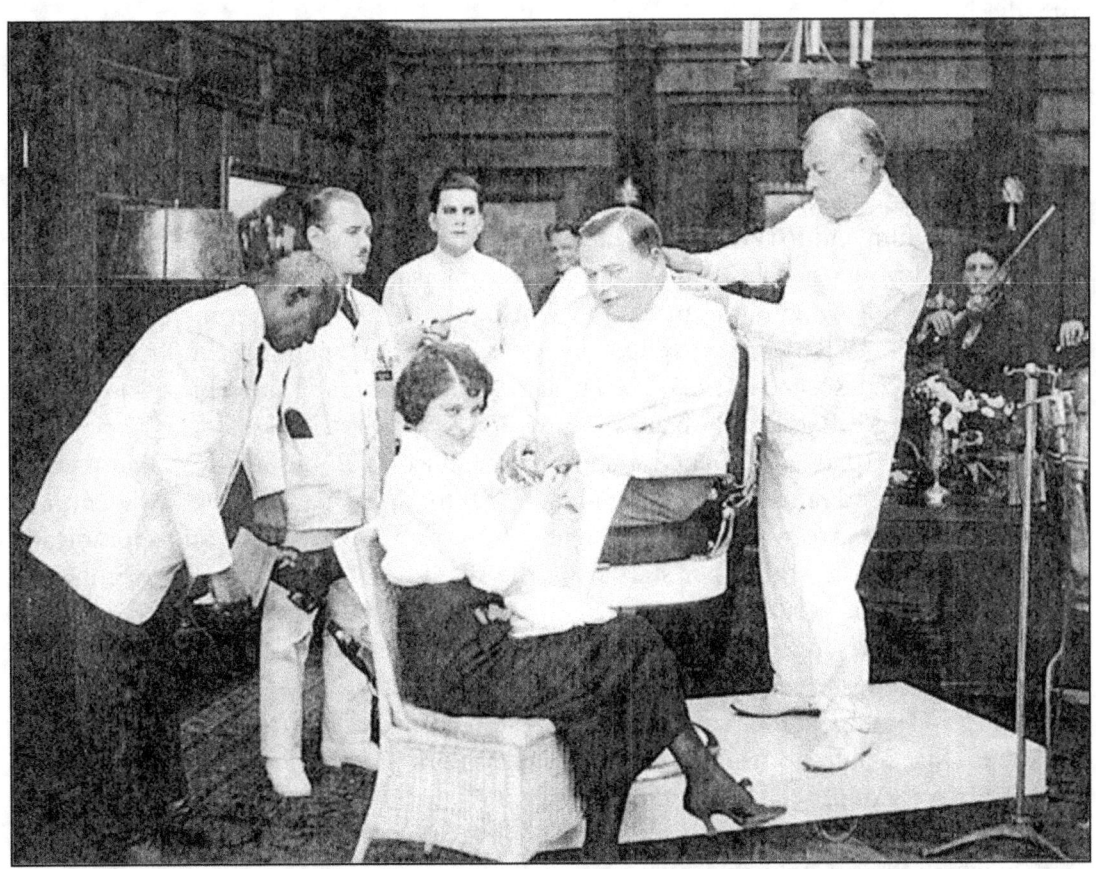

Roscoe getting his hair and nails done under Horace Haine's (right) supervision in *The Other Man* (1916).

The Other Man marked the last appearance of Roscoe and Minta Durfee. Since coming to the East Coast a great deal of Minta's time had been spent taking care of Mabel Normand, which is why she didn't appear in *He Did and He Didn't* (1916). She did comeback in *The Bright Lights* (1916), and when Mabel returned to California she had bigger parts in *His Wife's Mistake* and *The Other Man* (both 1916). After the shooting of *The Moonshiners* (1916) Mack Sennett sent for Minta to come back to California to be part of Mabel's first feature *Mickey*. In addition to acting in the film he wanted her to look after Mabel again as she was holding up production with chronic headaches and by just being difficult (to get back at Sennett).

Roscoe stayed in the East to make *The Waiter's Ball* and *A Reckless Romeo*. The couple was already having marital problems, but Minta later said that this separation was a critical moment as while she was gone Roscoe talked to Joseph Schenck's people and made the deal for his own production company. Minta had always taken care of his business, and she felt that she was being left out of this arrangement with Schenck. At the same time Roscoe was becoming a big star, so she may have secretly resented his growing celebrity status. Once Roscoe began his Comique shorts the couple lived separately, and Minta's last work for Mack Sennett was *Mickey* (1918). Outside of her supporting role in the feature *The Cabaret* (1918) her career slowed down, and she had been inactive for a while when she received an offer in 1920 to headline in an independently made series of comedy shorts.

The *Minta Durfee (Mrs. Roscoe Arbuckle)* series was made by Truart Pictures, with distribution through the recently formed Plymouth Pictures, Inc. Five two-reelers—*The Wives Union*, *He, She, and It*, *When You Are Dry*, *Whose Wife*, and *That Quiet Night* (all 1920) —were shot in Providence, Rhode Island. Despite talented collaborators such as Billy Quirk, Agnes Neilson, and director Charles H. France, the enterprise didn't raise a blip on the film industry's E.K.G. screen, and they're all sadly lost today. Although long separated Minta stood by Roscoe during his manslaughter trials—appearing in the courtroom and posing with him in photos. During the 1920s she did some stage work in shows such as the Will Morrissey revue *The Newcomers*, plus spent time in France where she finally divorced Roscoe in 1925. They're said to have remained amicable, although she did occasionally go after him for back alimony.

In the early 1930s she opened a shop on Hollywood Boulevard for "Fountain of Youth Toiletries" and ran ads for her old film friends to "drop in and say hello." Eventually she returned to the screen as an extra, keeping busy from 1935 to 1971, and sporadically appeared on the radio with other stars from the silent days, sometimes performing old time melodramas such as *East Lynn* or *Ten Nights in a Barroom*. Having never re-married Minta remained Mrs. Roscoe Arbuckle in the public's mind and got a certain amount of attention from reporters and journalists who would occasionally interview her, plus she'd sometimes appear with other veterans on television programs like *The Merv Griffin Show* and others that would do tributes to the silent film era. Her last days were spent at the Motion Picture Country Home, and she passed away in 1975.

Variety (April 28, 1916): "The show closed with a two reel Keystone, "The Other Man, in which Roscoe Arbuckle, by the aid of double exposure, plays two distinct roles. It is excruciatingly funny and shows "Fatty" at his best."

Motion Picture News (May 6, 1916): "'The Other Man,' the first comedy to grace the screen at Rothapfel's Rialto, features Roscoe Arbuckle in a duel [*sic*] role. The humor is in the consequence of no thrilling chase or comical feats—Arbuckle has reserved the right to take the laugh-making burden on himself almost exclusively. To be sure there is an automobile wreck, but this is startling without being funny.

"Being introduced to the spectator in two different parts, the fat comedian manages to make the picture very funny. It is mild humor, but Arbuckle's rotundity and seemingly sunny disposition and his clean business, which is in such contrast from that of other comedians, places the picture in the class of good ones.

"Arbuckle is the lover and at a masque ball his engagement with the girl is going to be announced. But Fatty is slightly banged up in an automobile accident and he is late in attending. A fat tramp makes his way to the ball and the girl believes him to be her lover. But Fatty frightened by the thought of an operation and the sudden appearance of a carpenter who is fixing window shades, hies himself to the ball in his nightgown and then things start to hum and they are made more amusing by the introduction of a pair of society crooks. A chase results, the tramp gets an unexpected reward for capturing the light-fingered couple, while Fatty and his sweetheart are united.

"This story, which is subordinated to its star, is worked out after a good fashion, although some time is consumed before real action is introduced.

"There are new tricks of business and old ones, and both kinds achieve the desired results."

The Moonshiners

Released May 14, 1916. Produced by Mack Sennett for the Keystone Film Co. Distributed by the Triangle Film Corp. Directed by Roscoe Arbuckle & Ferris Hartman. Assistant director Dave Anderson. Working title: **Kentucky Moonshiners**. Two reels. Extant: clips at LOC. Filmed at the Eastern Triangle Studio in Fort Lee, New Jersey and on location. With Al St John, Alice Lake, Horace Haine, Joe Bordeaux, James Bryant, Bert Frank, Mike Eagan, H. J. Thompson.

Al is an assistant baggage smasher in a small town train depot who falls asleep on top of a pile of trunks reading a dime novel. He dreams that he's a famous detective who while out hunting rescues a girl and gets captured by her moonshining family. Spoofing typical moonshining melodramas, Al brings the shiners to justice and wins the girl, but is finally awakening by the falling trunks.

The Moonshiners marked a number of firsts for Arbuckle and company. It was Roscoe's maiden voyage as a director without himself as the star player (depending on how one feels about the *Tillie's Punctured Romance* rumors). According to the May 13, 1916 *Moving Picture World*:

> *Roscoe Arbuckle, who is taking a short rest from the dual activities of starring and directing will produce the new feature. Arbuckle, St John and the supporting company left Fort Lee last night for Dover, N.J., where they found the right locations for the story which has a Kentucky mountain atmosphere.*

Joe Bordeaux, Horace Haine (left) and other hillbillies get the drop on Al St John and Alice Lake in *The Moonshiners* (1916). Courtesy of The Museum of Modern Art.

Working with Ferris Hartman as co-director Roscoe fashioned the first Al St John comedy, transitioning Al from sidekick to star. Later, when Roscoe was setting up his Comique Company in 1917, Al and Hartman kept busy at Keystone turning out a few St John one-reelers such as *The Grab Bag Bride, Her Cave Man, A Self-Made Hero,* and *A Winning Loser,* and again in 1919 with Roscoe moving into features the pair established Al full-time in the star capacity with shorts for Warners/Paramount and Fox.

The film is also pretty Alice Lake's first work with Arbuckle. Born in Brooklyn in 1897, she had gone from amateur dancing and pantomime theatricals to the local Vitagraph Studio. Her debut was 1912's *The Picture Idol,* and her other Vitagraph titles included *Who's Who in Hogg Hollow* (1914), *Insuring Cutey,* and *Levy's Seven Daughters* (both 1915). After a brief stint with Thanhouser she hooked up with the Arbuckle unit and also appeared in the East coast-made *The Waiter's Ball* and *A Reckless Romeo* (both 1916) before heading out West with them.

In California she did the unfinished *A Cream Puff Romance* (1916) and a couple of Triangles before becoming a regular in Roscoe's Comique Comedies such as *Out West, The Bell Boy, Moonshine, Good Night Nurse!,* and *The Cook* (all 1918). On her own she worked for Mack Sennett in *Whose Little Wife Are You?, Rip and Stitch Tailors*, and *East Lynne with Variations* (all 1919). From there she made the jump to dramatic features and became a popular star in the early 1920s with features like *Shore Acres* (1920), *Hole in the Wall* (1921), *Broken Hearts of Broadway* , and *The Unknown Purple* (both 1923), but her career waned by the end of the decade and by the time sound arrived she was limited to background work. In an interview, Olivia de Havilland spoke about her first days in Hollywood and mentioned being surprised to see Lake as an extra, as she had been a great favorite of hers as a girl.

According to reviews Roscoe played the moonshine melodrama parody with a straight face, as he would do in shorts like *The Iron Mule* (1925). At the moment *The Moonshiners* is only represented by a minute-long fragment of Al clowning around with the trunks at the railroad depot that has turned up in the collection of the Library of Congress

Motography (June 17, 1916): "The story of the city detective in search of the hidden still in the mountains who by virtue of his determination and a little courage finds both the outlaw's stronghold and a girl with whom he falls in love, is amusingly burlesqued in the latest Triangle-Keystone offering. This plot which has done such valiant service since the beginning of photoplays, requires not the usual broad comic treatment to be entertaining. And the scenario writer and director apparently realized the fact, for once the mountains are reached the spectator is presented with the old familiar romance with the pursued girl and rescuing hero and with the occasional lapse into the real Keystone slapstick, "The Moonshiners" has no difficulty in holding attention and keeping the audience diverted.

Al St John, whose effective clowning in many Keystone Comedies has earned him the right to feature position in this picture. He is the expressman's assistant who reads dime novels and places himself in the role of the famous detective. While out hunting he meets the girl. Her suitor, the young moonshiner, who has not shaved for two days, attempts to embrace her, and rather than have this, the girl jumps over the cliff. Al rescues her and he is captured by the outlaws, but the girl intercedes. The rest of the story follows the course of many moonshine melodramas."

Motion Picture News (June 17, 1916): "Picturegoers who have been accustomed to expect rapid-fire comedy in Keystone pictures will probably be somewhat puzzled by "The Moonshiners." There is a small amount of preliminary slapstick, centering about Al St John, who as a country boy, is employed as a baggage agent in a small town. After dodging trunks for a few scenes, he goes to sleep reading a dime novel, entitled "The Moonshiners," and the main action that follows occurs in his dream, with himself as the hero pitted against a gang of moonshiners.

Evidently intended as a burlesque of "illicit still" melodrama, the latter action has twice as many serious moments as it has comic ones, and the spectator has little or no occasion for laughter. Curiously enough, the melodrama is quite realistic, even to the killing of some of the villains, and their final capture by government officers.

Some of the exteriors, taken in a forest, are beautiful, and there are some admirable lighting effects,"

The Waiter's Ball

Released June 25, 1916. Produced by Mack Sennett for the Keystone Film Company. Distributed by the Triangle Film Corp. Directed by Roscoe Arbuckle & Ferris Hartman. Assistant director Dave Anderson. Filmed at Eastern Triangle studios in Fort Lee, New

Roscoe overhears Corrine Parquet making another date for *The Waiter's Ball* (1916).

Jersey. Two reels. Extant: Friuli, LOB, GEM, LOC, DAN, ACAD, ESM. With Roscoe Arbuckle, Al St John, Corinne Parquet, Robert Maximillian, Kate Price, Alice Lake, Joe Bordeaux, Horace Haine, James Bryant, Edward Earle.

The pretty cashier of a cheap restaurant has two ardent suitors—Fatty the cook and Al the waiter. This rivalry causes a lot of friction between the wheels of the dining room and the kitchen, and innocent bystanders such as the proprietor and the customers get caught in their crossfire.

All the employees are anxiously anticipating the evening's Waiter's Ball, which is a strictly full-dress affair. Al is ready to escort the cashier to the ball but it turns out that he does not have the dress suit. Fatty does, so he and Corinne set the date for the festivities which sends Al on a murderous rampage.

The outcome of the fracas has Al "appropriating" Fatty's dress clothes and endin4g up with Corinne at the ball. With his suit gone Fatty borrows the fancy gown of the large Irish dishwasher and goes in drag. While busy dancing and becoming "the Belle of the Ball" Fatty discovers Al wearing his pilfered suit and all hell breaks loose. With the ball goers for an audience Al and Fatty rip off each other's stolen outfits, battle with the musician's instruments for weapons, and finally get arrested. The last shot has the boys wearing barrels while being trundled off to jail.

The Waiter's Ball is one of the best-known and best loved of Roscoe's films. It's also his ultimate restaurant comedy—with the first use of his giant magic stewpot that everything comes out of and everything goes into. Some of the wonderful kitchen gags include a really fresh fish that refuses to be cooked and goes on a rampage, Al St John as the waiter taking orders and screaming things like "Singe a Fish" and "One Grunt with a Thousand on a Plate, "and the ripe limburger cheese that scoots around on the counter while Roscoe gasps for air trying to cut it. Add to this Roscoe's acrobatic pancake flipping and knife tossing, as well as a motley crew of diners who would be at home in David Lynch's *Eraserhead* (1977). Many of these culinary routines would see later variations in outings like *The Cook* (1918), *Hey, Pop!* (1932), and *In the Dough* (1933).

Another classic Arbuckle routine is the dueling broom battle between Roscoe and Al, which would get rebooted in *Love* (1919), and even Buster Keaton's 1934 *Grand Slam Opera* (although the Keaton's did this bit in vaudeville). The final button for the broom duel is missing in most circulating prints. While the boys are whacking each other their boss Robert Maximillian walks in and gets knocked over in the fray. Another missing sequence involves Joe Bordeaux's appearance as Corinne Parquet's thug brother (Bordeaux also turns up at the end as the cop that arrests Roscoe and Al). This very brief sequence came at the beginning of the second reel and does exist in Lobster Films' copy of the film.

One of Roscoe's most important collaborators during this period on the East Coast was his old mentor Ferris Hartman. Really nothing has been written about Hartman's contribution to silent comedy as a writer and director. Like Clarence Kolb and Max Dill he was a West Coast theatrical institution at the beginning of the Twentieth Century who headed up a top comedy and light opera company. Making his name at the Tivoli Opera Company (not grand opera but musical comedy) in San Francisco, Roscoe and Minta were part of his troupe on a tour of the Orient in 1912 and early 1913. Other people who passed through Hartman's shows include Walter Catlett, Snub Pollard, Francis White, Robert Z. Leonard, Anna Little, and Lon Chaney (who worked as a property man). As he had done with Walter C. Reed, Roscoe brought Hartman to movies.

It appears that Hartman joined the Arbuckle unit as early as May of 1915 as he can be spotted on screen in *Mabel's Wilful Way*. He worked with Roscoe on all the Eastern-made shorts and returned with the comedian to California, where he assisted him for the last time on the mysterious *A Cream Puff Romance*. When Roscoe embarked on his Comique Comedies contract Hartman stayed with Mack Sennett and became a busy comedy writer and director. He helmed a number of shorts with Al St John, such as *The Stone Age*, *A Self-Made Hero*, and the surviving *The Grab Bag Bride* (all 1917), as well as other Triangle comedies like *A Royal Rogue*, *Dangers of a Bride*, and *A Clever Dummy* (all 1917). After moving on to the Charles Gunn features *A Phantom Husband* and *Framing Framers* (both 1917) he spent some time in 1918 at L-Ko directing Asian comedian Chai Hong before returning to the stage.

He came back to films by re-joining Al St John. Although not credited on any of Al's solo comedies for Warner Brothers photos exist of Hartman directing on the set of *Ship Ahoy* (1920), and he moved with the comic to the Fox Studios to helm *The Simp*, *The Big Secret*, *The Hayseed*, and *The Happy Pest* (all 1921). From here Hartman returned permanently to the stage but by the late 1920s his fortunes took a downward turn and in 1931 he was found on the floor in a hotel room in Oakland. Suffering from malnutrition, a benefit was organized on his behalf but he died just before it took place. Although soon forgotten, his son Paul Hartman carried on the family tradition as a Tony Award winner, popular dancer, and as Emmett Clark on *The Andy Griffith Show* and *Mayberry RFD*.

Roscoe's leading lady is the attractive Corinne Parquet, a novice actress whom very little is known about. According to an item in August 5, 1916 *Motion Picture News* she was from Rochester, New York and had won a contest conducted by the Victoria Moving Picture Theatre. This led to a trial with the Keystone Film Company. After a tiny role

Portrait of Ferris Hartman on the left, and Hartman (sitting) directing Al St John and Norma Contero in *The Big Secret* (1921) on the right. Courtesy Robert Arkus.

in *His Wife's Mistake* (1916) she became Arbuckle's heroine in *The Waiter's Ball* and *A Reckless Romeo* (shot in 1916 but released in 1917). She told the *News*:

> "We are now on our third weeks' work of 'Waiter's Ball,' writes Miss Parquet, "in which I have the part of a cashier in a third-rate restaurant. Roscoe Arbuckle enacts the role of a chef and Al St John that of a waiter. Had it not been for the bad weather, which necessitated the retaking of many scenes, we would have finished much sooner."
>
> "My role in this picture has been an easy one. Inasmuch as I am a newcomer, they have not made me jump over the bar or be walked upon—as yet. Mr. Arbuckle and Mr. St John are responsible for some real funny stuff in the restaurant and also in the ball room. Kate Price does some funny stunts, this being her first picture with this company."

Although very charismatic with a pleasing personality, *A Reckless Romeo* was Ms. Parquet's last known screen credit. The opposite has to be said for the aforementioned Kate Price, who was a film comedy stalwart for more than twenty years. Price personified the tough Irish woman—often a cook as she is here in *The Waiter's Ball*—but also landladies, maids, laundry women, housekeepers, and mothers, all with last names like Sullivan, Mulligan, or Maloney. Born in Cork, Ireland in 1872, the family emigrated to Pawtucket, Rhode Island when she was two (where her younger brother, comedian Jack Duffy was born) and she ended up in vaudeville with her husband Joseph Price Ludwig. His illness led her to try films in 1910 for the Vitagraph Studio near their home in Brooklyn, and she quickly became a regular part of the Vitagraph family—playing all sorts of stock characters such as widows or wives sorely tried by their husbands.

Besides supporting John Bunny, Flora Finch, and Sidney Drew, the studio even initiated a "Kate" series with pictures like *Fisherman Kate, Cabman Kate* (both 1914), and *Conductor Kate* (1916). Leaving Vitagraph she did this appearance with Roscoe and then headed to Florida to make comedies for Vim and Sparkle Comedies with the likes of Oliver Hardy and Billy Ruge. Finally she ended up in Hollywood in big features such as *Amarilly of Clothes-Line Alley* (1918), *Little Lord Fauntleroy* (1921), *The Perfect Clown (1925)*, and *Irene (1926)*, and even occasional shorts like Roscoe's *Goodnight Nurse* (1918) and Buster Keaton's *My Wife's Relations* (1922). Her biggest and best role in features was as Mrs. Kelly, in *The Cohens and Kellys* (1926), which continued with *The Cohens and Kellys in Paris* (1928), *The Cohens and Kellys in Atlantic City* (1929), *The Cohens and Kellys in Scotland*, and *The Cohens and Kellys in Africa* (both 1930). She worked until the late 1930s and died in Los Angeles in 1943.

Also on hand as the proprietor of the restaurant is the overlooked character man Robert Maximillian, a forgotten East Coast player, who had an engaging comic look with his large nose, moth-eaten mustache, and spindly body. He takes a lot of physical abuse from Roscoe and Al, and would take some more in *A Reckless Romeo* (1917). In the early 1920s he became a regular in the Toonerville Trolley comedies which were produced by the Betzwood Film Company and shot in Pennsylvania. Based on the comic strip *Toonerville Folks* by Fontaine Fox, the stars were Dan Mason as the Skipper and Wilna Hervey as the powerful Katrinka. Maximillian appeared in support as the terrible tempered Mr. Bang in shorts such as *The Skipper's Narrow Escape* (1921), *The Skipper's Policy*, and *Toonerville Trials* (both 1922). After the Toonerville comedies his last credit is the 1922 Lee Kohlmar feature *Breaking Home Ties*.

Motography (January 19, 1918): "The best Arbuckle comedy ever produced. We have run it three times."

Motion Picture News (August 3, 1918): "Following the feature the orchestra plays "Eugene O'Negrin" and then comes the comedy, a re-issue, and one of the funniest that has ever been made, "Fatty" Arbuckle in "The Waiter's Ball." We remember distinctly that when it was first issued we sat through it on three successive evenings and then on a return booking saw it twice."

A Reckless Romeo

Released May 21, 1917. Produced by Mack Sennett for the Keystone Film Co. Distributed by Paramount Pictures. Directed by Roscoe Arbuckle. Assistant directors Ferris Hartman and Dave Anderson. Working title: **His Alibi**. Two reels. Extant: NOR, LOB. Filmed July 9 through September 13, 1916 at the Eastern Triangle Studio in Fort Lee, New Jersey. With Roscoe Arbuckle, Corrine Parquet, Agnes Neilsen, Alice Lake, Al St John, James Bryant, Robert Maximillian, Edward Earle.

Fatty, arriving home from the club at 3 a.m. in a rather hilarious condition, attempts to sneak into the house but is caught and upbraided by his wife. In order to square himself he promises to take her and her mother for a holiday at the amusement park. While visiting the different concessions in the park, Fatty manages to lose the wife and mother-in-law and start a flirtation with a pretty girl. But the unexpected arrival of her sweetheart on the scene, who proceeds to thrash Fatty within an inch of his life, puts an end to Fatty's romance. After vainly searching for Fatty, the wife and mother-in-law go home and wait for him. When Fatty arrives home with a beautiful black eye, his wife demands an explanation and he tells her that while defending a blind beggar woman he was beaten by a gang of thugs. All is forgiven and that night the happy family goes to a moving picture show. They are thoroughly enjoying themselves when the animated weekly news flashes on the screen: a movie of Fatty flirting with the pretty girl and the fighting with her sweetheart is part of the newsreel. Fatty starts to flee but is captured by wife and mother-in-law who threaten him with dire punishment upon arriving home. To escape them Fatty throws a brick through a window, is arrested by a policeman and cheerfully goes to jail in preference to home and mother-in-law.

A Reckless Romeo was Roscoe's last East Coast-made short for Sennett/Triangle. For reasons unknown it was never released by Triangle—it was shelved, along with Arbuckle's next short *A Cream Puff Romance*. Triangle eventually sold *Romeo* to producer Joseph Schenck, where it became the second of the Comique releases. A re-working of *Fatty at San Diego* (1913), which would be dusted off again for the Al St John Tuxedo comedy *Never Again* (1924), production went from July through September of 1916, and the September 30, 1916 *Motion Pictures News* described the elaborate theatre set:

Roscoe standing in as a hall tree for Corinne Parquet (left) and Agnes Neilsen (right) in *A Reckless Romeo* (1917). Courtesy Marc Wanamaker/Bison Archives.

> *The entire studio was transformed into the interior of a theater, and the setting for the stage, proscenium arch and all, was the equal of most any moving picture theater in New York. Besides an orchestra of twenty pieces partially hidden behind a bank of palms at one side of the stage, a stream of running water poured down a paper mache mountain on the opposite of the stage.*
>
> *Close to four hundred extra people were employed for the scenes taken in the theater, and that too, comes close if it doesn't actually establish a record for the number of extra people employed in the making of a comedy.*

The amusement park scenes were shot at the Palisades Amusement Park in Fort Lee, New Jersey. Palisades was owned by Joseph and Nicholas Schenck, who had some important negotiations with Roscoe while he was in New York which would make them important players, particularly Joe, in the comedian's subsequent career and life. When *A Reckless Romeo* was finished shooting Roscoe headed back to California and announced to the press:

Al St John has at Roscoe as Agnes Neilsen (right) and Corinne Parquet (left) try to prevent the blood bath in *A Reckless Romeo* (1917). Courtesy Marc Wanamaker/Bison Archives.

Arbuckle To Be Independent
Heavyweight Comedian to Have His Own Company After Jan. 1.

Roscoe "Fatty" Arbuckle is on his way to California, tired of New York and eagerly awaiting the end of the year, when his contract expires with the Keystone company. To-day, a few hours after his arrival in Chicago from the East, he departed for Los Angeles.

"I was in New York altogether too long," he remarked, "and I am happy to return West."

On Jan. 1 Mr. Arbuckle is to begin producing comedies for his own company under the brand name of Comique.

"I have organized a producing concern with Joseph and Nicholas Schenk, two New York theatrical men," the comedian told the interviewer, "and I'll begin work one minute after my contract with Mr. Sennett expires."

Other than Al St John, Arbuckle has not decided upon any player whom he will engage under regular contract.

"I will put my money in writers instead of actors," and the comedian assumed a businesslike air. "Five or six men will do nothing else but smoke tobacco and dream funny situations for the public's enjoyment. Outside of Mr. St John, I expect to engage a leading woman permanently, although I have not decided who she will be."

Joseph M. Schenck was born in Rybinsk, Yaroslavl Oblast in Russia, and immigrated to New York City at the age of seventeen in 1893. He and his younger brother Nicholas went into the drugstore business, but used their profits to move into amusement parks—operating the concessions at New York's Fort George Amusement Park and buying Palisades in 1909. Film pioneer Marcus Loew bought one of their parks, and the Schencks got into the film business through him, becoming partners in Loew's movie house chain. In 1916 Schenck married actress Norma Talmadge and was poised to get into film production. Roscoe and Schenck connected during Roscoe's East Coast stay, and an arrangement was made for when Roscoe's Mack Sennett contract expired. In early 1917 Schenck launched the Norma Talmadge Film Corporation for features to star his wife, and the Comique Film Corporation for two-reelers with Roscoe.

According to the people who knew him and worked for him, people like Roscoe, Buster Keaton, and Anita Loos, Schenck was a mensch—a person of integrity and honor, who was a warm individual and a true friend. These qualities were combined with an acute business sense, the mix of which made him well-liked in the film industry. Over the years Schenck remained a major Hollywood player—a second president of United Artists, helping to set up Twentieth Century-Fox and acting as its first chairman, and was even instrumental in launching the career of Marilyn Monroe.

In some simplistic accounts of Buster Keaton's career Schenck sometimes gets a bad rap for Buster being moved from his own studio to MGM. This was because Joe was getting out of independent production, and his intent was to take care of Buster. As he had done successfully with Roscoe and Paramount, Schenck secured a place for Keaton (his brother-in-law) at the most prestigious studio in Hollywood at a tremendous salary. Schenck, not being a creative type, wasn't aware that the assembly-line nature of MGM would create problems for Buster. Joe would help Keaton out through some tough times in the 1930s, just as he stood by Roscoe in the dark days of the early 1920s.

Portrait of Roscoe's producer and good friend Joseph M. Schenck.

Moving Picture World (May 26, 1917): "Roscoe "Fatty" Arbuckle, who made such a tremendous hit in his first Paramount comedy "The Butcher Boy," will be seen this week in "A Reckless Romeo," a modern version of the world's greatest lover. Far more hilarious are the scenes in this production than in the first Paramount comedy. "A Reckless Romeo" is filled with action from start to finish, plenty of heart interest and a sufficient amount of comedy suspense."

Motography (April 20, 1918): "An excellent comedy that kept the audience in a continual laugh. Fatty is a good drawing card."

A Cream Puff Romance

Not released. Shot in Oct. and Nov. of 1916 in Los Angeles. Produced by Mack Sennett for Keystone Film Co. Distributed by Triangle Film Corp. Directed by Roscoe Arbuckle. Assistant director Ferris Hartman. Two reels. With Roscoe Arbuckle, Al St John, Alice Lake, Mai Wells, Walter Wright.

This film remains an unsolved mystery in Roscoe's career. It began shooting almost immediately after *A Reckless Romeo* (1916) and then sat on Sennett's shelf. Unlike the former film, *A Cream Puff Romance* doesn't seem to ever have been released and may not have been completed. It's possible that the film may have seen daylight under another title later through W. H. Productions or Tower Film Corp., but there's no evidence to support that. There's not even a synopsis available, although the plot seems to have concerned the usual hijinks in a train yard, and then a bakery and luncheonette. At the moment the only info available on the film are shooting descriptions from the trade magazines such as:

> *Los Angeles, October 28. Roscoe Arbuckle, Al St John and Alice Lake have taken up filming of a railroad comedy, or at least one which has numerous scenes of railroad properties, and are working at local yards. In two instances transcontinental trains were delayed in departing to make possible the shooting of a Keystone comedy scene.*
> – **Motion Picture News**—November 11, 1916.

> *Los Angeles, November 1. A quarter section of the mammoth Keystone open air stage is occupied by a mammoth set built for the first Roscoe Arbuckle comedy to be made since the heavyweight comedian returned to the coast. The set is a marvel for detail and contains a bakeshop, kitchen, retail salesroom and a luncheonette and a soda fountain of a delicatessen. There are tubs and tubs of dough, piles of sacks filled with flour, hundreds of pies, cakes, cookies and luscious French pastry, all in place waiting the call of action. Arbuckle will be the part of the cook, Al St John and Alice Lake taking the other principal parts. In the direction Arbuckle will be assisted by Ferris Hartman.*
> – **Motion Picture News** –November 18, 1916.

> *At the Triangle studios out on the coast active work is about completed on the new Roscoe Arbuckle comedy, "A Cream Puff Romance." Alice Lake is being*

Roscoe and Alice Lake do a little spooning in the never-released *A Cream Puff Romance* (1916). Billy Rose Theatre Division, the New York Public Library for the Performing Arts.

featured in support of "Fatty," and most of the amusing incidents in which they figure take place in the bakery and about the soda fountain set that are used in the story. Several barrels of flour, and numerous drayloads of bakers' and confectioners' supplies have also been utilized in giving atmosphere to the Arbuckle vehicle, despite the high cost of foodstuffs.

"Fatty" is said to have evolved much novel business in his handling of the various cream puff and chocolate sundae episodes that characterize the

plot. Throughout most of the picture he is garbed in a large plaid shirt and the apron and cap considered in keeping with a culinary comedy.

Spectators who witnessed the filming of this new feature declare that "Fatty" has achieved his most laughable effects since he romped through the various complications of "The Waiters Ball."

– *Moving Picture World*—December 9, 1916.

Taking a break from shooting *A Cream Puff Romance*, Roscoe harmonizes on the Sennett lot with (L-R) Reggie Morris, Gloria Swanson, and Bobby Vernon.

Roscoe Arbuckle with his high power auto, his high power bulldog and his high power humor is once again under way in a new high power Triangle-Sennett-Keystone comedy.

It would be unfair to divulge too much at present but this much may be stated, that a large portion of its action occurs in a restaurant and candy shop; further it may be revealed that two hundred pounds of flour—not two hundred press-agent pounds, but two hundred actual pounds as measured out by the Flour Trust—were moved into the scene to provide the dough and the batter that will figure largely in the production of the comedy.

In addition there is a complete assortment of perfectly good pies bought from the Los Angeles pie baking company, some puddings ditto, and a great assortment of saucepans, pots, pans, broilers, kettles, beaters, stirrers, forks and ladles for all the intricate purposes of high class cookery for which Roscoe Arbuckle is to become responsible when he starts in to play the comedy.

– *The Triangle*—November 11, 1916.

A Cream Puff Romance was Roscoe's last work for Mack Sennett. While he had benefited greatly from his four years at Keystone—learning the basics of filmmaking and becoming a world-renowned star—it was time to move on to bigger and better things.

Chapter 6
Comique Comedies

ROSCOE SIGNED WITH PRODUCER Joseph Schenck who set up the Comique Film Corp. to make shorts that would be released through Paramount. Although his late Sennett films had become more sophisticated, for his initial Comique releases Roscoe returned to roughhouse on such a grand scale that they became slapstick ballets. Having brought nephew Al St John along with him from Keystone, Roscoe added former vaudevillian Buster Keaton to the mix, and with the three best tumblers in show business many of the shorts seem like a contest to see who can out-stunt the others. Once the exhalation of freedom settled Roscoe returned to the old finesse with shorts like *Camping Out* (1919) and *The Garage* (1920), as well as developing his gift for parody with *Moonshine* and *Out West* (both 1918).

1917

The Butcher Boy

Released April 23, 1917. Produced by Joseph M. Schenck for the Comique Film Corp. Distributed by Paramount Pictures. Directed by Roscoe Arbuckle. Story by Joe Roach. Photographed by Frank D. Williams. Edited by Herbert Warren. Two reels. Extant: LOC, MoMA, LOB, ACAD. With Roscoe Arbuckle, Josephine Stevens, Al St John, Buster Keaton, Agnes Neilson, Arthur Earle, Luke.

Fatty is the butcher boy who's in love with the cashier, the pretty daughter of the grocery store owner. Also employed in the store is Al, who has his own feelings for the girl. Fatty sends love notes to his adored one by the cash conveyor and this arouses Al's wrath, which leads to an all-out war in the store with broken crockery, swinging brooms, molasses, and flying bags of flour with all the customers in the line of fire. This is too much for the girl's father so he sends her away to a young ladies' seminary. Fatty follows, and shows up at the school dressed in a dress, blonde wig, and a sash of blue as the "new girl." His sweetheart recognizes him and all is fine, until Al has the same idea and shows up in a dress, glasses, and pigtails that stick out on either side of his head. The head mistress puts the two "new girls" in a room together, where they soon recognize each other and resume their battle royal. When Fatty is

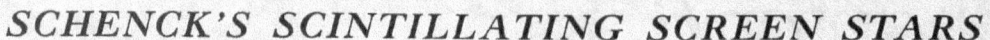

Norma Talmadge and Roscoe as Joseph Schenck's main attractions.

Roscoe and Josephine Stevens pitch a little woo in *The Butcher Boy* (1917) as Luke stands guard.

made to go stay in the room with the instructress, Al's confederates show up at the dormitory and try to kidnap the heroine. Ultimately they are thwarted by Fatty and the headmistress who turns out to be very handy with a pistol. Fatty and his love make their escape and head for the nearest minister.

The Butcher Boy was one of the most important productions in Roscoe's career. Having just left Sennett to embark with his own company, a lot was riding on its success. As it turned out there was nothing to worry about as the picture was a smash hit, immediately establishing Comique as a comedy force to be reckoned with. It still holds up today. Everything that Roscoe had accumulated about comedy filmmaking is on parade in *The Butcher Boy*—the fast pace with a gag a minute, Roscoe in drag, and all the usual stunts.

Although such a pivotal film in Roscoe's development, it is much better remembered today as the screen debut of Buster Keaton. One of the greatest comedy creators in film history, Keaton had been "born in a trunk" and became a regular member of his parents' vaudeville act at the age of three. It wasn't long before Buster became the main attraction of The Three Keatons, which was often referred to as the roughest act in vaudeville. By 1917 Keaton was a young adult and about to go out on his own as a solo performer. Cast in the upcoming Broadway revue *The Passing Show of 1917*, Buster was working out his routines when he had a fateful meeting on the street:

> *But just a day or two before rehearsals were to start, I ran into Lou Anger, a Dutch comedian, who had worked on vaudeville bills with us many times. Anger was with Roscoe (Fatty) Arbuckle, the screen comedian. As he introduced us, he explained that Arbuckle had just broken away from Mack Sennett to make two-reel comedies of his own. Joe Schenck was producing them, and Anger had quit vaudeville to be Joe's studio manager.*
>
> *I had seen some of Arbuckle's work in Sennett comedies and greatly admired him. He said he'd caught our act many times and always liked it.*
>
> *"Have you ever been in a movie, Buster?" he asked.*
>
> *When I told him I hadn't, Roscoe said, "Why don't you come over to the Colony Studios tomorrow morning? I'm starting a new picture there. You could try doing a bit in it. You might enjoy working in pictures."*
>
> *"I'd like to try it," I told him.*
>
> **– My Wonderful World of Slapstick**, Doubleday, 1960

So with such a casual meeting began one of the great careers in film. Buster was always justifiably proud of his debut, done without any retakes, and was very fond of the "nickel in the molasses" routine that he and Roscoe do. He would revive it a few times on early television.

The Colony Studios was a big loft in Manhattan on East 48th Street. Joseph Schenck had been using it to make his Norma Talmadge features and Roscoe set up shop there. The space was around for years, later becoming a parking garage before eventually being demolished.

Besides adding Keaton to the mix, Roscoe had brought along Al St John and Joe Bordeaux. Another returnee that oddly didn't work out was William Jefferson, who had

A Paramount pressbook depiction of Roscoe on his way to theatres.

been a major presence in Roscoe's New Jersey-made Triangle productions such as *He Did and He Didn't*, *The Bright Lights*, *His Wife's Mistake*, and *The Other Man* (all 1916). Jefferson can be spotted at the very opening of the film, but gets drug off and never returns. According to the October 17, 1918 *Film Daily* Jefferson was hired to be part of the new Comique Company, but things didn't work out:

W. W. JEFFERSON SUES COMIQUE CO.

> *William W. Jefferson has filed suit in the Supreme Court against the Comique Film Co., and Roscoe Arbuckle for $3,480 damages for breach of contract of employment. The plaintiff alleges that he was engaged by the corporation through Mr. Arbuckle as president on March 5, 1917, and was discharged on June 18 without cause. The defendant admits the employment but alleges that Jefferson was discharged because he was found to be incompetent to perform the duties for which he was engaged.*

The reasons for the dismissal and the outcome of the suit have been lost to time.

Moving Picture World (April 28, 1917): "If one laugh weighed an ounce "The Butcher Boy," the first two-reel comedy made for Paramount by Roscoe Arbuckle, would weigh as much as "Fatty" himself. Crammed full of laughs and chuckles, the offering justifies the wide pre-showing bookings of the Arbuckle comedies. Surrounded by a group of expert funmakers, "Fatty" comes up to even the most optimistic expectations. Evident all through the film are the comedy touches that have made Arbuckle a comedy name to conjure with."

Variety (April 20, 1917): "The first of the Arbuckle series has set a good mark to aim at. While there is some slapstick, the comedy is recommended."

Chicago Daily Tribune (April 24, 1917): "Attendance at theaters showing 'The Cure,' Mr. Chaplin's latest vehicle, was rivaled yesterday by the crowds flocking to see 'Fatty'

Arbuckle in his new comedy, 'The Butcher Boy'.... Anybody who can make people laugh as did Mr. Arbuckle yesterday...deserves a nice fat contract here and a harp over yonder.

"The plot has to do with the advent of two deadly rivals for the hand of a maiden into a select seminary. One of the rivals being Fatty dressed as a girl in short skirts and curls. Fatty's precocious bull pup is also on the job, so you can imagine things move."

The Rough House

Released June 25, 1917. Produced by Joseph M. Schenck for the Comique Film Corp. Distributed by Paramount Pictures. Directed by Roscoe Arbuckle. Story by Joe Roach. Photographed by Frank D. Williams. Edited by Herbert Warren. Two reels. Extant: Buch, MoMA, GEM, FRANC, LOB, ACAD . With Roscoe Arbuckle, Al St John, Agnes Neilson, Buster Keaton, Josephine Stevens, Arthur Earle.

All is not well in the house of Mr. Rough, in particular because of his domineering mother-in-law. After smoking in bed and causing a fire Mr. Rough is in the dog house, but to make matters worse he's caught flirting with the maid. Next he gets involved in a battle between his cook and a delivery boy, which lays waste to the kitchen, dining room, and living

Agnes Neilsen surveys *The Rough House* (1917) wreckage with Roscoe, Al St John, and Josephine Stevens. Courtesy Marc Wanamaker/Bison Archives.

room. When his wife and mother-in-law return Rough gets blamed for all the wreckage, and even worse is caught flirting with the maid. Not only is she promptly dismissed, but Rough is forced to take her place and that of the cook.

A lunch party has been set up with a couple of visiting dignitaries, who are actually crooks, and Rough embarrasses his family to no end with his maid skills—serving the soup from a sponge, regluing one of the guest's toupee with butter, and seasoning the roast with gasoline which causes a big conflagration. In the uproar one of the crooks takes the opportunity to sneak in a bedroom and pilfer a pearl necklace, but he's been secretly observed by a private detective who calls the cops. In the meantime the detective deputizes Mr. Rough and gives him a pistol. The film ends with much gunfire, and the cops finally arrive to take the pair of crooks away.

This was the second Comique production, but the third release. As mentioned earlier *A Reckless Romeo*, the unreleased New Jersey-made Sennett Triangle short, was purchased by Joseph Schenck from Mack Sennett and was slotted into the second spot to help fill out the Comique release schedule. A partial re-working of *Fickle Fatty's Fall* (1915), *The Rough House* is certainly that—a rough and rowdy slapstick fest, where everyone, especially Buster Keaton and Al St John, seem to be seeing who can top who. Buster and Al lay waste to the kitchen and dining room, with some of their business, involving the kitchen table and brooms, having their origins in the Keaton family vaudeville act. Roscoe gave free rein to the pair, and Keaton later said in his autobiography that Arbuckle:

> …would turn you loose. Because he didn't care who got the laughs in the pictures. He wanted them in there.

After his experience on *The Butcher Boy*, Keaton was sold on movies. He later told interviewer Christopher Bishop:

> I was very interested in it—the mechanics of it. I wanted to know how that picture got put together through the cutting room, and the mechanics of the camera, which fascinated me the most.
> What part did you play?
> Oh, in those two-reelers, they didn't bother to give you any character or name or anything, things just started happening.
> They were shooting this in a studio—not on location?
> Yes, but in good weather we did sneak out and shoot exteriors.
> How many were there in the Arbuckle company at that time?
> Oh, there'd be a standard troupe. Your cast were always your leading lady, your villain, and you always carried a handful of bit people—they were cops or whatever you wanted them to be—you certainly had two or three in the scenario department helping you lay out the picture, you had a cutter, you had a camera man—two camera men. It's just done on a bigger scale today, that's all.

– ***Film Quarterly***, Autumn, 1958

With his fate sealed, Buster had gone back to his agent Max Hart and got out of the commitment to *The Passing Show of 1917* to join Arbuckle. Hart, a very powerful theatrical agent, was very understanding about Buster going from $250 a week on the stage to $40 in the movies, as he happened to also be Roscoe's agent. He advised Keaton:

> *Learn everything you can about the business, Buster," he said, "the hell with the money. Movies are the coming thing, believe me.*

In the midst of all the furious physical knockabout Roscoe does include some delicate and offbeat touches. He repeats his methodic "trying to put out a fire with small cups of water" routine from *Fatty's Plucky Pup* (1915), and at one point during the dining room fracas with Buster and Al, Roscoe gets clocked and literally sees stars—and takes a moment to happily count them as they hang in the air in front of him. Roscoe also has two fun bits with food. The first involves entertaining the maid by sticking forks into two dinner rolls and making them imitate Charlie Chaplin's shuffling gate (much has been made about this bit and how it may have influenced the Oceana Roll dance in Chaplin's 1925 *The Gold Rush*). The other kitchen business involves him matter of factly slicing potatoes by shoving them through the spinning blades of an electric fan.

Maid Josephine Stevens and Roscoe get friendly in *The Rough House* (1917).

On hand besides Buster and Al are Agnes Neilson as the over-bearing mother-in-law, Robert Maximillan as the oddly mustached and eyebrowed police captain, and Arthur Earle as the toupee-wearing dinner guest. Earle was a long-time vaudevillian, as a solo performer and in an act with his wife Vera Barrett, who was an old friend of Roscoe and Minta Durfee's. His first film appearance appears to have been the diner who makes eyes at Alice Lake in *The Waiter's Ball* (1916), but he would be very busy in the Comiques with big supporting roles in *The Butcher Boy* and *His Wedding Night*. After his work with Arbuckle he appeared in a few New York-made features such as *The Dark Star* (1919) and *Salvation Nell* (1921), but died in 1926.

Returning from *The Butcher Boy* and playing the flirty maid is dark-haired leading lady Josephine Stevens. Stevens came from a prestigious Philadelphia theatrical lineage—her father having been Benjamin D. Stevens, a longtime manager for producers Klaw & Erlanger, and her mother actress Helen Beresford. She began her own stage career at age seventeen in *The Argyle Case*, and soon followed with other productions such as *Daddy Long Legs* with Henry Miller and *Captain Kidd Jr*. Her screen debut came in *The Butcher Boy*, and after *The Rough House* she made one feature, *Oh, You Women* (1919), and then disappeared from movies. She returned to the stage for shows like 1923's *GoGo*.

The success of *The Butcher Boy* and *A Reckless Romeo* was so big that Paramount had to increase the number of prints for this third release. Lost for many years, *The Rough House* was rediscovered by Raymond Rohauer in the 1980s, but because of all the kitchen related comedy it was initially misidentified as *The Cook* (1918). Eventually, both films turned up and the proper titles were sorted out.

Motion Picture News (June 30, 1917): "'A Rough House' not only should 'get the money,' but may said to fairly earn it as being in a peculiar class by itself of appealing to intelligent audiences beyond the mere 'action' of the slapstick."

Motography (September 8, 1917): "If you want a comedy that will keep them laughing book this. Star is great."

Moving Picture World (June 30, 1917): "'Fatty' Arbuckle will give many a laugh in 'Rough House,' a Paramount picture in two reels. The astonishing attention he gives to a conflagration in his bed room will be a new laugh producer. There is no unoccupied moment, and while there is much in the picture that is old, none of it is slow. Nearly all of it good."

His Wedding Night

Released August 20, 1917. Produced by Joseph M. Schenck for the Comique Film Corp. Distributed by Paramount Pictures. Directed by Roscoe Arbuckle. Story by Joe Roach. Photographed by George Peters. Edited by Herbert Warren. Two reels. Extant: MoMA, LOB, EYE, ACAD, Buch, Budapest. With Roscoe Arbukle, Al St John, Alice Mann, Buster Keaton, Arthur Earle, James Bryant, Emma Reed.

Fatty is the "boy-Friday" at the Koff & Kramp drugstore and soda parlor. He and the proprietor's daughter are in love, but Fatty has a terrible rival in Al. Fatty has many misadventures with various people at the drugstore, but when Al finds out that Alice and her father have accepted Fatty as her husband-to-be he takes drastic action. He and two cohorts

Al St John gives Roscoe and Alice Mann the evil eye in this *His Wedding Night* (1917) lobby card. Courtesy Matt Vogel.

plot to kidnap Alice, but accidentally abduct Buster the messenger boy who was modeling the wedding gown for Alice. The plotters load their captive into a buggy and take off, closely followed by Fatty and the girl's father in a wagon. Alice herself sees the chase and jumps on to a bicycle to bring up the rear. They all arrive at the minister's house where Buster is discovered, Al is vanquished, and Fatty and Alice are wed.

With *The Butcher Boy* and *The Rough House* under his belt Buster Keaton began his movie apprenticeship in earnest and quickly became an integral part in the creation of the Comique shorts. In 1958 he recalled for interviewer George C. Pratt:

> [There was] no script. We simply talked over what we're goin' to do and we got our ideas, and went to work. Arbuckle was his own director and I'd only been with him probably about three pictures when I was his assistant director. In other words, I was sittin' alongside the camera when he was doin' the scene. And he taught me the cutting room also because he was his own cutter.

His Wedding Night had originally been announced in April as the follow-up to *The Butcher Boy*, to be written by Herbert Warren and the eventually discharged William Jefferson (see *The Butcher Boy*), but ended up on movie screens as the fourth Comique release. The plot repeats Al's rivalry for the girl but substitutes a drugstore for *The Butcher Boy's* general store, and has plenty of room for Roscoe to clown around making sodas, spraying ladies with chloroform, and doing some wildly inappropriate physical comedy with a recalcitrant mule that sits on his head. One bit of business ended up being trimmed to satisfy a well-known stage producer:

"Lift" Removed

> The scheduled suit for injunction and damages threatened by Flo Ziegfeld against Jos. M. Schenck for the alleged "lift" of a section of "business" created for "The Follies" and employed in that production by W.C. Fields, has been called off, Schenck having voluntarily eliminated that portion of the film from the "Fatty" Arbuckle picture, "His Wedding Night," where the scene was duplicated.
>
> That no intention of piracy existed was made clearly evident by Schenck's prompt action while in addition it was known that Schenck previous to picturing of "His Wedding Night" attempted to locate the source of the scene, understanding it was common property and not created especially for "The Follies" show.
>
> – **Variety,** September 21, 1917

The routine in question was said to have been the *One Man Bar* scene in the bit known as *Trenches on Broadway*.

Longtime comedy cameraman Frank D. Williams, a veteran of Keystone, Sterling, and L-Ko Comedies, had shot the first two Comiques, but left the company under not the

The "interior exterior" of *His Wedding Night's* (1917) Koff & Kramp drugstore at New York's uptown Biograph Studio.

best circumstances:

> **Camera Man Sues Arbuckle**
> Suit was brought against Roscoe Arbuckle, the film star, last week by Frank Williams a motion-picture cameraman, who claims Arbuckle broke his contract with him. The camera man asked for $1, 820.18, in addition to salary which he claims is due him. Williams says that he signed a contract to work for Arbuckle on March 1, 1917, and was discharged June 1917.
> – **New York Clipper,** November 19, 1919

His replacement was George B. Peters, who began his career as a newspaper photographer, and worked for Biograph, Metro, and Clara Kimball Young productions. Peters' experience as an aviator and dangerously filming the 1912 Dayton, Ohio flood while with Selig, suggests that he had the proper stamina for shooting physical comedies. Peters stayed with the unit through 1918's *The Cook*, and then moved on to dramatic features. In the 1920s he shot three Johnny Hines comedy features—*The Brown Derby*, *Stepping Along* (both 1926), and *All Aboard* (1927), but retired in 1931.

A new leading lady was also added in the person of comedy ingénue Alice Mann, who started her career at Lubin Films supporting comics like Davey Don and Billie Reeves in shorts such as *Limberger's Victory* (1915), *Otto the Soldier*, and *Millionaire Billie* (both 1916). After a stint at the Mittenthal Studio in Yonkers for some *Heinie & Louie* shorts, she joined the comedy unit at Vitagraph and worked with Hughie Mack and Jimmy Aubrey in outings like *Hash and Havoc* (1916) and *Rips and Rushes* (1917) under Larry Semon's direction. Her best known work is the three Comique shorts with Roscoe—*His Wedding Night*, *Oh, Doctor*, and *Coney Island* (all 1917). Following these, she sporadically appeared in mostly independent features on the order of *Scrambled Wives* and *The Family Closet* (both 1921) until 1925.

Among the supporting people is Emma Reed, a chubby black actress, who comes into the drugstore asking for make-up and is given charcoal. New York-based in the teens, Reed has been spotted in the recently rediscovered unfinished Bert Williams *Lime Kiln Club Field Day* rushes that were shot by Biograph in 1913. Later locating to the West Coast, she played Farina's mother in three *Our Gang* shorts: *Saturday's Lesson* (1929), *The First Seven Years*, and *When the Wind Blows* (both 1930).

Exhibitors Herald (September 8, 1917): "With pleasant memories of 'The Butcher Boy,' 'His Wedding Night' is something that might well be anticipated with expectancy. The production might be best described as being a 'scream' from beginning to finish."

Moving Picture World (September 8, 1917): "This comedy will get a laugh out of everyone."

Oh, Doctor!

Released September 30, 1917. Paramount-Arbuckle Comedy No. A-3105. Produced by Joseph Schenck for the Comique Film Corp. Distributed by Paramount. Directed and written by Roscoe Arbuckle. Scenario by Jean Havez. Scenario editor Herbert Warren.

Gag shot of Roscoe and Buster Keaton medicating Edward Earle in *Oh, Doctor!* (1917).

Photography by George Peters. Two reels. Extant: LOB. With Roscoe Arbuckle, Buster Keaton, Alice Mann, Al St John, Joe Bordeaux. (Filmed at the uptown Biograph Studio at 807 East 175 Street in New York; and at Coney Island amusement park.)

Roscoe is a well-to-do doctor who takes his wife and annoying son to the horse races. He meets a pretty woman sitting next to him and to flirt with her he distracts his wife by sticking his son with a pin. He overhears Al, the woman's boyfriend, make a "sure bet" on the race, and does one of his own. Their horse not only is last but runs in the wrong direction. Dejected the family returns home, where Roscoe vents all his frustrations on his son. Meanwhile the mysterious lady and Al hatch a scheme to take advantage of Roscoe. Since he gave her his card she calls him and gets him to come over. On the way Roscoe sees a man selling an antibacterial soap on a street corner that is billed as "eliminating the need for doctors." He gets out of his car and rolls it into the crowd, then passes out his business card to the injured.

When he finally shows up at the woman's apartment, he mixes them drinks out of his doctor's bag as a remedy to her "illness." While this is happening Al shows up at Roscoe's house and steal his wife's necklace. This is observed by the son who follows in pursuit when Al takes it on the lam. The woman gets Roscoe to make another bet, and while he's gone Al brings her the necklace which the son sees and calls his mother. Roscoe returns while Al and the woman are packing to run, and at the same time Roscoe's wife shows up for her necklace. Roscoe hides in the kitchen where he finds a policeman's uniform. The shady lady and the wife tussle for the necklace, with the wife ending up locked in a closet. Roscoe comes out disguised as a cop and chases Al up to the roof, etc. The wife gets loose, gets back the necklace and runs into Roscoe. Sonny shows up with real cops in tow. The crooks try to take it on the lam, but are nabbed. Roscoe finds out that the bet he made is winner, and when he shows up to claim his winnings in the cop uniform he empties the place out. All alone he helps himself to the available money, but is taken in hand by his wife and dragged home.

Roscoe gets chummy with the vamp in an exhibitor ad for *Oh, Doctor!* (1917).

This film was lost for many years and turned up around 2002 thanks to Serge Bromberg and Lobster Films. It's a very unusual Arbuckle production in that Roscoe is not at all likeable. He mistreats his wife and son, slams his car into innocent pedestrians, and is ready to make time with a woman of questionable background. This character is completely callous—in sharp contrast to the regular fun-loving and innocent Fatty, so it seems that perhaps Roscoe wanted to try something a bit different and more sophisticated. There is also a very convoluted and complicated plot (i.e. the long synopsis), made up of elements from domestic and crime dramas.

While not entirely engaging due to the main character's lack of appeal, it's a very handsome production—very well shot and edited—and benefits from much location work in New York. The atmospheric scene of Al and the vamp trying to sneak out through a back alley almost looks like something out of D.W. Griffith's *The Musketeers of Pig Alley* (1912). The exterior scene of the soap salesman and crowd was shot outside the uptown Biograph studio in the Bronx. Buster is very funny and takes much abuse as the annoying kid, and Al is perfect as the shady and excitable grifter.

Exhibitors Herald (October 20, 1917): "Roscoe (Fatty) Arbuckle in his role of Doctor I.O. Dine, in his latest production, is funny. Many of the situations are time-worn, but portrayed by this inimitable fat man they should bring laughs wherever the film is shown. Mr. Arbuckle has surrounded himself with a cast that appreciates humor, and plenty of it has been injected in this picture.

"Undoubtedly exhibitors will find that this picture will cause as many laughs as any of Mr. Arbuckle's previous farces."

Moving Picture World (September 29, 1917): "Paramount's weightiest comedian, Roscoe 'Fatty' Arbuckle, has been caught in the toils of a beautiful but unscrupulous vampire, accomplice of a crook. But luckily, this only occurs in 'Oh, Doctor!' a Paramount-Arbuckle comedy which will be released following 'His Wedding Night.'

"The susceptible individual is Dr. I.O. Dine, otherwise Mr. Arbuckle, and the character gives 'Fatty' one of the greatest laugh-getting parts he has been called to play in some time."

Fatty at Coney Island

Released October 29, 1917. Produced by Joseph M. Schenck for the Comique Film Corp. Distributed by Paramount Pictures. Directed by Roscoe Arbuckle. Photographed by George Peters. Edited by Herbert Warren. Two reels. Extant: Friuli, GEM, LOB, BFI, UCLA, DAN, Berk, ACAD, EYE. With Roscoe Arbuckle, Alice Mann, Al St John, Buster Keaton, Agnes Neilson, James Bryant, Joe Bordeaux.

At the beach Fatty endeavors to get away from his hen-pecking wife and does this by burrowing into the sand and watching her maneuvers by using a pipe as a periscope. After she is out of the way he heads for the Coney Island rides and arcade, where he meets a girl. Getting rid of her date they take a ride on the chutes and get a good dunking. Deciding to go in swimming, Fatty is unable to get a suit big enough for him, but he manages to steal a large one belonging to a fat woman. Thanks to the suit and some long curls he pretends to be a woman and becomes a favorite with the men. Wifie appears, still looking for her errant

Luna Park makes a nice backdrop for Alice Mann and Roscoe in *Fatty at Coney Island* (1917). Billy Rose Theatre Division, the New York Public Library for the Performing Arts.

husband, and soon figures out why the fat woman looks so familiar. Finally everything hits the fan, and Fatty and the girl's rival end up in jail after the cops get involved.

Coney Island is one of Roscoe's most commonly seen films. Thanks to Keaton's presence it's often included in repertory screenings and is bountiful on YouTube. Perhaps the ultimate in Arbuckle's series of beach/amusement park shorts that includes *Mabel's New Hero* (1913), *A Bath House Beauty*, *The Sea Nymphs*, *Zip the Dodger* (all 1914), *Fatty and Mabel at the San Diego Exposition* (1915), *A Reckless Romeo* (1917), and *The*

Cook (1918), the Coney locations, such as the Wild Waves ride and Shoot the Chutes, are well-used in the comedy stunts, and become like characters in the film. Roscoe also has one of his longest and most involved drag sequences, and also repeats the gag of asking the camera to tilt up so he can remove his trousers. Al and Buster, who is seen broadly laughing, clapping, and crying, give some of their most energetic support, and Joe Bordeaux and Jimmy Bryant chip in with multiple roles.

Agnes Neilson is one of the film's chief assets as Roscoe's virago of a wife. Having made her Arbuckle debut in *A Reckless Romeo*, she provided yeoman's service as well in *The Butcher Boy* and *The Rough House*, and could be always counted on to provide the proper

Al St John and his "lady friend" snuggle in *Fatty at Coney Island* (1917).

amount of menace to develop the needed comic tension. She was said by Minta Durfee to have been an old friend from vaudeville, and although plain and small she excelled at playing domineering wives and mother-in-laws. Having been part of the Neilson Sisters, a singing and dancing act that toured from 1894 to 1920, she was based on the East Coast and became a regular in Roscoe's Eastern-made Sennett and Comique shorts.

She also appeared in Billy West's New Jersey-shot *The Goat* (1917), some of Victor Moore's eastern Klever Komedies such as *Adam and Some Eves* (1918), and Minta Durfee's starring 1920 shorts for Truart Pictures. She also turned up in the features *The Girl Who Didn't Think* (1917), Marion Davies' *April Folly* (1920) and *Insinuation* (1923). Later focusing on the stage, she had small parts in Mae West's *Diamond Lil* (1928) and *The Jayhawker* (1934) with Fred Stone. At the time of her death in 1936 she was in rehearsals for the WPA Theatre Project's "Living Newspaper" production *Crime*.

Most of the circulating prints of *Coney Island* end with Roscoe and Al coming out of the police station and swearing off women. At that point a cute woman walks by and Al says "Every man for himself" and follows her off. Roscoe stands there surprised for a moment until another woman comes by and he then follows her. This is where the usual version ends but in the original cut (seen courtesy of Lobster Films) Roscoe follows the woman but when he gets up to her he finds out that she's black, which causes him to do a big reaction and run off. This original racist button gag was most likely trimmed when the film was recirculated in the 1960s and 1970s.

Motography (January 19, 1918): "A big hit, with one laugh after another."

Photoplay (February, 1918): "His latest Paramount outgiving 'Fatty at Coney Island' is typical of his form of elephantine joy. His success is due, less to situations and novel stunts, than to his clever capitalization of his physical peculiarity. His smooth, bland childlike countenance never fails to awake a reflected smile."

Motion Picture Magazine (March 1918): "Very suggestive. We took it off the program after the first show. Not fit for ladies and children in a high-class theater. A splendid picture for downtown but not in a neighborhood house."

A Country Hero

Released December 10, 1917. Produced by Joseph M. Schenck for the Comique Film Corp. Distributed by Paramount Pictures. Directed by Roscoe Arbuckle. Photographed by George Peters. Edited by Herbert Warren. Two reels. Extant: Buch.With Roscoe Arbuckle, Al St John, Buster Keaton, Alice Lake, Joe Keaton, Natalie Talmadge.

In the berg of Jazzville Fatty and Cy Klone, the garage owner, are rivals for the affections of the pretty school teacher. A city slicker comes to town and unites the two rivals in a common cause against him when he tries to steal the school teacher from them. The stranger takes the girl to the city and there he is followed by Fatty and Cy who finally rescue her from the unscrupulous villain.

At the writing of this book *A Country Hero*, along with *The Sheriff* and *A Desert Hero*, is an unavailable film. Although there have been rumors of material existing in foreign archives so far nothing has turned up, but since rarities like *Oh, Doctor!* (1917), *The Cook* (1918), and *Camping Out* (1919) have resurfaced, there's still hope.

Alice Lake gets courting in stereo from Roscoe and Al St John in *A Country Hero* (1917). Courtesy Marc Wanamaker/Bison Archives.

After the shooting of *Coney Island* Roscoe and the company headed out West, and would stay in California for the rest of the series. Space was obtained at the Balboa Studio in Long Beach, where a country town, called Jazzville, was built. Not only was the town built but a good deal of it was said to have been demolished in an elaborate stunt where an auto collided with a train. Roscoe told the March 1918 *Motion Picture Magazine*:

> We wrecked two Ford cars getting this incident—no this is not another new Ford story—and had the cars completely demolished in a wreck with a real locomotive which also drew a large salary for accommodating us by thwarting the villain's dark designs. That part of the comedy cost us thousands of dollars because of the necessity of going over certain parts time and time again. This picture probably made greater demands on our exchequer than any we have made in some time.

Other elaborate aspects of the film included a big masquerade party and a free-for-all in a nightclub where furniture is smashed and Roscoe uses an upright piano as a giant club. An item from the December 8, 1917 *Moving Picture World* describes that action scene not going quite as planned:

Roscoe and Alice Lake have a quiet moment with some ducks in *A Country Hero* (1917). Courtesy Marc Wanamaker/Bison Archives.

Roscoe's Breakaway Didn't Break

In filming a scene recently for "The Country Hero," which is being staged at the Balboa studio in Long Beach, "Fatty" Arbuckle had two chairs and an upright piano broken over him while carrying on a stage fight with five men. The furniture was of the "breakaway" type, but, as frequently happens, it failed to break properly and Arbuckle was nearly knocked out. The camera kept grinding out the scene, however, and no one suspected the comedian was hurt. As he is his own director, and instigator of most of his scenarios, he continued to fight, continued to direct and continued to be funny, although he was reeling from the blow. When the scene had been finished Arbuckle was led to the studio hospital and treated for a contusion the size of a hen's egg which had appeared on his head.

Alice Lake rejoined the outfit, and not only is *A Country Hero* the first Comique shot in California, it was also the film debut of Joe Keaton, the irascible real-life father of Buster Keaton. One-third of the famous vaudeville act The Three Keatons, Joe generally didn't like the movies, and is quoted as saying in horror to William Randolph Hearst, when the newspaper magnate proposed to bring the Keatons to the screen in a 1913 series based on the comic strip *Bringing Up Father*— "We work for years perfecting an act, and you want to show it, a nickel a head, on a dirty sheet?"

Joe did like Roscoe, and was talked into doing this short where he's said to have demonstrated his legendary high-kicking prowess. When asked if he liked movie-making in the May 3, 1918 issue of *Variety* Joe groused:

> Oh, it's all right if Arbuckle wouldn't tell me how to kick my boy. Shucks (or its equivalent), ain't I been kicking him all his life?

Only appearing in pictures directed by Arbuckle or Buster, Joe's other films included *The Bell Boy* (1918), *Neighbors* (1920), *Day Dreams* (1922), *Our Hospitality* (1923), *The Bonehead* (1924), and *The General* (1926). Described as "a hard guy" by his daughter-in-law Eleanor Keaton, Joe passed away at seventy-eight in 1946.

Joe wasn't the only Keaton to work in this missing film. According to the March 1918 *Photoplay* a future member of the Keaton family appeared as well:

> Natalie Talmadge, sister of Norma and Constance, plays with Fatty Arbuckle in "A Country Hero." The young lady is also Arbuckle's private secretary.

Moving Picture World (December 8, 1917): "A two-reel farce comedy, which presents a wealth of amusing slapstick business with many original touches. The comedy is clean and can be easily used on the children's program."

Al St John and Buster Keaton share a holiday exhibitor ad.

Motography (March 30, 1918): "All I have to do is advertise the night and Arbuckle fills the empty seats."

Moving Picture World (December 8, 1917): "It is extremely funny and remarkable as it may seem to those who have been forced to yawn at the monotony of old tricks this comedy has actually discovered one or two new ones."

1918

Out West

Released January 20, 1918. Produced by Joseph M. Schenck for the Comique Film Corp. Distributed by Paramount Pictures. Directed by Roscoe Arbuckle. Scenario by Natalie Talmadge. Photographed by George Peters. Edited by Herbert Warren. Two reels. Extant: MoMA, LOB, ACAD, EYE. With Roscoe Arbuckle, Al St John, Buster Keaton, Alice Lake, Bill Hauber, Joe Keaton.

Fatty is a tramp stowing away in the water tank of a freight train travelling through the desert. Stealing the train men's breakfast from the caboose gets him chased and thrown off

Roscoe surveys his isolation in 1918's *Out West*.

the train in the middle of nowhere. In nearby Mad Dog Gulch things are rocking at the Last Chance Saloon. Bill Bullhorn is the owner of the saloon and has a hard time keeping the gamblers and bandits like Wild Bill Hiccup in line.

Back out in the desert Fatty is suffering fom extreme thirst—he's literally spitting cottonballs and seeing mirages. After drinking the entire contents of a watering hole he's attacked by hostile Indians. Running from the redskins, Fatty falls down a cliff and tumbles into the saloon just in time to rout Wild Bill and his desperados. Bill Bullhorn, impressed with Fatty's gun-slinging prowess, hires him to work in the saloon as the bartender.

When a young black shoeshine boy is tormented and made to dance by the cowboys in the bar, he is protected by a Salvation Army girl that Fatty takes a shine to. Wild Bill Hiccup and his gang decide to return and when the bandit starts manhandling the Salvation Army girl both Fatty and Bill Bullhorn shoot him and break bottles over his head to no effect. They find out that he's ticklish and get rid of him by tickling him senseless.

Still out for revenge, Hiccup lassoes and kidnaps the girl with Fatty in hot pursuit. Taking her to his deserted shack he tries to make her drink, when she throws it in his face Fatty sneaks in and tickles him. Getting the girl out, Fatty then pushes the shack off the side of a cliff, which finally puts Wild Bill out of commission. Fatty and the girl have a final embrace.

With the move to California it was a no-brainer that Roscoe would soon revisit western subjects like *Ben's Kid* (1909) and *Fatty and Minnie Hee-Haw* (1914). The western town set, called Mad Dog Gulch, was built in a small canyon near Long Beach, California, and the production took six weeks, including the location work in the desert.

The resulting short is an anything-for-a-laugh western spoof with lots of cartoon gags, such as Roscoe literally spitting cottonballs when he's dry in the desert, and the hands of the saloon's clock jumping to 12 when Hiccup orders everyone in the saloon

Roscoe suffers from a mirage in *Out West* (1918).

to put up their hands. Joe Keaton and Bill Hauber from Keystone days show up in small parts in the train opening, and everyone seems to be having a great time, particularly Al St John, who's a completely indestructible villain until it's discovered that he's ticklish. One sequence that's difficult for modern audiences to view is where the black shoeshine boy is tormented in the saloon. Black stereotypes and the abuse of black characters regularly turned up in films of the silent era, especially comedies, and other examples in Roscoe's films include *Zip the Dodger*, *That Minstrel Man* (both 1914), *His Wedding Night* (1917), the original ending of *Coney Island* (1918), and the talkie *Pete and Repeat* (1931) which starred the blackface team of Bud Harrison and Peenie Elmo. Of course every ethnicity was fair game in the silent days, but it's still unsettling to see these moments today.

Due to Roscoe's extreme popularity his return to the West Coast started something of a bidding war among the local communities to host a studio for the company:

> *Since it has been announced that Roscoe Arbuckle is looking for a studio site, practically every city of any size in Southern California has been confronting his office with offers. Santa Ana started first with an exceptionally attractive offer, and up to date it leads the field because of a more definite and concrete proposition. They will erect a studio to cost $100,000, to be used solely for the Comique Film Corporation, of which Joseph M. Schenck is president and Roscoe Arbuckle, vice-president. Architects and engineers are working on the plans for the Santa Ana Chamber of Commerce, and will be presented to Arbuckle this week. Delegations of business men from Long Beach, where Arbuckle is located; from Santa Ana who hope to get him, and from Redlands, Riverside and Anaheim, who are also in the race, will attempt this week to prove to the satisfaction of Arbuckle exactly why he should take up a permanent residence in their city. Although Jacksonville, Florida is too far away to send a delegation, with their usual progress they have kept the wires warm with their messages, and have made several alluring offers.*
>
> – **Motion Picture News**, March 9, 1918

Things didn't work out for Santa Ana, Redlands, Riverside, Anaheim, or even Jacksonville. After moving around from Balboa, Diando, and Henry Lehrman's new studio, Comique finally established a facility in Culver City in 1919. But only *The Hayseed* (1919) and *The Garage* (1920) would be shot there before Roscoe moved into features.

At the beginning of 1918, W.H. Productions, a state rights outfit owned in part by former Mutual president Harry Aitken, began reissuing earlier Keystone shorts, including a large swatch of Roscoe's comedies (see Appendix One). Often re-titled to suggest new films, the older Arbuckle shorts were particularly popular and other outfits soon followed suit, leading Roscoe to end up competing with himself.

When Roscoe and company moved to California Joe Schenck's business manager Lou Anger came along with the unit as their business manager. As mentioned before it was Anger who introduced Roscoe and Buster Keaton, as he had known the Keatons in vaudeville. Born in Philadelphia in 1878, Anger entered showbusiness in burlesque as a "Dutch" comedian with various partners. Playing broad stereotypes of German characters

Portrait of former vaudevillian and Arbuckle studio manager Lou Anger. Billy Rose Theatre Division, the New York Public Library for the Performing Arts.

came easy to Anger since his father was from Prussia and his mother Bavaria. In 1908 he struck out as a solo with a monologue act called *The German Soldier*, which was billed as "a humorous satire on war topics." This was pretty successful until the start of World War I, when he changed the act to *The Neutral Soldier* and described what would happen after the war.

He also appeared in stage musicals such as *The Gay Hussars* (1910) and *The Honeymoon Express* (1913) where he worked with the likes of Al Jolson, Fanny Brice, and Gaby Deslys. During the run of *The Gay Hussars* he met and married singer Sophye Barnard. They toured together in an act, but in 1916 he moved to the business end when he began working for Joe Schenck. Over the next thirty years he would be business manager for the Arbuckle company, and then the Buster Keaton company, produce a few comedy shorts with Clyde Cook, become active in California real estate, and work for Schenck at United Artists. Always a strong supporter of Roscoe, Anger died in Hollywood in 1946, and was vice-president of United Artists at the time of his death.

Motography (February 9, 1918) "Fatty Arbuckle's latest is a dashing, slashing, shooting tale of the west. Fatty literally falls in on an isolated town in the Western desert and routs the bandit who is about to loot the place. The bartender is shot in the fight and Fatty gets his job. His quickness with the gun and ability to shoot gains him the respect of the townsmen.

"This is bound to be a sure fire hit. It is a departure from what the big comedian has done in the past, and its burlesque on the familiar dance hall with its two-gun man, made even the sometimes hard-hearted and unrelenting reviewers and critics laugh. When this can be done the subject must, indeed, be a humorous one."

Motion Picture News (February 9, 1918): "In 'Out West' Fatty Arbuckle offers a burlesque on the Western melodrama that possess many laughable features. William S. Hart is the main target of Arbuckle's comedy. For instance, he rolls a cigarette in one hand with miraculous ease and rapidity, volunteers to reform for the sake of a Salvation Army lassie and proceeds to rescue her at the last moment from the villain, Heartless Bill, by tickling him into unconsciousness. These points and additional clever burlesque on the 'typical' barroom scene make for the general good of the comedy."

Variety (January 25, 1918) "'Out West' is the newest Fatty Arbuckle comedy and hits a better comedy tempo than any of his recent productions. 'Out West' is really a satire on the typical western photodrama with its lively café dance halls, gun play, etc.

"Good camera work aids the comedy."

The Bell Boy

Released March 18, 1918. Produced by Joseph M. Schenck for the Comique Film Corporation. Distributed by Paramount Pictures. Directed by Roscoe Arbuckle. Photographed by George Peters. Edited by Herbert Warren. Two reels. Extant: CNC, LOB, FRANC, ACAD, NAZ, ITAL. With Roscoe Arbuckle, Buster Keaton, Al St John, Alice Lake, Joe Keaton, Charles Dudley.

In the community of Ouch Gosh, Pennysyltuckey Fatty and Buster are bell boys at the Elk's Head Hotel. Making their life difficult is Al, who is combination manager, hotel clerk, and transportation head. Busy in the lobby with their cleaning chores, a demonic-looking gentleman comes in and frightens the boys, but it turns out that he just wants a haircut and shave. Since Fatty also fills in as barber, he takes care of him—with some well-placed snips

Alice Lake gets familiar with Roscoe to Al St John and Buster Keaton's amazement in *The Bell Boy* (1918). Courtesy Mike Hawks.

turning him into different famous people. First he's Ulysses S. Grant, then Abraham Lincoln, and finally Kaiser Wilhelm, which causes Fatty to slap him in the face with shaving cream.

A new group of guests arrive at the hotel, including a cute manicurist. The boys vie for her attentions, with Buster winning out. Problems with the elevator propel the manicurist to the top of the Elk's head high up on the lobby wall. Fatty and Buster come to the rescue, but when Buster's pants are snagged on the Elk's antlers Fatty leaves him to hang there while he takes Alice out for a buggy ride.

The hotel has its regular Saturday night dance. Fatty's all dolled up to impress Alice, and enlists the aid of Buster and Al to pretend to rob the local bank, so Fatty can stop them and be the hero. They hadn't counted on real robbers hitting the bank at the same time, and Buster and Al have a hard time fighting off the crooks. When Fatty comes in to "save the day" he joins the battle with the real thugs, who are finally routed thanks to the hotel trio. Fatty turns out to be a real hero, and wins Alice's admiration.

The Bell Boy was Roscoe's eighth Comique and is one of the most frequently shown today, a regular item in the numerous Buster Keaton festivals of the past few decades. By this time the unit was a well-oiled machine, giving Roscoe the freedom to riff on any subject that popped into his head. *The Bell Boy* in particular is like a grand slapstick ballet, with Roscoe, Buster, and Al trying to see who can outdo the other in stunts and falls. The film breaks down into big physical comedy setpieces—such as Roscoe giving Charles Dudley his transformational shave (a spoof of vaudeville celebrity imitation acts), the gag sequence with the stalled elevator and elk's head, and the big, climatic bank robbery free-for-all. An appreciation of the type of sight gags that were the stock-in-trade for Roscoe and his contemporaries to make audiences laugh was penned in the September 1918 issue of *Photoplay*:

> *Any tired business man will chuckle himself into state bordering on hysteria at the sight of a plate of hot soup overturned on an unsuspecting victim's head or a close-up of somebody else's silk hat overflowing with water or broken eggs. "Fatty" Arbuckle used both of these in "The Bell Boy" as he has in many other two-reelers. They have been favorites with Chaplin and in the Sennett comedies.*
>
> *Sliding or falling unexpectedly on a slippery floor or pavement is another accident which audiences like to see. Chaplin made his tobogganing on a hardwood floor a large percentage of the action in "One A.M." He did it, too, in "Shanghaied" and "The Immigrant." "Fatty" Arbuckle knows how funny he looks when he slides and had the floors well covered with soapy water when he made portions of "The Rough House" and "The Bell Boy."*

In later years silent comedy performers and directors never talked much about the "tricks of their trade"—preparations or techniques that were used behind the scenes to create maximum comic effect in the cinemas. They generally kept to themselves on things like wire work, oiling or soaping streets to make cars skid during chases, and undercranking—cranking the camera slower so less film was exposed, which meant the action on screen would be faster. Undercranking in particular was an important tool, as complicated or

Charles Dudley gives Roscoe and Buster Keaton the devil in a lobby card for *The Bell Boy* (1918).

dangerous physical routines or stunts could be performed in a measured tempo but would appear to be lightning paced when shown. This insured the clean timing and precision that are hallmarks of American silent comedy.

A new addition to the Comique acting ensemble is the imposing, six-foot tall Charles Dudley. Roscoe takes advantage of his physical presence, having him look like the devil himself, which quickly turns around with his "nancy" gestures and posturing. Dudley was born in Arizona in 1883, and started his career on stage in comic opera, including Gilbert & Sullivan shows. In 1913 he left the stage because of vocal problems and made his film debut for the Balboa Company in Long Beach. He worked on and off for Balboa for many years, and was comfortable switching back and forth between dramatic and comedic roles. He also spent time at L-Ko, Fox, and Century Comedies in slapstick shorts like *Cupid in a Hospital* (1915), *Roaring Lions on the Midnight Express* (1918) and *Oh! Nursie* (1923), plus was support in dramatic features that included *Steelheart* (1921), *Purple Riders*, and *The Fighting Guide* (both 1922) before leaving films in 1924.

An important, but overlooked, member of Roscoe's Comique Comedy crew was scenario department head Herbert Warren. Starting his career in vaudeville in 1907, he toured as a performer with the Valerie Bergere Company. Bergere was a popular stage actress who had starred in David Belasco's famous production of *Madame Butterfly*. Warren was

Au natural portrait of character player Charles Dudley.

leading man for Bergere, and they toured in one-acts such as *Billie's First Love* and *A Bowery Camille*. Warren began writing their playlets, such as *Don't Walk in Your Sleep*, and in 1917 became the scenario head on *The Butcher Boy*, Roscoe's first independent production. He stayed with the company through the next ten shorts, leaving after *The Cook*.

Having married Valerie Bergere, Warren's plan was to have his own picture company, to make comedies with a noted comedian, but when this didn't happen he and his wife started touring on stage again. It was announced that they were returning to Hollywood to make movies, but that didn't happen either. For the rest of his career Warren acted in vaudeville, in films, and in the 1930s Broadway plays like *Light Wine and Beers* and *The Guest Room*. While working in New York on the Broadway stage he traveled to Brooklyn and appeared in a number of Vitaphone shorts, sometimes billed as Herb Warren, including *How've You Bean?* (1933) with his former employer Arbuckle. He retired from acting, and nothing is known about him after his registering for the draft in 1942.

Motion Picture News (March 30, 1918): "This two reeler, Roscoe Arbuckle's latest for Paramount, reaches the very heights in this type of comedy which gave him his reputation. There is originality in the gags and plentiful opportunities for both Arbuckle and his excellent supporting team, Buster Keaton and Al St John.

"A better comedy than 'The Bell Boy' would be hard to find and this statement may be taken to include the Chaplins and the Sennetts."

Variety (March 29, 1918): "Roscoe 'Fatty' Arbuckle's latest screen comedy, released this week, 'The Bell Boy,' is excruciatingly funny.

"The rapid, acrobatic comedy of these three slapstick comedians had the audience in hysterics at the Rialto Sunday afternoon."

Moving Picture World (March 30, 1918): "It takes two reels to hold the Paramount-Arbuckle comedy 'The Bell Boy,' but no one will realize this from watching the picture.

"Fatty Arbuckle is a living example of how to be nimble though fat, and his fertility of invention supplies him with the right piece of business for every situation. Al St John as the hotel clerk, Buster Keaton as the assistant bell boy, and Alice Lake as the manicurist are a trio whose acting ability is equaled only by their disregard of life and limb."

Moonshine

Released May 13, 1918. Produced by Joseph M. Schenck for the Comique Film Corp. Distributed by Paramount Pictures. Directed by Roscoe Arbuckle. Photographed by George Peters. Edited by Herbert Warren. Two reels. Extant: MoMA, GEM, NAZ, LOB. With Roscoe Arbuckle, Buster Keaton, Al St John, Alice Lake, Charles Dudley, Joe Bordeaux.

Fatty is a revenue officer, and he and his assistant Buster are sent into the Blue Ridge Mountains of Kentucky to put a stop to illegal traffic in moonshine. Al and his father Charles are the main offenders. Pa in particular has the reputation of being the most daring feudist and moonshiner in the Blue Ridge country. He is a desperate man, but this fact does not dampen the spirit of Fatty and Buster. They have a mission to perform and come what may the trick must be turned.

The arrival of the officers in the neighborhood of the moonshiners causes a sensation and plans are immediately set on to stamp them out. The plotters get the upper hand at the start, but the tricky officers turn the tables and the outlook takes a different hue. Fatty gets distracted from his mission when he falls for Alice, the ragged mountain girl, and practically forgets what he's there for. This enrages Al, the girl's mountain boyfriend, who's determined to get rid of Fatty so he can claim Alice for himself. Fatty finally finds the means to defeat Al and the moonshiners, and also win the hand of Alice.

Alice Lake and Roscoe are sure that Al St John is ready to plug him in *Moonshine* (1918).

Moonshine is Roscoe's first full-out genre spoof—the forerunner of his later classics *The Iron Mule* and *Curses* (both 1925). Taking a chance to do something a bit different is always a tricky proposition, and not long after Roscoe had this to say to the June 1919 *Photoplay* about some of the subtler bits of business in the film:

> *The average person watching a comedy on the screen does not want to be compelled to think—to figure out a piece of business—so that there is always a little hesitancy in dealing with satire and the little subtleties that are enjoyed by clever people.*
>
> *An illustration of satire that didn't "get over" with the masses is furnished by the scene in "Moonshine" of the elaborately furnished underground retreat of the moonshiners. The travesty was carried a little too far. Take again the scene of the moonshiners donning evening clothes for dinner. It "went" great with those that are familiar with social customs and slipped completely over the heads of those who were not. Yet the kids invariably "got it" for they immediately sensed the incongruity of the roughneck mountaineers putting on "soup and fish."*
>
> *But as a piece of business it scored a failure on the whole because it required thought to grasp the satire; somehow it was out of rhythm.*

Another notable bit of business was the trick shot of a score of revenuers endlessly filing out of Roscoe's car. This playing with the camera is a definite forerunner for Buster Keaton's technical gags in *The Playhouse* (1921) and *Sherlock, Jr.* (1924).

To represent the Blue Ridge Mountains setting, Roscoe and company went on location, which didn't work out as smoothly as hoped for:

> **Arbuckle and Company are Marooned on Location**
> *Roscoe "Fatty" Arbuckle and company are still at San Gabriel Canyon, Cal., where for four weeks they have been marooned much of the time, flooded by heavy rains while attempting to make exteriors for the new Paramount-Arbuckle comedy "Moonshine."*
> – ***Motion Picture News***, April 27, 1918

Returning to the fold behind the scenes was Roscoe's old mentor and stage partner Walter C. Reed. After being brought to films by Roscoe (see 1915's *Miss Fatty's Seaside Lovers*), Reed became an assistant director to Edwin Frazee, and ended up part of the stable of directors for Foxfilm Comedies. Following 1917 shorts like *Social Pirates*, *Love and Logs*, and *An Aerial Joyride* he stopped directing and joined the Arbuckle staff:

> *Walter Finnigan Reed, a famous Irish comedian known from one end of the coast, to another as a fun-maker, has been added to the Arbuckle scenario staff, of which Herbert Warren is editor. Fatty and Walter are old partners in musical comedy and the jovial "Finnigan" promises to introduce some of their old stage gags in the Paramount Arbuckle comedies.*

Roscoe taking a break while on location for *Moonshine* (1918).

Motography, March 2, 1918

In the 1920s Reed would continue to be part of Roscoe's brain trust, writing gags as well as playing roles in Reel Comedy and Educational shorts such as *Dynamite Doggie, The Iron Mule, Curses* (all 1925), and *Home Cured* (1926).

Motion Picture Magazine (August 1918): "'Fatty' Arbuckle has as good a time leaping around mountains and hanging perilously over cliffs in this, his newest comedy, as the redoubtable Doug himself. 'Moonshine' is a take-off on Kentucky mountain dramas with their everlasting secret stills. Many deliciously funny and original comedy stunts are

Roscoe and Walter C. Reed during their touring days.

interpolated. For instance when 'Fatty' hangs his side-partner by his toes to dry after his ducking in the rapids. Because of equally funny bits of business, this is the best comedy "Fatty" has done in some time."

Moving Picture World (May 25, 1918): "If the last reel of 'Moonshine' were as full of comic points as the first this Paramount-Arbuckle comedy would have great speed. The picture is an amusing burlesque of the Blue Ridge Mountains of Kentucky, a drama of 'still' life, and 'Fatty' Arbuckle makes a handsome heavyweight revenue officer.

"The locations are picturesque enough for a five-reel feature, and the titles are examples of real wit. Aside from being a complete departure from the usual style of story used for the Arbuckle ribticklers the picture has many mirth-provoking moments."

Good Night, Nurse!

Released July 6, 1918. Produced by Joseph Schenck for the Comique Film Corp. Distributed by Paramount Pictures. Directed by Roscoe Arbuckle. Photographed by George Peters. Edited by Herbert Warren. Two reels. Extant: MoMA, ACAD, LOB, DAN, EYE. With Roscoe Arbuckle, Buster Keaton, Al St John, Alice Lake, Kate Price, Dan Albert.

Fatty is trying to make his way home in a terrible rainstorm after a night out on the town. Having trouble lighting his cigarette in the deluge, he meets another happy pedestrian—happy, but in a sad condition. Fatty gets some stamps and sends the pickled one home parcel post. He finally arrives at home with an organ grinder, a pretty girl dancer, and a monkey he picked up on the way. Ready to party on, his exasperated and long-suffering spouse throws Fatty's new friends out and puts him to bed. The next morning she takes him to a sanitarium for the "cure."

Fatty has a tough time and many weird experiences at the sanitarium. Doctors greet him holding knives dripping with blood, a beautiful patient flirts with him and wants his help, and after he eats a thermometer the staff decides they have to cut it out. Fatty's taken to the operating room and is administered ether. The next thing he knows he's waking up in his room and the pretty girl patient gets him to help her escape. After they finally get outside

The clientele gives Roscoe second thoughts about the No Hope Sanitarium in *Good Night, Nurse!* (1918). Courtesy the Lobster Collection.

she wants to go back in so Fatty gives up on her, and while the staff is combing the grounds for him he puts on the heavy nurse's uniform and flirts with the head doctor. When the nurse suddenly returns from her break the jig is up, and in the ensuing fracas Fatty gets stripped to his shorts and undershirt. Running outside he ends up in a cross-country footrace, and wins the first prize. The staff catch up with him and drag him back to the sanitarium—but at this point he wakes up on the operating table and finds that not only were most of his misadventures an ether dream, but that he's now "cured."

Good Night, Nurse! is probably the most surreal of the Comique comedies. Besides being a re-do of Roscoe's early Selig short *A Robust Patient* (1911), his recent experiences with a nasty leg carbuncle may have possibly fueled some of this nightmarish take on sanitariums. Along the way Roscoe works in his drag routine, recycles a gag with a garden hose from his early Keystone *A Noise from the Deep* (1913), and uses a climatic footrace that would be repeated six years later when he directed Al St John in *Stupid But Brave* (1924). The title *Good Night, Nurse* was a popular one for silent comedy shorts as "Smiling Billy" Mason used it in 1913, Neal Burns in 1916, Alice Howell in 1920, and Lupino Lane in 1929.

The scenes of the sanitarium, its grounds, and the footrace were shot on location. According to the June 8, 1918 *Motography*:

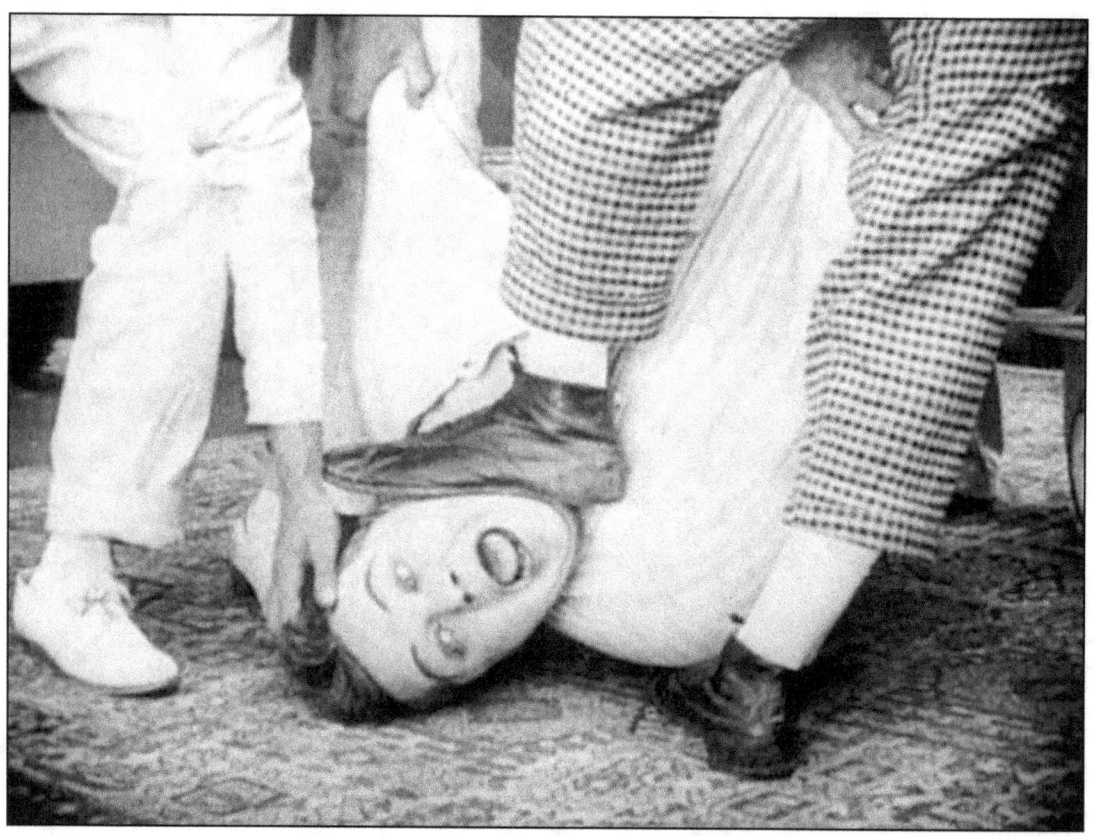

Roscoe getting TLC from the sanitarium staff in *Good Night, Nurse!* (1918).
Courtesy the Lobster Collection.

Accordingly, the portly comedian and his supporting fun creators descended upon Arrowhead Hot Springs, which is just about the most famous health resort in Southern California.

Instead of resting, Fatty immediately plunged into the finishing touches of the picture. With the hundreds of health seekers as "extras," the sanitarium and the mud baths for atmosphere, and the wild mountain scenery for the beauty eye of George Peters, the cameraman, Arbuckle promises to get so much fun out of the sanitarium that you may have to go to a sanitarium after seeing the film.

In addition to the regular Comique crew Irish character comedienne Kate Price is on hand so that Roscoe can wear her clothes as he did in *The Waiter's Ball* (1916). Roscoe's butler/valet (who also doubles as a sanitarium attendant) is played by Dan Albert, an overlooked silent comedy veteran who specialized in bit parts and working behind the scenes as an assistant. His background was the stage and he started his film career at Keystone in 1914. Some of his films are *Dough and Dynamite*, *His Musical Career* (both 1914), *He Wouldn't Stay Down*, and *Court House Crooks* (both 1915). In 1916 he's credited as Charles Parrott's assistant director on *Hearts and Sparks*, and moved over to Hank Mann's unit at Foxfilm

Alice Lake watches Roscoe flirt with Buster Keaton as Kate Price has a moment of déjà vu in *Good Night, Nurse!* (1918). Courtesy Robert Arkus.

Comedies. During a short span he worked at Roach in at least two Stan Laurel comedies, *Hoot Mon!* and *No Place Like Jail* (both 1918), at Comique with Roscoe, and was employed at L-Ko in 1919 when he died at age twenty-nine of meningitis.

Motion Picture News (July 6, 1918): "'Good Night, Nurse,' Fatty Arbuckle's latest picture, is varied and contains a great amount of excellent comedy. The opening scenes are some of the funniest he has ever given the screen. A heavy wind and rain storm is raging and Fatty is out in it trying to run between the rain drops. His constant attempts to light a cigarette in the downpour are uproarious and the gags that the wind and wet provided are surprisingly natural as well as funny. The scene then shifts to a sanitarium where Buster Keaton is the physician in charge. He makes his appearance with a knife dripping molasses. Fatty thinks it's blood. Under the effects of ether he indulges in a thoroughly funny nightmare. Keaton and Al St John are in evidence through the hospital scenes and Alice Lake as the 'nut' is cute. 'Good Night, Nurse' ranks well up in the list of Arbuckle comedies."

Moving Picture World (July 6, 1918): "There are plenty of laughs all through both of the two reels of this release, not so much at the farcical incidents as at Arbuckle's characterization. Really an acrobat of great natural strength, in spite of his rotundity, a born comedian as well, the mere contrast of his physique with the role of a sanitarium patient evokes laughter, and his antics do the rest.

"Arbuckle's efforts to light a match in a driving rain storm while under the influence of liquor, his good-natured submission to adverse circumstances, his boyish face and manner, above all, his keen sense of humor, compel laughter from the first. He tears along through ridiculous incidents from then on like a baby elephant out for a romp and careless of consequences. The story is naturally funny, one of the few of its kind, and it will prove a welcome relief to those which labor hard without spark of real humor in them. A winner."

The Cook

Released September 15, 1918. Produced by Joseph M. Schenck for the Comique Film Corp. Distributed by Paramount Pictures. Directed by Roscoe Arbuckle. Photographed by George Peters. Edited by Herbert Warren. Two reels. Extant: DAN, EYE, NOR, GEM, LOB. With Roscoe Arbuckle, Buster Keaton, Al St John, Alice Lake, John Rand, Bobby Dunn, Luke.

Fatty is the cook at a beachside café and Buster is the waiter. Buster gets in trouble with the café owner when he tries to make time with Alice the pretty cashier. Fatty and Buster spend most of their time tossing food orders to each other, in between Fatty flipping knives, bouncing eggs, and getting all the food items out of the same mysterious pot. The floor show with an Egyptian dancer sends Buster, and then Fatty, off into their own versions. Fatty, wearing pots and pans, does the full Salome routine, even having an asp (a link of weenies) bite him for the climax. Everyone in the place wildly applauds as the large chef takes multiple curtain calls.

Tough thug Al descends on the café and forcibly makes Alice dance with him. The owner, Buster, and Fatty are unable to take care of the yegg, but luckily Fatty's dog Luke comes to the rescue and chases Al out of the café and across town. Al have been taken care

Bad man Al St John holds up Roscoe, Buster Keaton, Alice Lake, and John Rand (right) in 1918's *The Cook*.

of the restaurant staff enjoys a lunch of spaghetti, and all find their own variations on how to eat it.

In the afternoon everyone heads off to the amusement pier—Fatty and Luke to fish, and Buster and Alice to ride in a goat cart. Troublemaker Al shows up at the park and chases Alice onto the rollercoaster tracks. Finally to get away from him she dives into the ocean. Luke returns to take care of Al again, leaving Fatty and Buster to rescue Alice.

Missing for many years, *The Cook* was initially thought to have been found by Raymond Rohauer in the 1980s. What Rohauer turned up was actually *The Rough House* (1917), which was also lost at the time. Eventually the real *The Cook* was located and preserved in Norway by their Norsk Filminstitutt in 1998, and an English version was made by the George Eastman Museum. A few years later additional footage was discovered at the EYE Filmmuseum in Amsterdam, and in 2003 Milestone Films released on home video an "improved version" that incorporated the new scenes with the original Norwegian material. Since then this has become the "official" version.

Part restaurant comedy and part amusement park romp, *The Cook*'s antecedents include *Fatty's Day Off* (1913), *A Bath House Beauty* (1914), *Fatty and Mabel at the San Diego Exposition* (1915), *A Reckless Romeo*, *Coney Island* (both 1917), and particularly *The Waiter's Ball* (1916). The scenes at the amusement pier were filmed at Long Beach on its famous Long Beach Pike and Silver Spray Pier, and takes good advantage of the Jackrabbit Racer Rollercoaster and Goatland cart rentals. Parts of Harold Lloyd's *Number Please* (1920) and Keaton's *The High Sign* (1921) were also shot there.

One unusual aspect of *The Cook* is the presence of comic character actor John Rand as the owner of the café. Rand is best known for the twenty years he spent working with Charlie Chaplin—from 1915's *The Bank* through *Modern Times* in 1936. Although he's chiefly remembered as part of Chaplin's stock company, in reality he spent a lot of time working all over the silent comedy map. Born in New Haven, Connecticut in 1871, his early days were spent as an acrobatic clown with Adam Forepaugh's Circus, a major three-ring touring circus. He later had a vaudeville act with his wife Lillian Byron, and entered films in 1913.

Before ever working for Chaplin, he appeared at Majestic, Universal, and L-Ko in support of Chester Conklin, Billie Ritchie, and Bobby Fueher (as Universal Ike Jr. and later known as Bobby Ray). Hooking up with Chaplin at Essanay, Rand worked steadily but on and off for Chaplin, so he continued to turn up with other comedy units such as Kalem, George Ovey's Cub Comedies, Larry Semon, and here with Roscoe.

1919 saw him settle in at Mack Sennett Comedies for a few years in shorts such as *When Love is Blind* (1919), *Fickle Fancy* (1920), and *Officer Cupid* (1921), as well as the

Buster Keaton insists that Roscoe have a word with John Rand in *The Cook* (1918).
Courtesy Mike Hawks.

features *Down on the Farm*, *Love, Honor and Behave* (both 1920), and *A Small Town Idol* (1921). Showing up with Chaplin in *The Idle Class* (1921), *Pay Day* (1922), *The Circus* (1928), and *City Lights* (1931), he can also be seen in Fox Sunshine Comedies like *The Two Johns* (1923), the Jack White Comedies *Dizzy Daisy*, *Fast and Furious* (both 1924), *Red Pepper*, and *Baby Blues* (both 1925), and the Biff Comedy *His Taking Ways* (1926). In the sound era he pops up in features, a few Sennett shorts, and his last work in the later 1930s was for Columbia Pictures in shorts with the Three Stooges and Andy Clyde, in addition to their features like 1938's *Blondie*, until his death in 1940.

The rest of the supporting crew consists of the regular Comique rank and file of St John, Alice Lake, and Luke. Buster Keaton was drafted in June of 1918 and was soon sent overseas. *The Cook* would be his last Arbuckle release for a full year—until *Back Stage* in September of 1919. One return to the Arbuckle fold was Roscoe's old Keystone companion Bobby Dunn, who turns up as the kitchen's dishwasher. Often included in the group of "original Keystone Cops," Dunn was born in Milwaukee in 1887. He started in show business at age nine doing high diving stunts. Appearing for many years with Dr. Carver's Diving Horses, it's said that he lost his front teeth, and even an eye, due to repeated impact with water. His glass eye sometimes gave him a cockeyed look, which would often be used for comic effect.

His first films were for Universal's Sterling Comedies in 1914 where he supported Ford Sterling, William Wolbert, and Max Asher. Joining Keystone the next year, he was busy playing cops and being general support, but was finally teamed up with Slim Summerville (see the Summerville section in 1914's *Leading Lizzie Astray*). Bobby soon moved to L-Ko, but then hooked up again with Slim in Fox Sunshine Comedies like *Mary's Little Lobster* and *Pretty Lady* (both 1920).

That same year Dunn began a starring series of Mirthquake Comedies, which were produced by Eddie Lyons and distributed by Arrow. Looking very Chaplinesque, with a little moustache and derby, this series was the peak of his career. It ended in 1924, and he hooked up with Summerville again, this time at Universal, for a year's worth of one-reelers mostly directed by Slim. Titles included *My Little Brother*, *Easy Work*, and *Green Grocers* (all 1924). For the rest of the 1920s Dunn turned up in various shorts and played support in features like *The Thrill Hunter* (1926) and *Neath Western Skies* (1929). The sound era saw him decline to mostly bit roles, frequently at the Hal Roach Studio, where he turns up in *Me and My Pal* (1933), *Tit for Tat* (1935), and *The Lucky Corner* (1936) before his death in 1937.

Moving Picture World (September 14, 1918): "Although the list of dishes concocted by the fat chef in the new Paramount-Arbuckle comedy is a long one, the principal and favorite food served in 'The Cook' by Roscoe Arbuckle is food for laughter. It is not at all necessary to set down all the doings, high jinks and comic stunts that fill the two reels of the comedy with unconfined joy.

"'The Cook' is one of 'Fatty's' best releases."

Exhibitors Herald and Motography (November 23, 1918): "Feature this comedy. It is worth it. Supporting cast is very good. Contains many laughs. Buster Keaton's Salome dance will make any grouch laugh. Kids will stay and see it twice."

Motion Picture News (September 14, 1918): "'The Cook' contains many of the same gags as one of Fatty's previous releases, 'The Waiter's Ball.' It is really a revised edition of this earlier picture, and happily, many of the gags and quips have been improved upon. It is never tiresome what with Fatty and his fine support. Buster Keaton gave a fine performance for his last one, and Al St John and Alice Lake help the fun along. There is a lot of trick juggling, etc., that is always effective."

Scraps of Paper

Released October 1918. A Victory Loan Appeal. Produced by Famous Players-Lasky Corp. and Joseph M. Schenck. Directed by Roscoe Arbuckle. Scenario by Adam Hull. ½ reel. Extant. OTT. With Roscoe Arbuckle, Glen Cavender, Al St John, Monty Banks.

Fatty calls at the palace in Berlin and refuses to be "raused" by the guards. Entering, he confronts the Kaiser and "Clown Quince," asks about their treatment of Belgium and shows them "scraps of paper" from America (Liberty Bonds). They attempt to escape, but are barred by the Italian, English, French and American armies. Fatty introduces "the boys you said were afraid to fight" rising from the midst of the scraps of paper which makes a snowstorm. The Huns plead for mercy.

America entered World War I on April 6, 1917, and soon Hollywood and its denizens were doing their bit for the war effort. Publicity items stated that Roscoe was deemed too overweight to serve, but he still did what he could. The May 11, 1918 *Moving Picture World* reported:

Roscoe tries to reason with the Kaiser (Glen Cavender) and the Clown Quince (Al St John) in *Scraps of Paper* (1918). Courtesy Robert Arkus.

> ***Arbuckle Subscribing Heavily to Loan***
>
> *Roscoe "Fatty" Arbuckle, the motion picture comedian, this week subscribed $50,000 to the third Liberty Loan. This amount is credited to the First National Bank of Long Beach, California, of which team Mr. Arbuckle is a member. This subscription is the comedian's third one, his total in bonds representing a splendid amount. Mr. Arbuckle and his team associates are planning a series of events in Long Beach, boosting the sale of the bonds.*

Besides money from their own pockets, the various studios and performers put out a series of "Liberty Loan Specials," shorts designed to inspire and encourage the populace to buy Liberty Bonds. The films ranged from dramatic subjects with stars such as Lillian Gish, Dorothy Dalton, Sessue Hayakawa, and Norma Talmadge, to more light-hearted fare with Mr. & Mrs. Sidney Drew, Douglas Fairbanks, and Mack Sennett's Keystone crew. The best known of these little propaganda items is Charlie Chaplin's surviving *The Bond* (1918), and also surviving is Roscoe's contribution *Scraps of Paper*.

> *Roscoe "Fatty" Arbuckle has been a busy man during the past few weeks, for, in addition to making the picture "Scraps of Paper," which is his contribution to the National Association's Liberty Loan Committee, he is now nearing the completion of "The Sheriff," his newest comedy for Paramount release.*
> – **Moving Picture World**, October 12, 1918

Unavailable for many years, the short resurfaced in 2005, in an edition that was put out for the Canadian War Loan. Written by Famous-Players Lasky publicity man Adam Hull, Roscoe put aside his schedule, and with his regular actors and crew put together an entertaining split-reeler.

After the war the February 1919 issue of *The Photo-Play Journal* gave an apt summation of Roscoe's contribution to the war effort:

> *The country owes a lot to "Fatty" Arbuckle, the portly comedian. Why? Simply because he kept a big portion of the populace chuckling when real chuckles were needed to offset the depressing effects of the terrorizing war. Such roaring farces as Mr. Arbuckle generally presents surely act as an efficacious boon to many weary souls even in peace time. Throughout the dark belligerency period he offered laugh-provokers and side-splitters galore and many a heart must have become quite immune to aches as a result of witnessing his amusing capers in a variety of funny situations.*

Moving Picture Weekly (September 28, 1918): "Of an entirely different character was the Fatty Arbuckle picture. It was a gem of comedy with the desired effect of creating a determination to buy Liberty Bonds to the extent of one's ability."

Film Daily (September 22, 1918): "Fatty Arbuckle combined a little burlesque comedy with his lesson and showed the Kaiser and his son snowed in by an avalanche of Liberty Bonds, contracting the Kaiser's scraps of paper with the scraps of paper bought by

Having been adopted as their mascot, Roscoe entertains the boys of Company C at San Diego's Camp Kearny. Courtesy Robert S. Birchard.

the American people. At the finish, the Potsdam beasts found themselves halted at each exit by the representatives of the Allied Nations."

The Sheriff

Released November 24, 1918. Produced by Joseph M. Schenck for the Comique Film Corp. Distributed by Paramount Pictures. Directed by Roscoe Arbuckle. Two reels. With Roscoe Arbuckle, Betty Compson, Mario Bianchi (Monty Banks), Ernie "Sunshine Sammy" Morrison, Luke, Mildred Reardon, Glen Cavender (?).

Fatty is a western sheriff who models himself on the exploits of Douglas Fairbanks and William S. Hart, and wants to live up to them at every opportunity. His deputies are Luke, his dog, and Snow Ball, an eight-year old black child. One day when the law keepers are taking a nap a desperado comes into town and kidnaps the local school teacher with whom Fatty is in love. The bad man ties her up in a cabin, and rigs a pistol, so it points at her and will fire when the clock reaches a certain time. Fatty and company trail the bad men to their lair, and the faithful dog burrows his way into the cabin and unties the heroine. It's the villain who receives the fatal shot when the gun goes off, and Fatty proves himself a credit of his

Roscoe in the lobby card for *The Sheriff* (1918).

community as well as to his motion picture heroes.

Over the last three decades many of Roscoe's missing *Comique Comedies* such as *The Rough House, His Wedding Night, Oh Doctor!* (all 1917), *Out West, The Cook* (both 1918), and *Camping Out* (1919) have been found—a number of them by the late Raymond Rohauer in his quest for Buster Keaton's films. The still A.W.O.L. *The Sheriff* reworked the climax from *Fatty's Plucky Pup* (1915) and was remade by Roscoe in 1924 as *The New Sheriff*. The descriptions of the original's western parody suggests a very breezy style with specific spoofs of some of Roscoe's movie contemporaries:

> **Arbuckle Burlesques Confreres**
>
> *Roscoe "Fatty" Arbuckle's newest comedy "The Sheriff," which will be released at an early date under the Paramount trade mark, is said to offer much in entertainment for those who like to laugh. Unlike most of Arbuckle's recent pictures this comedy is straight burlesque, the comedian emulating in a most ludicrous manner Douglas Fairbanks and William S. Hart in a series of astonishing stunts. He climbs a lofty steeple with the characteristic agility of Fairbanks and duplicates the two-gun exploits of Hart.*
>
> – **Moving Picture World**, November 23, 1918

For *The Sheriff* Roscoe moved his operations to the Diando Studio in Glendale, California. The Diando outfit was making the films of Baby Marie Osborne. Originally formed in 1917 as the Lasalida Film Company, it was soon re-organized as Diando, with the name coming from founders Leon Osborne (Baby Marie's papa) and W.A.S. Douglas (the "D" and "O"). Having taken over the old Kalem Studio, besides turning out Baby Marie features like *Captain Kiddo* (1917) and *Daddy's Girl* (1918), they rented out space. Reporter and future Mack Sennett writer A. H. Giebler observed Roscoe at work at the studio in his *Rubbernecking in Filmland* column in the September 28, 1918 *Moving Picture World*:

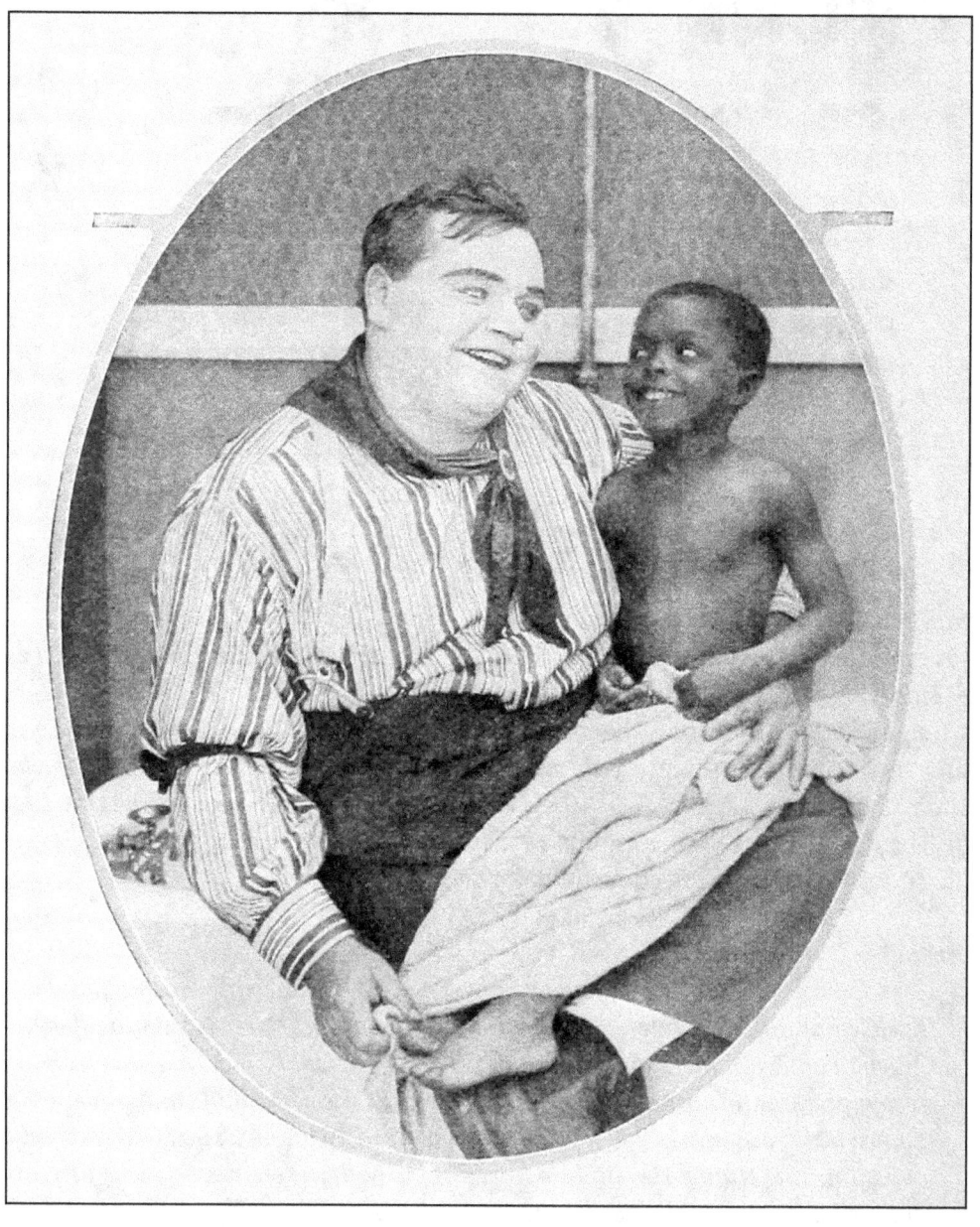

Sunshine Sammy Morrison as Roscoe's sidekick and assistant in *The Sheriff* (1918).

> *Mr. Arbuckle is not a member of the Diando players, but as the studio is very large and Fatty is no infant in size it naturally appealed to him when he was looking around for a place after he left the Balboa Studios at Long Beach.*
>
> *Mr. Arbuckle as you can see is his own director. He not only tells the other players what to do, but gives himself tips on how to be funny and gets away with both propositions.*
>
> *The set represents a school house, and the beautiful blonde at the teacher's desk is Mildred Reardon. Among the bad boys in the seats you will readily recognize Al St John, known wherever people laugh themselves sick at Arbuckle comedies which is equivalent to saying—everywhere.*

Renting the space at Diando gave Roscoe the opportunity to take advantage of and use one of the companies' regular players. The column went on to say:

> *Folks, meet Ernest Theodore Roosevelt Morrison, or Sunshine Sammy, the youngest Afro-American actor in the movies.*
>
> *Little Ernest Theodore is just five years old and has been shining on the screen for over two years. To give you an idea of how important this chap is, he is in two plays at the same time. He has a role in "The Sawdust Doll" with Little Miss Osborne, and at the same time he is supporting Fatty Arbuckle in the comedy being made on the stage we just looked at a minute ago.*
>
> *The elderly colored lady is Sunshine Sammy's grandmother and chaperon. She is very proud of her grandson and wants him to be a preacher when he grows up.*

Best-known today for his films made for producer Hal Roach, Ernest Frederic Morrison was the son of a chef and born in 1912. He entered films in 1917 and got a good deal of attention as the comic relief in the Baby Marie features. In addition to working with Roscoe in *The Sheriff* and supporting May Allison in her Metro Pictures like *Peggy Does Her Darndest* (1919), he appeared in a few shorts of his own, known as the *Sambo* series. The August 24, 1918 *Motion Picture News* reported:

> *The first two-reel Pathé-Diando Comedy featuring the little Negro who is known as Sunshine Sammy has been completed under the direction of Walter McNamara, and is titled "Black Cupid."*

Hal Roach signed him in 1919, making Sammy the first black performer to be signed to a long-term Hollywood contract. Most black players in silent comedies were rarely allowed to do anything but be scared or whip out giant razors, but on the Roach lot Sammy was allowed to be what he really was—a tough, smart kid with an infectious personality and smile. At first his time at Roach was spent giving Snub Pollard, Eddie Boland, Paul Parrott, and even Harold Lloyd a run for their money with his crack comic timing, but in 1922 the producer decided to star the youngster and ended up building *Our Gang* around him.

Starting with *One Terrible Day* (1922) *Our Gang* became the most popular kids series ever made, and Sammy starred in *Gang* classics like *Young Sherlocks* (1922), *The Champeen*, *Dogs of War* (both 1923), *The Buccaneers*, and *Cradle Robbers* (both 1924).

Leaving the Roach organization and movies in 1924, Sammy headlined in his own vaudeville act. Billed as "Sunshine Sammy—Our Gang Star," he sang and danced his way across the country. With the exception of an MGM musical short, *Stepping Along* (1929), Sammy didn't return to the screen until 1940 to spend three years as part of another gang—the *East Side Kids*. After a number of cheaply-made adventures like *Spooks Run Wild* (1941) and *Clancy Street Boys* (1943), he joined the army and entertained the troops during World War II as part of the USO. Later leaving show business, he spent the last part of his life being feted for his contributions to black film history.

Monty Banks fumes as Roscoe serenades senorita Betty Compson in *The Sheriff* (1918).

Besides Sammy, Roscoe had support from his regulars like Luke, as well as Mildred Reardon and Mario Bianchi (more on them in *Camping Out*). Making her only appearance with Roscoe as his leading lady is Betty Compson, who would go on to be a big dramatic star of the 1920s. Eleanor Luicime Compson had a difficult childhood with an indigent father, and it was her study of music that led to a show business career. Playing the violin to silent movies and acts was her entry into vaudeville, which consisted of tours of the West Coast. Returning to Los Angeles, she got an introduction to producer Al Christie, and it wasn't long before she got a name change and became a Christie star. Working with male comics like Eddie Lyons, Lee Moran, and Neal Burns, from 1915 to 1918, Betty starred in shorts like *The Quiet Honeymoon* (1915), *The Deacon's Waterloo*, *Those Primitive Days* (both 1916), *Love and Locksmiths* (1917), and *Betty's Adventure* (1918).

On her own she moved around—this work with Roscoe, a serial, western features, and Baby Marie Osborne's *The Little Diplomat* (1919). What set her feature career on course and really made her a star was *The Miracle Man* (1919), a huge hit which co-starred her with Lon Chaney and Thomas Meighan. During the 1920s some of her better-known pictures were *The Little Minister* (1922), *Paths to Paradise*, *The Pony Express* (both 1925), *The Docks of New York*, and *The Barker* (both 1928). Married to Roscoe's pal and supporter James Cruze, she did his sound film *The Great Gabbo* (1929), but the bulk of her talking appearances were routine and by the mid-1930s she was playing supporting roles. After retiring from films in 1948 she made a few stage appearances, ran a cosmetics business, and also started Ashtrays Unlimited, which supplied personalized ashtrays to hotels and restaurants. She died in 1974.

Moving Picture World (November 16, 1918): "Roscoe Arbuckle may not be as handsome as Bill Hart nor as lithe or svelte-like as Doug Fairbanks, but when it comes to doing stunts he is more than willing to take the chance with either or both of them. In his latest picture, 'The Sheriff,' he shows that his confidence in himself is founded on something more substantial than conceit. Trick riding, steeple climbing, headlong dives out of windows, pistol play, hot-footing it down the pike, love-making—nothing is too swift or daring for the heavyweight comedian.

"The story, written by Roscoe, is a frank admission of the yearning ambition that has been eating at his heart in secret. He has longed to emulate the deeds of the two Apollos of the screen and fill the feminine breast with admiration for a new movie hero. His love scenes with a Mexican belle are models of fervent passion, and it is not his fault if any of the spectators choose to laugh at him. Later on he transfers his affections to a pretty schoolma'am and rescues her from a band of bad men with all the dash and bravery of his rivals, if not with all their grace. A little darkey, who supports the name of Snowball, and a willing and intelligent dog who answers to the name of Luke, do their best to fill Buster Keaton's place, and make a good showing by their efforts. Al St John is as useful as ever."

Variety (November 29, 1918): "All of which may sound very thrilling and melodramatic, but the manner in which it is depicted is ridiculously farcical and certainly laughable."

1919

Camping Out

Released January 5, 1919. Produced by Joseph M. Schenck for the Comique Film Corp. Distributed by Paramount Pictures. Directed by Roscoe Arbuckle. Two reels. Extant: EYE. With Roscoe Arbuckle, Al St John, Mildred Reardon, Mario Bianchi (Monty Banks).

Fatty's wife spends so much time at her Household Duties Club that she's unable to take care of their home and neglects her hubby. When he comes home to their empty house he has to gather cold meals from the icebox. Cobwebs cover the dishes in the sink and, when poor Fatty tries to use the oven a proud house cat and her three kittens emerge. That's the last straw, and Fatty writes a note saying that he's going camping where he can do his own cooking.

Armed with various books about cooking and housekeeping, Fatty boards a steamer for Catalina Island. On the ship Fatty meets annoying husband Al and his neglected wife. After bouts of seasickness, Al gets jealous of his wife's attempts to comfort Fatty, and when he begins to strangle her, Fatty tosses him overboard.

Getting to the island Fatty gets a tent and begins cooking and keeping house. In the meantime his wife has come home to discover that he has eloped to Catalina with her cook

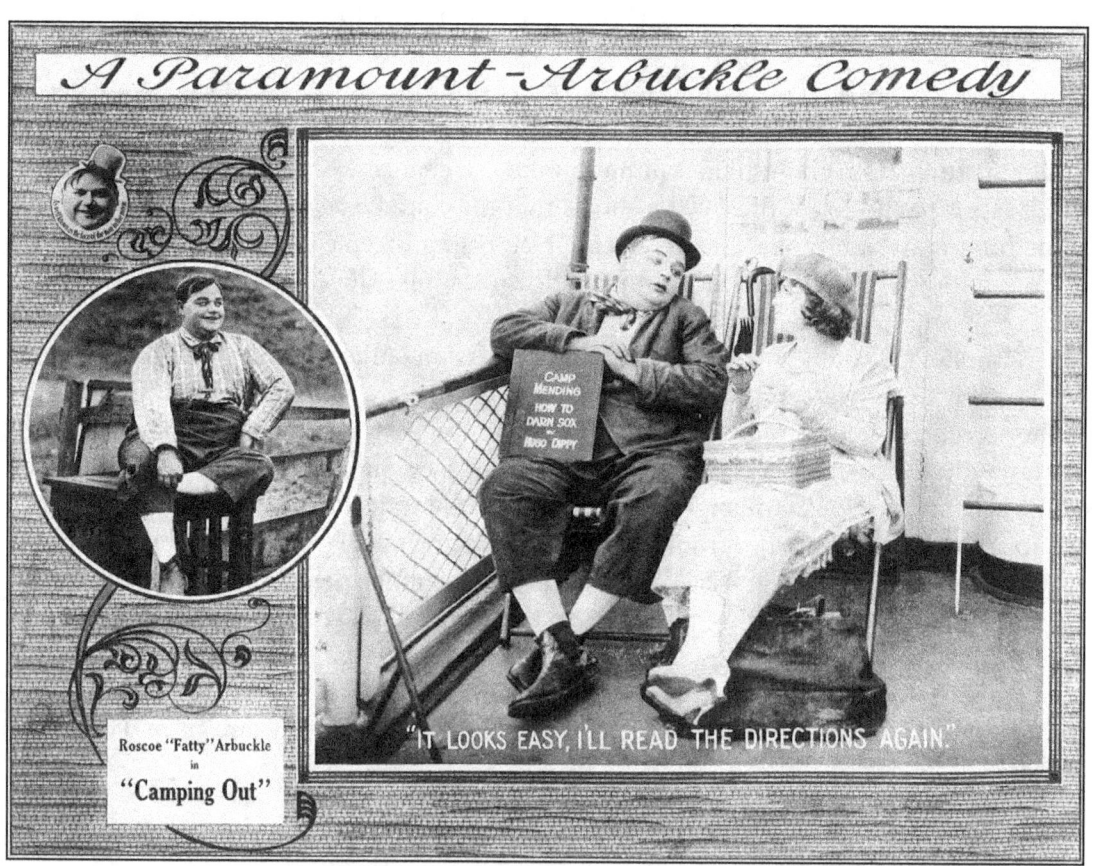

Mildred Reardon and Roscoe share a boat ride to Catalina in *Camping Out* (1919).

books. *Setting off after him, she meets a dejected Al on the Catalina dock. Befriending him, they set out to find their spouses. From the top of a rugged mountain they can see the camp of tents, and observe Fatty and the wife being friendly.*

The deserted wife and the jealous husband charge the camping grounds, and the matrimonial fray is on. Al has at Fatty again, but when the two women start to battle the two husbands escape to the sea in a small boat, and eventually dive overboard.

Having been missing practically since its original release, *Camping Out* was found in 2002. Separate reels turned up at the EYE Filmmuseum in the Netherlands and Italy's Cineteca del Friuli. The preservation, combining of the prints, and final restoration was supervised by Elif Rongen-Kaynakci and Simona Monizza of the Filmmuseum. So far it's played in festivals in Europe and America, but hasn't had a wide release on home video.

The picture's few interior scenes were shot at the Lasky Studio, with most of it being made on location on Catalina Island—in the streets of Avalon, on its dock, and ferry ship. The sea trip inspires a lot of gag material, such as an officer spitting tobacco into the wind from an upper deck. When it hits Roscoe below he assumes it was a "delivery" from the circling sea gulls. Roscoe also takes a cue from Chaplin's *The Immigrant* (1917) for some seasickness gags, but where Chaplin used it for throwaways Roscoe devotes a lot of time to it, developing a whole routine where first Al St John and then Roscoe himself gets ill. Not everyone was happy with this material—censors in places like Spokane, Washington demanded cuts, and some critics carped:

> *He never misses a chance to get in a vulgar or suggestive touch. If it is not a surgeon who has just performed an operation, appearing with his white clothes smeared with blood, or a man trying to get into a woman's bedroom, or peeping into her bath-house, and too conspicuously displayed human forms divine, or mistaking rank cheese for his socks, and so on, it is an exhibition of vomiting from seasickness as in "Camping Out."*
> – **Motion Picture Magazine**, April 1919

Roughing it on the island leads to clothes-line gags similar to those in *Mabel and Fatty's Wash Day*. Al St John plays his usual comic gremlin, as well as a peg-legged old man who rents tents on Catalina. While cooking Roscoe uses the man's peg-leg to make holes in donuts, and to mash potatoes that the comedian has carefully lathered and shaved with his straight razor. Another food gag has Roscoe going to an outdoor market for more supplies. Irritating the owner (Monty Banks) by taking bites out of and rejecting a good deal of the fruit, Roscoe finds that he's forgotten his money so he's kicked out. As he leaves he dumps a watermelon on Bank's head, which causes Monty to retaliate by throwing fruit at Roscoe, who fills his empty basket with the projectiles and gets all that he needs for free. Roscoe would rework this routine in the second reel of his "comeback" short *Hey, Pop!* (1932).

Monty Banks had joined the Comique unit when Buster Keaton had left for the army. As Roscoe was one of the biggest comics of the day Banks' appearances—in *Scraps of Paper*, *The Sheriff*, *Camping Out*, and especially *Love*—gave his burgeoning career a boost. He would go on to be a busy and popular star of the 1920s. Born Mario Bianchi

Mack Sennett visits the *Camping Out* (1919) location on Catalina. Billy Rose Theatre Division, the New York Public Library for the Performing Arts.

in Italy, in 1916 the non-English speaking Bianchi did whatever bits parts he could to break into the movie business. He later credited Roscoe's old mentor Henry Lehrman with being a big help in getting him established. Banks barely survived a stunt he did in an L-Ko Comedy and landed in the hospital. This impressed Lehrman, who let all the other comedy producers know he "could take it." It wasn't long before he was turning up in Triangle and Fox shorts, but a big role in Universal's *The Geezer of Berlin* (1918) got him noticed and may have put him on Roscoe's radar.

During his early days he was variously billed as Mario Bianchi, "Frenchy" Bianchi, or even Mario Bromo, but according to Robert S. Birchard in his 2015 *Monty Banks 1920-1924 Filmography* it was Roscoe who helped the young comic settle on an appropriate screen name:

> Arbuckle told Bianchi he needed to change his name if he was to get anywhere in the picture business, but the actor protested he couldn't change his name because he had just ordered underwear with his initials "MB" embroidered on them. "With all the mountebanks you've been playing," Arbuckle is said to have responded, "you should change your name to Monte Banks, then you wouldn't have to change your underwear." So Mario Bianchi became Monte

Banks first—then shortly thereafter the "Monte" was further modified to "Monty."

Taking a lot of physical punishment in the Arbuckle shorts, Banks followed this up with a stint in some *Bulls Eye Comedies*, and joined the ranks of headliners in 1920 with his own series of *Welcome Comedies* for Warner Brothers. The basic Monty Banks character was a dapper, somewhat pudgy guy always in trouble because of a beautiful woman, and he was busy in two-reelers like *A Rare Bird* (1920), *Squirrel Food* (1921), *F.O.B. Africa* (1922), *Six AM* (1923), and *Wedding Bells* (1924).

By the mid-1920s all the big comics were starring in features so Banks formed his own production company, and with release through Pathé made the leap to full-length films. Doing well with features like *Atta Boy* (1926) and *Play Safe* (1927) Monty relocated to England at the end of the silent era and made a smooth transition to sound as an actor and director. In 1936 he directed comedienne Gracie Fields in *Queen of Hearts* and they soon married. During World War II they moved to Hollywood where Banks directed Laurel & Hardy in *Great Guns* (1941). After the war the couple spent much of their time abroad and Monty passed away, after having been taken ill on the Orient Express, in 1950.

The pretty, down-trodden wife that Roscoe meets on the boat is played by Mildred Reardon, making her last of two appearances with the large comic. Reardon was a former *Ziegfeld Follies* girl, and in addition to working with Roscoe she supported Stan Laurel at the Hal Roach Studio in *Just Rambling Along*, *Hoot Mon* (both 1918), *Hustling for Health*, and *No Place Like Jail* (both 1919). She had a brief vogue in features such as *Number 17* and *Silk Husbands and Calico Wives* (both 1920), with her best known film Cecil B. DeMille's *Male and Female* (1919), but her career petered out and her last appearance was in 1927's *His Rise to Fame*.

Exhibitors Herald (March 12, 1921): "For comedy this exceeds anything I have ever shown. If you want to get the laughs book this picture. Pleased them all."

Moving Picture World (January 25, 1919): "Arbuckle is an acrobat, ingenious, and a fine actor, but he seems to overlook the best part of his own interesting personality, that which always sets an audience laughing, the pure humor of mental revelations.

"This is not to say that 'Camping Out' is not amusing, but it ranks far below other vehicles for Fatty's laughable psychology. He is largely in evidence every moment, and therefore not sufficiently in contrast with other characters to enforce the fun on his own. He does not need this prominence—it would be accorded him without solicitation on his part, and he is so rarely good in comedy of human nature that he ought to give more time to the quality of his medium and less to directing its presentation. He will get more than one laugh in 'Camping Out,' but not near so many as he has received in farces more naturally funny."

Motion Picture Magazine (April 1919): "Roscoe Arbuckle's latest is no better nor worse than his previous releases, and not much different in character. He is the same 'Fatty' in whatever he plays. It will amuse and entertain many thousands and disgust many of them. Not many will go to sleep when 'Camping Out' is on, for it is a continuous performance of funny incidents, mostly of the slap-stick order.

"While I personally seldom get a laugh out of the Arbuckle comedies, and am always stirred hilariously by everything that Chaplin does, some people are affected quite the opposite, because I hear considerable laughter in every theatre where Arbuckle is showing. While there are many clever and ingenious devices and incidents in all the Arbuckle farces, I would say, while Chaplin is a genius, Arbuckle is merely a clown."

The Pullman Porter

Announced for Release on February 16, 1919. Produced by Joseph M. Schenck for the Comique Film Corp. Distributed by Paramount Pictures. Directed by Roscoe Arbuckle. Two reels. With Roscoe Arbuckle, Winifred Westover.

Along with *A Cream Puff Romance*, *The Pullman Porter* is one of the main mysteries of the Arbuckle canon. Announced in Paramount publicity:

> Some of the joys of riding on the McAdoo railroads are depicted in Fatty Arbuckle's new comedy, "The Pullman Porter," which the portly comedian has just finished. Winifred Westover, a talented ingénue who has been starred in a number of Fine Arts Pictures, plays opposite Fatty in the new picture, which is said to be a radical departure from other comedies in which the great laughmaker has appeared.
> – 1919 Paramount and Artcraft Pressbook for *The Winning Girl*

It was listed as a February 16, 1919 release on the upcoming Paramount schedules in the trade magazines, but with no copyright info, no assigned Paramount-Arbuckle comedy number, and no reviews it appears that *The Pullman Porter* was never completed or released. Winifred Westover would be the leading lady in Roscoe's next opus.

Love

Released March 2, 1919. Produced by Joseph M. Schenck for the Comique Film Corp. Distributed by Paramount Pictures. Directed by Roscoe Arbuckle. Scenario by Vincent Bryan. Two reels. Extant: Friuli, DAN, LOB. With Roscoe Arbuckle, Al St John, Winifred Westover, Frank Hayes, Mario Bianchi (Monty Banks), Fanny Kelly, Pat Kelly.

Fatty is smitten with Winnie, a pretty country girl, but her farmer father decides she's going to marry Al. His father owns all the farm land adjoining, and the marriage will consolidate the two properties. Fatty is told to leave the premises, and when Winnie declares to her father that she loves Fatty and refuses to marry Al she's locked in her room. Winnie and Fatty try to elope, but their plans fail. Fatty gets another idea and schemes to get the large-sized cook fired. When an advertisement is placed for a new cook, Fatty, in drag, answers the ad and gets the job as the new "hired girl."

The time comes for Winnie to marry but because the young minister is nervous and inexperienced Fatty (as the cook) suggests a rehearsal and stands in for Al during the ceremony. The young minister unknowingly marries Winnie and Fatty, and when the time comes for Winnie to marry Al, Fatty reveals his true identity and the fact that he and Winnie have already tied the knot. Winnie's father and Al finally give up, and Fatty and Winnie end the film with a kiss and embrace.

Winifred Westover and Roscoe in two poses on the lobby card for *Love* (1919).

This short, Roscoe's farewell to barnyard comedy, was unavailable for almost eighty years. The only known surviving materials were two separate incomplete prints—one at La Cineteca del Friuli in Italy and the other with the Danish Film Institute. For the 2005 DVD collection *The Forgotten Films of Roscoe "Fatty" Arbuckle*, producer Paul E. Gierucki was able to access the prints and create a video restoration. Miraculously the combined footage made ninety-nine per cent of the film. After the Italian and Danish intertitles were translated, news articles, reviews, and pressbook material for the short were gathered up by Andy Coryell, Cole Johnson, Bruce Lawton, David B. Pearson, and yours truly so that new English titles in the style of the originals could be made. After all the hard work a close approximation of *Love* was now available, but only on this DVD. Plans were afoot for a proper restoration on film, but it never happened.

The film is a re-telling of 1914's *Those Country Kids*, with the same parental problems, and with the dunkings down the well enlarged and expanded into quite an elaborate sequence. Three of the characters end up in the drink, and much footage is devoted to the process of trying to haul them out. For the inside-of-the-well shots of the actors plummeting down an extremely clever set was built where the walls would shoot up around the suspended performers, creating the illusion that they were falling. The interior of the well and the farmhouse were shot at a studio that Roscoe knew very well:

Comique Film Leases Part of Sennett Studio

A large portion of the Mack Sennett Studio located on the opposite side of Allesandro Street from his main plant, has been leased to the Comique Film Corporation, and Roscoe Arbuckle is now at work there on a subject titled "Love."

*– **Motion Picture News**, January 11, 1919*

The story of finding and using the location for the farm and its house was told in the July 1919 issue of *Picture-Play Magazine*:

"Land Sakes! So you make these moving pictures I've heard so much about? Do you know, I've never seen one."

Roscoe taking a moment's pause from the action in 1919's *Love*. Courtesy Cole Johnson.

> *It was hard to tell who was the more surprised, Fatty Arbuckle or Mrs. Mary G. Dodge, at whose farm, near Glendale, California, Fatty and his company had stopped a few weeks ago, having noticed that it was just the sort of old-fashioned rural setting they were looking for.*
>
> *"Well, you can see one made," answered Fatty, "and that's more than most people have ever done."*
>
> *So all day they worked on the farm, only stopping to eat luncheon under the broad branches in the barnyard. As for Mrs. Dodge, she was quite agog, as she watched them work, only she couldn't seem to quite understand it.*
>
> *"They just seem to have a lot of people run around, and Mr. Arbuckle—isn't he fat? —fell down into a water trough or something that they rigged up, and that was all," she said. "They do say that when it's all cut up and pieced together with some other parts, like a puzzle picture, that it's real good. But it looked to me like a lot of nonsense."*
>
> *Fatty promised that if she could ever get to town he'd see to it that she sees one of his complete pictures.*

Despite Roscoe's extreme popularity at the box office, he was still at the mercy of the local exhibitors as far as how his films were presented. Earlier we had mentioned censorship issues for a few pictures like *Rebecca's Wedding Day* (1914), but footage could be trimmed for other reasons, as illustrated by this report form New York's Rialto Theatre that appeared in the March 3, 1919 *Motion Picture News*:

> *On account of the length of the program the second orchestral number is omitted, and for the same reason the comedy, Fatty Arbuckle in "Love," has been decidedly trimmed. The old duel stuff with the brooms, which, we believe, was seen in "The Waiter's Ball," and the scenes in the well have been cut out, but we cannot say that these excisions have hurt the comedy in the slightest.*

Love benefits from the services of Vincent Bryan, a Broadway play and songwriting veteran, that settled into movies with Mack Sennett in 1915. Part of Charlie Chaplin's crew on his Mutual Comedies, Bryan worked with Chaplin on *The Floorwalker* (1916) through *The Cure* (1917), and then went on to Marie Dressler's shorts at Goldwyn. Besides this one-time assignment for Roscoe, he also did single shots for *He's In Again* (1918) with Billy West, and Max Linder's feature *Be My Wife* (1921), plus co-directed the Harold Lloyd shorts *Pay Your Dues*, *Soft Money*, and *He Leads, Others Follow* (all 1919). The nomadic quality of his employment may have been caused by his drug use, which led to his arrest and serving time in prison in the early 1920s. This put a damper on his writing assignments, and he had been out of the business for about eight years when his body was found in "an obscure hotel" in 1937. His death at fifty-seven was ascribed to by the police as "an overdose of sleeping sedative."

Frank Hayes makes a welcome return to the Arbuckle universe as the irascible father, who's not above flirting with the new "cook." Al St John and Monty Banks turn in their customary solid support, with Banks having the largest and best role of his Arbuckle appearances. Here he's definitely filling in for Buster Keaton, and even wears a pork pie hat to seal the deal. Rotund Fanny Kelly, who plays the disgruntled cook, was a Mack Sennett veteran making her only appearance with Arbuckle. Although usually playing Irish characters she was of Scottish descent, and came from vaudeville with her husband Pat Kelly. The pair worked for Sennett for many years, and some of Fanny's appearances include *Sheriff Nell's Tussle* (1918), *Hard Knocks and Love Taps* (1921), and *Romeo and Juliet* (1924), plus the features *Yankee Doodle in Berlin* (1919), *Love, Honor and Behave* (1920), and *The Extra Girl* (1923). She also turned up as Mickey Daniels' mother in *Giants vs. Yanks* (1923) and the *Telephone Girls* Comedy *Sherlock's Home* (1924) before her early death in 1925.

Leading lady Winifred Westover was a blonde ingénue who began her career at Triangle with D.W. Griffith's Fine Arts Company doing bits in *Intolerance*, *The Matrimaniac* (both 1916), and *Jim Bludso* (1917). In 1918 she became a comedy lead for Fox Sunshine Comedies opposite male comics like Billie Ritchie, Hugh Fay, and Jimmie Adams in shorts like *The Son of a Gun, Are Married Policemen Safe?*, and *Her Husband's Wife* (all 1918). By 1919 she moved on to being a western heroine with William S. Hart, Buck Jones, and Harry Carey, and has good supporting roles in films like *Is Life Worth Living?* and *Anne of Little Smoky* (both 1921). That year she married cowboy star William S. Hart and retired from the screen, although she did return in 1930 with the lead role in Herbert Brenon's sound feature *Lummox*.

New York Tribune: "At the Rialto there is a Roscoe Arbuckle Comedy called 'Love' which is the funniest one the plump comedian has yet presented."

New York Times: "The comedy at the Strand and also at the Rialto is 'Love,' with 'Fatty' Arbuckle and his company of broad comedians. It is funny; uproariously funny in places."

The Bank Clerk

The Bank Clerk, like 1916's *A Cream Puff Romance* and more recently *The Pullman Porter*, is a film that was started but never released and likely never completed. Announced in the trade magazines with photos of Roscoe and Molly Malone, the April 12, 1919 *Motion Picture News* previewed:

> **Arbuckle Washes Windows**
>
> *The earlier part of "Fatty" Arbuckle's forthcoming Paramount-Arbuckle comedy requires that he starts washing windows in a banking institution before climbing to the top.*

But it seems that things didn't gel on the production as a month later the May 3, 1919 issue announced:

> **Arbuckle Changes Plans**
>
> *Owing to weather conditions which have held up work on the Paramount-Arbuckle comedy, "The Bank Clerk," and also because the script will need*

A Big Help to the Cameraman.
The pair of 'em, Fatty Arbuckle and Molly Malone in the Paramount comedy, "The Bank Clerk."

revision, "Fatty" Arbuckle has decided to temporarily suspend work on this particular film and make a Western subject for his next comedy release.

The western subject referred to became *A Desert Hero*.

A Desert Hero

Released June 1, 1919. Produced by Joseph M. Schenck for the Comique Film Corp. Distributed by Paramount Pictures. Directed by Roscoe Arbuckle. Scenario by Jean

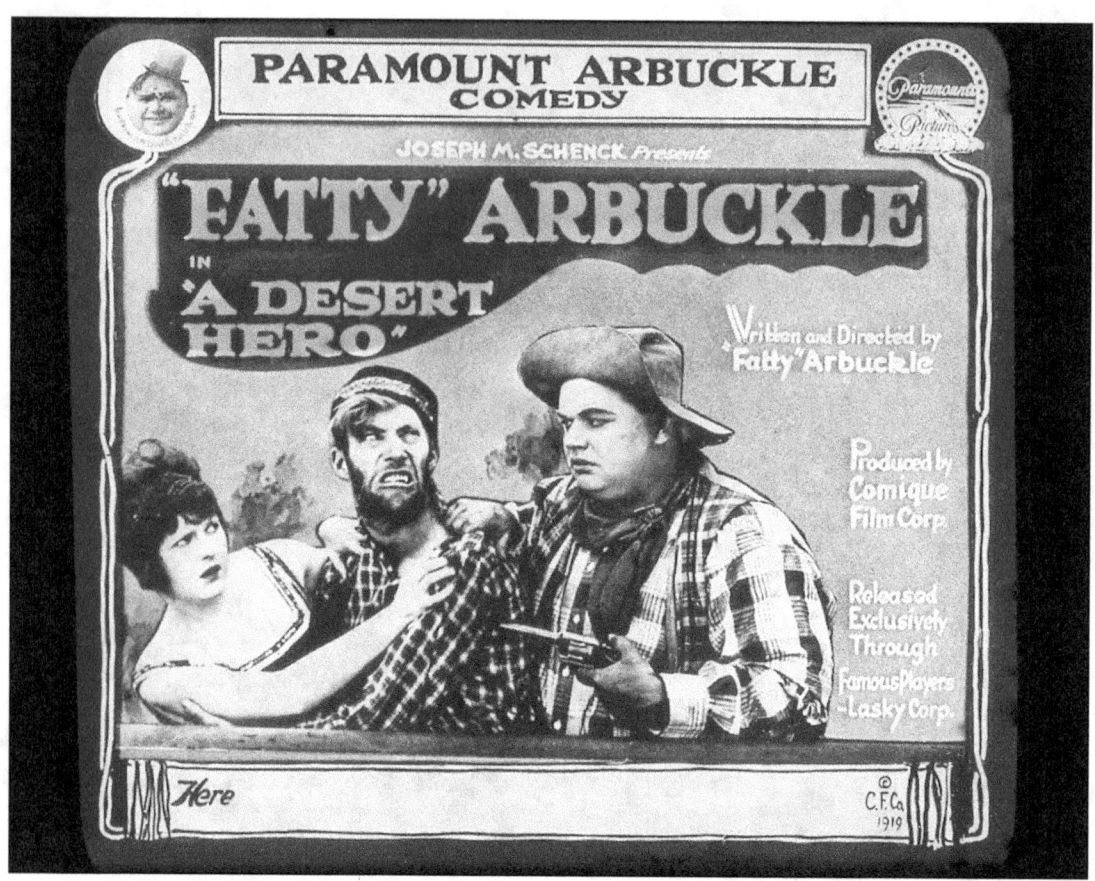

Roscoe stops Al St John from manhandling Molly Malone on the glass slide for *A Desert Hero* (1919). Courtesy Matt Vogel.

Havez. Two reels. With Roscoe Arbuckle, Al St John, Molly Malone, Monty Collins Sr., Edgar Kennedy, Charles "Buddy" Post, Rube Miller.

The scene is a wild and western town where sheriffs are killed every ten minutes by the boisterous population whose hangout is a dance hall of which a giant bully is proprietor. Fatty, introduced via title card as "A long, gaunt son of the desert," has made a fortune in a desert mine and goes to the town to enjoy himself. He enters the dance hall to change his gold into currency and discovers a hotbed of crookedness.

The proprietor wants to separate Fatty from his money, but the star dancing girl refuses to enter into the crooked scheme, and she gets thrown out into the street. Fatty takes care of the crook with a wonderful exhibition of prowess, and is elected sheriff by acclamation.

Molly, the former dancing girl, introduced as "so innocent that she's afraid to pick wild flowers," is welcomed into the Salvation Army, and while she and a band of the Salvationists are engaged in a meeting in front of the dance hall the giant owner makes trouble and disparaging remarks, which sheriff Fatty resents. The two then have a terrific battle, using boxing gloves instead of guns. Although at a disadvantage with the seven-foot-tall proprietor, Fatty is victorious.

Like 1918's *The Sheriff*, *A Desert Hero* is a western burlesque that at the moment is considered to have vanished without a trace. Reports from the trade magazines suggest that the parody was done on a grand scale:

> *Fatty Arbuckle is rapidly nearing the completion of his latest two-reel Paramount-Arbuckle comedy, "A Desert Hero." The production is being made in the hills near Glendale, Cal., where one of the biggest sets ever used in the making of a western picture has been erected to serve as saloon and dance hall.*
>
> – ***Motion Picture News**, May 19, 1919*

The May 17, 1919 issue of *Exhibitors Herald and Motography* added:

> *One hundred and fifty people have been working for the past ten days in what is probably the largest interior set ever erected for a western picture.*

Although described as a travesty on the conventional wild and woolly western dramas, the October 1919 *Picture-Play Magazine* relates that Roscoe introduced some serious elements in the picture. While they didn't approve of it, they did give a description:

Edgar Kennedy and Charles "Buddy" Post are put on the spot by Roscoe, Molly Malone, and Al St John in *A Desert Hero* (1919).

> *There is no doubt about Fatty scoring here. It is a picture that makes one almost ready to believe that contract of seven figures he is said to possess with Paramount. But, he, too, approaches the serious in a manner totally out of place when he introduces a Salvation Army scene. It is not burlesque, it is an attempt at drama, and it has no more business in "A Desert Hero" than Theda Bara would have in it. I wish our comedians would polish up a bit on their perspectives.*

Al St John plays a bad western hombre, Charles "Buddy" Post the enormous dance hall proprietor (more on him in *Back Stage*), and a photo in the June 28, 1919 *Moving Picture World* shows Roscoe's old Keystone colleague Edgar Kennedy as a roulette operator at one of the dance hall's gambling tables. The leading lady is Molly Malone, who started working with Roscoe on the unfinished *The Bank Clerk*.

Born in Denver, Colorado, Malone was a model and made her film debut at age nineteen with the West Coast Vitagraph Company. She was soon an ingénue in serious films for Lasky, Lubin, and Universal, and was teamed with cowboy star Harry Carey in the early John Ford-directed westerns *Straight Shooting, A Marked Man, Bucking Broadway, The Scarlet Drop, Thieves Gold*, and *The Phantom Riders* (all 1917). While at Universal Malone began cutting her comedy teeth in shorts such as *To Be or Not to Be Married* (1917) with Eddie Lyons and Lee Moran, and *Adventurous Ambrose* (1918) opposite Mack Swain. A move to the National Film Corporation saw her become the leading lady for "Smiling Bill" Parsons in two-reelers like *Widow's Might, Birds of a Feather*, and *Matching Billy* (all 1918).

A brief stint at Christie Comedies preceded her appearances with Roscoe, for whom she made a spirited and peppy love interest. With something of a rag doll look—delicate features, button eyes, and unruly hair—she was not above slapping Harry McCoy when he gets too fresh or pushing Roscoe into a water tub. When Roscoe moved into features Malone starred in her own brief series that Al Christie produced for the Southern California Producing Co. under the brand name *Supreme Comedies*. Titles included *Molly's Millions, Molly's Mumps, Her Doctor's Dilemma*, and *Come into the Kitchen* (all 1920). From here she was in demand for features, and appeared in a wide variety of comedies and westerns like *It's a Great Life* (1920), *An Unwilling Hero, A Poor Relation* (both 1921), *Little Johnny Jones* (1923), and *Battling Bunyon* (1924).

She returned to shorts in 1923 with Roscoe on the aborted *Handy Andy*. When it was continued under Roscoe's direction with Poodles Hanneford, Molly resumed her role and stayed working with the unit on *The New Sheriff* and *The Bonehead* (both 1924). Back at Christie Comedies she supported Neal Burns, Bobby Vernon, Jimmie Adams, and goofy gob Billy Dooley in outings such as *Court Plaster* (1924), *Love Goofy, Don't Pinch* (both 1925), *Whoa Emma*, and *A Dippy Tar* (both 1926). She finished the decade mostly in independent western features and bounced around in single shorts for Bray, Jack White, and Universal. Her last known film is 1929's *The Newlywed's Pest*, after which she left the screen. An undated clipping from the mid-1930s talks about her working in the photo department of MGM, but her 1952 *Variety* obituary lists her passing away at age sixty-three under the name Mrs. Edith Greaves.

Starting with *A Desert Hero* Roscoe got the regular services of one of the most important writers in early film comedy: Jean Havez. Born in Baltimore in 1872, after college he became a newspaper reporter and entered show business as the advertising man for Lew Dockstader's Minstrels, one of the biggest and most famous minstrel troupes. He began writing for them, penning skits and comic songs like *Everybody Works but Father*. Besides touring the United States the troupe had shows on Broadway like *Bull Durham* (1908) which Havez wrote. He began freelancing in 1910 and teamed with Leo Donnelly to write monologues, sketches, and songs for performers such as Al Jolson. He also worked with comic Bert Williams, co-writing numbers for his *Ziegfeld Follies* appearances, and became a charter member of ASCAP.

In 1915 he moved to Los Angeles and began working at Keystone on shorts like *Dizzy Heights and Daring Hearts* (1915), *Better Late than Never*, and *A Dash of Courage* (both 1916). Moving back and forth between Los Angeles and New York, he first worked with Roscoe on *Oh Doctor!* (1917). Still busy working on musical shows like *Yip, Yip, Yaphank* (1918), *Poor Mamma* (1919), and *The Satires of 1920*, he signed a contract with Joseph Schenck to join Roscoe's team and then stayed on to work for Buster Keaton.

Part of the team on Keaton's shorts as well as the features *The Three Ages*, *Our Hospitality* (both 1923), *Sherlock, Jr.*, *The Navigator* (both 1924), and *Seven Chances* (1925), Havez also found the time to co-write Harold Lloyd's first four features *A Sailor-Made Man* (1921), *Grandma's Boy*, *Dr. Jack* (both 1922), and *Safety Last* (1923), in addition to some *Hallroom Boys* comedies and Monty Banks' debut feature *Racing Luck* (1924). Havez may have been involved on the early script work on Keaton's *Go West* (1925), but died of heart failure on February 12, 1925.

Keystone writing staff circa 1916 with Jean Havez (bald in center), Harry Williams (left), scenario head Hampton Del Ruth (with cigar), Clarence Badger, unknown, Vincent Bryan (seated), Harry Wulze (in back), and Charles Reisner (right).

Moving Picture World (June 28, 1919): "A welcome burlesque of those dramas laid amid a shabby group of shacks, supposedly a mining town, where everybody shoots everybody else, and winds up with reform, the Paramount-Arbuckle product 'A Desert Hero,' is a laugh from the start and might be to the finish but for an effective bit of contrast, a few really serious moments. The reform is not burlesqued; at least not to an offensive degree. Of course Fatty Arbuckle provides most of the fun in the characterization of a 'desert hero,' so lucky as never to get a scratch amid all the shooting, such a remarkable shot himself that he hits the cuckoo in a clock and causes it to drop into a glass of beer below, converting it to a cocktail.

"'A Desert Hero' is a timely burlesque with a point that will be appreciated, admirably done at every stage of the game."

Exhibitors Herald and Motography (July 5, 1919): "Satire, the very best form of slapstick comedy, has been the aim of the rotund comedian in the present performance and the result is the most thoroughly diverting contribution that has come from his workshop in easy memory. There will be those that claim it the best work of the stout humorist's career."

Back Stage

Released September 7, 1919. Produced by Joseph M. Schenck for the Comique Film Corp. Distributed by Paramount Pictures. Directed by Roscoe Arbuckle. Scenario by Jean Havez. Photographed by Elgin Lessley. Two reels. Extant: LOB, EYE. With Roscoe Arbuckle, Buster Keaton, Al St John, Molly Malone, Jack Coogan, Rube Miller, Monty Collins Sr., Charles "Buddy" Post.

Fatty and Buster are stage hands at a vaudeville theatre, and are getting things ready for the arrival of a new company. Fatty is also the chief bill poster, and while he's out posting he ends up pasting a local boy who gets in his way on a wall. The new troupe arrives and consists of an old ham actor, an effeminate eccentric dancer, and a bad-tempered strongman. The weight-lifter is a giant who mistreats his poor, overworked female assistant, and the stage hands get together and decide to put him in his place. Since slugs and axes don't faze him, they surprise him with an electrified barbell which does the trick.

The performers become disgruntled and quit, so the pretty assistant convinces the boys to put on their own show. Fatty, Buster, and Molly do a parody of fruity ballet dancing and Salome enactments—with Fatty as the king and Buster as his voluptuous dancing girl. Another sketch has Fatty serenading Molly, who's up in a houses' second floor window, but Buster loosens the support for the house flat and it falls on Fatty. Luckily he just happens to be standing where the open window passes and he's unscathed.

The strongman is out in the audience watching the show, and getting angrier and angrier as it progresses. Finally he takes out a pistol and fires, hitting Molly in the shoulder. Fatty and Buster, with the help of Al and Rube, leap into action and drag him onstage. Al and Buster fight with him to keep him busy, while Fatty and Rube ultimately take care of him by loading all his heavy weights in a trunk and dropping it on him. The film ends with Fatty visiting the recovering Molly in the hospital and absentmindedly eating the apple he brought for her.

Back Stage revisits some of the settings and themes that Roscoe used in Keystones such as *A Small Town Act* (1913), *That Minstrel Man*, *Fatty's Debut* (both 1914), and *Fatty and the Broadway Stars* (1915). The vaudeville theatre and gags for this film (plus Molly Malone) would be dusted off and reused with Poodles Hanneford in *The Bonehead* (1924).

In typical Arbuckle fashion the laughs are spread around amongst the large cast. Roscoe has surrounded himself with a crack selection of supporting comics. Newcomer Jack Coogan (more on him in *The Hayseed*) acts the nance and demonstrates a lot of his eccentric dancing, while Rube Miller returns from the Keystone days as Roscoe's fellow stage hand. Miller would also turn up in *The Hayseed*, and would only appear in films for another year or so before disappearing from the screen. Making his last silent film appearance with his uncle Roscoe, Al St John pops in and out of the film, but makes sure to turn up for the big action climax.

Two unsung comedy regulars are also on hand. The old Shakespearian ham actor in the top hat is played by Monty Collins Sr. (sometimes Monte). An old vaudevillian, Collins started doing film bits in the late teens, and had his most memorable moments in Buster Keaton's films. He can be seen as Kate Price's tough Irish father in *My Wife's Relations* (1922), and the minister in *Our Hospitality* (1923), but his best role comes as

Buster Keaton reclines, as Roscoe, Molly Malone, and Al St John emote in *Back Stage* (1919). Courtesy Annichen Skaren.

one half of the one-armed civil war veterans who can't agree on what to applaud for in *The Playhouse* (1921). Also providing atmospheric characters in features like *Tumbleweeds* (1925), *The King of Kings* (1927), and *The Wind* (1928), his son Monty Collins Jr. (as just plain Monty Collins) became a comedy regular in silent and sound films —even starring in three Arbuckle-directed shorts (see 1932's *Keep Laughing*). The elder Monty passed away in 1929.

The gigantic strongman is Charles "Buddy" Post, who because of his enormous height specialized in unusual and usually menacing characters. Born in Salt Lake City, Utah, he performed in stock companies for two years before entering pictures in 1917. After working with Roscoe in *A Desert Hero* and *Back Stage* he got his own short-lived series of starring shorts in 1920. Titles such as *Mum's the Word*, *A Counterplot*, and *A Money Mix-Up* (all 1920) were made by the National Film Corporation and released through Goldwyn. Not catching on as a lead comic, he continued working as a character player and was busy with roles in features like *Wild Oranges* (1924) and *The Satin Woman* (1927), as well as shorts such as Charley Chase's *Are Brunettes Safe?* (1927). His career tapered off after 1933, but he returned with other silent comedy veterans in the 1940 picture *Lil' Abner*, where he played the heavy Earthquake McGoon. Occasional bits followed until his death in 1952.

A new addition to the Comique team was cameraman Elgin Lessley, who, along with Rollie Totheroh, Walter Lundin, and Hans Koenekamp, was one of the great silent comedy cinematographers. As a young man he had discovered photography and won numerous amateur contests before starting his film career in 1911 in the camera department of the

Charles "Buddy" Post as the mean strongman in *Back Stage* (1919) with a more neutral portrait. Courtesy Sam Gill.

Melies-Star Company. After filming many of Gaston Melies' westerns and travelogues, Lessley's comedy career commenced when he joined Keystone. During his time there he worked on various Arbuckle shorts like *Mabel and Fatty Viewing the World's Fair in San Francisco* (1915) and *He Did and He Didn't* (1916), plus others comedies such as *A Royal Rogue* and *A Clever Dummy* (both 1917). Lessley also did the Al St John's solo comedies *The Grab Bag Bride, Her Cave Man, A Self-Made Hero*, and *A Winning Loser* (all 1917).

Lessley shot the final three Comique shorts—*Back Stage, The Hayseed*, and *The Garage*—and then became chief cameraman for Buster Keaton, shooting masterworks such as *One Week* (1920), *The Boat* (1921), *Cops* (1922), *Our Hospitality* (1923), *The Navigator* (1924), and *Go West* (1925). Keaton also benefitted from Lessley's mastery of special photographic effects for the mind-blowing multiple exposures of *The Playhouse* (1921) and *Sherlock, Jr.'s* (1924) split-second scene shifting.

In 1926 Lessley was lured away to work for Harry Langdon, who had just embarked on his own starring features. Lessley's expertise helped insure Langdon hits like *Tramp, Tramp, Tramp, The Strong Man* (both 1926), and *Long Pants* (1927), and to Langdon's more personal features he brought beautiful snow-bound vistas in *Three's A Crowd* (1927) and clever traveling shots that follow Harry from room to room in *The Chaser* (1928). Returning to Keaton, Lessley's last credited film was *The Cameraman* (1928), Buster's first feature for MGM. The film's ingenious elevator shots of Buster running up and down his tenement building stairs while trying to answer a phone, and the detailed Tong war scenes, allowed Lessley to go out in style. A combination of personal problems and bad health curtailed Lessley's activities, and he died in 1944 at age sixty.

Another addition to the company took attention over the others:

Buster Keaton Back in Arbuckle's Company
Work has been started by "Fatty" Arbuckle's company at the temporary studio in Glendale on the next Paramount-Arbuckle comedy, which bears the working title, "Back Stage." "Fatty's" supporting cast is again headed by Al St John, Molly Malone and Buster Keaton. The latter arrived a few days ago from New York, after spending two months in a hospital there under treatment for an unusual ailment which he contracted in the Flanders trenches.

"I was deaf as a post," says Buster, "not from the racket of bursting shells, as you might suppose, but due solely to the climate. The army doctors said they had never seen a case like mine, and I guess they were telling the truth, for none of them were able to do anything for me.

An operation was finally performed that gave me back my hearing."
  *– **Motion Picture News**, July 5, 1919*

Buster said that he became practically stone deaf due to prolonged exposure to dampness and floor drafts overseas, and while the treatments helped he never fully regained his hearing. After a period of re-adjustment, he returned to the Comique Company:

The moment I could get to a telephone I called my girl at her home. Joe Schenck's office was nearer the receiving hospital so she asked him to hurry

Gag photo of Roscoe, Buster Keaton, King Baggot, and an unidentified leading lady. Courtesy Robert S. Birchard.

over. When he saw me Joe looked as though he was going to cry.

"You look terribly peaked Buster," he said. "You've lost so much weight. I never saw you look so sick and miserable."

"Why shouldn't I look miserable—with my beauty gone forever?" I asked. But I wasn't fooling Joe Schenck with wisecracks— "Of course you haven't any money," he said. He took out his wallet and gave me all of the money in it.

Before I was out of uniform I received two $1,000-a-week offers. One was from Jack Warner, the other from the William Fox Company. But I preferred to resume working for Joe Schenck at my old salalry of $250. I couldn't see how I could go wrong stringing along with a square shooter like him who had been so kind to my family. I had never met a finer man in show business. I haven't yet.

– *My Wonderful World of Slapstick,* Doubleday, 1960

Variety (October 10, 1919): "The latest Paramount-Arbuckle release entitled 'Back Stage' is one of the best comedies the hefty comedian has appeared in for some time. At the

Rivoli this week it was the strongest point in favor of the screen entertainment that was offered, overshadowing the feature. It is all the old slapstick stuff imaginable, but it is so presented that it pulls laughs readily.

"It is a real comedy scream from first to last."

Motion Picture News (October 11, 1919): "Just as 'A Desert Hero' was a corking good burlesque on the screen melodrama of the wild and wooly west, 'Back Stage' is a sure fire travesty on the small town show appearing at the 'Opry House.'

"Yes, there is plenty of slapstick, but it is clean, and this comedy will generally entertain everybody wherever it is shown."

Exhibitors Herald (September 13, 1919): "Not as good as the best Fatty has made, but reasonably close.

"It will hold its own without a doubt."

The Hayseed

Released October 26, 1919. Produced by Joseph M. Schenck for the Comique Film Corp. Distributed by Paramount Pictures. Directed by Roscoe Arbuckle. Scenario by Jean Havez. Photographed by Elgin Lessley. Two reels. Extant: ITAL, CNC, MoMA, BFI, GEM, LOB, ACAD. With Roscoe Arbuckle, Buster Keaton, Molly Malone, Luke, Jack Coogan, Kitty Bradbury, Rube Miller.

Buster is the sales clerk at the Grimes General Store, and Fatty is the head of the post office. When delivering the mail Fatty has much help from Luke, and when they end up at the house of his girl Molly a round of hide-and-seek is in order. Fatty has a rival for Molly in the person of the town sheriff. To get Fatty out of his way, the sheriff steals a letter containing $300 with the aim of framing the large mail clerk with the theft.

Thanks to having ingested onions, Roscoe's soulful tones brings tears to the eyes of Luke, Molly Malone, Buster Keaton, Kitty Bradbury, Rube Miller, Jack Coogan, et al, in *The Hayseed* (1919).

The sheriff uses the pilfered money to buy Molly a real diamond engagement ring, but she prefers Fatty's imitation stone (it's much bigger). The whole town convenes at a big party at the general store. Buster does magic tricks, the sheriff some eccentric dancing, and then it's Fatty's turn to sing. Having trouble with his voice Buster suggests he eat a bunch of onions to give his voice strength—and thanks to the fumes his singing literally brings the audience to tears. At the end of his song the sheriff publicly accuses him of stealing the money, and when Fatty appeals to his friends for support thanks to the onions they all turn away from him. Finally Buster speaks up and says that he saw the sheriff steal the money, and for the happy ending the crook is chased out of town by an eager Luke.

Coming as the next to last Comique short *The Hayseed* tends to get lost in the shuffle—which is a shame as it's one of the most charming films in the series. Although not ground-breaking or particularly innovative, it's thoroughly entertaining and relatively subdued (for a Comique). The comedy is done with a very casual air—very unhurriedly—but with a snap and precision that succinctly puts everything over. There's no trying to top each other—without Al present Roscoe and Buster work as a tight unit, and everyone seems to be having fun. After moving around to different facilities such as Balboa and Henry Lehrman's studio, the Comique unit settled into a new studio:

Arbuckle in New Studio

> *Fatty Arbuckle is now safely installed in his new studio at Culver City with plenty of room, all modern facilities and fine sunlight.*
>
> *He has already commenced work upon "The Hayseed," his new Paramount-Arbuckle comedy.*
> –***Exhibitors Herald and Motography*** (August 30, 1919)

The earlier July 26, 1919 issue of the same magazine had given more details on the new facility:

> *The new studio has one stage which measures 70 by 220 feet and is equipped with modern dressing rooms, cutting and assembling rooms, etc. —indeed all that is necessary to the making of thoroughly up-to-date, high-class comedies.*

A new face in films is the long and skinny one of eccentric dancer and vaudeville comic Jack Coogan. Having made his debut in *Back Stage*, Coogan fills in as the villainous sheriff in this picture. Born in Syracuse, New York, he was the stage struck son of a local pharmacist, who as a kid entertained the communities' Rotary Club and Chamber of Commerce. Hitting the road in 1908, he toured around the country as a solo and with partners, cracking jokes and doing his athletic eccentric line of dance (a good example can be seen in *Back Stage*). He eventually teamed up with and married Lillian Dolliver, and in 1914 their son John Leslie Coogan was born. Soon he was part of the act, doing a little shimmie number, and the Coogan's played the West Coast in 1919.

Roscoe and Minta were old friends of the Coogans, and Roscoe thought that Jack Sr. should try Hollywood. At the same time Charlie Chaplin saw Jack Jr. at the Los Angeles Orpheum, and soon both father and son started working in films:

> *Jack Coogan, who appeared in the New York Winter Garden shows and with Annette Kellerman, has left the vaudeville stage to join the Fatty Arbuckle Company. Jack takes Al St John's place with Roscoe's company. Laugh-provoking tendencies seems to run in the family as Jack Coogan Jr., aged four, recently entered into a contract with Charlie Chaplin Company at the highest salary ever paid such a youthful actor.*
> – **Exhibitors Herald and Motography** (August 30, 1919)

Of course little Jackie's career hit the stratosphere with the success of *The Kid* (1921), so Jack Sr. stopped performing to manage his son's career and produce his films. The Coogan's most successful years were 1921 to 1927 through hits like *Peck's Bad Boy* (1922), *Daddy, Circus Days* (both 1923), *Little Robinson Crusoe* (1924), and *The Ragman* (1925). Getting older, Jackie still starred in features such as *Tom Sawyer* (1930) and *Huckleberry Finn* (1931), and father and son did a vaudeville tour together, but Jack Sr. died at age forty-two in a 1935 car accident.

A prosperous-looking Jack Coogan with his super-star son Jackie. Author's collection.

Also on hand as Molly Malone's mother is Kitty Bradbury, an angelic-looking white-haired actress best known to silent comedy fans for playing Edna Purviance's ailing mother in Charlie Chaplin's *The Immigrant* (1917). Always one of the leading players' mother or aunt, Ms. Bradbury made other comedy appearances such as in Buster Keaton's short *The Goat* (1921) and his feature *Our Hospitality* (1923), as well as Chaplin's *The Pilgrim* (1923). Having started in films around 1916 she also appeared in the dramatic pictures *Intolerance* (1916), *The Brand of Lopez* (1920), and *The Man Between* (1923), before she disappeared from screens in the mid-1920s.

Motion Picture News (December 20, 1919): "We cannot remember when Fatty Arbuckle has had a more rollicking comedy than 'The Hayseed.' The big filmmaker is particularly partial to rural life in his subjects and he has made such a study of it that it seems genuine even though it is richly burlesqued. Fatty himself still takes the role of a humorous half-wit and that he is an artist of the first order can not be denied in the easy assurance which marks his performance."

Wid's Daily (December 16, 1919): "Fatty Arbuckle has provided a comedy that will credit any bill in 'The Hayseed.' He gets in a lot of original business and his supporting company headed by Buster Keaton and Molly Malone works like a smooth machine in helping along the comedy tricks."

Exhibitors Herald (November 1, 1919): "There are many more laughs in store for the admirers of Fatty Arbuckle. His new production 'The Hayseed' is quite up to standard."

1920

The Garage

Released January 11, 1920. Produced by Joseph M. Schenck for the Comique Film Corp. Distributed by Paramount. Directed and written by Roscoe Arbuckle. Scenario by Jean Havez. Photography by Elgin Lessley. Two reels. Extant: CNC, QEB, FRIU, DAN, MoMA, ACAD, Berk, LOB, ITAL. With Roscoe Arbuckle, Buster Keaton, Molly Malone, Dan Crimmins, Harry McCoy, Charles Dorety, Monty Banks, Luke, Polly Moran.

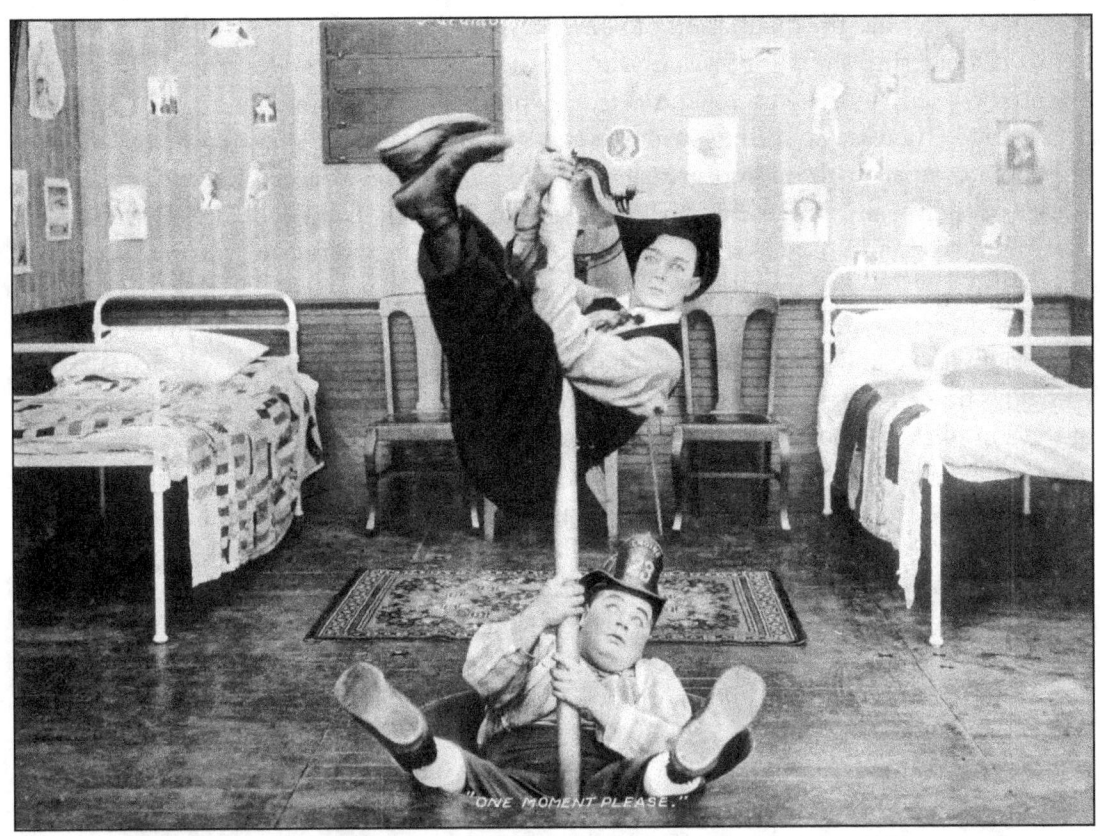

Buster Keaton causing a fire pole bottle neck in 1920's *The Garage*. Courtesy Mike hawks.

Fatty and Buster work in a garage/ fire house, and when their fighting makes everything a shambles they get in bad with the garage owner. Various clients come in and the pair do their slapstick best to satisfy their demands. The village dandy drops by to see the owner's daughter and his fancy clothes and flowers get covered with oil. The boys hose the dandy down with gasoline and eventually clean him up.

To get the girl alone the dandy sics Luke on Fatty and Buster under the pretense that he has rabies. Alone with Molly he gets into a fight with her, and when Fatty and Buster return too soon he sets off a false alarm fire to get rid of them (as they double as the fire department). Locked in the garage/fire house after they head out to the fake fire, the dandy tries to break the door lock with a blow torch but only succeeds in setting the place on fire. Harry's trapped inside and Molly's upstairs taking a bath when she notices the smoke.

Fatty and Buster's fire crew return to the garage to put out the fire, but their hose has too many holes for Fatty to sit on at the same time. Harry appears in a window gasping for help so the group sets up their net. Just as the dandy's about to jump Molly appears at another window so the group runs to her with the net leaving the dude to crash on the ground. Molly jumps but bounces off the net onto some telephone wires. Fatty and Buster climb up the pole, shimmy over to her, and make a human ladder and safely drop her in her father's arms. The pair then have their own trouble getting down, but Molly drives by in car so Fatty and Buster can drop into the back seat.

The Garage has the distinction of being Roscoe's last starring silent short, and would be his last starring short for twelve years until *Hey, Pop!* (1932). It's a very loose, gag-oriented comedy where Roscoe and Buster explore all the possible material to be found in a garage. There's a spinning turntable (a prop just made for silent comedy) and lots of people covered with oil and grease. With Al St John again gone, Roscoe and Buster work as a tight team, and grace notes amid all the slapstick include Charles Dorety's self-destructing car and Roscoe kissing a photo of Mabel Normand on the wall before settling into bed.

Harry McCoy and Polly Moran, two former Keystone cohorts, turn up in the cast, and also briefly Luke and Monty Banks. Charles Dorety, the chap with the walrus mustache who buys the self-destructing auto, was a workman-like comic who turns up later in some of the sound shorts Roscoe would direct for Educational and RKO. Molly's father/Fatty's boss is played by Dan Crimmins, a silent comedy veteran making his only appearance in an Arbuckle film. Born Alexander M. Lyon in England, he migrated to America, and with his wife Minnie became a popular vaudeville team as Dan Crimmins and Rosa Gore.

They toured the globe with their act *What are the Wild Winds Saying?*, and appeared in the stage version of *The Wizard of Oz*. They also joined films together, making their debut for Vitagraph in 1914. Very busy with East Coast comedy units, they worked for Pathé and Reliance, and became regulars in *The Mishaps of Musty Suffer* series with Harry Watson Jr., as well as the Yonkers-made *Heinie & Louie* comedies that starred Jimmy Aubrey and Walter Kendig. Heading to the West Coast around 1919 Crimmins remained busy in comedy shorts and features such as *The Two Twins* (1923), *Pretty Ladies* (1925), *Chilly Days* (1927), and *White Zombie* (1932) until 1936.

Roscoe's Comique comedies had been a smashing success, with *The Garage* the peak of their box office clout:

> **Arbuckle Plays Four Houses**
> For the first time in motion picture history, a comedy was featured last week simultaneously in New York's four biggest picture theatres. "Fatty" Arbuckle in the Paramount-Arbuckle comedy "The Garage" held the screen at the Rivoli, the Broadway, the Strand, and the Capitol.
> –**Moving Picture World**, January 24, 1920

With the completion of *The Garage* Roscoe would set up shop at Paramount, and Buster Keaton inherited the Comique unit. Buster began production quickly on *The High Sign* (not released until 1921) and *One Week* (1920), with Roscoe helping out in publicity photos and trade items to get Keaton securely launched as a solo star.

Exhibitors Herald (February 7, 1920): "The whole history of slapstick comedy contains no funnier comedy than 'The Garage.'

"'A Dog's Life' and 'Shoulder Arms,' alone in slapstick history, may be set down as funnier than 'The Garage.' And age operates to the advantage of these.

"It is certain that Arbuckle has never done anything in the past to compare with his present effort. He has made more pretentious comedies, more costly ones, but never a more amusing one."

Roscoe takes time from shooting *The Garage* (1920) to talk to L.A. Times social columnist Virginia Wood. Courtesy Marc Wanamaker/Bison Archives.

Wid's Daily (February 1, 1920): "Photographed and staged in fine style, the slapstick comedy bits that make up this two reel comedy will draw round after round of laughter. The star gives a most satisfactory exhibition, and there are numerous bits of business that are distinctly novel."

Exhibitors Herald (June 19, 1920): "All of these Paramount Arbuckle's are good, and Fatty is my best puller. This one is one of the best."

Screen Snapshots (Series 1, No. 3)

Released June 20, 1920. Produced by Jack Cohn and Louis Lewyn for the C.B.C. Film Sales Corp. One Reel. Extant. With Muriel Ostrich, James Corbett, Pauline Frederick, Viola Dana, Roscoe "Fatty" Arbuckle, Charles Murray, Sessue Hayakawa, Bessie Love, Elaine Hammerstein.

Roscoe's great success with his Comique series solidified his position as a major star—which not only led to feature films but also made him a ready subject for publicity. Audiences couldn't get enough of the comedian and he was soon a regular in short movie newsreels.

Exhibitor ad for the long-running *Screen Snapshots* series.

From the beginning of his work with Sennett, Roscoe became a film icon and his round figure was readily identifiable. Popular in the Sennett comedies his image turned up in animated films. In 1916 Roscoe, Mabel Normand and Charlie Chaplin were depicted in a series of cartoons that were produced by the Movca Film Service and distributed on the independent states rights market. Made by John G. Terry and H. M. Shields, whom the exhibitor ads called "World Renown [sic] Cartoonists," titles included *Charlie the Chef*, *Charlie's Busted Romance*, and *Charlie the Busy Barber* (all 1916).

By 1920 motion pictures had become an institution and films about films began proliferating. One of the first series was *Screen Snapshots*, one reelers produced by the C.B.C. Film Sales Corp., which was founded by Jack Cohn, Joe Brandt, and Harry Cohn. *Screen Snapshots* ran until 1958, long after CBC had morphed into Columbia Pictures. This was an early entry in the series, which exists today, where Roscoe is prominently featured in a little impromptu sketch with Sessue Hayakawa and his former Keystone cohort Charles Murray.

At the time the trio was appearing in an all-star production of the play *Arizona* for the benefit of the Hollywood Post of the American Legion. The June 26, 1920 *Moving Picture World* covered the production and detailed:

> *Roscoe Arbuckle was Dr. Fenlon, the army surgeon. Fatty played the big audience on his knee and dandled it up and down and played with it. The crowd was "his baby" every time he had the stage.*
>
> *Charlie Murray got away with the part of Sergeant Kellar, German accent and all, in fine shape. His make-up was great, and like Fatty, the house was all his all the time he was on the stage.*
>
> *Sessue Hayakawa was Sam, the Chink cook. Gus Thomas didn't write many lines for Sam in "Arizona" But you can't keep a good actor down. Sessue made up for the lack of lines with pantomime, he pulled some clever stuff with a wine bottle that got one of the biggest hands of the evening.*

The segment appears to have been shot on the show's set, and the three come out in their costumes. Roscoe and Murray see who can dance the best, and the sequence ends with a terrific pratfall from Roscoe, followed by Murray and Hayakawa getting him upright again.

WID's Daily (9/1/1920): "For the average screen fan an issue of this type, added to the bill, will have the value of frosting added to the cake. Taking the spectator behind the scenes at picture studios and giving him intimate shots of picture celebrities will undoubtedly hold attention, especially so with this production which is titled in splendid style and generally up to the mark."

Screen Snapshots (Series 1, No 6)

Released August 10, 1920. Produced by Jack Cohn and Louis Lewyn for the C.B C. Film Sales Corporation. One reel. With Sessue Hayakawa, Tsure Hoki, Eddie Polo, Blanche Sweet, Ned Flannagan, Neely Edwards, Billy Bitzer, Mary Anderson, Clara Kimball Young, Jack Holt, Fatty Arbuckle, William Duncan, Dustin Farnum, Bessie Barriscale.

On the eve of being a feature film star, Roscoe makes another appearance as himself for *Screen Snapshots*.

WID's Daily (September 5, 1920): "To close, they show a group including Clara Kimball Young, Hayakawa, Jack Holt, Fatty Arbuckle, William Duncan, Dustin Farnum, Bessie Barriscale and others. As a whole, this is up to the standard set in the previous issues of the series."

Chapter 7
Starring Feature Films

THE COMIQUE SERIES had been a cash cow for their distributor Paramount, so much so that Vice-President Jesse Lasky later wrote:

> *Arbuckle's two-reel comedies were produced by Joseph Schenck and released through Famous Players-Lasky, but they did so well that we wanted all three hundred pounds of him for ourselves. When his contract was up for renewal, we outbid Schenck, and proceeded to launch him in feature-length comedies. He made at least a dozen for us, all of them high-grossing hits. Arbuckle was conscientious, hard-working, intelligent, always agreeable and anxious to please. He would invent priceless comedy routines and also had a well developed directorial sense.*
> – *I Blow My Own Horn*, Doubleday, 1957

Roscoe had long been a star of his comedy shorts, but short subjects were on a somewhat low rung in the Hollywood hierarchy. Now his new contract with Paramount made him a full star of prestigious features. After the first, *The Round-Up* (1920), which was a serious western with a basically straight role for Roscoe, they were polite drawing room comedies. Deciding to go for more prestige, Paramount brought in name directors like James Cruze and Joseph Henabery, but it's obvious that Roscoe was an active participant and that he had definite ideas about pepping up the polite comedy with well-placed and frequent bits of physical business. He was one of the first slapstick comics to move into full-length films, but we'll never know how his starring career would have continued to develop as it came to a sudden stop in September 1921.

1920

The Round-Up

Released October 10, 1920. Produced by Famous Players-Lasky Corp. Distributed by Paramount Pictures. Directed by George Melford. Scenario by Tom Forman. Based on the play by Edmund Day. Photographed by Paul Perry. Art titles: Lon Megaree. Seven

Now that he's a feature star Roscoe passes on Oscar Smith's pies for movie ammunition.
Courtesy of The Museum of Modern Art.

reels. (Shot between December 22, 1919 - February 11, 1920) Extant: LOC. With Roscoe Arbuckle, Mabel Julienne Scott, Irving Cummings, Tom Forman, Jean Acker, A. Edward Sutherland, Wallace Beery, Guy Oliver, Jane Wolfe, Lucien Littlefield, Fred Huntley, George Kuwa.

When engineer Dick Lane fails to return from Arizona, his fiancée Echo Allen assumes that he is dead and agrees to marry Jack Payson. On the night of the wedding ceremony, Dick returns and Jack sends him away after collecting the three thousand dollars owed to him by the engineer. Meanwhile, outlaw Buck McKee has robbed the express office and sees Jack's windfall as an opportunity to throw suspicion upon the bridegroom. In order to clear himself, Jack confesses Dick's return to Echo and then rides off in the desert after him. As he overtakes Dick, the two are attacked by Indians and Dick is mortally wounded. Slim Hoover, the sheriff, comes to the rescue, and the U.S. Calvary arrives in time to hear Dick's dying confession, which exonerates Jack from all accusations. He then returns home to his wife, who finds it in her heart to forgive him.

Roscoe had become such a huge star around the world with his slapstick Comique Comedy shorts that Paramount Pictures hired him right away and… put him in a dramatic western. Although it seems a strange choice to do with one of the reigning

Roscoe taking a moment from shooting *The Round-Up* (1920).
Courtesy Marc Wanamaker/Bison Archives.

kings of comedy, in 1920 there had been very few full-length slapstick comedies made. Mack Sennett had produced the famous *Tillie's Punctured Romance* in 1914, but had only occasionally followed it up with longer comedies like *My Valet* (1915), *Yankee Doodle in Berlin* (1919), and *Down on the Farm* (1920). There had been sporadic slapstick features made by other producers, such as Lubin's *Tillie's Tomato Surprise* (1915) with Marie Dressler, but they were very rare.

Mabel Normand beat Roscoe into features, and her initial feature for Samuel Goldwyn was originally set to be the World War I drama *Joan of Plattsburg* (1918). *Joan* proved to be a difficult production and its release was held up, but Mabel's first releases like *Dodging a Million* and *The Floor Below* (both 1918) were heavily-structured Cinderella stories with Mabel having to work around the plot to insert smidgens of comedy business. Mabel and Roscoe's type of comedy shorts, while loved by audiences, didn't get much respect in the film industry itself, where they were often treated like poor step-children. To be taken seriously one had to appear in drama, so it seems the idea of putting them into more serious fare was a move to "legitimize" them as movie stars.

Roscoe does very well in *The Round-Up*, adding some needed comic relief, and playing the serious aspects of his role deftly while leavened with much good humor. The

Cowboy Roscoe on location for his first feature *The Round-Up* (1920). Courtesy of The Museum of Modern Art.

film was based on the 1907 hit play of the same name which oddly enough had starred Maclyn Arbuckle, who was no relation to Roscoe (as he repeatedly let the press know during Roscoe's infamous trials). The play was adapted to the screen by Tom Forman, who also plays the role of Jack Payson. A busy actor and director, Forman worked on popular films such as *Shadows* (1922) and *Kosher Kitty Kelly* (1926), but took his own life in 1926.

Leading ladies Mabel Julienne Scott and Jean Acker were popular in the early 1920s, with Acker having the distinction of being the first (and short-termed) wife of Rudolph Valentino. Future comedy director A. Edward Sutherland is young Bud Lane, and would also support Roscoe in 1921's *The Dollar-a-Year Man* (more on him there). The direction was by George Melford, a workman-like pro, whose best-remembered films are *The Sheik* (1921) starring the aforementioned Rudolph Valentino and the Spanish language version of Universal's *Dracula* (1931), which is regarded today as more atmospheric and cinematic than the Bela Lugosi/Tod Browning telling.

The two villains in the cast would become longtime movie veterans. The evil halfbreed Buck McKee is Wallace Beery, who's remembered today for 1930s MGM classics like *The Champ* (1931) and *Dinner at Eight* (1933). His film career began in 1913 for the Essanay Company, and most of his early work was in slapstick, most memorably playing a big lummox Swedish girl in the *Sweedie* comedy shorts. Besides a brief stint with Mack Sennett, Beery even directed comedies for Essanay and Universal until 1920 when he became in demand as a character actor. Big pictures such as *Robin Hood* (1922), *So Big* (1924), *The*

Lost World (1925), and *Old Ironsides* (1926) followed, as well as a comedy partnership with skinny Raymond Hatton in *Behind the Front* (1926) and its seven sequels. The arrival of sound saw him become something of a superstar with movies like *The Big House* (1930) and *Grand Hotel* (1932).

Irving Cummings, who plays the cad Dick Lane, was an actor from the Broadway stage who had worked with Lillian Russell and began his film work around 1910 at companies like Powers, Pathé, and Champion. Also busy in shorts for Reliance and Imp, he graduated to features in 1914 and was a leading man for many years with outfits such as World, Paramount and Metro, plus in the early 1920s had his own production company where he produced, directed and starred in shorts as Corporal Jim Campbell of the Northwest Mounted Police. After 1923 he primarily switched to directing, and was active until 1959 helming popular titles like *In Old Arizona* (1929), *Curly Top* (1935), *The Story of Alexander Graham Bell* (1939), *Down Argentine Way* (1940), and *The Dolly Sisters* (1945).

A good luck token for Roscoe's first feature is a cameo by Buster Keaton as an on the warpath Indian who's shot by Roscoe and has a spectacular running and flying in the air death scene. Keaton always maintained that he met up with *The Round-Up* company by accident, which seems unlikely considering how close Keaton and Arbuckle were, but here's what Buster told Kevin Brownlow for *The Parade's Gone By* (Knopf, 1968):

> *Right after* The Saphead, *I was up hunting at Long Pine, on the edge of Mojave Desert. It's good quail country, and I went up there to shoot. And there's Arbuckle, on location. Now I had no connection with the picture—it was Paramount—but they had a scene to make and Arbuckle said, "Put make-up on Keaton and let me shoot him."*
>
> *George Melford, the director, says "All right," so they get me in Indian make-up and they put the camera shooting over Arbuckle's head. You could see him take aim at me and shoot....when he shot, I died. But I was going at top speed, and when he hit me I sailed through the air and then plowed the dirt—right over a fifty foot cliff. Ever see a rabbit hit in the back of the head—what it does to him? Well, that's what it looked like it did to me.*
>
> *The silly part of it was that my mother, living in Muskegon, Michigan, went to see it because she liked Arbuckle, and remembered the show from Broadway. When the Indian died on the screen, she said, "That's Buster." How in God's name she could pick me, I don't know. No one told her I was in the picture, and I never thought of writing. It was just a long shot of an Indian. But she knew it was me. "Nobody else could do that," she said.*

Wid's Daily (September 12, 1920): "'The Round Up' is first to be noted because it introduces Roscoe 'Fatty' Arbuckle as a feature star. As has been the case with other good comedians, Arbuckle has often shown in his hilarious two reelers, that he is capable of playing in a more serious vein. He again displays this talent in the role of the jovial sheriff in 'The Round Up,' playing his part in the dramatic sequences of the story with a sincerity and effect that completely disarms those who would laugh at his figure. On the other hand, the producers have shown the good judgement to let him loose in some regular hilarious comedy scenes and in these he shines as of old. The sequence in which he bursts out of his new suit, the one in which he attempts to play at romance with the flirtatious Polly, and his actions at the wedding are all very funny.

Picture-Play (August 1920): "While 'The Round-Up' lacks a theme to make it memorable, it is invigorating entertainment for the hour. Roscoe 'Fatty' Arbuckle, who has been capitalizing his corpulence in two-reel comedies, turns to serious drama as the sheriff. He seems funnier than when he was expected to be funny, which may be the reason he is. He's quick on the draw of both guns and grins—quick as Hart or Chaplin. Mr. Arbuckle might never have carved immortality in custard, but as the sheriff he puts his notch in the hilt of film fame."

Motion Picture News (September 18, 1920): "'The Round Up' reminds us of the Westerns which established the name of Thomas H. Ince. It abounds in action and whooping cowboy stuff. Desperados are present to supply conflict. Guns are toted, villains are chased, and romances figure to some extent. When the serious moments take leave for a brief spell at times, when Fatty Arbuckle comes into the scene and executes some peculiar trick of gesture which accounts for the dash of humor. This note of it strikes us could have been used more effectively. There is no denying that the picture is a first class western—one which is abundant in atmosphere and highly colorful backgrounds."

The Life of the Party

Released December 12, 1920. Produced by Famous Players-Lasky Corp. Distributed by Paramount Pictures. Directed by Joseph Henabery. Scenario by Walter Woods. Based on the Saturday Evening Post story by Irwin S. Cobb. Photographed by Karl Brown. Assistant direction by Dick Johnson. 5 reels. (Shot between April 15 – May 22, 1920) Extant: LOC, EYE, GOS. With Roscoe Arbuckle, Viora Daniel, Winifred Greenwood, Roscoe Karns, Julia Faye, Frank Campeau, Allen Connor, Frederick Starr, Ben Lewis, Lucien Littlefield.

Roscoe plays Algernon Leary, an impoverished lawyer without any clients. Milly Hollister, the secretary for the Better Babies League, consults Judge Voris in her fight against the milk trust not knowing that Voris is in collusion with the trust. To sidetrack Milly he sends her to Algernon, as he regards him as an incompetent lawyer. Algernon is so smitten with Milly that he accepts the case for nothing, but when the case comes to trial under Judge Voris, Voris makes Algernon seem ridiculous and throws the case out of court. Algernon denounces Voris and the women nominate him as a mayoral candidate to run against Voris, the candidate for the trust. To discredit Algernon, Voris and the trust hire a notorious woman, French Kate, to compromise and discredit him. The scandal alienates Milly, who announces her betrothal to Voris. After a series of misadventures, Algernon is vindicated and wins both Milly and the election.

As *The Round-Up* had been a dramatic western with some humorous overtones from Roscoe, *The Life of the Party* marked his first real feature-length comedy. This, and the

Roscoe in a quandary on a lobby card for *The Life of the Party* (1920). Courtesy Mike Hawks.

seven Paramount features that would follow, were polite, drawing room comedies based on popular stories, novels, or plays. *The Life of the Party* had been a story by popular Kentucky-born humorist Irvin S. Cobb, who wrote numerous stories and titles for films, as well as had his own career as an actor as a sort of fill-in for Will Rogers. Almost all of the source materials were adapted by Walter Woods, and then livened up by Roscoe with well-placed and frequent bits of business. Most of the slapstick and bits of old routines (dodging a cop, disguising himself as a chair, etc.) occur late in the film when Roscoe gets stranded out in the snow in a child's costume and ends up hiding in an apartment building. Although he had been directing his shorts for some time the studio seems to have decided that for features he needed a "real" director, so people like Joseph Henabery and James Cruze were brought in to fill the bill.

Having started his career as an actor, along the way playing Abraham Lincoln in D.W. Griffith's *The Birth of a Nation* (1915), Joseph Henabery became an assistant to Griffith on *Intolerance* (1916). Eventually he became a full director under the master's tutelage, and was soon helming Douglas Fairbanks vehicles like *Say! Young Man* (1918) and *His Majesty the American* (1919). After his stint directing Roscoe he remained on Paramount's payroll and piloted three Mary Miles Minter comedies for their subsidiary company Realart, and spent the rest of the 1920s directing mostly light-hearted features with Bessie Love, Glenn

Hunter, Alice Day, and Monty Banks' *Play Safe* (1927). When sound arrived Henabery directed all kinds of dramatic and musical shorts for eight years at the Vitaphone Studio in Brooklyn, and although he and Roscoe were there at the same time they didn't work together again. His career wound down in the very beginning of the 1940s.

Henabery's memoirs, *Before, In and After Hollywood*, was published in 1997, with a whole section on his recollections of working with Roscoe. Very much told from his point of view, he was very candid on his thoughts on Roscoe and the work they did together:

> *About 1919 or 1920, Paramount signed Roscoe "Fatty" Arbuckle to make feature comedies. "Fatty" had been a tremendous box-office draw in his two-reel slapstick comedies. He had ability, great determination and experience (before he even worked in pictures he had been on the stage, mostly with stock companies or with traveling musical shows). A company he worked with for a long time had traveled extensively along the West Coast and in Asia with success, and it ran for months at a second-rate theatre in Los Angeles. I never saw any of their shows, but judging by the lengths of their runs, they must have been pretty good.*

Henabery claims that when he heard that the front office was picking a dramatic western for Roscoe's debut feature he was sure that it was bad idea, and told many of the powers that be so:

> *They made the film, I believe it was called* The Round Up *[1920], and it was a terrific flop. Exhibitors rated the picture at twenty-seven out of a possible one hundred percent. Arbuckle was so disturbed that he asked to be let out of his contract. He wanted to go back to two-reel comedies. They finally got Arbuckle calmed down and convinced him that the first picture was a fluke, that he would fare better in the future, and that he would be given more latitude to do his stuff.*
>
> *Apparently, Frank Woods remembered my outburst in regard to Arbuckle's first picture, and I was asked about working with Arbuckle for a while. I said okay, provided everybody understood one thing—I was going to be boss. I wanted to be sure Arbuckle had not been given some authority that might later cause friction. I made it known that anything I didn't like would not be shot. I made three pictures with Arbuckle, and we got along together well. Sometimes he made suggestions I liked and we would shoot accordingly. With suggestions I didn't like, I'd explain why I thought they should not be used. He was cooperative and we had no trouble.*

Henabery also talks a bit about a stunt sequence where Roscoe tumbles backwards out of a window, but like most movie veterans doesn't reveal how it was really done. The sequence is broken up into quick shots, so all could be safely done by Roscoe. One very brief shot where he hangs out of the window by one arm with the street below in sharp

Roscoe in Harold Lloyd territory in a frame grab from *The Life of the Party* (1920). Courtesy the Library of Congress.

focus was done the way Harold Lloyd did his famous climb up the side of a building in *Safety Last* (1923) —with a set of the window built on the roof of a building. Since the set was near the edge of the roof, the angle of the camera puts Roscoe hanging in the same frame with the real street and traffic that's behind him. Although this pre-dates *Safety Last*, the technique was in wide use with Harold Lloyd already using it in *Look Out Below* (1919) and *High and Dizzy* (1920).

Roscoe's love interest is played by Viora Daniel, a California-born brunette who began her career with Paramount in 1920. *The Life of the Party* was only her fifth film, and after appearing with Max Linder in *Be My Wife* (1921) she became a regular in Christie Comedies. Working with Neal Burns, Bobby Vernon, Jay Belasco, and Earl Rodney she appeared in two-reelers such as *Let Me Explain*, *In for Life*, *A Pair of Sexes* (all 1921), *A Barnyard Cavalier*, *Cold Feet*, and *The Son of a Sheik* (all 1922). After this she turned up sporadically in features like *Old Shoes* (1925), *Quarantined Rivals*, and *Bulldog Pluck* (both 1927), and left pictures in 1927.

Julia Faye appears as the "other woman" who's out to blackmail Roscoe on behalf of the milk trust. Faye was born in Richmond, Virginia, and after college became a fashion model where it's said that she was discovered by Cecil B. DeMille (she spent the bulk of her career working for DeMille). Her first known appearances were tiny parts in Fine Arts Productions supervised by D.W. Griffith such as *The Lamb* and *Don Quixote* (both 1915), and she also spent time in Mack Sennett and Triangle comedies like *His Auto-Ruination, Bucking Society, The Surf Girl*, and *A Lover's Might* (all 1916). Her first DeMille production was 1917's *The Woman God Forgot*, which led to more like *Old Wives for New* (1918), *Don't Change Your Husband* (1919), *Something to Think About* (1920), and *Saturday Night* (1922).

She was also co-starred with light comic Bryant Washburn for Paramount's *Venus in the East, A Very Good Young Man, It Pays to Advertise*, and *The Six Best Cellars* (all 1919). Through the 1920s while appearing in DeMille dramas like *The Ten Commandments* (1923), *Triumph* (1924), *The Road to Yesterday* (1925), and *The Volga Boatman* (1926), she still had time for many comedies like *Changing Husbands* (1924), *Bachelor Brides, Meet the Prince* (both 1926), *Turkish Delight,* and *Chicago* (both 1927). In the sound era she continued to work for DeMille, but was mostly seen in uncredited bit parts in features and on television until 1963.

Julia Faye vamps Roscoe in an original glass slide for *The Life of the Party* (1920). Courtesy Matt Vogel.

Algernon's buddy, Sam Perkins, is played by another movie Roscoe—Roscoe Karns. Well-known for his memorable sound film appearances in classics like *It Happened One Night* and *Twentieth Century* (both 1934), it's generally overlooked that Karns also had an extensive silent film career. Born in San Bernardino, California in 1891, Karns began working on the stage in San Diego as leading man to actress Marjorie Rambeau. Appearing in stock for fifteen years all over the Pacific Coast, he got his first film work in 1915 for the Lubin Company under Romaine Fielding. In 1918 he began appearing in Christie Comedies like *Beans for Two*, *Know Thy Wife* (both 1918), *Brides for Two*, and *Sally's Blighted Career* (both 1919).

It was a short stop to featured roles in features and through the 1920s he turned up in *The Family Honor* (1920), *Conquering the Woman* (1922), *The Overland Limited* (1925), *Ritzy*, and *Wings* (both 1927), with a few Century Comedies like *Down to the Ships to See* (1923) made in between. Sound films really brought him to prominence, and he was busy in pictures like *Night After Night* (1932), *Alibi Ike* (1935), *His Girl Friday*, *They Drive By Night* (both 1940), and *Woman of the Year* (1942) until 1964. His television work included *Rocky King, Detective* (1950-1954) and *Hennesey* (1959-1962).

Moving Picture World (December 4, 1920): "Arbuckle has long been 'The Life of the Party' from the time he first appeared in Keystone farce, an actor who needs neither make-up nor strained grimace to be amusing—he is just 'naturally funny.' Not withstanding his admirable and well-balanced support, Arbuckle centers attention by overpowering force of personality. 'The Life of the Party' as shown at the Rivoli Theatre, is a gem of its kind, suited to all audiences, high and low, inasmuch as it is pure entertainment of the finest quality."

Motion Picture News (December 4, 1920): "This should be a great picture for the children. Those in the Rivoli, New York chuckled with glee. The grown-ups had a good time, too. This type of picture is just the thing for Arbuckle. It doesn't tax his capabilities and ask him to do the impossible. He is the Fatty Arbuckle of the short comedy. Which means he is at his best."

Wid's Daily (December 5, 1920): "The biggest feature of 'Fatty' Arbuckle's second Paramount is that it's such a vast improvement over his first. The comedy moments are well distributed and there are several mighty good laughs. The star is the life of the picture as well as the party. His efforts to amuse are sincere and he makes a good deal out of a rather limited role.

"The actual story material isn't conspicuous enough to attract much attention but the situations afford good opportunities particularly suited to Arbuckle's personality, and he never misses a chance to make good. Perhaps the biggest laugh of the picture comes when 'Fatty' as a lawyer who only pretends to be busy, is smitten with a pretty face in such a bad way that he sinks into a swivel chair near a window, the chair inclines backward and the hero turns a somersault out the window with the next flash showing him hanging on the ledge for life. This all happens so spontaneously that it brought a score of 'ohs' at the Rivoli.

"Other good bits that register are the 'busy' lawyer's safe which contains a desirable assortment of 'kickey' beverages. 'Fatty' in one place sits on the desk buzzer and all the 'help' come running in for orders from the boss and again when his prim stenographer interrupts one of his 'nips,' he holds the bottle in back of him, with his back to the window. A window cleaner on a scaffold outside, relieves him of the bottle. The titles are well written and get a good share of the laughs in themselves."

1921

Brewster's Millions

Released January 4, 1921. Produced by Famous Players-Lasky Corp. Distributed by Paramount Pictures. Directed by Joseph Henabery. Scenario by Walter Woods. Based on the book by George Barr McCutcheon and the play by Winchell Smith. Photographed by Karl Brown. Art direction by Wilfred Buckland. Assistant direction by Dick Johnston. Supervised by Frank E. Woods. Six reels. (Shot between July 29 – Oct 20, 1920) With Roscoe Arbuckle, Betty Ross Clarke, Fred W. Huntley, Marian Skinner, James Corrigan, Jean Acker, Charles Ogle, Neely Edwards, William Boyd, L.J. McCarthy, Parker J. McConnell, John McFarland, Walter A. Coughlin.

The two grandfathers of Monte Brewster, Messrs. Brewster and Ingraham, argue as to how the fatherless boy shall be brought up. Brewster wants him to work, Ingraham doesn't and the mother says she will bring him up to suit her own ideas. At twenty-five Monte is

Roscoe at the ship's controls in *Brewster's Millions* (1921).

clerk in a steamship office. Grandfather Brewster gives him one million dollars, so that he need not work. Ingraham proposes to Monte that if he will spend the million in one year, be absolutely broke and contract no matrimonial alliance, he will hand him five million dollars in stock at the end of the period. Monte starts to spend the million, his three friends McLeod, Harrison and Pettingill, not aware of the circumstances try to reform him. They persuade Peggy Gray to take a job in Monte's office, and she succeeds in turning away many promoters after his money. One of Peggy's wise investments is the purchase of silver mines from the Peruvian Government, which must be worked within a certain time or revert to the government. Monte refuses to work the mines. They all start for a yachting cruise to Peru, but Monte brings about a breakdown in the boat's engine. Peggy confesses to him that she was trying to save his fortune. He decides to wed her, go to Peru and save the money at which the mines are valued. The engine is repaired, a steamer in distress signals for help. Monte gives up the Peru project and tows her into port. Ingraham tells him he has broken his contract by marrying Peggy. He loses the Ingraham money, but gets a million salvage for the steamer and all ends happily.

Brewster's Millions is one of the hardiest properties ever created. It was originally a novel written in 1902 by George Barr McCutcheon (as Richard Greaves), and was adapted into a hit Broadway play in 1906. The success of the play led to the fledgling Paramount Company purchasing the story for movies, and making three versions of it. The first was directed by Cecil B. DeMille in 1914, next came Roscoe's, and the studio finished by dusting it off and adapting it as *Miss Brewster's Millions* (1926) for their female comedy star Bebe Daniels. Other American screen tellings are the 1945 and 1985 versions with Dennis O'Keefe and Richard Pryor respectively, and overseas it's been done in England, India, and Brazil, with a Broadway musical adaptation, *Three on a Spree*, done in 1951. At the writing of this book there's yet another film, *Brewster's Billions*, in pre-production.

Right now Roscoe's version is not known to exist, but director Joseph Henabery had some remembrances of the film and its making in his memoir:

> *The story began when the Arbuckle character was a baby. Arbuckle's face and figure were ideal for a baby or child makeup. We opened the picture with a scene at a large dinner table. Roscoe was supposed to be about one or one-and-a-half years old. Two rival wealthy grandfathers were present and bickering about which family the baby resembled. For the long shot, we had a real baby in a highchair, seated with his back to the camera. I had ordered an oversized highchair built for Arbuckle. We took front view close-ups of Roscoe in this chair. In relation to the giant chair, Arbuckle's bulk made him appear baby-size. He looked great in a baby dress.*
>
> *Probably the most amusing bit in this sequence was after we arranged for the real baby to get a hold of the bowl that held cube sugar. The baby pulled it on to the tray of the highchair and took out several cubes. In the reverse close shot of Arbuckle in the oversized chair, he had the two cubes of sugar in his hand and then rolled them as if they were dice. It was a big surprise, and a terrific laugh.*

Baby Roscoe early in *Brewster's Millions* (1921).

Henabery also talked about some elaborate trick photography that was done by cameraman Karl Brown (more on him on *The Traveling Salesman*):

> *I did another sequence in this picture with Roscoe as a child of four or five years of age. The scenes were designed to show that Roscoe was a mischievous little boy. We did the job with split-screen photography.*
>
> *Practically all trick photography in those days was done in the camera. The cameraman had to be careful to insure that each half of a split screen would have the correct placement, otherwise the special effect would draw attention to itself and destroy the illusion.*
>
> *In these scenes, one half of the scene was occupied by the grandparents in natural size as they stood by a sideboard drinking tea, while the other half of the screen was occupied by Roscoe, made to appear as a little four-or-five-year-old kid preparing to devil the old folks.*

> To make Roscoe look small on his side of the screen, everything was built about four times natural size. The furniture was so elaborate that several pieces had to be reproduced photographically, because the cost of building oversize furniture of this type would have been too great. We enlarged the photographs four times the furniture's natural size. Then we made cutouts from the enlargements, placed them in upright positions, and dusted in shadows on the floor where the natural shadows would have been.
>
> One particularly tricky piece of work in this episode required careful timing. The kid shot a stone with a slingshot from the enlarged half of the split screen to break a teacup in the hands of his grandfather in the natural half of the split screen. In other words, these scenes were shot separately, but when viewed on the screen, the stone from the enlarged scene was timed so perfectly that the cup in the natural scene was broken at exactly the right second. I believe we made 23 takes before we felt sure we had a match.

The big climax of *Brewster's Millions* took place on a ship at sea. A large rocking stage was constructed. The delay caused while the set was built started a precedent of Roscoe working on more than one Paramount production at a time:

> **Arbuckle Kept Busy on Two Productions**
>
> Roscoe Arbuckle is leading a nice quiet life these days, being so absorbed in his work that he doesn't have time for anything else. For the last few days the rotund comedian has been engaged on two different pictures for Paramount. The moment one director finishes with him the other puts up a call sheet summoning him to work in the other production.
>
> For scenes in "Brewster's Millions," which is almost completed, a massive setting some sixty or seventy feet high and of an equal length, provided with a double system of rockers and representing the complete deck and cabin exteriors of a yacht, had to be constructed. As this occasioned a few days delay during which Mr. Arbuckle would be idle, Director James Cruze, who was all set to launch production work on "The Dollar-A-Year Man," the next picture in which Mr. Arbuckle was to star, decided to begin work right away. The call went up and soon the popular "Fatty" was portraying his role of amateur detective in the new picture.
>
> – ***Motion Picture News***, November 13, 1920

Taking advantage of Roscoe's strong work ethic, the studio would soon have him making back to back pictures. Henabery gives some details on the storm at sea sequence:

> On this large rocking stage, we erected different sets at various times. A deck set was used several times for scenes when big waves, dropped from 20,000 gallon tanks, were to hit the ship and nearly wash people overboard. Then we had a dining room with long family tables deliberately designed

to allow the diner's food to slide back and forth the length of the tables as the ship rolled. Each time Roscoe started to eat, his food would slide away, then return and slide away again. We had a porthole that was forced open by a huge wave that swept in a big fish (dead). Roscoe convincingly played around with the fish as if to catch it and put it out the porthole. The audience loved this action.

In one instance we went too far to get a comic effect. I had a 20,000 gallon tank of water that was released onto the deck set to hit Arbuckle and send him rolling. Since I thought the scene looked weak because the water on the deck appeared shallow, I had them put in another 20,000 gallon tank alongside the first. We remade the shot. The two tanks were released, and the torrent of water shot Roscoe down the deck out of sight into a passageway out of camera view. When Roscoe disappeared from sight, I ran down the deck, still flooded with water, to the passageway. Roscoe, still under several feet of water, had been trapped under the platform but had managed to hold his breath. On the screen, the scene wasn't a bit funny, and I eventually used the first shot. It's no fun to see someone swept away to God knows where.

Roscoe and the others are having a rough voyage in *Brewster's Millions* (1921).

Supporting Roscoe on screen are solid character players such as Jean Acker, back from *The Round-Up*, Charles Ogle, and leading lady Betty Ross Clarke (see *The Traveling Salesman*). One silent comedy regular in the cast, playing Brewster's friend McLeod, was Neely Edwards. Having started in vaudeville as part of a comedy team with Edward Flannigan in the popular sketch *On and Off*, the pair broke into films in 1919 starring in the *Hallroom Boys* Comedies for Harry Cohn's C.B.C. Film Sales Corp. Eventually moving their antics to the National Film Corporation for a few *Flannigan and Edwards* shorts, Edwards also headlined in shorts for the Special Pictures Corporation and Arrow's *Speed Comedies* as well as support in features like this and *Green Temptation* (1922). 1922 saw him starring as "Nervy Ned" in a series for Universal. Ned was a gentleman tramp, who, with comic Bert Roach as his hobo valet, scrupulously avoided work and looked for easy money.

By 1924 the series added Alice Howell and morphed into a domestic series with Edwards and Howell as a comfortably middle-class married couple that had Roach gumming up their lives as their goofy butler. Edwards continued on in shorts and features through the early days of sound, but eventually slowed down. He started a new leg of his career when he joined the cast of the popular stage show *The Drunkard* in 1933 and stayed with it during its legendary run of twenty-five years. He continued doing occasional bit parts in films, but retired when *The Drunkard* closed in 1959.

Exhibitor's Trade Review (January 29, 1921): "Score another decisive feature comedy hit for the rotund and irrepressible Roscoe Arbuckle, better known as 'Fatty' throughout the confines of filmland. Arbuckle is fast achieving his pet ambition to register as something more than a mere slapstick performer, his latest screen vehicle offers intensely amusing straight comedy without a single dull moment in its mirthful action and the star has never been seen to better advantage. Cleverly phrased, snappy subtitles help the action along amazingly, there are no end of amusing farcical situations in evidence and an atmosphere of clean, wholesome fun dominates the entire production. Arbuckle's portrayal of dollar-burdened Monte is laughable in the extreme. The episodes showing the big fellow in various stages of growth from babyhood up are a certain comic cure for the blues and 'Fatty' proves himself a genuine artist in every instance."

Moving Picture World (December 5, 1921): "Roscoe Arbuckle, erstwhile 'Fatty,' now a full-fledged comedian, while bound to please by sheer force of personality works a little too hard in 'Brewster's Millions' to be at his best. It is not at all necessary for him to interpolate any of the horseplay of farce in order to win in pure comedy. His expressive face is far more effective than his physical agility, and he need not fear to give larger development to other characterizations in his plays, if only for the sake of variety. Scenarist and director have done well in their amplification of the original story, and the whole production moves along the lines of good craftsmanship. As shown at the Rialto Theatre, 'Brewster's Millions' is bound to prove a highly amusing entertainment."

The Dollar-A-Year Man

Released April 3, 1921. Produced by Famous Players-Lasky Corp. Distributed by Paramount Pictures. Directed by James Cruze. Scenario by Walter Woods. Photographed by Karl Brown. Five reels. (Shot between October 16 – November 6, 1920) With Roscoe

Roscoe under duress on the glass slide for 1921's *The Dollar-A-Year Man*. Courtesy Matt Vogel.

Arbuckle, Lila Lee, Winifred Greenwood, J. M. Dumont, A. Edward Sutherland, Edwin Stevens, Henry Johnson, Arthur Thalasso.

Laundryman Franklin Pinney, the owner of the only speedboat of the Santa Vista Yacht Club, is requested not to attend the club's reception for a visiting prince. Franklin meets the prince in a haunted house after a band of anarchists have plotted to kidnap him and have absconded with a South American diplomat by mistake. Discovering that his sweetheart's father is a Secret Service man on the track of the anarchists and is detailed to act as a bodyguard to the prince, Franklin and the prince overcome the blackguards, and, invited to the reception, the laundryman is welcomed as a hero and son-in-law by his sweetheart's father.

The Dollar-A-Year Man marked the start of Roscoe's professional and personal relationship with director James Cruze. The pair became fast friends, and according to cameraman Karl Brown shared a couple of common interests—alcohol and partying. One of the major directors of the 1920s, Cruze is remembered for epics because of the survival of *The Covered Wagon* (1923) and *Old Ironsides* (1926). His signature work was satirical and idiosyncratic comedies, but practically all of these films have disappeared today. Born

James Cruze Bosen on March 27, 1884 in Ogden, Utah, he became stage struck when he saw a traveling tent show at age sixteen, and left his Danish Mormon family to join the theatre. Hoboing his way to San Francisco he worked as a fisherman and in hotels while he pursued theatrical work. Eventually he appeared in medicine shows, vaudeville and stock companies on the road.

In 1908 he switched to films when he joined the ensemble of the Thanhouser Company in New Rochelle, New York. He became one of their popular stars, and in addition to some of their more important shorts such as *The Cry of the Children* (1912) and *When the Studio Burned* (1913), he headlined in their serials *The Million Dollar Mystery* (1914) and *Zudora* (both 1914). Working for Paramount in 1918 he moved behind the camera after breaking a leg and became Wallace Reid's director for nine consecutive films—from *Too Many Millions* (1918) to *Hawthorne of the USA* (1919). After more comedies with Bryant Washburn and Wanda Hawley he hooked up with Roscoe. 1923's *The Covered Wagon* was an immense critical and box office hit, and made Cruze a star director.

At his peak through the 1920s, he set up his own production company and devoted himself to offbeat comedies such as *Beggar on Horseback*, *The Goose Hangs High* (both 1925) and *On to Reno* (1928), while still turning in an occasional big budget historical epic like *The Pony Express* (1925) and *Old Ironsides* (1926). The arrival of sound found him a bit more on shaky ground as a director, but he still turned out some very interesting

Director James Cruze (right) poses with Roscoe, and *Gasoline Gus* stories writer George Patullo (left). Courtesy The Museum of Modern Art.

pictures like *The Great Gabbo* (1929), *Mr. Skitch* (1933) *David Harum* (1934) and *Sutter's Gold* (1936). His last films were programmers for Republic Pictures, and he retired in 1938. Always a true friend to Roscoe, Cruze stood by him during the worst days of the trials. Afterwards he continued to push for Roscoe to be reinstated in pictures and would put him under contract with his own company. Cruze was eventually side-lined by poor health and died in 1942.

Future comedy director A. Edward Sutherland supports Roscoe as he did a year earlier in *The Round-Up*. The British-born Sutherland came from a prominent theatrical family—his aunt Blanche Ring was a big American stage star—and he began in films as an actor, appearing in many of the Triangle-made Keystone Comedies such as *Won by a Foot* and *The Ring and the Girl* (both 1917). Eventually he became a young leading man, but after being an assistant director to Charlie Chaplin on *The Kid* (1921), *A Woman of Paris* (1923), and *The Gold Rush* (1925) he became a full-time director in 1925 and until the late 1950s was known for comedies such as *It's the Old Army Game* (1926), *Tillie's Punctured Romance* (1928), *Palmy Days* (1931), *Poppy* (1937), *The Flying Deuces* (1939), and *The Boys from Syracuse* (1940).

The other interesting supporting player is Arthur Thalaso, who plays the large anarchist. Thalaso has been completely neglected even though he was a regular foil for big name comics like Harry Langdon, Monty Banks, and W. C. Fields. Born Arthur Thallassoff Schultz, he was brought to films by no less than Charlie Chaplin:

> *Charlie Chaplin recently engaged Arthur Thallasso said to be a double of Chaplin's old time favorite foil, Eric Campbell, who was killed in an auto accident. Chaplin states that if Thallasso proves to be as good as he looks, he will certainly be a winner.*
> – **Exhibitors Herald and Motography**, August 23, 1919.

Chaplin appears to have been looking for a big heavy to take Campbell's place and discovered Thalaso. There are brief glimpses of make-up tests of Thalaso in Campbell get-up done at the Chaplin Studio that appear at the end of the 1996 documentary on Campbell, *Chaplin's Goliath*. His first film appears to have been *A Day's Pleasure* (1919) where he plays the large woman who runs for the embarking boat and gets caught hanging between the boat and the pier. Chaplin also used him as the crook who with his partner Albert Austin steals the car with the baby in the back seat in *The Kid*. The pair leaves the baby in an alley where he's found by Chaplin and grows into Jackie Coogan.

Working for Chaplin was a great way to jump start anyone's career, so Thalaso was immediately in demand for features such as *La La Lucille* (1920) with Eddie Lyons and Lee Moran, and Mary Pickford's *Little Lord Fauntleroy* (1921). His large size and blustery personality put him in good stead as a heavy for small star comics, and he fulfilled that position for Monty Banks in *Sailing Along* (1922), *Horse Shoes* (1927), and *A Perfect Gentleman* (1928), as well as Harry Langdon in *The Strong Man* (1926), *Three's a Crowd* (1927), and *Skirt Shy* (1929). Roscoe used him again in the Lloyd Hamilton short *The Movies* (1925) and *Gigolettes* (1932). After sound arrived his last memorable appearance was as the man who wants a stamp from the very middle of the page from

Arthur Thalasso acting as the heavy for Monty Banks and Ruth Dwyer in the 1927 feature *The Perfect Gentleman*. Courtesy Jim Kerkhoff.

W. C. Fields in *The Pharmacist* (1933). Although his subsequent roles were brief and uncredited, often as cops, bartenders, or train conductors, he remained extremely busy until 1947.

Moving Picture World (April 2, 1921): "In 'The Dollar a Year Man' you are not obliged to take anything seriously—not even the serious scenes. But this will not hurt your enjoyment of the picture in the least. It's a five-reel farce and the story doesn't count—much. The plot is merely a peg on which to hang all the funny business invented or remembered by the author and the director. Roscoe Arbuckle is the biggest thing about the picture, literally and as a source of entertainment. He puts over every good piece of business that comes his way with deftness of a sleight-of-hand performer. When there is nothing provided by the scenario writer he puts something of his own over and makes a dozen laughs grow where the director would have been delighted to get one. His fight with a gang of crooks is a yell of delight for the spectator but must come within an inch of sure death for the bunch of kidnappers—when 'Fatty' cheerfully cast his bulk from over the stair rail on top of six or more of their numbers.

"Lila Lee acts the sweetheart of Roscoe and does the most delightful comedy work of her screen career. She has developed into a vivacious and accomplished ingénue."

Exhibitors Herald (April 9, 1921): "Arbuckle to the rescue of a weak vehicle. He is ninety per cent of the picture's entertainment value. Lila Lee makes a clever foil for the star. James Cruze directed.

"This feature proves beyond question that Roscoe Arbuckle is a splendid comedian whether indulging in polite light comedy or throwing custard pies. Walter Woods is responsible for the story and the continuity and he has a lot to answer for. Even with the aid of Mr. Arbuckle the story is not clear at times. Another technical fault that mitigates against the story's merit is found in the titles. These are not masterpieces of humor and besides they tell most of the story. And yet despite all these things Mr. Arbuckle actually pitches in, and with the aid of director James Cruze, makes the complete production better than the usual farce solely because of his ability as a 'gag' artist supreme."

Camera! (April 9, 1921): "If Douglas Fairbanks thinks that his last offering was the utmost in 'nuttiness' we wish that he would make it a point to witness Roscoe Arbuckle in his latest Paramount release, 'The Dollar a Year Man.' We believe that he would learn thereby much that he has never even suspected heretofore about that which lurks in the corners of a rampant comedy imagination. We did!

"Never has farce or slapstick either (this production is a combination of both) boasted an insaner plot. Because the picture contains much clever laugh-producing material, however, the story is saved for the amusement of many and the rare joy of not a few.

"The photography is good generally and some of the now rather popular tinting is utilized advantageously."

Screen Snapshots (Series 2, No.1 – F)

Released June 1921. Produced by Jack Cohn and Louis Lewyn for the C.B.C. Film Sales Corporation. Distributed by Federated Film Exchange. One Reel. With Max Linder, Lina Cavalier, Lucien Muratore, May Allison, Doris May, Wallace MacDonald, Cecil B. DeMille, Dorothy Dalton, Fatty Arbuckle, Bebe Daniels, Mary Pickford.

> *"Screen Snapshots", produced by Jack Cohn and Louis Lewyn, will portray in a highly effective manner—in their work, in their homes and engaged in their favorite recreations—virtually every picture star and popular pictures favorite working in the country, as well as occasional glimpses of those working in the big studios abroad.*
>
> *– **Exhibitors Herald**, September 2, 1922*

Roscoe was becoming a regular in these news items, and in addition to the American-made entries he was also turning up in European equivalents. British Pathé and French Gaumont footage of the comic on a European tour exist. Both have him doing gags with a cigarette—swallowing it, blowing smoke out of his nose, and eventually coughing it up again. Roscoe's growing international fame made these appearances as popular as his domestic ones.

Film Daily (June 5, 1921): "Fans will find this number of 'Screen Snapshots' above the average of the series."

Moving Picture Age (September, 1921): "The informality of this series makes it a pleasant change from the usual type of one-reeler."

The Traveling Salesman

Released June 5, 1921. Produced by Famous Players-Lasky Corp. Distributed by Paramount Pictures. Directed by Joseph Henabery. Based on the play by James Grant Forbes. Scenario by Walter Woods. Photographed by Karl Brown. 5 reels. (Shot between June 10 – July 12, 1920) Extent: GEM. With Roscoe Arbuckle, Betty Ross Clarke, Frank Holland, Wilton Taylor, Lucille Ward, Jim Blackwell, Richard Wayne, George Pearce, Robert Dudley, Gordon Rogers.

Bob Blake, a traveling salesman, falls asleep on the train and his drummer friends, by a ruse, get him off the train at a lonely country crossing, leading him to believe it is his destination. He spends the night in an unoccupied house, with a sheriff's sale sign tacked on the door. The next day he arrives at Grand River, his destination, and falls in love with the girl who owns the house. Martin Drury, an unscrupulous politician, conspires with Franklin Royce to obtain the property at a cheap price, knowing that the railroad wants the land. Bob beats Royce to the sheriff's sale and pays the taxes. Beth thinks he has duped her. Drury and

Roscoe made tongue-tied by Betty Ross Clarke in *The Traveling Salesman* (1921). Courtesy Sam Gill.

Royce give her $10,000 for the place and she signs it away. Mrs. Babbitt suggests to Bob that under the state law a wife cannot sign the deed without the signature of her husband, and Bob grasps the idea and marries Beth.

The Traveling Salesman is one of three surviving but unavailable Arbuckle features. The only known print resides at the George Eastman Museum in Rochester, New York, and while it hasn't been properly restored as yet, it is being preserved and maintained. What the Museum has is a four-reel German release version, which is slightly cut down from the five-reel American release. American movies were often modified for overseas release—sometimes shortened but in other cases expanded according to the preferred tastes of the target audience. Since Roscoe's films were purged in America the survival of his features is more likely from European sources. *Salesman* was filmed before *Brewster's Millions* and *The Dollar a Year Man*, but not released until after both. It was Roscoe's last released work with director Joseph Henabery. Although the pair would end up at Brooklyn's Vitaphone Studio in 1932 they never worked together again.

A key member of the Arbuckle feature unit was cameraman Karl Brown, who shot six out of seven of Roscoe's features. In addition to being a cinematographer, Brown would be a director, screen writer, and memoirist for over fifty years. His parents were actors,

Roscoe has second thoughts on sharing with George C. Pearce (left) and Frank Holland (middle) in *The Traveling Salesman* (1921). Courtesy Sam Gill.

and Brown's first job in films was as a sixteen year old lab man for the Kinemacolor Co. of America. When they went belly-up the teenager got a job taking stills at Selig on the big hit *The Spoilers* (1914), but having difficulty getting more still-taking work, he heard that D.W, Griffith was permanently moving his entire company to California. Setting his sights on assisting Griffith's famous cameraman, Billy Bitzer, Brown won the older man over and ended up working for the Griffith unit until 1919. During that time he was involved on the director's great productions, like *The Birth of a Nation* (1915), *Intolerance* (1916), and *Broken Blossoms* (1919) as well as others he produced and supervised.

After World War 1 service he worked again for Griffith but soon moved over to being a chief cinematographer at Paramount. He joined Roscoe's unit in 1920 with *The Life of the Party*, and Brown soon began working with director James Cruze, photographing all his films through 1926's *Mannequin*. Sadly most of these pictures are missing today, but *The Covered Wagon* (1923) and *Beggar on Horseback* (1926) show an astonishing range—one showcasing detailed location work and the other expressionistic and stylized studio settings. In 1927 Brown left cinematography and began directing. Taking his cue from James Cruze, his first two productions were very non-traditional by Hollywood standards.

Jim Blackwell brings the refreshments for Roscoe, George C. Pearce (left), and Frank Holland (middle) in *The Traveling Salesman* (1921). Courtesy Sam Gill.

Stark Love (1927) was a simple story set in the Carolina Hills shot on location with a largely non-professional cast, and *His Dog* (1927) chronicled a down and outer who finds a stray dog, with the dog being the most important character. Brown continued directing in sound films, but they were program pictures for independents and smaller studios like Republic and Monogram. After 1938 he continued writing, again more lower-budgeted pictures for Columbia and Monogram like *Before I Hang* (1940) and *The Ape Man* (1943). His last work in the industry was writing some 1960 episodes of the television series *Death Valley Days*, but in his later years he was rediscovered by Kevin Brownlow, who included his firsthand accounts in his documentary series *Hollywood* (1980) and *D.W. Griffith Father of Film* (1993). Brown also published the memoir *Adventures with D.W. Griffith* in 1976, before his death in 1990.

In the supporting cast is Lucille Ward, who had last worked with Roscoe at Keystone in 1914's *An Incompetent Hero*, and black actor Jim Blackwell. The older Blackwell was a very dignified presence, and specialized in playing old family retainers in films like Buster Keaton's *Our Hospitality* (1923) and *Hand's Up!* (1926) with Raymond Griffith. Doing her second turn as Roscoe's leading lady is Betty Ross Clarke. Born in Langdon, North Dakota, Clarke was primarily a stage actress who began working in touring stock. She made her Broadway debut in 1917 in the play *The Family Exit*, and was tapped for films in 1920. Besides *Brewster's Millions* and *The Traveling Salesman* with Roscoe, her other early 1920s films include *If I Were King* (1920), *Mother O' Mine* (1921), and *At the Sign of the Jack O' Lantern* (1922). Having married British-born banker Arthur Collins, the couple moved to England where Ms. Clarke performed on stage and in European films such as *The Cost of Beauty* and *Um Eine Million* (both 1924). She returned to America and Hollywood films in 1931, but for the most part her roles were small and uncredited. She left the industry in 1940.

Motion Picture News (May 7, 1921): "Fatty Arbuckle in his latest picture 'The Traveling Salesman,' seems to have caught his stride again after a dismal effort in 'The Dollar a Year Man.' His newest release, like 'Brewster's Millions,' is an adaptation of a successful play, both of which have been picturized before. The picture, insofar as its characterization is concerned, is ideally suited to Arbuckle's personality, although some will say it is not entirely sure-fire because he is expected to furnish exaggerated hokum. There is no striving to put over the comedy. Those who remember 'Brewster's Millions' may have some grievance in the fact that there are no moments of broad slapstick. Perhaps had the star exaggerated his efforts it would hit a higher mark. What Arbuckle does here can be duplicated by any heavyweight actor. So it might have been better had he supplied his own brand of comedy—a brand which cannot be imitated. 'The Traveling Salesman' affords good entertainment, is capably interpreted and directed."

Moving Picture World (May 7, 1921): "It is upon the personality and acting of Roscoe (Fatty) Arbuckle that the Paramount picturization of the stage play, 'The Traveling Salesman,' depends mostly for its appeal. While it cannot be called Arbuckle's best picture, it makes an amusing vehicle for the corpulent star, affording him plenty of chances for a display of his unique style of fun-making. 'Fatty' interpolates some comic touches unknown to the stage play. He has the character of the breezy, good natured, good hearted traveling salesman down pat, and as each situation requires, a vast variety of amusing expressions flit across his rotund countenance, all prone to tickle the risibilities. Although the picture starts off slowly and drags a little in one or two places, there is more than enough comedy in it to make it a worthwhile attraction."

Crazy to Marry

Released August 28, 1921 (sources give other dates in mid-August). Produced by Famous Players-Lasky Corp. Distributed by Paramount Pictures. Directed by James Cruze. Scenario by Walter Woods. Story by Frank Condon. Photography by Karl Brown. Five reels. (Shot between January 17 – February 19, 1921) Extant: GOS, BRUS. With Roscoe Arbuckle, Lila Lee, Laura Anson, Edwin Stevens, Lillian Leighton, Bull Montana, Allen Durnell, Sidney Bracey, Genevieve Blinn, Clarence Burton, Henry Johnson, Charles Ogle, Jackie Young, Lucien Littlefield.

Dr. Hobart Hupp, who believes he can cure criminals by surgery, is about to experiment on Dago Red, who has been promised freedom if the operation is successful. Ready to do the surgery Dr. Hupp is reminded that it is his wedding day. Estrella De Morgan, daughter of a socially prominent family, is waiting to become his bride, although she is actually in love

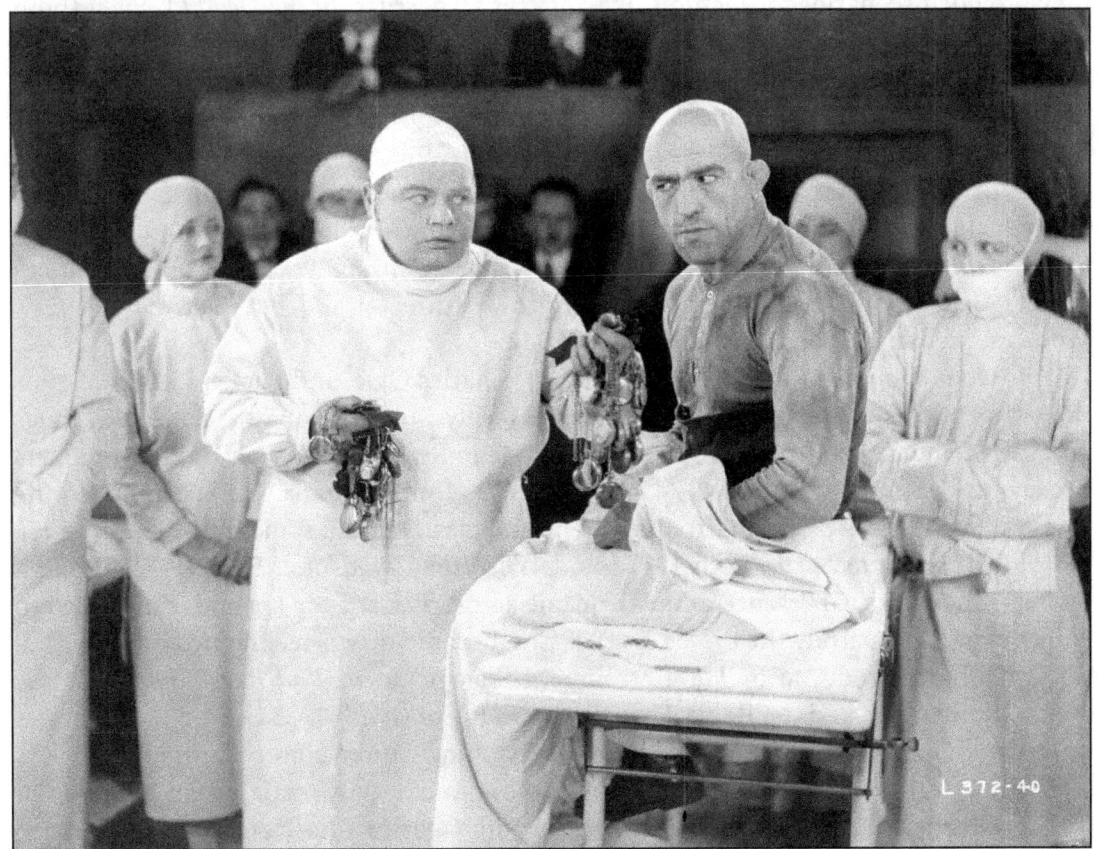

Roscoe having surgically removed Bull Montana's (right) pilfered goods in *Crazy to Marry* (1921). Courtesy Marc Wanamaker/Bison Archives.

with young Arthur Simmons. En route, Hupp is mistaken by the charming Annabelle Landis for her chauffeur, and deciding to desert the waiting bride, he drives Annabelle to her home 300 miles away. There she is halted by her parents who want her to marry another man. Dago Red now appears to rescue the doctor, and with a minister and Annabelle they row to an island. There they find Estrella, who has eloped with Arthur, and the parents arrive to find them all married.

Released in August of 1921, *Crazy to Marry* was only in theatres for about a week when Roscoe's Labor Day party scandal hit the newspapers. Yanked out of theatres, its fate and that of three features still in the can, were left on hold as Roscoe started the first of his manslaughter trials. *Crazy to Marry* hasn't been viewed since, and although it exists in European archives and has been transferred to safety film, it remains unavailable.

For the screenplay Walter Woods adapted the Frank Condon story *Three Miles Out*. With the exception of *The Round Up*, all of Roscoe's features were written by Woods. Starting his career on stage as a leading man, Woods was also a director/manager of stock companies in St. Louis, Cincinnati, Richmond, and Massachusetts. While barnstorming around the country he began writing, and authored numerous plays such as *Billy the Kid*, *Girl of Eagle Ranch*, *Within Four Walls*, and *The Sunset Gun*.

Woods started his film career writing for Lubin and Universal, and while at "Big U" he formed a partnership with fellow writer F. McGrew Willis. Known as Willis-Woods, they provided scenarios for pictures like *Society's Hypocrites*, *In the Dead O' Night* (both 1916), *Won by Grit*, and *The Flame of Youth* (both 1917). In 1917 they went their separate ways – Willis to Fox and Woods to Paramount. There Woods was writing for Houdini, and also the light-hearted Wallace Reid vehicles *The Love Burglar* and *Hawthorne of the USA* (both 1919). At this time he hooked up with director James Cruze and became his steady collaborator until 1936. In addition to Roscoe's pictures, Woods work with Cruze includes *One Glorious Day* (1922), *Ruggles of Red Gap* (1923), *Beggar on Horseback* (1925), *Old Ironsides* (1926), *The Mating Call* (1928), *Salvation Nell* (1931), and *Sutter's Gold* (1936). Also writing cameraman Karl Brown's directorial debut *Stark Love* (1927), Woods retired in 1938, and passed away in 1942.

Roscoe's supporting cast includes Lila Lee, Charles Ogle, and Lucien Littlefield, plus three new additions to his character circle. Pug-ugly Bull Montana specialized in mugs and thugs, and here plays the comic criminal Dago Red. Born in Italy, Luigi Montagna became a wrestler and toured the United States as Bull Montana. He began appearing in films around 1917, working frequently in Douglas Fairbanks' pictures like *In Again, Out Again*, *Down to Earth* (both 1917), and *When the Clouds Roll By* (1919). Although an imposing physical presence, Montana came across as just a big lug and leaned toward comedy and self-parody. In the early 1920s he became a two-reel comedy star with a series of shorts produced by Hunt Stromberg that included *Glad Rags*, *The Punctured Prince* (both 1922), and the Robin Hood spoof *Rob 'Em Good* (1923).

Also in demand for features he played everything from a comic Cardinal Richelieu in Max Linder's *The Three Must-Get-Theres* (1922) to a heavily made-up missing link in *The Lost World* (1925). Frequently turning up with Charley Chase and other Hal Roach comics, *The Uneasy Three* (1925), *On the Front Page* (1926), *The Sting of Stings* (1927), and *The Fight Pest* (1928) were some of his appearances on the Roach lot. Sadly the changeover

Roscoe checks out Bull Montana's facial fuzz for *Crazy to Marry* (1921).
Courtesy of The Museum of Modern Art.

to sound films wasn't kind to Montana. Not really an actor, and with a thick Italian accent, his roles plummeted to unbilled walk-ons, such as in the serial *Flash Gordon* (1936) where he's on screen for just a few moments as a feral monkey man. Retiring from films in 1937, he passed away in 1950.

Roscoe's annoying prospective mother-in-law was played by the heavy-set Lillian Leighton, who had the market cornered on combative wives and matrons. A newspaper

Lillian Leighton (left) and Laura Anson are on hand in *Crazy to Marry* (1921) to create comic complications for Roscoe.

woman before embarking on the stage, Leighton toured the country with a self-written sketch, in addition to appearing in stock and even managing her own company. Her movie career began in 1911 with the Selig Company in Chicago, and right away she was playing mothers, cooks, and hotel keepers in shorts like *His First Long Trousers*, *Getting Married* (both 1911), *Mistaken Identity*, and *Murray the Masher* (both 1912). She also played "mamma" in the studio's film version of *The Katzenjammer Kids* comic strip, which included the titles *They Go Tobogganing*, and *Unwilling Scholars* (both 1912). Eventually she moved to Selig's West Coast studio, where Roscoe had started his film career, and there she was a regular as Mrs. Plum in their 1915 comedy series *The Chronicles of Bloom Center*.

When the series ended she had a brief stint at Vogue Comedies, and then joined the E&R Jungle Film Company as the human co-star to the simian team of Napoleon and Sally, supporting them in entries such as *Some Detective!* and *Uncle's Little Ones* (both 1916). She made the leap to features and was in demand for "A" pictures such as *Joan the Woman* (1916), *Male and Female* (1919), *Peck's Bad Boy* (1921), *Ruggles of Red Gap* (1923), and *Tumbleweeds* (1925). Like Bull Montana, in the late 1920s she began making semi-regular appearances at the Hal Roach Studio, and lent her comic expertise in *Your Husband's Past*, *Be Your Age* (both 1926), *Flaming Fathers* (1927), *Blow by Blow*, and *Fair and Muddy* (both 1928). While there she worked with Charley Chase, Max Davidson, and Our Gang. Still busy in the early days of sound, she continued to turn up as aunts, teachers, and pioneer women in *Feet First* (1930), *The Bitter Tea of General Yen* (1933), *Millions in the Air* (1935), and *Trapped by Television* (1936) until 1937.

Sidney Bracy was a familiar face in pictures until 1942. Usually seen in sound films as butlers or valets, he had a wider variety of roles in the silent days. Born in Melbourne, Australia in 1877, he started his stage career there at age sixteen, and worked for J.C. Williamson. During his extensive stage years he performed in Gilbert & Sullivan operettas, and supported the stars Kyrle Bellew, Nat C. Goodwin, and Nazimova. He entered pictures in 1910 with Kalem through director Sidney Olcott, but was soon appearing with the Vitagraph Company. 1913 saw him become a regular in the Thanhouser Film Company's stable of actors, and was busy for them in dramas and comedies on the order of *Robin Hood*, *The Hoodoo Umbrella* (both 1913), *Mrs Pinkhurst's Proxy* (1914), *God's Witness*, and *The Baby Benefactor* (both 1915). Making the jump to feature films, he began turning up in good supporting roles for films made at Universal, Fox, and finally Paramount. For Roscoe he would be in *Crazy to Marry* and *Leap Year*, and continued on with good roles in pictures such as *Merry Go Round*, *Ruggles of Red Gap* (both 1923), *Her Night of Romance* (1924), and *The Blackbird* (1926).

The peak of his career was 1928 with roles in high profile pictures like *The Crowd*, *The Cameraman*, *Home, James*, *The Wedding March*, and *Show People*. Unfortunately the arrival of sound changed the playing field for Bracy and he was oddly demoted to uncredited roles, usually as butlers, for the next decade. Occasionally he'd have more to do in shorts, such as the *Our Gang* comedies *Second Childhood* (1936) and *Three Smart Boys* (1937), but he mostly did walk-ons as manservants in features that include *A Star is Born*, *Easy Living* (both 1937), *Merrily We Live* (1938), *The Old Maid* (1939), and *You Belong to Me* (1941) until his death in 1942.

The Billboard (August 13, 1921): "A fifty-minute comedy with an abundance of laughs.

"In 'Crazy to Marry,' Roscoe Arbuckle is deprived of his usual comedy costume, but the fact that he is stylishly dressed does not detract from his ability to get laughs, and as that is without doubt the purpose of this picture, it fulfills its mission. There is not much of a story, but the ludicrous situations which follow each other with almost bewildering rapidity prevent the picture from becoming tiresome. The action is rapid and the uncertainty as to what is going to follow keeps interest alive. But it is regrettable that Director Cruze considered it necessary to give Roscoe a bath in wet cement; it is a dirty piece of business which strikes a discordant note without adding to the laughs."

Variety (August 5, 1921): "To attempt to describe in cold, unfeeling print the story of a 'Fatty' Arbuckle comedy is well-nigh futile task. And if, perchance, some descriptive writing genius succeeded, he would only be spoiling a bunch of fun for those unfortunate to read it.

Arbuckle's newest pre-release is 'Crazy to Marry,' a Paramount five-reel production, written by Frank Conden, scenario by Walter Woods, directed by James Cruze. No effort will here be made to relate this tale, but it is only fair to state that it is one of the funniest 'jazbo' slaps-stick affairs ever conceived. Not only are the inimitably ludicrous mannerisms of the obese comedian uproariously funny, but there is a plot of no mean caliber. It is sufficient to make for a rip-roaring stage farce—one of those in-and-out-of-doors, fast-moving affairs originated by the French at which you laugh out loud and then feel like kicking yourself for not being sufficiently blasé to restrain yourself."

Los Angeles Herald (August 2, 1921): "Sid Grauman is to be thanked for the splendid variety of numbers on the bill at his Million Dollar house this week. First is the Famous Players-Lasky picture, 'Crazy to Marry,' with Fatty Arbuckle as the crazy one, then Bull Montana in person….

"The picture, 'Crazy to Marry,' has not much of plot, but a fine cast and many comedy situations that only Fatty Arbuckle knows how to handle make it a laugh feast. Lila Lee is the foil for Fatty's nonsense, and is very clever in handling her part. Others who deserve credit for their work in the cast are Bull Montana, Charles Ogle, Lillian Leighton, Clarence Burton, Lucien Littlefield, Allen Durnell, Edwin Stevens and Laura Anson.

"The plot is twisted around the shape of Bull Montana's head. He appears as a thief with a longing to go straight, but prevented from doing so by a disease called mesencephalon, and Fatty Arbuckle, as Dr. Hupp, is to operate on him, but is delayed by his wedding. Montana is good in his part, and pulls some very clever stunts in his determination to be operated on. One where he changes his bicycle for a cop's motorcycle, then a Ford and lastly a big car brought down the house."

Exhibitors Trade Review (September 17, 1921): "Excellent. Splendid picture, splendidly played to splendid audiences. Fatty is very popular with film fans here and always welcomed for return dates."

Exhibitors Herald (August 20, 1921): "The production, 'Crazy to Marry' is as good a picture as 'Fatty' Arbuckle has appeared in and his characterization of the love-bitten surgeon is humorous. The closing scene puts the punch in the picture and Arbuckle's pantomime at the luncheon table during this chapter is one of the cleverest bits he has ever done.

"Bull Montana who plays the part of the thief is entitled to special commendation. James Cruze directed the picture and has made good entertainment out of the light material."

Gasoline Gus

Made in 1921 but never released in the United States. Produced by Famous Players-Lasky Corp. Distributed by Paramount Pictures. Directed by James Cruze. Based on the Saturday Evening Post story by George Patullo. Scenario by Walter Woods. Photographed by Karl Brown. Five reels. (Shot between March 21 – Aprl 14, 1921) Extant: GOS, BRUS. With Roscoe Arbuckle, Lila Lee, Charles Ogle, Theodore Lorch, Wilton Taylor, Knute Erickson, Fred Huntely.

Gasoline Gus is the "village boob" who runs the neighborhood garage, and besides playing the trombone he loves Sal Jo Banty, the belle of their little Texas berg. Two con artists, Nate Newberry and Dry Check Charlie, breeze into town and swindle Gus into buying some barren land and getting all the locals involved in the scheme too. It looks bad for Gus when the sham is discovered and everyone thinks they've lost all their money, but luckily oil is struck on the property, making Gus a hero to his girl and the whole town.

Gasoline Gus was originally slated to be part of Paramount's October 1921 release line-up, but ended up in distribution limbo due to Roscoe's court troubles. Following *Gasoline Gus* Roscoe had shot *Leap Year* and *Fast Freight* in rapid succession. Jesse Lasky remembered in his autobiography:

Roscoe having a bad hair day in *Gasoline Gus* (1921). Courtesy Sam Gill.

I recalled the time I had taken over Caruso's eight-week contract from Schenck and made his high salary do double duty by rushing through two pictures instead of one. It would have been a master stroke of economy if the first picture hadn't flopped so badly we couldn't release the second one at all. I thought we wouldn't be taking such a chance on Arbuckle, whose drawing power at the box-office was firmly established. So I schemed with Ben Schulberg to go even further—and make three Arbuckle pictures in a row, without a day lost between them. The fat comedian was passed from the first director right to the second, with still another director impatient to call "Camera!"

It would be hard to imagine more strenuous work than making three old-fashioned lightning-paced comedies. I don't know of another star who would have submitted to such extortionate demands on his energy. But Fatty Arbuckle wasn't one to grumble. There were no temperamental displays in his repertoire. He went through the triple assignment like a whirling dervish, in his top form. They were the funniest pictures he ever made. We were sure they would reap a fortune. Schulberg and I congratulated ourselves on pulling a fast one that would save the company untold overhead. Three Arbuckle pictures in the vault at one time was like a cache of gold.

Although the shooting schedule wasn't quite as non-stop as Lasky remembered, and all three pictures were directed by James Cruze (a marathon for him as well), it was still a grueling pace for Roscoe to keep up. Paramount would basically do the same thing with Wallace Reid, and keep him filled with morphine to do it. *Gasoline Gus* was to have a special pre-release engagement at Sid Grauman's Million Dollar Theater in Los Angeles beginning on Labor Day, September 5. Sadly, everyone's plans were derailed by the events of that holiday weekend:

> *Exhibitors in some parts of the country are cancelling contracts on Arbuckle pictures and withdrawing them during showings.*
>
> *Members of the Motion Picture Theatre Owners of Southern California have adopted a resolution favoring the withdrawal of the films. This action was taken after Sid Grauman withdrew "Gasoline Gus," Arbuckle's latest comedy from his Los Angeles theatre.*
>
> – **Moving Picture World**, September 24, 1921

Gasoline Gus was based on two *Saturday Evening Post* stories by author George Patullo—*Drycheck Charlie* and *Gasoline Gus*. Besides other stories like *Boy Howdy* and *The Liberator*, Patullo was known for his articles about World War I. The adaptation and scenario was the work of the ever-present Walter Woods, but this time he had the help of an old Arbuckle collaborator:

> *Jean Havez has been signed to write Roscoe Arbuckle adaptations.*
> – **Motion Picture News**, March 26, 1921

But the partnership didn't last long:

> ### Jean Havez's Switch
> *Jean Havez walked out of the Lasky lot, where he was supplying the "gag stuff" for the Fatty Arbuckle picture "Gasoline Gus." It was a little too highbrow to suit Jean on Vine Street, so he moved his amiable personage over to the Special Pictures Productions on Santa Monica, where he is supplying material for Monty Banks comedies, the All-Star Comedies, with Chester Conklin, and Louise Fazenda and Neely Edwards productions*
> – **Variety**, April 22, 1921

Much of the picture was shot at the Lasky Ranch where an oil town was built, complete with a well to serve as a gusher. A number of scenes were also made on location in a small town theatre, which director Cruze had found after some excursions to nearby places. A crack supporting cast was assembled, starting with leading lady Lila Lee. Having made her debut with Roscoe in *The Dollar-A-Year Man*, Lee also appeared with him in *Crazy to Marry* and *Fast Freight*. The small and child-like Lee, nicknamed "Cuddles," was born in New Jersey in 1901 and began acting on stage at an early age. Discovered while playing on the street by performer/song writer Gus Edwards, she toured vaudeville with his *School Days* Company for ten years. Although she may have had a few sporadic early appearances, her film career began in earnest when Jesse Lasky brought her to Paramount in 1918.

After making a big impression in Cecil B. DeMille's *Male and Female* (1919), she became the light-comedy leading lady for Roscoe and Wallace Reid in popular features like *Hawthorne of the USA* (1919), *One Glorious Day*, and *The Ghost Breakers* (both 1922). With memorable dramatic performances such as Rudolph Valentino's sweet and long-suffering wife in *Blood and Sand* (1922), the early 1920s were the peak of her career. Although she continued to work for decades, a tempestuous offscreen life affected her career.

Most of her later work was routine, but highlights include *The Unholy Three* (1930) and Olsen and Johnson's *Country Gentlemen* (1936). After a break of more than a decade she returned to acting in the 1950s, and *The Emperor's New Clothes* (1966) and *Cotton Pickin' Chickenpickers* (1967) were her last films. In the 1920s she was married to actor James Kirkwood, and their son James became a writer who, besides two novels about Hollywood (*There Must be a Pony* and *Some Kind of Hero*, which included characters based on his mother), also wrote the play *P.S. Your Cat is Dead* and the book for the megahit musical *A Chorus Line*.

Lila Lee gives Roscoe moral support in *Gasoline Gus* (1921). Courtesy Sam Gill.

In 1959 Lee described *Gasoline Gus* and her impression of Roscoe to Columbia University's Oral History Research Office:

> *Lee: This was a charming sweet picture—a lovely story about this man. You see, they were trying to get Roscoe away from the slapstick thing, he was really a very fine actor, very fine.*
>
> Q: Was he an intelligent man?
>
> *Lee: Oh, yes. And a charming man—sweet, nice. This was the story of a big, fat man who ran a gasoline station. He falls in love with a very pretty young girl, and he cannot possibly believe that she would return his affections, because he'd always had this thing about himself—that he's just a great big hunk of nothing. The fact that she does fall in love with him—he just blossoms, and he still can't believe it. That was the gist of the thing.*

Roscoe also benefitted from the work of three scene-stealing character players. On hand as Drycheck Charlie is Theodore Lorch, who spent his film career specializing in comic heavies. After twenty years on the stage heading his own stock companies, appearing in vaudeville, and working with stars like Julia Marlowe, he made his film debut in Chicago for the Selig and Emerald Companies. At Emerald he supported Chaplin imitator Billy West in shorts like *Mustered Out* and *Cleaning Up* (both 1920), and when West moved back to California Lorch came along.

Soon he was a regular in features such as *The Last of the Mohicans* (1920), *The Sea Hawk* (1924), *The Man on the Box* (1925), *The Better 'Ole* (1926), and *Sailor Izzy Murphy* (1927), as well as turning up in shorts with Lloyd Hamilton and Charley Bowers. The transition to sound found the actor mostly in small uncredited roles, but he did have better parts in some Three Stooges shorts such as *Uncivil Warriors* (1935), *Goofs and Saddle* (1937), and most memorably *Half-Wits Holiday* (1947), where he wagers that the Stooges can't be turned into gentlemen. Also on the board of directors for the Screen Extras Guild, he worked until his death in 1947.

Charles Ogle portrays Nate Newburry, but his best-known film appearance is as the monster in the Edison Company's 1910 version of *Frankenstein*. Born the son of a minister in Zanesville, Ohio, all of his early education was geared to his becoming a minister as well, but an appearance at eighteen with a traveling show led him to give that up and go off with the company. Performing in opera, circuses, minstrel shows, and dramas for fifteen years, he took a break in 1899 and became a lawyer. He set up a practice in Chicago, but by 1904 the lure of the theatre was too strong and he went back to acting. This time he performed for the producers Klaw & Erlanger and sang with star Chauncey Olcott. He made his film debut for Biograph, and in 1908 joined the stock company at Edison Films.

During his six years with Edison he played doctors, kings, wardens, prizefighters, and even George Washington in dramas and comedies such as *The Minute Man* (1911), *How Washington Crossed the Delaware* (1912), *Mother's Lazy Boy* (1913), and *The Uncanny Mr. Gumble* (1914). In 1914 he left to make his home with Universal, and

Roscoe tries to give service with a smile in *Gasoline Gus* (1921). Courtesy Sam Gill.

continued his versatility for their Victor, Imp, and Rex Brands. 1917 saw him busy in numerous Paramount features like *Rebecca of Sunnybrook Farm* (1917), *The Whispering Chorus* (1918), *Treasure Island* (1920), *Miss Lulu Bett* (1921), and *Manslaughter* (1922). In addition to *Gasoline Gus*, he also supported Roscoe in *Brewster's Millions* and *Crazy to Marry*. Films such as *The Ten Commandments* (1923) and *Merton of the Movies* (1924) followed before he retired in 1926.

The role of "Scrap Iron" Swenson is played by the overlooked Knute Erickson, a long-time stage and film performer. Born in Sweden, Erickson began performing on stage in America in 1894, touring vaudeville for many years with the character of "Yon Yonson," and playing with comic Eddie Foy. His introduction to movies was in a series of 1915 shorts for the Harry Cort Comedy Film Company with the persona of "Daffy Dan." After a six year break he returned to movies with *Gasoline Gus* and spent the next fifteen years as support in features like *The Monster* (1925), *Johnny Get Your Hair Cut* (1927), and *Twin Beds* (1929). Most of his sound roles were small and uncredited, but he worked until 1936, and passed away in 1945.

After Roscoe was exonerated *Gasoline Gus* was slotted to mark his return to the screen in April of 1922, but as that was about to happen he ended up being officially banned and the film never came out in America. Like *Crazy to Marry* the film is unavailable but does survive from its European release. This lone review from the trade periodical *Camera!* seems to have been from an industry sneak preview:

Camera! (September 10, 1921): "This comedy, another crossing of slapstick and farce, is up to Arbuckle's high standard in entertainment value and correct presentation. James Cruze's direction is of just the right variety that is almost always to his credit. Karl Brown's photography is also above reproach.

"Roscoe himself is as usual—Fatty. Perhaps, at that, Gasoline Gus is a trifle more peppy than the bulkly comedian's characters customarily are, by which we do not intend an insinuation that they are not always more nimble of movement than an amateur observer would be liable to judge possible from Arbuckle's physical proportions. Seriously, Arbuckle is strictly at home as he slides easily through Gus's harrowing experiences right down to the very finish. He must be criticized for negligence in his make-up, however, which is inexcusably and unpleasantly ragged in various sequences.

"Lila Lee fits in remarkably well opposite the star. This time she appears in the role of Sally Jo Banty, a simple child of the village, whose unwavering loyalty to poor, abused Gus lends her considerable sympathy. We begin to think that Miss Lee has 'located' at last.

"Dry Check Charlie and Brother Newberry, the scheming crooks who do so much to 'ball things up,' generally are very well done by Theodore Lorch and Charles Ogle. They form a great combination."

Leap Year

Made in 1921 but only released in Europe in 1924. Produced by Famous Players-Lasky Corp. Directed by James Cruze. Working title: **Skirt Shy**. Scenario by Walter Woods. Story by Sarah Y. Mason. Photographed by Karl Brown. Assistant Director Vernon Keays. Five reels. (Shot between May 16 – June 9, 1921) Extant: UCLA, LOC, LOB. With Roscoe Arbuckle, Lucien Littlefield, Mary Thurman, John McKinnon, Clarence Geldart, Harriet Hammond, Allen Durnell, Gertrude Short, Winifred Greenwood, Maude Wayne, Sidney Bracey.

Stanley Piper is the scion of a wealthy family and lives in a mansion with his grouchy and woman-hating Uncle Jeremiah. Stanley is inflicted with a stammer that shows itself when he gets excited, especially when he's around girls. In love with his uncle's nurse, he proposes to her when the angry old man fires her, but she is concerned about his wandering eye for other women and turns him down. Stanley goes to Catalina to forget his nurse and stay out of trouble, but when he tries to get advice from three other women about his love for the nurse, they misinterpret what he says. All three think he's proposing to them, and quickly accept his accidental proposals. To get away he hightails it back to the mansion, but they all follow. Lots of going in and out of rooms and slamming doors ensue as he tries to keep the three women from seeing each other, and his nurse seeing any of them. Finally all the details get ironed out, and Stanley gets the girl he truly loves.

Leap Year, like *Gasoline Gus* and the ensuing *Fast Freight*, were shelved and never released in the United States. But they were distributed in Europe:

Leap Year (1921) sees Harriet Hammond with Roscoe in her clutches.

The Roscoe (Fatty) Arbuckle pictures are being released and shown generally in Europe where they are playing to surprisingly big business. The business turned in on these pictures at the London kinemas is phenomenally great.
– **Moving Picture World**, May 13, 1922

Luckily *Leap Year* has survived, and is readily available for appraisal. Comparing it to the early *The Life of the Party* the important difference is *Leap Year* is farce comedy instead of

Roscoe caught between Mary Thurman (left) and Harriet Hammond (right) in *Leap Year* (1921).

polite drawing room comedy. Farce better suits Roscoe's talents and gives him much more to react to. Based on the evidence of *Leap Year* it looks like Roscoe's unit had become a well-oiled machine—James Cruze's pacing is brisk and precise, Walter Wood's scenario is boiled down to the essentials, and Roscoe has found ways to work in more physical business—his stammering and bigger and bigger fits give the perfect opportunity for slapstick action. The Catalina Island location scenes at the hotel are a nice reminder of *The Sea Nymphs* (1914) and *Camping Out* (1919).

Beginning production under the titles *Should a Man Marry?*, and *This Is So Sudden*, an expert cast was gathered for Roscoe's support. Character actress Gertrude Short is the youngest of Roscoe's perspective wives (more on her in 1932's *Gigolettes*), and the other three are former Mack Sennett bathing girls. Leading lady Mary Thurman was a school teacher from Richfield, Utah who headed to Hollywood in 1915 and entered a Sennett bathing suit contest. She began working for Triangle and for three years was an ingénue for Chester Conklin, Ford Sterling, and Charlie Murray in shorts such as *A Bedroom Blunder* (1917), *Friend, Husband, Watch Your Neighbor*, and *Love Loops the Loop* (all 1918). In 1919 she left Sennett and moved into features, and the first four—*The Poor Boob*, *Spotlight Sadie*, *This Hero Stuff*, and *The Prince and Betty* (all 1919) were comedies, but she soon concentrated on dramas, working frequently with the well-known director Allan Dwan.

Some of her features for Dwan include *In the Heart of a Fool* (1920), *The Sin of Martha Queed*, *A Broken Doll* (both 1921), and *Zaza* (1923), where as Florianne, the rival of star and fellow Sennett alumnus Gloria Swanson, she has a knock-down, no holds barred cat fight with La Belle Swanson. *Leap Year* was a rare return to comedy for Thurman, and she sports a page boy hair-do, preceding Colleen Moore and Louise Brooks who were to make it very popular. For the next few years Thurman was kept busy in all types of dramatic features with co-stars such as Edmund Lowe, Helene Chadwick, and Hope Hampton. On location in Florida for *Down upon the Swanee River* (1925) she caught malaria. It seemed that she had fought it off so she continued working, but she developed pneumonia. During her last few days her mother and old friend Juanita Hansen were at her side, and she died in New York in December of 1925. Only thirty years old, her final film *The Wives of the Prophet* was released posthumously in January 1926.

Another Sennett alumnus was Michigan-born Harriet Hammond. Giving up thoughts of about being a concert pianist when she became a Mack Sennett girl in 1918, she spent four years in two-reel comedies such as *She Loved Him Plenty*, *The Village Chestnut* (both 1918), *Hearts and Flowers* (1919), *Great Scott* (1920), and *Astray from Steerage* (1921), as well as the Sennett features *Yankee Doodle in Berlin* (1918), *Married Life* (1920), and *Home Talent* (1921). With her great beauty and warm camera presence she moved into features—some dramas like *Bits of Life* (1921) and *The Golden Gift* (1922), others comedies such as *Leap Year* and *Confidence* (1922). While shooting a 1922 Buck Jones western a premature explosion resulted in injuries and burns to her face. She returned to films in 1925, having a role in the comedy *Man and Maid* opposite Lew Cody, and supported Harry Carey in the westerns *The Man from Red Gulch* (1925), *Driftin' Through*, and *The Seventh Bandit* (both 1926). After the 1928 silent *Queen of the Chorus*, she made one talking appearance in the short *The Chumps* (1930) and left movies.

The final Sennett bathing girl graduate was blonde Maude Wayne, who had joined Triangle in 1917 and was a leading lady in shorts such as *Won by a Foot*, *Innocent Sinners*, *The Camera Cure* (all 1917), *His Punctured Reputation*, and *A Playwright's Wrong* (both 1918). After a few Triangle features she spent 1919 working at Fox Sunshine Comedies in two-reelers like *Back to Nature Girls* (1919). The bulk of the rest of her career was spent in supporting parts in dramatic features, although her few later comedies include *Fixed by George* (1920) with Lyons and Moran, *The Bachelor Daddy* (1922), and *Leap Year*. She continued working in films until 1927.

Charlie in "Teeth"
J. G. Blystone-Fox

Brassett in "Charley's Aunt"
Scott Sidney-Christie

The Minister in "A Woman Who Sinned"—*Finis Fox*

Griggs in "Never Say Die"
George Crone—Douglas MacLean

Push Miller in "Checkers"
W. S. Van Dyke—Fox

LUCIEN LITTLEFIELD

GRanit 0886

Adonis in "In the Palace of the King"
Emmett Flynn—Goldwyn

Charley Winters in "The Deadwood Coach"—*Lynn Reynolds-Fox*

Matt Logan in "The Painted Lady"
Chester Bennett—Fox

A 1920's *Studio Directory* example of Lucien Littlefield's versatility.

As far as the men, Sidney Bracey plays the eccentric publicity agent for Harriet Hammond, and wanders mysteriously in and out of various scenes. Lucien Littlefield plays Roscoe's crotchety uncle Jeremiah Piper, and after appearing in four out of nine of Roscoe's features has his best role in *Leap Year*. Littlefield was something of the Lon Chaney of comedy character acting, playing a wide variety of types and ages during his forty year film career. Born in San Antonio, Texas on August 16, 1895, he first acted at age seventeen, and after attending military school went to Hollywood. Littlefield got in right away with Paramount in 1914 and spent the next ten years as their busy character man in features for Cecil B. DeMille and others like *The Warrens of Virginia*, *The Cheat* (both 1915), *Joan the Woman* (1916), *Hawthorne of the USA* (1919), and *Why Change Your Wife?* (1920).

In 1924 he began branching out to other other studios, which included highlights like *Charley's Aunt* (1925), *The Cat and the Canary*, and *My Best Girl* (both 1927), plus had a stint at the Hal Roach Studio where he appeared in two-reelers like *What Price Goofy?*, *Innocent Husbands* (both 1925), and *Your Husband's Past* (1926). Making the jump to sound films without a blink, he starred in a series of *The Potters* shorts for Vitaphone, and remained very busy in features like *If I Had a Million* (1932), *Sons of the Desert* (1933), *Ruggles of Red Gap* (1935), *Man on the Flying Trapeze* (1936), and *The Little Foxes* (1941). Although he never became a "name," his versatility and comedy prowess kept him extremely active, even becoming a regular face on TV shows like *Lassie*, *The Adventures of Superman*, and *The Abbott and Costello Show*, right to his death in 1960.

Fast Freight

Made in 1921 but never released in the United States. Produced by Famous Players-Lasky Corp. Directed by James Cruze. Story by Curtis Benton. Five reels. (Shot between July 18 – August 13, 1921) With Roscoe Arbuckle. Lila Lee, Nigel Barrie, Herbert Standing, Raymond Hatton, Mary Carr, Gertrude Short, Emily Gerdes.

Roscoe and Lila are newlyweds who go to Chicago for their honeymoon trip. While there, they buy the furnishings for their love nest back home, and, of course, have a lot of misadventures. Finally at the end of their stay, thanks to complications that always occur in comedies, Roscoe ends up wandering the streets in the wee hours of the morning, and is very nervous because of the thought of crime in the big city. When he thinks he hears something he backs into a telephone pole. The metal step of the pole sticks into his back. He thinks it's a gun, and believes that he's being held up. Too scared to look back, the strap of his change purse hooks on the step, and when he takes off running his purse remains with the telephone pole. He runs non-stop through the city all the way to the train yard where Lila is waiting for him. With the money that they had for their return tickets gone, the couple stowaway in the freight car containing their furniture, and set up housekeeping in the car for their long trip home.

This was Roscoe's last produced feature, and like *Gasoline Gus* and *Leap Year* it was never released in America. Not currently known to exist, *Fast Freight* hasn't been seen in almost a hundred years, and because of its non-release there are very few descriptions available. Based on a story by Curtis Benson, it was scenarized by Walter Woods and went

Fast Freight (1921) sees Roscoe and Lila Lee under the scrutiny of Raymond Hatton (glasses), Mary Carr (older lady), Gertrude Short (left), and Emily Gerdes (right). Courtesy of Matt Vogel.

through many title variations. Starting as *Via Fast Freight*, it became *Handle with Care*, then *Freight Prepaid*, before finally ending up *Fast Freight*. Interiors were shot at the Lasky Studio in Hollywood, but the company also spent some time in Chicago shooting scenes in its streets, department stores, and train yards.

Lila Lee returned as Roscoe's leading lady, and the supporting cast consisted of unsung film comedy veterans. Raymond Hatton was a busy character player who made his debut in 1909 in D.W. Griffith-directed Biograph shorts. He got a good training in comedy by appearing in a number of 1913 Keystone Comedies such as *Their First Execution*, *That Ragtime Band*, and *Barney Oldfield's Race for a Life*. By 1915, he had hooked up with Cecil B. DeMille, becoming a regular member of the director's stock company with important roles in *Joan the Woman* (1917), *Male and Female* (1919), and the starring lead in *The Whispering Chorus* (1918). In the 1920s he was a steady supporting actor in comedies like *Head Over Heels* (1922) with Mabel Normand, as well as dramas like *The Hunchback of Notre Dame* (1923).

Hatton got a taste of stardom when he was teamed with Wallace Beery. The mismatched duo was a box office hit in comedy features such as *Behind the Front*, *We're in the Navy Now* (both 1926), and *The Big Killing* (1928). Following their seven starring pictures

Hatton went back to the supporting ranks. Still busy in the early days of talkies, his roles got progressively smaller, and by the 1940s he'd become a fixture of low-budget westerns. He continued working in movies and television until his last appearance in *In Cold Blood* (1967).

Gertrude Short is back from *Leap Year* (see 1932's *Gigolettes*), plus Mary Carr and Emily Gerdes filled in the other character spots. Mary Carr was a long-time stage actress who specialized in mother roles in silent and sound features and shorts. Famous for her star performance in *Over the Hill to the Poorhouse* (1920), she played supporting maternal figures in comedies such as *A Self-Made Failure* (1924), *The Wizard of Oz* (1925), *Stop, Look and Listen*, and *Atta Boy* (both 1926). Her sound films include *Lights of New York* (1928), *One Good Turn*, with Laurel and Hardy, and *Stout Hearts and Willing Hands* (both 1931). She continued working until 1951, and lived to age ninety-nine.

Emily Gerdes was plain and skinny, and seems to have been the prototype for Miss Prissy in Warner Brothers' later *Foghorn Leghorn* cartoons. She got her start in Mary

Roscoe double-checks his train tickets in *Fast Freight* (1921).

Pickford pictures such as *Rebecca of Sunnybrook Farm* (1917) and *How Could You, Jean?* (1918), and spent the 1920s in numerous shorts and features. She worked with Lyons and Moran in *Heart Trouble* (1919) and *Oiling Uncle* (1920), Billy West in *Hello Bill* (1923) and *Fiddlin' Around* (1925), in addition to other shorts with Buster Brown, Charley Bowers, and Cliff Bowes. Her feature appearances include *Bell Boy 13* (1923), *Dynamite Dan* (1924), *Heir-Loons* (1925), and her most often-seen film *Ella Cinders* (1926), where she annoys Colleen Moore as Prissy Pill. She continued in sound films until 1940, mostly in walk-ons in features like *Banjo on My Knee* (1936) and *The Grapes of Wrath* (1940).

Paramount, under extreme public scrutiny due to the Arbuckle trials, as well as the scandals resulting from the murder of director William Desmond Taylor, and the morphine-related death of star Wallace Reid, made a big display of house-cleaning by firing Roscoe. Karl Brown also claimed that president Adolph Zukor ordered the destruction of the negatives of Roscoe's films (but not before prints were struck for Europe). Properties that had been gathered for future Arbuckle vehicles were re-assigned—*The Melancholy Spirit* was made as *One Glorious Day* (1922) with Will Rogers, Wallace Reid got *Thirty Days* (1922), and *The Man from Mexico* was retitled *Let's Get Married* (1926) for Richard Dix. *Are You a Mason?* was one that wasn't re-tooled, and the studio even tapped fat comic Walter Hiers to try and fill Roscoe's shoes with 1923 features like *Mr. Billings Spends His Dime* and *Sixty Cents an Hour* (see Appendix 2).

Chapter 8
Banishment

ROSCOE'S CAREER CAME to a screeching halt with the events that followed Labor Day, 1921. He threw the party at the St Francis Hotel in San Francisco to celebrate the finishing of the consecutive shooting of *Crazy to Marry*, *Gasoline Gus*, *Leap Year*, and *Freight Prepaid*. During the party a young woman named Virginia Rappe was taken violently ill and died a few days later at a hospital. Arbuckle was accused of raping her, and San Francisco's District Attorney, Matthew Brady, saw the case as a way to launch himself into national politics. The subsequent trials were a media circus with the newspapers, which printed rumors as facts and published doctored photographs, creating a public frenzy. After two mistrials Roscoe was completely exonerated, and the final jury issued an apology saying that the case should never have come to trial at all. However the Hollywood establishment, under pressure because of this, and the William Desmond Taylor and Wallace Reid scandals, made Roscoe the sacrificial lamb.

He was officially banned from the screen on April 8, 1922. Having been away from pictures since the scandal broke it seems that Roscoe stuck his first toe back in the cinematic waters by helping out his former apprentices Al St John and Buster Keaton. At the same time Roscoe's final trial ended, St John began directing as well as starring in his two reel Fox comedies, and some of the rare survivors like *Special Delivery* and *Out of Place* (both 1922) contain gags and big physical comedy set pieces that suspiciously have the kind of staging and split-second timing that was an Arbuckle specialty.

For Buster, Roscoe wrote the story for his two-reeler *The Frozen North* (1922). In the July 29, 1922 *Movie Weekly* article *"I'm Broke," Says Roscoe Arbuckle*, reporter Constance Palmer interviewed Arbuckle at the Keaton Studio and confirmed that he was writing for Buster:

> "They paid me a flat rate for the scenario. I was pretty glad to get it. I'm broke, you see, and in debt. I was cleaned out by the first trial.
>
> Everybody thinks I'm under contract with Mr. Schenck. But I'm not under contract or under salary to anyone. I stay around this studio in the capacity of author of Buster's current scenario."

The Frozen North

Released August 28, 1922. Produced by Joseph M. Schenck for Buster Keaton Productions. Distributed by First National Pictures. Directed by Buster Keaton & Eddie Cline. Written by Keaton & Cline (uncredited Roscoe Arbuckle). Photographed by Elgin Lessley. Technical direction by Fred Gabourie. Two reels. Extant: Friuli, UCLA, LOB, LOC, EYE, QUB, Buch. With Buster Keaton, Joe Roberts, Virginia Fox, Bonnie Hill, Freeman Wood, Eddie Cline.

Buster gets out of the last stop of the subway at the North Pole. Coming upon a gambling den he decides to rob the proceeds, and with the help of a cut-out of a gun man he holds everyone up. Unfortunately as he's gathering up the monies his ruse is detected and he's thrown out the window. He then returns home to find his wife making love to another man. After letting a few tears run down his cheek, he takes out his pistol and kills them both. At this point he realizes that he's made a slight mistake—it isn't his house or his wife—and quickly hightails it to his own home.

At home he treats his wife so brusquely that she screams which brings a Mountie to the house to check out the problem. Although his wife is unconscious he puts on a dance record and moves her around on the floor, which satisfies the Mountie that everything is okay.

Buster next decides to woo the woman in the next cabin when her husband is heading off on a trip. Unfortunately the husband comes back for something and catches Buster. When the husband goes off and takes his wife with him Buster summons his Nanook-like henchman and they follow them in the mountains.

After a break while they perform numerous snow and ice fishing gags, Buster fortifies himself with soda pop and goes after the wife again. While Buster confronts her in their cabin, her husband is attacked by and defeats Nanook. The husband then arrives at the

Desperado Buster Keaton has two guns ready to blaze in *The Frozen North* (1922).

cabin after Buster has had his way with the wife. As they fight Buster's wife comes by the window and fires in, shooting Buster in the back. As he's dying he takes out his gun to plug the husband and wife, but at that moment he awakes in an empty movie theatre with the janitor telling him "Wake up—the movie's over."

Roscoe wrote this as a parody of western star William S. Hart. The genesis came after Hart spoke out against Arbuckle during his trials—leading Roscoe and Buster to decide to even the score. After this deadly skewering of his screen persona Buster claimed that it was years before Hart spoke to him again.

The Frozen North turned out to be the most off-beat and unusual of Keaton's nineteen starring two-reelers. It even looks different than the rest of Buster's shorts, probably because of all the snow and cabin interiors. The exterior scenes were shot in Truckee, California where Chaplin would shoot some of the opening scenes for *The Gold Rush* (1925). The snow gives Buster plenty of material for ice fishing, igloo, and sleigh traffic gags.

Definitely a dry-run for Roscoe's later movie-genre parodies like *Curses* and *The Iron Mule* (both 1925), not to mention anticipating W.C. Fields' 1933 *The Fatal Glass of Beer*, this is, thanks to the unusual settings and the unlikeable version of the William S. Hart persona instead of Buster's usual character, the least shown or appreciated of Keaton's starring shorts.

Exhibitors Herald (November 25, 1922): "Here Keaton goes into burlesque, but the word isn't good enough to describe the product. Punch scenes from half a dozen pictures you have seen are parodied with screaming humor. Stars are lampooned with biting satire. Yet all this is incidental, the straightaway action of the subject constituting in itself semi-slapstick of the highest order."

Film Daily (September 24, 1922): "In selecting the drama of the northwest as the subject of his latest burlesque, Buster Keaton has hit the proverbial nail on the head. The subject is one which has not been satirized to any great degree and Keaton's antics have the advantage of novelty. There are several distinctly amusing episodes in the production."

On December 20, 1922, Will Hays lifted Roscoe's ban and he began work on a starring short:

Arbuckle Begins Production in Face of Protests

First Comedy Will Be "Handy Andy"- Reported Picture To Be Handled on States Right Market

After several weeks of preparation, Roscoe "Fatty" Arbuckle last week commenced production on a comedy which he hopes will carry him back into public favor. The picture, "Handy Andy," is a typical Arbuckle two-reel comedy which will be produced at a cost of $75,000, it is said. Production will require about six weeks.

Molly Malone, who played opposite "Fatty" in a number of productions prior to his enforced retirement from the screen several months ago will support the comedian in his newest creation.

The production is being financed by a group of San Francisco capitalists headed by Gavin McNab, the attorney who defended Arbuckle during his

> *trials in San Francisco. The concern is to be known as Screen Comedy Company, of which Jo Paige Smith, prominent vaudeville booking agent, is manager. Space has been rented at the Buster Keaton studios in Hollywood.*
>
> *"Handy Andy" was written by Arbuckle and Joseph A. Mitchell. It will be filmed under the direction of Herman C. Raymaker. No arrangements have been made as yet for the distribution of the initial Arbuckle picture but it is believed that it will be distributed on a states right basis.*
>
> – **Exhibitors Herald**, January 27, 1923

Unfortunately, as *Variety* reported, the outcry among "the reform element and uplift organizations" was so great in response to the lifting of the ban that it killed any thoughts of him returning to the screen. "Many cities have unofficially expressed sentiment through official channels concerning [Hays' decision]," the trade paper asserted. "Perhaps the most important has been the action taken by Mayor Cryer of Los Angeles.... Through pressure brought on him by civic bodies, Mayor Cryer pronounced against Arbuckle." Other cities swiftly followed suit.

Shooting on *Handy Andy* was stopped, but despite the hue and cry Roscoe did make one special film appearance.

Hollywood

Released August 19, 1923. Produced by Famous Players-Lasky Corp. Distributed by Paramount Pictures. Directed by James Cruze. Story by Frank Condon. Adaptation by Tom Geraghty. Photographed by Karl Brown. Eight reels. / **Cast the of the main story**: Hope Drown, Luke Cosgrove, George K. Arthur, Ruby Lafayette, Harrison Gordon, Bess Flowers, Eleanor Lawson, King Zany. **Stars and Celebrity Appearances**: Roscoe Arbuckle, Gertrude Astor, Mary Astor, Agnes Ayres, Baby Peggy, T. Roy Barnes, Noah Beery, William Boyd, Clarence Burton, Robert Cain, Edythe Chapman, Betty Compson, Ricardo Cortez, Viola Dana, Cecil B. De Mille, Charles De Roche, Dinky Dean Reisner, Helen Dunbar, Snitz Edwards, George Fawcett, Julia Faye, James Finlayson, Alec Francis, Jack Gardner, Sid Grauman, Alfred E. Green, Alan Hale, Lloyd Hamilton, Hope Hampton, William S. Hart, Gale Henry, Walter Hiers, Mrs. Walter Hiers, Stuart Holmes, Sigrid Holmquist, Jack Holt, Leatrice Joy, Mayme Kelso, J. Warren Kerrigan, Theodore Kosloff, Kosloff Dancers, Lila Lee, Lillian Leighton, Jacqueline Logan, May McAvoy, Robert McKim, Jeanie Macpherson, Hank Mann, Joe Martin, Thomas Meighan, Bull Montana, Owen Moore, Nita Naldi, Pola Negri, Anna Q. Nilsson, Charles Ogle, Guy Oliver, Kalla Pasha, Eileen Percy, Carmen Phillips, Jack Pickford, Chuck Reisner, Fritzi Ridgeway, Will Rogers, Sennett Girls, Ford Sterling, Anita Stewart, Gloria Swanson, Estelle Taylor, Ben Turpin, Bryant Washburn, Maude Wayne, Claire West, Lawrence Wheat, Lois Wilson.

Angela Whitaker, convinced by her friends that she is so pretty she can easily become a movie star, goes to Hollywood with her old uncle, who is ill and seeking a better climate. Angela is rebuffed at every turn while her uncle, because of his peculiar "beezer," is literally swept into pictures and is always in demand. Finally, the rest of the family and Angela's sweetheart, Lem Lefferts, come to Hollywood to see what has happened. Before long, Angela's

grandmother gets into pictures and so does her aunt, as both are pronounced types. In a spectacular stunt, which a scenario writer pulls to bring attention to himself and Angela, the plan goes wrong and results in Lem getting a job. He makes good, becomes a star, marries Angela, they have twins and they as well as the family parrot are requisitioned for pictures. So the whole family, except for Angela gets into the movies, but she finds contentment as the star's wife.

This satire on the California film industry had so many cameos that it amounted to a who's who of the movies in 1923. James Cruze, the director and Roscoe's good friend, decided to go out on a limb and include Roscoe as one of the cameos, and make a dramatic point with it. Although the film is lost today descriptions of Roscoe's brief turn say that the scene involved a large man who was walking with his back to the camera. He's heading toward the casting office's window, but when he gets near the man inside slams down the window which has the large sign "Closed." Stopping in his tracks the man turns to face the camera and it's Roscoe.

Pretty ballsy and admirable of Cruze, and it's also a surprise that Paramount allowed the scene to be included. The studio had dumped Arbuckle pretty quickly when the scandal hit, and perhaps this was a way to appease their consciences (or test the waters for a possible comeback for the comic so they could release and recoup on the product they had to shelve). At any rate Roscoe was there for the public to see, and this item from the August 1, 1923 *Film Daily* discusses the issue, and gives a little descriptive detail on the lost cameo from various critics:

> **Denies Hidden Motive**
> ***Famous Players Declares Presence of Arbuckle in "Hollywood" Carries No Special Significance***
>
> Officials of Famous Players deny that the flash of Roscoe Arbuckle in "Hollywood" carries any special significance with it. They declare that the Arbuckle contract with the company has been abrogated and that the fact that he appears in the picture is only "one of those things."
>
> In the reviews of "Hollywood" by the metropolitan newspaper critics, some interesting angles are discussed. Thus the critic of the Evening Journal said:
>
> "It is just a flash of Arbuckle that is presented. He looks well groomed. He shrugs his shoulders in a hopeless sort of way as he walks before the camera. Was it a subtle move by friends of Arbuckle to see how the public would receive him again?*** Or was it to show the public that Hollywood's motion picture people will have no more to do with him in films?***
>
> "This reviewer knows that the motion picture colony, as such needs no defense. But we asked certain Paramount people, after seeing the picture 'Hollywood' why Arbuckle was in it.
>
> "It just happened that he was in Hollywood when the picture was taken, and we took him along with the others, was the explanation."

The Herald said -

"The camera is then moved into a closeup and the audience sees Fatty Arbuckle reading that one word ("closed") over and over again.

"There are many perhaps, who will object to this. Well, let them. We can say that, from our point of view it is a marvelously telling touch. It is done with no semblance of false sentiment; it is not a palpable effort to arouse sympathy. It is nothing more than a remarkably eloquent example of moving pictures."

The Sun said -

"Nothing in the way of direct propaganda for the fair name of the film city is directly traceable to this picture, except a rather obvious attempt to restore Fatty Arbuckle to public favor, which met with the biggest hand of the picture last evening."

The Times said -

"Fatty Arbuckle is seen for a few brief moments in this film, but his appearance will not whet public desire for his reintroduction to motion picture enthusiasts. He is at the casting director's window, which is slammed down, leaving the obese comedian with naught to do but walk away with others for whom there is no work. However, none of the interest in this photoplay hinges on this incident, and nothing would be lost by its elimination."

It's very possible that some communities may have cut him out. A large part of the population was convinced he was guilty and did not want to see him on the screen. A few years ago some unedited newsreel footage of a 1927 Hollywood premiere came to light. James Cruze's wife, Betty Compson, arrives at the premiere and her escort was Roscoe. For a brief second he is visible standing next to Compson as she's being interviewed, but all of a sudden the camera shifts with a brisk jerk and the two-shot of Arbuckle and Compson becomes a one-shot of Compson. The cameraman simply realized that the footage was no good with Roscoe in it, and quickly remedied the problem.

James Cruze's brave move didn't affect any immediate changes in the industry's treatment of Roscoe, but he remained a loyal friend and supporter and his steady efforts over the years on Roscoe's behalf helped pave the way to his eventual comeback in the 1930s.

Motion Picture News (July 14, 1923): "The big outstanding feature of this production is that it is refreshingly different. It is a novel idea, and who is there to gainsay that this is not just what a jaded public is hungry for.

"All the Paramount celebrities are in it and the luminaries of many other companies, and, hold your breath, Roscoe 'Fatty' Arbuckle! The introduction of the rotund Roscoe is the big surprise. It is probably a bit of diplomacy. If Roscoe gets a hand every time the picture is shown and the folks thus show that all is forgiven—we believe that it will not be long before the fat funmaker will be in our midst again.

"James Cruze has put much effort into this production and he deserves much credit for the result. The continuity is masterfully done and it is very easy to follow the main theme in spite of the many asides—as we visit the stars and studios. This is a production that is sure to be a box office magnet and everyone is going to like it—because it's out of the beaten path."

Moving Picture World (August 11, 1923): "There have been other pictures that dealt with this subject and showed numerous big players in the big Western film producing center, but this one approaches it from a different angle, for it is a sparkling comedy, a keen satire filled not only with good humor that will make anybody laugh but also with subtle wit and bright, clever touches that will appeal even to the highbrows. In fact it is one of the best made and most cleverly conceived and directed picture that has reached the screen. Every type of patron will like it; there is something in it to please any class of patronage. It ranks as one of the season's most entertaining productions. Don't hesitate to book it.

"Too much credit cannot be given James Cruze for the manner in which he has directed this picture. His work is excellent and unusually smooth. He has played up the human interest note and deftly handled the comedy situations."

A Return to the Stage

With performing in movies cut off to him, Roscoe returned to the stage. In mid-1923 he signed a year's contract with the Pantages Circuit and embarked on a series of performances. He would continue in various stage acts through the early 1930s, appearing around the United States and abroad. For some of these performances Roscoe created filmed preludes, little shorts that would chronicle his misadventures backstage before the show, or show his difficulties getting to the theatre. Buster Keaton and Al St. John appeared to add support and their slapstick expertise. The June 18, 1924 *Variety* gave a description of the opener short shown at the San Francisco Pantages Theatre:

> *He precedes his actual appearance with a picture showing him arriving at the stage door where he is handed his mail by the door keeper. On his way to the dressing room he encounters two stage hands, played by Al St. John and Buster Keaton.*
>
> *Here Arbuckle goes into several comedy "gag" stunts reminiscent of his Keystone days and finally gets to his dressing room. He proceeds to make up, the next film scene shows him attired in the "country boob" costume, a feature of his Keystone films; the loose, baggy trousers, suspenders over shirt and funny little derby hat. As he walks from the dressing room towards the stage the picture ends, the lights come up and "Fatty" walks into view of the audience.*

The following week's *Variety* gave an account of the entire act:

> *When the electric flashed for Arbuckle's turn, an applause storm broke loose and lasted for a full three minutes. The house was dark, as the picture screen had been lowered, but the applause kept up. Then the machine began*

working, and a real slap-stick comedy followed for about four minutes. Roscoe appeared, and another storm of applause broke loose. Arbuckle started in and told the folks that as a native son he was glad to get the real true home welcome, and launched into a series of gags about himself. His turn lasted 19 minutes after which he received another ovation and many floral pieces. For the basis of getting Arbuckle in front of an audience his material suffices. It is said that it was conceived by Lou Anger, Vince Bryan, Joe Mitchell and Jean Havez. The boys mixed a bit of "Will Rogers" into the offering for good measure, and probably will work on what they have given the film comic and round out some consistent "gags" to augment what he has now. However, regardless of what material "Fatty" may have, he ought to be a good time bet around the circuit.

It isn't known exactly how many of these stage shorts were made. A notice from a couple of years later has him appearing with a different film.

Roscoe "Fatty" Arbuckle made his first appearance in a motion picture house in Los Angeles last week since being banned from the screen. Arbuckle appeared in conjunction with a picture entitled "Screenland Beauties of 1925" in which he did some comedy work. Arbuckle did a talk and dance act on the stage.

– **Variety**, August 19, 1925

Roscoe in an unidentified photo with a bevy of actresses. Could this have some connection with *Screenland Beauties of 1925*? Courtesy Marc Wanamaker/Bison Archives.

There was a Fanchon and Marco novelty act of the same name in 1925, but it's unknown if that had anything to do with this film. Sadly, none of these little prelude films are known to survive. Only one or two nitrate prints would have been made for use, and the original negatives are also long gone. In addition to doing his own act Roscoe would sometimes be master of ceremonies for the entire bill. He later did a regular act at his Plantation Club in the late 1920s, and in the early 1930s he would appear with Addie McPhail, who would sing and dance, and sometime be a plant in the audience. He would also work with Jack Shutta as a foil.

Despite a few problems with an occasional local community wanting to keep him off their stage, Roscoe was generally welcomed. The critical reactions were fairly mixed—some were less than impressed:

> *Fatty was in the big trousers, little hat, and sport clothes in general, and would have gotten over very well if only appearance counted. His first attempt to get his act over was a song. Voice and number poor. His constant references to his ostracism proved tiring.*
> – **Exhibitors Herald and Moving Picture World**, June 16, 1928

> *His comedy is puerile. His gags are the hoary ones he used on the screen a generation ago. And like a beggar, he makes a crude play for public sympathy, during his duties of master of ceremonies by constantly referring to his hard lot in recalling, with mock humor and much self-pity, his experiences in the courts.*
> – **Picture Play**, April 1929

But others found him a wow:

> *Roscoe Arbuckle, ably aided by Franklin Batie, drew perhaps the biggest ovation tendered him since his eastern vaude debut. Applause was so long and spontaneous all Fatty could do was just to stand there and feel good over it.*
> – **Variety**, February 8, 1928

> *A riot of laughter and fun, with Addie McPhail of the film comedies assisting, as well as a "plant" in the audience. Arbuckle sings "Something to be Thankful For," and then dances to "Narcissus" with a comedy fall.*
> – **Motion Picture Herald**, May 28, 1932

Chapter 9
Reel Comedies, Inc. – Round One

STILL EMOTIONALLY SHATTERED from his ordeal, and in debt from legal fees, Roscoe needed movie work. A group of friends that included Joe Schenck, Lou Anger, Eddie Mannix, producer Jack White, and Roscoe's trial lawyer Gavin McNab formed Reel Comedies, Inc., a production company for shorts that Roscoe could direct anonymously. In a statement given to trade magazines like the February 10, 1923 *Exhibitors Trade Review* Roscoe said:

> *I signed today a contract with Reel Comedies, Inc., to direct comedies. I am done with acting. My great ambition is to make the world laugh and I can do this best as a director of comedies.*
>
> *This is my chance to make good in the right way and in the business that I know and love, and in a way that should meet the approval of all. I will start work at once and from now on you will not see me or hear from me except through the comedies that I direct.*

Given the brand name Tuxedo Comedies, the shorts were distributed by Educational Pictures.

Educational gets a bad rap today because of its poverty-stricken sound shorts, but in the 1920's it distributed some great comedy from the likes of Jack White, Al Christie, Lloyd Hamilton, Larry Semon and Charley Bowers. The company was formed in 1915 by E.W. Hammons with the intention of making educational films for schools, although when this didn't pan out Hammons began distributing short subjects—travelogues, cartoons, but mostly comedy shorts—and for some reason hung onto the name Educational. This usually gets a chuckle today, as does the company's Aladdin's lamp logo with the motto "The Spice of the Program." In Hammon's defense that's exactly what shorts were considered at the time, as the regular section that covered shorts in *The Moving Picture World* was titled "The Pep of the Program."

In his surviving January 27, 1923 contract with Reel Comedies, Roscoe is designated as "Producer" of the series, and it states that;

> *Producer agrees to personally supervise and direct said comedies and to furnish necessary story, cast and each and every thing necessary to properly produce the said motion pictures.*

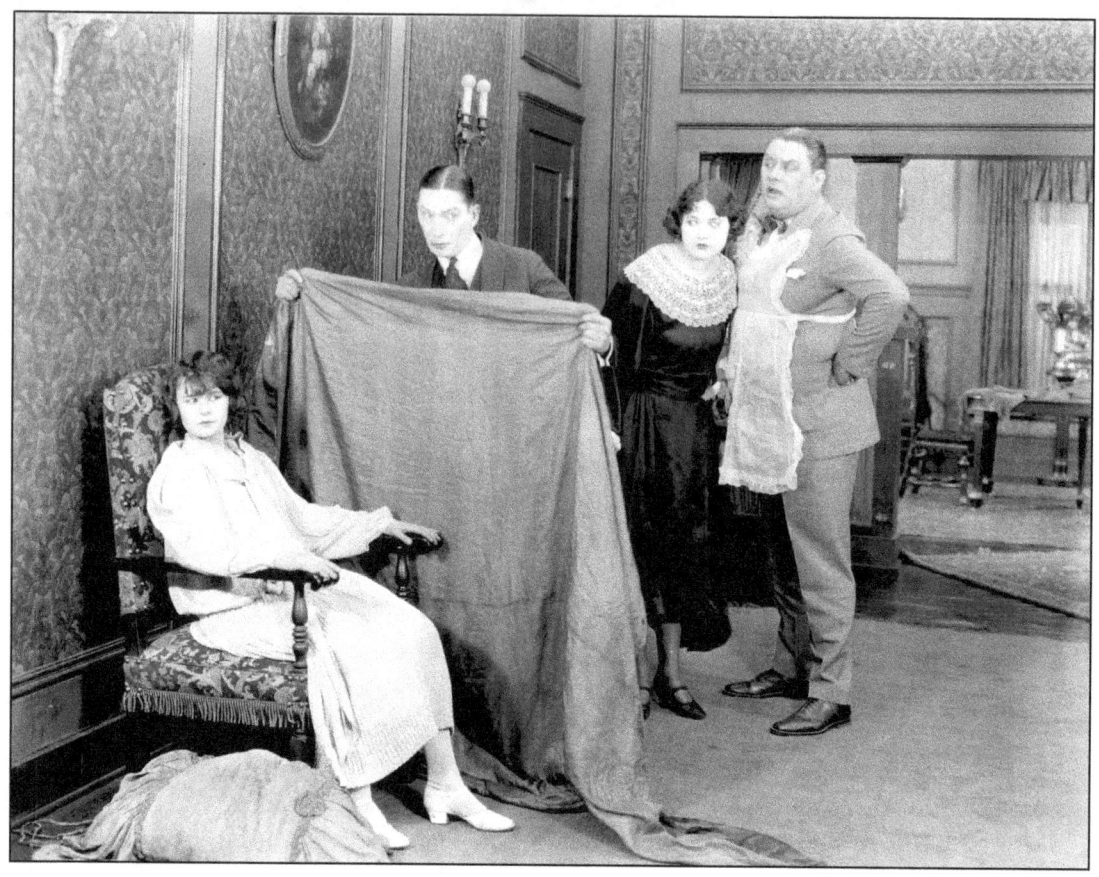

Ned Sparks attempts to hide Marion Harlan from Harry Tighe and Doris Deane in *Easter Bonnets* (1923). Courtesy Sam Gill.

Production began in February of 1923, with Roscoe's salary said to have been $1,000 a week. Stage comics, mostly new to films, were recruited to star. In this first series of six Tuxedo Comedies, two starred well known vaudeville comedians Harry Tighe and Ned Sparks. The other four shorts starred clown and trick equestrian rider Poodles Hanneford.

Not only did this company jumpstart Roscoe's movie work, it also started the careers of others. A June 2, 1945 *Motion Picture Herald* profile on Republic Pictures head Herbert J. Yates revealed:

> But the best place to begin is at the beginning, when Fatty Arbuckle wanted $80,000 to finance a series of eight two-reelers. He went to Yates, a young man who had demonstrated his flair for business by rising rapidly to the top in the tobacco manufacturing business, but who had yet to reveal the instincts of a gambler. Now he revealed them. Arbuckle got his $80,000 on a handshake; Yates got it back with the release of the first two-reeler.
>
> That started the saga of Yates in pictures.

Easter Bonnets

Released August 26, 1923. A Tuxedo Comedy. Produced by Reel Comedies, Inc. Distributed by Educational Pictures. Two reels. With Ned Sparks, Harry Tighe, Doris Deane, Marion Harland.

A pair of newlyweds is plagued by an overabundance of hats.

An article announcing the new Tuxedo Comedies, in the August 4, 1923 *Moving Picture World*, gives this description of the series:

> Ned Sparks is known on the stage as well as in pictures. He has appeared in a number of stage plays under Al Woods' management and has prominent roles in Constance Talmadge pictures.
>
> Harry Tighe is best known as a member of the vaudeville team of Tighe and Clifford. Both Miss Harlan and Miss Dean are members of Pacific Coast stock company, and are making their debut before the camera.
>
> The pictures will be produced by Reel Comedies, Inc., and will endeavor to present a series of polite farce comedies somewhat after the style made popular by the late Sidney Drew and his wife.

Ned Sparks, Harry Tighe, and Doris Deane are the star trio of *Easter Bonnets* (1923). Courtesy Sam Gill.

As noted above Harry Tighe was a long-experienced vaudevillian, but *Easter Bonnets* was not his movie debut. He had been hired in 1917 to make some comedy shorts for Vitagraph with Adele DeGarde, and his early features included *Red Foam* (1920) and *A Wide Open Town* (1922). The latter part of his career saw him back on stage, and busy in radio before his death in 1935.

Ned Sparks is a movie icon today thanks to his deadpan appearances in early 1930s Warner Brothers musicals like *42nd Street* and *Gold Diggers of 1933* (both 1933). He made a lot of silent films, but never made a real movie impression until audiences could hear his monotone drone of a voice. After beginning his career singing in honkytonks and acting with stock companies, he worked his way up to being a Broadway regular in shows such as *Little Miss Brown*, *Nothing but the Truth*, and *My Golden Girl*. Being a leader in the Actor's Equity strike of 1918 caused him to be blackballed by producers.

With the stage cut off he moved into films, and besides the shorts with Roscoe he also appeared in *Good References* (1920) with Constance Talmadge, *Seven Keys to Baldpate* (1925), *Mike* (1926), and *On to Reno* (1928). Busy after making his splash in sound pictures, he continued his dour character in *Blessed Event* (1932), *Sing and Like*

Ned Sparks and Marion Harlan dine in *Easter Bonnets* (1923). Courtesy Sam Gill.

It (1934), *Wake Up and Live* (1937), and *Stage Door Canteen* (1943). Also a smash on radio, in guest appearances and his own show *Grouch Club*, he was later inactive due to bad health and died in 1957.

Motion Picture World Straight from the Shoulder Report (May 3, 1923): "The first one for us of the Tuxedo comedies. It went across good for us and had some funnybone ticklers in it."

Motion Picture World (December 22, 1923): "Here's a clever comedy of the refined type. There's nothing objectionable in it as one finds in so many comedies and everybody seems to thoroughly enjoy it. Has good moral tone and is suitable for Sunday."

Front! (Handy Andy)

Released October 17, 1923. A Tuxedo Comedy. Produced by Reel Comedies, Inc. Distributed by Educational Pictures. (Originally released as **Handy Andy**). Two reels. With Poodles Hanneford, Molly Malone, George Davis, Si Jenks, Jerry Mandy.

Poodles is the handy man at a rural hotel, who has to take on everybody's work when all the help quits.

As the jack-of-all-trades porter of *Front!* (1923) Poodles Hanneford fumbles with Jerry Mandy's suitcase. Courtesy Cole Johnson.

> **"Poodles" Hannaford New Educational Star**
>
> Edwin "Poodles" Hannaford, famous New York Hippodrome clown, equestrian and juggler, will soon make his debut in motion pictures in Tuxedo Comedies, released through Educational Film Exchanges, Inc. "Poodles" is of the fifth generation of circus clowns in the Hannaford family, which has been in the circus business in England for the last 150 years.
>
> Hannaford's first picture will be titled "Handy Andy." "Poodles" will be supported by George Davis, another circus and vaudeville clown, and Cy Jinks and Molly Malone.
>
> – ***Motion Picture News***, September 22, 1923

The British-born Edwin "Poodles" Hanneford as stated above came from a legendary circus family that endures to the present, and became famous for a comedy riding act that was full of laughs and dangerous stunts. He came to America in 1915, worked in circuses and became a vaudeville favorite at the New York Hippodrome (the only New York stage large enough for a team of horses). Tapped to star in Tuxedo Comedies, the idea for his first release appears to have been to salvage as much as possible of Roscoe's aborted *Handy Andy*.

Poodles Hanneford, Molly Malone, and a baby in *Front!* (1923). Courtesy Joseph Yranski.

Although this film is missing today Molly Malone was brought back as leading lady, and in surviving photos Poodles is dressed in Roscoe's signature plaid shirt, suspenders, high-water pants, and derby, in addition to looking somewhat padded. Interestingly, descriptions of the film talk about a long sequence in the second reel where Poodles performs with his back to the camera:

> *An especially effective bit of pantomime and comedy is shown when "Poodles" endeavors to hook up a short hammock on a short rope. This sequence is played with Hannaford's back to the camera, a particularly difficult position from which to register comedy, but his gift of excellent pantomime make the scenes highly effective.*

1923 Educational Pictures pressbook

> *Any comic who can have his back turned to the audience for a couple of hundred feet and hold attention is worthy of being watched, for he is a comer. "Poodles" does just that.*
>
> – *Motion Picture News*, October 6, 1923

The question is whether there were any long shots with Roscoe kept from the original and used in the new release version. Sadly this will remain a question until the time the actual short turns up.

This new version of *Handy Andy* was released under the original title in October of 1923, but to perhaps cover its origin, by the end of the month its title was changed to *Front!* Getting uniformly excellent reviews, *Front!* was warmly received and made an auspicious kick off for the Hanneford series.

Motion Picture News (October 6, 1923): " 'Poodles' Hannaford, for years one of the most famous mimics that clowned at the New York Hippodrome, has finally invaded the screen, and the latter can be thankful that he has, for he is an artist in every sense of the word. Tuxedo Comedies signed him for a series of two-reel comedies that Educational will release. 'Front!' is the first. And it is a wow. It is one of the truly funniest comedies it has been the pleasure of this writer to see. Here is a clown who can be funny without the utilization of age-worn tactics. He is original."

Moving Picture World (October 6, 1923): "The action moves slowly at first, but once it gets under way there are plenty of laughs. 'Poodles' does good work, including some clever acrobatic work in his character as handy man at a hotel who tries to do everybody's work when the help leaves. His attempts to hang a hammock should cause a young riot with the average audience. It is a scream."

No Loafing

Released November 25, 1923. A Tuxedo Comedy. Produced by Reel Comedies, Inc. Distributed by Educational Pictures. Two reels. Extant: 2nd reel. With Poodles Hanneford, Big Joe Roberts

Poodles Hanneford and Big Joe Roberts have an up in the air lunch in *No Loafing* (1923). Courtesy David Wyatt.

Reginald Rosewater is a tramp who comes into town in the middle of a "work or jail" reform movement, and with a persistent cop on his heels Reginald tries to look busy. All his pretenses of work fall through, and it looks like he's going to end up in the jug when he finally connects with a job moving furniture.

As an assistant to Big Joe, they are working to deliver furniture to an apartment. A piano has to be hoisted up the side of the building to the apartment, and the pair is riding up on it when a noon whistle blows. They stop and enjoy their lunch up in the air, but soon return to work setting up the furniture. Joe goes out, leaving Poodles alone to demolish the apartment in his attempts to bring the swinging piano in through the window and to catch a distracting butterfly.

Big Joe tries to fix everything up cosmetically, but when the owner of the stuff shows up, who, of course, just happens to be the cop who had followed Reginald around earlier, the wrecked furniture is discovered. The boys get away and keep ahead of the police, and finally lose them when they go through some gates and close them before the cops see them. What the boys don't know is that they have escaped—right into the local penitentiary.

Of the four shorts that Roscoe directed with Poodles Hanneford only the second reel of this one is known to survive today. It turned up in England under the title *The Gentle Furniture Movers*, and initially generated much interest due to the presence of Big Joe

Roberts in a non-Buster Keaton appearance. In the early 1920's Big Joe moonlighted in shorts with the Hallroom Boys, Fox Sunshine Comedies, and Clyde Cook, and it makes sense that Roscoe would take advantage of his menacing presence and excellent comic timing. It's probable that Roscoe would have continued to use Big Joe, but he passed away on Oct. 28, 1923, just a month before this short was released.

Hanneford has a different look in this short than in the surviving stills from *Front!* Here he has a bushy moustache, and is outfitted in a bowler hat, flowing tie, and outsized baggy pants and vest. Big Joe is of course the bullying boss, and Poodles is his innocent and child-like helper. Roscoe directed all of the physical mayhem in a subtle and leisurely style, giving Hanneford plenty of footage to show how his mind doesn't work, and to have his troubles believably snowball out of control. The framing of the slapstick action is very effective, and long takes gives Poodles room to do his stuff.

And finally, since we don't have the entire film for reference, the Educational Pictures pressbook points out a rather unusual aspect of this short:

> *Another feature of this comedy, "No Loafing," is that there isn't a woman in a single part of the picture.*

Moving Picture World (November 24, 1923): "Most of the amusement in this Tuxedo comedy lies in a familiar stunt—suspending the hero at a precarious height where thrills are combined with laughter. It is effectively done, although the idea will not be new to the average patron. At times it gets very exciting. The star is a good comedian and an expert tumbler."

MPW Straight From the Shoulder Report (May 5, 1924): "Best two-reel comedy we have run for months. Equal to 'Safety Last' for thrills. Pleased everybody" **and** "Funny, I'll say so! It brought plenty of laughs and made the women scream at the piano moving stunt. Some slick gags in this one."

One Night It Rained

Released January 20, 1924. A Tuxedo Comedy. Produced by Reel Comedies, Inc. Distributed by Educational Pictures. Two reels. With Ned Sparks, Harry Tighe, Doris Deane, George Davis.

A prosperous young doctor and his wife have the latter's male relative come to visit them. The doctor, jealous of the actions of the other two, makes a number of implied threats as to what is to happen in the course of the night. As the trio retires these threats are apparently carried out in reality, amid some exciting activity. A telephone call brings the doctor out in a wild rainstorm and he finds the call is to a vacant house. This convinces him of the unfaithfulness of his wife and he returns to murder her and her relative. After the deed is accomplished the three awake from a dream and find that the lobster eaten for dinner is responsible.

The reviews and plot synopsis for this lost film show that Roscoe reworked the basic idea and story of *He Did and He Didn't* (1916), again concentrating on a very polite, plot driven style for the comedy. This time around Roscoe's original part was taken

An uneasy dinner party with Harry Tighe (left), Ned Sparks (right), and Doris Deane in *One Night It Rained* (1924).

by Harry Tighe, with Doris Deane as the wife, Ned Sparks as the visiting relative, and George Davis replacing Al St John as the crook. Doing regular slapstick knockabout in the Poodles Hanneford shorts, it seems that Roscoe used the Ned Sparks/Harry Tighe films for a more sophisticated approach. It's hoped that this picture will eventually be recovered as it would be fascinating to compare and contrast with the *He Did and He Didn't* blueprint. This is the last of the two shorts that Sparks and Tighe did with Roscoe.

Moving Picture World (January 12, 1924): "Educational's newest Tuxedo comedy, introducing two prominent vaudeville players to the screen, Harry Tighe and Ned Sparks, differs from the majority of short comedies of the present day. It belongs to the type in which situations are depended on to produce the laughs logically with no resorting to slapstick. The story, involving a jealous husband who has a terrible dream after eating lobster, is essentially melodramatic and has considerable appeal along this line. At the same time the comedy element has not been overlooked and is uppermost in the ending. It is a comedy that should appeal especially to patrons who do not care for slapstick and should satisfy the average audience."

Exhibitors Trade Review (March 15, 1926): "Originality of treatment. Harry Tighe and Ned Sparks show the effects of eating lobster at night and husband's jealousy. The sort of stuff that chuckle rather than laugh."

Moving Picture World (May 2, 1925): "A splendid comedy, but too high class for children and roughnecks. Tone good. Sunday, yes. Good audience appeal."

The New Sheriff

Released March 16, 1924. A Tuxedo Comedy. Produced by Reel Comedies, Inc. Distributed by Educational Pictures. Two reels. With Poodles Hanneford, Molly Malone, Doris Deane, George Davis, Robert Jenkins, Pal.

Robert Jenkins (middle) objects to Poodle Hanneford's and George Davis' playing in *The New Sheriff* (1924). Courtesy Matt Vogel.

Poodles the new sheriff has been reading too many western dime novels. He wants to be a combination of Broncho Billy and Buffalo Bill, but his weakness is women. When in the Mexican quarter of town he sees a wooer serenading his lady by strumming a guitar. Poodles decides that he can do a better job with a slide trombone. The Mexican lover doesn't take kindly to the interference and starts shooting, leading Poodles to take refuge on the telegraph wires.

Next the schoolmarm gets his attention. Poodles, his dog, and pal "Snowball" decide that he needs an education, so they show up in the classroom and end up disrupting the village school system. The schoolmarm has also been noticed by desperado Bleary Eyed Bill, who's so tough that he drinks fusel oil with tabasco sauce for a chaser. Bill kidnaps the teacher, so it's up to Poodles and company to rescue her. They get on the trail and find the deserted cabin where the villainous gang have her captive. Poodles' dog tunnels into the cabin and manages to untie the girl, while Poodles besieges the gang and lays waste to them. The little teacher embraces her hero and promises that Poodles shall be her scholar for life.

The missing *The New Sheriff* is an out and out remake of Roscoe's equally missing 1918 Comique *The Sheriff*, even to replacing Sunshine Sammy Morrison with Robert Jenkins (as the sidekick "Snowball") and Luke with popular dog star Pal. Poodles' two leading ladies are Molly Malone and a relatively new face, Doris Deane. A former dancer who began her film career at Universal, Deane was "discovered" by Roscoe and after

Poodles Hanneford holds George Davis (right) and another cowpoke at bay with coming and going pistols in *The New Sheriff* (1924).

appearing in most of the Reel Comedy Tuxedo shorts became his second wife on May 16, 1925. Sadly their relationship was tumultuous and ended in divorce in 1928, but Deane later turned up in Roscoe's 1931 sound short *Marriage Rows*, and also did some brief television work in the 1950s before her death in 1974.

In addition to Poodles Hanneford's abilities as a trick rider, juggler, tumbler, and dancer, *The New Sheriff* took advantage of his wire walking skills in, according to the original Educational Pictures pressbook, "a series of scenes with him taking refuge from a mob by climbing telegraph poles and walking the wires. He dodges the bullets by bouncing around on the wires and succeeds in outwitting his pursuers." Definite echoes of *Their Ups and Downs* (1914) and *Fatty's Tintype Tangle* (1915).

Moving Picture World (March 8, 1924): "Some audiences may not consider this Tuxedo release on a par with Poodles Hanneford's usual work. It's not Hanneford's fault, if such is the verdict. The plot contains a lot of material long believed in the so-called "best of circles" to be obsolete. However, it is a comedy and should get by at that. Poodles' dog does some great work."

Exhibitors' Trade Review (March 8, 1924): "Poodles Hanneford, the clown comedian, is featured in this Tuxedo comedy. His pantomime as well as that of another character in this comedy, bearing the name of Bleary-eyed Bill 'a bad egg,' is superb and sure to be appreciated by the sort of audience that doesn't always appreciate slapstick.

"Hanneford as the sheriff falls in love with a Spanish senorita but when he sees the new school teacher, education's the thing for him. A pickaninny and a dog figure in the case and all do their bit to rescue the teacher from Bleary-eyed Bill. Sure to get many laughs and to hold the interest throughout."

What a Buster

Sherlock, Jr.

Released April 21, 1924. Produced by Joseph M. Schenck. Distributed by Metro Pictures. Directed by Buster Keaton (uncredited Roscoe Arbuckle). Written by Jean Havez, Clyde Bruckman and Joseph Mitchell. Photography by Elgin Lessley and Byron Houck. Technical direction by Fred Gabourie. Five reels. Extant: LOC, GOS, MoMA, UCLA, FRIU, LOB, EYE. With Keaton, Kathryn McGuire, Ward Crane, Ford West, Joe Keaton, Erwin Connelly, Christine Francis, Steve Murphy, Doris Deane, Tom Murray, Walter C. Reed, Horace "Kewpie" Morgan, Jane Connelly, John Patrick, Ruth Holly.

Buster, the projectionist/janitor at the local movie theatre, is an amateur detective thanks to a correspondence course. When his girlfriend's father's watch is stolen by his rival Buster gets blamed. Dejected, he goes to the cinema, and while projecting the film he falls

Buster Keaton practicing his sleuthing in *Sherlock, Jr.* (1924). Courtesy Robert Arkus.

asleep and dreams that he is the great detective Sherlock, Jr. While Buster is sleeping his girlfriend solves the mystery, and he wakes up to find himself her choice.

Today *Sherlock, Jr.* is considered one of Buster Keaton's masterworks—a combination of ambitious comedy concepts, perfectly realized special effects, and audacious slapstick. The big question for this book is exactly how much did Roscoe contribute to the production—did he direct the entire film or just the early part of the shoot? It's definite that Roscoe started the picture, which is confirmed in the recollections of participants and observers, as well as trade magazine items. The tricky issue is determining just how long he stayed on the production.

In his 1960 autobiography *My Wonderful World of Slapstick*, Buster Keaton offered that Roscoe was "down in the dumps and broke," so Buster arranged with his manager Lou Anger for Arbuckle to direct *Sherlock, Jr.* But "the experiment was a failure. Roscoe was irritable, impatient, and snapped at everyone in the company. He had my leading lady, Kathryn McGuire, in tears a dozen times a day." To get out of the situation Keaton claims that he went to Marion Davies and suggested that Roscoe would be a perfect director for her next film *The Red Mill*. Davies agreed and Roscoe went off to helm that.

The main problem with this scenario is that *The Red Mill* was still three years in the future. Also Buster makes no mention that Roscoe had already been busy directing the first season of his Reel Comedy shorts (on the Keaton lot) with Ned Sparks and Poodles Hanneford, which seem to have gone along swimmingly. An alternative reason for a possible Arbuckle exit from *Sherlock, Jr.* was given by Keaton and Arbuckle's close friend Viola Dana, in a 1974 conversation with author Stuart Oderman:

> *There were never any problems between Roscoe and Buster until Peg Talmadge showed up and demanded to know why Roscoe was there, and who was paying and how much. And then Roscoe would take it out on poor Kathryn McGuire, a lovely girl, a trained dancer. Kathryn was no Mabel [Normand] and she never could do what Mabel could do.*
>
> *Buster, always the diplomat when it came to dealing with Roscoe, thanked him for his help and told him he now had a handle on the film.*
>
> *Roscoe, equally polite, knew better than to question Buster's judgement. It was after all Buster's film. It was better to remain friends.*
>
> *Which they did.*

The earlier scenes in *Sherlock, Jr.* do have more of an Arbuckle feel, especially the shy courting scenes of Buster and Kathryn McGuire, which have echoes in *Dynamite Doggie* (1925), *My Stars* (1926), and the possible Arbuckle production *The Live Agent* (1925). There are also numerous Roscoe "regulars" in the cast such as Doris Deane describing a dollar bill that she's lost, Walter C. Reed as the pawnbroker who identifies Ward Crane to Kathryn McGuire, and Christine Francis as the girl in the candy shop. It's possible that Roscoe helped out at the beginning and then went back to his Reel Comedy shorts, or he could even have helped out from time to time. We'll probably never know. Even if Peg Talmadge did raise a fuss, the industry knew that Roscoe was involved in the film, made clear by this mention in the July 1924 *Photoplay*:

Christine Francis sets Buster straight price-wise in *Sherlock, Jr.* (1924). Courtesy Robert Arkus.

> *It is not generally known that Arbuckle directed Buster Keaton's "Sherlock Holmes Jr."[sic] His name as director appears on the screen as Will B. Good! Thus adding a comedy touch—if you get it.*

Roscoe was directing the Reel Comedy shorts anonymously, but it's from this time period that the joke about him directing as "Will B. Good" originated. Another example is in the February 16, 1924 *Exhibitors Trade Review*:

> *Fatty Arbuckle, since he is no longer an actor, is to cast his line in the directing sea. He will direct Buster Keaton comedies under the name of Will B. Good (we wonder if this is a promise).*

In his autobiography Keaton claimed he suggested "Will B. Good" for Roscoe's directorial nom de plume, and perhaps he made this as a joke to the press. Ultimately Roscoe would adopt William Goodrich.

Screen Opinions (May 15-31, 1924): "Sherlock, Jr." is one of the most original farce-comedies that has come to the screen in some time…The picture teems with amusing situations. The exhibitor cannot afford to miss this one."

Film Daily (May 11, 1924): "Comedy, but not just plain comedy—a comedy-riot fits it better. Buster Keaton has made many fine comedies before but never has he had a story with so many original stunts and new comedy gags as he offers in "Sherlock, Jr." To describe the laughs in the picture is impossible. They have to be felt to be enjoyed."

Exhibitors Trade Review (May 17, 1924): "When a reviewer says of a motion picture comedy that it is uproariously funny, it would seem to add anything further is to dabble in the superfluous.

"However in the case of 'Sherlock, Jr.,' after pronouncing it a barrel of fun, the writer feels that much more can be said without encumbering his opinions with redundancies.

"The picture is a winner! Pleasurable entertainment for the family; laughs galore for the case-hardened. Fun for young and old alike. It's just the prettiest piece of feature comedy work the writer has seen in many weeks of movie-going."

Photoplay (July 1924): "Comedies are like oases in a celluloid world, rare and refreshing, and you don't want to miss Buster with his immobile face and unique composure in his new setting."

The Bonehead

Released May 18, 1924. A Tuxedo Comedy. Produced by Reel Comedies, Inc. Distributed by Educational Pictures. Two reels. With Poodles Hanneford, George Davis, Molly Malone, Joe Keaton.

Poodles Hanneford poses onstage as part of the weight lifter's act in *The Bonehead* (1924).

Poodles gets involved with a troupe of traveling ham actors that comes to his small town. He, of course, messes up the show that they put on, but also gets to wow the audience with his bareback riding. The crooked manager of the troupe steals the admission money from the opera house owner. Poodles goes after him, which leads to a big chase with autos narrowly escaping collisions with trains, etc. Finally capturing the villain Poodles becomes a hero.

Although a missing film, the reviews and descriptions of *The Bonehead* suggest more than a few echoes of Roscoe's 1919 *Back Stage*, with Poodles as a prop man at a local theatre who gets mixed-up with the various acts and interacts with characters like George Davis, Molly Malone, and Joe Keaton. The theatre setting also gives the opportunity to commit Poodles' famous bareback riding act to film. It wasn't its first filming as Hanneford was making shorts for the Fox studio at the same time, and 1923's *The Riding Master* beat them to it. Variations on the act would end up on the screen over the years in shorts and features like *Circus Daze*, *The Circus Kid* (both 1928), *Our Little Girl* (1935), and *The Riding Hannefords* (1946).

This was Poodles last work with Roscoe, and besides the silent shorts for Fox he did more two-reelers for Jack White and Weiss Brothers Artclass Pictures which included *Plumb Dumb* (1927), *Deaf, Dumb and Blonde*, and *Why Detectives Go Wrong* (both 1928). In the sound era his film appearances became more sporadic, often as himself or as a character player in westerns like *Springfield Rifle* (1952). His last film was *Billy Rose's Jumbo* (1962), but he had always continued his stage and circus work, and finished his career at an amusement park in New York State, Frontier Town, where he clowned and played the part of The Old Prospector until he passed away in 1967.

Motion Picture News (May 24, 1924): "Here's a funny two-reeler with 'Poodles' Hanneford strutting a lot of comedy stuff that is bound to get laughs from any audience. As a bareback rider he's a knockout and he's a real hero when it comes to capturing the villain who escapes with the finances of the troupe. It is just a hodge podge of comedy stuff that makes for laughter."

Moving Picture World (May 10, 1924): "The Tuxedo Comedy, 'The Bonehead,' released by Educational and presenting 'Poodles' Hanneford, manages to be satisfactorily funny though it follows conventional lines. The chase is well staged and offers several real thrills when automobiles narrowly escape collision with trains. The acting is, of course, broad burlesque, and it is generally effective."

Exhibitors' Trade Review (May 10, 1924): "Don't miss 'Poodles' Hanneford in this Tuxedo Comedy. He is a hit. As a jack of all trades around a theatre he is called upon to do an unlimited number of things. He also acts as assistant to the actors and is also chief scene shifter and property man.

"The best scene is that of a riding act in which 'Poodles' acts as the assistant to the bareback rider. He performs daring stunts that will make your hair curl. He is an accomplished rider and his comedy in this particular scene is excellent.

The story deals with a roughneck theatre manager who decides to rob the theatre safe. He takes the bareback rider into his confidence and after cracking the safe they escape on a horse. 'Poodles' comes to the rescue and after a good chase scene he captures the robbers and wins his sweetie."

Chapter 10
Reel Comedies, Inc. – Round Two

THE FIRST SERIES OF Tuxedo Comedies had worked out smoothly and were a success for Educational. Years later, in interviews with author David N. Bruskin (*Behind the Three Stooges: The White Brothers*, DGA 1990), Jack White commented about Roscoe:

> He hadn't lost his talent because of the trouble he was in. We were afraid he might not pull out of it, but he did. When he had a problem, he was like any other director on the lot; he would come to my office and seek advice.

On June 21, 1924 the *Moving Picture World* announced:

> ***In Tuxedo Comedies***
> Al St John, formerly starred in Fox Sunshine Comedies, has been added to the list of stars appearing in Tuxedo Comedies. His first picture with the new affiliation will be "His First Car" and will be on the July program of releases of Educational Film Exchanges, Inc.
> He will be supported by Doris Dean [sic], who was leading lady to "Poodles" Hanneford, and by George Davis, the well known circus and stage clown, who also appeared with "Poodles" in many of his pictures.

The short *Dumb and Daffy* (July 1924) ended Al's three-year stint with Fox, and this re-teaming with Roscoe got rid of the last remnants of Al's old country boob character. For this second season of Tuxedos he became a clean-cut (but still bumbling) man-about town or young hubby.

All seven shorts of the series are known to survive, and give a good look at how Roscoe's directing skills continued to develop. His films go about their business cleanly, crisply, and efficiently, and he unerringly puts the camera in just the right place to capture the physical action. A restrained and low-key approach to his material allows the slapstick to grow logically out of the situations. Roscoe gets very natural performances from his actors, and to support Al he put together a crack stock company of comics that included: George Davis, Blanche Payson, Doris Deane (the second Mrs. Arbuckle), Glen Cavender,

Al St John, Doris Deane, Leon Holmes, Donald Hughes, George Davis, and Blanche Payson at the end of an imperfect day from *His First Car* (1924). Courtesy Sam Gill.

Florence Lee, Johnny Sinclair, Christine Francis, and Walter C. Reed. The directorial credit on this group was given to either Al or writer Grover Jones.

His First Car

Released July 27, 1924. A Tuxedo Comedy. Produced by Reel Comedies, Inc. Distributed by Educational Pictures. Directed and written by Al St John. Two reels. Extant: LOB, ACAD. With Al St John, Doris Deane, George Davis, Blanche Payson, Leon Holmes, Donald Hughes.

Al plunks down the payment on his first car, and he's prouder than the father of twins. His wife and son are just as proud when he brings it home, and his neighbors are impressed and just a bit jealous. Al has a brainstorm and proposes that both families use the new car and go on a camping trip.

They start out the next morning with great expectations and the car piled high with camping equipment. Trouble lands its first blow when they run out of a gas on a lonely spot on the road. While George is dispensed to walk to the nearest station and fetch a new supply, the rest decide to make the best of the situation and have a picnic lunch. Al discovers that they also have a blowout and while the whole crew is helping to fix the tire the family dog eats the laid-out lunch.

All gassed and patched up they set off again and end up completely lost. They decide to camp where they are but find that they have no food or water, and this sets family against family—complete with physical blows by the men and hair pulling from the women. Finally peace is restored, but a huge storm blows away their tents and nearly drowns them. The next morning they start home cold, wet, and hungry. They stop at a roadside restaurant and as they sit and eat they watch the car get bumped and sail over a cliff in stunned disbelief. All that remains of the first car is unpleasant memories—and nineteen more payments to be made.

Roscoe kicks off the new season of Tuxedo Comedies with a very simple tale about a family and their new car—basically a shaggy dog story where everything that could go wrong does go wrong. The bickering family motif is similar to what Hal Roach was doing in his *Spat Family* Comedies, except much funnier, and all the issues with the new car foreshadow Harold Lloyd's *Hot Water* (1924) which would come out in three months. Even Al and company's departure on the trip, with the whole neighborhood turning out to see them off, is reminiscent of scenes in Laurel & Hardy's *Perfect Day* (1929) and W.C. Fields' *It's a Gift* (1934).

Doris Deane, Leon Holmes, and Al St John are left out in the cold in *His First Car* (1924). Courtesy Sam Gill.

Except for the brief shot at the beginning where Al signs for the car at the dealership the entirety of the short was shot outdoors, where nature becomes a main character—a tireless adversary to the struggling families. There's even a flatulence gag—very rare in "silent" films. It occurs when the family has car trouble and finally determines that it's out of gas. The two boys are sitting in the back seat. Leon Holmes turns to his buddy to say (via title card) "Pop's never outta gas" and holds his nose.

The cast works together like a well-oiled unit. One of the standouts is the aforementioned Leon Holmes as the son of Al and Doris Deane. Holmes was one of the freckled-faced urchins to follow in the popularity of Our Gang's Mickey Daniels, and although something of a poor man's Spec O'Donnell, Holmes was a genuinely funny kid and very busy from 1925 to the end of the silent era. Besides lots of comedy two-reelers he also appeared in features like *Poker Faces* (1926), *The Shamrock and the Rose*, *The King of Kings*, and *The Jazz Singer* (all 1927), and continued working into the 1940s.

The other is former stage clown George Davis who appeared in important supporting roles in more Reel Comedy shorts than anyone else—nine out of the total thirteen. Amsterdam-born and the fourth generation of a theatrical family, Davis played around the world in pantomimes and musical revues, in addition to early films for Pathé and

Al St John (left) and George Davis (right) stay in each other's way in *His First Car* (1924). Courtesy Sam Gill.

Éclair. After coming to America and making a big hit at the New York Hippodrome, one of his first jobs in Hollywood was coaching Lon Chaney in clowning for *He Who Gets Slapped* (1924). At the same time he became a regular in Roscoe's Reel Comedies, and continued in the Arbuckle-directed comedies for Jack White and on into his sound shorts such as *Idle Rumors* (1931) and *Keep Laughing* (1932).

By 1927 Jack White was headlining Davis in his own two-reelers like *Nothing Flat* (1927) and *Stage Frights* (1928), where he was usually a tall and gangly goof who was a magnet for misfortune. In addition to this series he also turned up in Universal and Fox shorts, and had nice parts in *The 4 Devils*, and Chaplin's *The Circus* (both 1928), where he plays the magician whose tricks Charlie keeps messing up. After the arrival of sound he kept busy in shorts and features, and though his parts got smaller, he did have occasional nice roles such as Pierre, the taxi driver who squires Marilyn Monroe and Jane Russell around Paris, and has a nice bit with co-star Tommy Noonan, in *Gentlemen Prefer Blondes* (1953). Davis worked non-stop in character bits until the early 1960s.

Motion Picture News (July 19, 1924): "Here is one of the funniest two-reelers seen this season. It fairly sparkles with humor and contains a laugh for every foot of film. It is funny for the man who does not own a car, but funnier for the one who does. Al St John is the featured player and he gets the most out of every situation."

Moving Picture World (July 5, 1924): "'His First Car' certainly impresses as one of the best Tuxedo comedies yet presented by Educational. Al St John wrote and directed this laugh-maker, and takes the leading part as well, proving that such an exhibition of versatility is occasionally possible without resulting in a vehicle expressing only an individual's conceit. He made a good job of it, for it not only has more than a two-reeler's usual quota of laughs, but it has coherence and unity. The subtitles are simple and well done, fitting the mood of the picture to a 'T.'"

Never Again

Released August 24, 1924. A Tuxedo Comedy. Produced by Reel Comedies, Inc. Distributed by Educational Pictures. Directed and written by Al St John. Two reels. Extant: LOB. With Al St John, Doris Deane, Blanche Payson, Johnny Sinclair, George Davis, Christine Francis, James Bryant, Chick Collins, Rosalind Byrne, Carmencita Johnson.

Al plays a henpecked husband of a big amazon who, when left alone in the park, flirts first with a blind girl and then with a married woman. He gets into a fight with the woman's husband and ends up with a black eye. He ingeniously explains it to his wife with a wild yarn where he appears as the hero. Later they go to a movie, which the married woman and her husband also attend, and see a newsreel that captured Al flirting and fighting. Between his wife and the irate husband Al ends up in the hospital resolved never to flirt again—until he gets better.

The only known surviving print of *Never Again* has been preserved by Lobster Films in Paris, and through the generosity of their Serge Bromberg I was able to view the film. A total re-working of *Fatty at San Diego* (1913) and *A Reckless Romeo* (1917), *Never Again* has a definite Keystone feel as much of it was shot in Echo Park, home for so many Sennett park comedies. The climax takes place in a movie theatre, which is the same cinema set

Doris Deane orders Al St John to swim out of her car in *Never Again* (1924). Courtesy Sam Gill.

from Keaton's *Sherlock, Jr.* (1924) re-dressed and relit. Roscoe's three versions of this story would be the prototype for Laurel & Hardy's *We Faw Down* (1928) and *Sons of the Desert* (1933). As usual the male comics like Al, George Davis, and Johnny Sinclair are on view, but since they always outnumber the women and get more attention it's a good opportunity to highlight *Never Again*'s ladies—Blanche Payson and Christine Francis.

Payson was definitely the tallest of the silent comediennes, and at 6'4" very few of the male comics matched her in height making her the living embodiment of the phrase "large and in charge." Said to have been a sweetheart in real life, she worked with practically everyone at every studio, and became one of the most ubiquitous faces of silent comedy. Getting some publicity for her early work as a lady police officer she was "discovered" for movies by Mack Sennett, and made her debut in 1916's *Wife and Auto Trouble*.

Playing William Collier's bad-tempered Amazon wife, she was a natural—projecting just the right amount of menace to give an anchor for the comedy. From here the die was cast—for the next thirty years she would slow-burningly henpeck husbands, screw up her face into a knot of hostility, and pop people who deserved it in the eye or nose. Over the years she made screen life difficult for the likes of Al, Billy West, Larry Semon, Montgomery & Rock, Baby Peggy, Lloyd Hamilton, Buster Keaton, Our Gang, the Three Stooges, and Harry Langdon in shorts and features until 1946.

Turning up in a small bit role as one of the girls Al flirts with is Christine Francis, a cute brunette from Tacoma, Washington. Francis was a friend of Doris Deane and an

Al St John in fear of Blanche Payson in *Never Again* (1924).

aspiring actress who had appeared in a tour of *Abie's Irish Rose*. Most of her movie work was in films directed by Roscoe or Buster Keaton. She was the leading lady in *The Broncho Express* (1924, and shot on the Keaton lot), and *Dynamite Doggie* (1925), can also be seen in *Stupid But Brave* (1924) and *Be Careful, Dearie* (1926), and is most frequently on view as the candy shop girl in Keaton's *Sherlock, Jr.* (1924). She also worked as a script/continuity girl on *The Iron Mule* (1925) and *The General* (1926), and in 1938 married well-known aviator and Hollywood stunt flier Dick Grace.

Motion Picture News (August 2, 1924): "Here is a real comedy chock full of funny situations well acted with a story that moves rapidly and smoothly from start to finish. Al St John is the star and he doesn't miss a chance for a laugh. It's a comedy that will go well with any kind of audience."

Moving Picture World (August 2, 1924): "As author, director and star, Al St John has certainly provided himself with a crackerjack comedy vehicle in 'Never Again,' his second for Educational under the Tuxedo brand. There are a lot of clever situations, good gags and, combined with Al's stunts, the result is a comedy that is decidedly above the average. Any audience that likes rough and tumble stuff should be thoroughly satisfied with this comedy, for it is high in amusement value and will cause a lot of spontaneous laughter."

Stupid But Brave

Released October 26, 1924. A Tuxedo Comedy. Produced by Reel Comedies, Inc. Distributed by Educational Pictures. Directed and written by Al St John. Two reels. Extant: FRIU, MoMA, UCLA, ACAD, LOB. With Al St John, Doris Deane, George Davis, Johnny Sinclair, Eugene Pallette, Christine Francis, "Kewpie" Morgan, Steve Murphy.

Al is a member of the idle class (a.k.a. a hobo) and living in the park, but is looking for work. When he sees a likely looking ad in a newspaper he realizes that he needs a shave and a haircut to make a good impression. Al finds a barbershop that seems to be staffed by refugees from Al Capone's gang and almost gets more than his hair cut, but manages to end up looking all neat and clean for his interview.

The president of the banana company giving the interview is looking for someone who is not afraid of anything to become the manager of his South American banana ranch. To test his interviewees he plans to shoot off a gun to startle them. Because of a chronic ear ache, Al has cotton stuffed in his ears and doesn't hear the gun shots. Impressed by his nerves of steel, the president gives Al the position provided that he can get to San Francisco on his own to catch the boat to South America.

Since he has no money for fare he tries to travel via freight train but gets thrown off his "side-door Pullman" by the railway watchmen. Setting off on foot Al gets entangled with a

Al St John, Doris Deane, and Eugene Pallette set out for a drive in *Stupid But Brave* (1924). Courtesy Annichen Skaren.

work gang of convicts, one of whom changes clothes with him. Forced to join the gang, he finally makes a break with the local sheriff in hot pursuit. Getting rid of his convict stripes leaves Al in his undershirt and shorts, but this works out for him when he literally stumbles into a cross-country running race, and with impetus from the sheriff at his heels, Al wins the race and the $100 prize.

His luck continues to hold when he rescues a beautiful girl from bandits and she turns out to be the daughter of the president of the banana company. She happens to motoring across the country to meet her father at the boat—and all ends happily when Al is invited to join her.

The main set-piece in *Stupid But Brave* is the five-minute sequence of Al in Tony Toenaili's Tonsorial Parlor. Led to believe that they give free shaves to men in need, Al finds out that he's been tricked the moment he's in the barber chair and gets a look at pug-ugly barbers Jimmy Bryant, Steve Murphy, Johnny Sinclair, and Kewpie Morgan. Morgan begins to operate on Al, and a number of times twists his head completely backwards for better cutting access. This startling scene is probably the closest thing to an animated cartoon that Roscoe ever directed—when Morgan twists Al's head around it immediately spins back—and although it's easy to see how it was done (someone else is in the barber chair covered with the apron to be Al's body and arms as Al sticks his head up from

Al St John tries to pull the wool over sheriff George Davis in *Stupid But Brave* (1924).
Courtesy Annichen Skaren.

behind the chair) it's still initially a surprise and very impressive. Definitely a variation on the shaving routine in *His Wife's Mistake* (1916), another gag re-working that contributes substantially to the chase in the second reel is *Good Night Nurse*'s (1918) footrace sequence.

Doris Deane is on hand as the pretty woman in need, and besides Arbuckle regulars Jimmy Bryant, Johnny Sinclair, Christine Francis, and George Davis there's a few other silent comedy stalwarts that should be mentioned. Prominent in the barbershop are Steve Murphy and Kewpie Morgan. Murphy, known as "Broken Nose Murphy," was an ex-boxer who settled into pictures in the teens and came in handy for features with underworld or seedy settings such as *Broken Blossoms* (1919), *Outside the Law* (1920), and *Justice of the Far North* (1925). Also in demand for comedies with Billy West, Harold Lloyd, and Laurel & Hardy, he was a favorite of Buster Keaton's and was put to good use in *Cops*, *The Electric House* (both 1922), and *Sherlock, Jr.* (1924), but is probably best-remembered as the pickpocket who battles with Charlie Chaplin in the opening of *The Circus* (1928).

Jumbo-sized Horace "Kewpie" Morgan is the barber who works Al over, and was a silent comedy veteran best known for his work as a heavy for Billy Bevan and Ben Turpin in shorts like *Love and Doughnuts* (1921), *Gymnasium Jim* (1922), *Ice Cold Cocos*, and *Wandering Willies* (both 1926). In the teens he entered films for Lubin and Universal, and co-starred in a series of Clover Comedies with Bud Duncan and Dot Farley. Besides playing Old King Cole in Laurel & Hardy's *Babes in Toyland* (1934), he appeared in many features and shorts with comics on the order of Lloyd Hamilton, Larry Semon, Charley Bowers, and Clark & McCullough until 1936.

When Al goes to the banana company for his interview the president is Eugene Pallette. Known today for his bullfrog voice and rotund figure in sound comedies such as *My Man Godfrey* (1936), *The Lady Eve* (1941), and *The Gang's All Here* (1943), Pallette had started out as something of a leading man in silent films. Entering movies in 1913 he was busy in dramas, even turning up in D. W. Griffith's Fine Arts Company and having a major role in *Intolerance* (1916). By the 1920s he was transitioning into a character player, and spent some time as a stock member at the Hal Roach Studio in shorts like *Jewish Prudence*, *Fluttering Hearts*, *Barnum & Ringling, Inc.*, and *The Battle of the Century* (all 1927). When sound arrived the addition of his gravelly voice made the transition complete and he was a busy and popular supporting player until 1946.

Film Daily (September 14, 1924): "A Real Comedy. Here is another peach of a comedy of which Al St John is the star, author, and director. The work he is doing in these comedies is consistently funny and good. It isn't so much what he does, but the way he does it, although there is a chase in this that is one of the funniest things seen in a long time."

Moving Picture World (September 20, 1924): "The Al St John Tuxedo comedies for Educational are going great guns and this latest release exceeds its predecessors in real entertainment values. There are hearty laughs right at the start where Al, as the down and outer gets fixed up in Tony Toenaili's Tonsorial Parlor, and these are provoked regularly throughout the two reels. Play this subject if you want to give your audiences a real treat. It ought to make a hit with any kind of audience."

Lovemania

Released December 28, 1924. A Tuxedo Comedy. Produced by Reel Comedies, Inc. Distributed by Educational Pictures. Directed and written by Al St John. Two reels. Extant: BRUS. With Al St John, Doris Deane, George Davis, Johnny Sinclair, Joan Hoff, James Bryant, Chick Collins.

Al has just married Doris. Immediately following the wedding he receives a telegram from his rich Uncle George saying that he is bringing with him a million dollars for Al that afternoon—provided his is still single. A scheme is hatched were Al pretends that his inability to marry has driven him mad, while Doris takes the role of his nurse and the best man as his doctor. When Uncle George arrives each time love is mentioned Al throws conniptions and raises the roof. Eventually uncle is won over to Al being married and even proposes himself to Doris' mother. When he hands over the million-dollar check guards rush in and capture him since he's really an escaped lunatic who likes to give away phony checks.

A difficult rich uncle is a familiar figure in comedy films. Always dangling an inheritance over a nephew or niece by dictating that in order to get his dough they must be wed, or must not be married, when he arrives for a visit. Their reasons are usually completely frivolous, but the star comedian is sure to jump through whatever hoops necessary to comply in shorts such as *One Too Many*, *His Wooden Leg* (both 1916), *Max*

Doris Deane causes Al St John's pulse to race in 1924's *Lovemania*. Courtesy Sam Gill.

Wants a Divorce (1917), *365 Days* (1922), *Uncle Sam* (1923), *Welcome Uncle* (1924), *That's My Wife* (1929), and many more. Sometimes the comic manages to secure the money, but usually, as in *Lovemania*, the uncle turns out to be an escaped lunatic and all the struggles have been for nothing. Roscoe uses the crazy uncle at the end of his Vitaphone short *Close Relations* (1933).

Al St John, Doris Deane, George Davis, and Jimmy Bryant provide their regular sterling service alongside an overlooked member of the Reel Comedies stock company. Johnny Sinclair appeared in six of the seven shorts in this second series, as well as many other film comedies. A friend of Al St John's, Sinclair spent a number of years working with him. Having started with bit parts in Al's Fox comedies, he got larger roles in this Tuxedo series, playing the irate husband in *Never Again* (1924), Christine Francis' unwanted suitor in *Dynamite Doggie* (1925), and in *Curses* (1925) Al's second-bandit in command. Sinclair also appeared in the Al St John shorts that came out through Biff Comedies (more on these soon) and starred in his own Biff shorts like *Hollywouldn't* and *The Starvation Hunters* (both 1925).

At this point he seemed to be on the rise, getting comic relief roles in features on the order of *The Goat Getter* (1925) and *Rapid Fire Romance* (1926), working as support for

Al St John acts crazy for the benefit of Joan Hoff, Doris Deane (left), Johnny Sinclair, and George Davis in *Lovemania* (1924).

Lloyd Hamilton, and even doing his own starring Jack White Cameo Comedy *High Spirits* (1927). But in early 1927, he was involved with Lloyd Hamilton in a barroom brawl that resulted in the death of boxer Eddie Diggins. As a result Hamilton spent a year banned from the screen and it seems to have put the kibosh on Sinclair's rise in the industry. After being relegated to very small bits and stunt work, he saved W. C. Fields' life in October of 1927 after an on-the-set accident during the making of *Two Flaming Youths* (1927). From here, he spent the next eight years working for Fields as a gagman and stunt double (also getting a memorable shave from W. C. in 1933's *The Barber Shop*) through *Poppy* (1936). Having married former Sennett bathing girl and comedienne Thelma Hill, Sinclair did uncredited bits until his death in 1945.

Motion Picture News (December 27, 1924): "Al St John is featured in this good story, which he is also credited with writing and directing. He is a very versatile man, this St John, for his work in the picture is even better than his story and direction. He is a comedian, a gymnast and a little bit of about everything. It is a picture that is good for laughs with any class of audience."

Moving Picture World (December 27, 1924): "Al St John wrote and stars in this Tuxedo Comedy and it is thoroughly entertaining from the word go. There is a lot of good fun in this subject and it ought to please most audiences. It is lively and well acted and the story has surprises."

Dynamite Doggie

Released March 22, 1925. A Tuxedo Comedy. Produced by Reel Comedies, Inc. Distributed by Educational Film Exchange. Directed by Grover Jones. Two reels. Extant: LOB, EYE. With Al St John, Christine Francis, George Davis, Pete the pup, Johnny Sinclair, Walter C. Reed, Glen Cavender.

Al has a sweetheart whose father hates him. The father's dog also hates Al and attacks him whenever he sees him. Trying to get the dog to like him Al buys meat at a butcher's shop, and while there ends up in possession of an anarchist's time bomb. When Al gives the dog the meat he also feeds him the bomb, which has been set to explode in 15 minutes. Thinking his canine worries will be over once the bomb goes off, Al gets a rude awakening when he finds that the Pup now loves him and won't leave his side. The rest of the short details Al's attempts to get away from the dog, and eventually ends happily as all the physical activity causes the dog to lose his lunch and the bomb at the last minute.

For many years this short has been a rare item. Never available or in circulation, it wasn't definite that the film even existed—until recently. In 2002 a nitrate copy was found in a collection at the Nederlands Filmmuseum in Amsterdam, but it turns out that a 35mm print had already been restored and preserved by Lobster Films and shown on European television. Serge Bromberg of Lobster generously passed along a screening copy.

Roscoe's firm hand can be seen in the direction of this short, with gag sequences from *Love* (1919) and *Sherlock, Jr.* (1924) repeated, as are all the early films that featured his dog Luke. Luke (1913-1926) was around 12 years old when this film was shot, but the young Pete the Pup is an excellent replacement and gets more screen time and business

Al St John and Pete the pup have a love/hate relationship in *Dynamite Doggie* (1925). Author's collection.

Roscoe recycles Buster Keaton and Kathryn McGuire's *Sherlock, Jr.* (1924) awkward courtship via Al St John and Christine Francis in *Dynamite Doggie* (1925). Courtesy the Lobster Collection.

than he did in any of the Our Gang comedies that he's remembered for. As always, Roscoe films and frames all the action in a tight and economical style, and fills out the cast with regular supporting players: George Davis (*His New Car*, *My Stars*, *The Fighting Dude*, etc.), Christine Francis (*Stupid But Brave*, the candy shop girl in *Sherlock, Jr.*) and Johnny Sinclair (*Never Again*, *Curses*).

All in all, *Dynamite Doggie* is an excellent addition to the surviving films of Al St John and Roscoe Arbuckle, and is more evidence that Arbuckle's ability to make audiences laugh had survived his ordeal intact.

Motion Picture News (March 21, 1925): "Al St John is always good for a laugh and he doesn't fail in this one, which has more than the usual number of humorous incidents. A well trained dog is of material aid to the success of the picture. The dog belongs to the girl Al is wooing, and is none too friendly disposed toward her suitor. This should be good for laughs from almost any type of audience."

MPW Straight From the Shoulder Report (February 6, 1926): "Al St John uses some of his famous bicycles in this and thereby gets some hearty laughs. A dandy comedy and no mistake."

The Iron Mule

Released April 12, 1925. A Tuxedo Comedy. Produced by Reel Comedies, Inc. Distributed by Educational Pictures. Directed by Grover Jones. Two reels. Extant : MoMA, GEM, LOC, UCLA, ACAD, Berk, LOB, EYE. With Al St John, Doris Deane, George Davis, Glen Cavender, Billy Franey, Walter C. Reed, Lotus Thompson, Florence Reed, Buster Keaton.

Back in the days of 1830, Al is the engineer and brakeman on the railway line between Likskillett and Sassafrass. The conductor is so honest that he turns in all his collections to the

Roscoe poses with the cast and crew of *The Iron Mule* (1925). Courtesy Annichen Skaren.

company, and the passengers are brave pioneers—they have to be for a ride on the railroad is one of the dangers of the age.

The train leaves Likskillett on time, and starts out on its journey through the danger-haunted wilds of the day. Cows block many tracks as the travelers tear through the country side at the zipping rate of eight miles per hour.

At a backwoods station a woodsman boards the train and tethers his horse to the caboose. When the horse refuses to move, the train doesn't move either—its wheels spinning in place—and when the passengers get out to push the horse the rope is undone and the train takes off. The problems with the horse distract the riders from their transportation, and when they find that the train has gone they have to run to catch it. Next they reach the raging river but logs are lashed to the sides, and, with Al manning long oars, the engine and coaches are ferried downstream.

Finally they arrive in Indian country, and when the train strikes an obstruction of logs piled on the tracks the redskins swoop in to massacre the riders. But they have not reckoned on what tough pioneer stuff the passengers are made of. Soon the Indians are routed and their scalps saved as the train and its passengers continue on their way.

Behind the scenes look at Roscoe and company shooting *The Iron Mule* (1925).
Courtesy Annichen Skaren.

The titular train of *The Iron Mule* is the same engine and cars used in Buster Keaton's 1923 feature *Our Hospitality*, and it's just as difficult, balky, and slow as it is in the Keaton picture. It's possible that the thought of taking it out of mothballs was the impetus for *Iron Mule*, but it's not the only Keaton item in the film. Buster himself is on hand as the Indian who's picked up along the way, and does some signature business and falls with a lasso. Also, in the long shot where the old couple is chasing the train and falling all over each other in the best Comique style it's pretty certain that they're being doubled by Buster and Al St John. Although perhaps a working vacation for Buster, the film was an opportunity to bring he, Al, and Roscoe together again, and the resulting film, which has the leisurely tempo of the train itself, is a unique, tongue-in-cheek spoof of "olden days" and westerns such as John Ford's *The Iron Horse* (1924).

The cast looks great in their period costumes, especially Al as the stoic and wooden-headed train engineer. The credited director on *Iron Mule*, as well as *Dynamite Doggie* and *Curses*, is Grover Jones. A long-time slapstick veteran with a sharp and original sense of the absurd, Jones was probably writing on the series when his name was put on as director, but he had already directed numerous shorts, and, as the films show, was an excellent collaborator for Roscoe. Born in Indiana in 1893, Jones' first job was as a sign painter, and when he noticed that labeling was needed for movies ("janitor" printed on hats, or "dynamite" on boxes) he headed to Hollywood. At first doing scene painting and working on set crews, he began making suggestions for the comedy shorts he was working on, and in 1919 became a gagman. It wasn't long before he was bumped up to director, and he was soon directing and writing shorts for Milburn Moranti, Billy Franey, and George Leroi Clarke like *Kick*, *The Cameraman*, *The Snip* (all 1920), and *In the Trenches* (1921).

Right from the beginning Jones had his own offbeat sense of humor, and would often have jokes about how the films were made, or a character who would step out of the film and comment on the proceedings. He moved on to directing low-budget and light-hearted action vehicles for Richard Talmadge and Frank Merrill, and even *Thrilling Youth* and *Oh Billy Behave* (both 1926), two of former Chaplin imitator Billy West's starring features. He made his real mark as a writer. After stints at the Hal Roach and Sennett studios he began writing "A" features such as *She's a Sheik* (1927) with Bebe Daniels, and the Wallace Beery/Raymond Hatton opus *Partners in Crime* (1928). Doing even better after the arrival of sound, he wrote classics such as *Trouble in Paradise* (1932), *The Lives of a Bengal Lancer* (1935), *The Milky Way* (1936), and *Abe Lincoln in Illinois* (1940). He died at the age of forty-six while still very busy in 1940, and some of his screenplays were adapted for later films like *The Kid from Brooklyn* (1946) and *Soldier's Three* (1951).

Moving Picture World (June 19, 1926): "This laugh hit has become a film comedy classic having been accorded some of the highest praise by motion picture critics that has ever been showered on a short feature."

Exhibitor's Trade Review (April 18, 1925): "A travesty on one of the most successful pictures of the year, 'The Iron Mule' offers some really subtle humor. It is a pleasing burlesque more calculated to extract a smile than a howl, but nevertheless excellent entertainment. It is somewhat reminiscent of Buster Keaton's earlier production of 'Our Hospitality,' depicting the journey of the first train across the plains. It is far removed from slapstick, and offers a theme altogether different from the majority of screen comedies… 'The Iron Mule' is a picture we unhesitatingly recommend to the most discriminating exhibitor."

Motion Picture News (April 18, 1925): "The train is a knockout and one marvels at how long it holds together for the duration of the too-long journey. Al St John is the featured player as well as the engineer and conductor of the train, and as usual Al is good for numerous laughs. He goes through his full repertoire of gymnastic stunts and falls, which should be entertaining to nearly any type of audience. The picture is well worth while aside from St. John, for a sight of that train and its peculiar gyrations. And to add to that there are a set of subtitles that get away from the usual wisecracks and inject some real humor."

Curses

Released May 17, 1925. A Tuxedo Comedy. Produced by Reel Comedies, Inc. Distributed by Educational Pictures. Directed by Grover Jones. Two reels. Extant: LOB. With Al St John, Bartine Burkett, Walter C. Reed, Johnny Sinclair.

A smashing, crashing, blood-curdling, hair-raising thriller in three side-splitting episodes:

"*The Teeth of Death*"
"*The Clutching Claws*"
"*Saved by a Sneeze*"

Our Story
Way up in the great Northwest lived Little Nell and her old father Buckwheat Ben. All was peaceful in their little cabin, but in the hills lurked Buttonshoe Bill, a bold, bad, bloodthirsty villain—literally a man with two left feet. Bill confronts Buckwheat Ben in his cabin and demands "the papers," and when Buckwheat refuses Bill knocks him senseless by beaning him with heavy flapjacks snatched from the stove.

Bill absconds with "the papers," and Little Nell returns to find her unconscious father and the flapjacks. As she implores the fates for someone to save them from the freak-footed flapjack felon we see Rodney Hemingway, the sinewy, sunburned sheik of the Sierras hurrying to her rescue. Despite his steely presence Little Nell is abducted by Bill and his confederates and taken to a sawmill where he lashes her to a log. He turns on the saw and the teeth get closer and closer—but of course in the nick of time she is rescued by Rodney.

Although they escape from the mill the dastardly crew again captures the devoted pair and handsome Rodney is tied to a tree and is made to sneeze with snuff so that he lets loose a huge rock which comes rolling down the mountain at him. Closer and closer the big rock comes, threatening to

Lobby card for *Curses* (1925) featuring Al St John, Johnny Sinclair (left), and Bartine Burkett. Courtesy Annichen Skaren.

crush the brave lad to smithereens. But using the snuff backfires on Bill as Rodney produces another huge sneeze which sets the rock on an opposite path so that it lands on the scheming gang.

Again the lovers make their escape and return to the cabin and revive Little Nell's father. Bill and the villains are right behind, and when their attempts to rout the little family fail, Bill grows desperate and pours gasoline around the cabin and sets a match to it. But as he happens to be sitting on the gasoline can the flames go around the cabin and ignite the can, spending Bill into orbit.

When our heroes come out to explore the damage they find Bill in the crater in which he's landed from his flight, and he finally surrenders "the papers," which are cigarette rolling papers, and then throws in the tobacco. Now free from Bill's vengeance, Little Nell, Handsome Rodney, and Buckwheat Ben cover Bill with dirt for the final "The End."

One of the most sophisticated spoofs in silent comedy, *Curses* burlesques western serials to a tee. Roscoe had done tongue-in-cheek parodies before in *The Bright Lights* (1916), *Moonshine* (1918), *The Frozen North* (1922), and *The Iron Mule* (1925), but reaches new surreal heights with this one. Al St John heads an on-the-money cast that alternates dead panning and over-the-top emoting for maximum comedy effect. Johnny Sinclair appears around the edges of the plot as Al's goofy henchman; Walter C. Reed, who returned in front of the camera in *The Iron Mule*, is back as Little Nell's elderly father who's repeatedly lambasted with Nell's deadly flapjacks, and there's even a giant boulder that probably saw duty in Buster Keaton's *Seven Chances* (1925).

Heroine Nell is played by Bartine Burkett, best known to silent comedy fans for Buster Keaton's *The High Sign* (1921), a comedy ingénue who worked at a number of different studios for a variety of well-known comics. Although prolific, most of her films are lost so her work is largely unknown. When her family moved to Hollywood from Shreveport, Louisiana in 1914, the sixteen year-old Bartine began making the rounds of the studio casting offices and became active at the Lasky Studio, as well as at Universal in their Joker, Star, and L-Ko Comedies. Working with Stan Laurel, Mack Swain, Lyons & Moran, and Chai Hong, her career got a boost when she landed the female lead in the Century Comedy "special" *The Geezer of Berlin* (1918).

Continuing at L-Ko, she moved over to Fox Sunshine Comedies, and right after working with Keaton in *The High Sign* she was back at Universal and headlined in a series of Star Comedies. These were short and sweet domestic comedies like *Kid-ing the Landlord*, *The Nuisance*, and *Cards and Cupid* (all 1920). The rest of the 1920s saw her working all over the silent comedy universe—supporting Charles Dorety and Harry Sweet at Century, turning up in CBC's Hallroom Boys Comedies, and many features. In 1926 she left films, but after a fifty-year retirement she returned to work in the early 1970s and was again busy in movies and television.

Playing sweet little old ladies in films like *Galaxina* (1980) and *The Devil and Max Devlin* (1981), she was all over television—on programs like *The Mary Tyler Moore Show*, *The Rockford Files*, and *Adam 12*, plus appeared in tons of commercials, such as the hip motorcycle riding granny in a series of spots for Boone's Farm Strawberry Hill wine. She also talked about working with Keaton in Kevin Brownlow and David Gill's 1987 documentary *Buster Keaton: A Hard Act to Follow*, and had made it to the ripe age of ninety-six when she passed away in Burbank in 1994.

Sadly original prints of *Curses* aren't available today, and for many years it only circulated in a 16mm version put out by the Glenn Photo Supply Company. Retitled *The Last Serial*, it was credited as a "Mack Sennett Comedy" with all the original title cards removed and very rudimentary new title cards added. A video version closer to the original was put together by producer Paul E. Gierucki, with help from Cole Johnson, David B. Pearson, Richard M. Roberts, Steve Rydzewski, and yours truly, for the 2005 DVD set *The Forgotten Films of Roscoe "Fatty" Arbuckle*. Using the Educational Pictures pressbook and other contemporary materials, it gives a much closer approximation of the tone and spirit of the original, but is not a true restoration and is only available on video.

Film Daily (May 24, 1925): "This is one of the funniest comedies seen in a long time. A title says that they called the picture 'Curses' because they couldn't think of any other name, but after you see it you can call it any name you like. It's a burlesque on all the motion picture serials, with the blood-curdling, hair-raising thrills, etc. Al St John, the featured player, is very funny as the bad man with two left feet. However the titles are

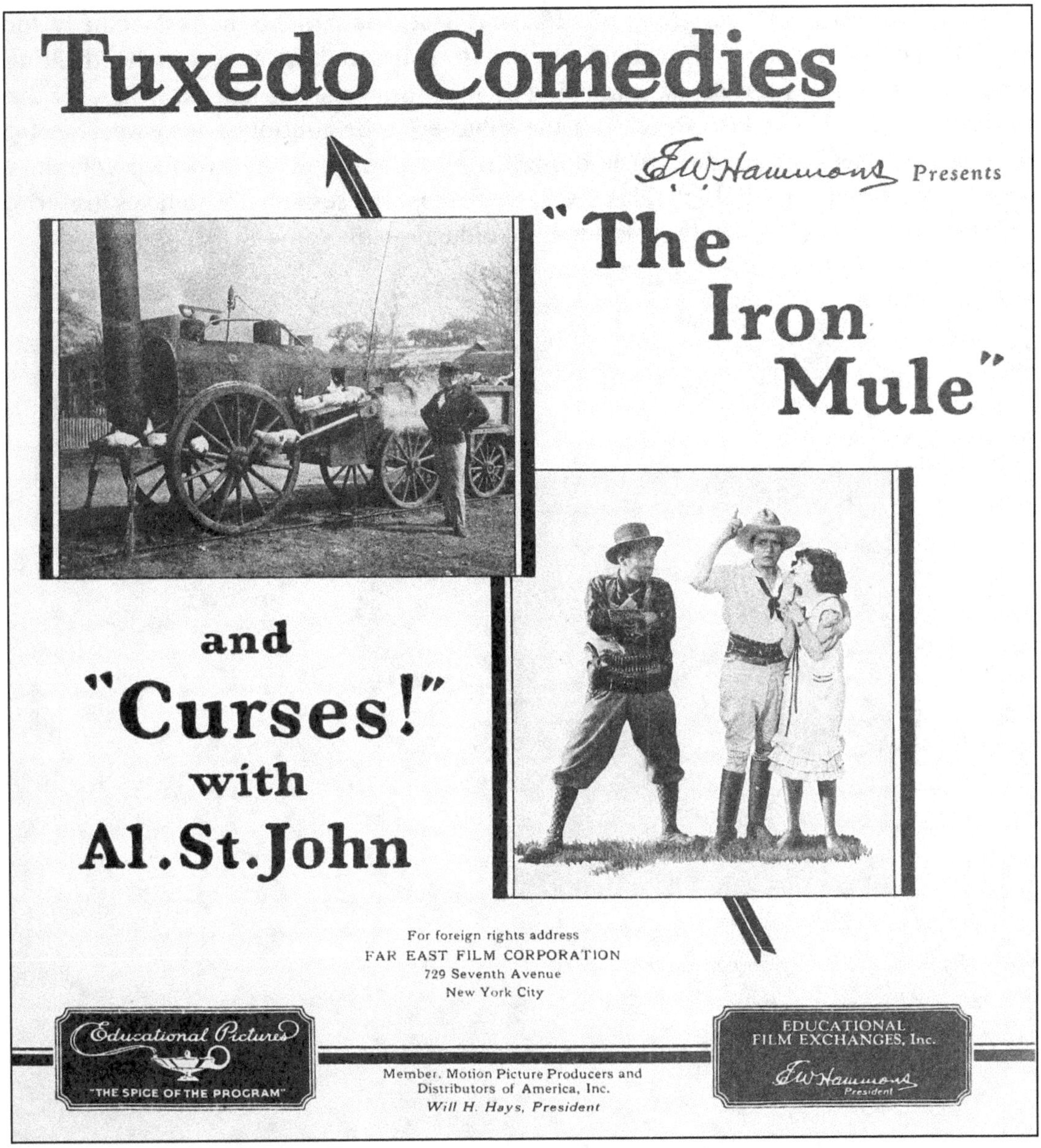

Exhibitor ad for *Curses* and *The Iron Mule* (both 1925).

probably the funniest of their kind. Don't let this get by you. Get it. They've got all the serial stuff burlesqued—even to the 'Continued Next Week' title."

Motion Picture News (May 23, 1925): "Here is a very cleverly arranged travesty on the serial, done in two reels with all the thrill of the serial and with an abundance of real comedy in which Al St. John is the central figure.... all the thrill and reality of the serial with some of the richest travesty that has been seen in a long time. This looks like a sure two-reeler that will be thoroughly appreciated by any type of audience not above laughing at situations that when analyzed are altogether ridiculous."

Moving Picture World (May 30, 1925): "Al St. John in his newest comedy for Educational has sprung a new one, for this is a broad burlesque on the thrilling melodramatic type of serials, even to being divided into episodes and carrying over the suspense in the middle of a thrill with the subtitle 'To be continued next week.' A lot of cleverness has been used in burlesquing the situations, and the two reels contain a number of good laughs and chuckles. Everyone, except the serial fan who takes his serial so seriously he objects to having it kidded, should enjoy this comedy."

Chapter 11
The Mystery of "Biff Thrill Comedies"

IN 1925 ROSCOE AND AL St. John both, although separately, began working for Educational Pictures proper. The accepted version is that *Curses* was Reel Comedies, Inc.'s last film. But scattered and tantalizing bits of information exist that suggest that at least two obscure Al St. John starring shorts, released in late 1925 into 1926, could have

Al St John and Bartine Burkett recreate *Sherlock, Jr.*'s (1924) sofa courtship routine in *The Live Agent* (1925). Courtesy Mark Johnson.

possibly been Reel Comedies productions that for whatever reasons weren't released by Educational. A small independent outfit, Bischoff, Inc., released four St. John titles—*The Live Agent* (1925), *His Taking Ways*, *Rain and Shines*, and *Service* (all 1926)—under the banner of their *Biff Thrill Comedies*.

Trained as a Certified Public Accountant, Samuel Bischoff had worked as a film exchange man in Boston before deciding to get into distribution himself. His first project as an independent producer was a 1925 Stan Laurel short *Mixed Nuts*, which had been cobbled together by G. M. Anderson from large chunks of Laurel's first film *Nuts in May* (1917) and outtakes from 1922's *The Pest*. Anderson sold the short to Bischoff, who set up his Bishoff, Inc. organization and launched three shorts series—*The Biff Thrill Comedies*, *Gold Medal Comedies*, and H. C. Witwer's *Classics in Slang*. Many of these shorts were supplied by people like Ernest Van Pelt and Trem Carr, and starred the likes of Chester Conklin, Cliff Bowes, Al Alt, Jack Cooper, Dot Farley, Billy Franey, and Arbuckle and St. John sidekick, Johnny Sinclair. Titles like *Hollywouldn't* and *Working for the Rest* (both 1925) gave Sinclair the opportunity to star on his own.

The Al St. John *Biff Comedies* came out at the same time as Al's films for Jack White/Educational, with publicity and exhibitor magazine coverage being extremely scant. They were released without attention and were forgotten. Missing for many years, recently all four shorts have turned up, and two of them have striking and suspicious similarities to the Reel Comedies.

The first St. John Biff, *The Live Agent* (1925), has the director credit of Grover Jones, who had been the directorial name on *Dynamite Doggie*, *The Iron Mule*, and *Curses* (all 1925), and co-stars Al with Bartine Burkett, the leading lady of *Curses*. Having the opportunity to view a nitrate print at the EYE Filmmuseum in Amsterdam, there are numerous stylistic similarities and material borrowings from the Reel Comedies including a new variation of the awkward courtship routine on a sofa that appears in *Sherlock, Jr.* (1924) and *Dynamite Doggie* (1925). The plot of the short has Al as a fledgling insurance agent who must sell a record number of policies to satisfy his boss, who also happens to be his girl's father. Dad won't give his permission to their marriage unless Al makes good.

The other potential Reel Comedies Biff release is *Rain and Shines* (1926). This one exists with a private collector and reworks chunks of *His First Car* (1924). Al buys a new car, but when he and his wife go out for their first ride they have nothing but trouble—they lose a wheel, and the car speeds off without them. Finally they get caught in a raging storm, and take refuge in a house where the black owners think they are ghosts. ("Shines" was a derogatory term for black people, hence the title *Rain and Shines*), One definite Arbuckle sequence is a reworking from *Fatty and Mabel's Simple Life* (1915) where their car runs amok and chases a fat man down the street, eventually backing him up against a tree and repeatedly bouncing off his ample stomach.

At the moment the possibility of these two *Biff* comedies having been written and directed by Roscoe is just theory and conjecture (or perhaps wishful thinking). Although Joseph Schenck was involved in the creation of Reel Comedies, Inc. a perusal of the Schenck papers turned up nothing on Reel Comedies or Bischoff, Inc. Although there's no concrete proof, there is circumstantial evidence that points to Roscoe's involvement in the *Biff Comedies*.

Al St John and Bartine Burkett in a few frame grabs from *The Live Agent* (1925). Courtesy EYE Filmmuseum.

Here's a couple of trade reviews for *The Live Agent*:

Film Daily (August 2, 1925): "*The Live Agent*—A Splendid Comedy. Al St John is starred in this comedy which deal with the harassed life of an insurance agent. St. John is excellent. Besides really good "straight" work, he takes a lot of throwing around, being kicked out of doors, time without number. There are many new gags and the action is fast and continuous. Should be a fine number for any house. Grover Jones is responsible for the good direction."

Exhibitor's Trade Review (August 22, 1925): "*The Live Agent*—This is a good product and should be good for a lot of laughs from any type of audience. Al St. John is the agent, and the ludicrous adventures that befall him call forth many a chuckle.

"The climax is when he stumbles on a crew of men who are blasting a hill away. He explains the terms of his accident policy and they all interchangeably sign up. Then, leaving for their shack, one leaves a trail of powder that leaks from a keg he carries. Al nonchalantly tosses a cigarette into the powder, and the entire crew are blown sky high. On his rapid way hence he corrals a pastor, and thrusting the signed policies and premiums into his prospective father-in-law's hand, he has the ceremony performed without further ado. The crew crash in just too late, and, of course, in a slapstick battle, Al lays them all low."

Shooting *His Private Life* (1926) on the Educational Studio's lot, Roscoe is surrounded by production staff that includes Virginia Vance, Lupino Lane (right of Roscoe), Walter C. Reed (sitting lower right), Glen Cavender (standing upper right), and Jimmy Bryant (sitting extreme left). Courtesy Sam Gill.

Chapter 12

Enter William Goodrich

W. G. and the Spice of the Program

With the finish of the St John shorts, Reel Comedies, Inc. appears to have been liquidated. The series did so well that Roscoe began working directly for Educational in the fall of 1925. At that time he adopted the pseudonym of William Goodrich for his directorial efforts. Over the years many different people claimed to have given him the name, or that it was a less-obvious variant on Will B. Good, but Roscoe took the name from his father, William Goodrich Arbuckle. He piloted ten shorts for three of Educational's popular stars: Johnny Arthur, Lloyd Hamilton and Lupino Lane.

These were under the auspices of Jack White Comedies. White had of course appeared with Roscoe in *Fatty Joins the Force* and *His Sister's Kid's* (both 1913) when he was an office boy at Keystone. As mentioned earlier he was fired by Sennett for inadvertently delivering a rival job offer to Ford Sterling. White then spent the next few years working for Henry Lehrman—learning to edit at L-Ko and directing Fox comedies by age nineteen. At Fox he met and formed a partnership with comic Lloyd Hamilton, and became a full-fledged producer at age twenty-one in 1920 when they began distributing their shorts through Educational Pictures.

After proving that he could deliver with the Reel Comedy two-reelers, Roscoe had been hoping to direct features under his own name. Having worked his way up from shorts to features as a performer, the two-reelers seemed like a step back, but directing features wasn't in the cards at the moment—explained by Roscoe to Minta Durfee in an April 1, 1925 letter:

> I had a year's contract to direct all ready to sign with Universal but some busy body women heard about it and went to Carl Laemmle and made a squawk about it and he got cold feet and backed out, so I don't know what I am going to do now. Every producer seems afraid to give me work on account of the fact that someone is liable to holler, so it looks like the best I will be able to do is to direct two reelers for some unimportant company where I can change my name and direct.

Despite his reluctance the three years that Roscoe would spend working on these comedy shorts would not only give him much-needed cash, but also prove that his ability to create comedy hadn't been snuffed out. They gave him a chance to regain his slapstick sea legs and rethink his place in, and approach to, film comedy. His success with these shorts finally led to offers to direct features.

1925

The Tourist

Released September 20, 1925. A Tuxedo Comedy. Produced by Jack White Comedies. Distributed by Educational Pictures. Directed and written by William Goodrich. Photographed by Byron Houck. Two reels. With Johnny Arthur, Helen Foster, Joy Winthrop, Glen Cavender, George Davis.

Johnny is traveling across the country in his beat up old flivver. After rising in the morning he converts the car into a stove and cooks his breakfast on its various parts. He later gives a lift to a girl walking back from an auto ride who invites him to dine with

Johnny Arthur is a "knight of the road" to Helen Foster in *The Tourist* (1925). Courtesy Robert S. Birchard.

her folks. Also dining with the family is a pair of crooks who discover the value of a well on the property. Helen's parents find out that unless the back taxes on their property are paid that very day it will be forfeited. When Johnny overhears the crooks plotting to get to the tax office first, he and Helen get in his car to try to get to the office before them. In the mad dash to get there both cars have difficulties, but even though his ancient auto actually ends up without a motor Johnny and Helen still arrive first and save the day.

Roscoe's first film for Jack White took the name brand Tuxedo Comedies, perhaps as a nod to his previous Reel Comedy shorts, and launched a newcomer to the unit—Johnny Arthur. Best remembered today for playing Darla Hood's prissy father in the Our Gang shorts *Night 'n' Gales* (1937) and *Feed 'Em and Weep* (1938), Arthur had spent more than twenty years on stage in New York and London working with stars like William Collier and Lou Tellegen before he made his film debut in 1923's *The*

Educational Pictures portrait of Johnny Arthur. Author's collection.

Unknown Purple. He went on to *Daring Love* (1924) and scored a big hit in *The Monster* (1925) with Lon Chaney. From there he was hired to star in his own two-reel comedies with Roscoe laying the blueprint for the series by directing the first four entries—*The Tourist, Cleaning Up* (both 1925), *My Stars,* and *Home Cured* (both 1926). The character developed for Arthur was that of a fussy milksop, usually an aspiring suitor or a henpecked husband, who though initially a lamb proves himself to be a lion when provoked.

Motion Picture News (August 15, 1925): "This is the first of the series of Tuxedo comedies starring Johnny Arthur and if it is indicative of what is to follow the series should be a profitable one for all hands. By way of a change in these short comedies here is one that tells a real story with some form of continuity and that does not side-track itself in interspersing an abundance of good comedy gags. Both the gags and the comedy work into the story naturally. William Goodrich has done a splendid job with the direction and the cast does the rest with the good story. Unfortunately there are not enough comedies of this type. There is a touch of melodrama to its great quantities of comedy and enough suspense to keep the interest at a high pitch."

Moving Picture World (August 15, 1925): "Gags and situations rather than slapstick have been relied upon to furnish the laughs and have succeeded, and this film should prove thoroughly entertaining for the majority of patrons. Much of the comedy is based on 'stunts' with a flivver, but they are all good for laughs or smiles, for Director Goodrich has introduced an entirely new lot of Ford gags. Johnny Arthur is a capable comedian of the quiet, unobtrusive type, who is pictured here as having plenty of spunk when he is aroused."

New York Morning Telegraph: "Here is the best two-reel comedy that has been turned out this season. It is a charming trifle, and there is every indication that in its star, Johnny Arthur, Educational has a real find. He is a delightful personality—he creates a character rather than merely submitting his person to the thuds of the slapstick. There is very little rough stuff of any kind in 'The Tourist,' but there is actually human interest—a rare quality in the two-reelers. Arthur plays a worthy tourist who has considerable trouble keeping his ancient flivver intact."

The Movies

Released October 4, 1925. Produced by Hamilton Comedies. Distributed by Educational Pictures. Directed and written by William Goodrich. Photographed by Byron Houck. Two reels. Extant: GEM, UCLA, LOB. With Lloyd Hamilton, Marcella Daley, Arthur Thalasso, Glen Cavender, Frank Jonasson, Florence Lee, Robert Brower, Charles Force, Charles Dudley. (Filmed at Montmarte Café on Hollywood Boulevard, outside the Chaplin Studios, and at the Educational studio in Los Angeles).

A young country boy decides to go to the big city to make good, but promises his parents that he'll stay away from the movies. In the city he has difficulties with traffic cops and a big burly chap of which he's gotten on the wrong side. After falling for an actress that he meets while dining at the Montmarte Café, it's found that he's the dead ringer for comedian Lloyd Hamilton. Hamilton has hurt his leg and can't finish a picture, so the country boy agrees to fill in so he can be near the actress. Things proceed alright at the studio, until the burly guy shows up on the set and goes after our hero. Having had enough of the movies and the city, our hero heads home to the bosom of his family.

This is the first of three silent shorts that Roscoe piloted for Lloyd Hamilton, and sadly the only one of the group known to exist. Roscoe's often sardonic take on the frailties of life fit right in with Hamilton's, as many of Hamilton's stories were as fatalistic as Buster Keaton's with titles like *No Luck* (1923), *Lonesome* (1924) and *Nothing Matters* (1926).

An extremely popular clown who almost made the jump to top stardom, Hamilton's screen character was that of a poor bumbler continually dogged by bad luck. This was unfortunately all too similar to his real life where his off-screen troubles stymied his career. After first finding fame in the teens with tiny Bud Duncan as half of the team of Ham and Bud, Hamilton then went to work for Henry Lehrman at Fox Sunshine Comedies where he met director Jack White. In 1920 they created their own company, releasing through Educational and developing the character that Hamilton made famous and would use for the rest of his career. Best described as a sort of overgrown mama's boy, he was prissy and courtly in a flat, checkered cap, with a swishy duck-waddle walk that became his trademark.

Lloyd Hamilton and Marcella Daly have trouble shooting their big love scene in *The Movies* (1925).

Although his screen style was always dry and underplayed, Hamilton was in private life a terrible alcoholic and was in and out of court due to divorce battles and drunken brawls. One such brawl ended up in the stabbing death of a boxer, and although Hamilton was not really implicated he was banned from the screen from mid-1928 into 1929. This makes Roscoe and Hamilton probably the only persons to actually have been banned in the 1920's. Ham would return to films, and working with Roscoe, in the early days of sound.

Since *The Movies* is set in Hollywood we get to see some of the local spots like the Montmarte Café and behind the scenes at the Educational Pictures lot, as well as Lloyd Hamilton in "character" and out of character as himself. An interesting footnote

Lloyd Hamilton, one of the most popular clowns of the 1920s. Billy Rose Theatre Division, the New York Public Library for the Performing Arts.

was discovered by film historian John Bengtson for his book *Silent Traces* (Santa Monica Press, 2006). Turns out the location for the hospital where Hamilton knocks out heavy Arthur Thalasso was part of the Tudor-style façade of the Charlie Chaplin Studio. Not a surprise considering that Roscoe and Charlie were old friends, and that Chaplin was said to have been fond of Hamilton's work.

Moving Picture World (September 26, 1925): "A clever bit of camera work has Hamilton leaving the vine-clad cottage, walking out into the middle of the road and finding himself in one of Los Angeles busiest streets. This is good trick work, mystifying and amusing. An excellent bit, sure to get a laugh is where his aged mother leaps through the air to embrace him. 'The Movies' is thoroughly entertaining."

Screen Snapshots (Series 6, No. 2)

Released October 15, 1925. Produced by Jack Cohn and Louis Lewyn for the C.B.C. Film Sales Corporation. One reel. With Enid Bennett, Vilma Banky, Lew Cody, Monte Blue, Roscoe Arbuckle, Doris Deane, Douglas Fairbanks, Mabel Normand, William Desmond, Wanda Hawley, Mary Pickford, Jack Pickford, Hank Mann, Jack Holt, Marilyn Miller

Because of the scandal and his court cases, Roscoe was all over the news media, but it ended his appearances in these entertainment news reels. By 1925 enough time had passed for them to note that the comedian had remarried and to include footage of Roscoe and Doris Deane.

Another Buster

Go West

Released November 1, 1925. Produced by Joseph M. Schenck for Buster Keaton Productions. Distributed by Metro-Goldwyn Mayer. Direction and story by Buster Keaton. Scenario by Raymond Cannon. Photography by Elgin Lessley and Bert Haines. Seven reels. Extant: Friuli, LOC, GEM, UCLA, ACAD, LOB, DAN. With Buster Keaton,

Buster Keaton and Brown Eyes in *Go West* (1925). Courtesy Robert Arkus.

Brown Eyes, Kathleen Myers, Howard Truesdale, Ray Thompson, Roscoe Arbuckle, Babe London, George Davis, Glen Cavender.

Friendless Homer Holiday leaves his home and drifts out West where he finds employment on the Thompson ranch. He befriends Brown Eyes, a cow, who reciprocates by saving his life. When she is included in a shipment of cattle bound for the stockyard, Friendless goes along to look after her. Tom Jackson, a rival rancher, attacks the train, and while the Thompson and Jackson men are fighting, Friendless commandeers the train and takes the cattle through town to deliver them. In gratitude, Thompson offers him anything he has as a reward, and instead of asking for his daughter's hand Friendless picks Brown Eyes.

Roscoe's second wife Doris Deane told author David Yallop that he contributed freely to Buster Keaton's mid-1920s films. Today we really don't know the extent of Arbuckle's participation in features like *Sherlock, Jr.* (1924), *Seven Chances* (1925), or *Battling Butler* (1926), but he does appear briefly on screen in 1925's *Go West*.

In the latter part of the film when Buster is trying to herd the cattle through downtown Los Angeles, there's a scene with the steers piling into a department store. Among the characters reacting to the animals are a fat woman and her fat daughter (Babe London). In the initial longshot it's Roscoe as the mother reacting and jumping around, but in closer shots around the elevator and in posed stills it's a large woman. The actual woman is shorter than daughter Babe London, but in Roscoe's shots they're the same height.

The other bystanders in the scene are played by Arbuckle pals such as George Davis, Johnny Sinclair, and Glen Cavender, who would have been sure to keep Roscoe's cameo to themselves. With its echoes of *Out West* (1918) and *A Desert Hero* (1919), it's likely that Roscoe was involved in some parts of *Go West*'s shoot, leading to this on screen in-joke.

Moving Picture World (November 7, 1925): "Our hat is off to Buster Keaton! In 'Go West' for Metro-Goldwyn-Mayer in which he quadruples as author, director, scenarist and star, by using a quadruped, a mild-faced cow, as the center of interest, he has injected an entirely new personality in screen comedy. Now who ever had a cow in a leading role when not on the other end of a string?"

Exhibitors Trade Review (November 7, 1925): "Some ridiculously funny things happen when Buster attempts to lead his thousand head of steers through city streets to the stock yards. The animals enter shops of various kinds and create havoc. Buster, unaware of the commotion he is causing, calmly marches ahead, and with 'Brown Eyes' finally brings the herd to harbor in time to save the day."

Film Daily (November 1, 1925): "As a whole some fine laughs and original comedy gags in Keaton's latest. A satire on the overwhelming lot of westerns."

Cleaning Up

Released November 22, 1925. A Tuxedo Comedy. Produced by Jack White Comedies. Distributed by Educational Pictures. Directed and written by William Goodrich. Photographed by Byron Houck. Two reels. With Johnny Arthur, Helen Foster, George Davis, Mark Hamilton, Napoleon.

Johnny and his wife quarrel when he loses his job for oversleeping. He tells her how easy it is for her to have nothing to do but care for the house and she volunteers to let him do it for the day, retiring to her mother's in a huff. Johnny makes a mess of everything and eventually the fire department is called in, completing the destruction he has started. The wife returns and finds the disaster, but Johnny manages to blame the calamity on her brother.

Unfortunately *Cleaning Up*, like the previous Arthur comedy *The Tourist*, is currently considered lost, but both films were well received by audiences and reviewers, getting the series off to a good start. With Johnny's screen persona of a fussy milquetoast, the gender reversal plot of having him stay home and take care of the house seems like a solid springboard for comedy business.

Helen Foster returned from *The Tourist* to play Johnny's fed-up wife. Kansas-born and from a theatrical family, she began her film career in independent westerns such as *Reckless Courage* and *The Bandit's Baby* (both 1925), and for a couple of years was a busy ingénue in Educational shorts that also included Lupino Lane's *Maid in Morocco* (1925) and *Move Along* (1926) with Lloyd Hamilton. In the late 1920s she was on contract to Universal, where she appeared in westerns and serials, and in 1929 was a WAMPAS Baby Star. She continued in minor roles until 1956.

The fire chief is played by long and lanky silent film character actor Mark Hamilton. Often billed as "Slim" Hamilton, he specialized in western types. Born in Washington, D.C., he had worked as a miner before starting in films in 1919. Turning up in numerous

Johnny Arthur and Helen Foster have a few husband and wife issues in *Cleaning Up* (1925).

comedy shorts and features, a selection of his two-reelers includes *The Hound of the Tankervilles*, *Daffy House* (both 1921), *Uncle Bim's Gifts* (1923), *Crushed* (1924), *Dizzy Daddies*, and *Fool's Luck* (both 1926). A few of his features are *Barbara Frietchie* (1924), *Riders of the Purple Sage* (1925), *Sparrows* (1926), *White Gold* (1927), and *Heart Trouble* (1928). His career wound down when sound arrived, and before his passing in 1963 he was involved in college and community theatre, and worked for Washington State's Department of Transportation for eighteen years.

Moving Picture World (November 14, 1925): "Johnny Arthur's first starring comedy for Educational was a corker, and although of an entirely different type, his second is just as funny. It is not so much the fact that Johnny has new material, for in the first he got his laughs largely out of a flivver and in this one he shows what happens when a husband tries to clean house, but it is his amusing personality and the clever gags that have been provided for him. There are some witty subtitles and plenty of real good laughs in this comedy. All classes should find it amusing, but the married folks and especially the wives will discover that it is especially so, for they can appreciate the situation."

Motion Picture News (November 14, 1925): "It is one of those comedies that just makes a complete mess of a house even to the calling out of the fire department, which as usual, floods it with water and thereby all but destroys most of the furniture as well as the occupants. It affords a lot of knock-about comedy, some of which is good and some not so good. Napoleon, a big Newfoundland dog, is a well trained animal and shares the honors of the picture with Arthur."

The Fighting Dude

Released December 6, 1925. Lupino Lane Comedies. Produced by Jack White Comedies. Distributed by Educational Pictures. Directed and written by William Goodrich. Photography by Byron Houck. Two reels. Extant: Moma, GEH, UCLA, MoMA, Buch. With Lupino Lane, Virginia Vance, Wallace Lupino, George Davis, Glen Cavender, Phil Dunham, Dick Sutherland.

Nip is a pampered wealthy sap very much in love with a young beauty. She invites him to a house party, where he sticks out like a sore thumb and finds that a clubman athlete is his rival for the girl. The athlete thrashes Nip, embarrassing him in front of the girl and her guests. Before he slinks out of the party the girl's father advises Nip that in order to impress women you have to be a rough and ready he-man. Dedicated to putting his rival in his place Nip begins working with a tough trainer at a gymnasium. After six lessons he thinks he's ready and confronts his rival, but gets himself another beating. Finally an official bout is arranged for them at a local boxing club, and since the club is men only the girl has to pose

Lupino Lane (left) about to get a boxing baptism of fire from sparring partner Dick Sutherland (left) and trainer Glen Cavender (middle) in 1925's *The Fighting Dude*.

in drag to get in. After a terrific battle Nip is still defeated. Later while jogging on the golf links he catches the rival trying to take advantage of the girl, and when coming to her rescue finally beats him senseless. But after his victory he finds that the girl has gone off with two suitors, so he joins his foe in collapse on the grass.

Lupino Lane was one of the greatest acrobats to ever grace the screen. Born in 1892 to a famous British theatrical family (Ida Lupino was a second cousin), as a child he was known as "Little Nipper" on stage. He began appearing in films in England as early as 1915. After coming to America in the early 1920s and headlining on Broadway and in the Ziegfeld Follies, he found time to venture to Hollywood and make a few shorts for the Fox Studio. In 1925 he came West again and started a series for Jack White/Educational where he was teamed with his brother and partner Wallace Lupino. His surviving films are marvels of comic action, with Lane as a diminutive dervish that sets all the other elements spinning.

His onscreen character was usually a befuddled innocent who stumbles his way to success, often a milquetoast who has to prove himself to impress a girl, which left room for lots of physical action and stunts. Roscoe worked with him on three shorts—*The Fighting Dude*, *Fool's Luck*, and *His Private Life*—all of which still exist, and present Lane as a pampered rich boy who has to learn to rely on his own resources and be a man.

Wallace Lupino (center left) and Lupino Lane (center right) are both down for the count in *The Fighting Dude* (1925). Courtesy Robert Arkus.

As mentioned above Lupino Lane's "partner in crime" in this series of shorts was his brother Wallace Lupino who plays Nip's smug rival in *The Fighting Dude*. While Lupino Lane was pure clown, Wallace was a versatile comic character actor, and besides his role here he played Moroccan sheiks, fiery gauchos, and in *Listen Sister!* (1928) even a boarding school head mistress. In addition to supporting his brother and other comics, Jack White starred Wallace in some of his own one and two-reel comedies, such as *Hard Work* and *The Lost Laugh* (both 1928), which garnered good reviews and praise for Wallace.

The brothers continued to work together on stage and in films into the 1940s, plus Wallace also appeared with cousin Barry Lupino, and turned in excellent character performances in *The Man Who Could Work Miracles* (1937) and *Waterloo Road* (1945). He later teamed with his nephew Laurie Lupino Lane in a club act, but after finding that the onset of arthritis made physical knockabout too painful, he retired.

Motion Picture News (December 5, 1925): "If all two reelers were a chock full of entertainment as this one which features Lupino Lane they would make it tough for a lot of feature pictures. There is not much that could be put into a comedy that is lacking in this one, for it is hard to imagine anything of a humorous nature Lane cannot do well. He is given full scope for the display of his talents and that means at least a laugh a minute.

"The comedian goes through some exceptionally humorous antics in a gymnasium where he has gone to learn something of boxing, but these only serve to get you in the right mood for the fight in which he engages with the popular clubman athlete. Wallace Lupino plays the latter role and between them they stage one of the funniest scraps ever seen on the silver sheet.

"This is an exceptionally good two-reeler with more humorous action in it than ordinarily is found in half dozen short comedies. It tells a good story and reveals Lupino Lane as one of the best all-around comedians seen on the screen."

Moving Picture World (December 5, 1925): "Lane certainly takes a lot of hard knocks and uses his acrobatic ability to advantage. He is a finished artist in his work and gets the most out of every situation. A corking good comedy that will cause a lot of genuine laughter and should convulse any audience."

1926

My Stars

Released January 17, 1926. Tuxedo Comedies. Produced by Jack White Comedies. Distributed by Educational Pictures. Directed and written by William Goodrich. Photographed by Byron Houck. Two reels. Extant: GEM, FRIU. With Johnny Arthur, Virginia Vance, George Davis, Florence Lee, Glen Cavender.

Johnny is a timid young man whose mother is a dress maker. The girl he's devoted to is crazy about movie stars. He tries to emulate them to please her, but her favorites change everyday when she gets a new star photo in the mail. When Johnny shows up as a sheik she's now moved on to Douglas Fairbanks. Finally when she's enamored of Harold Lloyd, Johnny impersonates him and has the gumption to take the girl through some daring stunts. This makes her decide that she really likes just plain Johnny.

My Stars (1926) sees Virginia Vance more interested in movie actors than just plain Johnny Arthur. Courtesy Robert Arkus.

This is a clever short in which Roscoe keeps the action brisk, and seems to have a great time poking fun at many friends in the industry. Not only does Johnny do on-the-money spoofs of Douglas Fairbanks and Harold Lloyd, but Roscoe gets in another jibe when the butler brings his mistress the new picture that's come in the mail and dares to tell her "My favorite is Buster Keaton." Her taken aback and puzzled reaction, and his embarrassed retreat puts the topper on this wonderful in-joke.

Johnny has two love interests in this picture—the movie-crazy object of his affections and his supportive mother. It's Virginia Vance that he's carrying the torch for, and at that moment she was Roscoe's leading lady of choice, as she appeared in five of his Arthur and Lupino Lane shorts. Vance was a pretty blonde who entered films in 1922 as support to Jimmie Adams and then Cliff Bowes in a huge amount of Jack White-produced Cameo Comedies. In 1925 she graduated to two-reelers, and, in addition to Arthur and Lane, she supported Al St John and Lloyd Hamilton in titles like *Fair Warning* (1925), *Live Cowards*, and *Here Comes Charlie* (both 1926). After a few features and changing allegiance to appear in Mack Sennett's *Dan the Taxi Man* series opposite Jack Cooper, she married actor Bryant Washburn and left the screen in 1928.

Arthur's mother is played by veteran actress Florence Lee, remembered today as Virginia Cherrill's grandmother in Charlie Chaplin's *City Lights* (1931). Lee, who was

Johnny Arthur telling George Davis to "step right up and call him Speedy" in *My Stars* (1926). Courtesy Robert Arkus.

married to neglected comedy director and actor Dell Henderson, specialized in playing "old ladies," always bringing a perfect combination of heart and moxie to the character. She spent the 1920's playing mother to adult comics like Lloyd Hamilton and Harry Langdon, and grandmother to screen tykes such as Malcolm "Big Boy" Sebastian and the *Our Gang* kids.

Motion Picture News (January 23, 1926): "Here's a first rate two reel comedy with Johnny Arthur as the star and it certainly ought to prove entertaining to the average audience. Some clever burlesque work is pulled by Arthur in his impersonation of several well known stars. Rest of the cast do good work."

Moving Picture World: A butler supplies a good bit of business by trying to do a Buster Keaton hand-spring. It is a Tuxedo Comedy and it should please all audiences."

Home Cured

Released March 14, 1926. A Tuxedo Comedy. Produced by Jack White Comedies. Directed by William Goodrich. Story by Donna Barrell. Photographed by Byron Houck. Assistant Direction by Vernon Keays. Two reels. Extant: LOC, GEM, UCLA, OTT. With Johnny Arthur, Virginia Vance, George Davis, Glen Cavender, Chick Collins, Robert Brower, Walter C. Reed, Frank Jonnason.

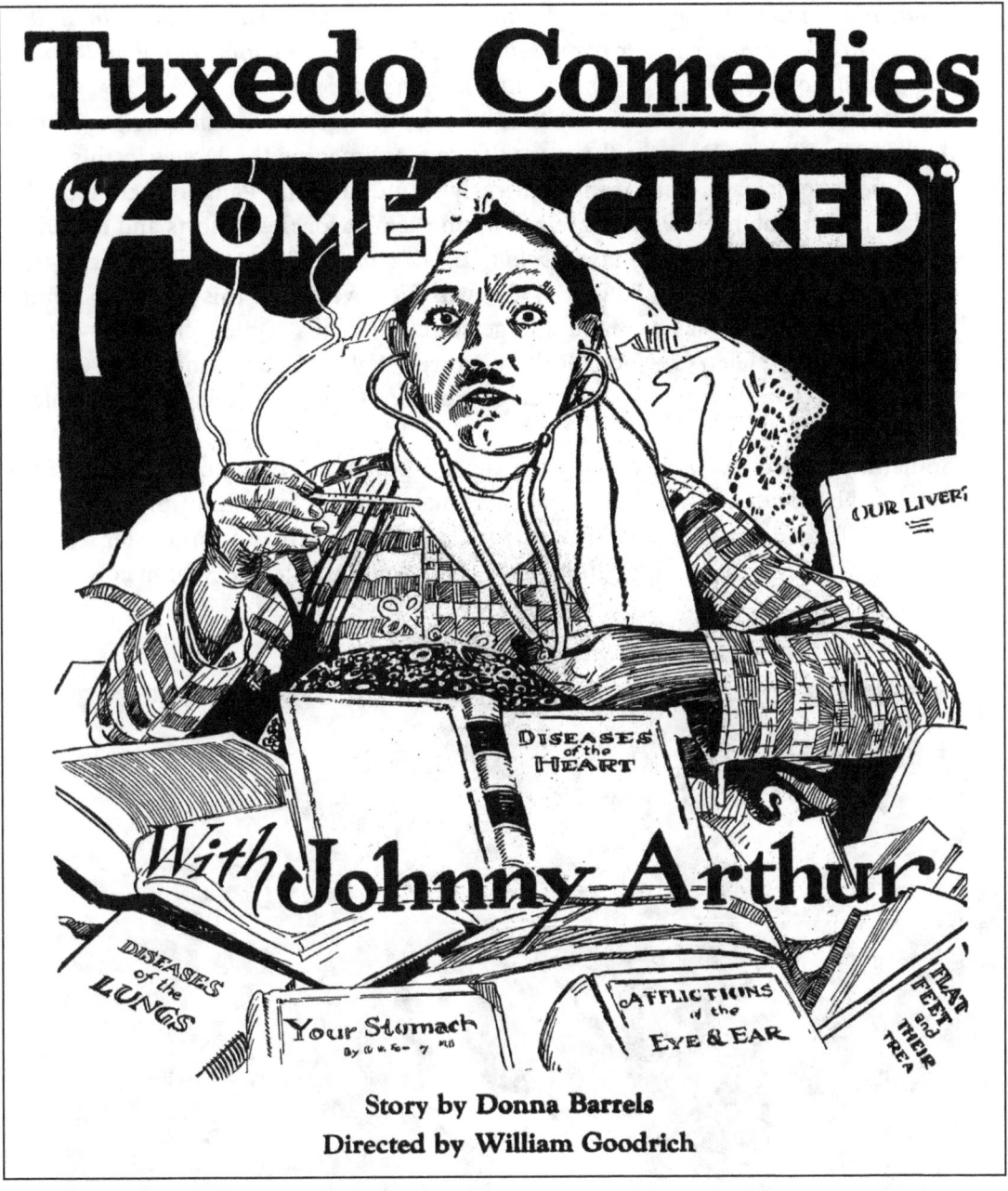

Johnny Arthur enjoying his hypochondria on the Educational Pictures pressbook cover for *Home Cured* (1926).

Johnny is a hypochondriac whose imaginary illnesses are driving his wife crazy. He won't even kiss her due to his fear of germs. After rushing out to take advantage of a fire sale of medicine and getting caught in a terrible rainstorm, he returns home to say that he's close to death's door. Having had enough, his wife conspires with the family doctor to cure him. The doctor examines him and gives the diagnosis that he only has four hours to live, then in quick succession a lawyer makes him sign a will, and an undertaker and grave-digger arrive to measure him. Finally the wife shows off what a beautiful widow she'll make, with his best friend ready to take his place in one of own suits. All of this snaps Johnny out of his "illness," and after chasing off his rival he announces that he is cured.

The story for *Home Cured* was written by Donna Barrell, who had written shorts for Mr. and Mrs. Sidney Drew in the teens. It's easy to imagine the Drews in this story, and Educational quickly re-used it for their early sound Franklin Pangborn comedy *The Crazy Nut* (1929). Columbia Pictures seized upon the plot for their shorts and remade it three more times—for Charley Chase's *Calling All Doctors* (1937), as well as *Doctor, Feel My Pulse* (1944) and *She Took a Powder* (1951) with Vera Vague. In this last of his Johnny Arthur comedies Roscoe has on hand a large selection of his regular character players such as George Davis, Glen Cavender, Robert Brower, Walter C. Reed, and Chick Collins, who, as the best friend that Johnny suspects is moving in on his wife, has the best role of his long movie career.

Sometimes billed as C.B. Collins, he was a stuntman and bit actor (and one of the founders of The Suicide Club with other stunters like Arbuckle pal Johnny Sinclair). After early work at Triangle in 1923 Collins was listed as stunt coordinator on Buster Keaton's *The Three Ages* and *Our Hospitality* (both 1923). No doubt due to the Keaton connection

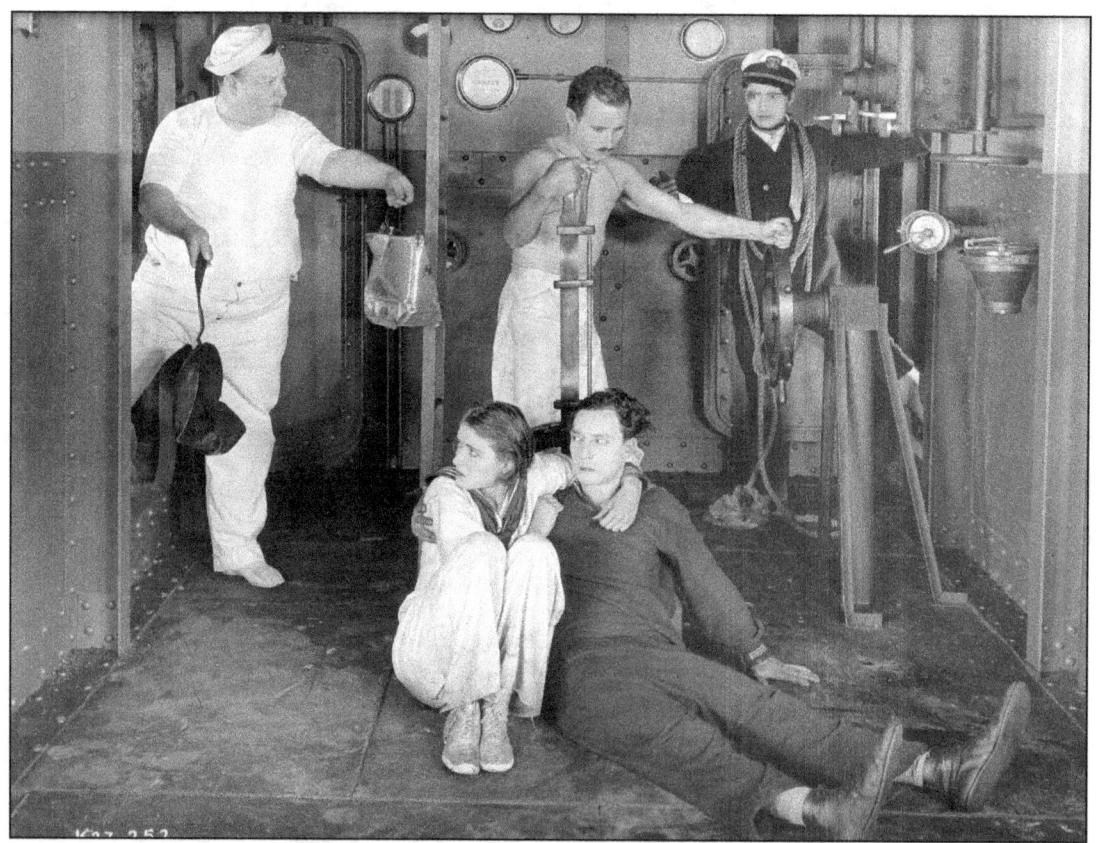

Commander Chick Collins (back right), Johnny Sinclair (middle), and cook Jean Havez (left) rescue Kathryn McGuire and Buster Keaton in 1924's *The Navigator* . Courtesy Robert Arkus.

he ended up working for Roscoe with bits in this, *His Private Life* (1926), *Peaceful Oscar* (1927), and others. In addition to doing stunts in features such as *Dr. Jekyll and Mr. Hyde* (1932), *My Man Godfrey* (1936), and *Singing in the Rain* (1952), he kept busy in uncredited roles in *Million Dollar Legs* (1932), *Sullivan's Travels* (1941), *Jitterbugs* (1943), and *The Good Humor Man* (1950) until 1965.

After *Home Cured* Norman Taurog took over the Arthur series, and Johnny fussed his way through 1928 for Educational. With his stage background Arthur was in great demand in early sound pictures and remained a character favorite into the 1940s.

Film Daily (March 28, 1926): "Here without doubt is one of the biggest laugh hits offered to the short subject field in this or any other season. Splendid situations, original comedy, great gags, fine direction and acting—a 100 per cent short with a riotous laugh punch. Shown cold in a projection room to the hard boiled gentry of the press, it had them snickering and guffawing all the way....Mark this one down right now and don't miss it. You can't afford to. You could run a flop feature, but this short screamer would be sufficient to send them out perfectly satisfied. Credit to director William Goodrich, Johnny Arthur, Virginia Vance and the entire cast for a peach of a comedy that hits the bull's eye plumb in the center."

Motion Picture News (March 27, 1926): "Action gags that shoot straight to the bullseye of laughter, and fine acting are the attributes which gives this Johnny Arthur comedy a high rating as entertainment for masses and classes. Indeed, 'Home Cured' seems to prove up to every test which can be applied to the judgement of what will or will not score with screen patrons. The story is credited to Donna Barrell and the direction to William Goodrich—both seasoned and accomplished specialists in their respective fields."

Exhibitors Daily Review (March 27, 1926): "Having been provided with an excellent cast, Director Goodrich gets the most out of every situation with the result that this two-reeler is rich in comedy value."

Fool's Luck

Released March 21, 1926. Lupino Lane Comedies. Produced by Jack White Comedies. Distributed by Educational Pictures. Directed by William Goodrich. Photographed by Byron Houck. Two reels. Extant: UCLA. With Lupino Lane, George Davis, Virginia Vance, Jack Lloyd, Mark Hamilton, Wallace Lupino, Glen Cavender, Bartine Burkett, Al St John (cameo as elevator boy).

Nip is a child of luxury and ease. He doesn't lift a hand for anything as long as his faithful valet George has two hands to do it with. George gets him out of bed, fixes his bath, adjusts his monocle—and even thinks for his master. Nip invites his girl Virginia and her father to have dinner in his rooms—but right after the invitation has gone out he finds that his rich uncle has cut off his allowance. The rent is due and without a dime to pay, Nip and George have to move everything out.

Their misadventures include dangling on a piano eight stories above the ground, and a wild ride on a driverless truck. Eventually it comes to a stop on a railway track, and although able to get it out of the way of an approaching train, another train coming from the other direction demolishes the truck and furniture. Luckily the claim agent of the railroad company

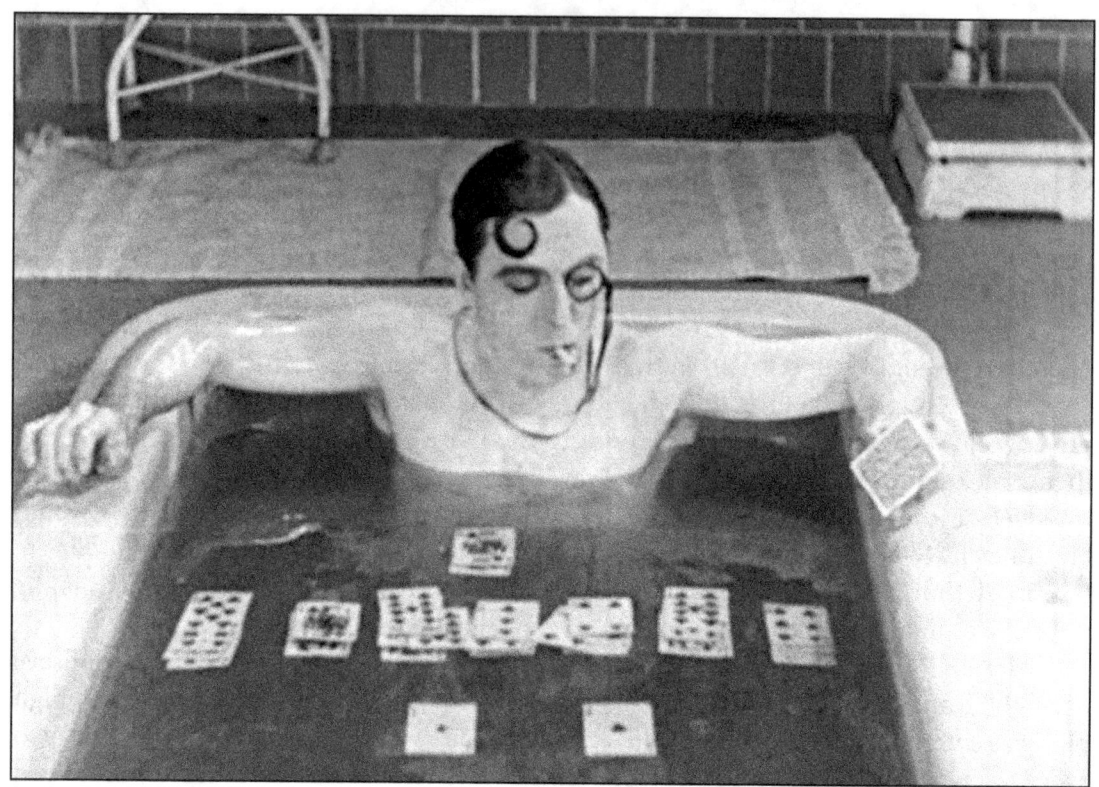

Lupino Lane deals a floating hand of solitaire in *Fool's Luck* (1926). Courtesy UCLA.

is on the train and settles the case with Nip for fifty thousand dollars. With this money he hurries back to the city. He moves back into his rooms and re-installs all his furniture just a split second before Virginia and her father arrive for dinner.

The character portrayed by Lupino Lane in *Fool's Luck*, as well as his other two shorts, *The Fighting Dude* (1925) and *His Private Life* (1926), directed by Roscoe, is a variation on Buster Keaton's pampered "poor little rich boy" from *The Navigator* (1924). Both Lane and Keaton can't do anything for themselves (Lane literally even needs his sissy valet George Davis' shoulder to cry on), and like Keaton, Lane ends up as a passive cog in some big slapstick thrill sequences. There are two in *Fool's Luck*—the first has Nip on a dangling piano eight stories up in the air that's a re-do from Poodles Hanneford's *No Loafing* (1923), and the other concerns a driverless truck full of furniture with Lane perched on top and unaware that the driver has fallen out.

The truck sequence is an adaption of Keaton's riding the front of the driverless motorcycle in *Sherlock, Jr.* (1924), and another Keaton borrowing comes for the big climax when the runaway truck finally comes to rest on a railroad crossing. Right away an oncoming train is bearing down—with the expected train missing the truck, but a surprise second train on the adjacent track appears and demolishes everything—just like the famous climax of *One Week* (1920).

On stage Lupino Lane was an amazing acrobat and athlete, doing all kinds of falls, tumbles, and flips, as well as being shot on stage from a star trap, but being a film comedian

Lupino Lane making a long distance phone call in *Fool's Luck* (1926). Courtesy UCLA.

was a whole other physical experience, as Lane related in the *Fool's Luck* pressbook:

> *First they dangled me out of an eight-story window above the pavement—and then they let me drop to a truck. Then I rode the truck when it ran away backward down a hill, and then, seeing that I was still on my feet, they allowed a fast train to knock the truck right out of my hands.*
>
> *Seriously, though, motion picture work is fascinating, but as for being easy—well, I've never been so tired in my life as I have been after working ten hours a day in the studio.*

Motion Picture News (April 3, 1926): "Another Lupino Lane comedy which will prove to be a first class attraction. The story and direction are by William Goodrich and the balance of the cast give Lane able assistance—the work of George Davis and Virginia Vance particularly standing out."

Moving Picture World (April 3, 1926): "There are a lot of laugh-getting gags in this comedy. Lane is excellent and George Davis as the sissy valet contributes a good performance. Altogether 'Fool's Luck' should go over well with the average audience."

His Private Life

Released May 16, 1926. Lupino Lane Comedies. Produced by Jack White Comedies. Distributed by Educational Pictures. Directed by William Goodrich. Two reels. Extant: MoMA, ACAD. With Lupino Lane, George Davis, Virginia Vance, Glen Cavender, Stanley Blystone, Chick Collins, Otto Fries.

Nip is a foppish young millionaire, the head of a big banking and brokerage firm. George is Nip's valet who meekly waits on him hand and foot—feeding, dressing, and waiting on his master. When war is declared George resigns as valet to join the army, but Nip attends to business as usual until his girl Virginia urges him to enlist (she envisions him as a handsome, dashing colonel). When Nip reports to training camp he finds that his former wimpy valet George is now a hard-boiled top-sergeant and is in charge of breaking in the new recruits.

The once master of finance is now nothing but a rookie private, and George makes it extremely tough for his former boss. Things go from bad to worse for Nip when he incurs the wrath of the commanding officer, and while assigned to watering the camp grounds the hose gets away from him and he drenches the staff from the Major General on down. Assigned to permanent K.P. duty he has major problems while baking in the kitchen, resulting in an

Lupino Lane is "nervous in the service" on the glass slide for 1926's *His Private Life*. Courtesy Matt Vogel.

all-out battle with flying dough and pies, and even the Colonel and Virginia get pasted in the melee. Nip is promptly ensconced in the guard house, and by the time he gets out the war is over.

Lupino Lane benefitted from Roscoe's years of experience in the three films they did together, and in his book, *How to Become a Comedian* (Frederick Muller, LTD, 1945), he talked about receiving his first Hollywood pie in the face while shooting *His Private Life*:

> *Roscoe (Fatty) Arbuckle insisted on throwing it himself. Unfortunately for me it was in a close up scene. Roscoe was well over six feet, weighed about twenty stone or more and was as strong as a bear. When I got the pie (it was a black currant one and weighed about half a pound), I went with it straight on to the flat of my back, to the delight of the onlookers. As I was about to wipe it off, I was told not to do so or the next shot wouldn't match up. Strangely enough, it was lunch time immediately afterwards and you can well imagine how I enjoyed my lunch with (it seemed) all the flies in Hollywood deciding to make their lunch off the remnants of the pie on my face. After lunch, I was told I could wipe it off as it had been decided to retake the shot! I realized then I had been put 'on the spot' to see what kind of sportsman I happened to be. Naturally I took it all in good part and when*

A mid-air candid shot of Lupino Lane working out a stunt for *His Private Life* (1926). Billy Rose Theatre Division, the New York Public Library for the Performing Arts.

the next shot came I noticed with glee that Roscoe was standing behind me right in the line of fire! When the pie came I ducked and he got it right in the neck. He enjoyed it as much as anybody, he was a loveable chap, and a master of slapstick.

After their films together Lane continued his Educational series into 1929, mostly working with director Norman Taurog until he began directing the shorts himself (as Henry W. George). Making a very successful transition to sound he appeared in *The Love Parade* (1929) and other big features. Homesick, he and his family returned to England where he continued making films and had his greatest stage success in the original production of *Me and My Girl*. He kept busy until his death in 1959.

Motion Picture News (June 12, 1926): "Interspersed with clowning and slapstick and abounding with funny situations Lupino Lane's latest comedy 'His Private Life,' will prove of mirth provoking in any house. Lane, beyond any doubt, is an excellent comedian. He is seen during the turbulent times of America's entrance into the war, as a rich and blasé young man who becomes inflated with patriotism and enters the rookie camp....They throw pies and everything in this picture and do it well too. Should prove satisfactory to most everyone."

Moving Picture World (June 12, 1926): "There is a 'play' upon the second word of the title of this Lupino Lane Comedy for it deals with his experiences during the war in the capacity of a private....There is considerable slapstick that is good for laughs. The idea is not by any means new and most of the gags and situations are familiar but they prove amusing nevertheless and the average audience should find this an entertaining comedy."

Screen Snapshots (Series 6, No. 17)

Released June 1, 1926. Produced by Jack Cohn and Louis Lewyn for the C.B.C. Film Sales Corporation. One reel. With Leatrice Joy, Enid Bennett, Mrs. Sidney Franklin, Mrs. Conrad Nagel, Maurice and Helene Costello, Richard Barthelmess, Sidney Olcott, Kathleen Key, Vilma Banky, Mary Philbin, Clara Horton, Douglas Fairbanks Jr., Roscoe Arbuckle, Doris Deane, Sol Lesser, Robert Z. Leonard, Rupert Julian, Edwin Carewe, Walter Hiers, Lillian Rich, Lloyd Hamilton, Gertrude Olmstead, Claire Windsor, Bert Lytell, Agnes Ayres.

Roscoe and Doris made the cut for another edition of this series. It's hard to determine exactly how many of these types of shorts that Roscoe (or his likeness) appeared in. For instance in July of 1926 his image was used in a Marcus *Hair Cartoon*—an entry of an animated series by the popular cartoonist Edwin Marcus where chunks of facial features and hair would be manipulated and moved around to make the faces of different celebrities and news figures.

Another group is the myriad of nostalgic reels that covered the early days of motion pictures or the "Roaring Twenties," which would often include clips of Roscoe in action. Titles include items like *Stars of Yesterday* (1931), *Memory Lingers On* (1936), and *Flicker Flashbacks* (1943). Roscoe would also turn up in examinations of the big scandals of the early 20th century.

Moving Picture World (August 14, 1926): "This issue upholds all the traditions of the popular 'Snapshots.'"

One Sunday Morning

Released December 12, 1926. Produced by the Lloyd Hamilton Corporation. Distributed by Educational Pictures. Directed by William Goodrich. Photographed by William Nobles. Two reels. With Lloyd Hamilton, Estelle Bradley, Stanley Blystone.

Ham plays a family man (with a wife and two kiddies) who buys an old Ford and manages to get it in front of his house. Since its Sunday he wants to take the family on a picnic, and the rest of the film details his attempts to get it running in spite of obstacles caused by neighbors and rain.

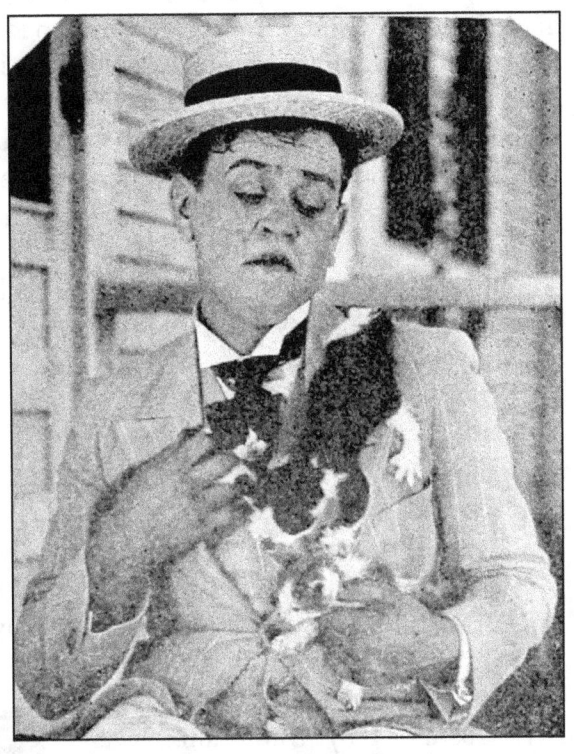

Rare image of Lloyd Hamilton as a human cat tree in the missing *One Sunday Morning* (1926).

Although missing at the moment, based on surviving reviews and descriptions *One Sunday Morning* appears to have been an exercise in auto frustration, and something of a blueprint for Laurel & Hardy's memorable *Perfect Day* (1929). Roscoe had previously explored problems with cars in outings like *Fatty and Mabel's Simple Life* (1915), *The Garage* (1920), and *His First Car* (1924), but of course the subject was fodder for all kinds of shorts such as *Get Out and Get Under* (1920), *All Wet* (1924), *Four Wheel Brakes* (1929), and many, many more.

Ham's leading lady Estelle Bradley was a former beauty contest winner who was Miss Atlanta in 1924 and a semi-finalist for Miss America. After a couple of bit roles in features she joined the ensemble in Jack White and Educational Comedies, making her debut opposite Lige Conley. Besides Hamilton, she also supported Al St John, Phil Dunham, Lupino Lane, and Monty Collins in shorts such as *Cheap Skates* (1925), *High Sea Blues* (1927), and *Three Tough Onions* (1927). Married to comedy director Charles Lamont, she retired in 1932. In 1987, at the Motion Picture Country Home, Ms. Bradley, Charles Lamont, and Anita Garvin spoke to film historian Edward Watz about the silent days. Ed reported:

> *Anita did not discuss Lloyd Hamilton, although Estelle Bradley sure did. She said he was the nicest guy in the morning but he always seemed preoccupied, and after lunch "he stank like a skunk from boozing." She said that on one*

occasion while filming a scene on a dirt road Ham stumbled and fell on top of her, into a ditch. She told me, "He was a big fellow, and all I thought was "Oh, no, I'm going to be squashed like a bug!"

Moving Picture World (December 25, 1926): "What happened to the owner of a new flivver who one Sunday morning decides to take his family on a picnic, furnishes the idea for this Lloyd Hamilton comedy. An amusing lot of gags have been worked into these two reels, some familiar and some new. Of course the thing won't start, then some of the parts become disconnected, there is a row with a neighbor and eventually a pouring rain with Lloyd unable to get the top up. At last he gives up in disgust and as his wife has already taken the kids to church he has a picnic on the lawn all by himself. Not as fast a comedy as some of the other Hamilton's, it should however prove generally amusing as there is considerable meat for the auto owner though of course the situations may have been exaggerated for comedy effects."

1927

The Red Mill

Released January 29, 1927. Produced by Cosmopolitan Productions. Distributed by Metro-Goldwyn-Mayer. Directed by William Goodrich (with uncredited assistance from King Vidor). Adaptation & scenario by Frances Marion. Based on the musical comedy by Henry Blossom. Titles by Joseph Farnum. Photographed by Hendrik Sartov. Settings by Cedric Gibbons & Merrill Pye. Costumes by Andre-ani. Seven reels. Extant: LOC, UCLA. With Marion Davies, Owen Moore, George Siegmann, Louise Fazenda, Karl Dane, Russell Powell, Snitz Edwards, William Orlamond, Fred Gamble, Madalynne Field, Ignatz.

Star Marion Davies as the Dutch girl slavey Tina in 1927's *The Red Mill*.

Tina, the general slavey at the Red Mill Inn who suffers from the extreme temper of her employer, Willem, falls in love with Dennis, a visitor to the Netherlands. Gretchen the burgomaster's daughter, is betrothed to the elderly governor, though she is actually in love with Captain Edam. Tina masquerades as Gretchen in order to help the lovers and to prevent the forced marriage, and in revenge Willem locks her in a haunted mill, where she is rescued by Dennis.

In the spring of 1926 it was announced in the trade magazines that William Goodrich had shot and completed *Over Night*, a Conrad Nagel comedy feature for MGM:

> *Fatty Arbuckle is to have a chance to earn some money at last. Metro-Goldwyn has engaged him to direct a new picture called "Over Night," which will feature Conrad Nagel.*
> – **Photoplay**, April, 1926

> *William Goodrich has completed "Over Night" with Conrad Nagel*
> – **Photoplay**, May, 1926

No Nagel feature came out with this title, and none were ever credited to William Goodrich. If the above items were correct one can assume that the picture may have been reshot and reworked by other hands, and released under a different title; not an uncommon event at a big studio like MGM. Working on the Nagel film probably led to Roscoe being considered for another MGM project—*The Red Mill* with Marion Davies.

Roscoe giving some long distance direction to Marion Davies during the shooting of *The Red Mill* (1927). Courtesy Matt Vogel.

Although director Marshall Neilan was originally announced at the helm Roscoe became the director. Loosely based on Victor Herbert's hit 1906 operetta, the film was planned as a more out-and-out comedy with plenty of slapstick and sight-gags, which made Arbuckle a good choice for the job.

Ironically he would be working for William Randolph Hearst, newspaper magnate, head of Cosmopolitan productions, and boyfriend of star Marion Davies, the man who may have profited the most from Arbuckle's early 1920's misfortunes. The Hearst organization sold untold papers and fanned the flames of public indignation during his trials with doctored photographs and rumors printed as facts. Since 1918 Hearst had been producing the films of his mistress Davies. Fate has played a dirty trick on Marion as modern impressions of her are based on the character of Susan Alexander, the concubine of Charles Foster Kane, in Orson Welles' *Citizen Kane* (1941).

In *Kane*, Susan Alexander is an untalented singer that the magnate tries to promote as an opera star. Although Davies did have the vast Hearst machine behind her, she was an excellent comedienne and a wicked mimic, and had the talents to warrant movie stardom on her own. Born Marion Cecelia Douras in Brooklyn in 1897, she followed her older sisters onto the stage as a dancer, and made her Broadway debut in 1914. Despite a life-long stutter, the *Ziegfeld Follies* and parts in popular shows like *Betty* and *Oh Boy* followed, as did her meeting and becoming the consort of the powerful Hearst.

Davies starting making films in 1917, and the next year Hearst formed the Marion Davies Film Corp. (which soon became Cosmopolitan Productions). Her early films were mostly

Roscoe working with Marion Davies and a child for *The Red Mill* (1927). Courtesy Matt Vogel.

light romantic comedies such as *Getting Mary Married* (1919) and *Enchantment* (1921), but she was soon starred in a series of lavish historical sagas like *When Knighthood was in Flower* (1922), *Little Old New York* (1923), and *Janice Meredith* (1924). A move to Hollywood and joining forces with MGM resulted in a new focus on her true strength—comedy. A series of peppy, girl-about-town comedies like *Tillie the Toiler* and *The Fair Co-ed* (both 1927) would ensue, but they would be proceeded by *The Red Mill* as a musical comedy romp.

The supporting cast includes former Sennett players and Arbuckle co-stars like Louise Fazenda and Owen Moore, in addition to seasoned scene-stealers such as Karl Dane, William Orlamonde, Russ Powell, and Buster Keaton regular Snitz Edwards. Despite all the talent the film is a bit of a mess—over-produced, unwieldy, and unfocused. There are four or five different plot strands—even veering into haunted house mode for the climax when Marion is locked in the "haunted" windmill by baddie George Seigmann. No doubt Roscoe's smooth handling of shorts such as *The Iron Mule*, *The Movies* (both 1925), *Fool's Luck* (1926), and others led to his promotion to features, but the shorts were handled with much more assurance and finesse.

It appears that Hearst hampered Roscoe on doing what he wanted with the material. After hiring him, it's known that the producer was concerned about Roscoe's lack of experience handling a feature, so he brought in director King Vidor to oversee the production. The July 7, 1926 issue of *Variety* justified it this way:

> *In rushing to finish the production of "The Red Mill" with Marion Davies starred, MGM officials assigned King Vidor and Ulrich Busch to help Roscoe Arbuckle in the direction of certain minor scenes.*
>
> *With most of the scenes with Marion Davies completed, there remained many interiors and exteriors with minor action still to be filmed.*
>
> *Rather than keep the large group of extras necessary on the pay roll for an unlimited length of time, the remaining scenes were split up between the three directors with Arbuckle taking those that required Miss Davies, while Vidor worked on the interiors.*
>
> *By this method the extras will be finished in one-third of the time, with the attending saving of money in addition to time.*

Later, King Vidor himself had this to say about the situation:

> *Hearst sent for me and persuaded me to go on the set and supervise and generally watch what was going on, keeping the film on agreed lines. It was an awkward situation for both of us.....I don't know what Hearst and the moguls were making a fuss about. The job [Arbuckle] was doing was all right.*

Hearst's main concern appears to have been that Roscoe would veer into too much out-and-out slapstick, something he didn't want for Davies. Silent star Colleen Moore, who was King Vidor's companion in their later years, added in a 1967 interview with author Stuart Oderman:

> *The intrigues on the set of "The Red Mill" would have made a good thriller. Everyone was aware that they were being watched. Arbuckle watched Marion. Vidor watched Arbuckle, and Mr. Hearst watched all three of them.*
>
> *Roscoe had a nice way of making everyone on the set feel relaxed. He was very workmanlike and had no problems communicating what he wanted his cast to do. I think he would have preferred a slapstick, since that was where he came from, but this was the assignment, and he was happy to get it. I don't think Mr. Hearst would have liked to see the girl of his dreams, his mistress, in anything that was rough and vulgar.*
>
> *Marion usually tensed up when Mr. Hearst was on the set. Sometimes Roscoe would whisper something to her, an off-color joke probably, and Marion would laugh, and Mr. Hearst would act like she was laughing at him. Which she probably did. I think all of us laughed at Mr. Hearst, but when Marion felt the joking was getting out of hand, she would defend him, and the joking would stop.*

In addition to having Vidor on the set, Marion Davies mentioned other directorial input in her autobiography *The Times We Had* (Bobbs-Merrill, 1975):

> But then they didn't like the rushes, so they put George Hill on. Then they didn't like George Hill's work, and they put Eddie Mannix on. And Eddie got fired.
>
> That picture had so many different directors I can't remember all their names. Everyday I'd have a different director.

Hearst's uncertainty, leading to Vidor's presence and the other directors' work, was not only a blow to Roscoe's confidence but created the potluck quality of the finished film. Later Hearst issues would cause what was set to be Davies' first talkie, *The Five O'Clock Girl* (1928), to never be released.

After *The Red Mill* King Vidor would later pilot two of Davies' best pictures—*The Patsy* and *Show People* (both 1928). There's even a rumor that Roscoe helped out on some of *Show People*'s comedy sequences. In spite of her stammer Davies made a smooth transition to sound and continued making good pictures until her retirement in 1937. Despite *The Red Mill*'s difficult shoot and mixed reviews, Roscoe now had a feature film directing credit, and another opportunity was soon in the offing.

Motion Picture News (February 25, 1927): "Not a very good job has been done by the screen version of 'The Red Mill,' which upon the stage was something to make a fuss over. The passing years haven't dealt kindly with Victor Herbert's operetta—the plot of which was weak, but which was strengthened by the composer's score. Upon the screen it looks trite even though it has been treated to a coat of slapstick. Apparently the director, William Goodrich ("Fatty" Arbuckle) realized it would never get anywhere under the straight conventional handling, so he's gone more or less burlesque with it."

Photoplay (April, 1927): "If there has been any doubt in your mind about Marion Davies' abilities as a comedienne, be sure and see 'The Red Mill.' The plot has as many holes as a mustard plaster, but what's a plot with Marion's capers and pantomime, plus Joe Farnum's wisecracking titles?"

Moving Picture World (February 19, 1927): "Money has been spent with lavish hand, and the cast includes such favorites as Owen Moore, Louise Fazenda, George Siegman, Karl Dane, and Snitz Edwards, and yet the result is a slapstick comedy that is more apt to appeal to the second and later run houses than to the discriminating first run patrons.

"Because the plot was thin; as most musical comedy plots are, the scenarist has sought to strengthen the story with slapstick ranging from the venerable limburger cheese gag to the old Weber & Fields 'changing light' bit, which convulsed Broadway nearly thirty years ago, though in this instance Miss Davies and Louise Fazenda, changing places on a balcony, replace the vari-colored lights.

"And since even with the slapstick there seemed to be a dearth of laughs, Joe Farnum has injected a large number of subtitles which should be sure fires on smaller circuits. These titles are put in merely to get laughs, not to explain the action, and sometimes there are two or three to the single scene."

Peaceful Oscar

Released January 30, 1927. Produced by the Lloyd Hamilton Corporation. Distributed by Educational Pictures. Directed by William Goodrich. Two reels. With Lloyd Hamilton, Blanche Payson, Toy Gallagher, Henry Murdock, Chick Collins, Billy Hampton.

A wistful Lloyd Hamilton and son on a glass slide for *Peaceful Oscar* (1927). Courtesy Matt Vogel.

Ham is henpecked by his large and domineering wife. He's also attracted to their cute maid, as are the chef and the butcher boy who get into a battle over her favors. The wife sends Ham to the kitchen to stop the fight and when he doesn't she physically throws them out. When she catches Ham comforting the maid she is promptly fired. Since wifie is having a reception that afternoon poor Ham is forced to take the place of the maid and kitchen staff, which he endures for as long as he can before he takes their small son and escapes to the beach. There he meets up with the maid and the two rivals, which leads to a series of escapades and battles—which include his son being taken aloft by a bunch of toy balloons. When the wife shows up looking for her errant husband, Ham decides that the ocean is the safest place for him to be.

A loose remake of *Fickle Fatty's Fall* (1915) and *The Rough House* (1917), much of the action for *Peaceful Oscar* was shot at Santa Monica Beach, and was Roscoe's last silent short with Lloyd Hamilton. Although this and *One Sunday Morning* are lost, the pair worked very well together, and at the time Hamilton described their loose working habits to the December 25, 1926 *Moving Picture World*:

> *Well, I get my gags this way. My director and I have a chat in the evening before we start shooting. The two of us can think of the funniest things.*
>
> *If we don't feel funny? Ah! Then I invite a few of my friends. They always provide me with material.*

It's possible that some kind of libations would accompany the friends but Ham didn't give any details on that. After a hiatus of three years (part of which time he was banned from the screen) Hamilton and Roscoe would resume their working relationship in the early days of sound.

Comedy battle-axe Blanche Payson makes a return here in an Arbuckle short, and she and Hamilton are supported by two overlooked silent comedy regulars. The cute maid who's the root of the commotion is Toy Gallagher, an Irish-born actress who came to Hollywood to write a series of articles for a New York newspaper on "Breaking into the Movies." The story goes that while interviewing Mack Sennett he offered her work in his pictures instead, which led to appearances under her real name of Louise in his 1924 shorts *Three Foolish Weeks* and *The Sea Squawk*.

Following a bit in Harold Lloyd's *The Freshman* (1925), plus western features such as *Action Galore* (1925) and *The Texas Terror* (1926), she settled in at Jack White Comedies, and was frequently paired with Phil Dunham in Cameo Comedies like *The Radio Bug*, *Plumb Goofy*, and *His Day Off* (all 1926). Later moving up to two-reelers with Hamilton like this and *New Wrinkles* (1927), as well as Lupino Lane's *A Half-Pint Hero* (1927), she ended her career with the arrival of sound in 1928.

The chef is played by Henry Murdock, a neglected fifteen-year veteran of silent comedy. A versatile comedy character actor par excellence, Murdock never developed a regular screen persona, so while in demand with the comedy units he was virtually unknown to audiences. After a background on stage in stock companies and vaudeville he made his film debut in 1915 for Kalem, and was part of their ensembles in Florida and California for their *Sis Hopkins*, *Ivy Close*, and *Ham & Bud* series. Playing whatever type of part that was needed for a story, Murdock often would go to absurd extremes, such as his rabid Bolshevik Krazy Killsky in Ham & Bud's *A Sauerkraut Symphony* (1916). From the late teens to the mid-1920s he worked non-stop for Century and Christie Comedies, and in 1926 took up residence in the Jack White and Lloyd Hamilton shorts for Educational, which included *My Kid* (1926), *Goose Flesh*, *His Better Half* (both 1927), *The Lucky Duck*, and *Cook, Papa, Cook* (both 1928). A little over a year after *Peaceful Oscar*'s release, while eating a meal, Murdock died from choking.

Exhibitors Herald World (May 4, 1929): "A very good comedy."

Film Daily (February 20, 1927): "A typical Lloyd Hamilton number, with plenty of slapstick, funny situations and gags. As usual Hamilton plays the part of an abused boob whom everyone takes advantage of. The famous Hamilton walk is played up for all it is worth. In this unique way of handling his feet the star is in a class all by himself. The Hamilton fans will like it."

Moving Picture World (February 5, 1927): "Several of the situations are familiar and there are not as many new gags as usual in a Hamilton comedy. Lloyd, however, is amusing as usual and Blanche Payson adds to the merriment as the wife.

Special Delivery

Released May 6, 1927. Produced by the Famous Players-Lasky Corp. Distributed by Paramount Pictures. Directed by William Goodrich (uncredited Larry Semon). Story by Eddie Cantor. Continuity by John Goodrich. Titles by George Marion Jr. Photography by Henry Hallenberger. Six reels. Extant. With Eddie Cantor, Jobyna Ralston, William Powell, Donald Keith, Jack Dougherty, Glen Cavender, Tiny Doll (Tiny Earles), Spec O'Donnell, Rosa Rosanova, Johnny Sinclair.

Eddie, a conscientious but blundering mail carrier, is in love with Madge the waitress, who is equally admired by Officer Flannigan, and Harrigan, a fireman, who are Eddie's roommates. The persistent efforts of Harold Jones, a promoter, to win Madge as his secretary unite the three rivals against Jones. They toss a coin to see who will escort Madge to the postal ball, and Eddie wins. Madge accepts Jones' job offer when the diner owner tries to force his attentions on her. At the ball, Eddie, who does not dance, leaves Madge to his rivals, but during a black bottom contest a piece of ice falls into his collar, and his wild gyrations win him the prize cup. Eddie is crestfallen to find that Madge has become engaged to Jones, but in delivering a package to Jones' home, he discovers that Jones is a swindler and with the aid of his roommates rushes to save Madge.

Cantor En Route to Coast

Eddie Cantor, left New York yesterday for Hollywood to prepare for work on "Special Delivery" for Paramount. The story was written by Cantor. Production begins Nov. 29.

– ***Film Daily,*** November 17, 1926

Stage star Eddie Cantor had made his film debut earlier in the year with *Kid Boots* (1926), which was based on his stage success. Eddie, with some help from Clara Bow, had a hit

William Powell (left), Jobyna Ralston, and a cartoon Eddie Cantor on a lobby card for *Special Delivery* (1927).

on his hands with *Boots*, and Paramount was ready for a follow-up. The idea of a mishap-prone mailman came from Cantor, and Roscoe was hired to helm the production. For many years *Special Delivery* was unavailable until a 16mm print turned up with the Cantor family. In 2006 we were able to show the film at the Museum of Modern Art, and even have the comedian's youngest daughter, Janet Cantor Gari, in attendance to introduce it.

It's a real crowd pleaser—a charming and effective vehicle for Cantor. There's plenty of funny moments for Eddie, the film moves at a lightning pace, and considering its somewhat turbulent production history it has a smooth and consistent narrative, something that was lacking in *The Red Mill*. According to Eddie Cantor in his autobiography plot changes were demanded after shooting had already started:

> Another serious alteration in the story was caused by the federal authorities. Our plot centered about a mail robbery, during which I, as a rookie postman, accidentally captured the robber singled-handed after a series of funny mishaps. This made me undeservedly a hero and won me the girl whose hand a fireman and a policeman also aspired.
>
> It was not until the picture had gotten well under way that we learned the government would not permit the showing of even a comical mail

Eddie Cantor and Jobyna Ralston in a dramatic moment from *Special Delivery* (1927). Courtesy Cole Johnson.

> *robbery on the screen. Had this been discovered before we started to shoot the picture, it would have altered all our plans and most probably we would have selected a different story altogether. But as it stood it was too late to turn back, and instead of the mail robbery we introduced a bucket-shop broker who used the mails to defraud. This switched the picture into conventional lines and diminished its strength considerably.*
>
> – ***My Life is in Your Hands***, (1928)

Aspects of the plot centering on the mail robbery were dropped, which included characters played by Victor Potel, Paul Kelly, and Mary Carr, all of whom are listed in the official cast list but are nowhere in the finished film. To help fill in any gaps comic and director Larry Semon was brought in and given eight days to do additions.

It's unclear exactly how much was shot by Semon, but two sequences seem certain. One is the business in the big chase climax where Eddie rides in the sidecar of a motorcycle. This is standard Semon material and almost matches shot-for-shot sequences in his shorts *The Show* (1922) and *The Cloud Hopper* (1925). The other is the scene where Eddie takes care of a lady's fussy baby (played by Tiny Earles, sister of *Freaks* (1932) star Harry Earles) and feeds it sausages. Photos have surfaced of Semon, Cantor, and Earles on the set. Other

Mailman Eddie Cantor turns crook William Powell (left) over to his father Louis Stern in *Special Delivery* (1927).

gag sequences where Eddie's leg is in a hole so people think he only has one leg and give him money, and another where he tries to make his girl jealous by flirting with a life-sized doll, could have been done by Semon but they are also things that Roscoe could have easily directed.

No matter what was added by Semon, the film works very well, with a fine performance by Cantor. Roscoe gets a lot of warmth and a touch of pathos from the actor and the supporting performances of Jobyna Ralston, William Powell, Jack Dougherty, and Donald Keith are all top notch. Silent comedy icon Spec O'Donnell has a couple of funny moments, and Arbuckle favorites Glen Cavender and Johnny Sinclair also make appearances. The subdued style of the direction and the logical integrating of the gags are all Roscoe, and certain familiar routines turn up, such as when Eddie is getting dressed to take Jobyna to the mailman's ball and finds that he has no cummerbund. A towel and shoe polish dots for buttons fills in as it does in *Fatty's Magic Pants* (1914) and *How've You Bean?* (1933). No matter who contributed what, the final result is a solid entertainment.

Film Daily (May 1, 1927): "Eddie Cantor offers his laughs by special delivery, also. This is good clean comedy and guaranteed to brighten the heart of anyone who enjoys laughing. The story isn't weighty, the gags aren't particularly important, but Cantor does it all so thoroughly well and his work is so interesting that the picture cannot but entertain them. The Paramount Theatre audience laughed throughout the picture and some of Cantor's highlight comedy bits were cause for mild uproar. The various tricks he pulls by way of delivering mail went over big and the preparation for the mail carrier's ball, with hero's makeshift evening suit, and finally his winning the black bottom contest, all hit the mark."

Picture Play (August, 1927): "There's no getting away from it, Eddie Cantor, in his second picture, "Special Delivery," takes his place among the foremost comedians of the screen. And now that he has won that place, it is hoped that he will keep it."

Photoplay (August 1927): "Eddie Cantor and a lot of gags, some new and some not so new. But a snappy evening."

Character Studies

Released November 20, 1927. Distributed by Educational Pictures. One reel. Extant: LOC, LOB. (a.k.a. ***Carter De Haven in Character Studies***) With Carter De Haven, Buster Keaton, Harold Lloyd, Roscoe Arbuckle, Rudolph Valentino, Douglas Fairbanks, Jackie Coogan.

Carter De Haven introduces himself on stage, and gives his quick-change impersonations of several Hollywood celebrities.

Educational Pictures exhibitor ad for 1927's *Character Studies*.

Character Studies is a curio in the careers of everyone who appears in it. It's a charming little parlor trick, a spoof of vaudeville "quick-change artists," and the camera sleight of hand is done simply and effectively. For many years it was unknown, until a print turned up at the Library of Congress. Its exact origins are still a mystery, but the film seems to have been privately made around 1925 due to the age of Jackie Coogan and that Rudolph Valentino appears in the an outfit from his film *Cobra* (1925). It's possible that it was made as a gift to Charlie Chaplin, who's conspicuously absent from the star line up. Everyone involved in the short was a Chaplin pal, particularly Carter De Haven who probably directed as well as starred. The film was eventually released theatrically by Educational.

Although forgotten today De

Haven was a big film name in the Teens and Twenties who directed and wrote many of his pictures. He entered films in 1915 after a successful career as a comedy juvenile on stage. In the late Teens he teamed with his real-life wife Flora Parker and began a series of two-reelers about an average married couple's trials and tribulations. In putting together his popular "Mr. & Mrs. Carter De Haven Comedies" De Haven collaborated with the likes of William Seiter, Charles Parrott (a.k.a. Charley Chase), Mal St Clair, Monte Brice and Robert McGowan—some of the cleverest and most polished practitioners of silent comedy. In the mid-20's De Haven retired and became involved in California real estate.

A side-note of his career is his role as a longtime friend and collaborator to Chaplin. Even at the peak of his own busy filmmaking the November 16, 1918 *Moving Picture World* reported:

> *Charles Chaplin has engaged Carter De Haven to assist him in directing a new comedy for the First National Exhibitors that was begun at the Chaplin studios the week of Oct 21.*

He can also be seen in Kevin Brownlow and David Gill's *Unknown Chaplin* (1983) in footage of Chaplin and his crew making an impromptu film with the Prince of Denmark on the sets of *Sunnyside* (1919). After his career wound down De Haven continued working with Chaplin, receiving assistant director credit on *Modern Times* (1936) and appearing as Jack Oakie's ambassador in *The Great Dictator* (1940).

Considering all of the above, it seems very likely that this short was made to entertain Chaplin, and may even have been shot at his studio. In the meantime many people have speculated on the creation of this film, and hopefully someday the full story will be revealed.

Outside of some newsreel footage, this was Roscoe's first film appearance since his special cameo in 1923's *Hollywood* (not including his uncredited sleight of hand in Keaton's *Go West*). Another film occasionally listed in Arbuckle credits is the Al St. John

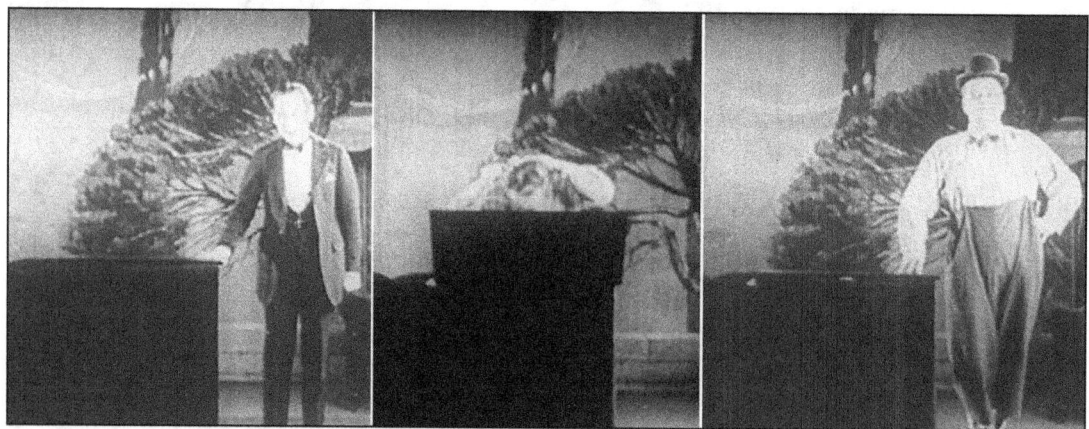

Carter De Haven (left) "changing himself" into Roscoe in *Character Studies* (1927). Courtesy the Library of Congress.

short *Listen Lena* (1927), thanks to a fat man who passes in front of the camera at one point suspiciously hiding his face. But the man in question is built very differently and is also much too tall to be Roscoe.

Motion Picture News (January 14, 1928): "Carter De Haven, whom exhibitors will remember as having appeared in comedies several years back, tries his hand at something new in this reel devoted to a sort of hoodwinking the fans with what are supposed to be a series of imitations of screen stars—Harold Lloyd, Fatty Arbuckle, Buster Keaton and others. De Haven will go through all the motions of making up his features and assuming disguises but when he has raised himself from a stooping position any one who knows the movie star can tell that the real character has assumed De Haven's place. You become convinced in your suspicions when you see the small figure of Jackie Coogan appear where a minute or two before had stood De Haven.

"The production is of a surprising type, and will serve as a novelty on an exhibitor's program."

Film Daily (January 15, 1928): "Carter De Haven pulls a novelty with a few make-up impressions of several popular screen players. Among them are Buster Keaton, Harold Lloyd, Roscoe Arbuckle, Rudolph Valentino, Doug Fairbanks and Jackie Coogan. The one of Harold Lloyd is best. But all are well done, and the act is a novelty that will prove a welcome diversion."

Andy Clyde and Daphne Pollard in an exhibitor ad for *Bulls and Bears* (1930).

Chapter 13
Goodrich In Sound

Out of and Back in the Movies
The studio interference on *The Red Mill* and *Special Delivery* were difficult experiences for Roscoe. At the same time in 1927 independent producer Abe Carlos approached him about a starring series of films that would be made in Germany, but when that fell through he turned his back on films. Throughout the 1920s, between directorial duties, he had been doing many live stage performances and short vaudeville tours, and decided to concentrate on that. In June of 1927 he opened in a Broadway play, *Baby Mine*, in which he appeared with future Hollywood regulars Humphrey Bogart and Lee Patrick. The run wasn't particularly successful, but Roscoe followed it up with European appearances and more vaudeville engagements. He also became the co-owner of the Plantation Café, a Culver City nightclub where he performed frequently. During this period Roscoe seemed to be doing fine without the movie industry—what brought him back was the Depression. After the stock market crash in 1929 he lost a $75,000 investment in the Montecito Inn, a luxury hotel, and eventually had to sell the Plantation Café. Roscoe found that Hollywood had ready work for him, and he started as a writer for his old employer Mack Sennett and at RKO.

Bulls and Bears
Released March 2, 1930. Produced and directed by Mack Sennett. Distributed by Educational Pictures. Story and dialogue by John A. Waldron, Harry McCoy, Earle Rodney, & William Goodrich. Photography by John W. Boyle & George Unholz. Two reels. With Andy Clyde, Marjorie Beebe, Daphne Pollard, Bud Jamison, Rosemary Theby, Hugh Saxon, Marshall Ruth, Jack Richardson, Patsy O'Leary, Doris Morton, Ethel Wood, William Searby.

Andy is partners in a grocery store with Bud. When Bud becomes a millionaire in the stock market it's all that thrifty Andy can do to keep his wife Daphne from investing all his money too. Ultimately Bud goes bust, but the careful Andy's kept his dough.

Arbuckle with Sennett
Roscoe Arbuckle, who is under contract to James Cruze Productions, Inc., has been loaned to Mack Sennett for a few weeks, during which time

> *he will act, write and direct for Sennett. Arbuckle is scheduled to direct and star in a film for the Cruze organization.*
>
> – **Film Daily**, December 4, 1929

Roscoe's first work on a sound picture was back for his old boss Sennett. It was also a reunion with his former Keystone cohort Harry McCoy, who was busy on Sennett's writing staff. Spending most of his time now writing, McCoy would also be on the writing crew for Roscoe's upcoming *Won by a Neck* and *Up a Tree* (both 1930). During this brief tenure with Sennett Roscoe penned the lyrics, and McCoy the tune, for the song *What Good Am I Without You?* which was eventually used in the short *Hollywood Zeppelin* (1930).

Having teamed up with Educational Pictures, Sennett dove into sound films relatively early with *The Lion's Roar* (December 9, 1928), but never completely adapted to the new medium. The December 27, 1930 *Exhibitors Herald* summed up some of the problem:

> *Educational does not seem to give us what we want. "Match Play," a golf comedy, is fair, "Bulls and Bears" is fairly funny. The trouble is with their action. It is slow, and the stunts are hooked up together in a slow, forced manner. Too much talk, not enough speed. Andy Clyde is in nearly every one, and we out here do not think Andy is a bit funny, which is just too bad for us.*

During the early 1920s Clyde had been Sennett's "Man of a Thousand Faces," playing all types of characters in all kinds of make-ups, sometimes two or three times in a single film. But by the end of the decade he developed the feisty old man persona that would take him through shorts for Sennett, Educational, and Columbia, roles in features, and into television up to 1967. Sennett had indeed picked Andy to be one of his main sound stars, and Clyde remained so until moving on in 1932.

Also on hand is another late 1920s Sennett star, Daphne Pollard. Starting her stage career at age eight in her native Australia as part of Pollard's Lilliputians child opera company, she took the last name Pollard and for years crisscrossed back and forth between stages in England and America. She finally made her film debut for Sennett in 1927 in a series of *Sennett Girl* Comedies like *Run, Girl, Run*, *The Campus Carmen*, and *Matchmaking Mama* (all 1928) where Carole Lombard supplied the sex appeal and Daphne the laughs. The 4'9" Pollard took to sound films like a duck to water, and besides her Sennett shorts was busy at RKO, Pathé, and Vitaphone. Her best-remembered work was as Oliver Hardy's most vicious and domineering screen wife in *Thicker than Water* (1935) and *Our Relations* (1936).

Although trade items said that Roscoe would "act, write and direct for Sennett," it appears that he only wrote for the producer. With the arrival of sound, Sennett himself returned to the director's chair. In certain films he may have had uncredited help from old pros like Alf Goulding and Harry Edwards, but it's unknown whether Roscoe contributed anything more than writing. Mack himself was branching into writing, according to an item from the February 8, 1930 *Motion Picture News*:

> *Mack Sennett, who glorified the bathing beauties, has turned songwriter. In collaboration with Harry McCoy, Mack has written two songs, "Sugar Plum Papa," which Daphne Pollard sings in the Sennett talking comedy of the same name and "The Same Old Thing Called Love," which is the theme of another Sennett comedy called "Bulls and Bears."*

Motion Picture News (February 22, 1930): "A Humdinger. Mack Sennett standard. Andy Clyde, as usual, provides enough mirth to chase away the blues—for 20 minutes, at least. Supported by Daphne Pollard, Marjorie Beebe, Bud Jamison and Rosemary Theby. Andy, a grocery store owner of the old school, refuses to sink his pile in the rapidly-rising stock market, despite urgings of his wife and friends. The latter are sitting on top of the world—until the crash comes and then all topple back to earth. Of course Andy eventually has the laugh on the bunch. He again delivers strong comedy material. Sennett directed and he did a good job. Running time 20 minutes."

Film Daily (February 23, 1930): "Good Stock Market Comedy. Timely travesty on the stock market shows how the speculating fever interferes with regular business and ends in disaster for the get-rich-quick boys. Andy Clyde puts over a good comedy job as the conservative store partner, who hangs on to his dough and stays behind while the other lad plunges into the ticker tape and achieves short-lived affluence. Mack Sennett has seen to it that the comedy is abundant and well distributed. Daphne Pollard, Marjorie Beebe, Bud Jamison and Rosemary Theby are the chief members of the cast."

Match Play

Released March 16, 1930. Produced and directed by Mack Sennett. Distributed by Educational Pictures. Story and dialogue by John A. Waldron, Earle Rodney, Harry McCoy, & William Goodrich. Photographed by John W. Boyle & George Unholz. Two reels. With Andy Clyde, Marjorie Beebe, Walter Hagen, Leo Diegel, Bud Jamison, William Searby, Kathryn Stanley.

Andy runs a country Club, but has a contentious relationship with mortgage holder Bud. Andy has a pretty daughter and Bud will settle the deed on the club if Andy lets Bud marry her. Instead Andy challenges Bud to a golf match—the winner gets the club. Bud shows up with golf pro Leo Diegel. Things look bad for Andy until he gets other master, Walter Hagen, to play with him.

Roscoe's second writing gig for Sennett is a golf comedy that was a showcase for the big time golf pros Walter Hagen and Leo Diegel. In addition to the comedy content is the illustration of virtuoso trick shots by the pros, which is almost a forerunner of the 1933 Bobby Jones' *How to Play Golf* one-reelers. Considered to be a "special" because of the presence of the high profile Hagen and Diegel, Sennett and Educational went out of their way to exploit *Match Play* with chain store and large department store window displays, golf merchandise tie-ins, marquee and lobby displays, radio, magazine and newspaper publicity, and novelty giveaways.

With the golf instructions in the hands of the pros, the comedy is provided by Andy Clyde (see *Bulls and Bears*), Marjorie Beebe, and Bud Jamison. Marjorie Beebe was being

Match Play's (1930) golf pros Leo Diegel (left holding club) and Walter Hagen (right pointing club) give some link pointers to Andy Clyde (left), Marjorie Beebe, and Bud Jamison (right).

groomed for comedy stardom in this Sennett series. Starting in films as a teenager in 1924, she worked her way up in shorts for Universal, Joe Rock, and Arrow to a starring role in Fox's *The Farmer's Daughter* (1928). Appearing for Sennett in shorts like *A Hollywood Star* (1929), *He Trumped Her Ace* (1930), and *Too Many Highballs* (1933), plus his feature *Hypnotized* (1933), she almost made the big time but her career lost steam when Sennett went bankrupt in 1933.

William Edmond Jamison, better known as Bud, made his film debut with Charlie Chaplin in *A Night Out* (1915), and worked at Essanay the rest of that year for Chaplin and in shorts directed by Hal Roach. In 1916 he became a regular in Roach's *Lonesome Luke* comedies and stayed on the lot supporting Harold Lloyd, Toto, and Stan Laurel until 1919. From there he spent the next twenty-five years all over, working for every unit turning out comedies in addition to supporting roles in features. Although best remembered for his appearances with The Three Stooges, he worked non-stop until 1944. Unfortunately, a gangrenous infection that he refused to treat (he was a Christian Scientist) may have led to the heart attack that killed him at age fifty.

New Movie Magazine (May 1930): "This Mack Sennett two-reel talkie is one of the two best short subjects of the year. The other is Christie's "Dangerous Females" with Marie

Educational Pictures/Mack Sennett exhibitor ad for 1930's *Match Play*.

Dressler and Polly Moran. This was a happy comedy thought, introducing Walter Hagen and Leo Diegel and some trick golf shots into a lively farce of the greens. Their amazing game will thrill the golf fans while there is enough reel comedy to get the lovers of screen laughter. Marjorie Beebe, who graces this month's rotogravure section, is prominently present. Watch for this short feature when it reaches your theatre. It shows the 1930 Mack Sennett at his best."

Screenland (June 1930): "This is a two-reel comedy that deserves feature rating and attention. It is a picture that will please those few die-hards who only go to the movies when they are dragged by other members of the family. If you have one of those crotchety uncles or hard-to-please papas, try to inveigle him to the theatre where "Match Play" is running. He'll be won over to our new little art of the sound screen, see if he isn't. There is no love triangle to bother him; no back-stage blues, no theme song. Just good, clean fun on the golf course, escorted by none other than Walter Hagen and Leo Diegel, mind you. Andy Clyde, the pivot of the piece, provides laughs in the best Sennett tradition; while Hagen and Diegel put on a show that will make you sit up and take notice whether you're a golf addict or not. Smooth and easy dialogue in which the famous pros participate, and Marjorie Beebe for heart interest. Swell! Please don't miss it."

The Cuckoos

Released May 4, 1930. Produced and distributed by RKO Radio Pictures. Directed by Paul Sloane. Adapted by Cyrus Wood from the Broadway musical *The Ramblers*, with music by Bert Kalmar & Harry Ruby, and book by Guy Bolton and Kalmar & Ruby. Gags (uncredited) by William Goodrich. Photography by Nicholas Musuraca. Art Direction by Max Ree. Musical direction by Victor Baravalle. Dance direction by Pearl Eaton. Eleven reels. Extant. With Bert Wheeler, Robert Woolsey, Dorothy Lee, June Clyde, Hugh Trevor, Ivan Lebedeff, Marguerita Padula, Mitchell Lewis, Jobyna Howland, Raymond Maurei.

Professor Bird and his assistant Sparrow are phony fortune-tellers at an exclusive summer resort in Mexico. A gypsy band nearby kidnaps a wealthy widow's daughter and our two heroes are hot on the trail. Sparrow is in love with a girl in the gypsy camp, and Professor Bird makes a play for Fannie, the rich widow. The kidnapped girl's sweetheart is also trying to rescue her. After outwitting the gypsies the entire group makes for the resort in a plane, but crash as they land. All reconciled, they go to Fannie's estate in San Diego.

In 1929 Radio Pictures (soon to be known as RKO) brought the Florenz Ziegfeld hit Broadway musical *Rio Rita* to the screen. Along with the property came the supporting comics Bert Wheeler and Robert Woolsey. Both were long-time veterans of stage comedy and made a decided hit in the film version. With *Rio Rita* making big money, the studio moved to put Wheeler and Woolsey in another production. *The Cuckoos* was based on the 1926 stage show *The Ramblers*, which had starred the team of Bobby Clark and Paul McCullough. The original book, with music and lyrics by Guy Bolton, Bert Kalmar and Harry Ruby, was adapted by Cyrus Wood for Wheeler and Woolsey.

Roscoe was brought in as a gag writer and would spend three months on the picture. Bert Wheeler is quoted in Edward Watz's *Wheeler and Woolsey: The Comic Duo and their Films, 1929-1937* as saying:

> *I think Fatty Arbuckle was three quarters responsible for Wheeler and Woolsey's success. Our second picture really set Wheeler and Woolsey up. We had another director, but Arbuckle worked on all our scenes. Sure, he was washed up, or he wouldn't have been "directing" us—and he wasn't even getting billed for it.*
>
> *Arbuckle was on the RKO payroll as what might be call a dialogue director. That man was really a clever man, and one of the sweetest men I've ever known in my life. He wasn't a pathetic sad character—never—even*

Caricatures of Bert Wheeler and Robert Woolsey on an exhibitor ad for 1930's *The Cuckoos*.

> *when it was the toughest. He had the greatest sense of comedy—just loved to laugh, and loved to live and loved people. It's a sad thing that anything like that had to happen to him—to a fine man like that. I always loved him.*

Roscoe's presence and input was needed as the credited director, Paul Sloane had been a director of melodramas with no experience with comedy. In the end *The Cuckoos* was another hit and solidified Wheeler and Woolsey as an ongoing movie team.

Variety (April 30, 1930): "Radio has a comedy hit in 'The Cuckoos.' It holds little besides the laughs, and doesn't need anything else. For this picture is apt to draw people back for another laugh spell. Through that it may become a holdover in the larger cities.

If comedy ever made a picture, it does here. Besides mixed up in the laughs or the comedy is plenty of s.a. or whatever you may wish to call offside remarks and business."

Exhibitors Herald-World (May 10, 1930): "The appropriately titled 'The Cuckoos' is that pure undiluted nonsense presented in a big way. Catchy songs, dancing girls, beautiful settings, and a couple of smart, smartcrackers keep it clicking. It slows down in spots only where the juvenile leads break into well regulated love making, foreign to the rest of the picture, and bits of singing and dancing in duet fashion. Lovely.

"'Cuckoos' is adapted from the stage 'Ramblers' and directed by Paul Sloane for RKO. Bert Wheeler and Robert Woolsey share laugh honors which is reminiscent of the Marx Brothers' 'Cocoanuts.' A few of the gags are a bit suggestive to evil minds but it's all in fun. No harm."

Talking Screen (July 1930): "If you like comedy in good heavy doses, for heaven's sake don't miss this picture. Bert Wheeler and Robert Woolsey certainly put this picture over in fun shape."

Half Shot at Sunrise

Released October 4, 1930. Produced and distributed by RKO Radio Pictures. Directed by Paul Sloane. Story & scenario by James Ashmore Creelman Jr. Dialogue by Anne Caldwell & Ralph Spence. Gags (uncredited) by William Goodrich. Photography by Nicholas Musuraca. Dance direction by Mary Reed. Ten reels. Extant. With Bert Wheeler, Robert Woolsey, Dorothy Lee, Hugh Trevor, Edna May Oliver, Eddie De Lange, E.H. Calvert, Alan Roscoe, John Rutherford, George MacFarlane, Roberta Robinson, Leni Stengel.

Colonel Marshall is with the U.S. Army in Paris. His duties are to oversee the delivery of important orders for a major offensive, but instead he's more concerned with keeping loveletters from the French flirt Olga a secret from his wife. The Colonel has two daughters— one who loves Lieut. Jim Reed against the Colonel's wishes. Tommy and Gilbert are buck privates who go A.W.O.L., and to escape the M.P.s they steal the Colonels car, complete with his younger daughter Annette. To get the boys in the Colonel's good graces Annette and Olga conspire to intercept the orders meant for Lieut. Reed so that the A.W.O.L. pair can go on the mission and become heroes. Things don't work out that way and the boys end up being apprehended by the army, but they're able to blackmail the Colonel with one of Olga's love notes.

Roscoe was re-hired by RKO in March of 1930 to work on *Half-Shot at Sunrise*. Following *The Cuckoos* (1929), Wheeler and Woolsey had been re-teamed with star Bebe Daniels and director Luther Reed for another big budget musical, *Dixiana* (1930). Now back on their own, Bert and Bob were again under Paul Sloane's direction. Wheeler felt that Roscoe was ultimately responsible for this new picture's success and said:

> *He would work on our comedy scenes and direct them to us. He didn't actually do it on the set, but he told us what to do. Paul Sloane was the director. He was a darned good director, but he was smart enough to let*

Bert Wheeler (right) and Robert Woolsey (left) give their undivided attention to Leni Stengel in *Half Shot at Sunrise* (1930). Billy Rose Theatre Division, the New Public Library for the Performing Arts.

> *Arbuckle, who knew better than he did, work with us. He wrote, too. He put a lot of great things in our pictures himself. We tried to keep Arbuckle. We would have had him with us the rest of our lives.*

The boys' physical business is crisp and funny, plus they have excellent support from Dorothy Lee, Leni Stengel and the great comic dragon Edna May Oliver. Now firmly established in depression audiences' affections with help from Roscoe's input, Wheeler and Woolsey would continue their cinematic misadventures until 1937. Along the way they would hit a real comic peak in their pictures, *Diplomaniacs*, (1933), *Hips, Hips Hooray*, *Cockeyed Cavaliers*, and *Kentucky Kernels* (all 1934).

Exhibitors Herald (October 18, 1930): "There is a boat load—make it a Leviathan—of tomfoolery and fun in this new Radio picture starring the team of Wheeler and Woolsey. If these two comics in 'Half Shot at Sunrise' don't make the audience howl, then the audience is at fault.

"As stated, it is all tomfoolery, but about the most pleasant and refreshing tomfoolery one could imagine. It brings the laughs that bring the tears to your eyes, and that should be sufficient comedy for anyone.

"It is the type of picture in which Wheeler and Woolsey excel—a picture which bothers little with the story, but is overflowing with situations. Give them the situations and they will take advantage of them 100 per cent.

"The picture moves rapidly, but the gags have been well timed and therefore none of the dialog is lost in the roars of the audience, a condition which is not avoided often enough in the audible film.

"Although there are a couple of good musical numbers in the picture, it should not be sold to the public as a musical comedy, for it makes no effort to be one. It should be exploited as one of the best farces to reach the screen thus far this season."

Motion Picture Committee of the Woman's University Club (October 1930): "The not unfamiliar theme is of two doughboys who go A.W.O.L. and quite stupidly and by accident, become heroes. The story is incidental to the slapstick antics of the well known comedians, whose rough humor is decidedly 'of the earth earthy.' Enjoyment is again a matter of taste."

Screenland (January 1931): "Bert Wheeler and Bob Woolsey hit the bull's eye again with their cuckoo comedy."

Sound Shorts 1930-1932

After his cinematic return as a writer, Educational Pictures soon welcomed Roscoe back to direct new shorts with Lloyd Hamilton, Al St John, Monty Collins, and Tom Patricola. He also directed two-reelers for RKO.

Shorts like *Idle Roomers* (1931), *It's A Cinch* (1932), and particularly *Bridge Wives* (1932) show that as a director Roscoe adapted easily to the new sound technology. He avoids the usual early talkie staticness with frequent and very fluid camera moves, and briskly paces the dialogue to keep everything moving along at a nice clip. It would have been interesting to see how he would have handled a feature at this time, but before that could happen Roscoe got the call for which he'd been waiting ten years.

Si, Si, Senor

Released September 21, 1930. Ideal Talking Comedies. Produced and distributed by Educational Pictures. Directed by William Goodrich. Two reels. Extant. With Tom Patricola, Joe Phillips, Chiquita De Montez, Glen Cavender, Carmen Guerrero.

Tom and Joe, a vaudeville team from Brooklyn, are in trouble again—and the sheriff is conducting them to the border where he emphasizes his orders for them to stay out of the country. As the emphasis is applied with a gun, the two boys start south into Mexico. After trudging for a while they find two men bathing in a lake, and promptly steal their clothes and proceed on their way. They arrive at a village, and because of the clothes they stole they are mistaken for Don Pedro and his friend, who no one has seen but is awaited to marry a local rancher's daughter, Chiquita.

Tom, sensing a full meal, a bath, and a place to sleep in the deal allows himself to be mistaken for the grandee—and soon falls in love with Chiquita. She returns his affection, and Joe has also found a sweetheart of his own. Chiquita's father has summoned a judge

Tom Patricola (left) and Joe Phillips (right) as partners in crime in *Si, Si, Senor* (1930).

to perform the marriage and as Tom doesn't speak any Spanish he says "Si Si Senor" to everything.

When the ceremony is over the real Don Pedro shows up and everyone realizes the boys are imposters. Joe takes it on the lamb, while Tom is seized and held. Chiquita tells everyone that Tom is her husband and that she is very much pleased with him. As she is the richest girl in the country Tom is in luck. Joe, unfortunately, is still being chased by the Indians. As he thinks they are after his scalp, he hastily strips off his toupee—and hands it to his pursuers.

Four Languages in Comedy Film

Yiddish, Spanish, Italian, and English are spoken in the Educational Ideal comedy, "Si Si Senor," which features Tom Patricola and Joe Phillips

Story was written around special talents of Patricola and Phillips, and a good share of the laughs are derived from introduction of the foreign languages, as used by the comedians.

– **Inside Facts of Stage and Screen**, September 27, 1930

Roscoe's return to directorial duties for Educational Pictures put him together with the eccentric comic, singer, and dancer Tom Patricola. A forgotten figure today, in 1930 Patricola was well-known as a 1920s mainstay of the *George White Scandals*, where he had introduced the Black Bottom with Ann Pennington. In addition to being the brother of vaudeville musician Isabella Patricola, he specialized in comedy, clog dancing, and strumming the ukulele (often doing all three at the same time). Hitting films when sound arrived in Fox musical features such as *Words and Music*, *Married to Hollywood*, and *Happy Days* (all 1929), he then settled into Educational shorts for most of the 1930s,

> 'Laugh Insurance' certificate used in connection with Educational's "Si, Si, Senor."

Make sure you sign the Laff Insurance Contract for *Si, Si, Senor* (1930).

and two others, *The Tamale Vendor* (1931) and *Moonlight and Cactus* (1932), were also helmed by Roscoe. The 1940s saw his career wane, and he died in 1950.

Patricola's sidekick is Joe Phillips, a very busy stage stooge of the 1920s on whom there's very little information today. Phillips was teamed for much of the 1920s with comic George LeMaire in popular sketches like *At the Dentist*. When sound came to films LeMaire was busy putting his sketches on film, and the short, bald, and deadpan Phillips turned up in *Joy Ride* (1928), *Dancing Around* (1929), and the Vitaphone short *Sitting Pretty* (1930). Always having been based in New York the June 11, 1930 *Variety* noted:

Phillips Takes a Chance

    Hollywood, June 10—Joe Phillips, vaud comic, arrived here this week from New York.

    He's on spec.

Si Si Senor is his only known Hollywood credit. In the latter part of his career he acquired and performed the stage act of Johnny Burke (known for a comedy act as a World War I doughboy) and according to his *Variety* obituary much of his income came from interest on investments he and other family members had made in the New York restaurant Frankie & Johnny's Steak House. He died in New York of a heart attack at age seventy-eight in 1966.

The UCLA Film and Television Archive has a brief clip of Roscoe on the set during the making of *Si, Si, Senor*.

Film Daily (September 14, 1930): "Good Comedy—Though framed to bring in some of Tom Patricola's dancing and strumming, this short develops a good comedy story and proves entirely satisfying on that basis aside from its musical enjoyments. Patricola and Phillips, a couple of desert tramps along the Mexican border, swipe the clothes of a couple of señors who are taking a swim just before calling on the daughter of a hacienda owner for matrimonial purposes. Neither the girl nor her father have ever met the suitor, so it's clear for Tom to pose as the awaited fiancée. After a few serenade numbers and some comedy business the irate señors turn up and expose the frauds. But the girl has taken a fancy to her musical American caballero and he cops the prize. Action is quite plentiful."

Won by a Neck

Released October 5, 1930. Lloyd Hamilton Talking Comedies. Produced and distributed by Educational Pictures. Directed by William Goodrich. Story by Harry McCoy and Walter DeLeon. Photographed by Dwight Warren. Two reels. Extant. With Lloyd Hamilton, Ruth Hiatt, Addie McPhail, Ed Brady, Dan Wolheim, William McCall, Glen Cavender, Al Thompson.

The city is in the grip of a crime wave. "One Shot Louie" and his gang are terrorizing the population and no policeman is safe on the streets. With the forces depleted, Percy, a recent detective correspondence school graduate, is chosen to help fill the ranks when he waddles into the police station. When the Chief of Police asks for a volunteer to capture "One Shot Louie" Percy can't find a seat and remains standing, so the Chief takes him as the volunteer and sends him off to get the gangster.

Percy ends up at the café where Louie and his gang hang out, and tries to keep a low profile. Sitting near an open window the cold air gives Percy a stiff neck, but at the same time he's recognized as a detective and locked in a storeroom. While Percy is making an escape by gassing his captors, Red Hogan, a rival gangster, is looking for "One Shot Louie" to settle a score.

After having escaped Percy's neck is worse, so he thinks he should see a doctor. Heading to what he thinks is the doctor's office it's actually "One Shot Louie's" apartment. "Louie" thinks that Percy is Red Hogan and starts strangling him. Percy thinks the rough stuff is part

Lloyd Hamilton and friend from *Won by a Neck* (1930).

Ruth Hiatt and Lloyd Hamilton scrutinize a scene in the early 1920s. Courtesy of Robert S. Birchard.

of the doctor's treatment for his neck. The real Red Hogan shows up, and when he mistakes Percy for "One Shot Louie" he repeats the "treatments" on him. When the gangsters finally discover each other they start fighting while the neighbors call the cops.

When the riot squad arrives, it finds that Percy has already arrested both of the criminals, and he is hailed a hero by his amazed comrades.

After his silent shorts *The Movies* (1925), *One Sunday Morning* (1926), and *Peaceful Oscar* (1927) with Roscoe in the director's seat, Lloyd Hamilton was banned from the screen for a year—from mid-1928 to mid-1929. Returning to films when sound arrived he was able to jump start his career, and was again in demand for features and shorts. Having both been away from pictures, Roscoe and Hamilton were back at Educational Pictures, and with *Won by a Neck* resumed their work together.

Hamilton's leading lady is Ruth Hiatt, a pretty blonde best-remembered today for Mack Sennett's series of *Smith Family* comedies. Ms. Hiatt had started her career in the early 1920s with Hamilton, as his regular co-star in shorts such as *The Educator* (1922), *The Optimist* (1923), and *My Friend* (1924), and then became a female-lead-in-residence for Jack White Comedies, where she was paired with Lige Conley, Cliff Bowes, and Lee Moran. She moved over to Sennett in 1925, and from 1926 to 1929 headlined in the *Smith Family* series—Sennett's stab at situational and domestic comedy. Hiatt played the young wife opposite Raymond McKee as her hubby and little Mary Ann Jackson as their scene-stealing baby. Following features like *The Missing Link* (1927) when sound arrived she returned to work with Hamilton in early talkies like *Grass Skirts* (1929), *Camera Shy*, and *Good Morning* (both 1930). From here she moved around doing small bits in shorts and features until the mid-1930s.

Film Daily (October 12, 1930): "A typical Lloyd Hamilton comedy with the star playing the part of a correspondence school detective. After most of the police force has been killed off, the chief picks Lloyd to go out single handed and capture One Shot Louie who has been terrorizing the city. In hunting for a doctor to cure his stiff neck, the amateur sleuth goes to the home of the gunman by mistake. The gangster beats him up, thinking he is a rival gunman. Hamilton thinks this is part of the doctor's cure, till the other gunman arrives, mistakes him for One Shot Louie, and beats him up all over again. It's a great gag, and good for plenty of laughs. Finally when the cops arrive on a riot call, the two thugs have beat each other up, and Lloyd is hailed as the hero for capturing them. Plenty of action, and Hamilton sends it in with his well known line of comedy antics."

Up a Tree

Released November 30, 1930. Lloyd Hamilton Talking Comedies. Produced and distributed by Educational Pictures. Direction and story by William Goodrich. Continuity and dialogue by Harry McCoy & Jimmy Starr. Photography by Dwight Warren. Two reels. Extant. With Lloyd Hamilton, Addie McPhail, Dell Henderson.

For the past year Elmer Doolittle has done little but sit around the house. He hasn't had a job, hasn't looked very hard for one, and his wife's patience is exhausted. He can't even do errands for her—when she sends him to the store for cream he returns with what he thinks is a cow, but it's actually a burro.

Lloyd Hamilton is devoted to his tree-sitting marathon in 1930's *Up a Tree*. Billy Rose Theatre Division, the New York Public Library for the Performing Arts.

Reaching the breaking point wifie goes after him with a rolling pin and to escape he climbs up their tree and refuses to come down. Elmer's good friend is a promoter who promotes endurance flights and marathon dancing—and he conceives the idea of having Elmer as his entry in an endurance tree sitting contest. Mrs. Doolittle is all for Elmer staying in the tree, and the promoter convinces her to enter a dance marathon.

Summer fades into winter and Elmer is still in the tree. He has installed all kinds of conveniences—a shower, an ice box, a radio, and other comforts of home. Over the radio he listens to the progress of Mrs. Doolittle's dance marathon. By the time spring rolls around the records are almost broken, and despite some last minute near-accidents and misadventures both the Doolittles are victorious with their endurance records.

Playing Hamilton's wife is Addie McPhail, who would soon end up playing that same role in Roscoe's real life. Born Addie Dukes in 1905 she did some stage work in Chicago before breaking into films in 1925 doing bits in Stern Brothers comedies. After appearing in some *Newlyweds and their Baby* shorts, she became a regular in the Stern's overlooked 1927-1928 *Keeping Up with the Joneses* comedies. Directed by Gus Meins, the series co-starred Harry Long, Stella Adams, and Gene "Fatty" Layman as the rest of the family in titles like *Keeping in Trim*, *Passing the Joneses* (both 1927), *A Big Bluff*, and *Reel Life* (both 1928).

She also appeared in shorts for Fox and Weiss Brothers such as Ben Turpin's *She Said No* (1928), and *Jack and Jilted* (1928) directed by Billy West, in addition to the early William Wyler-directed feature *Anybody Here Seen Kelly?* (1928). She made a smooth transition to sound and was co-starring with Hamilton, Al St John, and Andy Clyde. Addie later said that she really got to know Roscoe on the set of *Up a Tree*, and after working frequently under his direction the pair fell in love. They were married on the road while doing a vaudeville tour together in June of 1932. After being widowed a year later Addie tapered off her film work, and having re-married she retired in 1940. Later she worked as a volunteer nurse at the Motion Picture and Television Retirement Home in Woodland Hills, California, and passed away at age ninety-seven in 2003.

Also on hand in *Up a Tree* is the overlooked comedy director and player Dell Henderson. Canadian-born, Henderson was a long-time stage actor who switched to films in 1908 as part of D.W. Griffith's acting ensemble at Biograph. Originally more dramatic, he quickly gravitated to comedy and in 1912 became a full-time comedy director, eventually landing at Keystone. The comedy shorts he either wrote or directed include *A Dash through the Clouds* (1912), *Bertha, the Button-Hole Maker* (1914), *Those Bitter Sweets* (1915), *Wife and Auto Trouble*, and *A Bath House Blunder* (both 1916). By 1916 he was helming features of all kinds until *The Rambling Ranger* in 1927.

At this point he returned to acting, turning in excellent character performances in features such as *The Patsy*, *The Crowd*, and *Show People* (all

Portrait of the third Mrs. Roscoe Arbuckle, Addie McPhail. Courtesy of Matt Vogel.

1928). Having made a smooth move into sound he appeared in scads of talking shorts for Educational and Hal Roach, most memorably *The Laurel and Hardy Murder Case* (1930) and with Our Gang in *Choo-Choo!* (1932). He continued turning up in films like *It's a Gift* (1934) and *Ruggles of Red Gap* (1935) until 1950.

Screenland (April 1931): "A slapstick comedy about marathon dancing, tree-sitting and what have you, with Lloyd Hamilton cavorting."

Three Hollywood Girls

Released January 4, 1931. Ideal Comedies. Produced and distributed by Educational Pictures. Directed by William Goodrich. Story by Katherine Scola & Sherman L. Lowe. Continuity and dialogue by James Gleason, Ernest Pagano, & Jack Townley. Photographed by Dwight Warren. Two reels. Extant. With Rita Flynn, Phyllis Crane, Leota Lane, Edward Nugent, Florence Oberle, Ford West, Lillian Worth.

Our story is set in Hollywood; where every train disgorges ambitious youth, afire with yearning to shine on the silver screen; kids from the corn belt who think they could be Pickfords, Garbos, and Swansons if they could only get a chance.

At the gate of Mammoth Studios the guard tells the line of work-seeking extras that there will be nothing for them, and they all leave except one. Out of the studio pours a group of extras finished for the day. Phyllis has just found out that she's been given a small part in a big feature production. As she's happily telling the gateman her good fortune, she notices the crying girl that's stayed behind.

Phyllis listens to her story and takes her home to the room she shares with Rita, another aspiring actress, but one who refuses to do extra work—and is holding out for a $50 a day part. Their casting director friend Bill comes over to urge Rita to accept a lower paying roll, but she refuses. To convince her he has the three girls stage the big scene from "The Lighted

IDEAL COMEDIES

"THREE HOLLYWOOD GIRLS" was a real box-office appetizer, a "two-reeler", according to Photoplay, "with pace and dialogue that put many a feature in the shade."

Ideal Comedies exhibitor ad and image for *Three Hollywood Girls* (1931).

Lamp," and is impressed with the new girls, Leota's, ability. He renames her Beverly Wilshire and asks her to see him at the studio.

Three months later it's the big opening of the super feature "The Lighted Lamp." Tens of thousands of spectators jam the court of the theatre, to catch a glimpse of the sensational star of the picture, a small town girl who made good in Hollywood in three short months. A limousine drives up, the star steps out……and it's Beverly Wilshire!

Glamour shot of Rita Flynn

Phyllis and Rita are in the crowd cheering their friend. When they turn to go Phyllis comes across a girl crying and asks her what the trouble is. After hearing her story she asks the new girl to come home with them, and the Hollywood story continues on.

This is the initial entry in what would become a six-part series. Instead of the usual male-oriented slapstick this series focused on three young women trying to break into the movies with female-oriented slapstick, but still managed to incorporate some real insider details into the knockabout proceedings. The original trio of girls was made up of Phyllis Crane, Leota Lane and Rita Flynn, with only Ms. Flynn appearing in the entire run of shorts.

Born in 1905 as Edith Flynn, she was the 1925 Miss San Francisco and from there became a showgirl under the name of Mickey Flynn. When talkies hit pictures in 1929 she entered films as a chorus girl in productions like *Broadway* and *Fast Life* (both 1929). She got a lot of attention for the Alice White musical *The Girl from Woolworth's* (1929), and better parts followed in *Sweet Mama* and *Top Speed* (both 1930). Having changed her name from Mickey Flynn to Rita Flynn, as she didn't "think the [former] moniker is ritzy enough for picture work," she mostly headlined in the *Hollywood Girls* shorts until 1932's *Hollywood Luck*. In 1933 she married writer and sportsman McKinley Bryant and left show business.

Unlike Ms. Flynn, the brunette Leota Lane only appeared in this original episode. Oldest of the famous Lane Sisters (Priscilla, Lola and Rosemary), the family name was Mullican and Leota was the first one in show business. Discovered in her native Iowa by vaudeville impresario Gus Edwards, Leota was brought to New York and sang for Edwards, as well as appeared in the *Greenwich Village Follies*. In 1929 she was in the Broadway revival of *Babes in Toyland*. Venturing out to the West Coast she didn't find movie fame like her sisters Priscilla or Lola. Besides *Three Hollywood Girls* her only other film was another short, 1939's *You're Next to Closing*.

Getting a certain amount of attention from the movie fame of her sisters, Leota was serious about her singing and spent most of her time in New York. Although she appeared in the 1937 *Ziegfeld Follies* she aspired toward opera and studied at Julliard. During World War II she joined the WACs and was in charge of music for the 2nd Air Force. She later married and settled in California where she was a soloist and children's choir director at North Hollywood's Toluca Lake Methodist Church. She died at fifty in 1963.

The continuity and dialogue for *Three Hollywood Girls* is by the usual Educational Comedies' team of Ernest Pagano and Jack Townley, but with the addition of James Gleason. Remembered today as a crack comedy actor in films such as *Meet John Doe* (1941), *The Clock* (1945), *The Bishop's Wife* (1947), and especially *Here Comes Mr. Jordan* (1941), it's completely forgotten that Gleason was also a Broadway playwright and screenwriter.

As a young man he became an actor and toured around the country for many years, and eventually hit the big time in New York in 1914. In addition to performing on Broadway he wrote the shows *Is Zat So?* (1925), *The Fall Guy* (1925), *The Shannons of Broadway* (1927), *Rain or Shine* (1928), and even directed George S. Kaufman's hit *The Butter and Egg Man* (1926). He adapted *Is Zat So?* into a 1927 silent film for George O'Brien, but when talkies hit Gleason was all over the screen writing as well as acting.

Besides adapting his Broadway shows, he also worked on *The Broadway Melody* (1929), *Puttin' on the Ritz* (1930), *The Bowery* (1933), and *Change of Heart* (1934). Although he stopped writing in 1938, his busy career as a character actor lasted right up to his death in 1959.

Film Daily (December 28, 1930): "This one departs from the usual Hollywood comedy by giving some of the real inside dope on how the girls who come from the small towns manage to scrape along and live until such time as they land a studio job. It is well directed by William Goodrich, and the story shows an intimate knowledge of just how the screen-struck girls live in their little furnished rooms while they wait for Dame Fortune to smile on them. It is well gagged, and mixes the laughs with the natural situations. Should go over well, for it gives the flappers with screen aspirations a good idea of what they are up against, but does it with a smile."

Photoplay (March 1931): "A two-reeler with pace and dialogue that put many a feature in the shade. Leota Lane, Rita Flynn and Phyllis Crane are the girls. Aided by Eddie Nugent's flip antics, it's a travesty of girls who get to Hollywood via beauty contests."

Motion Picture Reviews (January 1931): "A light comedy about three aspiring movie stars who help each other with their meager resources until success is reached by at least one of them. It is above the average for this type of production."

Marriage Rows

Released January 18, 1931. Lloyd Hamilton Talking Comedies. Produced and distributed by Educational Pictures. Direction and story by William Goodrich. Continuity & dialogue by Walter Reed. Photography by Dwight Warren. Two reels. Extant: LOC. With Lloyd Hamilton, Al St John, Addie McPhail, Doris Deane, Al Thompson, Edna Marion.

Elmer loves his wife Winnie, but is the constantly jealous type. When the wife gets a telegram that Albert, her old sweetheart, is coming to visit, Elmer gets terribly worried and isn't particularly happy when Al shows up and Winnie gives him a big kiss for "old time's sake."

When wifie leaves the room Elmer confides in Al and asks him to pretend to make love to her so he can see if she is sincere. Al agrees to help but Winnie has overheard the scheme and decides to teach Elmer a lesson. When Elmer pretends to go to work Winnie begins to make violent love to Al. Elmer comes back, determined not to leave them alone together, but when they ask him to play piano so they can dance, they dance upstairs and into the bedroom. Elmer sees their shadows on the drawn curtain in what looks to be a compromising situation and assumes the worst.

Al had left his wife waiting outside in the car, and she comes in at this point to look for him. She also thinks that Al is making love to Winnie, and when the girls meet they begin a fight. When Elmer finds that Al is married he realizes that his jealousy was foolish, and as the women fight he makes peace with Al. The men go off arm in arm while the women battle.

The cast and crew for *Marriage Rows* make for an unusual type of "old home week" for Roscoe. It marks the first time he's worked with nephew Al St John since 1926, and contains wives past and future. Roscoe's ex-wife Doris Deane, in one of her last film appearances, plays Al's wife, and gets into it with Addie McPhail, Roscoe's soon-to-be

Marriage Rows (1931) chronicles Lloyd Hamilton's (right) jealousy over Al St John's attentions to his wife Addie McPhail. Courtesy Annichen Skaren.

wife. All that was needed was for Minta Durfee to play the maid, but that role is taken by comedy regular Edna Marion, best-known for her work at the Hal Roach Studio with Laurel & Hardy and Charley Chase. Even the dialogue and adaptation of Roscoe's story is handled by his old stage mentor and long-time supporting player Walter C. Reed.

Photoplay (March 1931): "Lloyd Hamilton is hitting his stride in talking comedies, and it's a fast one. This is a daisy, with Ham screamingly funny as a suspicious husband given to hysteria. Who should be "the other man" but our old pal Al St John. You really shouldn't miss this one."

Screenland (April 1931: "Lloyd Hamilton in a rib-tickling domestic comedy with Al St John and Addie McPhail."

Pete and Repeat

Released March 1, 1931. Ideal Comedies. Produced and distributed by Educational Pictures. Directed by William Goodrich. Story by George Jeske, Joey Mack, & A. Gold. Continuity & dialogue by Ernest Pagano & Jack Townley. Two reels. Extant: LOC.

Caricatures of Peenie Elmo (right) and "Bud" Harrison (left) in the Educational exhibitor ad for *Pete and Repeat* (1931).

With "Bud" Harrison, Peenie Elmo, Ed Brady, Robert Wilber, Dick Hatton, Baldwin Cooke.

Two convicts escape from the state penitentiary, but their flight is hampered by the heavy ball and chain which binds them together. Seben 'n' Leben have a blacksmith shop, and are having breakfast when the convicts arrive and ask the boys to remove the chains. They explain that they are working down the street at the local movie house ballyhooing a prison break picture. Seben 'n' Leben "buy" the job from the strangers, and throw in their nice clothes for the convict's striped outfits.

Seben 'n' Leben go to the movie house but the manager of the theatre assumes that they are the escaped convicts and calls the police. The boys hide in a delivery truck which just happens to be driven by the real convicts making their escape. Eventually they all end up back at the prison, where the real convicts are re-captured and the boys rewarded. They take their reward money and open an auto garage, but are convinced that cars are a fad and that horses are coming back.

This was an attempt to have the blackface characters of "Seben 'n' Leben" join those of Moran & Mack and Amos & Andy on the big screen. Bud Harrison and Peenie Elmo both had a background of fifteen years on stage in musical comedy and minstrel shows. They teamed up in the late 1920s and played vaudeville circuits such as Lowe Time, Balaban & Katz, and the RKO and Publix routes. In 1929 Moran & Mack had a huge screen success with their feature *Why Bring That Up?*, and its follow-up *Anybody's War* (1930). At the same time Amos & Andy became the biggest thing on radio, and made their jump to movies in *Check and Double Check* (1930).

Harrison and Elmo had done "Seben 'n' Leben" in the independent short *A Pair O'Dice* (1930) and an episode of the *Voice of Hollywood* series, so Educational Pictures decided to use them as their bid to get in on the momentarily lucrative blackface bandwagon. When

Pete and Repeat didn't start any fires there was no follow-up. Educational eventually got Moran & Mack on the rebound for a few two-reelers, and Bud Harrison and Peenie Elmo did a few movie bit roles through the 1940s. As one of the convicts, character man Ed Brady works with Roscoe again seventeen years after 1914's *Leading Lizzie Astray*.

Broadway and Hollywood Movies (February 1932): "Educational Films bring to the screen Bud Harrison and Peenie Elmo, the blackface team of vaudeville fame in a side splitting comedy, with situations abounding with the most logical humor we have seen in a very long time. Seben n' Leben, as the boys are called, pack a humor punch, which is a tonic in these days of discouragements. A real funny moving picture."

Photoplay (April 1931): "This short introduces a couple of blackface comedians to the screen. Their picture names are Seben and Leben and they hold promise of developing into sound laugh-makers, a pun."

Motion Picture Reviews (March 1931): "A fairly entertaining slaps-stick comedy. Two colored blacksmiths, unwillingly change clothes with two escaped convicts. A chase ensues which is lacking in art but not in humor. Family film."

Ex-Plumber

Released March 8, 1931. Lloyd Hamilton Talking Comedies. Produced and distributed by Educational Pictures. Direction and story by William Goodrich. Continuity and dialogue by Walter Reed. Photography by Dwight Warren. Two reels. Extant. With Lloyd Hamilton, Amber Norman, Mitchell Lewis, Addie McPhail, Stanley Blystone, Polly Christy.

Elmer's wife is jealous. She doesn't believe that all the phone calls that he gets at home are connected with his plumbing business. After a stormy scene at home he goes off to his shop. After he leaves their friend Addie drops by. She has just returned from Europe with a new husband and invites Elmer's wife to a dinner party in the evening.

When Addie returns to her home she finds a leak in the bathroom and calls Elmer, who comes and fixes it. While he is there Addie gets a phone call from Duke Ketchkoffski, a Russian nobleman, who has pursued her all over Europe professing his love for her. Addie tells him she is married but he says she is lying and is coming to see the husband, adding that he will kill her if there is no husband. Of course Addie's new husband has just gone off on a business trip so she hires Elmer to impersonate her husband at the dinner party to satisfy Ketchkhoffski.

That evening the Duke arrives and Elmer is introduced as Addie's husband. He nearly screws up several times, but the Duke thinks Elmer's slips of the tongue are just the American sense of humor. All is going well until Elmer's wife, who got tired of waiting for him, shows up at the party.

Although Elmer manages to avoid her the plot thickens when Addie's real husband appears, having missed his train. The appearance of the "second" husband convinces the Duke that he's been lied to, and Addie's husband is sure that Elmer is her lover, so they both insist on personally killing him. His wife wants a piece of him too, as she's sure he's been fooling around with Addie. As they fight over which of them will kill Elmer they break a steam pipe, and Elmer calmly reverts to his job and fixes the pipe while hot words and steam obscure them all from sight.

Exhibitor ad for Lloyd Hamilton's talking comedy series.

Although Hamilton had returned to films and was able to rekindle some of his popularity the depression brought financial reverses, and thanks to his drinking his health was shot. Able to work less and less, he died in 1935 of cirrhosis of the liver and stomach ailments. His hard luck even followed him after death as the negatives for his silent Educational shorts, including *One Sunday Morning* (1926) and *Peaceful Oscar* (1927), were destroyed in the famous 1937 Fox vault fire, with rare scattered prints only existing with collectors and archives.

Photoplay (May 1931): "Lloyd Hamilton again, but not so good this time. He just can't help getting involved with a lovely lady, and his wife is no great help to his peace of mind. Mitchell Lewis plays a comedy Russian count and Addie McPhail is the little wifie."

Screenland (May 1931): "Lloyd Hamilton is induced to pose as the husband of the lady where he is doing a plumbing job—and her real husband shows up and is very jealous! Giggles galore."

Crashing Hollywood

Released April 5, 1931. Ideal Comedies. Produced and distributed by Educational Pictures. Directed by William Goodrich. Story and continuity by Ernest Pagano & Jack Townley. Photographed by Dwight Warren. Two reels. Extant. With Virginia Brooks, Phyllis Crane, Rita Flynn, Edward J. Nugent, Bryant Washburn, George Chandler, Wilbur Mack, Walter Merrill, Charles Dorety, Frances Dean.

Phyllis and Rita are unemployed extra girls who haven't worked in weeks. Their total combined fortune is sixty cents, and the rent is due. Also due is Phyllis' cousin Virginia who's coming from Iowa for a visit. The girls aren't looking forward to taking care of what they think will be a country bumpkin, but they get a surprise at the train station when all the men in sight fall over Virginia and fight to carry her bags. She also manages to get a Rolls-Royce for their personal use, vamps a tough van driver out of repossessing their unpaid installment furniture, and gets mounds of food charged at the "Cash Only" grocery.

The girls take Virginia with them to the biggest studio in town and find that she met the studio owner on the train and turned down his repeated proposals of marriage because she

(L-R) Phyllis Crane, Rita Flynn, Eddie Nugent, and Virginia Brooks have a tense moment in *Crashing Hollywood* (1931).

wants to see "Hollywood wild life" before she marries. Phyllis and Rita realize that if Virginia marries Mr. Morgan they'll all get good jobs in the movies. With the help of Rita's boyfriend Eddie, they conspire to stage a wild party for Virginia in the hope that she will be cured and will marry Mr. Morgan.

Morgan is going to San Francisco, and as Eddie is his secretary they use his home to stage the party. Doubles are hired for all the big stars, the liquor bottles are filled with water, and when a signal is given the guests start a terrific fight which ends only when the police arrive. Unfortunately Mr. Morgan had cancelled his trip and returned in time to fire Eddie and tell the girls that they are through in the movie business.

Next morning the girls tell Virginia about the hoax and blame her for their predicament. They tell her that she'll have to marry Morgan to fix things up. Although Virginia is in love with Elmer, a country boy back in Iowa, she agrees.

At the wedding Rita and Phyllis congratulate themselves on the success of their scheme—with Morgan in the family their screen future is assured. At the altar the minister is beginning the ceremony when the sound of an auto horn is heard. It's Elmer, Virginia's country sweetheart, and she rushes out of the church and into his car. Phyllis and Rita see their dreams of a screen future waft away in the exhaust smoke of the departing car.

Charles Dorety (center holding beer) was part of the Bulls Eye film crew's wake at the passing of prohibition. Other mourners include Harry Mann, James Parrott, Leo White, and Charles Parrott. Courtesy of Robert S. Birchard.

This second entry in the *Hollywood Girls* series has the ladies getting no closer to stardom. Roscoe uses the party sequence to poke fun at friends like Chaplin and Keaton by having them imitated there, with the Charlie and Buster clones getting into a big fight. The ersatz Buster is Charles Dorety, who had a small bit with the collapsing automobile in *The Garage* (1920). Dorety had been a dancer and comedian in vaudeville, and after beginning his film career at Fox Sunshine Comedies, bounced around to Bulls Eye and Lehrman First National Specials before a stint headlining for Century Comedies.

Never developing his own comic style or identifiable character, he often imitated Keaton. Two surviving shorts, *A Twilight Baby* (1920) and *Third Class Male* (1921), show Dorety wearing the flat pork pie hat, complete with deadpan demeanor and stumpy body language. Later Dorety was teamed with Gene "Fatty" Laymon in Tennek/Sava Films such as *The Inventors* and *Are Golfers Cuckoo?* (both 1926) where they were working from the late teens Arbuckle/Keaton prototype. Lack of material and money doomed the films to obscurity, and Dorety's own lack of a definable persona and approach to comedy caused him to end up as an uncredited bit player, which he did until 1955.

Returning from the previous *Three Hollywood Girls* is the wisecracking leading man Eddie Nugent. Good looking, charming, and funny, Nugent showed a lot of promise in the early 1930s, but never made the leap to stardom. Coming from vaudeville he ended up in Hollywood in the mid-1920s, and broke into the studios working as a stunt man and property boy. Much of his film career was spent at MGM, where he contributed gags and finally got on screen in 1928's *Our Dancing Daughters*. His small bits in features generally saw him as collegiate or young sport characters, but in shorts he had bigger roles, usually as the comic sidekick to the leading man.

Some of his better roles in features came in *42nd Street* (1933), *Ah Wilderness!* (1935) and *Pigskin Parade* (1936). Giving up on Hollywood, he returned to New York in 1937 and appeared in a number of short-lived Broadway comedies on the order of *One Thing after Another*, *Snookie*, and *Round Trip* until 1945. Later directing 1950's television shows such as *The Arthur Murray Party* and *The George Jessel Show*, Nugent passed away in 1995.

Screenland (June 1931): "A miniature feature with many laughs and lots of Hollywood atmosphere. All three girls trying to crash the screen gates, with hilarious complications. The cast includes some players you have liked in features—Eddie Nugent, Phyllis Crane, Rita Flynn and Bryant Washburn. Nice to see Nugent again."

The New Movie Magazine (July 1931): "An amusing burlesque of Hollywood celebrities, including rather clever impersonations of Charlie Chaplin, Harold Lloyd and other studio personages."

Motion Picture Reviews (April 1931): "A wholesome and fun provoking short comedy. The picture is far more artistically done than most short subjects and is delightfully amusing throughout without descending to vulgarity."

Windy Riley Goes Hollywood

Released May 3, 1931. A Mermaid Talking Comedy. Produced and distributed by Educational Pictures. Directed by William Goodrich. Story by Ken Kling, based on his syndicated comic strip *Windy Riley*. Continuity and dialogue by Ernest Pagano & Jack

Townley. Photographed by Dwight Warren. Sound by W.C. Smith. Two reels. Extant. With Jack Shutta, Louise Brooks, William Davidson, Wilbur Mack, Dell Henderson, Walter Merrill, Al Thompson (in two roles), Burt Young, E. H. Allen.

Windy Riley, involved in a record breaking non-stop 72 hour drive from New York to San Francisco, accidentally finishes his trip in Hollywood. Not only is he in the wrong city, but after his car is repossessed it crashes into the car of a Hollywood producer, who forces Windy to work it out as an underling at his studio. Of course he disrupts everything. Actress Betty Grey is frequently getting bad press in the newspapers and is told that she needs to keep her name out of the papers or her contract will be terminated. Windy decides to take over her publicity and put her name on every front page in the country. To do this he kidnaps her director and hides him, making a sensational story. The ensuing publicity causes Betty to be in danger of losing her job when Windy shows up at the studio bragging about his bright idea. In the nick of time he's forced to retrieve the director and clear up the scandal. The head of the studio gives Windy a pummeling, which sends he and his car hightailing it back to New York.

While not one of Roscoe's better surviving talkies, *Windy Riley* does give some behind-the-scenes looks at the Educational Studios. A dance number even takes place on a blacksmith set left over from Lupino Lane's *Fisticuffs* (1928), while studio general manager E.H. Allen walks through the background. Although Roscoe tries to keep things moving, the trite plot and dull characters bog everything down, plus the lack of a background musical score creates a dead soundtrack.

Silent film icon Louise Brooks plays Betty Grey and looks great, but is given a completely humorless part with really nothing to do. Comedy regulars Del Henderson, Al Thompson, and Bert Young try to spice things up, as does Jack Shutta as Windy Riley. Shutta came from a show business family, his sister Ethel was a popular singer, and grew up on stage. Longtime in vaudeville as an eccentric tramp, in the early 1930s he was teamed with dancer/actor George Murphy. He started appearing in films in 1930, and worked in three of Roscoe's—*Windy Riley, Once a Hero* (1931), and *Hey Pop* (1932). Shutta was also a foil for Arbuckle in his stage act, and turned up in numerous movie bits until his death in 1957.

More annoying than funny, *Windy Riley* was a short-lived comic strip that thankfully didn't get a second chance on the screen.

Motion Picture Herald (April 11, 1931): "The auto record of Windy Riley from New York to Hollywood and the subsequent excitement at a studio when he works a fake publicity stunt, cannot be rated more than fair. The story by Ken Kling is not at all unusual. Jack Shutta, Louise Brooks, William Davidson, Dell Henderson, Wilbur Mack and Walter Merrill do their best but not very successfully."

The Back Page

Released May 24, 1931. Mermaid Comedies. Produced and distributed by Educational Pictures. Directed by William Goodrich. Story and dialogue by Ernest Pagano & Jack Townley. Two reels. Extant. With George Chandler, Virginia Brooks, Wheeler Oakman, George MacFarlane, Ethel Davis, Albert Austin.

George Chandler has Albert Austin signed and sealed in *The Back Page* (1931).
Courtesy Jim Kerkhoff.

Johnny Jones is the printer's devil for the Tribune who dreams of being a big time star reporter. When pleading with the editor for a chance leads nowhere, Johnny decides to get an interview with the gangland racketeer "Star" Palermo. Johnny is also in love with the editor's daughter who is being forced by her father to marry the visiting English nobleman Lord Atterbury. While out tracking down Palermo, Johnny has a car accident with him, and Palermo realizes he can use the green Johnny for his own purposes.

Palermo tells Johnny that he can find "Star" Palermo at the country club dance, and points out Lord Atterbury as the gangster. Gullible Johnny grabs Lord Atterbury, which is what Palermo had planned to begin with, and when he victoriously takes the "crook" back to the newspaper office he finds out he's been duped. After being thrown out of the office he comes upon the real Palermo again, and this time captures him and wins the girl's hand.

With its word play on *The Front Page*, this short is of course a spoof on the newspaper story cliché of the lowly cub reporter or office boy who gets a story and makes good. This plot was a standard and would serve many more comics at Educational, including Harry Langdon in *The Big Flash* (1932) and Buster Keaton in *Jail Bait* (1937). Speaking of Keaton, the Busterish hero of *The Back Page*, Johnny Jones, is played by George Chandler. Best remembered today as W. C. Fields' son Chester in *The Fatal Glass of Beer* (1933) and as Uncle Petrie on TV's *Lassie*, Chandler came from vaudeville where he was billed as "The Musical Nut," and made his film debut at Universal in a series of silent *Tenderfoot Thriller* two-reelers.

These shorts featured Chandler as a more than Keatonesque eastern dude, usually named Cuthbert or Bertie, who comedically had to prove his manliness out west in titles such as *Saps and Saddles* (1928) and *Two Gun Morgan* (1929). Described as "that engaging boob," sadly none of these are known to survive today, but existing photos and contemporary reviews referred to his "characterization (a la Keaton)" and that he was "featured in a Buster Keaton type of role." What do survive are these Arbuckle-directed sound shorts, which also include *Crashing Hollywood*, *The Lure of Hollywood*, and *Up Pops the Duke* (all 1931), that continued the Keaton cloning (he's sometimes even named Elmer). Chandler soon dropped the Buster mannerisms to become a ubiquitous character player and later president of Screen Actors Guild.

For support Chandler has Virginia Brooks, Wheeler Oakman, George MacFarlane, Ethel Davis, and regular Charlie Chaplin collaborator Albert Austin as Lord Atterbury. Well-known for playing multiple roles in Chaplin comedies, Austin was also a valuable asset to the comedian as a gagman and assistant director. Born in Birmingham, England, he first worked with Chaplin onstage in the Fred Karno music hall company, and joined the comic on screen in 1916 for his two-reelers for the Mutual Corporation. In the early 1920s Austin branched out his own—directing features for Jackie Coogan, Dinky Dean Riesner, and Monty Banks, in addition to shorts for Mack Sennett, Bull Montana, and Clyde Cook. He also freelanced around as a gagman, and by the end of the 1920s his career was waning, with his work often uncredited. His last known writing assignments are from the mid-1930s, and he ended his days as a guard at the Warner Brothers Studio.

Around this time a photo circulated in the trade magazines of Roscoe visiting Ford Sterling, Hank Mann, Chester Conklin and other former Keystone Cops during the making of the Masquers Club short *Stout Hearts and Willing Hands* (Universal, June 15,

Bill Patton (left) mistakes George Chandler for a more famous comedian in 1929's *Two Gun Morgan*. Billy Rose Theatre Division, the New York Public Library for the Performing Arts.

1931). This has led to some speculation that he was involved behind the scenes or in the direction of the short. There's no evidence that links Roscoe to the actual production, and in the photo itself he's very formally dressed in a three-piece suit as opposed to his regular "work clothes" of an open-collared shirt, sweater and slacks.

Motion Picture Reviews (May 1931): "Puerile, dull, badly acted short comedy."

The Lure of Hollywood

Released July 5, 1931. Ideal Comedies. Produced and distributed by Educational Pictures. Directed by William Goodrich. Story and dialogue by Ernest Pagano & Jack Townley. Two reels. Extant. With Virginia Brooks, Rita Flynn, Phyllis Crane, George Chandler, Bryant Washburn.

Still trying to break into pictures, the girls' luck has been bad and getting worse. Finally they land extra work on an "A" picture. Unfortunately they never get the chance to make a good impression as one of their boyfriends doesn't like the attention that the leading man is paying to his sweetheart, and starts a pie fight on the set.

This third installment of the *Hollywood Girls* series is a good opportunity to profile Phyllis Crane, who worked for Roscoe in the first three shorts of this series, as well as playing Monty Collins' love interest in *It's a Cinch* (1932). Born Phyllis Francis in Calgary, Alberta, Canada in 1914 her mother was involved in local theatre and had her daughter on stage with her by the time she was three. Busy acting, dancing, and singing, Phyllis excelled at recitations, and joined a performing group called the Calgary Kiddies. Appearing in vaudeville and in shows like *A Fool There Was* and *Shore Acres*, in 1926 Phyllis' mother decided it was time to move to Hollywood and get her daughter into the movies.

Phyllis Crane, Rita Flynn, and Virginia Brooks try to get noticed in *The Lure of Hollywood* (1931). Courtesy Richard Finegan.

Quickly after her arrival the actress was signed to MGM, and began getting experience with small bits in features such as *The Scarlett Letter* and *Tell It to the Marines* (both 1926). She also worked in comedy shorts for producer Joe Rock, and low budget features like *Racing Romance, One Minute to Go* (both 1927), and *The Battling Bookworm* (1928), all of this as a young teenager. In 1929 she was all over, in features such as *So This is College* and *The Forward Pass*, usually as college girls or dancers. Although she never rose above small bits in features, she had better parts in comedy shorts and until 1937 supported comics like Lupino Lane, Monty Collins, Andy Clyde, El Brendel and The Three Stooges. In 1937 she left Hollywood, moved to New York, and got involved in the perfume business. Settling in the East, she married, and passed away in 1982.

The vivacious Phyllis Crane.

Also on hand as the leading man in the film-within-the-short is former silent screen light comedy leading man Bryant Washburn. Very popular in the late teens and early 1920s in polite comedies like *Skinner's Baby* (1917), *The Poor Boob* (1919), and *What Happened to Jones* (1920), Washburn started his career in Chicago with Essanay in 1911. Working his way up from supporting people like Francis X. Bushman, he became popular enough as a lead at Essanay to move to studios like Famous Players-Lasky, Fox and Metro. After his career peak in 1920 he settled into supporting character roles, but the arrival of sound found his parts getting smaller. He appeared in many shorts, including *Crashing Hollywood* (1931), and *Keep Laughing* (1932) for Roscoe. Married to former Arbuckle and Lupino Lane leading lady Virginia Vance, Washburn continued to do bits in features. He also played major parts in serials such as *The Amazing Exploits of the Clutching Hand* (1936), *Jungle Jim* (1937) and *Adventures of Captain Marvel* (1941) up to 1947. Faring better than many other former movie stars, Washburn enjoyed a comfortable retirement until his death in 1963.

Photoplay (August 1931): "This picture is a comedy but it gives you a real tip that getting a job in the movies isn't all roses and fan mail. Three pretty girls have their troubles. Bryant Washburn, an old friend, makes a brief bow as the dashing matinee idol. A throwback to the old pie-slinging days is a bit regrettable. Some good laughs in spite of that, however."

Broadway and Hollywood Movies (December 1931): "E.W. Hammons presents this Ideal Talking Comedy, a short subject, by way of burlesque on what happens when you're Hollywood bound! Our old friend George MacFarlane appears with the shapely blonde, Virginia Brooks, Phyllis Crane, Rita Flynn, Geo. Chandler, Wilbur Mack, Bryant Washburn, and Ethel Davis. Educational knows how!"

That's My Line

Released July 13, 1931. Traveling Man Comedies. Produced and distributed by RKO Pathé Pictures. Direction, story, and adaptation by William Goodrich. Continuity by Ewart Adamson. Photographed by Harry Forbes & Robert Palmer. Supervised by Lew Lipton. Two reels. With Louis John Bartels, Paul Hurst, Doris McMahon, Gino Corrado, Bert Young, Al Thompson, Glen Cavender, James Bryant, Teddy Mangean, Billy Arnold, William Armstrong, Oscar Smith, William McCall, Gene Lewis, William LeMaire, Patricia Caron, Dorothy Granger.

A traveling salesman gets in trouble south of the border when he falls for a girl who's loved by a tough Mexican bandit. Things look bad for the salesman, but he manages to elude the bandido and his minions, and hightail it to the next town.

After writing and working with Wheeler and Woolsey at RKO in the early days of sound, the studio came back with new work for Roscoe.

Goodrich Farmed Out

William Goodrich, director-in-chief of the Educational Studios, was contemplating a few days vacation at his Malibu beach cottage, when RKO Pathé sent out an S.O.S. for a sure-fire comedy director, so through special

Louis John Bartels and Doris McMahon embrace in the 1931 RKO-Pathé short *That's My Line*.

arrangements with E.H. Allen, general manager of Educational, Goodrich took his megaphone to Culver City and got right on the job. He is scheduled to start a new Cameo Comedy in a few days, so the vacation was just a good idea gone wrong.

– ***Film Daily***, September 6, 1931

That's My Line is the first of five RKO-Pathé shorts that Roscoe would helm, and is part of their *Traveling Man Comedies*, a series built around the stage star Louis John Bartels. The shorts were designed to put Bartels in risqué situations with pretty wives and irate husbands. Forgotten today, Bartels was born in Illinois in 1895, and spent many years barnstorming around the country on stage. In 1924 he hit the big time as the star of the mega-hit comedy *The Show Off*. Running for over a year, all kinds of doors opened for Bartels, including movies. His film debut came in the 1927 feature *Broadway Nights*, and after one last Broadway show, *The Five O'Clock Girl*, he focused on movies and moved to Hollywood. In addition to supporting roles in features like *The Canary Murder Case* (1929), *The Floradora Girl* (1930), and *The Big Shot* (1931), he headlined in these *Traveling Man* shorts.

In *That's My Line* Bartels has support from Arbuckle and film comedy regulars like Glen Cavender, Al Thompson, Bert Young, and Gino Corrado, but his co-stars are Doris McMahon and Paul Hurst. A former *Follies* girl and singer, Doris McMahon made her movie

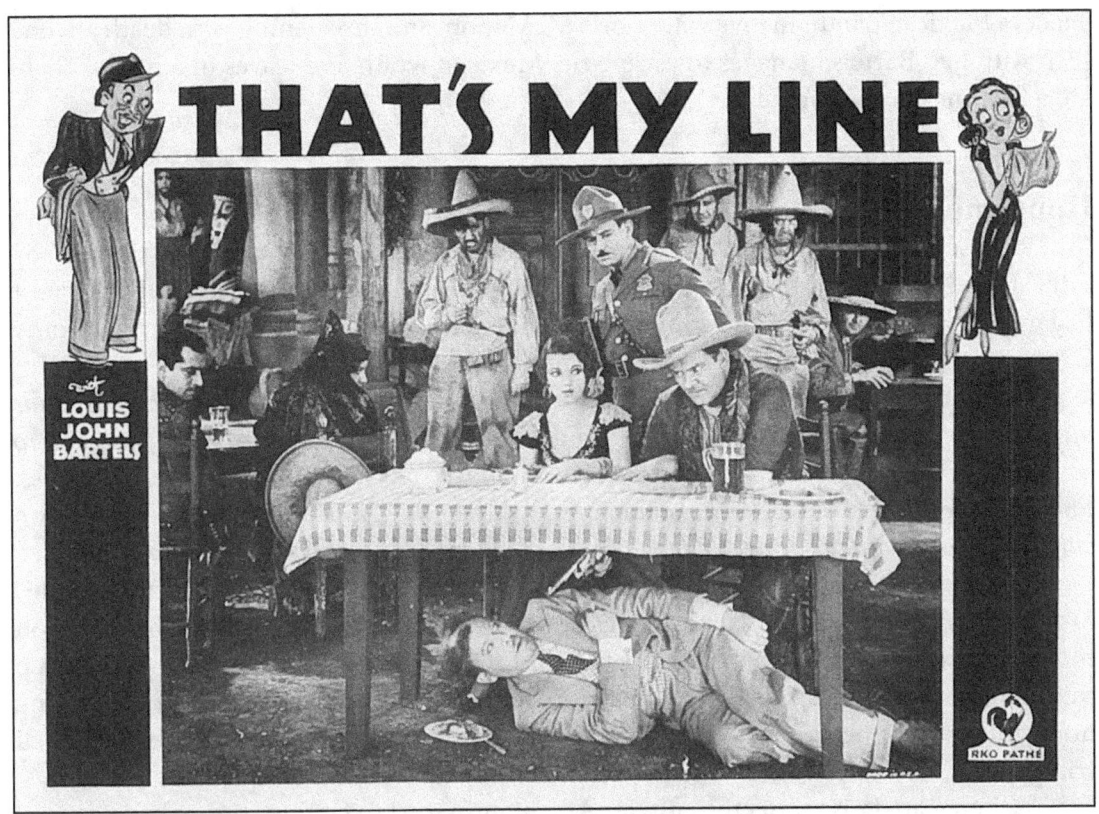

Bandido Paul Hurst draws a bead on Lewis John Bartels in *That's My Line* (1931).

debut in the New York-made two-reelers of George LeMaire. After shorts such as *Plumbers are Coming* and *Hard-Boiled Hampton* (both 1929) she moved to Hollywood. Small parts in a few features like *Madam Satan* (1930) and *Hips, Hips, Hooray!* (1934) followed, but she was mainly busy in shorts for Educational, RKO, Hal Roach, and Universal. *My Harem* (1930), *Pickin' a Winner* (1932), *Shrimps for a Day* (1934), and *Alibi Bye Bye* (1935) are some of her titles. She also appeared in the 1932 West Coast revue *Hang up Your Hat*, but in 1935 she married actor Hallam Cooley and retired from the screen.

Paul Hurst, who plays the Mexican bandit, was in films for forty years. Born in Traver, California in 1888, after moving to San Francisco he became involved in amateur theatricals, and entered movies in 1912 with the Kalem Company. Most of his early pictures were Kalem westerns, and as early as 1914 he began directing action films and oaters for Mutual and the National Film Corp. of America. While directing and writing he continued to play character roles, and during his long career appeared in big films such as *In Old Chicago* (1938), *They Drive by Night*, *The Westerner* (both 1940), and *The Ox-Bow Incident* (1943). His last picture was the 1953 John Ford-directed *The Sun Shines Bright*, but his best-remembered role is the Yankee scavenger whom Vivien Leigh shoots in the face in *Gone with the Wind* (1939).

Motion Picture Herald (June 6, 1931): "The first number of a new series, the Traveling Salesman comedies. Louis John Bartels plays the salesman, while Paul Hurst enacts a Mexican bandit in love with Doris McMahon, and threatening with death anyone seen with her. Bartels manages to escape the Mexican wrath and leaves in a hurry. There are a few lines in the comedy."

Honeymoon Trio

Released August 30, 1931. Cameo Comedies. Produced and distributed by Educational Pictures. Directed by William Goodrich. Story and dialogue by Ernest Pagano, Jack Townley, & Harrison Jacobs. One reel. Extant. With Al St John, Dorothy Granger, Walter Catlett, Bobby Burns, Al Thompson.

Dorothy and Al are just married. As they set off for their Honeymoon road trip, Al finds out that his former rival Walter is coming along to conduct the tour. Things go from bad to worse as Al is forced to ride in the rumble seat, and has to pay for numerous tickets and fines. Finally, in desperation Al locks the obnoxious Walter in the trunk and pushes the car over a cliff. Now alone with his bride she rewards Al with a punch in the jaw as the movie closes.

Honeymoon Trio is Roscoe's "road film"—a black comic version of *Detour* (1946) or *The Hitch-Hiker* (1953), as Al and Dorothy Granger head off on their honeymoon motor trip with former rival Walter Catlett in tow. Powerless to thwart or even shut up the obnoxious Catlett, Al is symbolically cuckolded as he's caught in a never-ending honeymoon from hell. Honeymoon Trio makes the first third of Roscoe's "domestic hell trilogy" that continues with *Bridge Wives* and ends with *Mother's Holiday*.

Walter Catlett is perfectly cast as Al's nightmare kibitzer—a megaphone-voiced blowhard who takes great relish in emasculating the hapless new husband. Specializing in fast-talking con men along the lines of Robert Woolsey and Lee Tracy, Catlett found a welcome berth in movies thanks to the arrival of sound. Born in San Francisco as the son

Walter Catlett and Dorothy Granger pucker up to Al St John's dismay in an ad for *Honeymoon Trio* (1931).

Walter Catlett (right) supports El Brendel (left) in the 1933 feature *Olsen's Big Moment*.

of a prosperous banker, Catlett was stage struck at an early age and began performing at thirteen in the kid's show *Brownies in Fairyland*. He also spent time as an usher, program boy, and water carrier on the orchestra floor before he became a full-time actor. After youthful work with Richard Mansfield and Fanny Davenport, and touring with Nance O'Neill, he eventually became a principal comedian, and like Roscoe, toured with Ferris Hartman's company.

His New York debut was in a 1911 revival of *The Prince of Pilsen*, which was followed by *Madame Sherry*, *So Long Letty*, and *Little Miss Simplicity*. Headlining in London in *Baby Bunting*, Catlett also toured the music halls in a girl act review titled *Keyhole Kameras*. He came back to New York to work for producer Florenz Ziegfeld opposite Marilyn Miller in the smash hit *Sally*, and continued on with more hits like *Lady Be Good* and *Rio Rita*. Having made a few sporadic appearances in silent films, Catlett really took up residence on screen in 1929. Never using elaborate make-ups, his main comic prop was a pair of horn rimmed glasses, which added an owlish air to his fast-talking con men.

He did a few shorts such as this and *One Quiet Night* (1931) for Roscoe, but was mostly seen in features. Some of the bigger titles he turned up in over the next thirty-six years include *A Tale of Two Cities* (1935), *Mr. Deeds Goes to Town* (1936), *Bringing Up Baby* (1938), *Yankee Doodle Dandy* (1942), *Ghost Catchers* (1944), and *Friendly Persuasion* (1956). Catlett isn't seen in Walt Disney's *Pinocchio* (1940), but voiced the character of T. Worthington Foulfellow and introduced the song *Hi-Diddle-Dee-Dee (An Actor's Life for*

Me). Considered a comedian's comedian, Catlett was even hired by Katharine Hepburn to coach her on the comedy bits in *Bringing Up Baby* (1938). In the 1950's he began appearing on television shows like *Make Room for Daddy* and *Walt Disney's Wonderful World of Color*, and his final role before his death in 1960 was playing New York governor Al Smith in Bob Hope's bio pic of Mayor Jimmy Walker, *Beau James* (1957).

Motion Picture Herald (September 26, 1931): "Amusing. Walter Catlett, Al St John and Dorothy Granger provide a number of laughs in this, which concerns the young bridegroom, who is shunted out of the wedding pictures and then into the rumble seat on the motor ride after the wedding. His anger rises and rises until, when the third party proposes that they sleep in the open, the bridegroom tosses him off the cliff. He tells his wife he is the boss and the finish laugh comes when she effectively swings her right against his jaw."

Photoplay (December 1931): "Two's company, but three's a crowd when it comes to a honeymoon! But sad-faced Al St John, as a much bullied bridegroom, finds it isn't always easy to lose a chaperone when he happens to be the bride's ex-suitor. Entertaining."

Up Pops the Duke

Released September 20, 1931. Mermaid Comedies. Produced and distributed by Educational Pictures. Directed by William Goodrich. Story and dialogue by Ernest Pagano & Jack Townley. Two reels. With George Chandler, Pauline Wagner, Helen Bolton, Bobby Burns.

When a Russian Grand Duke is unable to attend an important reception at his sweetheart's newly-rich aunt's house, George gets a false beard and disguises himself as the Duke to take his place. Unfortunately, Joe, a slick crook, has the same idea to try and rob the place. So two Grand Dukes end up at the party. While they are busy pulling off each other's whiskers the real Grand Duke arrives. The pandemonium reaches a climax when laughing gas is dispersed in the crowd.

Up Pops the Duke is Roscoe's last short with George Chandler, who went on to become a respected character actor and president of Screen Actors Guild. Around the edges of the film is Bobby Burns, former comedy star and longtime gag man, who turns up in a few of Roscoe's sound comedies. Burns came from vaudeville and musical comedy, where he played in big shows like *Babes in Toyland* and *The Wizard of Oz*. Onstage his forte was appearing in animal costumes (*Oz*'s the Cowardly Lion, etc.), but in 1911 he ended up in films with Lubin. Supporting Lubin's star comedienne Mae Hotley, Burns worked frequently with Walter Stull and George Reehem, and the trio moved on to their own split-reelers for Mutual's *Komic* and *Royal Comedies*. Eventually it thinned out to just Burns and Stull who became known as "Pokes and Jabs," and began making starring comedies for Sterling, Wizard, and finally *Vim Comedies*.

Vim was located in Jacksonville, Florida and was the most popular phase of "Pokes and Jabs" career, where they had the support of a young Oliver Hardy. In 1917 the team moved on to *Jaxon Comedies*, but went their separate ways by the end of the year. On his own Burns headlined for series like *Cuckoo Comedies* and was main support in Reelcraft's *Sun-Lite Comedies* and the Union Film Company's *Alt-Howell Comedies,* as well as frequently

George Chandler masquerades as a duke to help out his sweetheart in *Up Pops the Duke* (1931).

Imposter George Chandler and the real duke compare facial spinach in *Up Pops the Duke* (1931).

directing. Finally moving to Hollywood, Burns was a writer and character player in Jack White Comedies during the 1920s, and would do the same in Educational, Hal Roach, and Columbia shorts of the sound era. Burns also did uncredited bits in features, and was recently spotted quietly reading a book in the background of a library scene with Peggy Ann Garner in 1945's *A Tree Grows in Brooklyn*. Working until 1958, he died in Hollywood at age eighty-seven in 1966.

Motion Picture Times (October 20, 1931): "Your audience will go wild at the finish of this. Such hilarious laughter you've never heard before when some laughing gas is set loose."

Motion Picture Reviews (September 1931): "A slaps stick [*sic*] comedy sketched around a Russian title, false whiskers, player pianos, and laughing gas. However, no custard pies."

Beach Pajamas

Released September 28, 1931. Traveling Man Comedies. Produced and distributed by RKO Pathé Pictures. Direction, story, and adaptation by William Goodrich. Continuity by Henry R. Symonds, Hal Yates, Nick Barrows, E.A. Brown, & Charles Callahan. Photography by Dwight Warren. Supervised by Lew Lipton. Two reels. With Louis John Bartels, Addie

Addie McPhail (right) enjoying Louis John Bartel's trouble with Charlotte Mineau in *Beach Pajamas* (1931).

McPhail, Marion Douglass, Charlotte Mineau, Vernon, Dent, James Finlayson, Evelyn De Shields, George Billings, Charles Moore, Al Thompson, Claude Paton, Clarence Wertz, Bob Smith, Bert Young.

A traveling salesman gets in bad with the owner of a large department store when he flirt's with the man's fiancée. Desperate to get back in the owner's good graces so he can sell his goods, the salesman becomes an unknowing pawn in the fiancee's cousin's plot to keep her cousin out of a mistake of a marriage with the store owner. At the end the salesman remains on the outs with the store owner.

This is the second and last of the Arbuckle-directed *Traveling Man* comedies. Basically cleaned-up versions of the old traveling salesman jokes, star Louis John Bartels did four more entries with directors such as Edgar Kennedy and Ralph Ceder—*Selling Shorts* (1931), *Stop that Run*, *Blondes by Proxy*, and *A Perfect 36* (all 1932). The series came to an abrupt end when Bartels was found dead in his home from acute alcoholism in March of 1932. Roscoe also provided the story idea and screenplay for *Beach Pajamas*, and surrounded his star with a bevy of tried-and-true film comedy support. In addition to his regulars, wife Addie, Al Thompson, and Bert Young, the film is a showcase for three rocks of film comedy—Vernon Dent, James Finlayson, and Charlotte Mineau.

Louis John Bartels caught between Vernon Dent (left) and James Finlayson (right) in *Beach Pajamas* (1931).

A fixture in slapstick shorts from 1919 to the early 1950s, Vernon Dent was discovered singing in nightclubs by Hank Mann, and supported Mann in his 1919-1921 Arrow comedies. He soon moved on to his own starring series of *Folly Comedies* for the Pacific Film Company (see Appendix Two). After some freelancing Dent became ensconced at the Mack Sennett Studio where he supplied the comic gravity to counterpoint the antics of Harry Langdon and Billy Bevan. Always in demand, he did some late silent shorts teamed with Monty Collins, uncredited bits in silent and sound features, and many sound shorts for the likes of Educational, Sennett, and Vitaphone. In 1935 he joined the stock company at the Columbia Pictures shorts department where he stayed for over twenty years making screen life difficult for The Three Stooges, Andy Clyde, Vera Vague, Hugh Herbert, and El Brendel. His last appearance (via stock footage) was with the Stooges in *Guns A-Popping* (1957), and he died in 1963.

Probably the ultimate screen sourpuss, James Finlayson was born in Scotland and entered show business at an early age, touring the British Isles and music halls. Hooking up with the company of Sir Harry Lauder's brother Alec, Jimmy's big stage success was in Graham Moffat's hit play *Bunty Pulls the Strings*. This brought Fin to America, where it ran eighteen months on Broadway, and afterwards he toured vaudeville which brought him to California. Breaking into films in 1916 for L-Ko, Century, and Arrow, in 1919 he made his way to Mack Sennett Comedies, where in shorts like *Ma and Pa* (1922) he specialized in comic villains. In 1923 he moved to the Hal Roach lot and fulfilled a similar function for Snub Pollard and Stan Laurel.

Soon settling in at the top of the supporting comics heap, Finlayson was indispensable in the Roach comedies, particularly with Laurel & Hardy. He even found time to appear as support in some First National features like the hilarious *Ladies Night in a Turkish Bath* (1928). Sound revealed his Scottish burr, which only seemed to make him more irascible and blustery. Continuing in the Roach product, Fin also appeared in many RKO shorts and numerous features into the 1940s. He retired, due to ill health, a few years before his death in 1953.

The third comedy ace in the hole is tall and elegant Charlotte Mineau. After working for Selig, she joined the Essanay Company in Chicago in 1914 and appeared in their *George Ade Fables*, and *Sweedie* Comedies, plus had a featured role in Charlie Chaplin's first Essanay comedy *His New Job* (1915). Soon moving to the West Coast she joined Chaplin's Mutual Company and is seen in *The Floorwalker*, *The Vagabond* (both 1916), and *Easy Street* (1917) among others. From there she became a regular in Mack Sennett shorts until 1925, also working in the Sennett features *Love, Honor and Behave*, *Married Life* (both 1920), and *The Extra Girl* (1923). She appeared in a very different character role in Mary Pickford's *Sparrows* (1926), and became a member of the Hal Roach stock company in many shorts like *Baby Clothes*, *Should Husbands Pay?*, *Wise Guys Prefer Brunettes* (all 1926), and *Sugar Daddies* (1927). She later married character player Christian Frank, and her career wound down in the mid-1930s.

Motion Picture Herald (September 26, 1931): "One of the Traveling Man series, with Louis John Bartels in the title part of the traveling salesman who is in a tight scrape after trying to flirt with the fiancée of the owner of a large department store, whom he intended to sell. The girl friend of the fiancée cooks up the plan to save her cousin from an unwelcome marriage with the store owner. It succeeds, the salesman is the goat, and there is plenty of slapstick to prove it."

Take 'Em and Shake 'Em

Released September 28, 1931. Gay Girls Comedies. Produced and distributed by RKO Pathé Pictures. Directed by William Goodrich. Story by Beatrice Van. Continuity by Ralph Ceder. Photography by Ted McCord. Supervised by Lew Lipton. Two reels. With June MacCloy, Marion Shilling, Gertrude Short, Charles Judels, Arthur Hoyt, Frank Marlowe.

The girls have "borrowed" the apartment of a wealthy Frenchman who's away. When he comes back unexpectedly they're determined to stay, and hatch a scheme that one of them is sick. An operation is faked in the hospital for the benefit of the Frenchman.

Having directed two of their *Traveling Man Comedies*, Roscoe was also engaged by RKO to work on their *Gay Girls Comedies*. He would ultimately helm three out of the series of six. Starring June MacCloy, Marion Shilling and Gertrude Sweet, they weren't very far removed from his ongoing *Hollywood Girls* Shorts for Educational except that

This *Take 'Em and Shake 'Em* photo highlights the starring trio of RKO's *Gay Girls* series—June MacCloy, Marion Shilling, and Gertrude Short. Courtesy of Louis Despres.

this trio wasn't trying to break into the movies. Instead it was a borrowing from Warner Brother's *Gold Diggers* films, described in the RKO ads as "Just a trio of innocent gals out for ---- men's gold." *June First* (1931) was the initial entry quickly followed by *Take 'Em and Shake 'Em*. The shorts followed the common theme of the three girls trying to bilk or land some wealthy men, with a few songs provided by main star June MacCloy.

At 5' 7, 1/2 " the blonde MacCloy was statuesque, and her height and deep contralto voice set her apart from the usual Hollywood singing ingénue. Born in 1909, she began singing in vaudeville and made a name in New York in George White's 1928 Scandals doing an impression of star Harry Richman. Film offers soon followed, and she made her debut in *Reaching for the Moon* (1930) with Douglas Fairbanks Sr. She followed that up with the features *June Moon* and *The Big Gamble* (both 1931). Also appearing in many shorts, besides the six *Gay Girl* titles she was Eve to Leon Errol's Adam in *Good Morning, Eve* (1934), in addition to *Laugh It Off* and *Foolish Forties* (both 1932).

MacCloy returned to New York in 1932 to appear in the musical *Hot Cha* with Lupe Velez, Bert Lahr and Buddy Rogers, and spent the bulk of the 1930s singing with the orchestras of Ben Pollock, Jimmie Greer and Johnny Day. She did return to Hollywood in 1940 for *Glamour for Sale* and *Go West* which gave her some memorable scenes with Groucho Marx. Marrying California architect Neal Wendell Butler, she retired and raised a family. Living to the age of ninety-five, before her death in 2005 she told family friend Peter Mintun that "Fatty Arbuckle was a peach of a guy."

The story is by Beatrice Van, who had been the leading lady in four of Roscoe's earliest Sennett comedies (see 1913's *A Bandit*). Spending the 1920s as a busy screenwriter for features and shorts with Reginald Denny, Laura La Plante, Mr. and Mrs. Carter De Haven, and Mabel Normand, Van was nearing the end of her career, and after a few other projects retired in 1934. Working with her on the script was Ralph Ceder, a longtime film comedy veteran. Starting his career is 1917 as a writer for Triangle Comedies he moved over to the Hal Roach lot and began directing. Busy at Roach helming Snub Pollard, Stan Laurel, Paul Parrott, one-reelers, Ceder branched out to Fox Sunshine, Arrow, FBO, Paramount, Universal, Larry Darmour, and Weiss Brothers. After sound arrived he continued writing and eventually became a second unit director for Goldwyn, MGM, and Universal and shot chases for the W.C Fields features *The Bank Dick* (1940) and *Never Give a Sucker an Even Break* (1941). He remained in the industry until his death at fifty-four in 1951.

Gay Girls Comedies' headliner June MacCloy.

Motion Picture Herald (February 25, 1933): "Be sure you get an uncensored print of this, as you want the full effects to make it go over. Very good."

Film Daily (October 18, 1931): "Can't give this one very much, a Gay Girls comedy that crowds in a lot of mixed motives and incidents in a desperate attempt to create laughs. The comedy seems forced and strained to the cracking point at times. But it was due to no fault of the players. Charles Judels did wonders with his part of the foreigner who loaned his apartment to three stranded girls. The they try to frame him for a grand on his return, and the complications start by dragging in a hospital operation sequence that isn't a bit funny. June MacCloy, Marion Shilling and Gertrude Short are the girls who made the best of tough material."

That's My Meat

Released October 4, 1931. Cameo Comedies. Produced and distributed by Educational Pictures. Directed by William Goodrich. Story and dialogue by Ernest Pagano, Jack Townley, & Johnnie Grey. One reel. Extant. With Al St John, Lynton Brent.

Al is a butcher who is held up so regularly that he devises a scheme of pulling a lever when he is locked in the icebox which releases two bloodhounds. Burglars arrive again, but there's not enough money in the till to suit them so they start a sale, making Al attend the

Adrienne Dore, Al St John, and Lyton Brent in 1931's *That's My Meat*. Courtesy Cole Johnson.

customers while one of the crooks does some sidewalk spieling in front of the shop. Finally they get enough money and lock him up as he wishes. He pulls the lever and releases the hounds, but instead of going after the crooks they go after the meat in the shop and call in all their canine friends for a party.

Al's main nemesis in *That's My Meat* is Lynton Brent, who appeared in many of the Arbuckle-directed Educational shorts such as *Queenie of Hollywood*, *Idle Roomers* (both 1931), *Bridge Wives*, *Hollywood Luck*, and *Hollywood Lights* (all 1932). Generally nondescript, but with a bit of a hard-boiled quality, Brent had worked on stage in the 1920s and came to films with the arrival of sound. He was relegated to bit parts in features, but had larger roles in short subjects. Besides the Educational shorts he was also a regular in Columbia's two-reelers working many times with the Three Stooges as well as Harry Langdon and Charley Chase. In the 1940s he was also busy in western features, and kept working until 1950.

Variety (January 5, 1932): "Will serve as a comedy padder for any house."

One Quiet Night

Released October 25, 1931. Cameo Comedies. Produced and distributed by Educational Pictures. Directed by William Goodrich. Story and dialogue by Ernest

Walter Catlett reacting to things bumping in *One Quiet Night* (1931).
Courtesy Ben Model/Undercrank Productions.

Pagano, Jack Townley, & Harrison Jacobs. One reel. Extant. With Dorothy Granger, Walter Catlett, Richard Malaby, Al Thompson, Bobby Burns.

Father is so upset about the prospect of his daughter marrying Jimmy that he develops an ongoing case of the hiccups. His doctors recommend long-term rest and quiet, and take him to a deserted house to get the prescribed R & R. Right away odd things begin happening, and when father and his chauffeur have trouble sleeping in the middle of the night they wander the house. On their exploration they come across all kinds of strange things—a portrait whose eyes move, talking bear and lion skins, and a ghoulish guy in a long top hat walking around holding an equally long candle.

Daughter Dorothy is up wandering too and finally the scared trio is confronted by a ghostly apparition. When he falls down the stairs it turns out to be Jimmy in disguise. His idea was to scare the hiccups out of Father, but when it's found out that he had nothing to do with all the other scary events they run out of the house in a panic. At this point the doctor and staff come out of hiding and congratulate themselves on curing their patient, but the last shot has the group cowering outside, and are so scared by their experiences that they all start hiccupping.

With no time to spare Roscoe crams a lot of action into a brief ten minutes. Eschewing exposition, the plot rapidly jumps from—a) Father has the hiccups—b) the arrival at the spooky house—c) scary things happen—d) final denouement. A condensed version of horror comedies like *The Monster* (1925) and *The Cat and the Canary* (1927), Roscoe delivers the prescribed laughs and thrills, and along the way contributes nice touches of his own such as the talking animal skins, and the repeated image of groping hands coming into the film frame before the rest of the character enters the scene.

The expert cast supports the streamlined plot by skipping any frills and immediately getting down to the business at hand in each scene. Appearing as the somewhat maniacal doctor is Al Thompson, a long time silent comedy veteran who appeared in many of Roscoe's talking shorts. Thompson's early appearances were for the American Film Manufacturing Co, and he later became a member of Larry Semon's stock company where he was regularly blown up, dropped from high places, and covered with vats of goo in shorts like *The Suitor* (1920), *The Bell Hop* (1921) *Golf* (1922), and *Lightning Love* (1923).

In the mid-1920s he took up residence at Jack White comedies where he supported Al St John and Lloyd Hamilton and continued taking the brunt of physical punishment. During the sound era he turned up in all kinds of shorts, but by the late 1930s he was doing stunts in Columbia two-reelers and doubling for Andy Clyde. He also did tons of uncredited bits in features up to 1960.

Walter Catlett stars as father, working with Roscoe again after *Honeymoon Trio*. Also returning from that picture is Dorothy Granger, one of the busiest actresses to appear in sound shorts. Born in 1912, after winning a beauty contest at age thirteen she spent a few years in vaudeville and ended up in films in 1929. Almost immediately she began working for every shorts unit in California, and while she spent a lot of time at the Hal Roach lot she also was in demand with RKO, Educational, Paramount, and Columbia. Working with comics such as Laurel and Hardy, Charley Chase, W.C. Fields, Clark and McCullough, Andy Clyde, and Leon Errol, some of her more memorable appearances are in *Hog Wild* (1930), *The Pip from Pittsburgh* (1931), *The Chimp*, *The Dentist* (both 1932) and *The Gay Nighties* (1933).

Richard Malaby and Dorothy Granger plot against father on the left in *One Quiet Night* (1931), as Oscar Smith doesn't like hearing about ghosts on the right. Courtesy Ben Model/Undercrank Productions.

Working with Leon Errol for many years, Granger turned up in features like *When the Daltons Rode* (1940) and *The Women of the Town* (1943), and also worked on television shows such as the *Colgate Comedy Hour*, *I Married Joan*, *The Jack Benny Show*, and *Death Valley Days* before she retired in 1962. Because of her time spent at the Roach Studio she later became a regular guest at Sons of the Desert functions in the 1970s and 1980s, and she passed away in 1995.

An important part of the comedy is provided by Oscar Smith as Catlett's wary chauffeur. Like many of the black screen comics Smith had to work within the stereotypical roles available to him, but makes his character of the scared chauffeur genuinely funny. Smith first came to Hollywood as the valet of actor Wallace Reid, and after Reid's death set up a shoe-shine stand on the Paramount lot. At the same time he began appearing on camera. He can be spotted as chauffeurs in the Harold Lloyd films *The Freshman* (1925) and *For Heaven's Sake* (1926). A big break for the comic was a meaty role in the Richard Dix feature *Man Power* (1927). Playing Dix's sidekick Ptomain brought Smith a lot of attention and kept him busy onscreen. Making a smooth jump to sound in Paramount's *The Canary Murder Case* (1929), the actor maintained his boot blacking stand between pictures (like fellow character player Angelo Rossitto who kept a newspaper stand), playing train porters, valets, and soldiers in shorts and features like *Thunderbolt* (1929), *The Old Fashioned Way*, *Broadway Bill* (both 1934), *This Gun for Hire* (1942), and *Double Indemnity* (1944). Smith retired from the screen in 1944 and died in 1956.

Motion Picture Reviews (September 1931): "An inconsequential picture making a banal and feeble effort to be amusing."

Queenie of Hollywood

Released November 8, 1931. Ideal Comedies. Produced and distributed by Educational Pictures. Directed by William Goodrich. Story and dialogue by Ernest Pagano & Jack Townley. Two reels. With Virginia Brooks, Rita Flynn, Jeanne Farrin, Queenie the dog.

Lobby card for *Queenie of Hollywood* (1931).

The Hollywood girls are flat broke with no immediate prospects for landing jobs at the studios. They decide to take temporary jobs as chambermaids at a posh hotel. Through a telegram mix-up concerning Queenie, the pet pup of one of the girls, the hotel management thinks they are part of a royal family traveling incognito. So they set the girls up in a swell suite, and shower them with expensive service. Of course the hotel's mistake doesn't last forever, and the girls are finally found out.

This is the fourth example of the girls plugging away in Hollywood without getting any closer to success. The Queenie of the title is another in the long line of Roscoe's movie dogs along with Luke, Pete the Pup in *Dynamite Doggie* (1925), and others.

Virginia Brooks joined the trio with the second short, *Crashing Hollywood* (1931), and would finally end up appearing in five out of the six entries. She also worked for Roscoe as George Chandler's love interest in *The Back Page* (1931). Born in Twin Falls, Idaho, after her family moved to San Francisco she began acting at the Pasadena Playhouse, and moved on to vaudeville and shows like *Follow Thru*, *Hi There*, and *The Desert Song*. Movies naturally followed, and her first was *Crashing Hollywood*. Her career was short-lived and basically consisted of the *Hollywood Girls* series. Following 1932's *Hollywood Lights* she left the screen.

Also on hand is Jeanne Farrin. Not only is she a new girl in the series, but this is her only known picture.

Film Daily (October 25, 1931): "Unusual Comedy. An Ideal Comedy featuring Rita Flynn, Virginia Brooks and Jeanne Farrin. This one has more solid plot than the average comedy short, and works out into a highly amusing and very intelligent offering.

"Here is a 'different' comedy done with a lot of class."

National Board of Review (November 1931): "Three girls and a dog in Hollywood, and how Queenie, the dog, helped the girls to prosperity. Amusing."

Photoplay (January 1932): "Queenie, a small bull dog, is the cause of the hilarity in this comedy. Queenie herself isn't funny but her name gives three prospective hotel chambermaids a chance to masquerade as royalty. Entertaining."

Once a Hero

Released November 22, 1931. Mermaid Comedies. Produced and distributed by Educational Pictures. Directed by William Goodrich. Story and dialogue by Ernest Pagano & Jack Townley. Two reels. With Emerson Treacy, Frances Dean, Jack Shutta.

A bank teller unwittingly foils a robbery on the day before his wedding. Due to a mix-up the teller ends up in a jail cell with the crook where they are handcuffed together. The

Emerson Treacy (middle) and Jack Shutta (right) try to slip out while under the watchful eye of officer Pat Harmon in *Once a Hero* (1931).

crook doesn't recognize the clerk, but having sworn vengeance on the person responsible for his capture he escapes and drags the bank teller with him. Eventually the yegg realizes that his intended victim is actually handcuffed to him, but by this time the teller is able to subdue him and become a hero.

Abrasive Jack Shutta is back from *Windy Riley Goes Hollywood* as the inept crook, and Frances Dean (Betty Grable) makes her second appearance of three in an Arbuckle short as the hero's bride-to-be. Roscoe's lead in *Once a Hero* is Emerson Treacy, a stage and vaudeville performer who had recently made his film debut. Born in 1900, he came to prominence in the late 1920s as part of The Henry Duffy Players, where he was teamed with comedienne Gay Seabrook in a variation on George Burns and Gracie Allen—with Seabrook as the "dizzy dame" and Treacy as the frustrated and slow-burning husband or boyfriend. Much of their screen time in the 1930s was spent together, and they're best-remembered for playing Spanky McFarland's parents in the *Our Gang* shorts *Bedtime Worries* and *Wild Poses* (both 1933). The pair was also popular on the radio.

On his own Treacy had started appearing in shorts for Pathé in 1930, and had bits in features like *The Sky Raiders* (1931), *Two Alone* (1934), and *California Straight Ahead* (1935). He and Gay Seabrook stopped performing together at the end of the 1930s, and Treacy was offscreen for almost all of the 1940s. Coming back as a character player in 1949's *Adam's Rib*, he contributed funny little bits or more serious portrayals in movies and television shows such as *The Prowler* (1951), *I Led 3 Lives* (1953), *A Star is Born* (1954), *Alfred Hitchcock Presents* (1956), and *The Dark at the Top of the Stairs* (1960) until 1962.

Film Daily (November 22, 1931): "Peppy—A Mermaid Comedy with Emerson Treacy, Jack Shaw [sic] and Frances Dean. The hero is a bank clerk who captures a thief about to rob the bank where he is the paying teller. The next day is his wedding. He gets mixed-up in the cell with the robber, and handcuffed together, the yegg escapes, bent on wrecking vengeance on the bank clerk who caused his arrest, not realizing his intended victim is the one handcuffed to him. Works out in some swift comedy action that should please."

Motion Picture Herald (December 5, 1931): "Good—A bank cashier who inadvertently captures a robber becomes a hero."

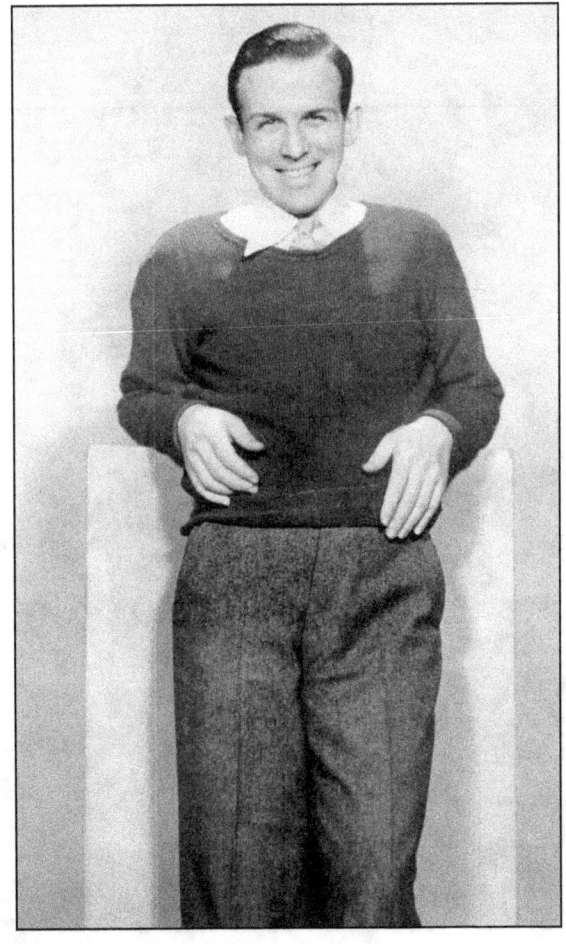

Character study of a casual Emerson Treacy.

The Tamale Vendor

Released November 26, 1931. Ideal Comedies. Produced and distributed by Educational Pictures. Directed by William Goodrich. Story and dialogue by Ernest Pagano & Jack Townley. Two reels. Extant. With Tom Patricola, Charles Judels, Al Thompson, Margaret Breen, Chiquita De Montez, Charles Dorety.

Tom and his pal are making their way through Mexico doing an instrumental double act. They rescue a señorita who would rather commit suicide than marry the middle-aged swain that her wealthy father has picked for her. Tom falls for her, and decides to help her out of her dilemma. Back at the hacienda Father and the heavy-set caballero are resistant to Tom's presence, and the two sides end up battling it out in a kitchen with food such as hot tamales and vegetables for ammunition. Tom wins the battle and the girl.

Tom Patricola is back working with Roscoe in another combination of comedy, singing, and dancing south of the border. One of his numbers in this short is the song *In a Little Spanish Town*, which is punctuated by crockery landing on Patricola's head as he performs the tune on his ukulele. This routine, which appears to have originated in vaudeville, would be borrowed by Buster Keaton for his British-made feature *The Invader* (a.k.a. *An Old Spanish Custom*, 1936) and it's two-reel remake *The Pest from the West* (1939).

Tom Patricola demonstrates some of his eccentric musical prowess in *The Tamale Vendor* (1931).

Besides getting in his usual line of eccentric musical interludes with remarkable tap dancing, the star has a great comedy foil in Charles Judels. Born in Amsterdam in 1881, Judels came to the United States when young and was soon involved in show business—touring around assisting magicians and appearing in burlesque. His first Broadway show was 1902's *A Trip to Buffalo*, and right from the start he specialized in comically excitable Europeans, just as he would do in the movies. Busy in shows such as *The Knickerbocker Girl*, *Flo-Flo*, *Old Dutch*, *The Slim Princess*, *Ziegfeld Follies of 1912*, *Twins Beds*, and *Mary*, he supported big names like Lew Fields, Elsie Janis, Madge Kennedy, Leon Errol, Anna Held, and even Marie Dressler in a West Coast tour of *The Merry Gambol*. In 1925 he began directing musicals and comedies, which included *Gay Paree*, *The Merry World*, *A Night in Paris*, and *Artists and Models*.

His stage fame led to some early appearances in New York-made films like *Old Dutch*, *The Commuters* (both 1915), and *Little Old New York* (1923), but the arrival of sound opened the floodgates. He

Stage character portrait of Charles Judels. Billy Rose Theater Division, the New York Public Library for the Performing Arts.

was in huge demand, and would remain so until 1949. During that time he was a comedy foil in shorts and features, almost always with a variation of some kind of blustery accent, in films that included *50 Million Frenchmen* (1931), *The Great Ziegfeld* (1936), *Swiss Miss* (1938), *Down Argentine Way* (1940), *The Chocolate Soldier* (1941), and *Samson and Delilah* (1949). Roscoe seemed to be very fond of him, and used him in five shorts—*Take 'Em and Shake 'Em*, *The Tamale Vendor* (both 1931), *Moonlight and Cactus* (1932), *Close Relations*, and *Tomalio* (both 1933). Today Judel's best-remembered performance is as the voice of Stromboli in Walt Disney's *Pinocchio* (1940), and he passed away in San Francisco in 1969.

Film Daily (August 28, 1931): "Take 'The Tamale Vendor'….with Tom Patricola puttin' over the Mexican atmosphere with a New Slant……a beaucoup combination of slapstick and the finished art of a trained trouper…..who strums a guitar and shakes his hoofs as only Tommy can do those two things……and all an Intrinsic Part of the story…….not just thrown in for a buildup for a piece of boloney that couldn't hang together without it….. which seems to be the general formula with some short comedy producers……and that mugg Charlie Judels….supporting Tom with his eccentric Mexican characterization……. deserves a series all to himself…..he's that good."

Film Daily (August 30, 1931): "Swell laugh number with Tom Patricola going over strong with his eccentric comedy guitar playing and fast stepping in a Mexican hacienda setting. One of the snappiest and funniest comedies of the season. It is an expert mixture of slapstick with fine characterization and classy artistry by this new comedy team. Can't Miss."

Idle Roomers

Released November 29, 1931. A Cameo Comedy. Produced and distributed by Educational Pictures. Directed by William Goodrich. Story & dialogue by Ernest Pagano & Jack Townley. One reel. Extant: LOC. With Frank Malino, Alfred Malino, Fern Emmett, George Davis, Al Thompson, Harriet Powell, Henry Cornelia, William McCall, Lynton Brent.

Two out-of-work vaudeville acrobats drive their landlady crazy by constantly practicing their stunts in their room. Sure that they are nuts, she sends for two psychologists to examine them. When the doctors arrive they humor the pair by learning the stunts. The booking agents that the acrobats were practicing for show up, and when they see the psychologists doing the stunts they promptly sign them up for a tour, while the crazy house attendants drag off the acrobats.

Fern Emmett spies on Frank and Alfred Malino practicing their acrobatics ad nauseum in 1931's *Idle Roomers*. Courtesy Robert Arkus.

Idle Roomers is a breezy little item about a pair of out of work vaudeville acrobats that are played by Frank and Alfred Malino, who had a long-time family act with their brothers Van and Mike. Besides little bits by Al Thompson, William McCall, and Lynton Brent, the two main supporting players are the Arbuckle favorites George Davis and Fern Emmett. Davis of course had been working for Roscoe since the Reel Comedy shorts in 1924, and was still busy in sound films. Although his roles were much smaller than the silent days, he continued working until 1963 and died in 1965. Fern Emmett was a new recruit to Roscoe's rep company, where she specialized in irritable landladies, town gossips, and put-upon wives (see *Mother's Holiday*).

Motion Picture Herald (November 7, 1931): "Two professional acrobats practice their act before an appointment with a booking agent. It is a fine piece of nonsense and good entertainment."

Film Daily (October 18, 1931): "Above Average—Snappy one-reeler Cameo comedy, featuring Frank and Alfred Malino in a fast acrobatic mixup. The boarding house landlady thinks the acrobats are a couple of nuts, and after the doctors arrive and start doing acrobatics to humor the supposed goofs, in walks the booking agent and signs the doctors for the big time. This one-reeler has more gags and speed than a lot of two-reelers."

Smart Work

Released December 27, 1931. Cameo Comedies. Produced and distributed by Educational Pictures. Directed by William Goodrich. Story and dialogue by Ernest Pagano & Jack Townley. Two reels. Extant: LOC. With Billy Dooley, Addie McPhail, Louise Glover, Mary Dunn, Lynton Brent, Charles Dorety.

Billy is a jealous hubby, who as a detective takes a case from a suspicious wife to trail her husband with another woman. The latter turns out to be Billy's wife who is just innocently buying a car from the man, who is a car salesman, to give to Billy as a birthday present. Thinking the man has given her the car for being his girlfriend, Billy smashes it to pieces. Just as he's finished with the destruction his wife appears and explains that the auto was for his birthday.

Smart Work was a return for silent comedian Billy Dooley who had spent the 1920's as part of producer Al Christie's stable of stars. From 1925 to 1929 Dooley's trademark was a sailor suit, and he was billed as Christie's "Goofy Gob" in shorts such as *A Briny Boob* (1926), *Sailor Beware* (1927), and *The Dizzy Diver* (1928). Although he came from vaudeville where he performed bicycle tricks and had double acts with Eddie Nelson and sexy Frances Lee, he left films with the arrival of sound, but the October 25, 1931 *Film Daily* announced:

> Billy Dooley (the Goofy Gob) interrupted his vaudeville engagements long enough to take another fling at pictures and has just made "Smart Work," an Educational-Cameo Comedy under direction of William Goodrich at the Educational Studios. He is now on another 42-week tour as the star of a Fanchon and Marco unit.

Detective Billy Dooley getting the details on a hot case in *Smart Work* (1931). Courtesy the Library of Congress.

Billy Dooley's neighbors have a ringside seat for his automotive revenge in *Smart Work* (1931). Courtesy the Library of Congress.

Dooley does a very nice job in the short, appearing very comfortable in sound, and looking like he shouldn't have any problem headlining in shorts again. Sadly this didn't resuscitate his starring career, and he was relegated to uncredited background work in features like *The Cat's Paw* (1934), *Little Lord Fauntleroy* (1936), and *A Star is Born* (1937) until his early death from a heart attack in 1938.

Photoplay (March 1932): "A very amusing marital quadrangle makes the plot of this very funny comedy. A lawyer unwittingly shadows the husband of a client to his own doorstep and wife! Billy Dooley and Addie McPhail head the cast."

Film Daily (December 20, 1931): "A good one reel Cameo comedy, featuring the return of Billy Dooley, the one-time goofy gob."

Motion Picture Herald (December 31, 1932): "A very good comedy."

Moonlight and Cactus

Released January 10, 1932. Ideal Comedies. Produced and distributed by Educational Pictures. Directed by William Goodrich. Story and dialogue by Ernest Pagano & Jack Townley. Two reels. With Tom Patricola, Louise Lorraine, Charles Judels, Renee Borden, Olive Borden, Charles Dorety.

Tom is the co-proprietor of a traveling medicine show down where the cactus grows and Romeos sing serenades in the moonlight. He falls for a young beauty, but finds that she's already in love with somebody else.

Tom Patricola's third and final film with Roscoe again has a south of the border setting. For the comedy element he's reteamed with Charles Judels, and Charles Dorety is mixed in for good measure. A very small part is played by Olive Borden, who had worked her way up from bit parts in comedy shorts to become a star at Fox in features like *Fig Leaves*, *Three Bad Men* (both 1926), and *The Monkey Talks* (1927). Sadly she was now working her way back down due to a falling out with Fox and a difficult and erratic personality. Her last film would be the 1934 Florida-made shoe-string production *Chloe, Love is Calling You*, and she would die in a skid row mission at age forty in 1947.

Tom's love interest is pretty brunette Louise Lorraine, a silent name who was trying to hang on in talkies. Having started her career as

Moonlight and Cactus (1932) star Tom Patricola.

an extra, she soon ended up in shorts for Century Comedies with Harry Sweet, Charles Dorety, and Baby Peggy such as *The Dog Doctor*, *A Bunch of Kisses* (both 1921), and *Sweetie* (1923). She was also in many western shorts and features, some with her first husband Art Accord, and later appeared in the comedy features *Exit Smiling*, (1926), *Rookies*, and *Legionnaires in Paris* (both 1927). After finishing the silent era as leading lady for comic Johnny Hines in *Chinatown Charlie* and *The Wright Idea* (both 1928), her sound films were this short and westerns before she retired in 1932.

Motion Picture Herald (December 26, 1931): "Good. Tom Patricola, playing the comedy lead, is sufficiently amusing in the manner in which he puts his material across to have the patrons indulging in more than a few hearty laughs and numerous surreptitious giggles. William Goodrich directed. A laugh-provoking comedy."

Keep Laughing

Released January 24, 1932. Mermaid Comedies. Produced and distributed by Educational Pictures. Directed by William Goodrich. Story and dialogue by Ernest Pagano & Jack Townley. Two reels. With Monty Collins, Addie McPhail, Bryant Washburn, Phyllis

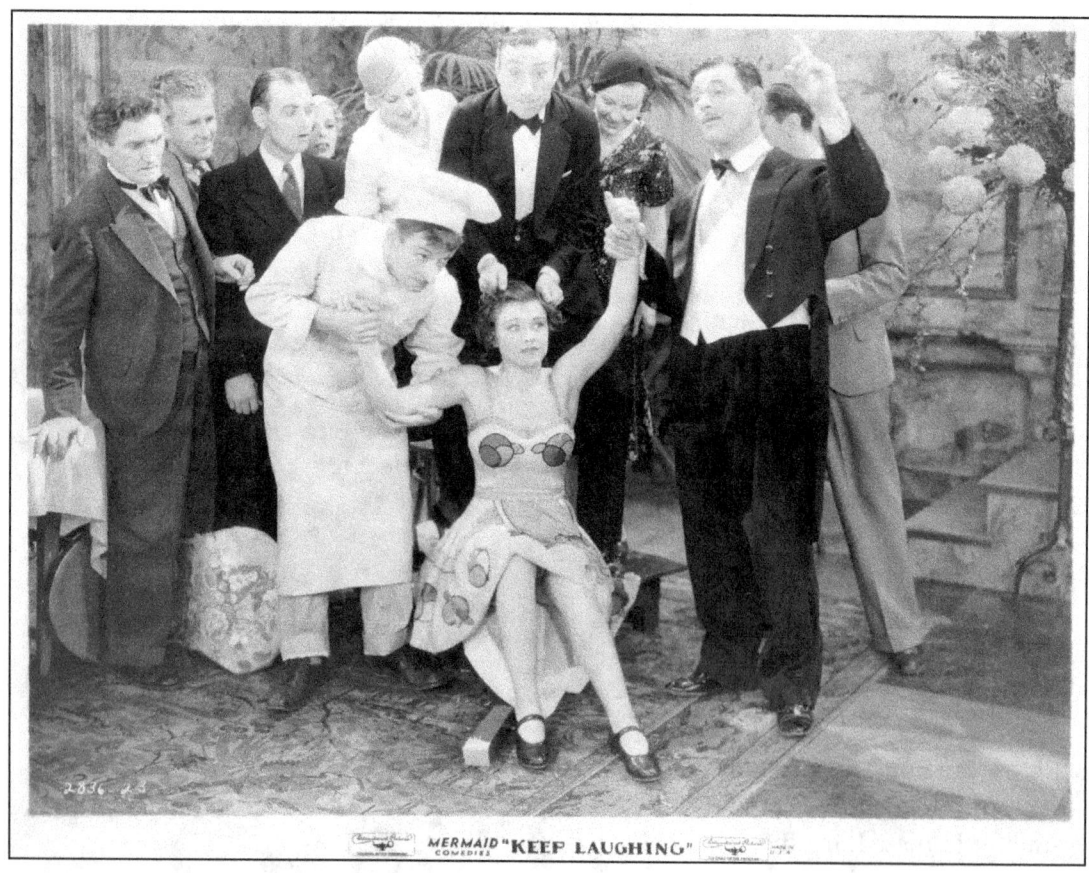

Monty Collins, George Davis, and Jack Shaw help the lady up as Bobby Burns and Harry Bowen observe from the left in *Keep Laughing* (1932). Courtesy Richard Finegan.

Crane, Jack Shaw, Dorothy Granger, Richard Malaby, George Davis, Hotel Roosevelt Blossom Room Orchestra.

Two ladies own a defunct nightclub and have an opportunity to sell it to some unsuspecting buyers, so to make the club look like a hotspot they plan a big floor show and hire a houseful of patrons. Unfortunately on the big night the cook, hat-check girl, and other members of the wait staff get into a battle which spills over into the show, and puts the kibosh on the hoped-for sale.

Keep Laughing is the first of three films Roscoe directed with the overlooked Monty Collins (sometimes Monte)—a comic who started in silents and kept busy until the late 1940s. This Monty is actually Monty Collins Jr., and the son of an old vaudevillian (Monty Sr.) who as previously mentioned had worked for Roscoe and Buster Keaton in the teens and twenties (see 1918's *Back Stage*).

Long overlooked comedy star Monty Collins.

Young Monty had his own stage background and began turning up in films in the mid-1920s. In 1927 Jack White began starring him in one-reel Cameo Comedies, and the next year promoted him to two-reelers where he was sometimes teamed with Vernon Dent. Usually cast as a henpecked husband, Collins was nervous and skinny with a long nose, bulging Adam's apple, and bowl-cut bangs. Continuing in sound films for Educational, he became a mainstay at the Columbia Pictures shorts department, where in the 1930s and 40s he supported Andy Clyde, Buster Keaton, Harry Langdon, and The Three Stooges (even in drag as their mother). His last credit, before his death from a heart attack in 1951, was as gagman on Laurel & Hardy's *Atoll K* (1950).

One reviewer gave Bryant Washburn a welcome back as an old movie friend, and another noted yet another use of Roscoe's favorite bottomless kitchen pot routine, saying "The best gag is a vat in the nightclub kitchen from which the chef draws "everything but the kitchen stove."

Film Daily (February 21, 1932): "Lively—A Mermaid Comedy, being the story of two dames who are trying to sell their nite club to a couple of prospects. But when the prospects drop in to look the place over, several numbers are injected into the floor show that were not on the bill. A riot and free-for-all follows, and the prospects walk out. Monty Collins as the cook, and Addie McPhail as the check gal, are responsible for the improvised numbers that bust up the show. A lively number with the laughs on the slapstick order."

Motion Picture Herald (February 20, 1932): "The frank slapstick that permeates this Mermaid comedy reaches a high point in a burlesque night club dance which would make any two-reeler well worth while, no matter what the qualifications of the remainder of the picture. The bored strong man at times frantically at his dainty partner to swing her around his waist and over and under him, then at the crucial moment forgets all about her, and there is a resounding thump as she plops to the floor. The hired help provide an unexpected after-dinner show, but their final free-for-all extinguishes the last hope of selling the restaurant."

Modern Screen (May 2, 1932): "Two reel comedy-slapstick in a night club. Very funny. Good—great for children."

Anybody's Goat

Released January 24, 1932. Cameo Comedies. Produced and distributed by Educational Pictures. Directed by William Goodrich. Story and dialogue by Ernest Pagano & Jack Townley. One reel. Extant: LOC. With Monty Collins, Fern Emmett, Philo McCullough, Lynton Brent, Richard Bishop, Lew Kelly.

A trio of crooks, passing through a small town, try to bilk a country girl with a bankroll by selling her a goat which they say has swallowed a large purse of money. Her station agent

Monty Collins and Fern Emmett at the train station of *Anybody's Goat* (1932).
Courtesy the Library of Congress.

friend discovers the truth, and saves the day by outwitting the crooks at their own game.

Monty Collins and Arbuckle-favorite Fern Emmett do the heavy comedy lifting in this short, where the action takes place in a small train station way out in the sticks. The con man leader of the three crooks is played by Philo McCullough, a performer with a fifty-seven-year-long film career. A local boy, raised in Los Angeles, McCullough entered pictures with the Selig Company in 1912. Early on he cornered the market on caddish and villainous second leads, and worked for Mutual, Kalem, and Balboa in the teens. Eventually graduating to features, he kept busy all through the 1920s, but didn't appear in any really outstanding films.

Lilac Time (1928) may have been the biggest, and in the early 1930s McCullough continued playing questionable characters in releases like *The Spy Spider* (1931) and *Tarzan the Fearless* (1933). Although he soon ended up in uncredited bit roles, McCullough remained extremely prolific and eventually moved to television programs like *Perry Mason*, *The Man from U.N.C.L.E.*, *The Monkees*, and *Here Comes the Brides* until 1969. He was eighty-seven when he died in 1981.

Motion Picture Herald (March 5, 1932): "This story centers on the activities of a trio of robbers who use a goat to further their crooked schemes. Amusing for all ages."

Variety (January 19, 1932): "The usual number of doors are slammed and prattfalls taken."

Motion Picture Herald (January 28, 1933): "Good comedy."

Bridge Wives

Released February 21, 1932. Cameo Comedies. Produced and distributed by Educational Pictures. Directed by William Goodrich. Story and dialogue by Ernest Pagano & Jack Townley. One reel. Extant. With Al St John, Fern Emmett, Billy Bletcher, Julia Griffith, Lynton Brent, Bert Young, Joe Young.

It's a tense moment at the end of a three-month contract bridge tournament. The press is there for the climax, and a radio commentator is providing a blow-by-blow account of the big finish. To follow the human interest element of the story a reporter interviews the husband of one of the players, and finds him near the breaking point having fended for himself for so long. At the sound of the gun the game is over but the judges find that it's a tie and that the game has to continue for another three months. The husband goes absolutely berserk with this announcement, and grabbing a handy fireplace poker chases everyone out of his house.

Later husband and wife are alone at home and since she can't play in the continuing tournament she decides to listen to it on the radio. Al refuses to listen to it, and the pair battle over control of the radio. Eventually the radio is thrown through the wall and Al, completely unhinged, decides to "kill it" and bury it in the yard. Fern, trying to stop him, finds that he's more than willing to make room for her in the grave as well, and in her horror runs off to get the police. Al, having buried the radio, goes in the kitchen, but when he turns on the water finds that he had put the radio next to the water pipe, and when he turns on the tap he hears the bridge broadcast. This sends him completely mad, and finding his wife playing bridge with the police in the living room, he flees from the house and takes refuge down an open manhole.

Al St John reaches the end of his rope in *Bridge Wives* (1932). Courtesy Robert S. Birchard.

An excellent example of Roscoe's sardonic take on marriage and relationships, *Bridge Wives* is also a clever spoof of the rage for contract bridge that was sweeping the country. Al St. John is literally driven mad having to fend for himself while his wife is in a three month bridge tournament. Outside of the opening tournament scenes, the short is a two-reel variation of Jean Paul Sartre's *No Exit* with Al and Fern Emmett giving tour-de-force performances locked into their domestic battleground. Al gets completely demented and Fern has good reason to fear for her life. This was Al's last Educational with Roscoe, and ends the group of films on a very high note.

In the opening tournament sequence Roscoe makes great use of crack character players such as Lynton Brent, Bert Young, and especially Billy Bletcher and Julia Griffith. Billy Bletcher was a ubiquitous face in silent and sound comedy—a fifty-year film veteran who started his career in 1915 and went on through to commercials in the 1970s. His first films were in the New York-made Wizard Comedies of Bobby Burns and Walter Stull, and Bletcher joined them in Jacksonville Florida in their ensuing shorts for Vim. He was also busy in Vim's *Plump and Runt Comedies* with Oliver Hardy and Billy Ruge, but soon headed back north to work for Vitagraph in one-reelers like *Hash and Havoc* and *Jane's Bashful Hero* (both 1916). In 1919 and 1920, under the name Billy Fletcher, he headlined opposite Violet Joy (aka Duane Thompson) in a series of *Spotlight Comedies* for producer

Fern Emmett is warned by hubby Al St John not to touch the radio dial in *Bridge Wives* (1932). Courtesy Robert S. Birchard.

Morris Schlank. He also did some *Universal Star Comedies* as Fletcher, but soon returned to Bletcher.

In the 1920s he was support in all kinds of films, but worked prolifically in Christie Comedies with Bobby Vernon, Dorothy Devore, and Neal Burns in shorts such as *Safe and Sane* (1923), *Call the Wagon*, and *Getting Gertie's Goat* (both 1924). Although only around five foot, sound revealed Bletcher's immensely deep voice, and in addition to features and shorts for Hal Roach he was in demand as a voice performer for Disney (as the Big Bad Wolf and Black Pete) and other cartoon producers. Never really retiring Billy worked into the 1970s, with some of his later work including playing Chief of the Keystone Cops in a memorable Shasta Root Beer commercial.

Fern Emmet's main bridge-playing rival is Julia Griffith, a tall, middle-aged blonde who specialized in dowagers in 1920s and early 1930s Mack Sennett comedies. Turning up as wedding guests, party guests, train passengers, or audience members, she came in handy for crowd scenes and can be seen in titles like *Don't Tell Dad* (1925), *A Blonde's Revenge* (1926), *Smith's Cousin* (1927) and *Love at First Flight* (1928). She can also be spotted in Roach and Educational shorts such as *Should Men Walk Home?* (1927) and *Honky Donkey* (1934), plus had more substantial roles in Weiss Brothers Art Class Comedies such as *Better*

Behave (1927) with Poodles Hanneford and Ben Turpin's *The Cockeyed Family* (1928). Besides shorts, she also appeared in features like *A One Man Game* (1927), *Vagabond Lady* (1935), and *Hellzapoppin'* (1941) through 1943.

Photoplay (May, 1932): "The famous Culbertson-Lenz bridge tournament is taken for a terrific ride in this hilarious comedy. Fern Emmett, the leading contestant in an all-female tournament, which has been going on for three months, has to retire from play because her husband goes bridge mad."

Film Daily (February 21, 1932): "Snappy Gags. A very good burlesque on the bridge craze, with Al St John as the distracted husband driven goofy by his bridge-crazed wife. She is a contestant in a marathon bridge contest held in his home. He finally throws the whole gang out, and proceeds to dig a grave for the radio which is still sending him news of the contest going on some place else. The windup is funny, for when he attempts to commit suicide to get away from it all, he finds he has to use a bridge. For a one-reeler, this crowds more material than a lot of two-reel comedies."

Frances Dean (a.k.a Betty Grable, top), Virginia Brooks (middle), and Rita Flynn (bottom) make up the trio of movie star wanna-bees in 1932's *Hollywood Luck*.

Hollywood Luck

Released March 13, 1932. Ideal Comedies. Produced and distributed by Educational Pictures. Directed by William Goodrich. Story and dialogue by Ernest Pagano & Jack Townley. Two reels. Extant. With Virginia Brooks, Addie McPhail, Rita Flynn, Fern Emmett, Frances Dean, Clarence Nordstrom, Lynton Brent, Dennis O'Donnell, Glen Cavender.

Still trying to crash into the studios, the girls try to get themselves regular positions in front of the camera by financing a newcomer who through dumb luck accomplishes more than they have been able to do in months. She gets herself married to a cowboy hero and becomes his leading lady.

This is the penultimate of the *Hollywood Girls* shorts, and had the biggest star to ever appear in any of Roscoe's Educational films. Frances Dean took as over one of the main trio in this episode. Previously she had had a bit in *Crashing Hollywood* (1931) and was Emerson Tracey's love interest in *Once a Hero* (1931). Better known today as Betty Grable, at the time the young actress was only fifteen years old, and was working her way up to stardom. Born in St. Louis, Missouri in 1916, she was singing and dancing in her home state under the watchful eye of her mother, and in 1929, when Betty was only thirteen, the pair moved to Hollywood to get her into the movies.

Chorus parts in musicals like *Happy Days* (1929) and *Let's Go Places* (1930) led to her becoming a Goldwyn Girl. Working in Goldwyn's big musicals like *Whoopee!* (1930), and *Palmy Days* (1931), she began moonlighting with roles in lower-budgeted comedy shorts under the name Frances Dean. Besides the shorts for Roscoe she also did bits in Mack Sennett comedies like *Ex-Sweeties* (1931) and *The Flirty Sleepwalker* (1932). Slowly but surely appearances in *The Gay Divorcee* (1934), and *College Swing* (1938), and a marriage to former child star Jackie Coogan, got her noticed.

After a solid turn on Broadway in the hit musical *DuBarry Was a Lady* she returned to Hollywood and started a string of hit musicals for 20th Century-Fox that included *Down Argentine Way* (1940), *Moon over Miami* (1941), *Springtime in the Rockies* (1942), and many more. Besides being the most famous G.I. pin-up during World War II, Ms. Grable continued making popular movies until 1955. Afterward she kept busy in nightclubs and on Broadway, but died young at fifty-six of lung cancer in 1973.

Over twenty of Roscoe's Educational Shorts were written by the team of Ernest Pagano and Jack Townley. Pagano was head writer for the studio and had been in vaudeville before working in Hollywood. He began contributing material in 1927, and some of his early films included *For Ladies Only* (1927), *The Matinee Idol* (1928), and *The Kid's Clever* (1929). Adapting the story and writing gags for Buster Keaton's *Spite Marriage* (1929) put him over as a film comedy regular, and it wasn't long before he settled in with a permanent berth at Educational. In addition to Roscoe's films he also penned Educational items for Monte Collins, Moran & Mack, Andy Clyde and Buster Keaton, like *Techno-Crazy*, *Hot Hoofs* (both 1933), *The Super Snooper*, *The Gold Ghost*, and *Allez Oop!* (all 1934).

1935 saw him leave Educational and become busy on more prestigious features at RKO such as *A Damsel in*

A young Betty Grable around the time that she was moonlighting for Roscoe as Frances Dean.

Distress (1937), *Vivacious Lady*, and *Having Wonderful Time* (both 1938). Now a feature comedy writer he moved over to MGM for Eddie Cantor's *Forty Little Mothers* (1940), and to Columbia for the Fred Astaire vehicles, *You'll Never Get Rich* (1941), and *You Were Never Lovelier* (1942). In 1944 he became a producer and writer with Michael Fessier at Universal of lighthearted B features such as *The Merry Monahans, San Diego I Love You* (both 1944) *That's the Spirit, The Night with You* (both 1945) and *Lover Come Back* (1946). Many of the above had nice character roles for his former star Buster Keaton. After 1947's *Slave Girl*, Pagano retired and died in 1953.

Film Daily (February 21, 1932): "The offering is bright and moves along at a fast pace, with the three girls proving to be a good comedy combination as well as a pleasing eyeful."

Photoplay (May 1932): "Those three extra girls who have such trouble crashing the Hollywood studio gates, are again embroiled in a series of escapades. Rita Flynn tries to hitch her wagon to a potential star in this one—quite unsuccessfully. Good fun."

Mother's Holiday

Released March 20, 1932. A Cameo Comedy. Produced and distributed by Educational Pictures. Directed by William Goodrich. Story by Walter Catlett. One reel. Extant. With Fern Emmett, Henry Roquemore, Broderick O'Farrell, Mary Jane Irving, Polly Christie, Teddy Mangean, Joe Young, Bert Young.

The family decides that mother works too hard and that she should have a holiday. Of course all the festivities and things that they do "for" mother end up causing her a lot more work than usual.

A good illustration of the dark and cynical view of family life and relationships that was always an undercurrent in Roscoe's films, and pops up in *Fatty and the Heiress* (1914), *That Little Band of Gold* (1915), *He Did and He Didn't* (1916), *A Reckless Romeo* (1917), *Never Again* (1924), *Home Cured* (1926), *Honeymoon Trio* (1931), and *Bridge Wives* (1932). The clever story is by actor Walter Catlett, and the insensitive family is made up of Henry Roquemore, former child performer Mary Jane Irving, Broderick O'Farrell, Polly Christie, and Ted Morgan. But

Roscoe's favorite character actress Fern Emmett has a rare starring role in *Mother's Holiday* (1932).

more than anything, *Mother's Holiday* is a showcase for character actress Fern Emmett.

Coming from the stage, she was married to supporting player Henry Roquemore (who plays father here), and they both began appearing in movies in 1927. Emmett's first films were two-reelers for Al Christie such as *Hot Papa*, *Mad Scrambles* (both 1927), and *Fighting Fanny* (1928) where she supported the likes of Neal Burns and "foxy grandpa" Jack Duffy. With the changeover to sound she became even busier, appearing in many comedy shorts, a number directed by Roscoe like *Idle Roomers* (1931), *Anybody's Goat*, and *Bridge Wives* (both 1932). She also turned up in horror pictures such as *The Vampire Bat* (1933), *The Mummy's Tomb* (1942) and *Dead Men Walk* (1943), plus countless other features and westerns right up to her death in 1946.

Motion Picture Herald (March 5, 1932): "Very good. With more than an atom of truth, this satirical short shows the farce of a 'Mother's Day' when mother is the victim of all the world."

It's a Cinch

Released March 27, 1932. Mermaid Comedies. Produced and distributed by Educational Pictures. Directed by William Goodrich. Story and dialogue by Ernest Pagano & Jack Townley. Two reels. Extant. With Monty Collins, Phyllis Crane, Tom O'Brien, Doris Carnes, Elinor Kingston.

Monty Collins puts his dancing students through their paces in *It's a Cinch* (1932).

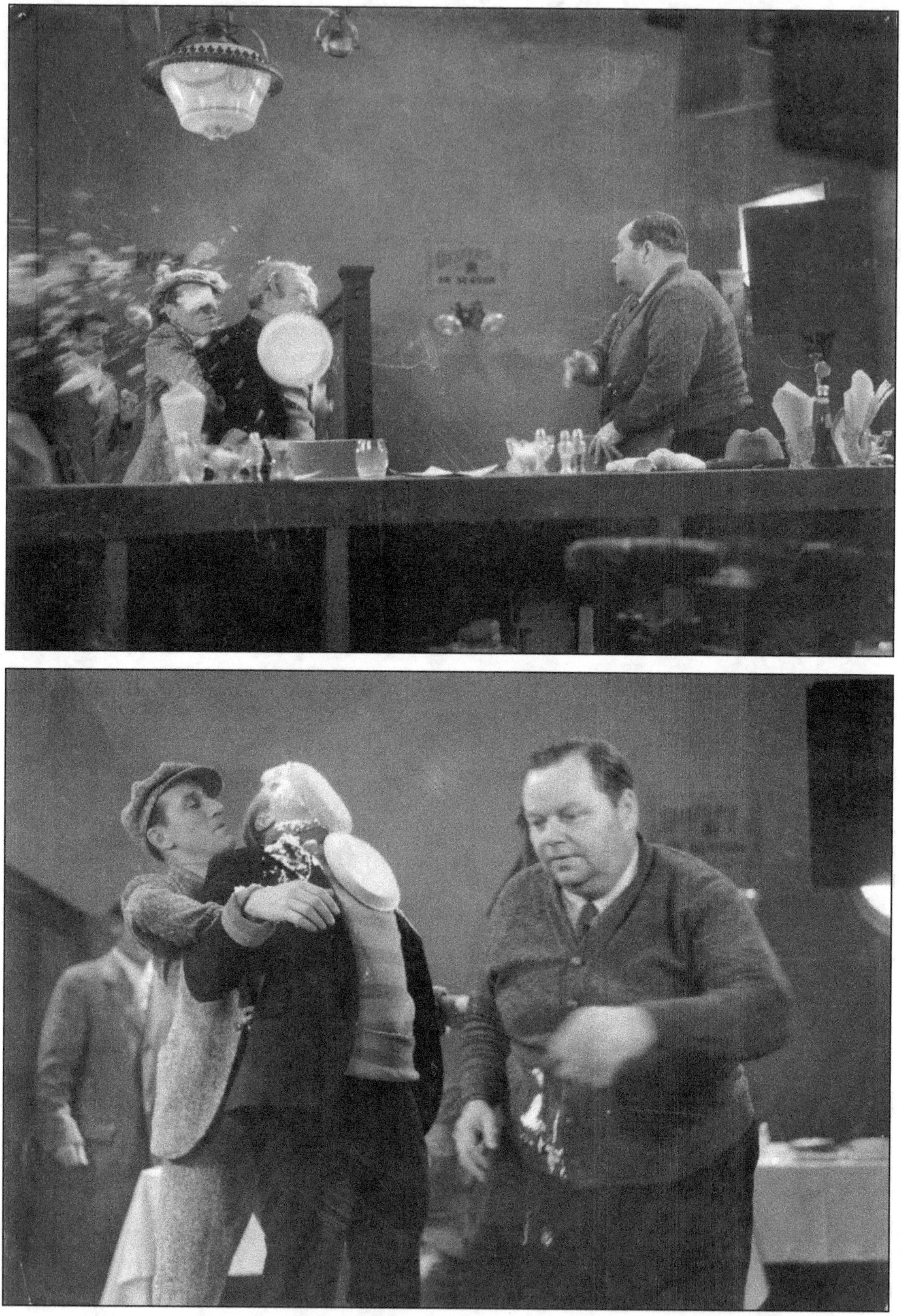

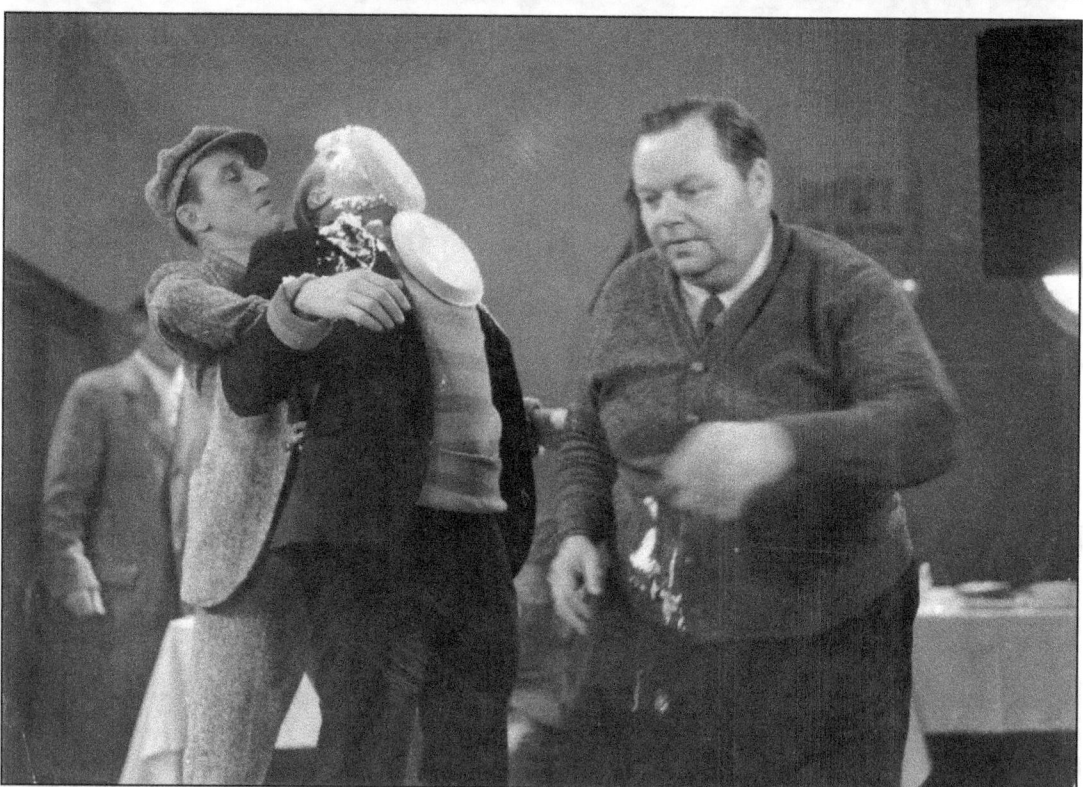

Roscoe demonstrating his pie-throwing prowess on the set of *It's a Cinch* (1932). Courtesy The Museum of Modern Art.

Monty is dancing teacher who gets in bad with a bruising boxer after the fighter comes on to Monty's waitress girlfriend. To avenge his humiliation of being hit with a pie, the boxer gets Monty to fight him in the ring, pretending he'll throw the fight so Monty will win the money prize. Things look bad as Monty's a failure at training, but he and his girl discover that the pug's big weakness is overeating. Right before the fight the girlfriend lures the fighter to her apartment for a big meal, and then when in the ring Monty repeatedly hits him in the stomach. The trick works, the pug goes down, and Monty is victorious.

This is Roscoe's last short with Monty Collins, who gets to show off his dancing skills when he instructs his female students early in the picture. He would soon move on to to be a regular in Columbia's short comedies, where he would sometimes be paired with big lug Tom Kennedy, but usually support The Three Stooges, Buster Keaton, and Harry Langdon. Phyllis Crane makes a welcome return as Monty's waitress girlfriend, and his adversary, Spike the boxer, is played by Tom O'Brien, a specialist in "tough Irish eggs."

O'Brien started his film career in 1914 in D.W. Griffith-supervised films for the Reliance and Majestic Companies. Shorts such as *Granny* (1914) with Dorothy Gish, and *The Runaway Freight* (1914) saw him typecast right away as crooks and mugs. This kept him in demand, and he moved on to support in features for Thomas Ince, William S. Hart, and Charles Ray. These appearances include *Square Deal Sanderson* (1919), *The Sagebrusher* (1920), *Scrap Iron* (1921), and *Flapper Wives* (1924), plus he also turned up in an occasional comedy short like *Pardon My Glove*, and *Glad Rags* (both 1922).

In 1925 O'Brien had a major role in one of the biggest films of the decade—King Vidor's *The Big Parade*. Playing John Gilbert's soldier buddy Bull led to the peak of O'Brien's career in the late 1920s where he had similar roles in big budget pictures like *Tin Hats* (1926), *Rookies*, *The Bugle Call*, *The Private Life of Helen of Troy*, and *That's My Daddy* (all 1927). Sound films still found him in demand, but better parts such as Starbuck in *Moby Dick* (1930) with John Barrymore, gave way to smaller bits in shorts and features as cops or boxers. In keeping with his tough guy image, O'Brien retired from films in 1934 and became a deputy sheriff. He died in Los Angeles in 1947.

Motion Picture Herald (April 9, 1932): "Monty Collins as the hopeful dance instructor who takes up boxing by accident or mistake, and cleans up through the brain work of his best girl, Phyllis Crane, does his best work here, but that is hardly more than fair. He becomes involved with a fighter, who frames him into thinking he will give Collins the fight. The girl saves the day by feeding the fighter heavily and forcing him into a collapse in the ring. A little slapstick is only that."

Photoplay (June 1932): "A lot of fun about a poor dancing professor who thinks that he'll win a lot of money fighting the champ boxer, who has promised to throw the fight. A spritely enough little comedy with Monty Collins and Tom O'Brien."

Screenland (July 1932): "What happens to a dancing teacher when he decides to turn prizefighter. Monty Collins finds it a tough life, but Phyllis Crane soothes his wounds. Amusing."

Hollywood Lights

Released May 8, 1932. Ideal Comedies. Produced and distributed by Educational Pictures. Directed by William Goodrich. Story and dialogue by Ernest Pagano & Jack Townley. Two reels. With Rita Flynn, Virginia Brooks, Tut Mace, Ted O'Shea, Fern Emmett, Lynton Brent, Jack Shaw, Bert Young, Joe Young, Kalla Pasha.

While looking for extra work one of the girls becomes a stunt double for a manly western star, who actually faints at the very thought of anything strenuous or dangerous. Doubling him jumping from a roof during a fire, she lands on the heroes' elderly horse instead of the fire net and ends up riding the worse-for-wear horse out of the picture and into the sunset.

This is the last installment in Roscoe's *Hollywood Girls* series, but the girls still don't get any closer to tinsel town success. It's also his final release for Educational Pictures, which had been his on-again/off again home for ten years.

Almost all of Roscoe's Educational sound shorts were co-written by Jack Townley, a seasoned veteran who would remain in the industry until 1957. His career began in the mid-1920s as a Hollywood columnist and picture editor for trade magazines such as *Hollywood News*. Going on to his own syndicated newspaper column, he broke into movies with stories for western shorts, but soon moved on to scenarios for comedy features such as Johnny Hine's *The Wright Idea* (1928) and *The Cohens and Kellys in Atlantic City* (1929). After sound features like *Father and Son* (1929), *The Last Dance*, and

Roscoe busy setting up the scene. Courtesy The Museum of Modern Art.

Tut Mace, Virginia Brooks, and Rita Flynn cozy up to movie cowpoke Ted O'Shea in *Hollywood Lights* (1932). Courtesy Richard Finnegan.

Divorce Among Friends (both 1930), he settled in at Educational and was teamed with Ernest Pagano.

Following this early 1930s stint at Educational, Townley continued comedy writing for another twenty years. More shorts followed at RKO and Paramount for the likes of Edgar Kennedy, Harry Langdon, and Leon Errol, and at the same time he branched into features. Outside of a rare drama or western like *Guilty Parents* (1934) or *The Last Outlaw* (1936) he was busy turning out comedy scripts for Wheeler and Woolsey, James Gleason and the Great Gildersleeve. He alternated between RKO and Republic Pictures, where he wrote seven vehicles for comic Judy Canova and some light-hearted Roy Rogers westerns. Townley's features include *Silly Billies*, *Mummy's Boys* (both 1936), *Should Husbands Work?* (1939), *Scatterbrain* (1940), *Puddin' Head* (1941), *My Pal Trigger* (1946), and *Oklahoma Annie* (1952). Television also beckoned and he was busy on series such as the *Abbott and Costello Show*, *Annie Oakley* and *The Millionaire* until he retired in 1957.

Joining Virginia Brook and Rita Flynn in this final entry of the series is the unusually named Tut Mace. This pretty brunette was a West Coast showgirl and dancer who started appearing in California hot spots and shows, like the *Music Box Review* in the late 1920s. Besides *Hollywood Lights*, she only made a couple of other small film appearances. Her

On the left Kalla Pasha takes a bite out of Charley Chase in *Chasing Husbands* (1928), while cop Bert Young hassles Gene Stone on the right in *Bumping Along* (1928). Courtesy Robert S. Birchard.

dancing career was also erratic, said to have been the result of a tumultuous relationship with her dancing partner and husband Gary Leon. After the pair was in and out of court in the 1940s, she left the stage and died in 1966.

In addition to favorites like Fern Emmett and Lynton Brent in support, Roscoe employs a trio of silent comedy veterans whose roles were reduced in size with the changeover to sound. Joe Young was the older brother of Robert Young, who started in walk-ons in 1924 at the Mack Sennett Studio. He worked his way up to larger bits and became a utility man on the lot playing everything—guards, henchmen, soldiers, and party guests. Sometimes he would play Alice Day's brother, but other times he would play her father. Shorts such as *Dangerous Curves Behind* (1925), *Gooseland*, *Her Actor Friend* (both 1926) and *Love at First Flight* (1928) gave him an occasional lead, and he moved over to Stern Brothers comedies where he would occasionally fill in as Mr. Newlywed in the *Newlyweds and their Baby* shorts, and took over the role of Mike in their *Mike and Ike* comedies. In sound he was demoted to uncredited bit parts, and changed his name to Roger Moore, but he remained busy until 1953.

An unsung player who toiled for many years without any kind of attention was another Young: Bert Young (no relation). Although he was anonymous to audiences he was a seasoned straight man, and the best description of him is that of "a mug." When a lazy brother-in-law, an irate customer, or a drunken lout was needed Bert filled the bill into the 1940s when he was busy in comedies for Jack White, Sennett, Educational, and Columbia. Last, but not least, is the burly Kalla Pasha who was a live-action version of Popeye's nemesis Bluto. One of the great comedy foils, Pasha's real name was the much less threatening Joseph T. Rickard. His background was a combination of stage, carnivals and circuses, plus professional boxing and wrestling, where he was billed as "The Terrible Turk." Beginning in 1919 he menaced all the comics on the Mack Sennett lot, and after 1924 began freelancing in Fox, Christie and Hal Roach comedies. His feature film appearances included Tod Browning's *The Wicked Darling* (1919) and *West of Zanzibar*

(1928). Sound moved him into the bit player category, and he soon began acting out some of his slapstick screen antics in real life. In a 1932 altercation with a streetcar conductor he broke an ink bottle over the man's head, but was found not guilty by reason of insanity and was committed to the Mendocino State Hospital. He died there a year later in 1933.

Broadway and Hollywood Movies (July 1932): "Educational Film with Rita Flynn, Virginia Brooks, Tut Mace, Ted O'Shea, Fern Emmett, and Lynton Brent. Crushing the movies is made to serve the purpose of comedy with a howl. In this every promising thing turns sour and the humor is found in the turn of events which prove disastrous to their hope. It is very good farce comedy."

Photoplay (July 1932): "A passive comedy without many laughs. Rita Flynn and her acrobatic legs do most of the work. It tells the story of the experiences of three girls in their search for employment at the movie studios."

Screenland (August 1932): "The adventures of three Hollywood girls in search of a break. They find it after several amusing adventures. Nice work by Rita Flynn, Virginia Brooks, and Tut Mace."

Gigolettes

Released May 23, 1932. Gay Girls Comedies. Produced and distributed by RKO Pathé Pictures. Directed by William Goodrich. Story by Beatrice Van. Photographed by H. Jackson. Supervised by Lew Lipton. Two reels. Extant. With June MacCloy, Marion Shilling, Gertrude Short, Roderick O'Farrell, Jerry Mandy, Charles Dorety, Bud Jamison, Heinie Conklin, Arthur Thalasso, Budd Fine, Herman Bing, Al Thompson, June Gittelson.

The girls, as always desperate for work, take on the running of a defunct and run-down night club.

Gigolettes is a reworking of Roscoe's Educational short *Keep Laughing* of only five months before. That script was by Ernest Pagano and Jack Townley, and *Gigolettes* is by Beatrice Van, so it seems likely that Roscoe may have engineered the "borrowing."

As the next-to-last of the *Gay Girls* series, *Gigolettes* is a good opportunity to profile the funny and overlooked Gertrude Short, who had previously supported Roscoe in his starring features *Leap Year* and *Fast Freight*. Little and slightly plump, Short specialized in playing off-beat friends of the leading lady. Born to a theatrical family she began appearing on stage as a child and often played boys, as she did in the popular 1909 production *A Man's World* opposite Mary Mannering. The Gender switch continued in her first films such as the 1914 *The Little Angel of Canyon Creek* where she played a Norwegian orphan named Olaf.

By 1920 there was no doubt that Gertie was definitely a girl, and she played bubbly characters all through the 1920s such as in the series *The Telephone Girl* as Alberta Vaughn's sidekick, not to mention features like James Cruze's *Beggar on Horseback* (1925), *Ladies of Leisure* (1926), and *Tillie the Toiler* (1927) with Marion Davies. Married to comedy director Scott (aka Percy) Pembroke, Gertie's roles became smaller in the early days of sound. Having dyed her hair blonde she still made memorable appearances in shorts and features like *The Thin Man* (1934). Eventually ending up in uncredited walk-ons, she left the screen during World War II to work for the Lockheed Corporation, remaining there until she retired in 1967.

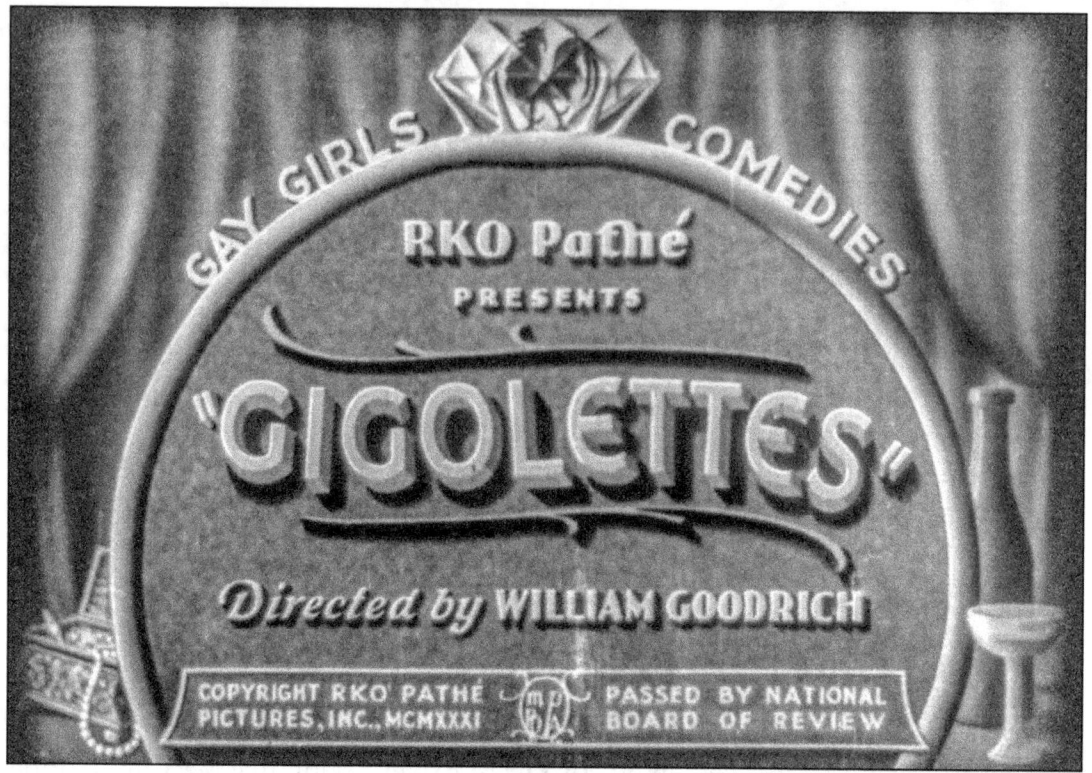

Courtesy of Ralph Celetano.

Gertrude Short (right) as the sidekick to Alberta Vaughn (left) in the *Telephone Girl* Comedy *The Square Sex* (1924). Courtesy Karel Caslavsky.

The supporting cast is a veritable "who was who" of silent and early sound comedy with stalwarts such as Bud Jamison, Jerry Mandy, Charles Dorety, June Gittelson, Al Thompson, Heinie Conklin, Arthur Thalasso, Bud Fine, and Herman Bing. The supervisor for the series was Lew Lipton, a long time comedy writer who had been born Hyman Herman Lipshitz. By 1920 he was Lewis Lipsky, and by 1921 Lew Lipton when he settled into films. In 1923 he was a production manager for the Dinky Dean Reisner feature *A Prince of a King*, and after writing two-reelers for Universal and Joe Rock he settled in for a five-year stint at MGM as resident comedy specialist. His pictures there include *Tin Hats* (1926), *Circus Rookies*, *The Cameraman* (both 1928), and *Spite Marriage* (1929), and although a couple of projects were announced with him as director none were released with that credit.

Leaving MGM in 1929, he got a berth at RKO and became the producing supervisor for their comedy shorts. In addition to the *Traveling Man*, and *Gay Girls* series that Roscoe worked on, Lipton also oversaw shorts with Benny Rubin, Edgar Kennedy, James Gleason, and Harry Gribbon. He gave the November 29, 1931 *Film Daily* his thoughts on sound comedy production:

> *During the past few months we have produced nearly half a hundred two-reel comedies at RKO Pathé and in these we have carefully balanced the action and dialogue giving the action a shade the better break. We have taken the comedy situation which is funny to the eye and placed dialogue with it that is calculated to enhance the humor. You cannot successfully photograph a stage comedy for motion pictures. Both been given a try and found lacking the proper ingredients for modern audience's tastes. Dialogue comedy is too slow for a group of people used to the old type of speedy comedy and of course no audience would accept only pantomime comedy in this day of sound.*

After 1932 he returned to writing, working on sporadic features for MGM and RKO like *Follow the Fleet*, *Mummy's Boys* (both 1936) and *Broadway Serenade* (1939). He was later publicity director for Trem Carr Productions at Monogram, and wrote a bit of television in the 1950s, but seems to have kept a somewhat low profile after his son was arrested in 1942 as part of a death threat and extortion plot against Lipton's old MGM boss Louis B. Mayer. He died in 1961.

Motion Picture Herald: (July 22, 1933): "Poor comedy for Sunday and not much anytime."

Niagara Falls

Released June 27, 1932. Gay Girls Comedies. Produced and distributed by RKO Pathé Pictures. Directed by William Goodrich. Story by Ewart Adamson. Photographed by Ted McCord. Supervised by Lew Lipton. Two reels. With June MacCloy, Marion Shilling, Gertrude Short, Eddie Nugent, Emerson Treacy, Jessie Perry, Ernest Hilliard, Isabelle Withers, Violet Barlow.

Niagara Falls (1932) is not only the last of Roscoe's *Gay Girls* Comedies, but also his final short subject directorial effort.

The girls are in financial straits again, and have to evade their stern landlady while they look for work. Trying to make the best use of June's singing abilities they attempt to get a job in a music store, but have issues with an amorous boss and his jealous wife. In the meantime a radio program man has heard June sing, and the girls are brought in to do a broadcast. They become a hit, and June marries the radio man.

After ten years of being a director for hire, *Niagara Falls* would be Roscoe's last directorial effort. While it's certain that he had creative input in his Vitaphone "comeback" shorts, they were helmed by the pros Alf Goulding and Raymond McCarey.

The third member of the *Gay Girls* trio, Marion Shilling, was a dark-haired beauty who began her career at the beginning of sound. Her first film was *Wise Girls* (1929) for MGM, and she also had contracts with Paramount and Pathé for *Lord Byron of Broadway*, *Free and Easy* (both 1930) and *Shop Angel* (1932). Not long after the *Gay Girls* series her career settled into B-Westerns, where she became leading lady for screen cowboys like Buck Jones, Tim McCoy and Hoot Gibson. Some of these titles included *The Red River* (1934), *Stone of Silver Creek*, *Gun Smoke* (both 1935), *The Idaho Kid*, and *Romance Rides the Range* (both 1936). Following her marriage to Philadelphia businessman, Edward Cook, she retired from films. In 2002 she received a Golden Boot Award from the Motion Picture and Television Fund for her contribution to the western genre and died at age ninety-three in 2004.

Emerson Treacy and Eddie Nugent, two of Roscoe's favorite sound comedy leading men, made a return in *Niagara Falls*, and the story is by short-subject regular Ewart Adamson. Having one of the most colorful backgrounds in film comedy history, Adamson was born in Dundee Scotland, served as a major in the Canadian Army during World War 1, and managed a tin mine in Perak, Malaysia. It appears he entered the film industry thanks to his brother Penrhyn Stanlaws (aka Stanley Adamson). A portrait painter and magazine illustrator, Stanlaws was working in Hollywood as a director. Ewart Adamson's first film project was doing the adaptation of his novel *South of Java* (1922) and he then did the scenario for *Pink Gods* (1922) and *Singed Wings* (1923), the last films directed by his brother. Besides authoring features for Rin Tin Tin, Mary Miles Minter, Buck Jones, George O'Brien, and Ranger the Dog, he spent a good deal of time working at the Mack Sennett Studio. Some of the shorts he wrote include *Don't Tell Dad* (1925), *Wide Open Faces*, *The Funnymooners* (both 1926), *The Girl Nowhere*, *The Campus Vamp* (both 1928), and *Taxi Spooks* (1929).

When sound arrived he continued working for Sennett, but soon moved on to write shorts for Educational, RKO and Columbia. Outside of a few features like *Annie Oakley* (1935), *The Walking Dead* (1936) and *The Gay Vagabond* (1941), the majority of the rest of his career was spent writing two-reel scripts for Buster Keaton, The

Portrait of Marion Shilling, who after the *Gay Girls* Comedies spent the rest of her career in Hoot Gibson and Buck Jones westerns.

Three Stooges, Andy Clyde, Moran and Mack, and Edgar Kennedy. In 1943 he wrote the novel *Haunted Harbor*, which was turned into a Republic serial the next year. Adamson passed away in 1945, but was kept working from beyond by producer Jules White, who recycled older Adamson scripts for Columbia shorts like *Innocently Guilty* (1950), *Blonde Atom Blonde* (1951) *Tooting Tooters* (1954) and *Scratch Scratch Scratch* (1955).

Variety (April 12, 1932): "Nicely paced short with an abundance of low comedy knockabout and custard-pie stuff, varied with interpolated song numbers in June MacCloy's female baritone voice.

"The three girls, who run through most of this series, give it a capital girly flavor, the low comedienne of the trio here taking an endless succession of rough falls for laughs. Production nicely dressed and unusually well plotted for a short."

Photoplay (November 1932): "June MacCloy's nice, huskily sung ditties save this from being just another comedy. The good old plot of three girls trying to evade the irate landlady while they find work, is dusted off again. Gertrude Short and Marion Shilling complete the trio. Only mildly amusing."

Chapter 14
Vitaphone Shorts

Comeback

In February of 1932, Warner Brothers approached Roscoe with an offer to star in a short. He made a total of six that were shot at the Vitaphone Studio in Brooklyn. For these films Roscoe seemed to turn back the clock, looking fit and hardly older than he had when his career was interrupted in 1921. He adapted easily to sound, which revealed

Producer Sam Sax signs Roscoe to his Vitaphone contract. Courtesy The Museum of Modern Art.

his soft, mid-western voice. While the directorial chores were handled by Alf Goulding and Raymond McCarey, the reworking of large amounts of old routines and bits in the finished films show that Roscoe was very much in charge.

Hey, Pop!

Released November 12, 1932. Produced by the Vitaphone Corporation. Distributed by Warner Brothers. Directed by Alf Goulding. Story by Jack Henley & Glen Lambert. Photographed by E. B. DuPar. Music by David Mendoza. (Shot between August 25 – 31 1932). Two reels. Extant. With Roscoe Arbuckle, Billy Hayes, Florence Auer, Jack Shutta, Dan Wolheim, Milton Wallace, Leo Hoyt, Herschel Mayall, Connie Almy, J.F. Lee.

Billy's mother abandons him in a restaurant where Fatty is cook, and while waiting for somebody from the orphanage to call for him, Billy appeals to Fatty for aid. Fatty hides the boy and sneaks him out of the place, unseen by the Orphanage inspector, thereby losing his job. The two become great pals.

Fatty's having a hard time finding a new job, and food is getting scarce. Fatty starts a throwing war with the vegetable vendor across the street, and since the receiving ammunition is carrots, potatoes, cabbages, and meat the boys end up with a fine feast. Unfortunately just as they've eaten the Orphanage officials show up for Billy, so the boys have to take it on the lam. Fatty changes clothes with a large lady and pretends to be Billy's "Ma." By accident they win a Pretty Baby contest with a $500 prize, but while Fatty is making the acceptance speech the officials get wise, and they have to take off again.

Roscoe busy cleaning some imaginary glass in his 1932 comeback short *Hey, Pop!*

Back before the camera making his first starring short since *Handy Andy* must have been a dream come true for Roscoe as well as a vindication. He's first seen in a white chef's hat doing the "polishing the imaginary glass routine" to the restaurant's kitchen door looking like it's 1921 with no time having passed in the meantime. Roscoe re-introduces himself with kitchen gags—casually flipping eggs and knives around with great aplomb, putting on a big fur coat to go into the freezer, and has the magic giant pot that everything and anything comes out of, including his hat and jacket when he and the kid take it on the lam—all familiar from shorts like *The Waiter's Ball* (1916), *The Butcher Boy* (1917), and *The Cook* (1918). In fact much of the short is a tour through Roscoe's gag book with items that include the vegetable throwing bit from *Camping Out* (1919) and an appearance in drag, although now he's more of a middle-aged matron than a flirty young thing.

Roscoe works very well with child actor Billy Hayes in a plot that has more than a little resemblance to Charlie Chaplin's *The Kid* (1921), but the theme is treaded on lightly and the little bit of sentiment is underplayed and honest. Billy Hayes (nee Heyes) had been starring in Vitaphone's *Penrod* series. Shorts such as *Batter Up*, *One Good Deed* (both 1931), *Penrod's Bull Pen*, and *Detectuvs* (both 1932) were based on Booth Tarkington characters, and Hayes also appeared in vaudeville:

> *Billy Hayes, Vitaphone's Penrod of the Booth Tarkington Juvenile Comedies, is almost ready to go on stage as the star of a vaudeville sketch written around him. His act was given an audition Thursday at the Warner Bros. home office by Walter Meyers, head of Artist's Bureau. Bill uses his dog "Duke" in the act and has with him two little girls, Anita Nunes and Judy Freeman. In the act Bill sings, dances and gives impersonations of Ted Lewis and Joe Penner.*
>
> – **Film Daily**, January 31, 1932

Hey, Pop! turned out to Hayes last movie. After serving in World War II he entered the aerospace industry and died in 2002.

As far as adapting his comedy to sound Roscoe goes about his business as he always did, so the dialogue comes where it should in a natural sort of way, and there are plenty of sight-gag sequences without talking where sound effects are used for punctuation, something that would be developed further in the next short *Buzzin' Around*.

Director Alf Goulding knew Roscoe from their early California theatre days, and was a long-time comedy pro who directed many of the most popular film comedy performers. One of the many graduates of Pollard's Lilliputians, a children's theatrical troupe that toured the world, he began his film career as a director and gagman for Hal Roach in 1917. After working on numerous Harold Lloyd and Snub Pollard one-reelers he switched to Century Comedies with Brownie the wonder dog and Baby Peggy. The latter 1920s found him making a few on screen appearances in films such as *The Lady* (1925) with Norma Talmadge, and directing many of the *Smith Family* comedies at the Sennett studio.

In the early sound era he worked for RKO, Vitaphone, and Universal, and then with the exception of Laurel and Hardy's *A Chump at Oxford* (1940) he spent much of the final leg of his career in England on films like *Dick Barton: Special Agent* (1948). His career wound down after making his Musty Suffer feature *Laffing Time* (1959), and he passed away back in Hollywood in 1972.

Overall Roscoe was given a very warm welcome back:

Billy Hayes as the baby to Roscoe's "mama" in *Hep, Pop!* (1932).
Courtesy Ron Hutchinson/The Vitaphone Project.

Arbuckle Short Clicks
  Fatty Arbuckle's first comeback short, "Hey Pop," produced by Vitaphone, was greeted with demonstrative applause in its first showings at the Ritz, Jersey City, and Fabian, Hoboken.
  – ***Film Daily***, October 10, 1932

There were a few critics that complained about old gags—but that seemed to be deliberate on Roscoe's part—a sort of picking up where he left off.
  Motion Picture Herald (March 4, 1933): "Fatty comes back strong. Many and loud were the laughs during the run of this comedy. Arbuckle will make good, and should be producing regular."
  Variety (December 13, 1932): "Arbuckle seems to be in fine trim. He looks little the older for the 10 years he has been away from pictures, a portion of it directing comedies under another name. He's agile and understands comedy values as applied to the screen.
  "About 78% of the short is pantomime, Fatty saying little throughout its 18 minutes. He wears the too-short balloon trousers and other accoutrements of another day and appears entirely familiar in every way. But no pie-throwing, though the fruit tossing suggests it."

Motion Picture Herald (April 1, 1933): "One of the best two-reel comedies we have played since Fatty quit making them. He is a funny fat man."

Buzzin' Around

Released February 4, 1933. Produced by the Vitaphone Corporation. Distributed by Warner Brothers. Directed by Alf Goulding. Story by Jack Henley & Glen Lambert. Photographed by E. B. DuPar. Music by David Mendoza. Two reels. Extant. With Roscoe Arbuckle, Al St John, Pete the Pup, Dan Coleman, Alice May Tuck, Tom Smith, Al Ochs, Harry Ward, Gertrude Mudge, Fritz Hubert, Donald MacBride.

Cornelius is a country boy who has created a solution that makes china unbreakable. He receives a telegram asking for a demonstration and sets off for the city, but in his haste he takes with him a bottle of cider that this buddies Al and Pete were drinking instead of the solution. After misadventures with bees, irate motorists, and cops, he gets to the china shop where he breaks some expensive pieces when his "solution" mysteriously won't work. Al and Pete arrive in the nick of time with the real solution, but at the same time the owner of the

Al St John and Roscoe break loads of crockery on Al Ochs in *Buzzin' Around* (1933). Courtesy Annichen Skaren.

shop shows up and just happens to be the guy whose car Cornelius caused to be demolished. A battle royal breaks out in the china shop, with the police called out in force, but in spite of the loss of Al's pants the three friends manage to make their escape.

Of Roscoe's six starring comedies for Vitaphone, *Buzzin' Around* most successfully recaptures the free-wheeling spirit of his silent shorts. The use of sound dubbed over action scenes shot silent gives the film the pace and rhythms of early slapstick, in addition to a kind of Jacques Tati flavor. It helps that more than half the short takes place in outdoor Brooklyn locations where Roscoe can really move and recreate routines from *Back Stage* (1919) and *The Movies* (1925).

Old cohorts Al St John and Pete the Pup are also on hand to add to the fun, with Al reprising his country hick character. Although they had continued to work together with Roscoe behind the camera, it's the first time in the fourteen years since *Back Stage* (1919) that they appeared on screen together. Sadly it turned out to be their last collaboration. From here Al became a western sidekick in low budget oaters. With a beard, and without his teeth, Al spent almost twenty years as "Fuzzy" St. John, where he reworked his old silent comedy bits to provide comic relief for the heroics of Buster Crabbe, Don "Red" Barry, and Lash LaRue. He retired in 1952, and passed away in 1963.

Roscoe waters down Dan Coleman in *Buzzin' Around* (1933).
Courtesy Ron Hutchinson/The Vitaphone Project.

The original Pete the Pup, who had appeared in *Dynamite Doggie* (1925), had died in 1930 and this Pete is one of his sons. Owner and trainer Harry Lucenay had had a falling out with producer Hal Roach, and brought Pete (or possibly Petes) to the East Coast where he appeared in other shorts and made publicity appearances. In addition to the veterans Pete and Al, Roscoe also has support from Fritz Hubert (see *How've You Bean?*) and Dan Coleman. Playing the pharmacist who helps Roscoe after he swallows the bee, Coleman was an old scene-stealer with a long vaudeville career. He had settled in at Vitaphone and was busy supporting Roscoe and Joe Penner in shorts like *Here, Prince* (1932), *Laughs in the Law*, and *In the Dough* (both 1933) until his death in 1935.

Another scene-stealer who might have ended up in the Vitaphones was Joe Besser. Having worked briefly in vaudeville with Arbuckle, in his 1988 book *Once a Stooge, Always a Stooge*, Besser said:

> *Fatty and I became such good friends during our two-week engagement together that before it ended he wanted to cast me in a new comedy series he was planning to star in for Vitaphone. The series didn't have a title yet, but I was going to play his kid brother. We were even going to dress identically. Fatty thought since our physiques and mannerisms were similar this would be a good gimmick.*

Unfortunately it didn't come to be, with Besser not becoming a film regular until the early 1940s.

Motion Picture Herald (September 9, 1933): "Too bad this comedian had to die as he was needed to put the laughs in comedies. A very few of the comedies are real funny nowadays. Comedians are born."

Variety (February 28, 33): "Slapstick is an important ingredient in 'Buzzin' Around,' as in first release, But in one sequence that has distinct originality and becomes very funny, the slight overindulgence in slapstick is counteracted. Strong laugh sequence occurs when Arbuckle, a farm boy going to town with a non-breakable chinaware invention, swallows a bee. When he opens his mouth, sound of a buzzing bee comes out. This business is carried forward to a showmanly point and then dropped.

"A freakish Model T figures for laughs, with a free-for-all in a class china shop for the big finish. In plot the two-reeler carries more originality than the average short of its kind.

"Al St John supports Arbuckle. He worked with Fatty many years ago in the pie-tossing days, and in 'Buzzin' Around' is of considerable laugh value.

"Photography and technical job excellent."

Motion Picture Herald (April 15, 1933): "Don't miss this great Arbuckle comedy. Good enough for any day. New stuff and clean. Will bring any house down."

Motion Picture Herald (July 29, 1933): "One of the best comedies we have seen in the past year. If the other Arbuckle comedies are as good as this one, we will be glad to get them. Al St John is very good also. Plenty of laughs and everybody enjoyed it. Vitaphone, let us have more like this."

How've You Bean?

Released June 24, 1933. Produced by the Vitaphone Corporation. Distributed by Warner Brothers. Directed by Alf Goulding. Story by Jack Henley & Glen Lambert. Photography by E.B. DuPar. Music by David Mendoza. (Shot between December 16 – 22 1932). Two reels. Extant. With Roscoe Arbuckle, Fritz Hubert, Mildred Van Dorn, Edmund Elton, Dora Mills Adams, Jean Hubert, Paul Clare, Charles Howard, Herbert Warren.

Abner and Willie are about to open their new grocery store. Their old army buddy Jimmy comes by to introduce his fiancée and ask them to be his best men at the wedding. The customers waiting outside the store think up a ploy to get their groceries for free, and end up cleaning the boys out. When an assistant to the mayor comes in to ask them for change the boys mistake him for a counterfeiter, and the scuffle ends in a huge flour-throwing free-for-all.

Later Abner and Willie arrive to be the best men at Jimmy's wedding. Out of place in the posh surroundings, they end up in the kitchen looking for food and come across a supply of beans (Mexican Jumping beans to be exact) and decide to cook some up to remind Jimmy of their days in the army. After cooking, the boys get ready for the wedding and are uncomfortable in the fancy clothes. When they put on their new shoes they cause them to

Mildred Van Dorn plays Roscoe's army buddies' bride in *How've You Bean?* (1933). Courtesy Ron Hutchinson/The Vitaphone Project.

Candid shot of Fritz Hubert and Roscoe. Billy Rose Theatre Division, the New York Public Library for the Performing Arts.

slip, slide and fall all over. *Jimmy and the bride are waiting for his father and the mayor to arrive before they start the wedding ceremony.*

When dad arrives he's covered with flour (it was he who had the encounter with Abner and Willie). While he gets cleaned up and they wait for the Mayor, the bride and groom decide to have their wedding dinner first. The boys make a spectacle of themselves with their bad manners and the troubles they have trying to eat asparagus and olives. Finally as a surprise they bring out and serve the cooked jumping beans. When dinner's over everyone proceeds to the ceremony, which goes along solemnly until the beans begin having their effect and make the group hop up and down. The wedding is off, and the boys hop off in their car.

How've You Bean? is a breezy short that takes another opportunity to tour Roscoe's gag book. Most of the older routines turn up in the first reel, with specific references to *The Butcher Boy* (1917). There's the grocery store and the flour fight, and at one point a little man comes in and does the "molasses and nickel" routine with Roscoe. This time the solution to getting the stuck on hat off his head is to hold him up and chop it off with the revolving ceiling fan. The highlight of the short is definitely the sequence of Abner and Willie slipping and falling in their new shoes. The boys take some tremendous falls, and the bit owes much to the stage act of Fritz and Jean Hubert.

Fritz Hubert plays the goofy Willie, filling in for Al St John, and in this and *Tomalio* becomes Roscoe's last screen sidekick. Hubert was a vaudeville favorite in an eccentric knockabout specialty act with his sister Jean titled *The Realistic Inebriates*. As dandified drunks in tuxedos and top hats the pair executed an amazing array of neck-breaking tumbles and falls. Jean, performing as a man, would reveal that she was a woman at the curtain call, and she can be spotted in *How've You Bean?* as the woman that Roscoe and Fritz knock over at the wedding party whose skirt goes up over her head. Starting in 1927 the Huberts toured their act in big venues like the Palace Theatre and the New York World's Fair, and even committed it to film in shorts such as *Fads and Fancies* (1934) and *Vaude-Festival* (1936). With the outbreak of World War II Fritz changed his professional name to Frank Hubert, but passed away young at age thirty-nine in 1945.

Film Daily (August 1, 1933): "A generally entertaining comedy. The main idea has to do with Fatty attending the marriage of an old war-time buddy. Planning to surprise the groom by cooking a mess of beans reminiscent of their service days, Fatty accidentally uses Mexican jumping beans which causes the guests to do a lot of hopping around. Fritz Hubert is Arbuckle's chief support."

Motion Picture Herald (October 21, 1933): "This is a very good comedy of the old slapstick variety. Just the type of comedy that made Arbuckle famous and the kind that everyone seems to enjoy. Full of laughs and should please both young and old."

Close Relations

Released September 30, 1933. Produced by the Vitaphone Corporation. Distributed by Warner Brothers. Directed by Raymond McCarey. Story by Jack Henley & Glen Lambert. Photography by E. B. DuPar. Music by David Mendoza. (Shot between May 22 – 27 1933). Two reels. Extant. With Roscoe Arbuckle, Charles Judels, Mildred Van Dorn, Harry Shannon, Shemp Howard, Hugh O'Connell, Jack Harwood, Herschel Mayall.

Eccentric millionaire and hypochondriac Ezra Wart sends for his doctor and charges him to locate all the surviving members of the Wart family so that he can decide who he wants to leave his money to. The Warts had married into the Mole family, and as old Ezra is convinced that there is insanity on the Mole side, he doesn't want to leave his dough to anyone with Mole blood.

Wilber Wart has received a telegram from his Uncle Ezra and is at the train station on his way to see the old man. A man that he gets in bad with at the station (accidentally smashing his suitcase and tearing his coat) turns out to be the other Wart relative—his cousin Harry.

They both arrive at Uncle Ezra's and while Harry endeavors to get his revenge on Wilber, they each must convince Ezra that they are not crazy to get their inheritance. Harry convinces Ezra that Wilbur is crazy, and Wilbur helps the story along by accidentally setting Ezra on fire, inflating him with helium, and forcing him to swallow a golf ball that he thinks is a pill. The final straw comes when Wilbur drops him down a well, but at that point Wilbur and Harry find out that Uncle Ezra, his doctor, and his nurse are all patients in an insane asylum, and there is no Wart fortune.

Roscoe ducks cousin Harry Shannon's punch in *Close Relations* (1933). Author's collection.

Close Relations is unusual in Roscoe's run of Vitaphone shorts in that it's more of a farce comedy, with an emphasis on plot and dialogue for its humor, as opposed to Roscoe's usual stock-in-trade physical slapstick. Also the entirety of the short being shot on interior sets gives it a very different feel than *Hey, Pop* or *Buzzin' Around*. Both had numerous sequences shot outdoors on the streets of Brooklyn which gave them more of a freewheeling feel of early Keystones. This may have been done on purpose to help launch Roscoe's series, but now that it was four shorts in it was settling into more of the standard Vitaphone groove.

The Vitaphone Corporation had been formed by Warner Brothers and the Western Electric Company in 1926. Production on sound shorts was started at that time in Brooklyn, New York at what had been the Vitagraph Studios. Warners did well with these sound shorts, and of course *The Jazz Singer* (1927) really put over sound features and made the Warners major players in Hollywood. Production of Vitaphone shorts started on the West Coast as well, but the plant in Brooklyn remained busy turning out short dramas, comedies, and musicals. This is where Roscoe reported for his "comeback" shorts.

Joseph Henabery, Roscoe's director on three of his features, had worked with independent producer Sam Sax in the 1920s. When Sax was placed in charge of production of the Vitaphones Henabery became a staff director. Although he and Roscoe were there at the same time, they didn't work together again, and in his memoir *Before, In and After Hollywood* Henabery gives a first hand account of the Vitaphone unit:

To begin with I could see the studio was being very efficiently operated. Sax was an excellent executive. Everything was in good balance. The directing staff consisted of three men. In general, one made the dramatic pictures, another specialized in musicals, and the third handled most of the comedies. Schedules were tight. When the director who had been shooting finished his picture, another director and all the departments of the studio were prepared to start the next. Sometimes the switch came at noon. Each director had time to prepare, shoot, and work with the film editors.

In support, we had a musical director, a dance director with a group of dancers and chorus girls steadily employed, scriptwriters, songwriters, casting department, costume department, property and set design departments, and a carpenter shop with a large staff, one—only one—full stage crew. We had adequate space for everything.

Everyone knew his job and each played his part in keeping the operation operating efficiently. Principally responsible from day to day was our stage manager, a veteran picture man, Phil Quinn, who started in the business in the pioneer days of Vitagraph. He really knew all the problems of picture making.

Close Relation's (1933) nuthouse nurse Mildred Van Dorn and Roscoe.
Courtesy Ron Hutchinson/The Vitaphone Project.

> The physical properties of the studio were always in use. There were two stages. When a company was shooting on one stage, scene-striking and erection of new sets took place on the other. Most two-reel pictures were shot in four days, and one-reel pictures in one or two days. We stopped work at five o'clock each day. No matter if all the scripted scenes had or had not been shot, when the five o'clock bell sounded on the last day of the schedule, it was absolutely the end of the shooting period for the picture—no overtime—no margin for error—no allowance for finishing touches—a discipline which forced everyone to concentrate.

A big advantage for the studio was its New York location, as it gave access to the nation's singers, bands, vaudeville acts, and actors. Many bands or acts that were between engagements were happy to pick up a one-shot job in a Vitaphone short. Future stars who did some of their early film work at the studio included Bob Hope, Burns & Allen, Jack Haley, Bert Lahr, Edgar Bergen, even Spencer Tracy and Humphrey Bogart. Roscoe was the old-timer amongst this new crop of talent. Two stage regulars seen to good advantage in *Close Relations* are Hugh O'Connell and Harry Shannon.

As the loopy Dr. Carver, Hugh O'Connell pilfers a lot of the laughs in the picture. Born in New York, he was orphaned and spent much of his early years on a farm near Green Bay, Wisconsin. Thanks to the acting bug he made his way to Chicago, and for seventeen years he toured the country in rep and stock companies. Landing in New York in 1921 he appeared in Broadway shows like *Twin Beds*, *Ballyhoo*, *The Racket*, and *Gentlemen of the Press*, but it was the Kaufman and Hart hit *Once in a Lifetime* that made him a name. When sound came to films he began turning up in the New York-made Vitaphone shorts, and began flirting with Hollywood in the early 1930s with films like *The Smiling Lieutenant* and *Personal Secretary* (both 1931). Despite an occasional show like *Ziegfeld Follies of 1936* and 1938's *Run Sheep Run*, he mainly focused on films with medium-sized parts in titles such as *My Favorite Wife* (1940) and *My Life with Caroline* (1941) before his sudden death from a heart attack in 1943.

Roscoe's combative cousin Harry Wart is played by Harry Shannon, a musical comedy regular who became a ubiquitous movie character player. As a stage-struck youngster in Saginaw, Michigan he ran away with a carnival show, and passed through burlesque and vaudeville before appearing in Broadway shows such as *Laugh, Clown, Laugh*, *Oh Kay*, *Hold Everything*, *Simple Simon*, and *Pardon My English*. While working on stage he began turning up in New York-made shorts for Vitaphone and Columbia, supporting stars like Roscoe, Bert Lahr, Leon Errol, and Shemp Howard. By 1940 he was in Hollywood and played small roles in films and television shows for the next twenty-three years. His features include *The Mummy's Ghost* (1944), *Champion* (1949), *The Jackie Robinson Story* (1950), and *High Noon* (1952), but his most memorable role was as Charles Foster Kane's abusive father in *Citizen Kane* (1941). He remained busy to his death in 1964.

Film Daily (August 19, 1933): "Situations and gags are effectively combined to make this a consistently laughable affair. Charles Judels plays the part of a gouty and obviously nutty old man with a wish to find his few remaining relatives so he can decide on the one who is to get his money when he dies. The only kin left turn out to be Fatty and a tough egg, who meet for a second time at the old man's place, after having become involved in a fight at the railroad station. Fighting and scrapping between these two continues, with Uncle Charley in between them being the innocent target for a lot of punishment. For the windup, it develops that Uncle is nuts and living in an asylum. Hugh O'Connell also helps the comedy along in the role of a doctor."

Motion Picture Herald (January 27, 1934): "Lots of laughs in this one. Will please children the most."

In the Dough

Released November 25, 1933. Produced by the Vitaphone Corporation. Distributed by Warner Brothers. Directed by Raymond McCarey. Story by Jack Henley. Photographed by E.B. DuPar. Music by David Mendoza. (Shot between June 22 – 28 1933). Two reels. Extant. With Roscoe Arbuckle, Marie Marion, Lionel Stander, Shemp Howard, Dexter McReynolds, Ralph Sanford, Fred Harper, Gracie Worth, Lawrence O'Sullivan, Ethel Davis, Dan Coleman, Bud Grey.

Roscoe in the kitchen with gangsters Shemp Howard (middle) and Lionel Stander (right) from *In the Dough* (1933). Courtesy Ron Hutchinson/The Vitaphone Project.

Schultz, the owner of a bakery shop, is advertising for a new baker. The unemployed Slim comes in and wins the position. Schultz has problems with the local gangsters, who are shaking him down for protection money. The thugs Skinner and Bugs come by and confront Slim in his bakery kitchen, which leads to a dough slinging match. The gangsters are chased off by the cops, but to get their revenge they sneak back and plant a bomb inside one of the cakes, which will explode when it is cut into.

Not long after Skinner's moll Maisie comes in for a cake and has Slim deliver it. Turns out it's for Skinner's birthday and although Slims tries to beat a hasty retreat, Skinner and his pals show up causing him to hide under the dining table. When Skinner cuts the cake it explodes. Slim runs back to the bakery followed by the blacken-faced Skinner and Bugs, and everything climaxes in a big pie fight between the store employees, the gangsters, and the police.

This was Roscoe's last film to be shot, and although he looks better than he does in *Tomalio* his timing of the physical business seems a bit sluggish. Some of this may be attributed to director Ray McCarey, who helmed Roscoe's last three shorts. The first three, directed by silent veteran Alf Goulding, have more snap and are better paced. Although McCarey piloted a number of shorts and features until 1948, and even worked at the Hal Roach Studio with Laurel & Hardy, he never rose above being routine. His main claim to fame was being the younger brother of the great Leo McCarey, one of the best comedy directors of the 1920s, 1930s, and 1940s. No doubt this opened many door for brother Ray, but while Ray got opportunities Leo got all the talent. Starting in pictures as a prop boy, Ray became an assistant at the Mack Sennett Studio at the time that Leo was making a name for himself working with Charley Chase.

He started directing shorts at Pathé in 1930, and a stint at Roach working on Laurel & Hardy's *Scram* and *Pack Up Your Troubles* (both 1932) led to his being hired by Vitaphone. Besides Roscoe's last three shorts, McCarey also worked with Jack Haley. After bouncing around doing shorts for RKO and Columbia, he settled in to making "B" features practically everywhere—Republic, Paramount, Fox, RKO, Columbia, and Universal. Leo McCarey was well-known for his loose sets and for shooting off the cuff, and according to the July 18, 1937 *Brooklyn Eagle* Ray thought that he should follow suit:

> *If a company engaged in making a comedy can't have a lot of fun while working, then the picture won't reflect the gay spirit the actors should feel.*
>
> *Light comedy is something that comes from within, bubbles out of you like champagne out of a freshly uncorked bottle. The comedian isn't at his best unless he feels gay inside.*
>
> *That's why in making "Love in a Bungalow" and every other comedy I've ever directed, I encouraged my cast and production crew to wisecrack, play jokes, and raise all manner of cain.*
>
> *We had a swell time making this picture and I'm convinced that as a result the public will see the very best comedy performances that the actors had in them.*

Unfortunately McCarey's pictures never realized the humor and spontaneity of his brother's. He turned out features such as *Love in a Bungalow* (1937), *Millionaires in Prison*

(1940), *It Happened in Flatbush* (1942), and *The Falcon's Alibi* (1946) right up to his death in 1948.

As far as support Roscoe had Dan Coleman return from *Buzzin' Around* as Mr. Schultz, the harassed owner of the bakery, plus had three new players on tap—two of whom would carve sizeable film careers for themselves. Forgotten today is Marie Marion, who plays the ditzy and stuttering Gal Friday of the establishment. Something of a poor man's combination of ZaSu Pitts and Gracie Allen, Marion was the grand niece of stage star Lotta Crabtree and was a long-time vaudevillian who toured the world with her straight man and husband Nelson Clifford in a skit tiled *Just Dumb*. Very popular on stage, the act was filmed by Vitaphone in 1929, and Marion was hired as support by the studio in 1932. In addition to *In the Dough*, she turned up in Joe Penner's *Here, Prince* (1932) and *Mushrooms* (1934) with Harry Gribbon. She appears to have retired from show business following a 1934 auto accident.

Roscoe's main antagonist in the film is the gangster Skinner played by Lionel Stander, who became a memorable supporting player in the 1930s and early 1940s, with his uniquely raspy voice and pugnacious personality. Stander was born in the Bronx, and may have done film extra work as a teenager. He began seriously acting in college, and made his professional debut at New York's Provincetown Playhouse in 1928. Some of early plays include *Him, Singing Jailbirds, Red Rust*, and *The House Beautiful*. Like many other New York stage performers he found his way to the Vitaphone Studio, where he worked with Roscoe, and in numerous other shorts like *Salt Water Daffy* (1933), *Pugs and Kisses, Smoked Hams* (both 1934), and *The Old Grey Mayor* (1935).

A nice part in the Ben Hecht/Charles MacArthur New York-made feature *The Scoundrel* (1935) led to him being in demand in other features. Moving to Hollywood he was soon ubiquitous in pictures like *The Milky Way, Mr. Deeds Goes to Town, Soak the Rich* (all 1936), *A Star is Born* (1937), and *Professor Beware* (1938). Because of his one-of-a-kind voice he was also popular on the radio, but his left-wing politics and outspoken personality found him on the wrong side of the entertainment industry's blacklists. The 1940s found it hard for him to get roles; besides a few good features like *Guadalcanal Diary* (1943), *Specter of the Rose* (1946), *The Sin of Harold Diddlebock* (1947), and *Unfaithfully Yours* (1948), he got by doing voices for Walter Lantz cartoons.

In the 1950s this all dried up after he was named and testified before the House of UnAmerican Activities committee. Much of his time after this was spent in Europe where he did turn up in films like *Cul-De-Sac* (1966), *A Dandy in Aspic*, and *Once Upon a Time in the West* (both 1968). Little by little he began appearing more often until his long 1979 to 1984 run as Max the chauffeur to Stephanie Powers and Robert Wagner in the very popular *Hart to Hart* television series. More television, bits in movies, and *Hart to Hart* television movies kept Stander busy to his death in 1994.

Shemp Howard had appeared in a silent role in *Close Relations*, but this time has a real role as gangster Stander's sidekick. Legendary today as part of the Three Stooges, Shemp also worked as a solo with Roscoe, Abbott and Costello, and W.C. Fields. Born in Brooklyn in 1895, Shemp and his older brother Moe got the acting bug early. Starting out in amateur shows and the lowest rungs of vaudeville, they got their big break in 1922 when they joined the act of Ted Healy. As Healy's "stooges" they appeared in the Broadway

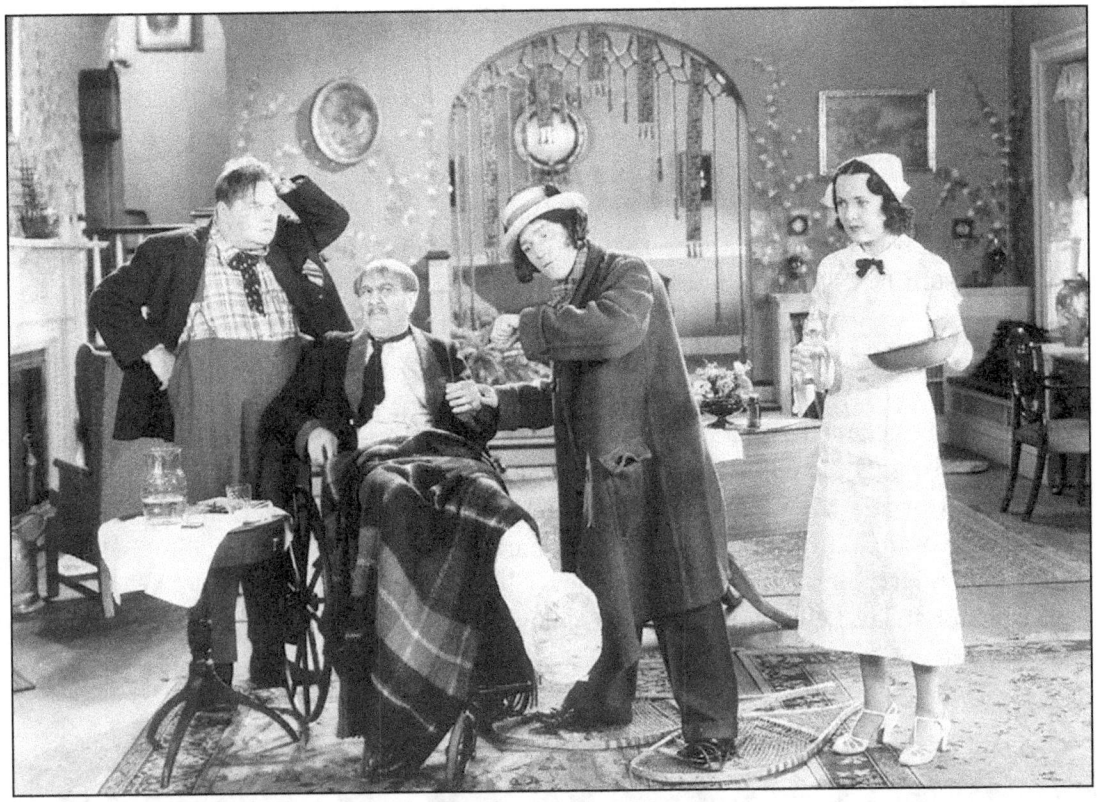

Charles Judels (wheelchair), nurse Mildred Van Dorn, and Roscoe observe Shemp Howard (middle) as one of the crazy Mole family in *Close Relations* (1933). Courtesy Cole Johnson.

shows *A Night in Spain*, *A Night in Venice*, and *The Passing Show of 1932*, as well as made their film debut in the Fox feature *Soup to Nuts* (1930). Following a falling-out with Healy, Shemp went out on his own and joined the Vitaphone unit in 1933, and was very busy with them until 1937.

Starting out as support to comics like Jack Haley, Ben Blue, and Harry Gribbon, he was soon starring in his own two-reelers such as *Smoked Hams* (1934), *His First Flame*, and *On the Wagon* (both 1935), plus was headlined as fight manager Knobby Walsh in the studio's *Joe Palooka* comedies. In 1937 Shemp moved to Hollywood, where he began doing bits in features and appearing in Columbia Pictures shorts (where brothers Moe and Curly were making *Three Stooges* comedies) most frequently with Andy Clyde. The 1940s saw Shemp on contract to Universal and making an impression in classics like *The Bank Dick* (1940), *Buck Privates*, *Hellzapoppin'* (both 1941), *It Ain't Hay*, and *Crazy House* (both 1943), as well as being teamed with Billy Gilbert and Slapsy Maxie Rosenbloom for a trio of Monogram-made ersatz *Three Stooges* features—*Three of a Kind*, *Crazy Knights* (both 1944), and *Trouble Chasers* (1945).

From there he went back to the real thing—rejoining the Stooges in 1946 following Curly's debilitating stroke. Most of the rest of his career was spent as the third stooge in shorts like *Brideless Groom* (1947), *Dopey Dicks* (1950), *Scrambled Brains* (1951), and *Goofs on the Roof* (1953). Although the budgets for the shorts were decreasing and corners were being cut, Shemp always turned in funny performances, and remained in harness right to his death in 1955 (and in fact after as producer Jules White used older footage of Shemp to make some of his final shorts like 1956's *Flagpole Jitters* and *For Crimin' Out Loud*).

Film Daily (November 4, 1933): "Instead of throwing pies, this comedy specializes in barrages of slushy dough. It gets a pretty fair amount of laughs, though it's pretty sloppy. Fatty takes a job as a baker in a shop that refuses to pay racheteers for "protection." Efforts of the gangsters to wreck the shop supply the main elements of the action."

Tomalio

Released December 30, 1933. Produced by the Vitaphone Corporation. Distributed by Warner Brothers. Directed by Raymond McCarey. Story by Jack Henley & Glen Lambert. Photography by E. B. DuPar. Music by David Mendoza. (Shot between April 7 -13 1933). Two reels. Extant. With Roscoe Arbuckle, Charles Judels, Fritz Hubert, Phyllis Holden, Phillip Rider, Jerry Bergen, Pierre de Ramey, Clyde Veaux, Clarence Rock, Aristedes De Leoni, John Barclay, Lew Kessler, Joe McCauley, Dermar Poppen.

Roscoe has a run-in with despot Charles Judels in *Tomalio* (1933). Courtesy of Ron Hutchinson/ The Vitaphone Project.

Wilbur and his buddy Fritz are trying to tour Mexico, but are having problems with the mule that's pulling their cart. They finally end up in a little town where the head man, General Garcia, is fond of executing his enemies with a slapstick firing squad. Since their aim is bad most of the supposed victims end up walking away. The General also likes music to put him in the proper mood for the executions so his personal army plays as well as shoots. Wilbur and Fritz get in bad with the General when the girl he intends to marry shows a fondness for Wilbur. Instead of shooting Wilbur the General challenges him to take part in the town's annual footrace, which the General always wins as the townspeople are afraid of his wrath. Wilbur plans to let him win, but a big spider that goes down his back makes him run like crazy, so he ends up winning the race and the girl.

Writers Glen Lambert and Jack Henley had trouble coming up with the right title for this short—first it was announced as *Cold Turkey*, then *Monkey Business*, and finally it came out as *Tomalio*. Lambert and Henley were responsible for Roscoe's series, as well as shorts for Jack Haley, Hal Le Roy, George Givot, and William Demarest. Before writing for Roscoe, Glen Lambert had a long career in silent comedy as a performer, writer, and director, but although it was a long and busy career it was always on the outside edges. Born in 1896, it's been said that he started his career as a juvenile actor for East Coast film companies like Biograph, Crystal, and Solax, and that he eventually became a cameraman.

In 1918 he hooked up with Harold "Josh" Binney (see Appendix Two) and began appearing with Nathan Dewing (a.k.a. Hilliard Karr) in Binney's *Funny Fatty Filbert Comedies* such as *Fabulous Fortune Fumblers* and *Fred's Fictitious Foundling*. The *Filberts* were made in Jacksonville, Florida, and Lambert continued working there, directing, writing, and starring in *Sunbeam Comedies* like *His Conscience, His Guide*, *A Concrete Dome*, and *A Dumbwaiter Scandal* (all 1919). During the 1920s he wrote gags for Chester, Century, and Stern Brothers Comedies, plus in 1927 he became supervisor and director of the Bray Company's *Skylark Comedies*. These consisted of *Weak Knees, Custard's Last Stand, Fresh and a Devil* (all 1927), and *Daze of '49* (1928).

Joining Vitaphone's stable of writers in 1931, he was busy with them through 1934, after which he joined Educational Pictures to work on shorts such as *The Palooka from Paducah* and *The Timid Young Man* (both 1935) for Buster Keaton. Lambert's last Hollywood credit was for additional comedy material for *Hillbilly Blitzkrieg* (1942), one of the Snuffy Smith programmers put out by Monogram Pictures. Moving back to Jacksonville, in the 1950s he was production manager of its Shamrock Studios, and made a series of shorts for Washington federal agencies. After a long career in film comedy he passed away in 1973.

Lambert's Vitaphone writing partner Jack Henley had a colorful and adventurous early life. Born in Ireland in 1896, he was a successful jockey in Ireland and England, bringing in forty-seven winners by 1913. During World War I he was part of the Royal Air Force, and spent four years in France without getting a scratch. Brought to America by statesman and financier Bernard Baruch to ride his horses, Henley eventually became a screen writer and found himself a spot at Vitaphone when talkies arrived.

Besides writing for Roscoe, he also wrote comedy for Harry Gribbon, Jack Haley, and Bob Hope, and after leaving Vitaphone in 1939 he went on to feature assignments. Some of his work included pictures for Monogram and Columbia, such as *Spooks Run*

Poster for Roscoe's Vitaphone series.

Wild (1941), *Mr. Wise Guy* (1942), *Reveille with Beverly* (1943), and *A Thousand and One Nights* (1945), followed by many entries in Columbia's *Blondie* series and Universal's *Ma and Pa Kettle* Comedies. Henley also wrote the screenplay for the sequel to the infamous *Bedtime for Bonzo* (1951), *Bonzo Goes to College* (1952), and retired in 1955.

> **Arbuckle's Death Not To Halt Three Releases**
> Death of Roscoe "Fatty" Arbuckle, whose funeral will be held today, will not affect Vitaphone release of his last three comedies. They are titled: "Tomalio," "Close Relations," and "In the Dough." Arbuckle had just finished work in the last-named two-reeler when his death occurred early Thursday morning.
> – **Film Daily**, July 1, 1933

Shot before *In the Dough* but released after, *Tomalio* was movie audience's last look at Roscoe. Although he had started the Vitaphone series looking relatively unchanged from the early 1920s, perhaps because of the strenuous nature of the second reel's footrace, it's clear to see that Roscoe wasn't exactly well. Sadly, he spends much of the race footage looking flushed and huffing and puffing. It's reported that he had already been experiencing heart issues which he kept to himself in order not to upset the Vitaphone people or his new wife. Even if he wasn't feeling tip-top he had waited too long to pass up this comeback shot, but it's probable that the rigorous shooting schedule of the series hastened his too early demise.

Film Daily (December 22, 1933): "Last of the Fatty Arbuckle comedies is a generally entertaining concoction in a Mexican locale. Slapstick, gags and other typical Arbuckle material combine to make the affair altogether satisfying."

Variety (December 19, 1933): "Fine production attention raises the screen value of "Tomalio" considerably. In a technical way, it represents a competent job all around."

Final Curtain

The Vitaphone shorts were a success and there was talk of a starring feature, but on June 28, 1933 Roscoe died quietly with Addie in their hotel room.

It seems unfair of fate to have chosen to take him then, but with his comeback in motion he probably died happy. What was unfair were the events that happened in 1921, and the neglect that has followed him to this day. With his career cut off early he never had the opportunity, like Chaplin and Keaton, to create mature comedy masterpieces where he might have been able to combine the refined style of his starring features with the grand slapstick of his earlier shorts. But for a short time he made the whole world laugh.

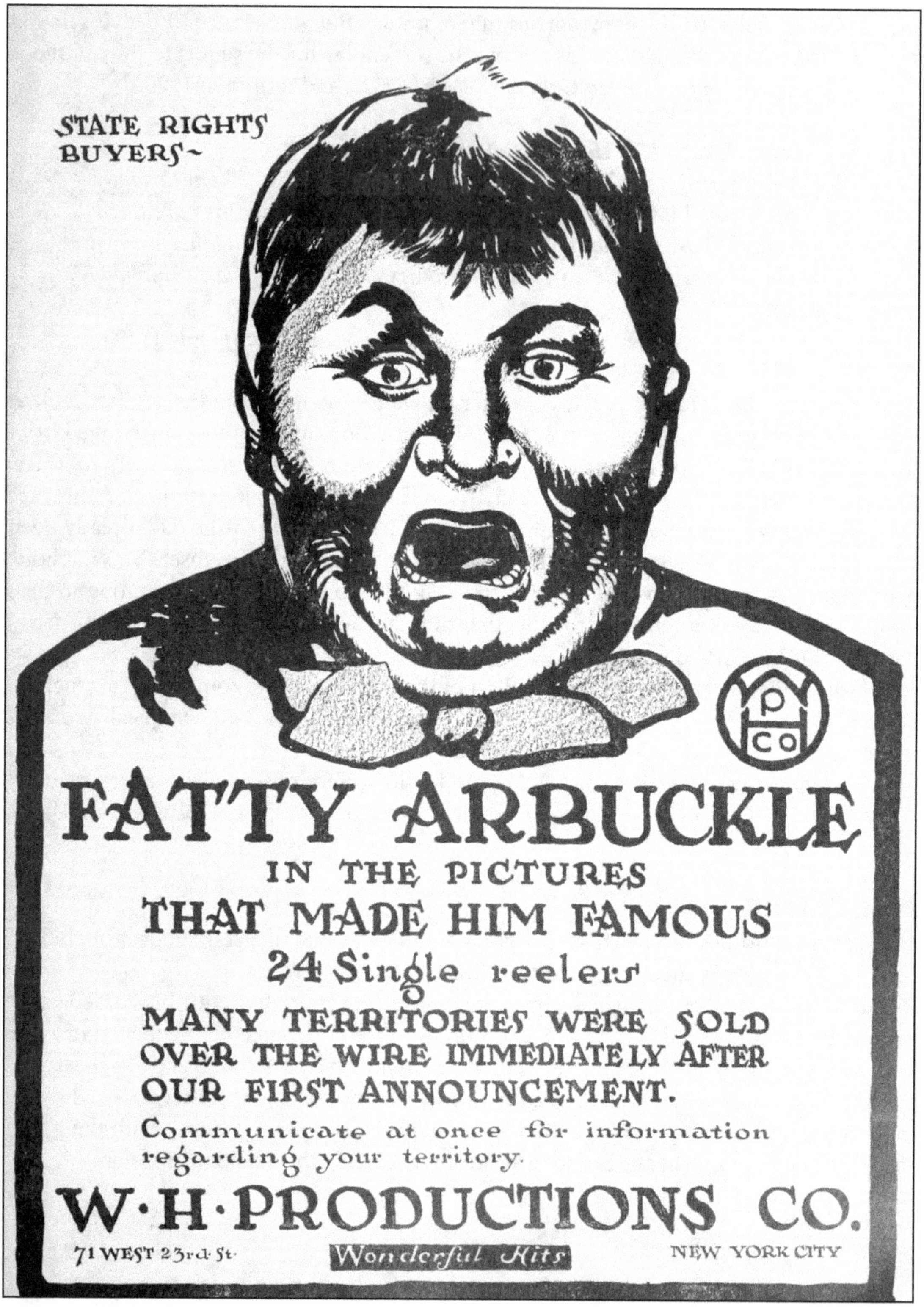

A 1918 exhibitor ad for W.H. Productions' Arbuckle reissues.

Appendix One

Seeing the Films Today

The good news is that a substantial amount of the Arbuckle films survive today—about one hundred and forty-five of the estimated two hundred and nineteen. But although certain titles exist they're not always readily available to the general public as they're housed at film archives—often unrestored and sometimes only in nitrate prints. None of his first films for Selig or Nestor are known to survive, and his very early 1913 and 1914 Keystones are very hit or miss. From 1915 on the bulk of his work is around, although with sporadic pockets of missing items. Considering the scandal and its aftermath of Roscoe's films being pulled from the screens, it's amazing that so much is still available.

By 1914 Roscoe was one of Mack Sennett's biggest and most profitable stars. Because of their immense popularity the shorts were constantly re-issued by various states rights companies such as W.H. Productions, Tower Film Corp., Tri-Stone Films, Majestic Pictures, Inc., and Unity Photoplays. These outfits would acquire the rights and repackage the films—often changing the titles and re-writing the intertitles. A W.H. Productions exhibitor ad in the December 28, 1918 *Moving Picture World* boasted:

> *Beyond a question they are the best one and two reel subjects on the market—re-edited, re-constructed, re-titled.*

Fatty and Mabel Adrift (1916) became *Cast Adrift—and How!*, *A Robust Romeo* (1914) recirculated as *Fatty the Homebreaker*, and *The Sea Nymphs* (1914) ended up as *His Diving Beauty*. Other retitlings included *Fatty's Timid Wife*, *Mabel's Speed Cop*, *A Small Town Bully*, and *A Lunch Room Romance*. During World War 1, W. H. Productions, citing the "importance of keeping before the public eye continually the great purpose for which we are fighting," even gave their series the patriotic brand names "Eagle Keystones" and "Liberty Keystones."

The Roscoe reissues reached a peak in 1920 just before the scandal, with canny producers using his new feature film status and popularity to recycle his old Sennett one and two-reelers. When the scandal hit the newspapers Roscoe's features were withdrawn from cinemas as were the earlier shorts, although according to the trade magazines there were a few enterprising exhibitors who showed Roscoe's pictures anyway and claimed to get good crowds despite the controversy. While curbed in America, Roscoe remained popular overseas and his films continued to circulate there, including his Paramount features.

The changeover to sound led to silent films being rarely shown, but a few of Roscoe's most popular titles were available in the home market. This is when the film archives became established and began their yeoman work preserving early cinema. Around the world many of Roscoe's films were found and saved. Without the archives' efforts we'd be missing key Arbuckle titles such as *The Gangsters*, *A Noise from the Deep* (both 1913), *The Butcher Boy* (1917), *The Round-Up* (1920), and *The Iron Mule* (1925), to name only a few.

One archival project that involved a substantial number of Roscoe's films was the Library of Congress' restoration of their paper prints. Not long after the birth of movies producers came up with a way of copywriting their films which involved sending a paper copy to the Library in Washington, DC. This started with a copyright application in 1894 for the *Edison Kinetoscopic Record of a Sneeze* (a.k.a. *Fred Ott's Sneeze*), and continued until 1915. The practice finally died out as a copyright law that specifically covered motion pictures went into effect in 1912. All the submitted paper copies remained at the Library, and although becoming dried and wrinkled over the years they were much more stable than nitrate film stock.

Roscoe feeds a bear at the Idora Park Zoo in the paper print of *Mabel's Wilful Way* (1915). Courtesy the Library of Congress.

In the 1940s a project was started to catalog and finally copy these paper prints back to film frame by frame. Completed in the early 1960s the films became available to scholars at the Library. A large chunk of Mack Sennett's Keystones were part of the collection, including almost all of Roscoe's 1915 output. So thanks to the paper prints we still have Arbuckle comedies such as *Fatty's New Role*, *Mabel and Fatty's Married Life*, *That Little Band of Gold*, *Fatty's Reckless Fling*, *Miss Fatty's Seaside Lovers*, and *Fatty's Plucky Pup*.

The 1960s saw Blackhawk Films offering a few home use Arbuckle titles like *Fatty and Mabel Adrift* (1916), *A Bandit*, *Peeping Pete* (both 1913), and *Fatty's Magic Pants* (1914) for sale in 8mm and 16mm prints. At the same time the revival of interest in the films of Buster Keaton brought with it residual attention to Roscoe. The demand for Buster created a new life for the Comique comedies, and while the focus was on Keaton, audiences that had never seen Roscoe were now getting treated to screenings of *The Butcher Boy*, *Fatty at Coney Island* (both 1917), and *Back Stage* (1919). The Keaton phenomenon was largely engineered and overseen by legendary film collector and pirate Raymond Rohauer, who was finding, restoring, and exhibiting many of the formerly missing Comiques for their Buster appearances. Young film students and buffs coming to the Keaton festivals for Buster, were taken with Roscoe and interested in seeing more.

Decades had passed since the scandal, and a cooler examination of the facts led to a re-evaluation of the case. These seeds of reinterest and rehabilitation were watered and fertilized by the home video boom of the 1980s. The previously mentioned Blackhawk Films put a few of their Arbuckle titles, like *Fatty's Tintype Tangle* (1915), on various VHS releases, but the first substantial home collection of Roscoe's films came in an eight volume series. Titled *The Original Keystone Comedies*, these were released by an outfit called Video Film Classics and produced by Kartes Video Communications, Inc. The bulk of the volumes featured Roscoe, with other units given over to Mack Swain and Syd Chaplin. The material for the series came from the previously described LOC paper prints. Since they were in public domain an outfit named Rhodes Productions packaged them for release, and for the first time a large swatch of Arbuckle was available for home consumption.

The next major release of Roscoe's films was Milestone Film and Video's 2003 set featuring *The Cook* (1918) and *A Reckless Romeo* (1917). Lovingly put together by Milestone, the set presents prints restored by the Norsk Filminstitut and EYE Filmuseum (along with Harold Lloyd's 1920 *Number Please?*), and was the first time that these Roscoe rarities were available for scholars and a general audience.

2005 saw the release of what remains the essential home video collection—Laughsmith Entertainment's *The Forgotten Films of Roscoe "Fatty" Arbuckle*. Distributed by Mackinac Media, this four-disc set gives a very comprehensive look at Arbuckle's career from his early Keystone days through the 1930s. Not just focusing on his work as a performer, there's numerous examples of his directorial efforts such as *The Movies* (1925), *My Stars*, *Fool's Luck* (both 1926), and *Bridge Wives* (1932). Also included are video "restorations" of hard to see films like *Love* (1919) and *Curses* (1925). Producer Paul E. Gierucki, with the assistance of silent comedy stalwarts such as Bruce Lawton, Andy Coryell, Robert Arkus, David B. Pearson, Richard M. Roberts, Brent Walker, and yours truly, put together what is still one of the best silent comedy releases ever put on the market.

Al St John has at Roscoe while Corinne Parquet (left) and Alice lake (right) try to avert the disaster in the rediscovered *A Reckless Romeo* (1917). Courtesy Marc Wanamaker/Bison Archives.

Two other important releases are Warner Home Video's 2012 *The Vitaphone Comedy Collection: Volume 1*, which contains all six of the Arbuckle comeback sound shorts (as well as thirteen with Shemp Howard) in beautiful transfers, and 2016's *Buster Keaton: The Shorts Collection 1917-1923*. This is a five-disc set from Lobster/Kino that includes very nice versions of all the surviving Comique shorts with Arbuckle and Keaton. Some lower-cost outfits such as Alpha Home Entertainment have put out sporadic public domain versions of *Fatty Joins the Force* (1913), *Fatty and Minnie Hee-Haw* (1914), and *Mabel, Fatty and the Law* (1915), but as of this writing the most recent set of note is Cinemuseum's 2017 release of *The Round-Up* (1920). Again producer Paul E. Gierucki has put together a high quality Arbuckle release, this time with very good remasterings of the 1913 Keystones *A Bandit* and *Peeping Pete*.

Finally, the latest phase of the re-exposure of Roscoe to the public at large has been the highlighting of his work on Turner Classic Movies. As part of their quality presentation of classic films, over the years the network has given focus to overlooked and underseen performers such as Marion Davies, Harold Lloyd, Warren William, and Roscoe. Having acquired the broadcast rights for the Paul Gierucki DVD sets, the Arbuckle films, including directorial efforts, have been shown frequently, and often in primetime spots. Their classy presentation, complete with detailed background and production information, has done much to keep Roscoe's legacy alive into the Twenty-First Century.

Specific Arbuckle Reissue Titles:

For the Love of Mabel (June 30, 1913) - *Fatty Foils the Villain* (Tower Film Corp)
A Noise from the Deep (July 17, 1913) – *Fatty's Bubble Trick* (W.H. Productions)
Mabel's New Hero (August 28, 1913) – *Fatty and the Bathing Beauties*
Mabel's Dramatic Career (September 8, 1913) – *Her Dramatic Debut* (W. H. Productions)
Two Old Tars (October 20, 1913) - *The Sea Dog*
The Speed Kings (October 30, 1913) *Teddy Tetzlaff and Earl Cooper; Speed Kings*
Wine (November 13, 1913) – *How Old Are You* (British release)
Ride for a Bride (December 8, 1913) – *Fatty, the Golfer* (Tower Film Corporation)
His Sister's Kids (December 20, 1913) – *Fatty's Naughty Nephews*
The Under Sheriff (January 8, 1914) – *Fatty Disturbs the Peace* (W.H. Productions)
Making a Living (February 2, 1914) – *A Busted Johnny* (W. H. Productions), *Troubles, Doing His Best, Take My Picture*
A Robust Romeo (February 12, 1914) – *Fatty the Homebreaker* (W.H. Productions)
A Film Johnnie (March 2, 1914 – *The Movie Nut, His Million Dollar Job*
Tango Tangles (March 9, 1914) – *Charlies' Recreation, Music Hall, A Tango Tangle* (British release)
His Favorite Pastime (March 16, 1914) – *His Reckless Fling* (W.H. Productions), *The Bonehead, Charlie is Thirsty*
Barnyard Flirtations (March 28, 1914) – *Fatty Disturbs the Peace*
The Chicken Chaser (April 2, 1914) *Fatty Chases Chickens* (W.H. Productions), *New Yard Lovers*
A Bath House Beauty (April 13, 1914) – *A Bathing Beauty* (British release)
A Water Dog (May 18, 1914) – *Fatty's Streak of Yellow* (Tower Film Corporation)
The Knockout (June 17, 1914) – *The Pugilist* (W.H. Productions), *Counted Out* (Maco Comedies), *The Fighting Demon*
Love and Bullets (July 4, 1914) *The Trouble Mender* (W.H. Productions)
The Masquerader (August 27, 1914) – *The Female Impersonator* (W. H. Productions), *Charlie the Actor* (Pathescope), *Putting One Over, The Picnic, Charlie at the Studio, The Perfumed Lady*
His New Profession (August 31, 1914) – *The Good-For-Nothing* (W.H. Productions)
The Rounders (September 7, 1914) – *Oh What Night* (W.H. Productions), *Revelry, Two of a Kind, Going Down*
Fatty's Debut (September 26, 1914) – *Fatty Butts In* (W.H. Productions)
Fatty Again (October 3, 1914) – *Fatty the Fourflusher* (W.H. Productions)
An Incompetent Hero (November 12, 1914) – *Fatty's Indiscretion* (Tower Film Corporation)
Fatty's Jonah Day (November 16, 1914) – *Fatty's Hoodoo Day* (W.H. Productions)
Fatty's Wine Party (November 21, 1914) – *Fatty's Wild Night* (W.H. Productions)

The Sea Nymphs (November 23, 1914) – *His Diving Beauty* (W.H. Productions)
Fatty's Magic Pants (December 14, 1914) – *Fatty's Suitless Day* (W.H. Productions)
Mabel and Fatty's Wash Day (January 14, 1915) – *Fatty's Flirtation*
Fatty and Mabel's Simple Life (January 18, 1915) – *The Joy Riders*
Fatty and Mabel at the San Diego Exposition (January 23, 1915) – *Fatty's Joy Ride* (W.H. Productions)
Mabel, Fatty and the Law (January 28, 1915) – *Fatty's Spooning Days* (W.H. Productions)
Fatty's Reckless Fling (March 4, 1915) – *Fatty Cleans Up* (W.H. Productions)
Fatty's Chance Acquaintance (March 8, 1915) *Fatty's Flirtation*
That Little Band of Gold (March 15, 1915) – *For Better or Worse* (W.H. Productions)
Fatty's Faithful Fido (March 20, 1915) *Fatty the Bouncer* (W.H. Productions), *Fatty's Canine Friend* (British Release)
Wished on Mabel (April 19, 1915) - *The Willful Flirt, What Happened*
The Little Teacher (June 21, 1915) – *A Small Town Bully* (W.H. Productions)
Fatty's Plucky Pup (June 28, 1915) – *Fatty's Canine Friend* (W.H. Productions), *Foiled by Fido*
Fatty and Mabel Adrift (January 1916) – *Cast Adrift—And How!*, *Mabel's Jealous Romeo*
His Wife's Mistake (April 2, 1916) – *His Funny Mishap*

Miscellaneous Titles:

A Lunch Room Romance, Fatty's Timid Wife, A Farmyard Romeo, Mabel's Speed Cop, Fatty the Masher, Fatty the Dodger, The Bouncer, Fatty's Wash Day, Fatty's Hard Day, At the Beach, The Tough Rube, Fatty's Busy Day, Fatty the Aviator

Appendix Two
"The Screen Must Have a Fat Comedian"

ROSCOE ARBUCKLE IS PROBABLY the best-known of the silent screen's plus-sized comedians, but he was just the tip of the very broad-bottomed fat comic iceberg. Since silent comedy was based on visual shorthand a round figure generally denoted humor, and there were numerous other oversized comics who frolicked before the cameras that have been forgotten today. This piece has been limited to the "everyman" type of big comedians. While

Jimmy Aubrey and his leading lady make snug use of Frank Alexander's balloon trousers in an unidentified comedy.

Portrait of early large everyman John R. Cumpson.

there were the large comic heavies such as Roscoe "Tiny" Ward, Wayland Trask, Tiny Sanford, Pierre Collosse, William Irving and others, they deserve a study of their own. Taking a good look at the playing field there were almost as many jumbo comics in silents as there were small ones with moustaches, and sadly one thing these large fellows almost all had in common, besides being funny, was a limited life span.

Most discussions of fat movie comics begin with John Bunny, but he was predated by the more than stout John R. Cumpson, who became popular with the Biograph Company in 1908. Cumpson came from the stage, and while details are sketchy he made his debut at Col. Sinn's Montauk Theatre in Brooklyn, starred in Frohman Brothers' productions doing German and Swedish dialect roles, and appeared in shows such as *Up State York* and Victor Herbert's *Song Birds*. In 1908 he joined D.W. Griffith's Biograph unit, and while doing both dramas and comedies for the master it was the comedies that he became known for.

One of his first films was *A Smoked Husband* (1908) in which he played a jealous husband who hides in a chimney to spy on his wife. Hubby gets his comeuppance for suspecting his spouse when the maid starts a fire in the hearth. The popularity of this film led to a series of *Jones Family* Comedies. One of the earliest film comedy series, with Mrs. Jones played by Florence Lawrence, it lasted from 1908 until Ms. Lawrence left Biograph in 1909. The focus was on the misadventures of a long-married couple, and Ms. Lawrence later told *Photoplay*:

> When we undertook the first picture there was no intention of making a series of comedy productions, but when the exchanges started asking for more and more "Jonesy" pictures, we kept it up until I left the Biograph Company. Mr. Cumpson was the most serious comedian I have ever known. Nothing was ever funny to him, and he never tried to be funny. When all the rest of the cast would laugh at something he had said or done he would become indignant, thinking we were making fun of him. What turned out to be the first of the "Jonesy" pictures was called "A Smoked Husband," a play in which groundless jealousy gets it just deserts. Instead of being called "Jones," Mr. Cumpson was called "Benjamin Bibbs," and how the public ever came to call him "Jonesy" is more than I know.

Titles included *Mr. Jones at the Ball* (1908), *Mr. Jones Has a Card Party*, *Her First Biscuits*, *His Wife's Mother*, and *Mrs. Jones' Love, or, "I Want My Hat"* (all 1909).

With his round figure and balding dome (which was often garnished with a toupee) the comic made a perfect put-upon everyman, and played that in other Biograph shorts such as *Schneider's Anti-Noise Crusade* (1909) where he's trying to write a speech but is distracted by all the noise his family is making around him. That night burglars come in the house, and when Schnieder finds that they're stealing all the noise making items he helps them get away. In *A Troublesome Satchel* (1909) Cumpson buys a bag and finds that it's filled with burglar tools. He spends the rest of the short trying his best to lose the bag, but it keeps being returned to him.

Leaving Biograph at the start of 1910 Cumpson joined his old colleague Florence Lawrence at Imp for a handful of pictures, such as the Jones Family clone *The Nichols on Vacation* (1910). Soon he settled in at Edison with a new series and character:

> *"There's Jones again!" a fan was heard to say in one of the local theatres on a recent evening while one of the Edison pictures was being run, and judging from the audible hum that swept over the audience at the same moment, he was not the only one who had made the same discovery.*
>
> *It was "Jones" all right. There was no mistaking that rotund figure and that good-natured, mobile face, so easily wreathed in smiles or the most convulsing of grimaces. "Jones" (stage name of course) is in a class all by himself when it comes to the interpretation of comedy roles before the camera. He was the most popular actor in that field of the motion picture*

Florence Lawrence and John Cumpson pucker up in front of Jeanie Macpherson (left) and Herbert Prior (right) in 1909's *Mrs. Jones Entertains*.

> *a year or two ago, and the Edison Company made a "ten-strike" when it brought him out of retirement to act for its films. So far he has appeared in two productions. "Fortune's Fool," released May 24, and "Bumptious on Birds," released June 7. The next of the series, "How Bumptious Papered the Parlor," will be released on July 15, after which comes "Bumptious as an Aviator," which will be released July 29.*
>
> *These short comedies of Edison's are making a decided "hit" with the patrons of moving pictures theatres. They are splendid "fillers" for use with the heavy dramatic stuff. Sometimes there is only one big humorous situation developed, and that as a climax to the story. That is true, however, only in the case of very short subjects. In the "Bumptious" series a laugh can be expected with every turn of the crank.*
>
> – **The Nickelodeon**, July, 15, 1910

Bumptious was Edison's bourgeois and somewhat self-important everyman. Some of his misadventures included *Mr. Bumptious on Birds, Bumptious Takes up Automobiling, Bumptious as a Fireman,* and *Bumptious Plays Baseball* (all 1910). Always considering himself to be a little smarter and a little wiser than the rest of the world, events in the films prove just the opposite. The most accessible of the Bumptious series today is *How Bumptious Papered the Parlor* (1910).

Coming into the parlor when a redecorator is giving his wife an estimate, Bumptious is aghast at the price and decides that he can easily do it himself. After picking up the needed equipment and wallpaper, he proceeds to make a huge mess of everything, covering the room, his spouse, the maid, and himself with paste and lopsided strips of wallpaper. Finally our hero sees the light and hires a professional, who does the job in double time as Bumptious relaxes in a chair with a good cigar.

Well promoted by the studio, the series and Cumpson were a big hit:

> *Perhaps no character in motion picture making is funnier than Bumptious.*
> – **Moving Picture World**, October 22, 1910

> *I have an ungratified and probably never-to-be gratified desire. I want to see John Bunny as a father and "Bumptious" as his son—give that pair the most "teary" comedy ever written and I would wager the hole in a doughnut against its rim, they get away with it.*
> –**Moving Picture World**, July 8, 1911

Later during his stint with Edison, Cumpson was teamed with the excellent comedy director C.J. Williams for titles such as *Ludwig from Germany, The Troubles of A. Butler, An International Heart Breaker,* and *John Brown's Heir*. At the very end of 1911 Cumpson returned to Imp to headline, and two of these shorts still exist in the Desmet Collection of the EYE Filmmuseum in the Netherlands.

Billy's Séance (1911) was his first release for Imp, and stars Cumpson as Billy, who follows a pretty girl into a spiritualist's parlor. After the medium reprimands him for flirting with the woman he gets the "spiritual bug" on seeing her table move on its own. Later, with a book he got at the parlor, he tries to call up spirits at his club, and becomes the laughing stock of his fellow club members. To get even with them he has his table electrified and hatches a plot. Plying the scoffing fellows with a couple of rounds of drinks he gets them to come to the table for a demonstration of his mystical abilities. He then turns on the juice and gets great pleasure from watching them bounce around and fry from the electrical current. All the commotion brings in a couple of cops, who decide

John Cumpson tries to pull a fast one on his wife Anne Taylor in *Mr. Smith, Barber* (1912).

to run in the whole group. Billy convinces them to let him just pay a fine which he puts on the table. When they reach for the cash he turns on the power again, and as they're helplessly stuck to the table Billy nonchalantly takes his money, puts on his hat and coat, lights up a cigar, and heads out on his way.

The other survivor, *Mr. Smith, Barber* (1912), shows Cumpson trailblazing in W.C. Fields territory. The film opens with Mr. Smith trying to enjoy his breakfast despite the nagging of his bossy wife. A friend comes into his barbershop with an invitation for an evening of fun at the Cozy Corner Club. In order to go Smith sends himself a telegram calling him out of town for an emergency. Pretending that he doesn't want to go, his wife insists that he must, so she packs him up and delivers him to the train station. Smith comes back out when she leaves and wends his way to the Cozy Corner where he joins his friend and two young ladies.

In Smith's absence his wife takes over the barbershop. Putting on his working jacket to shave a customer she finds the invite to the Cozy Corner in the pocket. Deciding to catch him in the act, she disguises herself as a man and heads to the Club. There she picks a fight with her hubby, and when they start to duel with swords she pulls off her moustache and reveals herself. At that point Smith realizes that his punishment is only just beginning.

Cumpson's series for Imp, which also included *The Wrong Weight*, *A Case of Dynamite*, and *Chappie the Chaperone*, was very popular, but complications from diabetes took him away from the screen in late 1912. He died of pneumonia a few months later on March 15, 1913.

While Cumpson led the way his place was soon taken by John Bunny, who quickly became the large-sized cinema superstar, as well as one of its first internationally known figures. According to legend, in 1910 the rotund actor presented himself at the Vitagraph Studio in Brooklyn looking for work. In a career that had encompassed twenty-two years, Bunny had appeared in minstrel shows, circuses, vaudeville, and worked with stage legends like William Brady, Lew Fields, and Raymond Hitchcock. Despite this long track record he had decided that movies were the coming thing and that "he would rather be behind the guns than in front of them." Bunny, who looked like Shakespeare's Falstaff and Sir Toby Belch come to life, made an immediate impression on moviegoers and became a favorite.

In 1911 he began working regularly with Flora Finch. The combination of the expansive Bunny with the severe Finch created an instant combative chemistry, and although their most popular films were made together it's been said that they had an active dislike for each other. Playing a variety of "salt of the earth" characters such as flirty husbands, old bachelors, crusty sea captains, etc., Bunny was a film actor years ahead of his time who got many of his laughs from a subtle look, or when a conflict of emotions would play across his broad face.

His films with Flora Finch were called "Bunnyfinches" by their fans, many of whom assumed the pair was married in real life. *The Subduing of Mrs. Nag* (1911) finds Finch as the henpecker of the title who objects to pretty Mabel Normand as her spouse Bunny's secretary. No matter how Mabel tries to homely herself up Mrs. Nag is still not satisfied, so finally Mabel pretends to be a boy in her brother's clothing and gets the old lady to flirt

Appendix Two: "The Screen Must Have a Fat Comedian" • 597

John Bunny ends up saving the game in *Hearts and Diamonds* (1914). Courtesy Louie Despres.

with "him." Husband Bunny is in on the scheme, and catching the missus in a flirtation he now has the upper hand to order her to keep her nose out of his business. In the famous *A Cure for Pokeritis* (1912) Bunny has sworn off playing poker to Flora, but is actually still indulging one night a week under the guise of it being a "Sons of the Morning" social club meeting. Flora gets suspicious when Bunny re-enacts the poker games in his sleep, and contacts her effeminate cousin Freddie. Following Bunny on his next evening out Freddie confirms the truth and conspires with Flora to have his bible class masquerade as cops and "raid" the next game. The following week the scheme goes through as planned and when Freddie and company are dragging the gamblers off to the hoosegow their wives conveniently show up and get them off the hook, leaving the miscreants in their custody and debt.

Bunny was a physical comedian, but unlike Roscoe was not a slapstick comedian—he didn't take falls or throw objects. One thing that Bunny and Arbuckle did have in common was their ability and frequency in appearing in drag. It wasn't long after Bunny's first films that he started turning up in crinoline and lace. *A Queen for a Day* (1911) starred the comic as Bridget McSweeney, an Irish cook who has come into an inheritance. Now that she has dough her old working-class boyfriend is no longer good enough for her, and she decides to marry nobility to get a title. Other examples include *Kitty and the Cowboys* (1911) where the comedian poses as his sister to trick a group of ranch hands, *Doctor Bridget* (1912) which has Bunny as another cook who this time decides that the

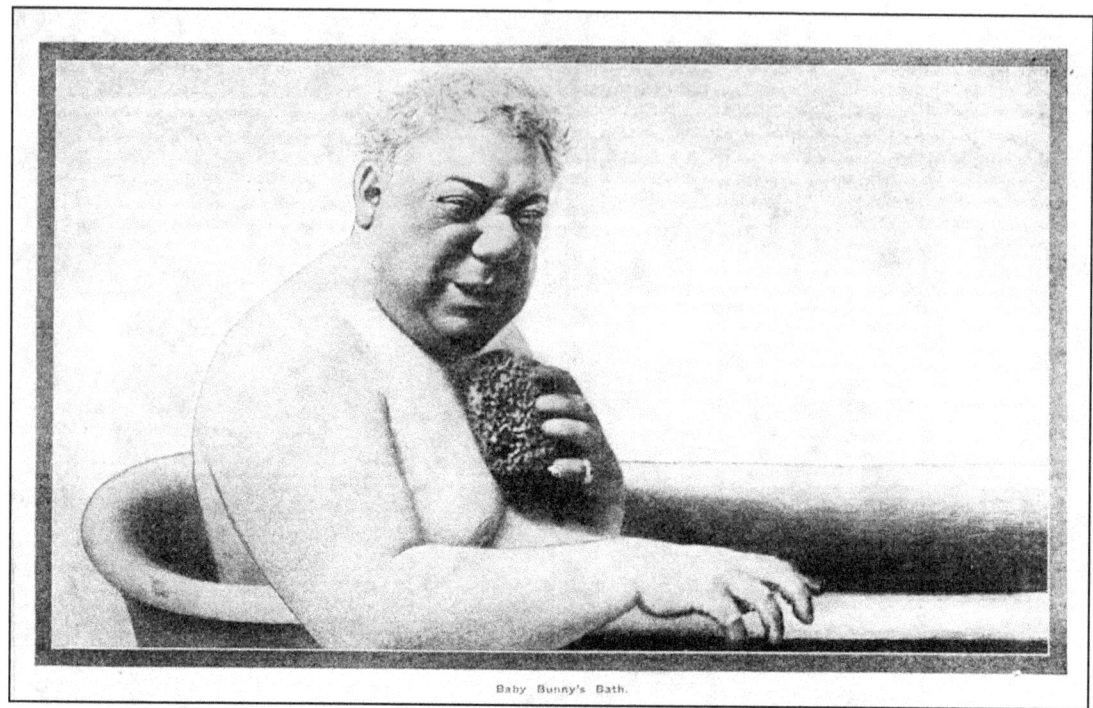

Once seen there are some things that can never be unseen—like this image of John Bunny in his bath from the souvenir program of his 1915 stage show *Bunny in Funnyland*.

way to cure the sickly and pampered son of her employer is to get rid of the fancy doctors and medicines and put him to good, old-fashioned work, and *Bunny's Honeymoon* (1913) where to teach wastrel Wally Van a lesson the comic poses as the wife that Van can't remember marrying on a drunken spree. The prospect of Bunny as his bride sobers Wally up pretty quickly.

Although physically filling the stereotype of the jolly fat man, it's rumored that Bunny was bad-tempered and egotistical, and, due to his extreme weight, narcoleptic, even able to snooze away in a complete standing position. In 1914, despite declining health, the comedian took on an extensive stage tour in his own show *Bunny in Funnyland*. Overwork, combined with kidney disease, caused his death on May 1, 1915. Tributes from around the world eulogized Bunny, predicting that he and his films would always be cherished by future generations, but sadly within only a few years the memory of him had dimmed and most of his films disappeared.

Not long after his death the remnants of Bunny's fame brought two George Bunnys to the screen—one was his brother and the other his son. The brother was large and resembled John, and had had his own stage career. He came to films at his brother's death and became a busy character actor. Starting out with the Eastern Film Company making features like *Cap'n Eri* (1915) and *Pelican Comedy* shorts such as *Hearts and Harpoons* (the shorts were eventually released in 1917 as *Jaxon Comedies*), more mainstream titles included *Friend Husband* (1918), *The Lost World*, *Lights of Old Broadway* (both 1925), and *Thrilling Youth* (1926). His work in sound films was mostly uncredited bits, but he

George Bunny the brother on the left with bald Dan Mason in *Hearts and Harpoons* (1917—courtesy Joseph Eckhardt) and George the son (with glasses) on the right in a slide for *Home Brewed Youth* (1921—courtesy Matt Vogel).

remained active right up to his death in 1952. George the son had a brief stint as the starring comic of his own series of two-reelers for Capitol Comedies such as *When Martin Gets Here* (1920), *Home Brewed Youth*, and *Why Worry?* (both 1921). As a comedian the younger Bunny made little impression, or as the December 5, 1920 *Film Daily* put it— "while he greatly resembles his well-remembered parent, he does not possess the same amount of comedy ability." Even before his father died George was involved in making and photographing films, and after his quick spell as a star he became an assistant cameraman for many years.

In the wake of Bunny's success Vitagraph seems to have decided to corner the market on fat comedians and hired three more—keeping them as "Bunny back-ups." Hughie (sometimes Hughey) Mack was born in Brooklyn in 1884 as Hugh McGowan. Originally an undertaker, thanks to an outgoing personality he became involved in amateur theatricals and became popular appearing at clubs and societies. It was while entertaining at a supper club that he was seen by an influential member of the Vitagraph staff, and soon ended up a member of the studio's supporting ensemble. Starting in 1912 he appeared with the likes of Bunny, Flora Finch, and Wally Van, and quickly gathered attention. Following Roscoe's popularity at Keystone, Mack was sometimes referred to as "Fatty" in vehicles such as *Fatty's Affair of Honor*, *Fatty on the Job* (both 1913), and *Fatty's Sweetheart* (1914), or even "Fat Boob" as he's billed in *The Dog House Builders* (1913).

Kept extremely busy by the studio, besides his starring shorts he worked frequently with Flora Finch, Kate Price, and William Shea in titles like *Sweeney's Christmas Bird* (1914), *A Pair of Queens*, and *Some Duel* (both 1915). Mack was able to bridge Vitagraph's transition from situation comedy to out-and-out slapstick. In 1916 he starred in a series of anything-for-a-laugh shorts directed by a young Larry Semon that included *Hash and Havoc*, *There and Back*, and *The Man from Egypt*. From here he moved on to Hollywood to headline at L-Ko and Century Comedies. At that time Roscoe was shooting on the East Coast, which led one wag to write in the November 1917 *Picture-Play Magazine*:

Lucille Lee Stewart is *Fatty's Sweetheart* (1914) to Hughie Mack.

> *Hughie Mack, the pulchritudinous comedian known to every motion-picture fan for his work in Vitagraph during a long period of time—almost since the formation of the company, in fact—is a Vitagrapher no longer. Hughie and his expansive wardrobe made their way cross country during August, and are now found in and about the sacred precincts of the L-KO studios in Los Angeles, where Hughie is now the featured star of the popular comedies released through Universal. With Hughie in "Los" and "Fatty" Arbuckle in New York, the balancing of the country seems complete—in fact, rumor has it that that was one of the inducements made Hughie to go West—the danger that with both he and Arbuckle on the Eastern edge of the country these United States might tip and slide into the Atlantic.*

After more shorts for Mack Sennett and Hal Roach he broke into supporting roles in features, becoming a favorite of director Erich von Stroheim, for whom he appeared in *Greed* (1923), *The Merry Widow* (1925), and *The Wedding March* (1928). Some of his other features include *Trifling Women* (1921), *Mare Nostrum* (1926), and *Four Sons* (1928), before he died of a heart attack at age forty-two in 1927.

The second of the "Big V" extra-large comics is the now-forgotten James Lackaye. A long-time stage veteran, and brother of the well-known Wilton Lackaye, before coming to films James made a name for himself in shows such as *Way Down East, New York State Folks, The Gentleman from Mississippi*, and *The High Cost of Living* with star Lew Fields. In 1913 he joined the Vitagraph family, and besides supporting work starred in his own series of *Bingles* comedies. Mr. Bingles was a bourgeois father and husband, and in misadventures such as *Bingles Mends the Clock, Bingle's Nightmare, or, If It Had Only Been True* (both 1913), and *Mr. Bingle's Melodrama* (1914) he was always in hot water with his wife, children, or servants. In 1915 Lackaye made the move to features in Vitagraph's *The Battle Cry of Peace*, and between stage engagements did a few more such as *York State Folks* (1915), *The Upstart* (1916), and *Pals First* (1918) before his death in 1919.

Portrait of James Lackaye. Author's collection.

The last of our hefty Vitagraph trio was Jay Dwiggens, plump, older, and balding, who was actually hired as a replacement for Bunny. As mentioned before Bunny and Flora Finch are said to have disliked each other, and after Dwiggens arrived at the studio Finch appeared with him and never with Bunny again. The switch was basically introduced in the short *Bunny's Little Brother* (1914), and afterwards he and Finch were busy in titles like *A Strand of Blonde Hair* (1914), *Whose Husband?, Strictly Neutral, The Starring of Flora Finchurch*, and *A Mistake in Typesetting* (all 1915). After Vitagraph he moved over to the Mack Sennett organization to play fathers or older husbands in *Secrets of a Beauty Parlor, Dangers of a Bride*, and *His Uncle Dudley* (all 1917), as well as Triangle Komedy shorts like *A Film Exposure* and *A Finished Product* (both 1917). Dwiggens found a welcome spot in features, especially the Douglas Fairbanks comedies *Bound in Morocco, He Comes Up Smiling* (both 1918), and *His Majesty the American* (1919). Also supporting Bryant Washburn and May Allison, his career came to a premature end with his death at fifty-two in 1919.

Vitagraph's good luck with large comics opened the flood gates for bringing full-figured comics to the screen. John Steppling came from an extensive theatrical career—working for producer Daniel Frohman and with star E. H. Sothern, in addition to appearing in the original production of *The Prisoner of Zenda*. He joined Essanay in 1911 and became a name with a series of *Billy McGrath Comedies*. The McGrath persona was a jovial everyman in the Bunny mold with misadventures like *Billy McGrath's Love Letters, Billy McGrath's Art Career* (both 1912), and *Billy McGrath on Broadway* (1913). After two

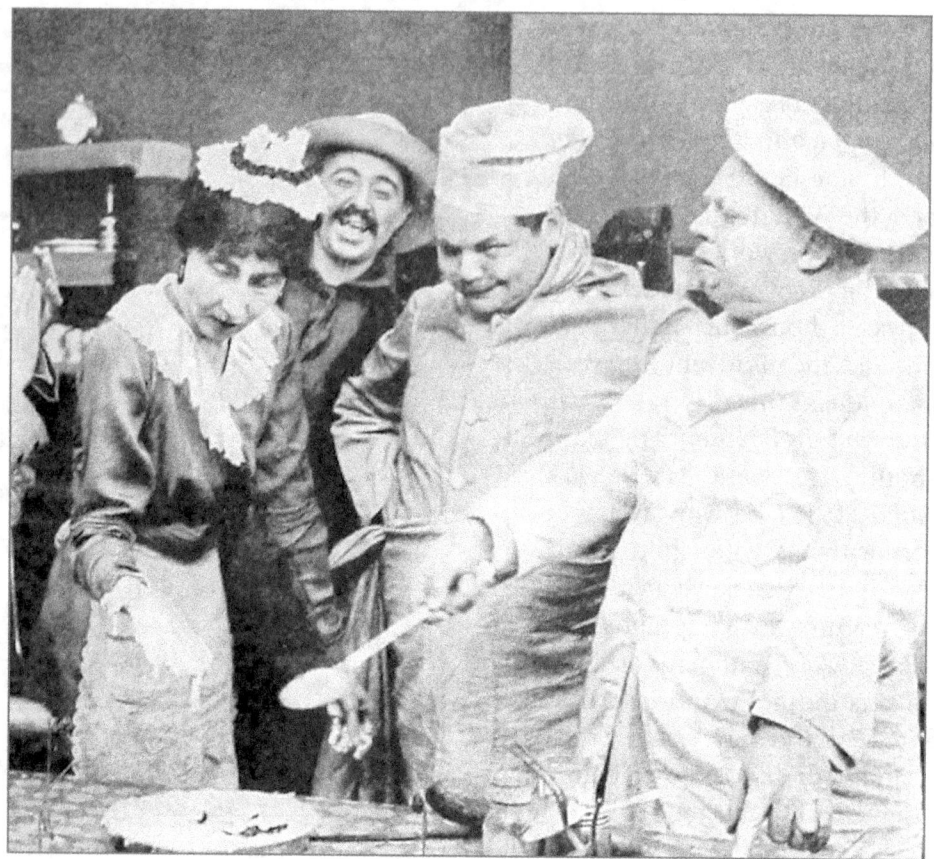

Jay Dwiggens (right) having trouble with Flora Finch in Vitagraph's *Strictly Neutral* (1915).

years Steppling moved on to a brief stint with Nestor before settling in at the American Film Manufacturing Company. At first he appeared in their general ensemble for dramas and westerns, but eventually he returned to comedy, headlining in their *Beauty Comedies* along with Beatrice Van, John Sheehan, and Carol Holloway.

In addition he directed shorts like *Uncle Heck, By Heck* and *What's in a Name* (both 1915), as well as dusted off his old Billy McGrath character under the new moniker of Billy Van Deusen for outings like *Billy Van Deusen, Cave Man* and *Billy Van Deusen's Egg-Spensive Adventure* (both 1916). In 1917 he supported Lloyd Hamilton and Bud Duncan in Kalem's last round of *Ham and Bud* shorts, and directed some Billy Mason comedies such as *A Charming Villain* (1916), *The Beauty Doctor*, and *A Box of Tricks* (both 1917) for the Victor Company. From this point on the rest of his career was spent as a supporting actor in features such as *Joanna Enlists* (1918), *Bell Boy 13* (1923), and Raymond Griffith's *Wedding Bill$* (1927) before he passed away in 1932.

Another stout, balding, and over-forty comic that made his mark at this time was John E. Brennan. Also a stage veteran, Brennan, while still in his teens in his native Springfield, Massachusetts, became an accomplished Irish clog dancer which led to his touring with minstrel shows, circuses, and even a side trip to playing baseball. Eventually he ended up in more legitimate theatrical fare—a long run as the stock comedian at the Keith Theatre in Boston, and touring with his own company in shows such as *The Ivy Leaf*, *An Irishman's Love*, *Tim the Tinker*, and *Bonnie Scotland*. His work attracted the attention of producer William A. Brady, who engaged Brennan to create the role of Hi Holler, the local yokel comedy relief, in the original production of *Way Down East*. More touring with his own company and revivals of *Way Down East* followed until Brennan entered the movies.

In 1912 Brennan became the star comedian of the Kalem Comedy Company and for three years played a variety of henpecked husbands, hungry hoboes, hicks, and ham actors with support from Ruth Roland, Marshall Neilan, Ethel Teare, Juanita Sponsler, Lloyd Hamilton, and Betty Teare in shorts like *The Rube Detective* (1912), *Parcel Post Johnny* (1913), *Reggie the Squaw Man*, *Sherlock Bonehead* (both 1914), and *Mr. Pepperie Temper* (1915). In addition to shorts built around his build such as *Fatty's Busy Day* (1913), *Fatty and the Shyster Lawyer* (1914), and *Fatty's Echo* (1915), like Bunny the short and round Brennan looked funny in women's clothes and did obligatory drag duty in *The "Fired" Cook*, *The Laundress and the Lady* (both 1913), and *Percy Pimpernickel, Soubrette* (1914). Movie audiences loved Brennan, and according to his statement in the July 1914 issue of *Blue Book* the feeling was mutual:

Character shot of John Steppling.

> "I might as well admit," says jovial Brennan, "that I have said goodbye to the stage forever. I enjoy every minute of my motion picture work. As my one aim in life is to make people laugh, I do not object to falling down three or four flights of stairs several times each day, providing I can produce laughter. Next to love, laughter is the greatest thing in the world."]

At the very end of 1914 Brennan became a headliner at Universal's *Sterling Comedies*. Ford Sterling had left the company named for him, and Brennan may have been brought in to fill the void—taking over the characters named Snitz and Heinze. During his brief five-month stay his comedies included *Innocent Dad* (1914), *Love and Dough*, *When Snitz Was Married*, and *The Battle of Running Bull* (all 1915). At this point he seems to have been tapering back his workload, and after doing comic relief in a couple of dramatic shorts for Centaur, he did occasional appearances in features such as *The Devil's Needle* (1916) and *Sooner or Later* (1920). The last was 1920's *The Hidden Light*; after spending the rest of his life in California, he died in 1940.

John E. Brennan in his starring Kalem Comedy *Fat Bill's Wooing* (1912).

Peter Lang was yet another corpulent theatre veteran who answered the call of moving pictures, but they remained only a sidebar of his overall career as forty-three of his sixty-five years were spent on stage. He made his debut in 1889 doing stock in Maine, and soon became a member of The Bostonians, a well-known group of musical players. He appeared in shows like *Robin Hood*, *The Forest Lover*, and *The Fortunes of the King*, where he worked for producers such as Daniel Frohman and appeared with names like James K. Hackett. He even worked with Roscoe in a 1910 Burbank, California production of George M. Cohan's *The Yankee Prince*. Entering films in 1911 at Lubin as a character player in dramas with Harry Myers, Ormi Hawley, and May Buckley, the studio launched him in his own one-reel comedy series in 1913 and ballyhooed to the press:

PETE LANG COMEDY SERIES
Do not, under any circumstances, allow yourself to be denied the series of roaring comedy pictures with jolly Pete Lang in the title role. He's a great big, healthy, fat fellow and will make you laugh whether you want to or not.
– **Moving Picture World**, March 1, 1913

Some of Lang's titles include *Peter's Pledge*, *Mayor's Waterloo*, *Pete Joins the Force*, and *The Heart Brokers*. The one known to exist of the group, *Auntie's Affinity* (1913), has Lang playing Pietro, the chef in a fancy hotel. On a walk in the park he meets a rich lady hotel guest and passes himself off as the wealthy Count of Montevidio. A romance ensues, but of course it's discovered that he's only the hotel chef, but in the nick of time a letter arrives from the Italian Counsel that certifies that Pietro is really a count and heir to a fortune, so the film ends happily.

Following the run of his own series Lang remained a comedy specialist for Lubin, becoming regular support in their *Patsy Bolivar* comedies. These starred Clarence Elmer as the frazzled everyman Patsy, and also included Patsy De Forest in entries such as *Patsy at School*, *Patsy's Elopement*, and *Patsy, Married and Settled* (all 1915). Lang also worked with British comic Billie Reeves in outings like *The Cello Champion*, *A Ready-Made Maid*, *The Election Bet*, and *Billie's Headache* (all 1915). After this he

1915 Lubin portrait of Peter Lang.

moved into feature film appearances for Lubin, Rolfe Photoplays, Fox, and Paramount, but really refocused on his stage career and only did sporadic films. Doing numerous Broadway shows such as *Honey Girl*, *It's a Boy*, *Glory*, *One Man's Woman*, and *Free for All*, his last film was the 1931 Joe Penner sound short *Making Good*, and he died in New York City the next year.

As mentioned in the beginning of this book hefty Fred Mace made his screen debut at Biograph in 1911 and soon became one of the top comedy screen stars as part of the original Keystone company (see *The Gangsters*). His exit from the Sennett fold made room for Roscoe, and his huge success reinforced the need that every comedy unit have a fat man. While some of the cinematic over-three-hundred-pounds club members that followed were basically used for the sight-gags inherent in their large sizes, many of them had the real goods and were great comics.

One of Keystone's main rivals was L-Ko Comedies. Founded in 1914 by Sennett's former right-hand man Henry Lehrman, their main star was the Charlie Chaplin-ish Billie Ritchie, and some fat men in the Arbuckle mold were also on the payroll. L-Ko's first heavyweight was Henry Bergman, ironically best remembered today for his years of working with Charlie Chaplin. Born in San Francisco, Bergman was taken to Germany as a child, and returned to America in 1883 as a tenor singer with the Metropolitan Grand Opera Company. Nine years with the Austin Daly Musical Comedy followed in which he appeared in shows such as *The Runaway Girl*, *San Toy*, *The Country Girl*, and *Cingalee*. In addition he spent three seasons in the *Ziegfeld Follies* and appeared with Blanche Ring

Henry Bergman became a fall guy for Charlie Chaplin starting with 1916's *The Pawnshop*.

in *The Yankee Girl*. His film career began with Pathé as part of the supporting ensemble in comedy one-reelers like *The Rise and Fall of Mickey Mahone* (1912), *An Itinerant Wedding*, and *There She Goes* (both 1913). In 1914 he moved over to another New York-based company, Universal's Crystal Films, and was busy in items like *Willie's Disguise* and *A Change of Complexion* (both 1914). It's said that his former Pathé co-star Paul Panzer introduced him to Henry Lehrman, who hired Bergman to be the main character man at L-Ko.

Love and Surgery (1914) was the first, and although Bergman was on call to support Billie Ritchie in shorts like *Partners in Crime* (1914), *Almost a Scandal*, *Poor Policy* (both 1915), and *Billie's Reformation* (1916), he still found time to star in his own pictures such as *The Blighted Spaniard* (1914), *Caught with the Goods*, and *The Butcher's Bride* (both 1915). One of them, *The Baron's Bear Escape* (1914), was even an unofficial remake of Roscoe's *He Would a Hunting Go* (1913) with Bergman repeating Roscoe's characterization of a foreign noble pretending to be a great sportsman. In early 1916 Bergman left L-Ko to join the Chaplin unit, and for the next thirty years he played multiple roles in numerous Chaplin films, as well as acted as gagman, assistant director, and personal confidant to the comedian until his death in 1946.

Dave Morris (right) working to make hamburger out of Fatty Voss' hand with Gertrude Selby's approval in *Dirty Work in a Beanery* (1916). Courtesy Robert Arkus.

Where Henry Bergman was an experienced character man, the Chicago-born Frank Voss had the earmarks of a deliberate Arbuckle clone. Henry Lehrman had a Chaplin doppelganger in Billie Ritchie, and it wasn't long after L-Ko was in business that this ersatz Arbuckle was added. Lehrman had directed Roscoe's first pictures for Keystone and must have felt he had a right to borrow his persona for the new company. First promoted as "the L-Ko Fat Boy," Voss even appropriated Roscoe's nickname and was billed as Fatty Voss. Debuting in 1915, most of Voss' shorts are missing, but the few that do survive, such as *Love and Sour Notes* and *The Child Needs a Mother* (both 1915), show that while proficient enough Voss was no match in funniness to Mr. Arbuckle. His career only lasted a brief two years, and at the time of his sudden death from heart failure in 1917 he was playing the heavy in Alice Howell's first Century Comedies like *Balloonatics*, *Automaniacs*, and *Neptune's Naughty Daughter* (all 1917).

Another full-figured L-Ko supporting player was Gene "Pop" Rogers, who joined the Lehrman ensemble in 1915 after twenty-five years on stage working as a comic in light opera troupes and touring vaudeville on the Orpheum Circuit. He told the March 25, 1916 *Universal Weekly*:

> *I have sung and played in every town of any importance on this continent and in a great part of Europe as well. Every name on the map is associated in my mind with some comic or tragic happening, but most of them are too personal to be of general interest.*

At five-feet, six-inches he was practically as big around as he was tall, and became a regular foil for the border-line psychotic Billie Ritchie. In shorts like *Silk Hose and High Pressure* and *Poor Policy* (both 1915) Rogers is Ritchie's sidekick and is continually backstabbed and taken advantage of by the aggressive British comic. Perhaps to get away from Ritchie the comedian moved over to the Mack Sennett Studio and spent the remainder of his career playing fathers for Peggy Pearce or Mary Thurman, as well as police captains, husbands, and judges in Sennett outings such as *A Scoundrel's Toll* (1916), *A Dog Catcher's Love* (1917), *Friend Husband* (1918), and *Rip & Stitch Tailors* (1919). Rogers died penniless of alcoholism and myocarditis in 1919, and it's said that comedian Charlie Murray took up a collection from his Sennett co-workers to give "Pop" a proper funeral.

The last larger-than-life L-Ko comic was Dan Russell, probably the most forgotten comedy star of the teens. From 1915 to 1919 Russell headlined in much of the L-Ko product, but today it's hard to discern what he was about, or what his "shtick" was, as only

Gene Rogers (left) gets put in his place by Alice Howell and Raymond Griffith (right) as Fatty Voss gasps in the background from *Under New Management* (1915). Courtesy Undercrank Productions.

one or two of his forty-plus films are known to exist. He was big at five-feet-nine and two hundred and seventy pounds, and Universal sometimes billed him as "L-Ko's Komical Irishman." Born Herbert Charles Dunn in England, his family ended up in California when he was young and he entered vaudeville with his first wife Blanche O'Neil. Their touring acts included *A Matrimonial Tangle*, *The Package Party*, and *The Matinee Girl*. Separating from O'Neil he took a new stage and life partner, seventeen-year-old Maggie Ray, who appeared with him on stage as Marguerite Ray. Tapped by L-Ko in 1915 and starting in *Father's First Murder*, Russell became a mainstay of the company and was regularly supported by Katherine Griffith, Vin Moore, Raymond Griffith, Billy Bevan, Bert Roach, William Irving, and his wife Marguerite, now billed as Marjorie Ray (and sometimes Mrs. Dan Russell).

Russell was even teamed with Fatty Voss in *The High Diver's Curse* (1916), and some of his other films included *A Scandal at Sea* (1915), *Blue Blood But Black Skin*, *Ignatz's Icy Injury* (both 1916), *Dan's Dippy Doings*, and *Where is My Che-ild?* (both 1917). He appears to have been off the screen in 1918, but came back the next year for a few more like *All Jazzed Up* (one of the few survivors) and *Sirens of Suds* (both 1919). Leaving Universal at this time he seems to have attempted to establish himself at the Sennett Studio, as he's been spotted mugging in the theatre audience scenes in *Salome Vs. Shenandoah* (1919)

Looks like the jig is up for Dan Russell (center) in *Dippy Dan's Doings* (1917).

"Smiling Bill" Parsons was the shining light of Capitol Comedies.

and can be briefly glimpsed in the complete version of the feature *Down on the Farm* (1920). Things must not have worked out with Sennett and he returned to the stage. Russell died in March of 1925 while out on the road doing a stage tour in Dallas, Texas, after an operation for ulcers.

Not to be outdone, the other studios began developing their own tons of fun. William Parsons, better known as "Smiling Bill" Parsons, was a plus-forty live-action version of Humpty-Dumpty—a round body that came to a peak with a big bald domed head that resembled a Rocky Ford cantaloupe. As the April 6, 1918 *Motion Picture News* put it he "seems built for comedy." Items about Parsons talk about his early days as an M.D. and insurance broker. There's no mention of any kind of theatrical background, but he entered films as an actor in 1914. For about a year he appeared as a character man in dramas for Vitagraph, Lubin, and Navajo, and then in 1915 he set up his own production company which became known as the National Film Corporation of America.

He launched into comedy with the three-reelers *The Tale of the Night Before* and *The Morning After* (both 1915) which established his comic persona of the henpecked husband or crotchety bachelor who seizes the opportunity to step out and prove that he's really "a gay old dog." While still doing occasional dramas, Parsons put out a series of shorts, some called *King Cole Comedies*, like *Beached and Bleached*, *The Little Puritan* (both 1915), *A Misfit Baron*, and *The Artful Dodger* (both 1916) through distributors like MinA and Pathé, a few with a young Constance Talmadge as his leading lady.

Temporarily cutting back on his performing to concentrate on producing, Parsons' National Film Corp. had a huge hit in 1918 with the feature *Tarzan of the Apes*, and its sequel *The Romance of Tarzan*. Returning to the screen in 1918, for the next two years he played his overweight everyman in a series of extremely popular two-reelers that were released through Goldwyn Pictures. Under the name *Capitol Comedies*, in shorts such as *Dad's Knockout*, *Bill's Sweetie*, *Birds of a Feather* (all 1918), *The New Breakfast Food*, *The Potum of Swat*, and *Chasing Rainbeaux* (all 1919) Parsons had directors such as

Alfred Santell and Louis Chaudet, and leading ladies that included Molly Malone, Teddy Sampson, and Billie Rhodes (whom he married).

Almost all of these shorts are missing. One rare survivor, *Bill's Opportunity* (1919), presents the comic as a downtrodden husband who's promoted from his position as an overworked department store bookkeeper to manager of the lingerie showroom. There he has to play the role of an exotic ladies' undergarment designer. Afraid to tell his stern wife (Billie Bennett) he pretends that he's invested in oil wells. So every morning he leaves the house in his oil worker overalls, goes to the department store lingerie showroom and dresses in fancy raiment to play the designer, and then to return home he puts back on his overalls and smears himself with oil for good measure. Making a fortune as the designer, his wife thinks it's due to his gushers, and of course eventually his double life unravels, but since his wife is happy being wealthy she allows him to continue presenting the ladies in the showroom.

In addition to his own shorts Capitol was putting out two-reelers with Mr. and Mrs. Carter De Haven, Neal Burns, and the team of Neely Edwards & Ned Flannigan, plus

William Parsons seems happy about the situation in a glass slide for *Bill's Predicament* (1918). Courtesy Matt Vogel.

Parsons was producing features with Henry B. Walthall, and his now wife Billie Rhodes. It all came to an end when Parsons died at age forty-one. Recently his last comedy, *A Much Needed Rest* (1919), has resurfaced and he looks terrible in it. His clothes are loose and his face is gaunt, plus the use of heavy white make-up to try and conceal his sunken-in eyes only looks strange. His obituaries generally gave his cause of death as due to a bad cold or pneumonia, but *Photoplay* elaborated that it may have been:

> …the effects of an accident which happened in the studio about a year ago. Parsons was doing a comedy scene at the time, in which large blocks of ice were used, and a heavy cake fell on his chest causing a hemorrhage.

Parsons died on September 28, 1919, with his last few shorts released posthumously. His final film appearance was in a dramatic supporting role in Mary Miles Minter's *Eyes of the Heart* (1920). Parsons' death brought "Smiling Bill" Jones to the screen in some one-reelers for Marion H. Kohn Productions in a brief attempt to capture the Parsons audience. Jones was bald, older, and a bit paunchy, but was relatively slim.

Roly-poly Victor Moore was one of the best loved and most famous clowns of the Broadway stage. With his large cue ball head, lumpy body, and timorous gestures and voice, Moore looked like a giant baby and always seemed to be wearing diapers under his

Victor Moore caught in between in 1917's *He Got There After All*.

trousers. After years in vaudeville with the sketch *Change Your Act, or Back to the Woods* with his stage partner and first wife Emma Littlefield, he hit the big time in 1906 when he co-starred with Fay Templeton in George M. Cohan's *Forty-Five Minutes from Broadway*. In 1915 he was one of the "famous players" brought to the screen by Famous Players-Lasky, for whom he starred in comedy features such as *Snobs* and *Chimmie McFadden* (both 1915), in addition to more dramatic fare like *The Clown* (1916).

The Klever Komedies organization was set up in 1916 to star Moore in one-reelers to be distributed by Paramount. Playing down the slapstick, this series concentrated on Moore as a befuddled everyman who experiences all kinds of complications in various domestic situations. *Flivvering*, *Camping*, and *Commuting* (all 1917) all chronicle the difficulties Vic and his family have going out for a drive, trying to enjoy the Great Outdoors, and going to and from work. *The Cow Jumped Over the Moon* (1917) has Moore concerned about the rising price of meat and trying to solve the problem by raising his own cow, but probably the most bizarre entry of the series, *Rough and Ready Reggie* (1917), has the effeminate Reggie trying to join an athletic club. After being terrorized by the he-man members of the club, Reggie's tough western uncle appears to him in a dream and inspires him to become an ultra alpha male, leading him to go on a rampage the next day at the club as he wrecks vengeance on his former tormentors.

Filming of the shorts originally began in Jacksonville, Florida before moving to the East Coast in the summer of 1917. After the end of the series in 1918, Moore's career continued unabated until his retirement in 1957, and along the way some of his successes included the stage shows *Of Thee I Sing* and *Anything Goes*, not to mention movies like *Swing Time* (1936) and *Make Way for Tomorrow* (1937).

A comic who came to the screen after Roscoe's success but was of the John Bunny ilk was George Bickel. Teamed for years on stage and in films with Harry Watson Jr., Bickel was a versatile and professional second banana, who did headline in a few of his own starring shorts in the late teens. Born in Saginaw, Michigan in 1863, the young Bickel was a musician and clown when he teamed up with Harry Watson Jr. in 1894, and when the pair didn't have much luck with a musical act or as "patter" comics they ended up with steady work as circus clowns, first for the Walter L. Main Circus and then Ringling Brothers. At Ringling the duo became part of the famous clown band and developed a popular "little German orchestra" routine with Bickel as conductor and Watson as disrupter. This became a signature piece for them which they used in vaudeville, in revue shows like *Me, Him and I*, and finally the *Ziegfeld Follies* in 1907. More *Follies* followed, but in 1912 they went their separate ways but were rejoined in 1915 when they were recruited for the big screen by producer George Kleine.

Bickel and Watson were introduced to movie audiences in the features *The Fixer* and *The Politicians* (both 1915). The first was a farce about mistaken identities and mishaps involving Mexican diplomats, and the other had the pair as dishonest NYC politicians who go to a small town to fix a mayoral election. The bald, fat, and forever middle-aged Bickel fit right in on the movie screen and his next appearance was again with Watson in episodes of the comedy serial *The Mishaps of Musty Suffer* (1916). Watson starred as the tramp Musty Suffer who lives the life of Job going from one disaster to another. Bickel plays his tramp buddy Willie Work in episodes like *Hold Fast!*, *Going Up*, and *Look Out*

George Bickel (right) supports Cissy Fitzgerald and Harry Watson Jr. in the *Musty Suffer* episode *Look Out Below* (1916). Courtesy the Library of Congress.

Below, and along the way the pair do their "little German orchestra" routine, as well as a popular boxing bit where Watson gets the worst from Bickel. Harry Watson went on to do two more editions of *Musty Suffer* for George Kleine, while Bickel did his own one-reelers for the producer.

Titles for Bickel's series include *Love, Luck and Loot* (1915), *A Mixed Color Scheme*, *The King of Cooks*, and *Nearly a Husband* (all 1917), which had him playing Willie Work or various tramps, crooks, and farmers. After these shorts Bickel returned to the stage and spent the 1920s in two editions of the *George White Scandals*, as well as comedies like *Paradise Alley* and the comic operetta *The Circus Princess*. When sound hit films he returned in front of the camera for the Clark and McCullough feature *In Holland* (1929), the Henry Lehrman-directed short *Sound Your 'A'* (1929), and a few other 1930s features. His last screen appearance before retiring was the 1933 Educational Pictures two-reeler *Pop's Pal*, and when he passed away in 1941 his body was sent for interment back to Saginaw, Michigan, where he had teamed up with Watson forty-seven years before.

Not long after the death of John Bunny Vitagraph decided to try and rekindle his success by recruiting a similarly round and craggy comic from the Broadway stage. Frank Daniels had been a larger-than-life purveyor of hilarity in the theatre for over thirty years, and had much in common with Bunny—small but wide, with a potato face, and a seemingly endless supply of expressions and reactions. The *New York Herald Tribune* referred to him as the "man of athletic eyebrows." Frank Daniels was born in Dayton, Ohio in 1860 and when young was apprenticed as a wood carver, but when his master continued to throw his finished carvings in the stove he decided he had nothing to lose in trying to be an actor.

Having appeared in amateur theatricals, Daniels became a professional at age nineteen when he joined George A. Jones' Boston Opera Company. He worked his way up steadily—creating the lead role in the original *Peck's Bad Boy*, touring in Gilbert & Sullivan—and had his first big success in 1884 in Charles Hoyt's *A Rag Baby*. Daniels went from one hit to another, which included *Little Puck*, *The Wizard of the Nile*, *Miss Simplicity*, *Sergeant Brue*, *The Office Boy*, *Roly-Poly*, and *Without the Law*. 1913 saw him retire from the stage after a thirty-three-year run, but in 1915 it was announced:

> **FRANK DANIELS IN "CROOKY"**
> *Frank Daniels, the comedian who has made thousands laugh during the days when he was the acknowledged king of the comic opera stage, will return to Broadway, this time in the silent drama, and will make his initial bow as an artist at the Vitagraph theatre, in a picture leading the list of features. Mr. Daniels will be seen in a five-part comedy entitled "Crooky."*
> *– Motography*, July 10, 1915

For *Crooky* (1915), the film neophyte Daniels was put in the hands of C. Jay Williams, a neglected but extremely talented early comedy film director. Williams had recently come from Edison where he had directed shorts like *A Proposal Under Difficulties* (1912), *All on Account of a Transfer*, *A Serenade by Proxy* (both 1913), and *Love By the Pound* (1914). The script was by Paul West, who had written the popular *Bill, the Office Boy* stories, and was about an escaped convict who rubs elbows in New York society as a supposed millionaire, but after endless complications and an old maid angling to get him to the altar is happy to return to his old jail cell.

The short, stout, and slightly pop-eyed Daniels made a hit on the screen, and Vitagraph was full steam ahead on more productions. The follow-up was another five-reel feature, *What*

Frank Daniels does some heavy mugging in an exhibitor ad for his Vitagraph *Kernel Nutt* Comedies.

Happened to Father (1915), and the comedian was then re-united with Paul West and C. Jay. Williams for his first series of one-reel shorts, *The Escapades of Mr. Jack* (1916). Based on the comic strip of James Swinnerton, creator of *Little Jimmy*, it was long on misadventures and laughs. Daniels had tip-top support in the persons of Kate Price, Ida Williams, and a recent recruit from Edison, Alice Washburn. Vitagraph knew they had a good thing, and kept putting the old wine into new bottles. Next came the *Kernel Nutt* series where, as the trades said, "Frank Daniels is seen as his usual funny self." In this series Alice Washburn played his crab apple wife, and it lasted through twelve episodes such as *Kernel Nutt and the Hundred Dollar Bill*, *Kernel Nutt and the High Shoes*, and *Kernel Nutt and Prince Tango* (all 1916).

Daniels' third and final group of films for Vitagraph was the *Captain Jinks* series. The studio entrusted another of their top directors, Van Dyke Brooke, to the enterprise and a whopping twenty-three entries were made. Unfortunately only a handful of Daniels' films have survived. Out of the known four only *Captain Jinks, the Cobbler* (1917) is readily available to be viewed. Seeing the comic in action there is a strong resemblance to Bunny—physically and in comic personae. His face was definitely what could be called a "mug," and this weather-beaten map with its bug-eyes, myriad of creases, bags, and multiple double-chins was made for the camera, where every flicker and nuance could be recorded. While some of his variety of expressions and takes are "broad," they are done with expert timing and genuine emotion.

The plot is a variation on *The Captain of Koepenick*. Jinks is a put-upon cobbler in a small village. When a soldier brings the top general's boots and uniform to the shop for sprucing up, Jinks can't resist the temptation to put them on and pose as the official. He struts around town brandishing his monocle, much of the time flirting with young Mildred Manning, and trying to avoid his shrewish wife who's out and about in the village. Accepted as the general, the burgermeister even awards him the officer's cash bonus for his lifetime of service. It turns out that the real general was napping while all this was taking place, and once he awakens the ruse is discovered and the jig is up for Jinks. Having returned to his shop and old clothes, Jinks is arrested and taken to jail. After a trial Jinks is given a choice—two years in prison, or going home with his hellish wife. This surviving print crashes just before Jinks makes his decision, but it's likely that he opts for the serenity of a prison cell. A good illustration of Daniels' screen work, the short moves along crisply and expertly with excellent support provided by Mildred Manning, director Van Dyke Brooke (playing the burgermeister), and especially Ann Brody as his combative wife.

Since joining Vitagraph Daniels had worked non-stop, but *Captain Jinks* brought that activity to an end. As his films were very popular with critics and audiences it must have been the comic's choice to slow down. His last verified appearance is a supporting role in the 1918 Dorothy Dalton feature *Flare-Up Sal*. Some filmographies for Daniels list him in five Harold Lloyd shorts—*Count the Votes, Soft Money, Pay Your Dues, His Only Father* (all 1919), and *Among Those Present* (1920). This seems very doubtful—considering he's nowhere to be seen in the circulating and available *Pay Your Dues* and *Among Those Present*. Daniels had amassed a sizeable estate (estimated at $200,000 at his passing) and spent a comfortable retirement spending summers at his home in Rye, New York and winters in West Palm Beach, Florida, where he died in 1935.

Dee Lampton (right) entertains Harold Lloyd, Sammy Brooks, and Slim Fitzgerald as Walter Lundin readies his camera in the background. Courtesy Richard Simonton.

A very strong resemblance to Roscoe brought the seventeen-year-old and two-hundred-and-eighty-five-pound Dee Lampton to Hollywood. Born in Fort Worth, Texas in 1898, this Arbuckle look-a-like spent most of his four-year career working for producer Hal Roach. Lampton first appeared at Essanay in 1915, and had a very good role as the mischievous fat boy that helps Charlie Chaplin harass the on-stage performers in *A Night in the Show* (1915). He also worked in some of the Essanay one-reelers such as *Fun at a Ball Game* (1915) that were directed by a young Hal Roach, and the next year after Roach had set up his own production unit with Harold Lloyd as star, Lampton became part of the regular supporting crew. In shorts like *Luke Does the Midway* and *Luke and the Bang Tails* (both 1916) the rotund Lampton specialized in annoying kids. *Luke Joins the Navy* (1916) has Snub Pollard rather enlist for sea duty than be with his obnoxious son Lampton and wife Margaret Joslin.

1917 saw Roach star Lampton in his own mostly split-reel series of *Skinny Comedies*. Survivors like *Schemer Skinny's Schemes* and *Skinny Gets a Goat* (both 1917) show that the Skinny character was basically Fatty Arbuckle junior—a younger version of the farm boy from the rural Keystone shorts. The shorts also have much in common with Essanay's *Snakeville Comedies*, especially since *Snakeville*'s Margaret Joslin and Harry Todd were

Lampton's main support in the series. After eight entries Roach discontinued the *Skinnys* and Lampton spent some time working for Mack Sennett in shorts like *Hula Hula Land* and *A Shanghaied Jonah* (both 1917). By 1918 he returned to the Roach lot and settled in as support to Harold Lloyd's new glasses character. Playing all types of roles, like Arbuckle, Lampton was good at drag and often turned up as a woman, even in blackface as in *The Marathon* (1919). Also working with Toto and Stan Laurel, Lampton continued supporting Lloyd up to his two-reelers from *Hand to Mouth* (1919) and *Haunted Spooks* (1920), but died suddenly from appendicitis at age twenty.

Edward Sedgwick is remembered today by comedy fans as a director, particularly of Buster Keaton's MGM features such as *The Cameraman* (1928), *Spite Marriage* (1929), *Free and Easy* (1930), *Speak Easily* (1932), and *What! No Beer* (1933). Like Keaton, Sedgwick came from a family vaudeville act, The Five Sedgwicks, that also consisted of his father, mother, and sisters Eileen and Josie. The Sedgwicks traveled across the country performing sketches, songs, and dances in tent shows, four-a-day vaudeville, and tab shows. The ill health of father Edward Sr. caused the troupe to leave the road and settle in the warm climate of California in 1913. No longer working on stage the younger Sedgwicks began doing bit parts at the various fledgling movie studios, and in 1914 they were hired by Romaine Fielding to be part of the ensemble at Lubin. Ed appeared under Fielding's direction, often opposite skinny Robin Williamson, in shorts like *Love and Flames*, *The Kid's Nap*, *A Cowboy Pastime* (all 1914), and *Green Backs and Red Skin* (1915).

Moving over to Universal's Imp brand he supported Victor Potel, Pat Rooney, Jane Bernoudy, and his sister Eileen in titles that included *Slim, Fat or Medium* (1915), *Hired, Tired and Fired*, *Ain't He Grand*, and *When Slim Was Home Cured* (all 1916) where he

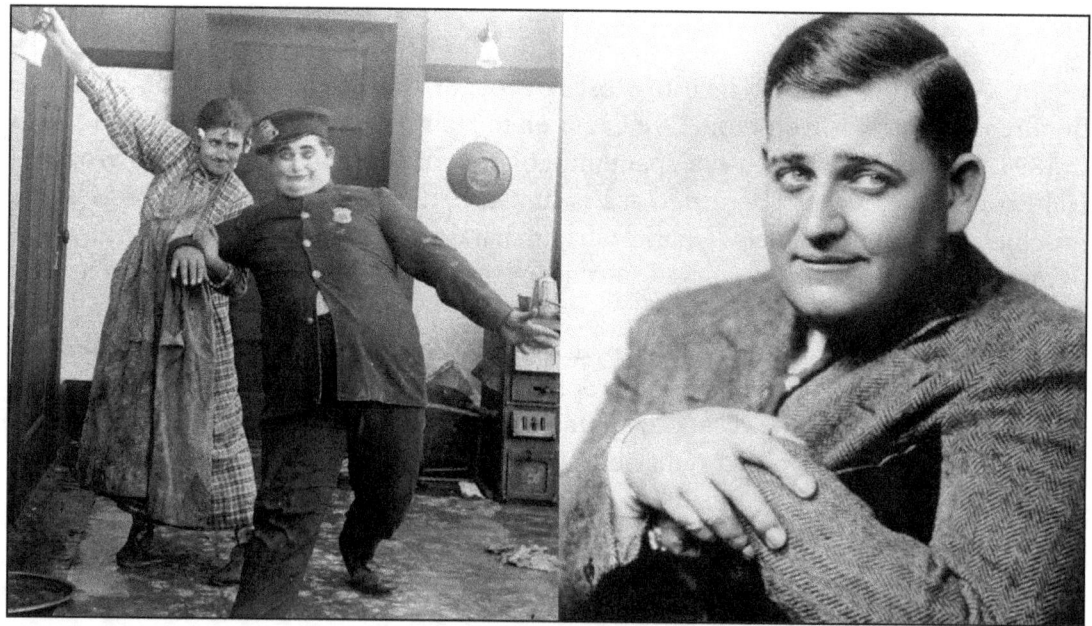

Edward Sedgwick does comic business with Jane Bernoudy in *Lizzie's Waterloo* (1919) on the left (courtesy Robert Arkus), and poses as a successful director on the right (Author's collection).

played characters named Heinrich Hippo, Hiram Hippo, or just plain Fatty. A short stint at Vogue Comedies had him working with Ben Turpin and Paddy McGuire, but he soon returned to Universal and was finally headlined in his own Arbuckle-esque series of shorts like *The Fascinating Model*, *Fat and Foolish*, and *His Golden Hour* (all 1916). *Married a Year* (1916) has Ed and Betty Schade having their first-year anniversary. Of course Ed has to stay late at work that night of all nights, and on the train home he reads a newspaper article that tells the evils of the modern wife. When he dozes off he has a nightmare where his wife is a complete shrew. At the same time at home Betty is waiting for Ed and reads another article about terrible modern husbands. She also falls asleep and has a dream about him as a carouser and ladies' man. The dreams shake them both up so much that they make a resolution to trust each other and begin a second honeymoon.

Although billing himself as "Big Ed Sedgwick—300 Pounds of Condensed Laughter," after this series Sedgwick wound down his on-screen appearances and concentrated on writing and directing. He piloted many light-hearted westerns for Tom Mix and Hoot Gibson before he moved over to MGM to specialize in comedy features like *Tin Hats* (1926), *Slide, Kelly, Slide* (1927), and *Circus Rookies* (1928). Following directing most of Keaton's MGM features he went on to helm some of the later films of Joe E. Brown and Laurel & Hardy such as *Pick a Star*, *Fit for a King* (both 1937), *Beware, Spooks* (1939), and *Air Raid Wardens* (1943). He spent a lot of time in the 1940s working on gags with Keaton for many MGM features, and at the time of his death in 1953 he was involved in the beginnings of *I Love Lucy*.

Odd little blips on the silent comedy radar screen are provided by the careers of "Smiling" Roland Hill and "Bumps" Adams. Both spent a few years bottom feeding on the outer edges of independent states' rights film production, and there's little information on them outside of their brief forays into the limelight. Roland Hill was a middle-aged, William Parsons wanna-be from Greensboro, North Carolina, who organized the Gate City Pictures Company to make comedies starring himself. The company rented space in Jacksonville, Florida at the Eagle Film Company's studio in the fall of 1916 and made shorts such as *Roland's Lucky Day*. Hill is said to have done some films in Chicago, and also to have appeared in some end-of-the-line Vim comedies in Florida with Kate Price and Billy Ruge. These were originally announced as *Amber Star Comedies*, but Amber Star became Jaxon and the films were released as *Sparkle Comedies*. The titles announced for the venture were *Home Made Horrors*, *Terrible Kate*, and *Thirty-Nine Sixty* (all 1917).

In 1917 it was announced that Hill was "discovered" by director Walter Richard Stahl, who set up the Hi-Ro Comedy Company to produce comedies with Hill to be made at a studio built in Greensboro. It's hard to say what became of this venture as by 1920 Roland Hill had stopped performing to become a successful film exhibitor in Greensboro for many years.

"Bumps" Adams was an Arbuckle clone who came out of nowhere and stayed on the screen for three years. He popped up in 1919, working with Dot Farley and Dorothea Wolbert in Romayne Super Comedy two-reelers like *Keyhole Reporter*, *Stale Eggs and Sweethearts*, and *Sewerside* (all 1920). The only one known to exist today is *Underground Romeo* (1920) which is a re-do of the second reel of Roscoe's *The Butcher Boy* (1917). Dot Farley is sent off to a girl's school, so her country lover "Bumps" shows up in drag as the new student. Dorothea Wolbert fills in for Agnes Neilson as the head of the school, and Dot and "Bumps" end up evading Dorothea and Dot's father to get to the minister's home to tie the knot.

In 1920 the trade magazines announced that Adams would be starring in comedies for Screen Crafts, Inc.:

> **FEATURING BUMPS ADAMS**
> *Work on the first two-reel athletic comedy featuring Bumps Adams started last week at the new studio of Screen Crafts, Inc. Maurine Chadwick is leading lady.*
>
> *Adams and DeWitte Hagar are co-directing and Jack Fuqua is behind the camera. The Adams comedies are being produced by Screen Crafts, of which Capt. H. M. Lawson, owner of cinema playhouses in Arizona and Northern California is president and general manager.*
>
> – ***Camera!**, May 1, 1920*

Screen Crafts, Inc. also announced that it would produce four Christian Science stories a year, but there are no known titles for those or for the Adams shorts. After this there's

Vivian Edwards tries to stop Fritz Schade from dousing Bill Hauber with water in *Only a Farmer's Daughter* (1915). Courtesy Sam Gill.

dwindling mentions of "Bumps." *Camera!* reports in 1922 that Kenneth J. Bishop was directing Adams in a burlesque of the Northwest Mounted Police, and another issues states that he had set up Adams Productions, a company through which he was producing and directing animated shorts with puppets named Billy and Betty. After this he flatlines on the cinema monitor screens.

Back at the Sennett Studio, Mack wasn't content to just have the most popular large comic on the screen under contract so he developed other heavy-set players. Portly Mack Swain became very popular with his character of "Ambrose" (see 1915's *Fatty's New Role*), and another was the more than pudgy second-banana Bert Roach, who made his name at L-Ko but took up residence on the Sennett lot in the late teens (see 1914's *Fatty's Magic Pants*). At five feet, two hundred pounds, Fritz Schade was a chunky forgotten funnyman that did yeoman work for Keystone from 1913 to 1917. Born in Germany in 1879 he had experience in German comedy theatre before he came to America to work in vaudeville and the Olympia Opera Comedy in California. Like Roscoe, Schade worked briefly at Universal before taking up residence on the Sennett lot at the end of 1913. At first he was kept active in small bit roles, and in 1914 he spent a lot of time supporting Roscoe and Charlie Chaplin in items like *The Property Man*, *Those Country Kids*, *Dough and Dynamite*, and *Leading Lizzie Astray*.

Schade came into his own in 1915 when he headlined in a series of one-reelers such as *Peanuts and Bullets*, *Love in Armor*, and *Settled at the Seaside* where he would be the also-ran for the leading lady, who always preferred young and handsome Charles Parrott. Usually playing excitable and exotic characters with names like Baron von Hassenfeffer and often sporting Germanic upturned moustaches, Schade took a good deal of punishment in the name of comedy art, and had his fair share of injuries:

> *In trying to save one of the Keystone diving girls from injury, Fritz Schade sustained a broken arm while playing in a scene at the edge of the large tank at the studio. This is the first real injury that has befallen this Keystone comedian—except the 942,670 bruises.*
> – **Motion Picture News**, July 22, 1916

Schade also did his duty in drag, donning female duds in *A Human Hound's Triumph* and *Love, Loot and Crash* (both 1915). During his days with Sennett, the comic was billed as, and signed his autographs, "Keystone Fritz Schade—Cute, Clever, Nifty." After two-reelers like *The Snow Cure* and *The Surf Girl* (both 1916), Fritz moved over to Triangle Komedies for shorts such as *A Prairie Heiress*, *Won by a Fowl* (both 1917), and *Ruined by a Dumbwaiter* (1918) before he finished his career at Fox Sunshine Comedies in *A Neighbor's Keyhole* and *A Tight Squeeze* (both 1918). Illness forced him to retire from pictures, and he died following brain surgery in 1926.

Jess Dandy was a versatile character player who spent a busy 1914 at Keystone. Born Jesse Danzig on the East Coast, as a young man he pursued a medical career, political campaigning, and sales before he entered vaudeville in New York. Touring around the country as a comedy monologist, often with a Jewish character although he wasn't Jewish, Dandy hit the big time in 1903 when he took over the lead role in the hit comedy *The*

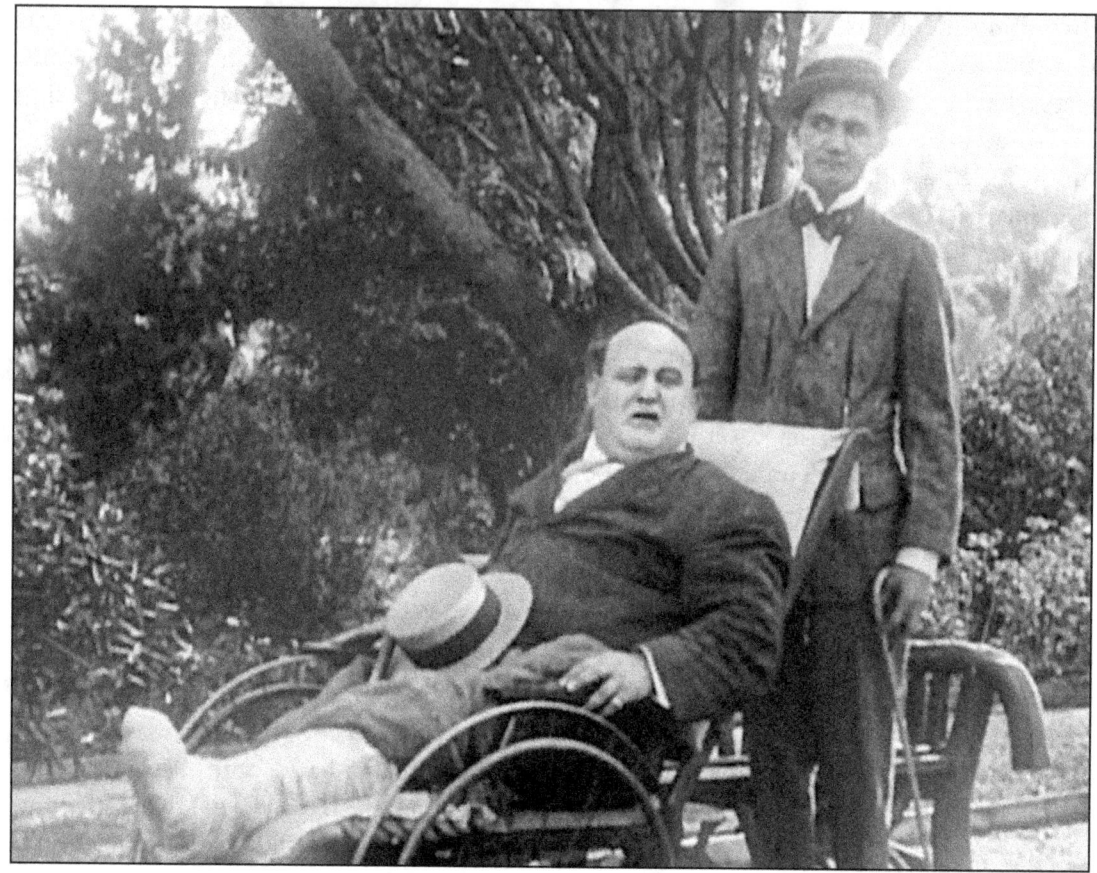

Charles Parrott has to put up with his gouty uncle Jess Dandy in the 1914 Keystone *His New Profession*. Courtesy Robert Arkus.

Prince of Pilsen. On and off for the next fifteen years Dandy played the German-American brewer of pilsner beer who is mistaken for the Prince of Pilsen while in Europe. The show even gave him the catch-phrase "Vas you effer in Zinzinnati?" In addition to *The Prince of Pilsen* he also appeared in shows such as *Marcelle* and *The Neverhomes*.

He was working in Los Angeles in the show *Auction Pinochle* when he joined Keystone. Appearing predominantly in Charlie Chaplin's shorts, Dandy was Garlico the Strongman in *The Property Man*, the invalid uncle that Charlie ends up pushing around in a wheelchair in *His New Profession*, and the bank president in *The New Janitor* (all 1914). Although only working at the studio for a few months, he made a strong impression and provided excellent support to Chaplin and the other comics with which he appeared. It may be he didn't enjoy filmmaking, for in 1915 he was back on the road again with *The Prince of Pilsen*. Other shows such as *Object Matrimony* and *Success* followed, and Dandy was in Boston performing in the play *Just Married* when he died of septic poisoning in 1923.

Harold J. "Josh" Binney was a large-sized bit player at many studios including Keystone, who became an independent producer of shorts that showcased other fat comics. Always on the outer edges of film production, Binney hung on and remained there for thirty-five years. Born in Kansas City, Missouri, he spent some time in vaudeville and stock before

Harold "Josh" Binney in drag with little Paul Jacobs in an unidentified Sterling Comedy. Courtesy Sam Gill.

he entered films with the Biograph Company in 1910. Moving on to Imp, he appeared in Sterling Comedies in shorts like *His Wedding Day* (1914) as support for stars Ford Sterling and little Billy Jacobs. The next two years saw him on tap at Keystone in shorts such as *A Submarine Pirate, Court House Crooks, A Janitor's Wife's Temptation* (all 1915), and *The Snow Cure* (1916). After a quick stint at Vogue Comedies in entries like *The Candy Cook* (1916), Binney struck out on his own into the independent states' rights film market as a producer. His first organization was Pacific Pictures Producing Company for a series of *Sunshine Films*, but according to his ad in the June 3, 1916 *Motion Picture News* it may have been more of a money-generating endeavor:

> *The bona-fide producer of legitimate photoplays who offers training, instruction and practical experience to the inexperienced people in moving picture acting. If you feel that you are talented call on or write him for full particulars.*

The next year Binney moved to Houston, Texas and set up the Masterpictures Company to make *Lion Comedies*. There weren't any actual lions in the pictures, only fat comic Nathan Dewing billed as "A Big Fat Funny Individual." Described as "a local man from Huston," surviving photos show that Nathan Dewing was the comedian better known as Hilliard Karr in the late teens and 1920s. Karr was indeed Houston-born, but it's not known whether Nathan Dewing was his birth name or just a moniker used for the *Lion Comedies*. After a couple of shorts such as *Nathan Busts into the Movies* and *A Village Villain* (both 1917), Binney and Dewing migrated to Jacksonville, Florida, reorganized as the Florida Film Corporation, and began making *Funny Fatty Filbert* two-reelers.

Known as *Josh Binney Comedies*, a number of shorts were made at Jacksonville's Klutho Studios, which included *Fabulous Fortune Fumblers, Freda's Fighting Father*, and *Fatty's Frivolous Fiancee* (all 1918). The only current survivor of the group is *Fred's Fictitious Foundling* (1918) which concerns Karr and Glen Lambert as a couple of hungry tramps who decide to bilk a wealthy childless couple by dressing Karr up as a baby and leaving him on their doorstep. Adopting him as their baby they spoil him and surround him with pretty nurses, while he sneaks food out the window for Lambert. Eventually the pair's scheme is discovered when they're caught trying to rob the house's safe, and they finally end up behind bars. Overall the short is a pretty standard slapstick opus for the time, with a wild chase in traffic in the middle, and a chase over the rooftops for the climax. Reviews for the series were pretty good, although the May 11, 1918 *Motion Picture News* gave this advice on *Fred Fictitious Foundling*:

> *This Filbert comedian is almost as large as Arbuckle and is possessed of a pleasing personality. For his own benefit, however, he should not show so much of his body. Huge rolls of fat are not funny.*

By 1919 Binney had left the Florida Film Corporation, although Hilliard Karr continued making shorts for the outfit (more on Karr soon). The 1920s saw Binney involved in various enterprises. In 1921 he was in Canada ballyhooing the Canadian Photo-Plays Productions, LTD, but being a by-the-seat-of-your-pants film promoter had its pitfalls, as illustrated by this item from the May 6, 1924 *Film Daily*:

Appendix Two: "The Screen Must Have a Fat Comedian" • 625

Harold "Josh" Binney and his staff in front of Pacific Pictures' office.

BINNEY JAILED
Promoter with Varied Career in Montana Prison for Period of Years

Seattle—Harold J. ("Josh") Binney, who has promoted production companies in many parts of the West Coast, has been sentenced to six years in the state penitentiary at Butte, Mont., for obtaining money under false pretenses in promoting the Vigilante M.P. Producers Co.

Binney was arrested in Santa Rosa, Cal., several months ago and taken to Montana for trial. He weighs 334 pounds and considers himself "the *biggest asset" of the company. He had stung ex-governor Sam Stewart and a number of others in his promoting scheme, according to the findings.*

Nothing if not tenacious, Binney was back on the fringes by the late 1920s. 1928 saw the announcements that he was director of the newly-formed Billie Rhodes productions all set to make two-reel travelogues with the former Al Christie star, and in 1933 there were items that he was directing Hal Byrnes in six cowboy song subjects for National Pictures. Neither series came to fruition. Binney did direct some Aircraft training films for the Bray Studios during World War II, and his last credits were as director for a number of low-budget all-black musical and comedy features. *Hi De Ho* (1947), *Boarding House Blues*, *Killer Diller* (both 1948), and *The Joint is Jumpin'* (1949) showcased performers such as Cab Calloway, Butterfly McQueen, and Moms Mabley. Binney died in Los Angeles in 1956.

Like most of the headlining comics, a great deal of the supporting comedy players got their start at Sennett as well. Once they finished their apprenticeship on the lot they ended up all over the silent comedy map. Another regular who was always used for his sight-gag value was Bert Gillespie. At five-foot, three-inches, but weighing three hundred and fifty-five pounds, this cannonball shaped performer started his career with the "King of Comedy" as part of the Keystone Kops Band, a motley group of minor players that appeared at publicity events. He began appearing on screen in 1916 and was always used for a quick weight-related laugh. If there was a swimming pool in a short Gillespie was usually floating around in it like his own little island. Comedies that he's seen bobbing around in include *The Snow Cure*, *The Surf Girl* (both 1916), and *The Punch of the Irish* (1921). In Hank Mann's *The Nickel Snatcher* (1920) Bert's a rotund lady passenger who has trouble boarding on the back of Hank's trolley. After much pushing and shoving Hank gets the lady aboard but her extreme weight tips the front of the trolley up in the air. Making the rounds of the comedy units during his six year career, he worked for Sennett, Paramount, Fox, Arrow, and Lehrman Specials. But like most of his fat brethren, Gillespie died young. He was only thirty-three when he passed in 1922.

Bert Gillespie poses with Ethel Burton (center) and an unknown actress during the making of Billy West's *The Scholar* (1918).

Probably the heaviest "heavy" of silent comedy was Frank "Fatty"

Appendix Two: "The Screen Must Have a Fat Comedian" • 627

Joe Rock is pulled in two directions by Frank Alexander (left) and Jack Lloyd (right) in *Too Much Dutch* (1923). Courtesy Jim Kerkhoff.

Alexander. Weighing in at three hundred and fifty pounds, the Washington State-born Alexander began his film career at Keystone in 1915. From the very beginning he was on the receiving end of much slapstick abuse, in particular from Syd Chaplin in shorts like *Gussle Rivals Jonah*, *Gussle Tied to Trouble*, and *A Lover's Lost Control* (all 1915). Besides helping to fill up the film frame, during his tenure with Sennett he played cops, harassed fathers, hotel porters, and headwaiters in support of Charles Murray, Harry McCoy, Fred Mace, and Chester Conklin. By 1917 he was branching out to other units like Fox and Roach, and in 1918 he became an integral part of Larry Semon's slapstick universe.

For almost a decade Alexander got blown up, took tremendous falls from high places, and was covered with various suds and goo in service to Mr. Semon. Some of their memorable encounters include the shorts *Bathing Beauties and Big Boobs* (1918), *The Star Boarder* (1919), *The Bakery* (1921), and *The Sawmill* (1922), as well as the features *The Perfect Clown* and *The Wizard of Oz* (both 1925). Between his work with Semon the big comic also found time to be the perfect fall guy for Joe Rock, Lige Conley, Cliff Bowes, and Oliver Hardy & Bobby Ray. In 1925 he had a fling at comedy stardom as the ringleader of A Ton of Fun (more on them coming up), and after the arrival of sound Alexander still turned up for a while in Hal Roach and Mickey McGuire shorts. His last appearance was in W. C. Fields' *The Barber Shop* (1933), and he passed away in 1937.

Marvin Loback was an adept comic foil who found a ready place in silent slapstick as his obese figure made him a walking sight-gag. Born in Tacoma, Washington, his earliest appearances were bits in Sennett, L-Ko, Triangle, and Harold Lloyd comedies. A good part in Universal's 1918 special short *The Geezer of Berlin* (as von Hindenboig—named after the zeppelin) gave him more visibility, leading him to become part of the regular stock company on both the Sennett and Roach lots. For the next five years he was kept busy supporting Charlie Murray, Billy Bevan, Paul Parrott, and Stan Laurel in shorts like *The Speakeasy* (1919), *Be Reasonable* (1921), *The Landlubber* (1922), *The Spoilers*, and *Hard Knocks and Love Taps* (both 1923), not to mention the Sennett features *Married Life* (1920) and *A Small Town Idol* (1921).

In 1924 Loback was unofficially teamed at Sennett with leading man Ralph Graves for a two-year series of light comedy shorts that were a distinct departure from the studio's usual fare of grotesque and absurd zanies. For the first time romance became an element of a Sennett comedy. Graves provided the love interest with leading ladies like Alice Day and Thelma Parr, while Loback was on hand as Ralph's buddy or shady business associate to bring the more sight-gag and traditional Sennett material to the films. After something like eighteen shorts together, which included *Breaking the Ice*, *Wide Open Faces* (both

Snub Pollard's piano playing is accompanied by Marvin Loback (right) and Tiny Lipson (left) among others while making a late 1920s Weiss Brothers short. Courtesy Robert S. Birchard.

1925), *Hooked at the Altar*, and *A Yankee Doodle Duke* (both 1926), the team went their separate ways.

Loback began circulating again, including some appearances in Christie Comedies, but soon settled in at Weiss Brothers Artclass Pictures. The economically-minded Weiss Brothers had moved into comedy shorts production and Loback supported many of their headlining series stars—he's particularly funny in drag as Poodles Hanneford's blimp girlfriend in *Why Detectives Go Wrong* (1928) —but was mainly hooked up with Snub Pollard in a bald attempt to cash in on the popularity of Hal Roach's Laurel & Hardy. Almost all of the Pollard/Loback shorts, such as *Double Trouble* (1927), *Men About Town* (1928), and *Here Comes a Sailor* (1929) pirated L&H material, but *Sock and Run* (19229) in particular is like a tour through Stan & Ollie's late 1920's gag book. The first reel alone recreates routines from *Putting Pants on Philip* (1927), *You're Darn Tootin'*, and *Should Men Go Home?* (both 1928), while the second plunders the prizefight material from the first reel of *The Battle of the Century* (1927).

The series with Snub was the final leading role for Loback. He was back to bits at the Sennett Studio in a slew of the producer's sound two-reelers like *Sugar Plum Papa* (1930), *In Conference*, *The Great Pie Mystery* (both 1931), *Billboard Girl*, and *Hatta Marri* (both 1932). When Sennett closed up shop in 1933 the comic turned up here and there—in features like *It Happened One Night* and *The Old-Fashioned Way* (both 1934), plus a few Columbia Pictures shorts like *Old Sawbones* and *Uncivil Warriors* (both 1935), before his death in 1938.

Many of the large supporting comics had little or nothing to do with Sennett Studio. Oliver Hardy made one isolated appearance for Sennett (1927's *Crazy to Act*) during the years that he was an ace featured player. Of course now he's one of the best loved and remembered fat comics thanks to his inspired teaming with Stan Laurel. Today Laurel & Hardy are considered a completely inseparable unit like "pork and beans" and "Sodom and Gomorrah," and it's amazing to discover what a sizeable solo career he had. Making his film debut in 1914 he appeared in more than two hundred and fifty films on his own as versatile support. Born Norvell Hardy in 1892 in Harlem, Georgia, he developed an early interest in singing, touring for a while with a minstrel show, and later, like Roscoe, singing to illustrated slides in theatres. By 1910 he was running a movie house and decided that he could do better, or at least not worse, than most of the comedians he saw on screen. So in 1913 he moved to Jacksonville, Florida, which at the time was a beehive of comedy filmmaking. Outside of a very brief foray to New York in 1915, Hardy's earliest film years were spent in Florida working for the Lubin and Vim companies. Having no stage training or background in comedy he learned the basics of film comedy by appearing in one or two split-reel or one-reel films a week, playing everything from kids to comic ladies in drag.

During his Jacksonville days Hardy acquired the nickname of Babe, and used it as his professional name for many years. At Vim in 1916, he was part of the ensemble that supported comics Bobby Burns and Walter Stull, who were known as "Pokes and Jabs." In their shorts Babe worked with a small comic named Billy Ruge, and before long he had his first screen partnership when they were spun off into their own one-reelers and dubbed "Plump and Runt." They made thirty-plus shorts together, but never caught on as the characters were sometimes rivals, sometimes pals, never really developing a

Oliver Hardy (left) with his papa James Levering in the 1915 Lubin short *Babe's School Days*. Courtesy Peter Bagrov.

screen relationship. After Vim closed at the end of 1916, Babe spent most of the next seven years as the main support for three different star comedians—Billy West, Jimmy Aubrey, and Larry Semon. All were small men, and Babe, with his height and heft, was perfect to be their comic adversary. Billy West had spent many years in vaudeville until a Charlie Chaplin imitation proved to be his ticket to success and the movies. In 1917 and 1918, West aped Chaplin for the King Bee Corporation, and Babe, often in big, bushy moustaches, was his Eric Campbell.

Jimmy Aubrey, who was a veteran of the English music hall and the Fred Karno Company, became a star in shorts for Vitagraph. Babe joined him in 1919 and again was the all-purpose heavy. Aubrey, a run-of-the-mill comic, was disagreeable and difficult, and Babe left his employ in 1921 to begin working for Vitagraph's top funnyman Larry Semon. One of the most popular clowns in pictures, Semon was an ex-newspaper cartoonist who brought the wild surrealism of comic strips to the screen, and Babe played the ultimate blustery villain. Around 1923, the big comics like Chaplin and Keaton made the jump to features, and Larry decided he should too. While continuing in the Semon features, Babe began freelancing and in 1924 re-joined his old boss Billy West in shorts for the Arrow Company. By this time West had dropped the Chaplin imitation and adopted a man-about-town persona. In addition to the shorts with West, Babe was teamed with goofy comic Bobby Ray in four West-produced shorts that are definite Laurel & Hardy forerunners. In *Stick Around* (1925) for example, the boys play paperhangers with Babe as the boss and Ray as the inept helper. Both are dumb, and although Babe is a bit brighter he's not as smart as he thinks he is. They even wear derbies.

After these West comedies, Hardy freelanced at Fox and finally with Hal Roach. Years before at King Bee and L-Ko, Babe had worked with director Charles Parrott (a.k.a. Charley Chase). Parrott had joined the Roach organization in 1921, eventually becoming director-general of the studio, and it wasn't long before Babe began showing up there as regular support. In 1926 Roach signed Babe to an exclusive contract to support stars like Mabel Normand and to be featured in their *All Star Comedies*. The Roach lot was the ideal place for Hardy. In his earlier comedies the pace was always too frenetic for a long exasperated look into the camera or a bashful tie twiddle. But at Roach they had slowed down the pace and developed more sophisticated story lines and characters. Babe was finally able to make full use of his natural acting abilities, and was working with some of the best comedy creators of the era—Chase, Leo McCarey, Clyde Bruckman, James Parrott, and Stan Laurel.

Laurel had re-joined Roach in 1925 and was working as a gagman and director. Having first met years before while making the short *The Lucky Dog* (1921), Laurel seems to have really appreciated Babe's scene-stealing abilities, using him regularly at Roach to great advantage. Soon Stan began performing again and the boys started appearing together in the *All Star Comedies*. Slowly, but surely, their chemistry together

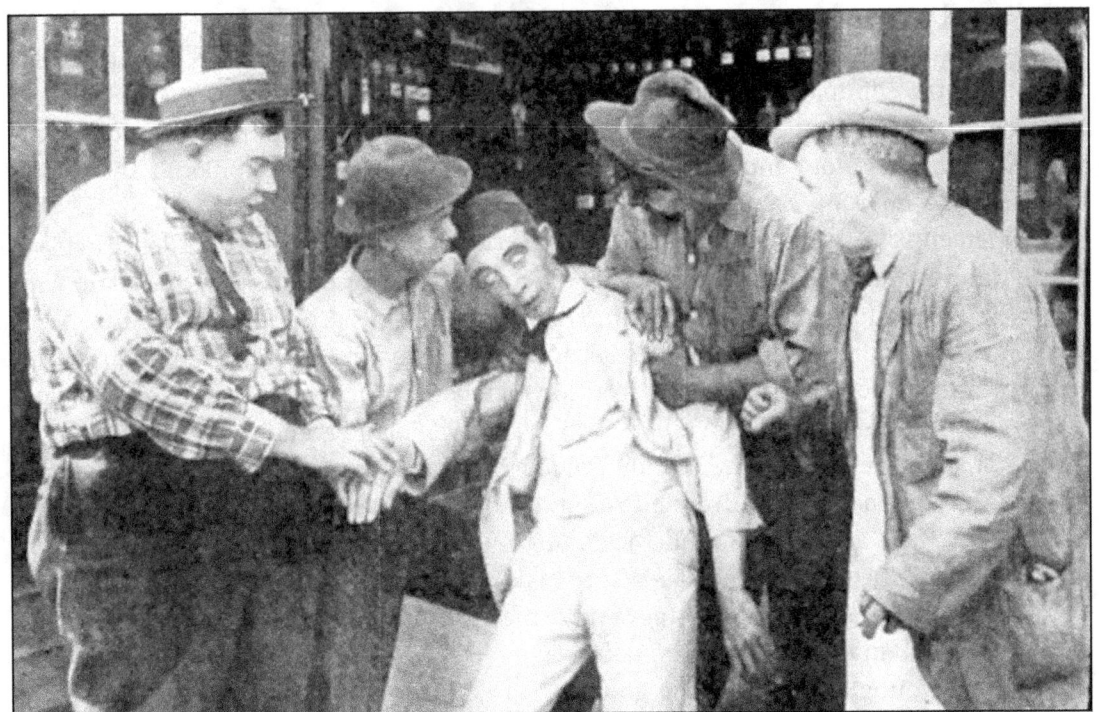

Ralph McComas (left) and the denizens of Bloom Center comfort Lee Morris (middle) in *The Comeback of Percy* (1915).

was recognized and developed by the Roach staff. The rest of course is cinematic history, and their teamwork would continue through their last films and even to live stage appearances in the 1950s.

Unlike Oliver Hardy, Ralph McComas is on the list of the fat, funny, and forgotten. Born in Los Angeles in 1889, McComas was a five-foot-eleven, two-hundred-and-ninety-pound local boy who made good in the early film industry of the teens. After attending the University of California, McComas began a business-oriented career working as a teller at L.A.'s Merchant's Bank and Trust Co., but succumbed to the lure of the stage. Entering vaudeville as a comic he played on the Pantages Circuit and in stock in San Francisco. Movies snagged him in 1914 when he joined the ensemble at *Joker Comedies* in the unit under the direction of Allen Curtis. McComas appeared with Max Asher, Louise Fazenda, Billy Franey, and Gale Henry in titles like *The Tender Hearted Sheriff*, *Schultz the Barber*, *He Married Her Anyhow* (all 1914), and *Fooling Fathers* (1915). Having gotten his foot in the door for comedy shorts he did a very brief turn with Fred Mace at Majestic, and then settled in at Selig to become a key member of their *Chronicles of Bloom Center* series of two-reelers.

Following the misadventures of the denizens of a small rural town, Selig announced the series as a "new idea in the Picture Play serial line," but it was suspiciously similar to Essanay's popular *Snakeville Comedies*. In Selig's carbon copy McComas played Chubby Green, the village prankster and bad boy who causes a lot of the machinations that fuels the plots. A dozen entries were made, and McComas' fellow performers included Sid Smith, Lillian Brown Leighton, John Lancaster, and Lee Morris in titles like *Landing the Hose Reel*, *A Thing or Two in the Movies*, and *No Sir-ee Bob* (all 1916). In 1916 and 1917, McComas was bouncing all over—making some West Coast Vitagraph comedies, working at the fledgling Hal Roach Studio for items like *Lonesome Luke's Lively Life* (1917), and becoming regular support for the chimpanzees Napoleon and Sally in their comedies produced by the E & R Jungle Film Company. Here McComas was re-united with his *Bloom Center* teammate Lillian Brown Leighton, and supplied the human element for the monks in shorts like *Stung*, *Father's Baby*, *In Dutch*, *Haunted*, and *Some Detective* (all 1916).

Nineteen-seventeen also saw him return to Universal and director Allen Curtis to turn out numerous comedies through their Victor and Nestor brands. Making a trio with Eileen Sedgwick (sister of aforementioned Edward Sedgwick) and little Milton Sims, McComas would often play a hapless husband named Duffer, Harold Dubb, or just plain Ralph, who was put-upon by Eileen in titles such as *It's Cheaper to be Married*, *A Bare Living*, *The Woman in the Case* (all 1917), *The Shifty Shoplifter*, and *The Butler's Blunder* (both 1918). Singled out by the *Motion Picture News* as "a fat man who is not vulgar," at this point McComas' career dropped off and he only made sporadic appearances. The short *Three Pairs of Stockings*, and the Maurice Tourneur feature *The Great Redeemer* (both 1921) are the last known films before his death at thirty-five in 1924.

Otis Harlan was a star of the stage and came to films as one, but it wasn't long before he transitioned into a much-in-demand character player. Born in Zanesville, Ohio in 1865, the young Harlan had the good luck to come to the attention of the popular playwright and humorist Charles H. Hoyt, who gave him his first starring role in his *A Hole in the Ground* in 1887. This established him as a star, and he appeared in subsequent

Otis Harlan (left) with Paul Hurst (middle) and Ken Maynard (right) in the early talkie feature *Mountain Justice* (1930).

Hoyt comedies such as *A Brass Monkey*, *A Black Sheep*, and *A Texas Steer*. Other successes included *The Vanderbilt Cup* opposite Elsie Janis, *Little Puck* where he was teamed with the aforementioned Frank Daniels, and he also appeared with Anna Held, Fay Templeton, and Weber & Fields. After twenty-two years on Broadway he was brought to the screen in Selig's 1915 film version of *A Black Sheep*. This was the first in Selig's series of *Hoyt-Farce Comedies*, all of which starred Harlan, and included *A Stranger in New York*, *Temperance Town*, and *A Milk White Flag* (all 1916).

Despite all the publicity, with Selig billing him as "the King of American Comedians," Harlan followed up the Hoyt comedies with a 1916 Edison short *The Resurrection of Dan Packard* and then returned to the stage. He finally settled in films in 1920 with two shorts, *Welcome Home* and *I'll Say He Forgot*, for Reelcraft Pictures' Royal Comedies series, and then continued on as a busy Hollywood character actor. The 1920s saw him in all types of features, but he remained a comedy specialist. In addition to supporting Edward Everett Horton and Laura La Plante in entries like *The Whole Town's Talking* (1926), *Silk Stockings* (1927), and *Dad's Choice* (1928), he was a regular in the features of Reginald Denny. The tall and handsome Denny was a light and nimble polite comedy leading man, and the round and cherubic Harlan made the perfect foil for him. Although close to the ground Harlan always walked on wobbly legs like he had sore feet, but it was likely due to being off-balanced by his weight and added to the sometimes crotchety demeanor of his characters.

Harlan appeared in eight features with Denny, including the overlooked gems *Oh, Doctor!* (1925) and *What Happened to Jones?* (1926). Making a solid transition to sound films he played Captain Andy in Universal's part-talkie filming of *Show Boat* (1929), as well as *Embarrassing Moments*, *Dames Ahoy* (both 1930), and *The Big Shot* (1931). The regularity of his appearances began tapering off, but he still had nice moments in *Life Returns* (1934), *A Midsummer Night's Dream* (1935), and as the voice of Happy in Walt Disney's *Snow White and the Seven Dwarfs* (1937). He retired in 1938 after suffering a stroke while rehearsing an appearance with Al Jolson, and died in 1940.

An overlooked foot soldier of silent slapstick is Frank J. Coleman, who was one of the most ubiquitous players in the genre. Plump and round, with a big bald head, his work went unnoticed by the public although they saw him constantly. A graduate of vaudeville with the Garden City Quartette, and the Bennett-Morton Stock Company on the West Coast, it was a small step to movies for Coleman, who made his first appearances in 1915. Turning up at L-Ko in shorts like *Love and Sour Notes* (1915) and some Rolin one-reelers, his most important early work was in Charlie Chaplin's Essanay comedies such as *The*

Frank J. Coleman (right) irritates Alice Howell and Phil Dunham with his bad table manners in *A Convict's Happy Bride* (1920). Courtesy Cole Johnson.

Bank, *A Night in the Show*, and *A Burlesque on Carmen* (all 1915). Chaplin must have appreciated Coleman's skills as he made him a core member of his Mutual stock company. Coleman appeared in eleven of the twelve Chaplin Mutual shorts, usually in more than one role, and played numerous policemen, most memorably in *The Adventurer* (1917), as well as firemen, restaurant managers, immigrant gamblers, and film directors.

Chaplin was the top of the silent comedy heap, and although Coleman never worked for him again, his time with the star led to stints with Mack Sennett and Fox Sunshine Comedies for titles that include *Sheriff Nell's Tussle, Love Loops the Loop, A High Diver's Last Kiss, Roaring Lions on the Midnight Express* (all 1918), and *His Musical Sneeze* (1919). At Fox he worked with the young director Jack White, and when White set up his own production company Coleman came along to play the mock villain or jealous husband in the organization's first shorts like *A Fresh Start, Nonsense* (both 1920), and *The Vagrant* (1921).

From this point on the large comic was a fixture in the silent comedy universe and worked everywhere—at Reelcraft with Alice Howell, a few of the Henry Lehrman First National Specials like *The Punch of the Irish* and *A Game Lady* (both 1921), Century Comedies, and with Larry Semon at Vitagraph. Often an authority figure, and sometimes in drag as a society matron, Coleman could always be counted on for sterling support and to get his laughs. Although anonymous to the public, Coleman was known in the industry as were the risks that silent comedy performers daily took in making these slapstick valentines. This led columnist Harry Burns (himself a comedy bit player and assistant director) to put this joke item in the August 9, 1919 issue of *Camera!*:

> *Frank Colemen was dragged along Cahuenga Pass for about a mile and he wasn't hurt at all. How did it happen? Why he was seated in his car, which had broken down and was being towed to a garage for repairs. No, I mean his car was. At any rate, I had you guessing.*

In 1924 Coleman had a brief return to the Mack Sennett fold when he played the heavy in the early Harry Langdon shorts *The First 100 Years* and *The Luck of the Foolish* (both 1924). The last few years of his career were spent back at Fox where he made screen life difficult for Jerry Madden, Ernie Shields, and Lige Conley in numerous *Imperial Comedies* like *Jerry the Giant, Honeymoon Hospital* (both 1926), and *Slippery Silks* (1927). Leaving films before the changeover to sound, he remained in Los Angeles until his death in 1948.

A fixture in Hank Mann's 1919-1920 Arrow comedies was little Jess Weldon, who usually played his boss or some other authority figure. Small enough to be sometimes described as a dwarf, he seemed to have been born old, and if you look up globular in the dictionary you'll find his picture. The *Motion Picture News* even mentioned that he "carries a vast amount of avoirdupois." Born in 1872, he first arrived on screen in 1917 and hit the ground running. That first year he was a regular in Triangle Komedies, and was busy at Fox, supporting Hank Mann in efforts like *A Domestic Hound* and appearing in Fox Sunshine Comedies such as the apocalyptic *Roaring Lions and Wedding Bells*. From there he was all over, working at Vitagraph, Century, Jack White, Reelcraft, and Joe Rock Productions for *Jazz and Jailbirds* (1919), *Footprints* (1920), *The New Member* (1921),

Dot Farley and Bull Montana (left) celebrate with Jess Weldon (right) and others in the Robin Hood spoof *Rob 'Em Good* (1923). Courtesy Robert S. Birchard.

and *A Howling Success* (1923), in addition to supporting big names like Larry Semon, Lloyd Hamilton, and Buster Keaton in *The Simple Life* (1919), *The Simp* (1920), and *The Playhouse* (1921).

Much of the above was done in between Hank Mann's one and two-reel series for Arrow, where the irascible Weldon gave Hank grief in entries like *Hopping Bells* (1919), *A Gum Riot*, *The Janitor*, *The Bill Poster*, and *When Spirits Move* (all 1920). Besides all the shorts he also made a few feature appearances, as in the Rex Ingram-directed *Trifling Women* (1922) and most memorably Douglas Fairbanks' *The Thief of Bagdad* (1924), where Weldon was the head of the palace eunuchs. His September 30, 1925 *Variety* obituary reveals that films weren't his only means of support:

FILM DWARF DIES

Los Angeles, Sept. 29

Jessie Weldon, who played the role of a dwarf in films, died at the General Emergency Hospital here on the eve of his trial for selling drugs, with two others, to narcotic agents.

The two other accomplices, Fernando Yskas and Romandy Duran, were convicted and sentenced to six months in the county jail.

Russell Powell was three hundred pounds of support during a thirty-year film career (he was also billed as Russ Powell and J. Russell Powell). Born in 1875, this Indiana native had eleven years on the stage—spent touring the Orpheum Circuit and being a legit bass singer in comic operas like *The Chocolate Soldier* and *The Madcap Duchess* on Broadway. He forsook the stage for the screen when he joined Biograph in 1914 for films such as *Bertha, the Button Hole Maker* (1914), *In the Boarding House*, and *The Boob and the Baker* (both 1915). It wasn't long before he branched out to supporting "Smiling Bill" Parsons (fat men in stereo) in *The Tale of the Night Before* and *The Morning After* (both 1915), as well as some MinA Comedies like *Kidding the Goats* and *The False Heir* (both 1915). His next move was to become part of the ensemble for the Vogue Comedy Company which had him rubbing elbows with Paddy McGuire, Priscilla Dean, Arthur Moon, and Lillian Brown Leighton in entries such as *Oh, for the Life of a Fireman*, *Love, Dynamite and Baseballs*, *Heaven Will Protect a Working Goil*, and *Bungling Bill's Peeping Ways* (all 1916), of which the *Motion Picture News* said; "Big, fat Russ Powell is the chief funny man, and pretty Priscilla Dean the leading lady. Nuff said! It's a scream!"

After a year's worth of the Vogues he re-located to Universal where he worked in their L-Ko and Century brands with funmakers like Alice Howell, Gale Henry, Merta Sterling, Hughie Mack, and Eddie Barry. Powell specialized in authority figures, replete with character names such as Maximilian Mudguard, in opuses on the order of *Fat and Furious* (1917), *The Blind Pig*, and *Choo Choo Love* (both 1918). In 1919 Powell broke into features and was

Merta Sterling draws a bead on Russ Powell, as Lee Morris and Babe Emerson cower in *The Donkey Did It* (1918).

very busy as a character player, alternating being officious and oafish, in pictures such as *The Slim Princess* (1920), *Head Over Heels* (1922), *A Boy of Flanders* (1924), and Arbuckle's *The Red Mill* (1927). Unfortunately by the end of the decade his roles were reduced to one-gag bit parts, with his last good role being in blackface as Kingfish in the 1930 Amos and Andy feature *Check and Double Check*. Powell remained very busy in features and shorts, making uncountable appearances until the early 1940s. During this time he's been spotted in *Modern Times* (1936), *A Day at the Races* (1937), *Son of Frankenstein* (1939), and *To Be or Not To Be* (1942). After retiring he passed away in 1950.

There were others—bit players who have been engulfed by obscurity, such as the two-hundred-and-eighty-four-pound Billy Joseph. In spite of a few appearances in some of the Vin Moore-directed *Lion Comedies* like *Howling Lions and Circus Queens* (1919) for L-Ko and Century, he never made a name for himself nor qualified for a footnote in film comedy history.

By the time the 1920s rolled around Roscoe was "the fat comedian" in most movie goers' minds, and the 1921 Labor Day scandal and his subsequent banishment from the screen left a void in their viewing pleasure. This led to a few enterprising producers attempting to take advantage of this situation by engaging large comics, some of whom had been in films since the teens, to be "Roscoe replacements" in an effort to fill Arbuckle's plus-sized trousers.

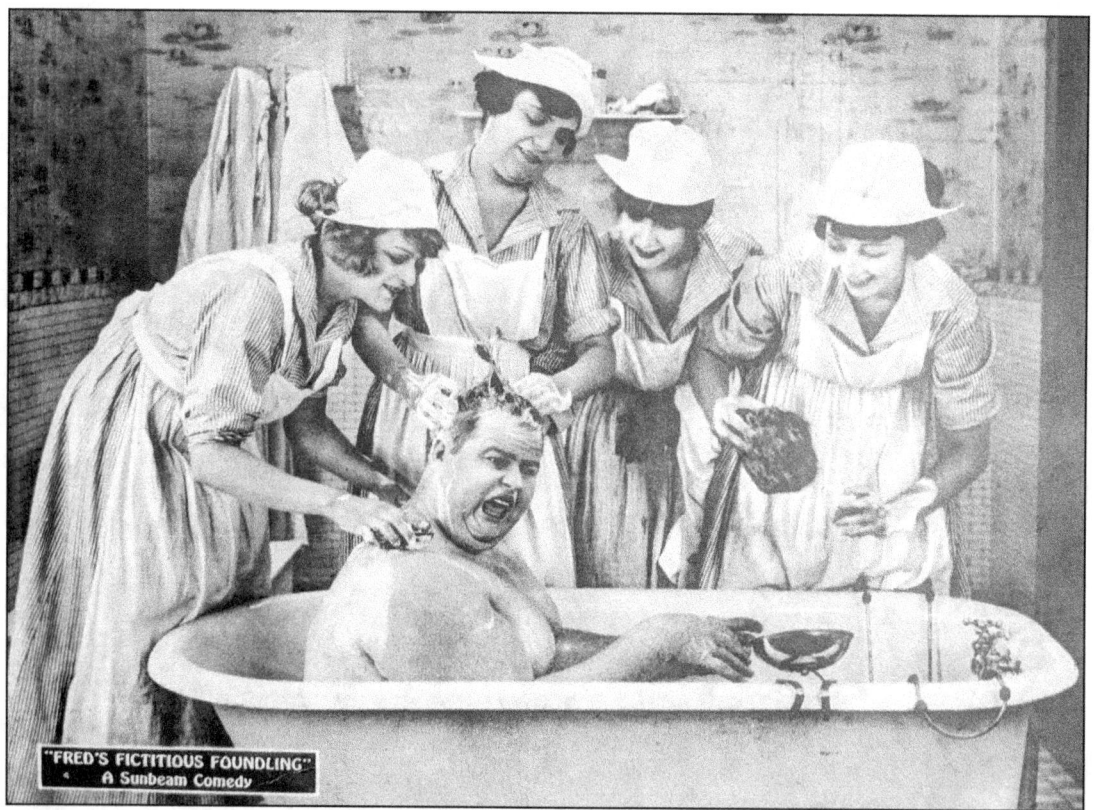

Hilliard Karr gets undivided attention in 1918's *Fred's Fictitious Foundling*. Courtesy Jim Kerkhoff.

As previously discussed, Hilliard Karr started his career as Nathan Dewing in Josh Binney's *Lion Comedies* and *Funny Fatty Filbert* shorts. Binney had set up the Florida Film Corporation to make the Filbert comedies, but by 1919 he had left the organization, and it was taken over by Glen Lambert who became director and manager of the outfit. Still based at the Klutho Studio in Jacksonville, they embarked on a series of *Sunbeam Comedies*, and Karr remained with the company to become part of the *Sunbeam*'s regular ensemble along with Bert Tracy and Gertrude Garretson. Titles like *A Pool of Peaches*, *His Muzzled Career*, and *Hot Sands and Cold Feet* (all 1919) were written and directed by Glen Lambert with distribution by the Arrow Film Corporation. Survivors such as *A Dumbwaiter Scandal*, *His Conscience, His Guide*, and *His Concrete Dome* (all 1919) show that the emphasis was on beaches and lots of pretty girls.

The *Sunbeams* were over before the year was out, and Karr moved over to another Florida company—Mark Dintenfass' *Cuckoo Comedies*. Again shapely women were the key element, and Karr was the main support for stars Bobby Burns and newcomer Jobyna Ralston in the shorts *Starting Out in Life*, *The Sultan of Jazz*, *The Shimmy Gym* (all 1919), and *Ball-Bearing But Hard Running* (1920). The series was advertised with the catch-phrase "Every One's a Bird." When this series ended Karr finally migrated to Hollywood. Besides appearing in features such as *Human Hearts* and *Big Stakes* (both 1922), he became an Arbuckle surrogate in a number of Al St John's comedies for the Fox studio.

Most of Karr's appearances with Al, in shorts like *Fool Days* and *Ain't Love Grand* (both 1921) are missing, but photos and the existing *Out of Place* (1922) show that he was working hard to fill in for Roscoe. In *Out of Place* not only is he dressed exactly in the country boy Fatty mode, but engages in a long knockabout sequence with Al where he's trying to help him straighten up after carrying a heavy box on his back that's right out of one of the Comique shorts. Karr also re-enacts some of Arbuckle's business from the early *Passions, He Had Three* (1913), sneaking and drinking all the milk that Al has just gotten from a cow, which suggests that Roscoe may have been behind the camera on this short.

After a brief hiatus to his career described in the June 9, 1922 *Variety*—

Fat Man Gets 30 Days

Hilliard S. Karr, 350-pound picture actor, was sentenced to 30 days on the county chain gang by Judge Shenk last week for running down and injuring Gussie Schuster and failing to stop and give her aid.

Karr is charged with driving away from the scene of the accident and returning later to find that someone else had taken the injured woman to the hospital.

In giving sentence Judge Shenk said : "The chart calls for a stretch on location. Prepare for a prolonged stay."

—it seems that the appearances in the St John comedies led to a more formal substitution for Roscoe:

"Fatty" Karr to be Featured
Comedian Will Be Starred in Series of Comedies to Meet Public Demand
> *Both Franklyn E. Backer of East Coast Productions and Bruce Mitchell of the T.R. Coffin Company, believe that the time is ripe for a series of two-reel comedies starring a fat comedian, as at the present time there is no such comedian on the screen. Exhibitors according to reports, have felt keenly the loss of a comedy unit of this nature since the departure of "Fatty" Arbuckle from the screen.*
> – **Motion Picture News** (September 16, 1922)

> *Hilliard (Fatty) Karr, who according to his producers, is to be presented as a successor of Roscoe Arbuckle, started work on his first picture this week at the Federal Studios under the direction of Bruce Mitchell. His first story will be "Weight for Me," and is built along the lines similar to those pictures in which Arbuckle appeared during his early career before the camera.*
> – **Exhibitors Trade Review**, November 25, 1922

The idea was to fill the void left by Roscoe's absence, and despite being called East Coast Productions, Inc., shop was set up in California. The shorts were made under the supervision of Bruce Mitchell, an actor who began directing comedies for MinA in 1915, and along the way worked with William Parsons and Norma Talmadge. Mitchell later mostly directed westerns and action films with the likes of Bob Curwood, Frank Merrill, and Kenneth MacDonald. In the sound era he did bit roles in features until 1945. A Pennsylvania beauty contest winner, Mary Jane Alden, was named as leading lady, and the rest of the production crew included:

> *Four "heavies" are supporting Karr in this new series, and their combined weight is 900 pounds. They are Bruce Mitchell, director, who weighs 240 pounds, "Tiny" Sandford, villain, 250 pounds, James F. Holleran, vice-president, 210, and Ward Hayes, gag man, 200.*
> –**Exhibitors Herald**, December 9, 1922

The only titles announced were *Weight for Me* and *Long Skirts*. There were numerous trade announcements in the fall and end of 1922, but when 1923 rolled around news grew quiet and it's not even definite that the films were actually released. After this stint as an Arbuckle stand-in Karr returned to the supporting ranks and was busy working at practically all the comedy units in Hollywood. He spent a lot of time at Century Comedies playing opposite Buddy Messenger, Edna Marion, and Wanda Wiley, likewise at Fox alongside Harry Sweet and James Parrott, in addition to side trips with Lloyd Hamilton and Billy West. In 1925 he became one of the literal "big three" in Joe Rock's *A Ton of Fun Comedies* (more on this coming up), which was the peak of his career. Afterwards he did some bit parts in shorts and features, but left the film industry in 1931. Moving back to his native Texas, he passed away there at age forty-six in 1945.

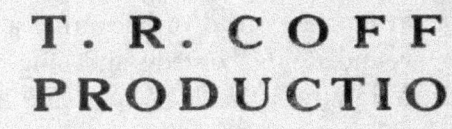

Exhibitor ad for Hilliard Karr's starring series.

Another hefty supporting player who was moved into a position to assume Roscoe's mantle of King-size King of Comedy (by Arbuckle's own studio of Paramount) was Walter Hiers. Born in Cordele, Georgia in 1893, after high school he enrolled at the military academy at Peekskill, New York, but because of his funny shape and outgoing personality he spent much of his spare time doing amateur theatricals and minstrel performances. Liking it so much, instead of becoming a career military man he entered vaudeville. Touring around doing comedy and singing, sometimes under the direction of Gus Edwards, and in the satire *The Villain Still Pursued Her*, Hiers began his movie career in New York. His first film is said to have been D. W. Griffith's 1911 *The Failure*, and Hiers was making extra money doing background and bits in other Biograph and Edison shorts.

> *Actors told me that the old Lubin company was seeking a fat boy for a good part. I scoffed at the movies—which proves that I began a long time ago, because in these latter days an actor may scuff to himself at the movies but the salaries can't be sniffed at.*
>
> *Salaries didn't count for much in those days, and I wasn't far enough along on the stage to consider the $50-a-week offered by Lubin beneath my dignity. I signed for a year, and was promptly sent to Florida for the winter, where I made one-reel comedies.*
>
> **– Educational Pictures pressbook for *Off His Beat* (1925)**

Spending about a year in Florida for Lubin, Hiers worked in shorts directed by Arthur Hotaling—some with people like Raymond McKee and Marguerite Ne Moyer, and others were black cast one-reelers starring John and Mattie Edwards. Returning to New York the young actor was comic relief in features such as *Just Out of College* and *The Labyrinth* (both 1915), and began working for the Thanhouser Film Company. Thanhouser was in New Rochelle, New York, and Hiers became a regular in their one-reel Falstaff Comedies. Often teamed with Riley Chamberlin in entries like *The Optimistic Oriental Occults*, *Rupert's Rube Relations*, and *The Professor's Peculiar Precautions* (all 1916), he even occasionally starred in items such as *Sammy's Semi-Suicide* (1916). Although busy at Thanhouser he still found time to appear at other New York studios like Wizard to support Bobby Burns and Walter Stull in their early efforts *A Quiet Game* and *How Ida Got Her Husband* (both 1915).

After Thanhouser he made the leap to good supporting roles in features. Pictures such as *Seventeen* (1916), *The Accidental Honeymoon* (1918), *When Doctor's Disagree* (1919), *What's Your Husband Doing?* (1920), and *The Speed Girl* (1921), had him playing characters named Tubby, Slim, and Fatty in support of Mabel Normand, Bebe Daniels, Bryant Washburn, Jack Pickford, and Constance Talmadge. Much of this supporting work was done for Paramount and its subsidiary company Realart. In 1922, during Roscoe's turmoil, Hiers was busy working for the company in *Bought and Paid For*, *Is Matrimony a Failure?*, and *The Ghost Breaker*, and when it became apparent to Paramount that Roscoe was no longer a viable star for them Hiers was tapped to following in his footprints.

Hiers was launched as a feature star in *Mr. Billings Spends His Dime* (1923), which was quickly followed by *Sixty Cents an Hour* (1923) and *Fair Week* (1924). All three have

Appendix Two: "The Screen Must Have a Fat Comedian" • 643

Paramount exhibitor ad for Walter Hier's starring *Mr. Billings Spends His Dime* (1923).

been unseen since their original release, but from synopsis and reviews it's clear that they were made in the Arbuckle feature mold—and even had Arbuckle regulars like Joseph Henabery and Walter Woods working behind the camera. Roscoe had been a tremendous draw for the studio, and while Paramount never publicized Hiers as an Arbuckle replacement it was clearly done to make exhibitors happy. Studio head Jesse Lasky said:

> *Mr. Hiers was made a star, you know, at the request of exhibitors, speaking through our Branch Managers at our last convention. The choice of the exhibitors was a wise one, for Mr. Hiers shows in "Mr. Billings Spends His Dime" that he is a master comedian.*
> – **Paramount Pep**, February 7, 1923

Exhibitors and audience reception of the pictures was decidedly mixed—

> *Although Mr. Hiers has his points...he is not Mr. Arbuckle. That he is fat, has an amiable smile and a genial friendliness are undeniable facts, but he does not have the inimitable mannerisms that made the dethroned obese star a success* —**Evening Journal**

> Walter Hiers, the comedian, is almost as fat, and almost as funny as Fatty Arbuckle used to be. —**Evening World**
>
> Does Mr. Hiers land in Arbuckle's place? And the answer is. He does. Or rather, he doesn't—for he goes beyond Arbuckle, higher or further, whatever way you choose to measure his distance. Mr. Hiers is a real comedian, which means that he is an actor. Arbuckle at his best was only an amusing clown with a foolish smile. Hiers, on the other hand, has the smile and a whole lot more. He ought to go much further than Arbuckle ever did. —**Times**
>
> It is possible that there are those who may be amused by the antics of Walter Hiers, as the ambitious soda dispenser in "Sixty Cents an Hour," but they'll certainly have to be easy to please and particularly mirthful if they find enough laughs in this one to make them thoroughly happy. —**Film Daily**

After the trio of films Paramount finished with Hiers, but his Arbuckle substitute days weren't quite over. Producer Al Christie, for whom the fat comedian had worked in *So Long Letty* (1920) and *Hold Your Breath* (1924), hired him to continue in series of two-reelers for distribution through Educational Pictures. Two years of shorts were made that included *A Fat Chance* (1924), *A Rarin' Romeo, Oh, Bridget, Hot Doggie* (all 1925), *Weak,*

Left to right Rosa Gore, Eddie Baker, Duane Thompson, Yola D'Avril, and Jack Duffy surround Walter Hiers in a *Hitchin' Up* (1926) lobby card. Courtesy Jim Kerkhoff.

But Willing, *Wireless Lizzie*, and *Hitchin' Up* (all 1926). Most had Duane Thompson as his love interest, and all gave him support from scene-stealing Christie regulars like Jack Duffy, William Irving, William Blaisdell, and Eddie Baker. The series showcased Hiers as a rotund everyman who often had to go to some absurd extreme to keep Duane and her family happy, in addition to exploring different professions such as cop, inventor, actor, and cowboy.

At the completion of his Christie series Hiers went back to supporting roles in features, but for lower-tiered studios such as Tiffany, Chadwick, and Gotham. Unfortunately his career went on a downward slide, and by 1928 he was the straight man for a tired and unfunny Larry Semon in his last short *A Simple Sap*. The changeover to sound films saw Hiers demoted to occasional uncredited bit roles, and he died of pneumonia while out on a personal appearance tour in 1933 at age forty-three.

Vernon Dent is well-remembered today by comedy fans—as support in many Mack Sennett comedies and as a long-time foil for the Three Stooges—but not for his 1921-1922 stint as an Arbuckle fill-in. Dent was a West Coast native, born in San Jose, California, who started his show business career in vaudeville and as a café singer. In 1919 star comic Hank Mann saw him singing and tapped Dent to be his foil in a series of comedies for Arrow release. For three years and almost thirty shorts Dent played a variety of dopey

Vernon Dent serenades Violet Joy (a.k.a. Duane Thompson) in the *Folly* Comedy *Coming and Going* (1921). Courtesy Cole Johnson.

co-workers, irritable bosses, and rivals for the favors of Madge Kirby, in titles such as *A Harem Hero* (1919), *Broken Bubbles*, *The Paper Hanger*, *A Gum Riot*, and *Don't Change Your Mrs.* (all 1920). On completion of the Mann comedies Dent went to work for the indie Pacific Film Company in Culver City and headlined in a series of Folly Comedies.

Looking at survivors such as *Up and at Em* (1921) and *Now or Never* (1922), plus photographs, Pacific was definitely capitalizing on Roscoe's absence from the screen with Vernon portraying an overweight and innocent boob dressed in the prerequisite bowler hat, plaid shirt, suspenders, high-water balloon trousers, and clod-hopper shoes. Pretty Violet Joy (later Duane Thompson) played his love interest, and thirteen one-reelers, with mostly rural settings and situations, were made with titles that included *Fat and Sassy*, *In at the Finish*, *Sleeping Sickness*, and *Slow but Sure* (all 1922). Not making much of an impact, the series only lasted a year, but Dent reprised his Arbuckle clone persona in the opening of the circus feature *Soul of the Beast* (1923).

After a bit of free-lancing for Larry Semon and Universal, Dent became one of the rocks of early screen comedy. In 1923 he became a fixture on the Mack Sennett lot and provided the comic gravity to counterpoint the antics of clowns such as Harry Langdon and Billy Bevan. Always in demand he appeared in features like *The Cameraman* and *Golf Widows* (both 1928), in addition to some late silent shorts for producer Jack White where he was teamed with Monty Collins. He continued in sound pictures without missing a beat, turning up in features and sound shorts for Educational, Sennett, Vitaphone, and Paramount. In 1935 he joined the stock company at the Columbia Pictures shorts department where he stayed for over twenty years making screen life difficult for The Three Stooges, Andy Clyde, Harry Langdon, Vera Vague, Hugh Herbert, El Brendel, Quillan & Vernon, and Bert Wheeler. His last appearance (via stock footage) was with the Stooges in *Guns A-Poppin* (1957), and he died in 1963.

Not wanting to miss their seat on the Arbuckle gravy-train, Universal found their own "Fatty" in the person of Karoly Huzar, a Hungarian comic who became better known in American films as Charles Puffy. Born in Budapest in 1888, after some early work as an insurance agent he ended up at the National Actors' Society school and made his stage debut in 1905. From then until the early 1920s he was very busy in all kinds of legitimate theatre productions, as well as cabaret. He became very popular as the star of a series of *Pufi Huzar* sketches (Pufi means Fatty in Hungarian), which no doubt strongly influenced his eventual screen persona. In Hungary he started appearing in little movie shorts which were based on the sketches, like the surviving *Pufi Cipot Vesz* (*Puffy Takes a Large* 1914), which details his difficulties in a shoe store. By the 1920s he was turning up in well-known German features such as Fritz Lang's *Der Mude Tod* (1921) and *Dr. Mabuse der Spieler* (1922). He began showing up in Hollywood films in 1924, although exactly how that occurred is open to debate. Some sources say that Universal president Carl Laemmle saw some of his work while on a business trip to Berlin, while others maintain that Puffy was already in Hollywood trying to break into the studios when Laemmle met him at a dinner party.

What is agreed upon is that Papa Carl was impressed with Puffy's performance in the feature *The Rose of Paris* (1924) and had the large comic set up shop at Universal for a series of one-reelers. Looking very similar to Roscoe, the resemblance was encouraged in the films. Most of his 1925 and 1926 shorts were directed and written by Richard Smith, with a few helmed by other well-seasoned comedy pros like Slim Summerville, Noel M. Smith, Scott Darling, and Zion Myers, and with screen support from Bud Jamison, Elsie Tarron, Billy Engle, and Mildred June. Puffy found himself in the usual slapstick predicaments of trying to avoid his irate wife (as well as other wives' irate husbands), being a tenderfoot out west, or having to disguise himself as a woman.

The films took a darker tone starting with *Not Guilty* (1926), when the bulk of the writing and directing was taken over by Harry Sweet. The surviving *Not Guilty* presents Puffy as a victim of circumstances who innocently goes to a courthouse with his girl Elsie to obtain a marriage license, but ends up in a slapstick version of Kafka's *The Trial* when he's charged with murder and painted as a savage killer. When the actual killer finally gives himself up and Puffy is freed, the end of the film has he and Elsie married with Puffy actually offhandedly killing her as he acts out

Chares Puffy in stylish drag—complete with saddle shoes.

one of the courtroom scenarios. Another Harry Sweet-directed short, *Smother O'Mine* (1927), co-stars Lydia Yeamans Titus as a sweet little old lady that Puffy helps out, but as it turns out there's nothing sweet about her and she becomes an albatross around the comic's neck.

Eventually bumped up to two reels, Puffy did help fill the void left by Roscoe's exit from the screen and became popular with audiences and exhibitors. The following are a couple of cinema manager's quotes about *Badly Broke* (1926) published in the April 10, 1926 *Exhibitors Herald*:

> *As I said before, I claim that this big tub of lard is very good and would take Arbuckle's place if they keep him in good stuff. This is a very good comedy with plenty of laughs.*

– **Trags Cinema, Neillsville, Wisconsin**

> *Charles Puffy is the best one reel bet that we have. Have used a number of these and they're all good.*
>
> **– Palace, Syracuse, Nebraska**

The shorts continued through 1928, and Puffy occasionally turned up as support in features such as *Mockery* (1927) with Lon Chaney and *The Man Who Laughs* (1928). With sound on the horizon Puffy moved back to Germany and hit the ground running in all kinds of feature films, the most famous being 1930's *The Blue Angel*. With the rise of Hitler, Puffy's life and career took a bad turn. Because he was Jewish he had to leave Germany in 1933. Returning to Hungary he was very busy in their film industry until the Nazis took over there as well. In 1940 he accepted an offer from MGM and tried to get back to the United States through Russia and Japan. From there it's not definite what became of him. It's reported in some places that he and his wife were arrested in Vladivostok, and imprisoned in the Spassky Prison Camp where he died of diphtheria sometime in 1941-1943. Other sources maintain that he died in Japan in 1942.

The bargain-basement ersatz Arbuckle was Gene "Fatty" Laymon, who was determined to fill Roscoe's plus-sized trousers in the lower levels of independent filmmaking, and was

Charles Puffy (front left) chows down on location with director Harry Sweet (fedora and striped tie), Bud Jamison (in blackface), and the rest of the crew. Courtesy Robert Farr.

proof that looking something like Arbuckle was not enough to have a career. Information is scarce on Laymon's early life, but he surfaced in films around 1920, appearing in the J. Stewart Blackton drama *The Forbidden Valley*. He seems to have been set on the road of Arbuckle mimicry when he was hired to pose as Roscoe for an exploitation campaign for the comedian's *The Traveling Salesman* (1921) that was detailed in the September 17, 1921 *Exhibitors Trade Review*. Edward D. Turner of the Greenwich Theatre in Connecticut had the idea to have a car drive around town and give the populace the impression that the real Arbuckle was there:

> *Step two was to proceed to New York and try to find "the needle in the haystack" in the shape of a man who would be similar enough to Arbuckle in appearance. In this matter he was very fortunate in finding the one man who is perhaps a counterpart of Arbuckle at leisure, Gene Laymon, who last appeared before the public in the comedy role of Forbidden Valley, Stewart Blackton's last release in this country, in which he worked with May McAvoy and Bruce Gordon. Turner managed to interest Laymon in the project from an advertising standpoint, so that it was not a case of dollars and cents, and therefore the cost was nominal. Laymon agreed to spend four days in Greenwich.*

What Laymon did was ride around town in the backseat of a banner-draped limo, and prompt the question in the town folk's minds of "Is that Arbuckle?" After detailing the success of the campaign the article added:

> *We'd not be at all surprised to see in the near future a series of comedies starring Hippo Gene Laymon, as Mr. Turner believes he has discovered a new laugh mine and a comedian of note who has somehow fallen by the wayside and been overlooked.*

Returning to New York, Laymon eventually turned up supporting Dedic Velde, another bottom rung comic, in his series of New York-made *Lightning Comedies* such as the surviving *Never on Time* (1923). At the end of 1925 the large comic incorporated the Laymon Co., Inc. and began making comedies at the Estree Studio on 125th Street in Manhattan to be distributed through the Tennek Film Corp. These two-reelers, billed as *Two Star Comedies*, paired the large and round Laymon with the short and skinny Charles Dorety. Earlier in some shorts for *Century Comedies*, Dorety had often imitated Buster Keaton, so the pair seemed to be going for the late teens Arbuckle/Keaton prototype, but existing examples such as *The Inventors* (1926) show a lack of basic ingredients—material, pacing, supporting players, and filmmaking know-how.

Are Golfers Cuckoo? (1926) is the most accessible of their films and really has absolutely nothing going for it. The story is vaguely that "Fatty and Cholly" are a couple of bums who try to get jobs as caddies at an exclusive country club, but it goes on and on without any laughs. Dorety has a couple of moments that are almost humorous, but Laymon has no personality and isn't funny. Roscoe was handsome and boyishly cherubic,

Gene Laymon fills up a full page ad for his Tennek Film Company Comedies with Charles Dorety.

but Laymon has an odd resemblance to British character actor Peter Bull, and often looks slack-jawed and disagreeable.

Other titles include *Hard to Hold, Radio Mad, Caught in the Act, Fatty's First Fancy*, and *Baby's Irish Nose* (all 1926), and by the latter part of the series Charles Dorety seems to have disappeared and it's Laymon solo, billing himself as "The King of the Fat Men." At some point the Tennek Film Corporation became Sava Films, Inc. with Laymon as president. Besides his pictures, Sava had a whole slate of six other series which headlined Sid Smith, Hank Mann, Eddie Gordon, and Eileen Sedgwick with Lightning the detective dog. Sava disappeared by the beginning of 1927, around the same time that Laymon embarked on the most upscale project of his career.

Keeping Up with the Joneses was a popular comic strip created by Pop Momand. Running in the New York Telegram and hundreds of other newspapers, it was optioned by the Stern Brothers to be added to their other big screen comic adaptations like *Buster Brown, The Newlyweds and their Baby*, and *Let George Do It*. Chronicling the McGinis family, with all their foibles and vanities, Laymon played Belladonna the clan's black cook. Like Roscoe in *That Minstrel Man* (1914), Laymon played the role in blackface and drag, shuffling around in a nappy wig and big muumuu dresses. Two years' worth of shorts were made which included *Keeping in Trim, Showing Off* (both 1927), *Indoor Golf*, and *McGinis vs Jones* (both 1928). The Stern Brothers released their shorts through Universal so this was the only mainstream Hollywood outfit that Laymon worked for.

When the series ended in 1928 it was back to the hinterlands for Laymon. He set up the independent H.I.L. Productions and announced the making of six features to star William Collier Jr. When these didn't happen, Charles Dorety reteamed with Laymon and together they became an itinerant production company who went to various small communities and made shorts that starred Laymon with local residents. Dorety would direct and edit the footage, which would have a "premiere" in the town at the end of the week. This enterprise seems to have ended once sound was added to the mix, or they were shut down by authorities, as this item from the October 18, 1930 *Motion Picture News* suggests:

"Rubber Check" Warning Is Sounded by Metzger

Ohio exhibitors have been warned against Gene Layman or Jean Laymon, alleged bogus check passer, in a message relayed by the state organization from Charles Metzger, secretary of the Associated Theatre Owners of Indiana. A warrant for his arrest has been issued at Brazil, Ind., says Metzger. A number of rubber checks were passed on Indiana exhibitors, it is stated. Layman formerly had a ballyhoo featuring a lion for theatres and more recently has sold films.

In this respect, and in spending most of his career on the fringes, Laymon has much in common with the previously mentioned Josh Binney, but Binney managed to make some decent films while Laymon's extent examples suggest the opposite. He either managed to beat or outrun this rap, as by 1933 he's back in the trades promoting a series of musical two-reelers starring himself and his old bottom-feeder associate Dedic Velde, with backup from "Gene's Gorgeous Girls," not to mention various action features. Of them all, two of the melodramas, *Twisted Rails* (1934) and *The Broken Coin* (1936), did come out. In 1937 he supported a young Billy Barty in a vaudeville tour. The November 11, 1937 *Variety* liked Billy, but had this to say about Laymon's contribution: "Fat" Laymon, 300-pound ex-film comic, as deucer, fails with his gags."

"King of the Fat Men" exhibitor ad for Gene Laymon's series of two-reelers for Sava/Tenneck Films.

Laymon steadfastly continued to plug around the edges of the film industry until his death at age fifty-six in 1946. One of the last trade mentions of him, still in the saddle, is this from the July 3, 1943 *Motion Picture Herald*:

A new film company, known as Majestic Pictures, Inc., has been formed in Sacramento with Gene Laymon as president, Charles Dorety and Charles Pratt, vice-presidents and John Rhyme, treasurer. The Talisman Studios will be used. The first picture, now in script form, is "I'm Shakespeare, Jr."

In addition to these adult "pretenders to the crown" were a few rotund children who were busy in comedy films. The most famous of these kids was Joe Cobb, who was a charming

Joe Cob (center) with Mary Ann Jackson, Jean Darling (both left), Harry Spear, and "Wheezer" Hutchins (both right) in the early Our Gang talkie *Lazy Days* (1929). Courtesy Robert Arkus.

miniature Arbuckle as the original fat boy in Hal Roach's popular *Our Gang* comedies. Born in Oklahoma in 1916, Joe told Leonard Maltin and Richard W. Bann for their 1977 *Our Gang: The Life and Times of the Little Rascals* (Crown Publishers) how he got started in pictures:

> *My dad and I were vacationing in Los Angeles. He thought we'd make the rounds of the studios, and of course we eventually stopped at Hal Roach's. We drove into the parking lot just as the noon whistle blew, and so the casting people took us right to lunch with them. That afternoon they put me through wardrobe upstairs, and I started immediately working on a picture called "A Tough Winter" with Snub Pollard, Marie Mosquini, and Jimmie Finlayson, who played the landlord—naturally evicting everybody. I played Marie's little brother.*

A Tough Winter (1923) was being directed by Charles Parrott (a.k.a. Charley Chase) who was also director-general of the studio, and when this short was finished he installed Joe as a regular in *Our Gang*. Starting with *The Big Show* (1923), the seventh Gang outing,

Cobb could be the prototype for Poppin' Fresh the Pillsbury Doughboy with his round white face and shy smile. He seemed to be all made out of circles and was as big around as tall in shorts such as *The Buccaneers* (1923), *The Sundown Limited* (1924), *Uncle Tom's Uncle* (1926), *Ten Years Old*, and *Baby Brother* (both 1927). Being one of the longest-lasting Gang members, Joe was generally good natured and it took a lot to rile him, but when it happened he was a wild man ready to lick the world.

After making the transition to sound with the series his advancing age (pushing thirteen) made it time for him to retire. His last regular short was *Bouncing Babies* (1929) and he went on to some vaudeville appearances with fellow *Our Gang* alum Scooter Lowry. Joe also turned up in later shorts like *Fish Hooky* (1933) and *Pay as You Exit* (1936) from time to time, and also worked as master of ceremonies for *Our Gang* publicity tours. He did small bits in feature films before quitting acting and joining the aviation industry. Pretty much remaining the same height he had been while in the Gang, Joe passed away in 2002.

Joe's popularity in *Our Gang* made it a prerequisite that all the other kids' series had to have their own fat boy. Three others that filled the bill and moved around between series and studios were Albert Schaefer, Bobby Newman, and Tommy Hicks. Schaefer and Newman were very interchangeable—they looked very similar and both turned up in features and the Stern Brothers' *Buster Brown* shorts. They also did duty in series like Jack White's *Juvenile Comedies*, *The McDougal Alley Kids*, and the *Winnie Winkle* shorts, and ended their careers in the early 1930s. Albert Schaefer did have more of a connection with Arbuckle as he played one of the children under Roscoe's direction in *The Red Mill* (1927).

Albert Witzel portrait of Tommy Hicks. Courtesy Sam Gill.

Tommy Hicks on the other hand had a definite personality—a funny, happy-go-lucky fat boy, always smiling and always with a mischievous twinkle in his eyes. Born in Fort Worth, Texas in 1916, Tommy made his film debut at age seven in 1923. He quickly became a regular in producer Jack White's *Juvenile Comedies*, starting out as part of the ensemble with kids like Ernest Butterworth, Peggy Cartwright, and Johnny Fox, eventually becoming the second lead with Jack McHugh in shorts like *Oh, Teacher*, *Dirty Hands* (both 1924), and *Wildcat Willie* (1925). Tommy's characters were almost always out for a good time, and ready with tricks and pranks to liven up any proceedings. He was also busy in other kids' series such as the live-action segments of Walt Disney's early *Alice in Cartoonland* shorts, and at Century Comedies. Making the rounds he also supported adult comics like Harold Lloyd, Lloyd Hamilton, and Cliff Bowes, and can be spotted in the features *Merry-Go-Round* (1923), *Life's Greatest Game* (1924), *Lightnin'* (1925), and *Speedy* (1928).

Tommy's mother Mamie Hicks, a large lady, was a bit player, and occasionally mother and son turned up together items like *Speed Boys* (1924) and *Smith's Modiste Shop* (1927). Not as prominently used as he got older, Hicks was still busy after the transition to sound in bit roles in *Side Show* (1931), *Wild Boys of the Road* (1933), *Modern Times* (1936), *Up the River* (1938), and *Sweater Girl* (1942). As an adult he weighed two hundred and sixty-five pounds and became a stand-in for actor Charles Laughton. Leaving films in the 1940s he passed away in 1984.

A duo of overlooked large fellows of the 1920s are Fred Spencer and Martin Wolfkeil. Thanks to this neglect little is known about either of them. Fred Spencer (Bretherton) was

Nitrate scan of Fred Spencer in the 1928 Fox Comedy *A Lady* Lion. Courtesy the EYE FIlmmuseum.

born in 1901 in Pueblo, Colorado, and is said to have come from the stage although no specific details have surfaced. He began appearing in comedy shorts in 1921 and quickly became a regular. Finding an early berth at Century Comedies, he was frequent support for stars such as Baby Peggy, Harry Sweet, and Buddy Messinger, but also headlined on his own in titles like *Speed Bugs* and *Spring Fever* (both 1923).

Referred to as "the genial fat man of Century comedies," Spencer tipped the scale at over 300 pounds, and looked something like a slapstick comedy version of 1940s actor Laird Cregar. Moving on, he was soon turning up at all the various comedy shorts units—Sennett, Fox, Educational—working with stars such as Lloyd Hamilton, Larry Semon, and Ben Turpin. He even had a small role in Frank Lloyd's 1924 swashbuckling feature *The Sea Hawk*. Spencer remained busy until 1929, but by the early 1930s disappeared from the screen and passed away in Hollywood in 1952.

Compared to Fred Spencer, Martin Wolfkeil was mostly treated like a prop, on hand whenever a fat man was needed for a group scene or a sight-gag. Born in 1900, he worked on the railroads before taking up a large chunk of space at the Hal Roach Studio. Nicknamed "Tonnage" by Will Rogers, he was busy on the lot from 1923 to 1926 in shorts like *Oranges and Lemons* (1923), *Short Kilts* (1924), and *Sure-Mike!* (1925) where he turned up in a sundry of bit roles that included orchard pickers, ranch hands, salesmen, mechanics, and Joe Cobb's father. According to census records he later had various jobs such as an engineer on a steamship. In the late 1930s he worked as a bodyguard for Stan Laurel, and sued the comic for nonpayment of services. Long out of films, "Tonnage" passed away at sixty-two in 1962.

Two overweight Jewish stage performers dipped tentative toes in the cinematic waters during the teens, and then returned to become busy players in the 1920s. George Sidney was a star on stage and became one in films. Born in Hungary in 1876, Sidney came to Manhattan at age five and grew up around Grand Street and the Bowery as Samuel Greenfield. His stage debut came at twelve in "amateur night" shows, and he made his first professional appearance at the Harlem Museum with his friend Lou Heyman. Billing themselves as "Hennessey and Gibbons," they rethought it and changed it to Lou Herbert and George Sidney. From there he was associated for four years with the famous composer Harry Von Tilzer in shows like *His Nibs, the Baron*, and also worked in the company of the comedy team of Ward and Vokes.

> *I've played every town, hamlet, gimlet, and omelette from Maine to California—I've seen America first, last and always—and after floundering around for eight years in medicine shows—side shows—minstrel shows—repertoire companies and burlesque, I became a star—and from 1901 to 1915 I toured the country at the head of my own musical comedy company—in the well-known "Busy Izzy" series.*
> – **1929 Motion Picture News Booking Guide**

Izzy was the stereotypical Jewish merchant who tries his hand at running a department store and a hotel with disastrous results. The *Izzy* shows (*Busy Izzy*, *Busy Izzy's Boodle*, and *Busy Izzy's Vacation*) toured around the country for fourteen years, and made the

Exhibitor ad with George Sidney for his 1915 film debut *Bizzy Izzy*.

five-foot-three, one hundred and ninety-pound Sidney a name. It also led to his first foray into films with a series to be produced by the Progressive Motion Pictures Corporation. The July 11, 1914 *Motion Picture News* announced:

> George Sidney, originator and producer of the "Busy Izzy" series, has just completed his first two reel release of that series, and is working on his second.

Despite the announcement, a series never materialized and a single Izzy film, *Bizzy Izzy*, was released on September 24, 1915 by the Gaumont Company as part of their Casino Star Comedy Series. Casino was headlining stage stars such as W.C. Fields, Cissy Fitzgerald, and John Daly Murphy, so Sidney fit right in. The plot of *Bizzy Izzy* has Sidney as a cloak maker who hires a more attractive model to show off his wares. The only problem is the new girl has a jealous husband who causes a lot of trouble for Izzy, so he eventually ends up back with his original scrawny and homely model. While the film is considered long lost, the reviews were very positive:

> *The comedy is of the eccentric sort, and the type of Jew portrayed by Sidney is somewhat different, and more pleasing than the ordinary picture type. Sidney's comedy is easy and refined, and the production which is in two reels will be amusing to most audiences.*
> – **Moving Picture World**, October 2, 1915

After this brief foray into pictures Sidney returned to the stage, and had one of his most popular appearances on Broadway with the play *Welcome Stranger* (1920-1921), and also turned up in *Oh Look!* (1918), *Why Worry?* (1918), and *Give and Take* (1923).

In 1923 Samuel Goldwyn transferred the popular play *Potash and Perlmutter* (1923) to the screen with its original stars Barney Bernard and Alexander Carr. This film about

George Sidney (left) and Charlie Murray (right) make noise in their silent comedy *The Life of Riley* (1927).

the trials and tribulations of two Jewish knights of the garment industry was a big hit and sequels were in the works. Barney Bernard died suddenly at age forty-six and a replacement was needed, so George Sidney was tapped to take over. *In Hollywood with Potash and Perlmutter* (1924) and *Partners Again* (1926) brought Sidney to the attention of movie audiences, but his stardom was assured with the release of *The Cohens and Kellys* in 1926. The film was a thinly-veiled rip-off of Anne Nichol's hit play *Abie's Irish Rose*, where Sidney was teamed with former Mack Sennett comic Charlie Murray as the battling heads of Irish and Jewish families whose oldest son and daughter fall in love and marry. Becoming famous together, Sidney and Murray were teamed in other features like *Sweet Daddies* (1926), *Lost at the Front*, *The Life of Riley* (both 1927), and *Flying Romeos* (1928). Sidney was also on hand for more silent *Cohen and Kelly* films (but without Murray) such as *The Cohens and Kellys in Paris* (1928) and *The Cohens and Kellys in Atlantic City* (1929).

At this point Sidney was a Hollywood star and also headlined in his own vehicles like *The Prince of Pilsen* (in the role made famous by Jess Dandy), *Millionaires* (both 1926), *The Auctioneer*, *Clancy's Kosher Wedding* (both 1927), and *We Americans* (1928). The arrival of sound made it possible to add a dialect to his "Jewish" mannerisms, and his first talking film was the one-reel short *Cohen on the Telephone* (1929) which details the difficulties a Jewish immigrant has trying to make a call. Charlie Murray rejoined Sidney for more *Cohen and Kelly* features like *The Cohens and Kellys in Scotland*, *The Cohen and Kelly's in Africa* (both 1930), and *The Cohens and Kellys in Hollywood* (1932). The last was *The Cohens and Kellys in Trouble* (1933), but he and Murray continued their feuding in a few Columbia Pictures shorts that included *Ten Baby Fingers* and *Radio Dough* (both 1934). Sidney was also busy in good character roles in features such *The Heart of New York* (1932), *Manhattan Melodrama* (1934), and *Diamond Jim* (1935). His last film appearance was in *Good Old Soak* (1937), and he did one last Broadway play, *Window Shopping* (1938-1939) before retiring. He passed away in Los Angeles in 1945.

Whereas Sidney was a popular star with roles in feature films built around his talents and fame, Jules Mendel was a West Coast vaudeville comic, who was busy in the teens but never became a "name." His schtick was German dialect comedy with a character named Heinz. Often he would be teamed with Al Frank who did an Irish bit, and they would be "Heinz and Brady" in vaudeville sketches such as *A Little of This, A Little of That, and Something Else*, *The Pawnbroker*, and *The Stolen Diamonds*, where they would have support from pretty choruses such as the Roly Poly Girls or future film comic Gale Henry. Movies, always on the lookout for new comic talent, came knocking, and the August 26, 1916 *Motion Picture News* announced:

> *The first comedy featuring Jules Mendel and Al Frank, well-known Pacific Coast comedians, has been made at the Universal under the title of "Down by the Sea." Many of the scenes are laid about the beach, and particularly in the dressing rooms of the bath house. The featured comedians appear as the baron and the count, who are in search of the "pappars." All the fast moving apparatus of the local beaches was used in the chase that ends this single reeler. The story was written by R.A. Dillon and directed by Mel Forrester.*

Appendix Two: "The Screen Must Have a Fat Comedian" • 659

Jules Mendel has second thoughts about putting Charley Chase out of his misery in *The Rat's Knuckles* (1924). Courtesy Robert Arkus.

Although mentioned in the various trades that more one-reel subjects were promised, *Down by the Sea* doesn't appear to have been released, and Mendel returned to the stage. In 1923 films came calling again, and this time Mendel settled in at the Hal Roach Studio. For the next four years he would be ubiquitous as a tough Jewish egg, always with a dead-eyed deadpan, and topped off with a derby and cigar. Turning up as used car salesmen, construction workers, or greasy diner proprietors, Mendel excelled at giving the fish-eye, and putting comic heroes like Charley Chase and Glenn Tryon in their place in outings like *Outdoor Pajamas* (1924), *The Rat's Knuckles*, *Whose Baby are You?*, *Looking for Sally* (all 1925), *Wandering Papas*, and *Don Key (Son of Burro)* (both 1926). After this spate of activity his portly figure disappeared from movies, and he died in Los Angeles in 1938.

Finally the piece de resistance of the larger-than-life comics was the three-way of high-caloried comedians featured in the Joe Rock-produced *A Ton of Fun* two-reelers. Rock had been a comedian, and started out as a producer with his own shorts. In 1924 he began branching out with comedies starring Jimmy Aubrey and Stan Laurel, and in 1925 teamed up Frank "Fatty" Alexander, Hilliard "Fatty" Karr, and Bill "Kewpie" Ross as the "ton" in this series for his Standard Cinema Corporation. A main component of silent comedy was physical grotesquery, and this series ran with the idea and never looked back—operating on the basic concept that if one fat guy was funny then three would be

The "ton of fun" of "Kewpie" Ross, Frank Alexander (middle), and Hilliard "Fatty" Karr (right) in *Three Fleshy Devils* (1927). Courtesy Cole Johnson.

a riot. Alexander and Karr have already been profiled here, and there's little known about third–wheel "Kewpie" Ross. Outside of his work as part of this trio his only other known appearance is a bit in the 1930 Sid Saylor short *Sid's Long Count*.

The usual format for the shorts consisted of putting the Fatties in situations and locations where fat men should fear to tread, and then milking all the weight-related gags possible. For example, their pacing on the deck of the boat in *The Vulgar Yachtsmen* (1926) causes the boat to careen and throw the occupants below from side to side. In trying to be football heroes in *Three Missing Links* (1927) they inadvertently tackle their coach during practice, and he emerges from the bottom of their cellulite pyramid with his head, hands, and feet poking out from an undisturbed lawn (like he was teleported there by their immense weight). The focus of their material is also reflected in titles like *Wanderers of the Waistline* and *Tanks of the Wabash* (both 1927). The premise of three extremely large buddies or siblings (the "Barrel Brothers") who hang out together reached a level of absurdity and almost surrealism in prime examples such as *All Tied Up* (1925), *Wedding Daze*, *Galloping Ghosts* (both 1926), *Three Missing Links*, and *Campus Romeos* (both 1927).

Thirty-six shorts were made from 1925 to 1928, and the leading lady in almost all of their misadventures was Lois Boyd. A former Mack Sennett beauty and busy ingénue for Roach, Fox and Monty Banks comedies, Boyd was petite and very game in taking numerous falls and much physical knockabout in support of her three fat funsters. Other support came from veteran players such as Gale Henry (who looked like an exclamation point in contrast to the Fatties' balloon shapes), Billy Engle, Joe Bonner, Jack Miller, Ella McKenzie, Dorothea Wolbert, and Budd Ross. The bulk of the series was directed by Gilbert Pratt and Albert Herman, but Harry Sweet, Slim Summerville, Marcel Perez, Scott Pembroke, and Earl Montgomery also contributed memorable entries. After four years of fun, the Fatties' hi-jinks came to an end at the close of the silent era, but they turned out to have a long lease on life, popping up to entertain kids thanks to 1950s and 1960s television shows such as *Howdy Doody, Comedy Capers,* and *Who's the Funny Mann.*

The switch to sound changed the nature of film comedy. No longer purely visual, movie comics didn't have to define themselves by just their physicalities. For many years the sole fat star comedian in sound film remained Oliver Hardy in his misadventures with Stan Laurel, with other large comics filling in as character players. Most of these full-figured supporting actors, such as Eugene Palette, Andy Devine, and Billy Gilbert, had funny voices to go along with their full forms. Over the years there have been occasional plus-sized comedians, such as John Candy and Chris Farley, who have made a name in films, but the real heyday for corpulent comics was in the silent era.

Bibliography

Periodicals – Trade Publications

Edison Kinetogram, 1911 – 1916

Educational Film Exchange Press Sheets, 1923 – 1932

Essanay News, 1915 – 1917

Exhibitors Trade Review, 1922 – 1927

Film Daily, 1919 – 1933

Kalem Kalender, 1914 – 1915

Motion Picture News, 1913 – 1933

Motion Picture News Blue Book, 1929 – 1930

Motion Picture News Booking Guide, 1922 – 1927

Motography, 1913 – 1917

Moving Picture World, 1910 – 1927

Paramount Pictures Press Books, 1918 – 1923

Photoplay, 1918 – 1933

The Photoplayers Weekly, 1914 – 1917

Picture-Play, 1917 – 1920

Reel Life, 1914 – 1916

San Francisco Dramatic Review, 1910 – 1913

Screenworld, 1930 – 1933

Selig Monthly Herald, 1915

The Triangle, 1916 – 1917

Roscoe is a busy blacksmith in 1917's *A Country Hero*. Courtesy Marc Wanamaker/Bison Archives.

Universal Weekly, 1913 – 1930

Variety, 1910 – 1933

Vitagraph Life Portrayals, 1910 – 1916

Periodicals –Articles

Berglund, Bo. *Does Buster Keaton Appear in A Reckless Romeo (1917)?*. Griffithiana# 65, August 1999.

———. *The Cook, the Lost Arbuckle-Keaton Comedy Found at Last*. Griffithiana #65, August 1999.

———. *Additions to the Arbuckle Filmography*. Griffithiana #65, August 1999.

Brown, Karl. *On James Cruze*. Films in Review Vol. 37, No. 4, April 1986.

Caslavsky, Karel. *American Comedy Series: Filmographies 1914-1930*. Griffithiana # 51/52, October 1994.

Jenkins, Henry. *Hey, Pop! Credits and Synopses of the Six Fatty Arbuckle Vitaphones.* Griffithiana #48/49, October 1993.

Oderman, Stuart. *The Abduction of Minta Arbuckle.* Films in Review Vol. 36, No. 8/9, August-September 1985.

Palmer, Constance. *"I'm Broke" says Fatty Arbuckle.* Movie Weekly, July 29th, 1922.

Starman, Ray. *James Cruze—Cinema's Forgotten Director.* Films in Review Vol. 36, No. 10, October 1985.

Books

Blesh, Rudi. *Keaton.* New York: Macmillan, 1966.

Blum, Daniel. *A Pictorial History of the Silent Screen.* New York: G.P. Putnam's Sons, 1953.

Brownlow, Kevin. *The Parade's Gone By.....*New York, Knopf, 1969.

Bruskin, David N. *The White Brothers: Jack, Jules and Sam White.* Hollywood: Scarecrow Press, 1990.

Cantor, Eddie. *My Life is in Your Hands.* New York, London: Harper & Brothers, 1928.

Dardis, Tom. *Keaton: The Man Who Wouldn't Lie Down.* New York: Scribner's, 1979.

Davies, Marion. *The Times We Had.* Indianapolis/New York: Bobbs-Merrill Co., 1975.

Edmonds, Andy. *Frame-Up!: The Untold Story of Roscoe "Fatty" Arbuckle.* New York: W. Morrow, 1991.

Foote, Lisle. *Buster Keaton's Crew.* North Carolina: McFarland & Co., 2014.

Fowler, Gene. *Father Goose.* New York: Covici-Friede Publishers, 1934.

Fussell, Betty Harper. *Mabel: Hollywood's First I Don't Care Girl.* New York: Ticknor & Fields, 1982.

Goodwins, Fred. *Charlie Chaplin's Red Letter Days: At Work with the Comic Genius.* Maryland: Rowman & Littlefield, 2017.

Henabery, Joseph. *Before, In, and After Hollywood: The Autobiography of Joseph E. Henabery.* Lanham, Maryland: Scarecrow Press, 1997.

Jura, Jean-Jacques and Bardin II, Rodney Norman. *Balboa Films.* Jefferson, North Carolina and London : McFarland and Co., 1999.

Keaton, Buster, with Samuels, Charles. *My Wonderful World of Slapstick.* New York: Doubleday, 1960.

Kerr, Walter. *The Silent Clowns.* New York: Alfred A. Knopf, 1975.

Lahue, Kalton C. *World of Laughter: The Motion Picture Comedy Short.* Norman, Oklahoma: University of Oklahoma Press, 1966.

——, and Brewer, Terry. *Kops and Custards: The Legend of Keystone Films.* Norman, Oklahoma: University of Oklahoma Press, 1967.

——. *Mack Sennett's Keystone.* South Brunswick: A.S. Barnes, 1970.

——., and Gill, Sam. *Clown Princes and Court Jesters.* South Brunswick: A.S. Barnes, 1970.

Lane, Lupino. *How to Become a Comedian.* London: Frederick Muller LTD, 1945.

Lasky, Jesse L., with Weldon, Don. *I Blow My Own Horn.* London: Gollancz, 1957.

Lloyd, Harold. *An American Comedy.* New York: Longman's, Greene and Co., 1928.

Louvish, Simon. *Keystone: The Life and Clowns of Mack Sennett.* London: Faber and Faber, 2003.

Maltin, Leonard. *The Great Movie Comedians.* New York: Harmony Books, 1978.

Massa, Steve. *Lame Brains and Lunatics: The Good, The Bad, and The Forgotten of Silent Comedy.* Georgia: BearManor Media, 2013.

——. *Slapstick Divas: The Women of Silent Comedy.* Georgia: BearManor Media, 2017.

Mast, Gerald. *The Comic Mind.* Indianapolis, Indiana: Bobbs-Merrill, 1973.

Merritt, Greg. *Room {1219}: The Life of Fatty Arbuckle, the Mysterious Death of Virginia Rappe, and the Scandal that Changed Hollywood.* Chicago: Chicago Review Press, 2013.

Mitchell, Glenn. *A-Z of Silent Film Comedy.* London: Batsford, 1998.

Montgomery, John. *Comedy Films.* London: George Allen and Unwin, 1954.

Oderman, Stuart. *Roscoe "Fatty" Arbuckle: a Biography of the Silent Film Comedian, 1887-1933.* Jefferson, North Carolina and London: McFarland and Co., 1994.

Reeder, Thomas. *Mr. Suicide: Henry "Pathé" Lehrman and the Birth of Silent Comedy.* Albany, Georgia: BearManor Media, 2017

Robinson, David. *The Great Funnies.* London: Studio Vista/Dutton, 1969.

——. *Chaplin: His Life and Art.* New York: McGraw-Hill, 1985.

Sennett, Mack, and Shipp, Cameron. *King of Comedy.* New York: Doubleday and Co., 1954.

Slide, Anthony. *Early American Cinema.* New York: Zwemmer/A.S. Barnes, 1970.

Turconi, David. *Mack Sennett, il "re delle Comiche."* Roma: Edizioni dell 'Ateneo, 1961.

Walker, Brent E. *Mack Sennett's Fun Factory*. Jefferson, North Carolina: McFarland & Co., 2010.

Watson Jr., Coy. *The Keystone Kid: Tales of Early Hollywood*. Santa Monica: Santa Monica Press, 2001.

Watz, Edward. *Wheeler & Woolsey: The Vaudeville Comic Duo and their Films, 1929-1937*. Jefferson, North Carolina: McFarland & Co., 1994.

Yallop, David A. *The Day the Laughter Stopped: The True Story of Fatty Arbuckle*. New York: St. Martin's Press, 1976.

Young, Robert. *Roscoe "Fatty" Arbuckle: a bio-bibliography*. Westport Conn: Greenwood Press, 1994.

Other Sources

Robinson Locke Collection of Theatrical Clippings 1870-1920. New York Public Library for the Performing Arts.

Media History Digital Library.

About the Author

STEVE MASSA is the author of *Slapstick Divas: The Women of Silent Comedy*, *Lame Brains and Lunatics: The Good, The Bad, and The Forgotten of Silent Comedy* and *Marcel Perez: The International Mirth-Maker*. He has organized and curated comedy film programs for the Museum of Modern Art, Library of Congress, the Museum of the Moving Image, the Smithsonian Institution, the Pordenone Silent Film Festival, and Bristol's Slapstick Festival. In addition to consulting with EYE Filmmuseum, Netherlands, the Cineteca di Bologna, the Royal Belgian Cinematheque, and other archives, plus contributing notes to the National Film Registry, the National Film Preservation Foundation, and the Criterion Collection, he is a founding member of Silent Cinema Presentations which produces NYC's Silent Clown Film Series. Steve has also provided essays and commentary tracks to many comedy DVD and Blu-Ray collections such as *The Forgotten Films of Roscoe "Fatty" Arbuckle*, *Harry Langdon: Lost and Found*, *Becoming Charley Chase*, Kino Video's *Buster Keaton: The Short Film Collection*, and *The Mack Sennett Collection*, Vol 1, as well as co-curated Undercrank Productions' *The Mishaps of Musty Suffer*, Volumes 1 & 2, the award-winning *Marcel Perez Collection*, Volumes 1 & 2, and *The Alice Howell Collection*.

Index

Numbers in **bold** indicate photographs

Acker, Jean 346, 348, 356, 361
Adams, "Bumps" 619-621
Adamson, Ewart 517, 559, 561-562
Alarm, The 130-132, **131**
Alas! Poor Yorick 26, **27**
Albert, Dan 133, 148, 150, 176, 198, 208, 301, 303-304
Alexander, Frank "Fatty" **591**, 626-627, **627**, 659, **660**, 660
Allen, E. H. **86**, 511, 518
Allen, Phyllis 79, **79**, **96**, 98, 99, 103, 123, **123**, 135, 137, **137**, 153, 154, 156, 157, 160, **160**, 163, 171, **171**, 176, 181, 182, 189, 205, 223, 227, 229, 233
Almost a Rescue 27-29, 163
Anderson, Dave **45**, 53, 64, 67, **67**, 70, 237, 240, 245, 248, 251, 255, 257, 262
Anger, Lou 271, 291-292, **292**, 399, 401, 414
Anson, Laura 371, **374**, 376
Anybody's Goat 544-545, **544**, 551
Are Golfers Cuckoo? 649
Arly see Arnold, Cecile
Arnold, Cecile 95, 148, 150, 153, 154, 171, 176
Arthur, Johnny 86, 445, 446, **446**, 447-448, **447**, 452-454, **453**, 456-461, **457**, **458**, **459**
Aubrey, Jimmy 172, 279, 340, **591**, 630, 659
Austin, Albert 512, **512**, 513, 364
Avery, Charles 32, **33**, 34, **35**, 41, 43, 45-46, **45**, **46**, 50, 52, 53, 55, **55**, 58, 61, 63, 64, **67**, 68, 70, 73, 76, 79, 84, 87, **88**, 91, 98, 109, 111, 113, 116, 117, **118**, 120, 122, 124, 128, 133, 135, 137, 163, 173, 200

Babe's School Days **630**
Baby Mine 483
Back Page, The 512-514, **512**, 533
Back Stage 156, 307, 328, 330-335, **331**, **332**, 336, 417, 543, 568, 587
Badger, Clarence **329**
Badly Broke 647-648
Baggot, King **334**
Baker, Baby Doris 128, **129**, 129

Baker, Eddie **644**, 645
Bandit, A 41-43, **41**, 528, 587, 588
Bank Clerk, The 324-325, **325**, 328
Banks, Monty 308, 310, **314**, 316, 317-319, 320, 323-324, 329, 338, 340, 352, 364, **365**, 378, 513, 661
Barnyard Flirtations 119-120, 589
Barrell, Donna 458, 460, 461
Bartels, Louis John 517, **518**, 518, **519**, 519, 520, 524, 525, **525**, 526
Bath House Beauty, A 8, **48**, 60, 118, 122-123, **122**, 283, 305, 589
Baumann, Charles 224, 242
Beach Pajamas 524-527, **524**, **525**
Beebe, Marjorie 483, 485-486, **486**, 487, 488
Beery, Wallace 346, 348-349, 388, 435
Bell Boy, The 256, 288, 293-296, **293**, **295**, 390
Ben's Kid 14-17, **15**, 20, 290
Bengtson, John 9, 450
Bennett, Billie 27, 135, 156, 160, 162, **162**, 163, 176, 195, 204, 204, **204**, 218, 220, 611
Bennett, Charles 135, **136**, 136, 137, 138, 160
Berglund, Bo 150
Bergman, Henry 95, 605-607, **606**
Bernard, Barney 657-658
Bernard, Sam 233, 234, 236
Bernoudy, Jane 618, **618**
Besser, Joe 569
Bevan, Billy 428, 526, 609, 628, 646
Bianchi, Mario see Banks, Monty
Bickel, George 613-614, **614**
Bill's Opportunity 163, 611
Bill's Predicament **611**
Binney, Harold J. "Josh" 581, 622-626, **623**, **625**, 639, 651
Birchard, Robert S. 10, 318-319
Bishop, Christopher 274
Bizzy Izzy **656**, 656-657
Blackwell, Jim 367, 369, 370
Bletcher, Billy 545, 546-547
Boggs, Francis 14, 16, **16**, 17, 20
Bombs and Bangs 155-156, **155**
Bonehead, The 288, 328, 331, 416-418, **416**, **417**, 589

Booker, Harry **30**, 233, **235**
Bordeaux, Joe 124, 160, **161**, 171, 176, 183, **186**, 187, 189, 193, 194, 195, 196, 198, 208, 210, 211, 212, 213, 214, 215, 216, 218, **220**, 220, 221, 222, 223, 225, 230, **231**, 233, 237, 239, 240, **241**, 242, **242**, 245, 246-247, 251, 255, **256**, 258, 259, 271, 280, 282, 284, 297
Borden, Olive 541
Bosworth, Hobart 20, 21, 23-24, **23**, 26, 60
Bowen, Harry **542**
Bowery Boys, The 124-125, **124**
Boyd, Lois 661
Bracy, Sidney 375
Bradbury, Kitty 335, **335**, 338
Bradley, Estelle 467-468
Brady, Ed J. 175, 176, **177**, 178, 495, 505, 506
Brand New Hero, A 84, 124, 150-151, 152-153, **152**
Brendel, El 516, **521**, 526, 646
Brennan, John E. 602-603, **604**
Brent, Lynton 529, 530, 538, 539, 544, 545, 546, 548, 554, 556, 557
Breslow, Lou 84, 87
Brewster's Millions 356-361, **356**, **358**, **360**, 368, 370, 381
Bridge Wives 4, 492, 520, 530, 545-548, **546**, **547**, 550, 551, 587
Bright Lights, The 40, 68, 124, 176, 244, 245-248, **246**, **247**, 250, 254, 272, 437
Broad, Kid 245, **246**
Brockwell, Billie 193, 200, 221, **222**
Brooks, Louise 385, 511, 512
Brooks, Sammy **617**
Brooks, Virginia 508, **508**, 512, 513, 515, **515**, 517, 532, 533, 534, 548, **548**, 554, **555**, 557
Brown Eyes **451**, 451, 452
Brown, Karl 350, 356, 358-359, 361, 362, 367, 368-370, 371, 372, 376, 382, 390, 394
Brownlow, Kevin 9, 349, 370, 438, 480
Bruskin, David N. 419
Bryan, Vincent 320, **329**, 399
Bryant, James 133, 173, 187-189, **188**, 195, 198, 200, 233, 237, 239, 240, 242, 245, 248, **252**, 255, 258, 262, 276, 282, 284, 423, 427, 428, 429, 430, **444**, 517
Bulls and Bears **482**, 483-485
Bumping Along **556**
Bunny, George 598-599, **599**
Bunny, John 261, 592, 594, 596-598, **597**, **598**, 599, 601, 603, 613, 614, 616
Burkett, Bartine 436, **437**, 438, **441**, 442, **443**, 461
Burns, Bobby 520, 522, 524, 531, **542**, 546, 629, 639, 642
Burns, Neal 29, 302, 315, 328, 353, 547, 551, 611
Burton, Ethel **626**
Busch, Mae 198, 233, 237
Butcher Boy, The 210, 244, 266, 269-273, **270**, 274, 276, 277, 278, 279, 284, 296, 565, 571, 586, 587, 619
Buzzin' Around 7, 565, 567-569, **567**, **568**, 573, 578

Camping Out 8, 269, 285, 311, 315, 316-320, **316**, **318**, 384, 565
Cantor, Eddie 475-479, **476**, **477**, **478**, 550
Capra, Frank 55-56
Carlos, Abe 483
Carlyle, Helen "Ollie" 195, 204, 205, 211, **212**, 212
Carmen, Jewel see Quick, Evelyn
Carr, Mary 387, **388**, 389, 477
Carruthers, Helen see Page, Peggy
Catlett, Walter 259, **520**, 520-522, **521**, **530**, 531-532, 550
Cavender, Glen 113, 133, 148, 150, **151**, 151, 158, **159**, 175, 176, 181, 193, 195, 196, 198, 199, 200, **201**, 202, 204, 205, **208**, 211, 213, 214, 216, **217**, 217-218, **218**, 223, 225, 227, 229, 233, 237, 308, **308**, 310, 419, 431, 433, **444**, 446, 448, 451, 452, 454, **454**, 456, 458, 460, 461, 464, 475, 478, 492, 495, 517, 518, 548
Ceder, Ralph 525, 527, 528
Chandler, George 508, 512, **512**, 513, **514**, 515, 517, 522, **523**, 533
Chaplin, Charlie 1, 3, 4, 5, 7, 31, 32, 38, 62, 64, 76, 80, 81, 89, 91, 105, 106, 111, 112-113, **112**, 114-117, **115**, 118, 133, 137, 138, 147-151, **148**, **151**, 153-155, **154**, 156, 157, 169, 172, 173, 178, 194, 198, 239, 250, 272, 275, 294, 296, 306, 307, 309, 317, 319-320, 323, 337, 338, 343, 350, 364, 380, 393, 423, 428, 435, 448, 450, 457, 479, 480, 486, 510, 513, 526, 565, 583, 605, **606**, 606, 607, 617, 621, 622, 630, 634, 635
Chaplin, Syd 46, 137, 171, **171**, 172-173, **172**, 178, 243, 587, 627
Character Studies 479-481, **479**, **480**
Chase, Charley (Charles Parrott) 3, 29, 90, 103, **104**, 133, 135, 141, 148, 150, 153, 163, 175, 176, 181, **181**, 182, 205, 208, 210-211, **211**, 303, 332, 372, 374, 460, 480, 504, **509**, 530, 531, **556**, 577, 621, **622**, 631, 652, 659
Chasing Husbands **556**
Chene, Dixie 98, 109, 137, 148, 153, 160, **160**, 176, 178, 181
Chicken Chaser, The 120-121, 589
Christie, Al 27, **28**, 28-29, 58, 91, 147, 195, 315, 328, 353, 355, 401, 475, 486, 539, 547, 556, 626, 629, 644, 645
Citizen Kane 470, 575
Clarke, Betty Ross 356, 361, 367, **367**, 370
Cleaning Up 380, 447, 452-454, **453**
Clifton, Emma 70, 76, 105, **106**, 106, 107, **107**, **108**, 108
Cline, Edward 3, 120, 153, 181, 195, 200, 205, 208, 392
Close Relations 430, 537, 572-576, **573**, **574**, 578, **579**, 583
Clyde, Andy 43, 87, 307, **482**, 483, 484, 485, **486**, 488, 499, 516, 526, 531, 543, 549, 562, 579, 646
Cobb, Irwin S. 350, 351
Cobb, Joe 651-653, **652**, **653**, 655

Cogley, Nick 21, 25, 32, **33**, 34, **35**, 37, 39, 41, **41**, 43, 46, 53, 58, 73-74, **74**, **75**, 79, 87, **88**, 233
Coleman, Dan 567, **568**, 569, 576, 578
Coleman, Frank J. 634-635, **634**
Collier Sr., William 136, 233, **233**, 234, 236, 424, 447
Collins Jr., Monty 332, 467, 492, 515, 516, 526, 542, **542**, **543**, 543, 544, **544**, 545, 549, 551, **551**, 553, 646
Collins Sr., Monty 326, 330, 331-332, 543
Collins, C.B. see Collins, Chick
Collins, Chick 423, 429, 458, 460-461, **460**, 464, 473
Comeback of Percy, The **631**
Coming and Going **645**
Compson, Betty 310, **314**, 315, 394, 397
Conklin, Chester 76, 105, 113, 114, 120, 137, 148, 149-150, **149**, 154, 160, 161, 169, 182, 231-232, 233, 306, 378, 385, 442, 513, 627
Contero, Norma **260**
Convict's Happy Bride, A **634**
Coogan Jr., Jackie 120, 130, 146, 336, 337, **338**, 364, 479, 481, 513, 549
Coogan, Jack 330, 331, 335, **335**, 336-337, **338**
Cook, The 210, 256, 259, 276, 279, 285, 296, 304-308, **305**, **306**, 311, 565, 587
Cooley, Frank 89, 90, 91, 99
Cooper, Earl 78, 79, 589
Country Hero, A 285-289, **286**, **287**, **664**
Crane, Phyllis 500, 502, 503, 508, **508**, 510, 515-516, **515**, **516**, 517, 544, 551, 553
Crashing Hollywood 508-510, **508**, 513, 517, 533, 549
Crazy to Marry 371-376, **371**, **373**, **374**, 378, 381, 391
Cream Puff Romance, A 256, 260, 262, 266-268, **267**, **268**, 320, 324
Crimmins, Dan 338, 340
Crooky **615**
Crosthwaite, Ivy 227, **228**, 229, 230, 233
Cruze, James 315, 345, 351, 359, 361, 362-364, **363**, 366, 369, 371, 372, 375, 376, 378, 382, 384, 387, 394, 396, 397, 398, 483-484, 557
Cuckoos, The 488-490, **489**
Cummings, Irving 89, 346, 349
Cumpson, John R. **592**, 592-596, **593**, **595**
Cure for Pokeritis, A **597**
Curses 68, 298, 299, 393, 430, 432, 435, 436-440, **437**, **439**, 441, 442, 587
D'Avril, Yola **644**
Daly, Marcella **449**
Dana, Viola 341, 394, 414
Dandy, Jess 148, 150, 153, 160, 621-622, **622**, 658
Daniel, Viora 350, 353
Daniels, Frank 614-616, **615**, 633
Darling, Jean **652**
Davenport, Alice 34, **35**, 39, **40**, 53, 58, 64, 70, 73, 98-99, **99**, 105, 109, 113, 128, 138, 144, 171, 173, **174**, 181, 182, **186**, 187, 193, 195, 205, 207, 213, **213**, 214, 216, **217**, 217, 234
Davies, Marion 285, 414, 468-473, **468**, **469**, **470**, 557, 588

Davis, George 405, 406, 409, 410, **411**, **412**, 416, 417, 419, **420**, 420, 422-423, **422**, 424, 426, **427**, 428, 429, 430, **430**, 431, 432, 433, 446, 451, 452, 454, 456, **458**, 458, 460, 461, 462, 463, 464, 538, 539, **542**, 543
De Haven, Carter 43, 211, 479-481, **479**, **480**, 528, 611
Dean, Frances 508, 534, 535, **548**, 548-549, **549**
Deane, Doris **402**, 403, **403**, 409, **410**, 410, 411-412, 413, 414, 419, **420**, 420, **421**, 422, 423, **424**, 424, 426, **426**, 428, 429, **429**, 430, **430**, 433, 450, 451, 466, 503
Del Ruth, Hampton 112, 114, 120, 178, 212, **329**
Dent, Vernon 217, 240, 525-526, **525**, 543, 645-646, **645**
Desert Hero, A 184, 285, 325-330, **326**, **327**, 332, 335, 452
Dewing, Nathan see Karr, Hilliard
Diegel, Leo 485, **486**, 487, 488
Dippy Dan's Doings **609**
Dirty Work in a Beanery **607**
Dodge, Mrs. Mary G. 323
Dolan, Frankie 133, 148, 163, 213
Dollar-A-Year Man, The 359, 361-362, **362**, 378
Donkey Did It, The **637**
Dooley, Billy 29, 328, 539, **540**, 541
Dore, Adrienne **529**
Dorety, Charles **211**, 338, 340, 438, 508, **509**, 510, 536, 539, 541, **541**, 542, 557, 559, 649, 650, 651
Dressler, Marie 74, 133, 136, 323, 347, 487, 537
Dudley, Charles 293, 294-295, **295**, 296, 297, 448
Duffy, Jack 261, 551, **644**, 645
Dunham, Phil 454, 467, 474, **634**
Dunn, Bobby 178, 189, 196, 200, 205, 216, 218, 221, 222, 225, 227, 304, 307
Durfee, Minta 14, **62**, 76, **77**, 79, 83, 84, 89, 91, **92**, 97, 98, 99, 103, 112, 113, 122, **122**, 125, **125**, 128, **132**, 133, 135, 138, 141-142, 145, **146**, 148, 153, 154, 156, 160, **160**, 163, **165**, 165, 167, 173, **174**, 175, **176**, 179, **180**, 181, **181**, 182, 183, 193, **194**, 195, 202, **203**, 204, 205, **208**, **208**, 220, 227, **228**, 230, 233, 242, 245, 248, **251**, 251, **252**, 254, 276, 285, 445, 504
Dwiggens, Jay 601, **602**
Dwyer, Ruth **365**
Dynamite Doggie 8, 210, 299, 414, 425, 430, 431-433, **432**, 435, 442, 533, 569

Earle, Arthur 248, 269, 273, 276, 276
Earle, Edward 258, 262, **280**
Earles, Tiny 475, 477
Easter Bonnets **402**, 403-405, **403**, **404**
Edwards, Neely 183, 343, 356, 361, 378, 611
Edwards, Ted 122, 167, 168, 176, 189, 193, 200, 202, 204, 205, 208, 211, **212**, 223, 225
Edwards, Vivian 148, 150, 176, 178, 181, 193, 200, 205, **620**
Elmo, Peenie 291, **505**, 505-506
Emerson, Babe **637**
Emmett, Fern 538, **538**, 539, 544, **544**, 545, 546, **547**, 548, 550, **550**, 551, 554, 556, 557

Emory, Mae 205, **207**, 207
Erickson, Knute 376, 381
Errol, Leon 14, 102, 528, 531, 532, 537, 555, 575
Ex-Plumber 506-508

Fairbanks, Douglas 34, 223, 234, 242, 244, 309, 310, 311, 315, 351, 366, 372, 450, 456, 457, 466, 479, 481, 528, 601, 636
Farley, Dot 83, **83**, 84, 93-94, **94**, 428, 442, 619, **636**
Farrin, Jeanne 532, 534
Fast Freight 376, 378, 382, 387-390, **388**, **389**, 557
Fatal Taxicab, The 68-70, **69**
Fatty Again 117, 160-162, **160**, **161**, 184, 589
Fatty and Mabel Adrift 7, 32, 41, 60, 144, 210, 224, 237-240, **238**, **239**, 585, 587, 590
Fatty and Mabel at the San Diego Exposition 187, 192-194, **192**, **193**, 201, 283, 305, 590
Fatty and Mabel's Simple Life v, 144, 189-192, **190**, **191**, 442, 467, 590
Fatty and Minnie He-Haw 183-185, **184**, **185**
Fatty and the Broadway Stars 229, 233-236, **233**, **235**, 331
Fatty and the Heiress 135-136, **135**, **136**, 137, 550
Fatty at Coney Island **188**, 282-285, **283**, **284**, 587
Fatty at San Diego 64, 79-80, **79**, 137, 262, 423
Fatty Joins the Force 64, 84-87, **85**, 152, 445, 588
Fatty's Chance Acquaintance 163, 182, 204-205, **204**, **205**, 590
Fatty's Day Off 63-64, **63**, 305
Fatty's Debut 158-160, **158**, **159**, 206, 331, 589
Fatty's Faithful Fido 60, 109, 178, 200, 208-211, **208**, 224, 590
Fatty's Finish 137-138, **137**, 182
Fatty's Flirtation 64, 81, 89-91, **90**, 101
Fatty's Gift 145-147, **146**
Fatty's Jonah Day 90, 168-171, **169**, **170**, 589
Fatty's Magic Pants 7, 178, 181-183, **181**, 478, 587, 590, 621
Fatty's New Role 116, 152, 196-198, **196**, **197**, 200, 210, 587, 621
Fatty's Plucky Pup 73, 137, 210, 223-224, **223**, 275, 311, 587, 590
Fatty's Reckless Fling 202-204, **202**, **203**, 587, 590
Fatty's Tintype Tangle 31, 49, 73, 159, 162, 169, 200, 225-227, **225**, **226**, 228, 239, 412, 587
Fatty's Wine Party 101, 171-173, **171**, 589
Fay, Hugh 221, 222, 324
Faye, Julia 350, 353-354, **354**, 394
Fazenda, Louise 95, 130, 178, 200, 225, **225**, 227, 378, 468, 471, 473, 632
Fickle Fatty's Fall 101, 227-230, **228**, **229**, 274, 474
Fields, Lew 138, 233, 234, 236, 473, 537, 578, 596, 601, 633 (see also Weber & Fields)
Fighting Dude, The 432, 454-456, **454**, **455**, 462
Film Johnnie, A 112-113, **112**, 149, 589
Finch, Flora 261, 596-597, 599, 601, **602**
Finlayson, James 394, 525, **525**, 526, 652
Fishback, Fred **86**, 138, **139**, 205
Fitzgerald, Cissy **614**, 656

Fitzgerald, Slim **617**
Flirt's Mistake, A 91, 99-101, **100**
Flynn, Rita 500, **501**, 502, 503, 508, **508**, 510, 515, **515**, 517, 532, 534, 548, **548**, 550, 554, **555**, 557
Fool's Luck 453, 455, 461-463, **462**, **463**, 471, 587
For the Love of Mabel 45-46, **45**, 589
Forman, Tom 345, 346, 348
Foster, Helen 446, **446**, 452, 453
Francis, Christine 413, 414, **415**, 420, 423, 424-425, 426, 428, 430, 431, **432**, 432
Franey, Billy 102, 433, 435, 442, 632
Frazee, Edwin 133, 171, 220, 298
Fred's Fictitious Foundling 624, **638**
Front! (*Handy Andy*) 328, 393-394, 405-407, **405**, **406**, 409, 564
Frozen North, The 391, 392-394, **392**, 437
Funkhouser, Metellus Lucullus Cicero 104-105, 152

Gallagher, Toy 473, 474
Game of Poker, A **72**
Gangsters, The 8, 29, 31, 32-34, **33**, 43, 60, 84, 100, 126, 152, 586, 605
Garage, The 73, 182, 210, 269, 291, 333, 338-341, **339**, **341**, 467, 510
Garvin, Anita 467-468
Gasoline Gus 363, 376-382, **377**, **379**, **381**, 387, 391
Gerdes, Emily 387, **388**, 389-390
Gierucki, Paul E. 8, 10, 321, 438, 587, 588
Gigolettes 43, 364, 385, 389, 557-559, **558**
Gilbert, Billy 64, 68, 73, 76, 78, 79, 84, 94, 103, **104**, 105, 112, 114, 116, 138, 140, **140**, 144, 148, 150, **151**, 151, 152, 153, 156, 157, 163, 164, 171, 176, 183, 189, 200, 205, 213, 214-215, **214**, 218, 227, 579, 661
Gill, David 438, 480
Gill, Sam 9, 42, 43, 98, 218
Gillespie, Bert 626, **626**
Gleason, James 500, 502-503, 555, 559
Glimpse of the San Diego Exposition, A 194, 201
Go West 329, 333, 450-452, **451**, 480, 528
Good Night, Nurse! 159, 301-304, **301**, **302**, **303**
Goodwins, Fred 116
Gore, Rosa 340, **644**
Goulding, Alf 215, 484, 561, 564, 565, 567, 570, 577
Grab Bag Bride, The **59**, 239, 256, 260, 333
Grable, Betty see Frances Dean
Granger, Dorothy 517, 520, **520**, 522, 531-532, **532**, 543
Gray, Betty 248, **249**, 250
Gribbon, Harry 193, 194, **194**, 195-196, **195**, 207, 233, 559, 578, 579, 581
Griffith, D.W. 38, 44, 46, 62, 81, 97, 98, 116, 199, 222, 228, 234, 282, 324, 351, 354, 369, 370, 388, 428, 499, 553, 592, 642
Griffith, Gordon 58, 60, 91, **92**, 92, 122, **122**, 129, 135, 203
Griffith, Julia 545, 546, 547-548
Griffith, Katherine 202, **203**, 203, 609

Griffith, Raymond 3, 370, 602, **608**, 609
Gypsy Queen, The 67-68, **67**

Hagen, Walter 485, **486**, 487, 488
Haine, Horace J. 248, 250, 251, 253, **253**, 255, **256**, 258
Half Shot at Sunrise 490-492, **491**
Hamilton, Lloyd 86, **86**, 146, **147**, 211, 218, 229, 364, 380, 394, 401, 424, 428, 431, 445, 448-450, **449**, **450**, 452, 457, 458, 466, 467-468, **467**, 473-475, **473**, 492, 495-500, **496**, **498**, 503-504, **504**, 506-508, **507**, 531, 602, 603, 636, 640, 654, 655
Hamilton, Mark "Slim" 452-453, 461
Hammond, Harriet 382, **383**, **384**, 385, 387
Hammons, E.W. **86**, 401, 517
Handy Andy see *Front!*
Hanneford, Poodles 8, 328, 331, 402, 405-409, **405**, **406**, **408**, 410-413, **411**, **412**, 414, 416-418, **416**, **417**, 419, 462, 548, 629
Hardy, Oliver 261, 484, 522, 546, 627, 629-632, **630**, 661 (see also Laurel and Hardy)
Harlan, Marion **402**, 403, **404**
Harlan, Otis 632-634, **633**
Harmon, Pat **534**
Harrison, Bud 291, **505**, 505-506
Hart, William S. 292, 310, 311, 315, 324, 350, 393, 394, 553
Hartman, Ferris 26, 31, 76, 216, 217, 240, 242, **242**, 245, 248, 251, 255, 256, 257, 259-260, **260**, 262, 266, 521
Hatton, Raymond 50, 349, 387, **388**, 388-389, 435
Hauber, Bill 32, **33**, 39, 41, 43, 46, 53, 58, 63, 64, 67, **67**, 68-70, **69**, 73, 76, 83, **83**, 84, **92**, 99, 112, 113, 114, 116, 120, 137, 138, 140, 150, 153, 163, 173, 183, 193, 195, 205, 289, 291, **620**
Havez, Jean 279, 326, 329, **329**, 330, 335, 338, 378, 399, 413, **460**
Hayes, Billy 564, 565, **566**
Hayes, Frank 26, **59**, 143, **143**, 144, 152, **152**, 156, **157**, 157, 160, **160**, 168, 171, **171**, 175, 179, 179, **180**, 183, 193, **194**, 195, 196, 198, 200, 202, 204, 205, 208, **208**, 209, 211, 221, 222, 225, 230, **231**, 233, 237, 239, 320, 323
Hayseed, The 156, 210, 260, 291, 331, 333, 335-338, **335**, 337
He Did and He Didn't 32, 124, 240-245, **241**, 250, 254, 272, 333, 409, 410, 550
He Would a Hunting Go 56, 89, 94-95, **95**, 116, 606
Hearst, William Randolph 287-288, 470-472
Hearts and Harpoons 598, **599**
Help! Help! Hydrophobia 32, 34, 37-39, **38**
Henabery, Joseph 345, 350, 351-352, 356, 357, 358, 359-360, 367, 368, 573-575, 643
Henderson, Dell 120, 138, 160, 458, 497, 499-500, 511, 512
Henley, Jack 564, 567, 570, 572, 576, 580, 581, 583
Henry, Gale 138, 227, 394, 632, 637, 658, 661
Hernandez, George 20, 21, **22**, 22-23, **27**

Hey, Pop! 259, 317, 340, 564-567, **564**, 573
Hiatt, Ruth 495, **496**, 497
Hibbard, Fred see Fishback, Fred
Hicks, Tommy 10, **653**, 653-654
Hiers, Walter 390, 394, 466, 642-645, **643**, **644**
Hill, "Smiling" Roland 619
Hill, George 472
Hippe, Louis 233, **235**
His Favorite Pastime 114-117, **115**, 589
His First Car 419, **420**, 420-423, **421**, **422**, 467
His New Profession 64, 150-151, **151**, 589, **622**, 622
His Private Life **444**, 455, 461, 462, 464-466, **464**, **465**
His Sister's Kids 48, 56, 60, 91-93, **92**, 589
His Wedding Night 188, 244, 276-279, **277**, **278**, 282, 291, 311
His Wife's Mistake 8, 32, 210, 244, 248-251, **249**, **251**, 253, 254, 261, 272, 428, 590
Hitchcock, Raymond 228, 230-231, **231**, **232**, 232, 234, 596
Hitchin' Up **644**, 645
Hoff, Joan 429, **430**
Holland, Frank 367, **368**, **369**
Hollywood 57, 394-398, **395**, 480
Hollywood Lights 530, 533, 554-557, **554**, **555**
Hollywood Luck 502, 530, 548-550, **548**
Holmes, Leon **420**, 420, **421**, 422
Home Brewed Youth **599**, 599
Home Cured 299, 447, 458-461, **459**, 550
Honeymoon Trio 4, 520-522, **520**, 531, 550
Horsley, David 28, 89, 98, 203
Houck, Tommy 245, **246**
How Bumptious Papered the Parlor 594
How've You Bean? 296, 478, 569, 570-572, **570**
Howard, Shemp 572, 575, 576, **576**, 578-580, **579**, 588
Howell, Alice 133, 137, 155-156, **155**, 157, 183, 302, 361, 607, **608**, **634**, 635, 637, 669
Hubert, Fritz 567, 569, 570, **571**, 571, 572, 580
Hunn, Bert 39, 41, 43, 46, 50, 64, 78, 79, 84, 98, 112, 113, 114
Hurst, Paul 517, 518, **519**, 519-520, **633**
Hutchins, "Wheezer" 652
Huzar, Karoly see Puffy, Charles

Idle Roomers 492, 530, 538-539, **538**, 551
In the Clutches of a Gang 84, 89, 101-102, **101**
In the Dough 259, 569, 576-580, **576**, 583
Incompetent Hero, An 167-168, **167**, 370, 589
Inslee, Charles 53, 58, 61, 62, **62**, 64, 67, 68, **69**, 70, 76, 77, 79, 83, **83**, 105
Iron Mule, The **5**, 68, 257, 298, 299, 393, 425, 433-436, **433**, **434**, 437, 438, **439**, **442**, 471, 586
It Pays to Exercise **149**
It's a Cinch 515, 551-553, **551**, **552**

Jackson, Mary Ann 497, **652**
Jacobs, Paul 53, 58, 60, 64, 78, 129, **623**
Jamison, Bud 217, 240, 250, 483, 485, **486**, 486, 557, 559, 647, **648**

Jefferson, William 240, **244**, 244, 245, 248, 250, 251, 271, 272, 277
Jenkins, Robert 410, **411**, 411
Jeske, George 73, 84, 89, 99, 102, **102**, 112, 113, 114, 504
Johnson, Walter 164-165
Jones, Grover 420, 431, 433, 435, 436, 442, 443
Joseph, Billy 638
Joslin, Margaret 17, 617-618
Joy, Violet see Thompson, Diane
Judels, Charles 527, 529, 536, 537, **537**, 541, 572, 575, **579**, 580, **580**

Karns, Roscoe 350, 355
Karr, Hilliard 581, 624, **638**, 639-640, **641**, 659, **660**, 660
Keaton, Buster 3, 4, 5, 7, 29, 31, 120, 121, 133, 187-188, 189, 210, 218, 259, 261, 265, 269, 271, 273, 274-275, 276, 277, **280**, 280, 282, 283, 285, 287-288, **288**, 289, 291, 292, 293, **293**, 294, **295**, 296, 297, 298, 301, **303**, 304, **305**, 306, **306**, 307, 308, 311, 315, 317, 324, 329, 330, 331, **331**, 333, **334**, 335, **335**, 338, **339**, 340, 349, 370, 391-394, **392**, 398, 409, 413-416, **413**, **415**, 424, 425, 428, **432**, 433, 435, 438, 448, 450-452, **451**, 457, 458, 460-461, **460**, 462, 471, 479, 480, 481, 510, 513, 536, 543, 549, 550, 553, 561, 581, 583, 587, 588, 618, 619, 630, 636, 649
Keaton, Joe 285, 287-288, 289, 291, 293, 413, 416, 417
Keep Laughing 332, 423, 517, 542-544, **542**, 557
Keeping Up with the Joneses 499, 650
Kelly, Eddie 245, **246**
Kelly, Fanny 320, 324
Kelly, Pat 230, **231**, 320, 324
Kennedy, Edgar 3, 32, 43, 46, **48**, 49-50, 53, 58, 59, 61, 64, 67, 68, 73, 76, 78, 84, 87, **88**, 94, 99, **100**, **101**, 102, 103, 105, 109, 111, 112, 113, 114, 116, 122, 133, 138, **139**, 140, **140**, 141, 167, **167**, 175, 176, 193, 196, 202, 205, 213, 214, 216, 218, **220**, 220, 223, 225, 326, **327**, 328, 525, 555, 559, 562
Kessel Jr., Ad 224, 242
Keystone Cops 53, 59, 92, 102, 129, 133, 144, 174, 179, 198, 215, 307, 513, 547
Kirtley, Virginia 53, 58, 61, 64, 67, 76, 87, 89, **89**, 91, 94, 99, 102, 103, 105
Knockout, The 64, 76, 109, 116, 132-134, **132**, **134**, 200, 210

Lackaye, James 600-601, **601**
Lady Lion, A **654**
Lake, Alice 100, 255, **256**, 256, 257, 258, 262, 266-267, **267**, 276, 285, **286**, **287**, 287, 289, 293, **293**, 296, 297, **297**, 301, **303**, 304, **305**, 307, 308
Lakin, Charles 122, 133, **134**, 163, 176, 196, 198, **199**, 199-200, 205, 208, 225
Lambert, Glen 564, 567, 570, 572, 580, 581-582, 624, 639

Lampton, Dee **617**, 617-618
Lane, Leota 500, 501, 502, 503
Lane, Lupino 86, 218, 302, **444**, 445, 452, 454-456, **454**, **455**, 457, 461-466, **462**, **463**, **464**, **465**, 467, 474, 511, 516, 517
Lang, Peter 74, 604-605, **605**
Langdon, Harry 3, 5, 333, 364, 424, 458, 513, 526, 530, 543, 553, 555, 635, 646
Lasky, Jesse 198, 308, 309, 317, 328, 345, 350, 356, 361, 367, 371, 376, 378, 379, 382, 387, 388, 394, 438, 475, 517, 613, 643
Laurel and Hardy 3, 4, 5, 29, 80, 87, 319, 389, 421, 424, 428, 467, 500, 504, 526, 531, 543, 565, 577, 577, 619, 629, 631-632, 661
Laurel, Stan 3, 4, 17, 102, 218, 304, 319, 438, 442, 486, 526, 528, 618, 628, 629, 631, 655, 659, 661 (see also Laurel and Hardy)
Lawrence, Florence 166, 592, 593, **593**
Laymon, Gene "Fatty" 510, 648-651, **650**, **651**
Lazy Days **652**
Leading Lizzie Astray 68, 124, 163, 175-179, **176**, 182, 200, 246, 307, 506, 621
Leap Year 7, 375, 376, 382-387, **383**, **384**, 389, 391, 557
Lee, Florence 420, 448, 456, 457-458
Lee, Lila 362, 365-366, 371, 372, 376, 378-380, **379**, 382, 387, **388**, 388, 394
Lehrman, Henry "Pathé" 31, 32, 34, 37, 38-39, **39**, 43, 45, 52, 53, 55, 56, 60, 73, 74, 78, 86, 87, 105, 106, 112, 113, 117, 118, 120, 129, 156, 291, 318, 336, 445, 448, 510, 605, 606, 607, 616, 626, 635
Leighton, Lillian 371, 373-374, **374**, 376, 394, 632, 637
Leonard, Robert Z. 29, 259, 466
Lessley, Elgin 330, 332-333, 335, 338, 392, 413, 450
Levering, James **630**
Life of Riley, The **657**, 658
Life of the Party, The 7, 350-356, **351**, **353**, **354**, 369, 383
Ligon, Grover 32, **33**, 63, 64, 94, 105, 112, 128, 133, 137, 156, 163, 176, 202, 204, 205, 208, 225, 230, **231**
Lipton, Lew 517, 524, 527, 557, 559
Little Teacher, The 116, 221-223, **221**, **222**, 590
Littlefield, Lucien 346, 350, 371, 372, 376, 382, **386**, 387
Live Agent, The 414, **441**, 442-443, **443**
Lizzie's Waterloo 618
Lloyd, Harold 3, 4, 5, 17, 62, 211, 215, 218, 219, **220**, 220, 306, 313, 323, 329, 353, 421, 428, 456, 457, 474, 479, 481, 486, 510, 532, 565, 587, 588, 616, **617**, 617, 618, 628, 654
Lloyd, Jack 461, **627**
Loback, Marvin 628-629, **628**
Look Out Below 86, 353, **614**, 614
Lorch, Theodore 376, 380, 382
Lorraine, Louise 541-542
Love 145, 259, 317, 320-324, **321**, **322**, 431, 587
Love and Bullets 138-140, **139**, 161, 589

Love and Courage 55-56, **55**
Love and Rubbish 52-53, **52**
Lovemania 429-431, **429**, **430**
Lover's Luck 145, 156-158, **157**, 210
Lover's Post Office 165-167, **166**
Lucas, Wilfred 63, 76, 78, 80, 97-98, **98**, 209
Lucenay, Harry 569
Luke **4**, **9**, **30**, 76, 97, 130, 133, 156, 187, 196, 208-210, **209**, 223-224, **223**, 237, **238**, 239, **239**, 269, **270**, 304-305, 307, 310, 315, 335, **335**, 336, 338, 339, 340, 411, 431, 533, 617
Lundin, Walter 332, **617**
Lupino, Wallace 454, 455, **455**, 456, 461
Lure of Hollywood, The 513, 515-517, **515**

Mabel and Fatty's Married Life 31, 198-200, **198**, **199**, 587
Mabel and Fatty's Wash Day 182, **186**, 187-189, 210, 317, 590
Mabel and Fatty Viewing the World's Fair at San Francisco 214
Mabel, Fatty and the Law 52, 101, 187, 194-196, **194**, **195**, 588, 590
Mabel's Dramatic Career 64-67, **65**, **66**, 149, 222, 589
Mabel's New Hero 61-63, **61**, 89, 174, 283, 589
Mabel's Wilful Way 216-218, **217**, 259, **586**
MacCloy, June 527, **527**, 528, **528**, 529, 557, 559, **560**, 562
MacDonald, Wallace 133, 138, 145, **146**, 153, 160, 161, 163, **165**, 366, 640
Mace, Fred 31, 32, **33**, 34, 49, 124, 141, 228, 233, 605, 627, 632
Mace, Tut 554, **555**, 555-556, 557
Mack, Hughie 279, 599, **600**, 600, 637
MacMahon, Doris 517, **518**, 518-519
Macpherson, Jeanie 394, **593**
Making a Living 62, 80, 89, 105-107, **106**, 589
Making It Pleasant for Him 20, **21**
Malaby, Richard 531, **532**, 543
Malino, Alfred and Frank 538-539, **538**
Malone, Molly 324, **326**, 326, **327**, 328, 330, 331, **331**, 333, 335, **335**, 338, 393, 405, 406, **406**, 407, 410, 411, 416, 417, 611
Mann, Alice 276, **277**, 279, 280, 282, **283**
Mann, Hank 43, 58, 64, 68, 70, 76, 84, 89, 90-91, **91**, **92**, 94, 101, **101**, 102, 109, 111, 112, 113, 120, 122, 124, 133, 137, 211, 233, 303, 394, 450, 513, 526, 626, 635, 636, 645, 650
Mannix, Eddie 163, 401, 472
Marion, Edna 503, 504, 640
Marion, Marie 576, 578
Marriage Rows 101, 412, 503-504, **504**
Mason, Dan 261, **599**
Masquerader, The 147-150, **148**, 178, 589
Match Play 484, 485-488, **486**, **487**
Maximillian, Robert 258, 259, 261-262
Maynard, Ken **633**
McCarey, Leo 3, 577, 631
McCarey, Ray 577-578

McComas, Ralph **631**, 632
McCoy, Harry 105, 109, 112, 113, 114, 133, 137, 148, 152, **152**, 163, 171, 173, 176, 181, **182**, 182-183, **184**, **186**, 187, 193, 194, 202, 204, 205, 208, 230, 328, 338, 340, 483, 484, 485, 495, 497, 627
McCullough, Philo 544, 545
McGuire, Kathryn 413, 414, **432**, **460**
McPhail, Addie 400, 495, 497, 499, **499**, 503-504, **504**, 506, 508, **524**, 525, 539, 541, 542, 543, 548
Melford, George 345, 348, 349
Mendel, Jules 658-659, **659**
Milk We Drink, The 80, **81**, 81
Miller, Rube 32, 34, **35**, 41, 43, 46, 54, 76, 91, **92**, **101**, 102, 113, 114, 116, 133, 145, 155, **155**, 156, 326, 330, 331, 335, **335**
Mineau, Charlotte **524**, 525, 526
Mintun, Peter 528
Misplaced Foot, A **96**, 97-98
Miss Fatty's Seaside Lovers 218-220, **219**, **220**, 298, 587
Mitchell, Bruce 640, **641**
Montana, Bull 371, **371**, 372-373, **373**, 374, 376, 394, 513, **636**
Moonlight and Cactus 494, 537, 541-542, **541**
Moonshine 68, 256, 269, 297-300, **297**, **299**, 437
Moonshiners, The 68, 253, 254, 255-257, **256**
Moore, Colleen 129, 385, 390, 471-472
Moore, Owen 221, **222**, 222-223, 394, 468, 471, 473
Moore, Victor 285, 612-613, **612**
Moran, Polly 200, 233, 338, 340, 487
Morgan, Horace "Kewpie" 413, 426, 427, 428
Morris, Dave **607**
Morris, Lee **631**, 632, **637**
Morris, Reggie 268
Morrison, Sunshine Sammy 310, **312**, 313-314, 315, 411
Mother's Boy 73-74, **73**, 162, 224
Mother's Holiday 520, 539, 550-551, **550**
Moulding, The 37
Mountain Justice **633**
Movies, The 364, 448-450, **449**, 471, 497, 568, 587
Mr. Smith, Barber **595**, 596
Mrs. Jones Entertains **593**
Mrs. Jones' Birthday 17-20, **18**
Much Needed Rest, A 612
Muddy Romance, A 62, **62**, 76
Murdock, Henry 473, 474-475
Murphy, Steve 413, 426, 427, 428
Murray, Charles 46, 81, 122, 137, 138, **139**, 148, 149, 150, **151**, 151, 154, 160, 161, 169, 178, 200, **201**, 201, 227, 233, 341, 343, 385, 608, 627, 628, **657**, 658
My Stars 414, 432, 447, 456-458, **457**, **458**, 587

Nagel, Conrad 466, 469
Neilan, Marshall 203, 470, 603
Neilsen, Agnes 262, **263**, **264**, **273**
Nelson, Eva 113, 117, **118**, 118
Nelson, Evelyn **211**

Never Again 80, 101, 262, 423-425, **424**, **425**, 430, 432, 550
New Sheriff, The 210, 311, 328, 410-413, **411**, **412**
Newman, Bobby 653
Niagara Falls 559-562, **560**
Nichols, George 79, 81, **82**, 83, 84, 85, 87, 89, 91, 93, **93**, 94, 98, 99, 101, 102, 103, 107, 109, 112, 114, 124, **185**
Nichols, Norma 168, 169-171, **170**, 225
No Loafing 8, 407-409, **408**, 462
No Luck **147**, 448
Noise from the Deep, A 8, 41, 53-54, **54**, 126, 187, 302, 586, 589
Normand, Mabel 31, 32, 39-41, **40**, 43, 45, **45**, 46, 51, **51**, 52, 53, **54**, 54, 55, 56, **57**, 58, 61-62, **61**, **62**, 64-66, **66**, 67, **67**, 68, 70, 71, 74, 76, 78, **78**, 79, 83, 89, **90**, 95, **96**, 97, 98, 108, 120, 130, 141, 144, 145, 148, 149, 158, 171-172, **171**, 173-175, **175**, 184, **185**, **186**, 187, 189-190, **191**, **192**, 192, 193, **194**, 194, 195, **195**, 196, **198**, 198-199, 200, 205-208, **206**, 213-214, **213**, 215, **216**, 216-217, **217**, 218, 221, **222**, 222, 223, 228, **232**, 234, 237-238, **238**, 240, 240-242, **241**, **242**, 243, 244, 245-247, **247**, 248, 254, 340, 343, 347, 388, 414, 450, 528, 596, 631, 642
Nugent, Edward J. 500, 503, 508, **508**, 510, 559, 561

O'Brien, Tom 551, 553
O'Connell, Hugh 572, 575, 576
O'Shea, Ted 554, **555**, 557
Ochs, Al 567, **567**
Oderman, Stuart 141-142, 414, 471-472
Ogle, Charles 356, 361, 371, 372, 376, 380, 382, 394
Oh, Doctor! 75, 279-282, **280**, **281**, 285, 634
Olsen's Big Moment **521**
Once a Hero 512, 534-535, **534**, 549
One Night It Rained 244, 409-410, **410**
One Quiet Night 4, 521, 530-532, **530**, **532**
One Sunday Morning 467-468, **467**, 474, 497, 507
Only a Farmer's Daughter **620**
Opperman, Frank 94, 98, **99**, 103, 107, **107**, 108, 109, 112, 113, 114, 116-117, **117**, 133, 144, 148, 160, **160**, 181, 196, 221, 222
Other Man, The 244, 250, 251-255, **252**, **253**, 272
Out West 68, 184, 256, 269, 289-293, **289**, **290**, 311, 452
Ovey, George 202, 203-204, 306

Pagano, Ernest 500, 502, 504, 508, 510, 512, 515, 520, 522, 529, 531, 532, 534, 536, 538, 539, 541, 542, 544, 545, 548, 549-550, 551, 554, 555, 557
Page, Peggy 113, 150, 179, **179**
Pallette, Eugene 426, **426**, 428
Palmer, Constance 391
Palmer, Frederick **242**
Parquet, Corinne 248, 250, **258**, 258, 259, 260-261, 262, **263**, **264**, **588**
Parrott, Charles see Chase, Charley

Parsons, William "Smiling Bill" 163, 328, **610**, 610-612, **611**, 619, 637, 640
Pasha, Kalla 394, 554, **556**, 556-557
Passions, He Had Three 34-37, **35**, 42, 639
Patricola, Tom 492, **493**, 493-494, 495, 536, **536**, 537, 538, 541, **541**, 542
Patton, Bill **514**
Patullo, George 363, 376, 378
Payson, Blanche 419, **420**, 420, 423, 424, **425**, 473, 474, 475
Peaceful Oscar 101, 229, 461, 473-475, **473**, 497, 507
Pearce, George C. 367, **368**, 369
Pearce, Peggy 76, 79, 93, **93**, 109, **110**, **111**, 111, 112, 113, 114, 116, 608
Peeping Pete 41, 43-45, **44**, 50, 587, 588
Pepper 130
Perez, Marcel 3, 97, 141, 215, 661
Perfect Gentleman, The 364, **365**
Pete and Repeat 178, 291, 504-506, **505**
Pete the Pup 210, 431-432, **432**, 533, 567, 568, 569
Peters, George 276, 279, 280, 282, 285, 289, 293, 297, 301, 303, 304
Phillips, Joe 492, **493**, 493, 494-495
Pickford, Mary 146, 203, 222-223, 364, 366, 390, 450, 500, 526
Pollard, Daphne 250, **482**, 483, 484, 485
Pollard, Jack 248, 250, **251**
Pollard, Snub **13**, 102, 211, 215, 250, 259, 313, 526, 528, 565, 617, **628**, 629, 652
Post, Charles "Buddy" 326, **327**, 328, 330, 332, **332**
Powell, Russell 468, 637
Powell, William 475, **476**, **478**, 478
Pratt, George C. 277
Price, Kate 258, 261, 301, 303, **303**, 331, 599, 616, 619
Prior, Herbert 593
Professor Bean's Removal 56-58, **57**, 141
Puffy, Charles 646-648, **647**, **648**
Pullman Porter, The 320, 324

Queenie of Hollywood 530, 532-534, **533**
Queenie the dog 532-534
Quick, Evelyn 32, 34, 43, 61
Quiet Little Wedding, A 76, **77**, 89, 209

Rae, Marvel **149**
Ralston, Jobyna 475, **476**, **477**, 478, 639
Rand, John 53, 304, **305**, 306, **306**
Rappe, Virginia 1, 38, 39, 391
Rastus and the Game Cock 43, 46, 48-50
Rat's Knuckles, The **659**, 659
Reardon, Mildred 310, 313, 315, 316, **316**, 319
Rebecca's Wedding Day 48, 103-105, **103**, **104**, 137, 152, 153, 323
Reckless Romeo, A 80, 100-101, 159, 254, 256, 261, 262-266, **263**, **264**, 274, 276, 283, 284, 305, 423, 550, 587, **588**
Red Mill, The 223, 414, 468-473, **468**, **469**, **470**, 476, 483, 638, 653
Reed, Emma 276, 279

Reed, Walter C. 76, 218, 220, 259, 298-299, **300**, 413, 414, 420, 431, 433, 436, 438, **444**, 458, 460, 503, 504, 506
Reisner, Charles **329**, 394
Ride for a Bride 87-89, **88**
Riot, The 48, 56, 58-60, **58**, 126
Ritchie, Billie 73, 118, 156, 172, 184, 306, 324, 605, 606, 607, 608
Roach, Bert 181, 183, 361, 609, 621
Roach, Hal 17, 28, 43, 46, 49, 62, 98, 102, 130, 169, 171, 200, 211, 219, 220, 250, 304, 307, 313-314, 319, 372, 374, 387, 421, 428, 435, 486, 500, 504, 519, 524, 526, 528, 531, 532, 547, 556, 565, 569, 577, 600, 617, 618, 627, 628, 629, 631, 632, 652, 655, 659, 661
Rob 'Em Good 372, **636**
Roberts, Big Joe 392, 407, **408**, 409
Robinson, David 115-116
Robust Patient, A **24**, 25-26, 73, 302
Robust Romeo, A 101, 107-109, **107**, **108**, 585, 589
Rock, Joe 178, 215, 486, 516, 559, **627**, 627, 635, 640, 659
Rogers, Gene "Pop" 607-608, **608**
Rohauer, Raymond 276, 305, 311, 587
Ross, Bill "Kewpie" 659-660, **660**
Rough House, The 73, 101, 224, 273-276, **273**, **275**, 277, 284, 294, 305, 311, 474
Round-Up, The 184, 345-350, **347**, **348**, 361, 364, 586, 588
Rounders, The 137, 153-155, **154**, 159, 589
Rural Demon, A 117-119, **118**
Russell, Dan 203, 608-610, **609**

Safe in Jail 50, **50**, 124
Sanitarium, The 21-24, **22**, 25, 73
Santschi, Tom 14, **15**, 17, **18**, **19**, 20, 26, **27**
Sax, Sam **563**, 573-574
Schade, Fritz 144, 171, 176, 196, 227, **620**, 621
Schaefer, Albert 653
Schaefer, F. G. 250
Scholar, The **626**
Scraps of Paper 8, 308-310, **308**, 317
Screen Snapshots 341-344, **342**, 366-367, 450, 466-467
Sea Nymphs, The 41, 173-175, **174**, **175**, 187, 283, 384, 585, 589
Sedgwick, Edward 618-619, **618**, 632
Selby, Gertrude 607
Selig, William 14, 17, 20, 21, 22, 23, 24, 25, **25**, 26, 29, 49, 73, 80, 83, 89, 137, 169, 178, 182, 279, 302, 369, 374, 380, 526, 545, 585, 632, 633
Semon, Larry 3, 64, 70, 141, 146, 171, 179, 214, 279, 306, 401, 424, 428, 475, 477-478, 531, 599, 627, 630, 635, 636, 645, 646, 655
Sennett, Mack 1, 28, 29, 31, 32, 34, 35, 37, 38, 39, 40, 41, 43, **44**, 44, 45, 46, 49, 50, 51, 52, 53, 54, 55, 56, 57, 58, 60, 61, 62, 63, 64, **65**, 66, 67, 68, 70, 73, 74, 76, 78, 79, 80, 81, 83, 84, 86, 87, 89, 90, 91, 93, 94, 95, 97, 98, 99, 101, 102, 103, 105, 106, 107, 108, 109, 111, 112, 113, 114, 116, 117, 118, 119, 120, 122, 123, 124, 125, 126, 128, 130, 132, 133-134, 135, 136, 137, 138, 140-142, 143, 144, 145, 146, 147, 149, 150, 152, 153, 154, 155, 156, 158, 160, 161, 162, 163, 165, 167, 168, 169, 171, 172, 173, 174, 175, 178, 179, 181, 182, 183, 187, 188, 189, 192, 193, 194, 195, 196, 197, 198, 199, 200, 201, 202, 203, 204, 207, 208, 211, 212, 213, 214, 215, 216, 218, 220, 221, **222**, 222, 223, 224, 225, 227, 228, 229, 230, 231, 233, **233**, 234, 235, 236, 237, 239, 240, 241, 242, 243, 244, 245, 247, 248, 251, 254, 255, 256, 257, 260, 262, 264, 265, 266, 268, 269, 271, 274, 285, 294, 296, 306, 307, 309, 312, **318**, 322, 323, 324, 343, 347, 348, 354, 385, 394, 423, 424, 431, 435, 438, 445, 457, 471, 474, 483-485, 486, **487**, 487, 488, 497, 513, 526, 528, 547, 549, 556, 561, 565, 577, 585, 587, 600, 601, 605, 608, 609, 610, 618, 621, 626, 627, 628, 629, 635, 645, 646, 655, 658, 661
Shannon, Harry 572, **573**, 575
Shaw, Jack 535, **542**, 543, 554
Sheriff, The 98, 184, 210, 285, 309, 310-315, **311**, **312**, **314**, 317, 327, 411
Sherlock, Jr. 298, 329, 333, 413-416, **413**, **415**, 424, 425, 428, 431, **432**, 432, **441**, 442, 451, 462
Shilling, Marion 527, **527**, 529, 557, 559, 561, **561**, 562
Short, Gertrude 382, 385, 387, **388**, 389, 527, **527**, 529, 557, **558**, 559, 562
Shotguns that Kick 179, **180**
Shutta, Jack 400, 511-512, 534, **534**, 535, 564
Si, Si, Senor 492-495, **493**, **494**
Sidney, George 200, 655-658, **656**, **657**
Simpkins, Joseph E. 130
Sinclair, Johnny 420, 423, 424, 426, 427, 428, 429, 430-431, **430**, 432, 436, **437**, 438, 442, 452, 460, **460**, 475, 478
Sky Pirate, A 140-141, **140**
Sloane, Paul 488, 489, 490-491
Small Town Act, A 56, 80, 81-83, **82**, 331
Smart Work 539-541, **540**
Smith, Oscar **346**, 517, **532**, 532
Smith, Sid **211**, 632, 650
Snookie's Disguise **111**
Some Nerve 93-94, **93**
Sparks, Ned 8, **402**, 402, 403, **403**, 404-405, **404**, 409-410, **410**, 414
Spear, Harry **652**
Special Delivery 8, 218, 391, 475-479, **476**, **477**, **478**, 483
Speed Kings, The 78-79, **78**, 589
Spencer, Fred 654-655, **654**
Square Sex, The **558**
St John, Al 8, 53, 58, 59-60, **59**, 73, 76, 80, 86, 91, 99, 101, **101**, 102, 113, 114, 124, **132**, 133, **134**, 137, 141, **142**, 143, 144, 153, 156, 165, **166**, 167, 168, 171, 176, 179, 181, 188, 189, 190, 195, 196, 198, 199, 200, **201**, 205, 208, **208**,

210, 211, 223, 227, 230, **231**, 233, 237, 238, 240, **241**, 242, 243, 245, **247**, 248, **249**, 251, **252**, 253, 255, **256**, 256, 257, 258, 259, 260, **260**, 261, 262, **264**, 264-265, 266, 269, 271, 273, **273**, 274, 275, **277**, 280, 282, **284**, 285, **286**, **288**, 289, 291, 293, **293**, 296, 297, **297**, 301, 302, 304, **305**, 307, 308, **309**, 313, 315, 316, 317, 320, 323, **326**, 326, **327**, 328, 330, 331, **331**, 333, 337, 340, 391, 398, 410, 419, **420**, 420, **421**, **422**, 423, **424**, **425**, 425, 426, **426**, **427**, 428, 429, **429**, 430, **430**, 431, **432**, 433, 435, 436, **437**, 437-440, **439**, 441-443, **441**, **443**, 445, 457, 461, 467, 480, 492, 499, 503, **504**, 504, 520, **520**, 522, 529, **529**, 531, 545, **546**, 546, **547**, 548, 567, **567**, 568, 569, 572, **588**, 639
Stander, Lionel 576, **576**, 578
Stanlaws, Penrhyn 561
Steadman, Vera **149**
Stengel, Leni 490, 491, **491**
Steppling, John 601-602, **603**
Sterling, Ford 32, 39, **40**, 43, 44, 45, 46, **47**, 48, 50, **50**, 52, 53, 56-58, **57**, 60, 62, 64, **66**, 68, **69**, 70, **72**, 72, 74-75, 78, **78**, 79, 81, **82**, 83, **83**, 84, 86, 90, 91, 93-94, **93**, 101, **101**, 102, 108, 111, 112, 113, **114**, 116, 120, 137, 141, 143, 158, 200, **201**, 205, **207**, 207, 220, 227, 307, 385, 394, 445, 513, 603, 624
Sterling, Merta 637, **637**
Stevens, Josephine 269, **270**, 273, **273**, **275**, 276
Stone, Gene **556**
Stout, George **242**
Strictly Neutral 601, **602**
Stupid But Brave 302, 425, 426-428, **426**, **427**, 432
Sullivan, Paddy 245, **246**
Summerville, Slim 99, 133, 138, **139**, 142, 144, 156, 157, 163, **165**, 167, 176, 178, 181, 183, 196, 200, 205, 233, 307, 647, 661
Suspended Ordeal, A 125-128, **125**
Sutherland, A. Edward 346, 348, 362, 364
Sutherland, Dick 454, **454**
Swain, Mack 76, 84, **92**, 98, 116, 133, 137, 171, **171**, 173, 175, 176, 182, 196, **197**, 197-198, 200, **201**, 205, 233, 328, 438, 587, 621
Swanson, Gloria **268**, 385, 394, 500
Sweet, Harry 438, 542, 640, 647, **648**, 655, 661
Swickard, Josef 144, 145, 156, 163, 167, 183, 189, 190, 195, 200, 225, 233

Take 'Em and Shake 'Em 43, 527-529, **527**, 537
Talmadge, Natalie 285, 288, 289
Talmadge, Norma 265, **270**, 271, 288, 309, 565, 640
Talmadge, Peg 414
Tamale Vendor, The 494, 536-538, **536**
Tango Tangles 113-114, **114**, 179, 589
Taurog, Norman 38, 461, 466
Tavares, Arthur 41, 43, 50, 53-54, **54**, 67
Taylor, Anne **595**
Teddy the Great Dane 130

Telltale Light, The 51-52
Tetzlaff, Teddy 78-79, 589
Thalasso, Arthur 362, 364-365, **365**, 448, 450, 557, 559
That Little Band of Gold 31, 41, 158, 187, 200, 205-208, **206**, **207**, 212, 222, 550, 587, 590
That Minstrel Man 48, 143-144, **143**, 291, 331, 650
That's My Line 101, 517-520, **518**, **519**
That's My Meat 529-530, **529**
Their Ups and Downs 73, 162-163, **162**, 412
Thompson, Al 495, 503, 511, 517, 518, 520, 525, 531, 536, 538, 539, 557, 559
Thompson, DeLloyd 212
Thompson, Duane 546, **644**, 645, **645**, 646
Those Country Kids 116, 144-145, **144**, 321, 621
Those Happy Days 141-143, **142**
Three Fleshy Devils 660
Three Hollywood Girls 500-503, **500**, 510
Thurman, Mary 382, **384**, 385, 608
Tighe, Harry 8, **402**, 402, 403-404, **403**, 409-410, **410**
Tillie's Punctured Romance 133-134, 136, 150, 255, 347, 364
Todd, Harry 14, 17, 617
Tomalio 537, 572, 577, 580-583, **580**
Too Much Dutch 627
Tourist, The 446-448, **446**, 452
Townley, Jack 500, 502, 504, 508, 511, 512, 515, 520, 522, 529, 531, 532, 534, 536, 538, 539, 541, 542, 544, 545, 548, 549, 551, 554-555, 557
Trask, Wayland 233, 237, 239-240, 592
Traveling Salesman, The 358, 361, 367-371, **367**, **368**, **369**, 519, 649
Treacy, Emerson 534, **534**, 535, **535**, 559, 561
Twixt Love and Fire 106, 109-112, **110**, 182
Two Gun Morgan 513, **514**
Two Old Tars 74-75, **75**, 87, **88**, 126, 589

Under New Management **608**
Under Sheriff, The 81, 98-99, **99**, 116, 589
Unknown Chaplin 480
Up a Tree 484, 497-500, **498**
Up Pops the Duke 513, 522-524, **523**

Van Dorn, Mildred 570, **570**, 572, **574**, 579
Van, Beatrice 34, **35**, 37, **38**, 41, **42**, 43, 527, 528, 557, 602
Vance, Virginia **444**, 454, 456, **457**, 457, 458, 461, 463, 464, 517
Vaughn, Alberta 557, **558**
Vernon, Bobby 29, 233, **268**, 328, 353, 547
Vidor, King 468, 471-472, 553
Village Scandal, The 227, 230-233, **231**
Voss, Frank "Fatty" **607**, 607, **608**, 609

Waiter's Ball, The 7, 32, 210, 217, 253, 254, 256, 257-262, **258**, **259**, 276, 303, 305, 307, 323, 565
Waiter's Picnic, The 39-41, **40**, 187
Walker, Brent 133-134, 587
Ward, Lucille 74-75, **75**, 167, **167**, 367, 370

Warren, Herbert 244, 269, 273, 276, 277, 279, 282, 285, 289, 293, 295-296, 297, 298, 301, 304, 570
Washburn, Bryant 354, 363, 394, 457, 508, 510, 515, 517, 542, 543, 601, 642
Water Dog, The 128-130, **128**, 589
Watson Jr., Coy 145, **147**, 147
Watson Jr., Harry 340, 613-614, **614**
Watz, Edward 467-468, 488-489
Weber & Fields 138, 233, 134, 236, 473, 633
Weber, Joe 134, 236 (see also Weber & Fields)
Weldon, Jess 635-636, **636**
Wells, Mai **59**, 225, 237, 239, 266
West, Billy 62, 179, 182, 184, 211, 214, 285, 323, 380, 390, 424, 428, 435, 499, 630, 640
West, Roland 34
Westover, Winifred 320, **321**, 324
Wheeler and Woolsey 120, 488-492, **489**, **491**, 517, 520, 555
When Dreams Come True 70-72, **70**, 109
When Hazel Met the Villain 123-124, **123**
When Love Took Wings 141, 211-213, **212**, 214
White, Jack 38, 84-87, **85**, **86**, 91, **92**, 92, 204, 211, 218, 227, 307, 328, 401, 417, 419, 423, 431, 442, 445, 446, 447, 448, 452, 454, 455, 456, 457, 458, 461, 464, 467, 474, 475, 497, 524, 531, 543, 556, 635, 646, 653

White, Leo 199, 200, **509**
Williams, Frank 279
Williams, Harry **229**
Windy Riley Goes Hollywood 510-512, **511**, 535
Wine 56, 83-84, **83**, 589
Wished on Mabel 31, 90, 213-215, **213**, 590
Wolfkeil, Martin 654, 655
Woman Haters, The 87, **88**
Won by a Neck 484, 495-497, **496**
Wood, Virginia **341**
Woods, Walter 350, 351, 356, 361, 366, 367, 371, 372, 375, 376, 378, 382, 387, 643
Wulze, Harry **329**

Yallop, David 9, 451
You're Darn Tootin' 3, 629
Young, Bert 511, 517, 518, 525, 545, 546, 550, 554, **556**, 556-557
Young, Joe 545, 550, 554, 556

Zabelle, Flora 230, **231**, 231
Zip, the Dodger 163-165, **164**, **165**, 182, 283, 291
Zukor, Adolph 390

www.ingramcontent.com/pod-product-compliance
Lightning Source LLC
Chambersburg PA
CBHW080934020526
44116CB00034B/2591